THEY CHANGED THE WORLD

200 ICONS WHO HAVE MADE A DIFFERENCE

BARBARA CADY

PHOTOGRAPHY EDITOR **JEAN-JACQUES NAUDET**

SPECIAL EDITOR **RAYMOND MCGRATH**

Tess Press

First Black Dog & Leventhal edition published 2003;
reprinted by permission of The Overlook Press, Peter Mayer Publishers, Inc.

Published by Tess Press, an imprint of
Black Dog & Leventhal Publishers
151 West 19th Street
New York, NY 10011

This material was originally published in the book entitled *Icons of the Twentieth Century* by The Overlook Press.

Manufactured in China

ISBN-10: 1-57912-590-5
ISBN-13: 978-1-57912-590-5

g f e d c b a

Library of Congress Cataloging-in-Publication Data

Cady, Barbara, 1942-
[Icons of the twentieth century]
Icons : 200 men and women who have made a difference / Barbara Cady ;
photography editor, Jean-Jacques Naudet ; special editor, Raymond McGrath.
p. cm.
This material was originally published in a book entitled Icons of the twentieth century, by the Overlook Press, 1998.
Includes bibliographical references.
ISBN 1-57912-328-7
1. Biography–20th century. I. Title.

CT120.C23 2003
920'.009'04-dc22

2003057779

To my husband,

Jean-Louis Ginibre,

for the patience, support, and unstinting love

he has shown me in a million different ways,

and to my children,

Stephanie, Jennifer, and Monica

—and my French son, Jean-Noel—

for their affection and encouragement

CONTENTS

JANE ADDAMS
MUHAMMAD ALI
WOODY ALLEN
YASIR ARAFAT
HANNAH ARENDT
LOUIS ARMSTRONG
NEIL ARMSTRONG
FRED ASTAIRE
JOSEPHINE BAKER
LUCILLE BALL
ROGER BANNISTER
BRIGITTE BARDOT
DR. CHRISTIAAN BARNARD
THE BEATLES
DAVID BEN-GURION
INGMAR BERGMAN
INGRID BERGMAN
HUMPHREY BOGART
MARLON BRANDO
BERTOLT BRECHT
HELEN GURLEY BROWN
MARIA CALLAS
AL CAPONE
RACHEL CARSON
HENRI CARTIER-BRESSON
FIDEL CASTRO
GABRIELLE "COCO" CHANEL
CHARLIE CHAPLIN
AGATHA CHRISTIE
WINSTON CHURCHILL
COLETTE
LE CORBUSIER
JACQUES COUSTEAU
MARIE CURIE
DALAI LAMA
SALVADOR DALI
BETTE DAVIS
JAMES DEAN
SIMONE DE BEAUVOIR
CHARLES DE GAULLE
DIANA, PRINCESS OF WALES
MARLENE DIETRICH
ISAK DINESEN
WALT DISNEY
ISADORA DUNCAN
BOB DYLAN
AMELIA EARHART
THOMAS EDISON
ALBERT EINSTEIN
DWIGHT D. EISENHOWER
SERGEI EISENSTEIN

T.S. ELIOT
QUEEN ELIZABETH I
QUEEN ELIZABETH II
DUKE ELLINGTON
FEDERICO FELLINI
ENRICO FERMI
HENRY FORD
FRANCISCO FRANCO
ANNE FRANK
ARETHA FRANKLIN
SIGMUND FREUD
BETTY FRIEDAN
YURI GAGARIN
INDIRA GANDHI
MOHANDAS GANDHI
GRETA GARBO
GABRIEL GARCÍA MÁRQUEZ
JUDY GARLAND
BILL GATES
ALLEN GINSBERG
JANE GOODALL
MIKHAIL GORBACHEV
BILLY GRAHAM
MARTHA GRAHAM
CARY GRANT
D.W. GRIFFITH
CHE GUEVARA
STEPHEN HAWKING
WILLIAM RANDOLPH HEARST
HUGH HEFNER
JASCHA HEIFETZ
ERNEST HEMINGWAY
KATHARINE HEPBURN
SIR EDMUND HILLARY &
   TENZING NORGAY
EMPEROR HIROHITO
ALFRED HITCHCOCK
ADOLPH HITLER
HO CHI MINH
BILLIE HOLIDAY
VLADIMIR HOROWITZ
DOLORES IBARRURI
   (LA PASSIONARIA)
MICHAEL JACKSON
MICK JAGGER
JIANG QING (MADAME MAO)
ELTON JOHN
POPE JOHN XXIII
MICHAEL JORDAN
JAMES JOYCE
CARL JUNG

FRANZ KAFKA
FRIDA KAHLO
HELEN KELLER
GRACE KELLY
JOHN F. KENNEDY
DR. JACK KEVORKIAN
BILLIE JEAN KING
MARTIN LUTHER KING, JR.
ANN LANDERS &
   ABIGAIL VAN BUREN
VLADIMIR LENIN
CHARLES LINDBERGH
SOPHIA LOREN
ROSA LUXEMBURG
GENERAL DOUGLAS MACARTHUR
MADONNA
MALCOLM X
NELSON MANDELA
MAO ZEDONG
THE MARX BROTHERS
MATA HARI
HENRI MATISSE
MARGARET MEAD
GOLDA MEIR
MARILYN MONROE
MARIA MONTESSORI
HENRY MOORE
EDWARD R. MURROW
BENITO MUSSOLINI
JOE NAMATH
GAMAL ABDEL NASSER
RICHARD M. NIXON
RUDOLPH NUREYEV
GEORGIA O'KEEFFE
SIR LAURENCE OLIVIER
JACQUELINE KENNEDY ONASSIS
J. ROBERT OPPENHEIMER
JESSE OWENS
EMMELINE PANKHURST
CHARLIE PARKER
BORIS PASTERNAK
LUCIANO PAVAROTTI
ANNA PAVLOVA
PELÉ
EVA PERON
EDITH PIAF
PABLO PICASSO
MARY PICKFORD
JACKSON POLLOCK
ELVIS PRESLEY
MARCEL PROUST

AYN RAND
RONALD REAGAN
LENI RIEFENSTAHL
JACKIE ROBINSON
JOHN D. ROCKEFELLER
ELEANOR ROOSEVELT
FRANKLIN D. ROOSEVELT
ETHEL & JULIUS ROSENBERG
WILMA RUDOLPH
BERTRAND RUSSEL
GEORGE HERMAN "BABE" RUTH
MARGARET SANGER
JEAN-PAUL SARTRE
ALBERT SCHWEITZER
GEORGE BERNARD SHAW
FRANK SINATRA
ALEKSANDR SOLZHENITSYN
STEVEN SPIELBERG
DR. BENJAMIN SPOCK
JOSEPH STALIN
GERTRUDE STEIN
IGOR STRAVINSKY
BARBRA STREISAND
ELIZABETH TAYLOR
SHIRLEY TEMPLE
MOTHER TERESA
MARGARET THATCHER
JIM THORPE
TOKYO ROSE
ARTURO TOSCANINI
HARRY S. TRUMAN
TED TURNER
RUDOLPH VALENTINO
WERNHER VON BRAUN
DIANA VREELAND
LECH WALESA
ANDY WARHOL
JAMES WATSON &
   FRANCIS CRICK
JOHN WAYNE
ORSON WELLES
MAE WEST
HANK WILLIAMS
TENNESSEE WILLIAMS
DUKE & DUCHESS OF WINDSOR
OPRAH WINFREY
VIRGINIA WOOLF
FRANK LLOYD WRIGHT
WILBUR & ORVILLE WRIGHT
BABE DIDRIKSON ZAHARIAS
EMILIANO ZAPATA

ACKNOWLEDGMENTS

MY DEEPEST GRATITUDE to my partner, the talented photo editor Jean-Jacques Naudet, to my agent and friend Lois de La Haba, who rescued and sustained me, and to my publisher, the iconic Peter Mayer, whose intelligence and vision helped refine and polish *They Changed the World.*

Sincerest thanks also to Overlook Editor Tracy Carns, and to Assistant Editor Albert DePetrillo, for their hard work and dedication to the project, and to Clark Wakabayashi for his superb production skills. Warm thank yous also to *They Changed the World* designer, Joel Avirom, whose contribution made the book come alive, Maura Carey Damacion, Beth Bortz, Murray Fisher, and Joy Parker, who always amazed and inspired me with their high level of professionalism and enthusiasm, and to my chief researcher and friend, Julie Rigby, who provided useful commentary and suggestions, and her assistants, Eve Rasmussen and Omar Le Duc.

Thanks also to my statistician, Morris Olitsky, whose help in developing the necessarily complicated but very efficient ballot sent to the prospective members of *They Changed the World* Board of Advisors was invaluable and whose interpretation of the returns was the single most important contribution, after the voting itself, to the selection process.

Heartfelt thanks also to Jacqueline O'Reilley, who typed my early manuscripts before Charlie Pancost and Rick Genzer acclimated me to the computer (and kept mine running), and to all the friendly and savvy people at Celebrity Services in Los Angeles who helped me locate *They Changed the World* Advisors. Bouquets to the helpful librarians at the University of Pennsylvania's Lippincott Library, the Philadelphia Public Library (especially the polite and competent mavens of its incredibly efficient information hotlines), and the reference desk staff of the 53rd Street Branch of the New York Public Library.

A low bow and a kiss to my friends and family who always listened: Wanda Celichowski, Patricia Prybil, Dr. Leslie Dornfeld and Grazia Dornfeld, Jay Cooper, Jack Wilkie, Greta von Steinbauer, Ann Thomson, Karen Kahn, Tom Drain, Sasi Judd, Dugald Stermer, Valerie Cavanaugh, Caryn Mandabach, Bonnie Turner, Marci Carsey (and all the other Sea Hags), Darren Clemens, the late Jay Allen, Chris Cannon, Fr. Frank Gambone, Karen Snyder McGrath (the gracious queen of patience), Barbara Flood, François Vincens, Erica Fletcher, Hester Beavington, Bernie Schleifer, Jenifer Wohl, Dan Marcolina, Jan de Ruiter, Bridget de Socio, Laura de la Haba, Joeseph Greco, Keith Estabrook, Dr. James R. Waisman, Joyce Cole, Tom and Jill Durovsik, Sharon Dorram, Dr. Joe Rogers, Ann Siefert, John Van Doorn, Molly Sheridan, Marie Moneysmith, Bonnie Carpenter, Adele Chatelaine, and Jessica Lauber and Firooz Zahedi.

THE TWENTIETH CENTURY—OUR CENTURY—may be remembered as one of immediacy, an instantaneous, globalized era in which almost every citizen was a witness to a shared history. In our age of overheated communication and celebrity, we have experienced first hand the mingling of reportage, public relations, and manufactured rumor into a new and unfamiliar form of media, a surfeit of information that by no means guarantees easy access to lasting knowledge. Entertained as never before, we are subject to the influences of a popular culture we do not often take seriously and cannot control. Today, we are wealthier or poorer immediately—and literally—thanks to electronic data transmissions systems. Press releases, job specs and instructions are phoned—or faxed or E-mailed—in, and a live satellite feed makes us hungrier for the next. Transfixed by our television and computer screens, we find ourselves both protagonists and pawns in an technological metamorphosis that—depending on one's viewpoint—is either enslaving or liberating. We are, as playwright and Czech president Vaclav Havel says about the end of this most transitional of epochs, in a "volatile chamber" where "everything is possible and almost nothing is certain."

They Changed the World takes its cues from the closing of this fast-forward, streamlined century, a point in time when the entire world will pause to review its one hundred years of magnificence and shame. As the title suggests—"icon" from the Greek *eikon* meaning "an image or representation"—*They Changed the World* is a photo gallery of those who defined the last hundred years. They are the visionaries, cult figures, revolutionaries, tyrants, trend-setters and opinion-makers who have shaped our group Zeigeist, stand-alones like Elvis Presley, Sigmund Freud, Walt Disney, Benito Mussolini, Princess Diana, the Dalai Lama, Mary Pickford, and Che Guevara. Cultural touchstones whose presence has never failed to draw crowds or to disturb the surrounding magnetic field, they are the harbingers of change: Men like Winston Churchill, Franklin D. Roosevelt, Mahatma Gandhi, and Charles de Gaulle; women like Margret Mead, Mother Teresa, Golda Meir, and Marie Curie.

Images of these men and women appear everywhere, their names and faces and words permeating the culture's communications, education, entertainment and arts. Interestingly, each of their own lives, in a kind of bizarre and fluid matrix, intersects more often than not with the others': Charles Chaplin and Albert Einstein, side by side in elegant tuxedos, on the cover of *Scientific American*; Mother Teresa making the acquaintance of Princess Diana; Charles Lindbergh posing proudly with Adolf Hitler; Billy Graham and Frank Sinatra, each

INTRODUCTION

ix

enjoying a succession of presidential photo-ops; Gabriel García Marquéz, sharing a cigar with Fidel Castro; Andy Warhol photographed with just about everyone. Many of these figures have become reflections of our own private obsessions; in turn, we have remade ourselves in their images, transformed them into *public* obsessions and, as such, into major components of a contemporary mythology.

With its rare and distinctive images—some negatively charged, some positively—*They Changed the World* is a showcase for the genius of modern photography, presenting the work of some of the most famous talents in the field: Henri Cartier-Bresson (himself one of the 200 chosen icons) Helmut Newton, Cecil Beaton and Robert Capa, to name a few. After five years of research, photo editor Jean-Jacques Naudet culled these unusual images from archives around the world; the result is a startling compendium which captures the century's unmistakable personalities in both posed and unposed moments. Here are the men and women who stimulated the imagination and inhabited dreams. They live on in our favorite movies, our history books, in television documentaries, in newspapers and on the sides of buildings and breakfast cereal boxes. Some icons have even been resurrected through new technologies in computer generated animation (in the unfortunate case of the late Fred Astaire, to dance with a vacuum cleaner in a TV commercial).

Here are the stars of Hollywood's—and other film capitals'—strange reality-altering process, the cinema immortals upon whom we have projected our fantasies and deceptions. Alongside Fred Astaire, alone in the high-stepping happiness of his musicals, are the great movie monuments: Humphrey Bogart, Marlon Brando, Cary Grant, James Dean, and John Wayne, the gritty loner who perhaps did more than anyone to shape the world's image of the true American hero. These edgy disturbers of the peace taught us how to snap the brim of a hat correctly, how to ride and shoot, how to light a lady's cigarette—and how *not* to drink. Equally important in this rarefied pantheon, for certain, are the goddesses: Greta Garbo, Marlene Dietrich, Marilyn Monroe, Elizabeth Taylor, Katharine Hepburn, and Brigitte Bardot. Directing the big screen's immortals

were Sergei Eisenstein, D.W. Griffith, Alfred Hitchcock, Orson Welles, Federico Fellini, Ingmar Bergman, Steven Spielberg, and Woody Allen, the medium's most celebrated auteurs.

In the midst of chronicling our loves and labors in celluloid we found ourselves looking at the world in a fresh, "modern" and radically new way. This vision flowered in the arts and literature, in the works of Pablo Picasso, Bertolt Brecht, Igor Stravinsky, Martha Graham, and James Joyce. The messages of this new movement, likes its messengers, were shocking and exhilarating. The artists, like the works they created, were studied endlessly by crowds both adoring and censorious.

Here also are the century's scientific intellects, from Watson and Crick, who discovered "the most golden molecule of all," to Thomas Edison, who lit our grandparents' parlors and gave their country cousins a radio to keep them company among the evening's crickets. Here are the pioneers of mass production, like Henry Ford, who put our parents in automobiles so they could colonize the suburbs; the courageous geniuses, like Orville and Wilbur Wright, who showed us that we could fly. Chief among the era's scientific geniuses was Albert Einstein, who made just about every major technological advance in the century possible, opening doors with the help of fellow physicists such as Enrico Fermi and J. Robert Oppenheimer, doors he later wished he had left shut.

Here are those that broke records and crossed barriers; in sports, legends like Roger Bannister, "Babe" Didrikson Zaharias, and Jackie Robinson; in politics, crusaders like Martin Luther King, Jr., Rosa Luxemburg, Nelson Mandela, Eleanor Roosevelt, and Betty Friedan; in medicine, the world's favorite pediatrician, Dr. Benjamin Spock and controversial figures like Dr. Christiaan Barnard and Dr. Jack Kevorkian; in architecture, pioneers like Frank Lloyd Wright and Le Corbusier; and in business, titans like John D. Rockefeller and Bill Gates.

In *They Changed the World,* amongst respected humanitarians such as Helen Keller and Albert Schweitzer, we find criminals like Al Capone. We also find dictators, like Joseph Stalin and Mao Zedong, who led nations—sometimes willing nations—to the edge of sanity and then ordered them to jump. Here—as far removed as possible from the secondary religious meaning of "icon" (in the Orthodox Eastern Church, "an image or picture of Jesus, Mary, a saint, etc.")—we see the maniacal ideologues who have terrified, manipulated, and decimated whole populaces—and then "reeducated" those who remained. First among them, without a doubt, is the scourge of the twentieth century, Adolph Hitler, who perpetrated such heinous crimes that many philosophers and historians consider him a completely unique form of evil. Others in this collection share aspects of Hitler's infamy, contemporary "saviors" known like rock and film stars by only one name: Lenin, Mussolini, Franco, and Mao.

The two hundred individuals included in *They Changed the World* were chosen with the help of a multinational Board of Advisors, respected leaders in the arts and sciences, in politics, publishing, education, fashion, entertainment and technology. Asked to base their deletions, nominations and rankings on their following definition of an icon: "Individuals whose names and faces have impacted us all and whose deeds—for good or ill—have literally shaped the course of modern history." When the ballots were tallied, about fifteen percent of the 200-name list—the nominations which garnered only a few votes each—fell at the thin end of the statistical bell curve. It was here that the combined efforts of the author, the publisher and the project's editors and researchers were called into service.

No grouping, of course, can ever be complete, nor can there be any objective criteria for hierarchical importance—not even for who is included and who is not. Questions will immediately arise: Why Nasser and not Khomeni? Why not Idi Amin, whose face came to symbolize the destruction of Africa in the post-colonial period, or Kwame Nkuma, whose independent Ghana initially offered a better hope for a continent in turmoil? Why not Konrad Adenauer, who out of the ruins of the Third Reich established the beginnings of post-World War democracy in Germany? And why Emperor Hirohito and not Tojo whose leadership of Japan may have had more to do with World War II in Asia than the imperial family? In the end, it would have been impossible to include *every* famous political leader of the century without eliminating key individuals in, say, music or literature. Acknowledging that in this century government leaders—whether mass executioners or sun-kings—ipso facto dominated the world stage, it was decided they would not overrun *They Changed the World*.

There were many others who made us think differently about our world—originals like Alfred Kinsey, Buckminster Fuller and Marshall McLuhan—who were not included. In some cases, it was because heir faces were simply not as recognizable as others, an important consideration because of the book's defining concept of *eikon*, or image. A similar point can be made for many of the century's innovators, individuals whose inventions—the television, the computer, the jet engine, the Pill, penicillin—are much more well known than they are. But *They Changed the World* was about people not things.

Given that the major categories of human endeavor were to be represented, choice was difficult when there were too many candidates in one category, which was often the case. Why Nureyev and not also Nijinsky or Balanchine? Why Billie Holiday and not also Bessie Smith and Ella Fitzgerald? Marcel Proust and not also Thomas Mann and William Faulkner? Why Babe Ruth and not Joe DiMaggio? Why not dozens of other high profile sports stars and performers, all iconic in their way due to the development of mass media in our century? Behind each inclusion and exclusion lie endless arguments. But the selection made at the end of the day is at best a selection.

If I worried about there being more men chosen than women, I know the proportionality identifies a fact of life, and that the balance will shift in the next century. Also, if there are more Americans chosen, it is because in many fields it was an American century. The next century may well be weighted differently. Regardless, the extraordinary subjects and the brilliant photography make their own statement. For myself, I hope in some small way that the profiles I have written take in not only our current cultural climate but reveal our changing sensibilities, perhaps providing intimations of the future. Very likely, given the speed of change, it will be a century that surprises everyone.

BOARD

OF ADVISORS

THE SELECTION OF THE TWO HUNDRED *Icons of They Changed the World* was a two-year project involving the formation of a Board of Advisors, a balloting procedure, a statistical evaluation of the procedure's results and a final polishing of the list by the author and publisher. The entire process began when a statistician was brought on board to help the author create a ballot, which featured a "seed list" of about 100 names. The author then began to compile another list: a thousand or so prominent and knowledgeable people all over the globe, international leaders in the arts and sciences, in politics, sports, publishing, fashion, education, entertainment and technology who might be willing to fill out the complicated and time-consuming ballot. A considerable effort was made by the author to insure that the potential board members be representative not only of various disciplines, but also of diverse cultures, races and nationalities. Variety of age on the Board of Advisors was also important in that the icons eventually chosen had to reflect the full historical span of the century, taking into account the judgments of all its generations—not just those of the current one. To this end Nobel and other honorary award lists were consulted, respected journals in the arts and sciences combed, and commemorative, survey and special topic issues of popular journals and newspapers collected. After a list of about a thousand potential board members had been compiled, the difficult task of locating them began. Using celebrity locator services and researchers, most were found; no where near all, to be sure, responded. To improve response, follow-up phone calls were made, agents contacted, duplicate ballots sent out and more names added to the on-going prospector list. When the last letter was stamped and mailed, it would be another year until all the ballots were ready to be analyzed.

The ballot required several steps. In addition to indicating agreement or disagreement with each of the author's suggested names and ranking them according to (1) most important and (2) "must-have," advisors were allowed to (1) eliminate names from the author's list and (2) replace them with their own nominations. The latter were also to be ranked in order of importance. (The ballot names were divided into the following categories: Politics, Science, Literature, Sports, Graphic & Plastic Arts/Design, Theater/Dance, Music, Philosophy/Theology, Film, Media, Humanitarian/Social Work, and Other.) Tabulation of the ballots by the statistician validated the author's "seed list" and, with the Board members encouraged to add their own nominations, many more interesting icon candidates surfaced.

The author extends her sincere thanks to all the board members. Their generosity of time, intellect and spirit made *They Changed the World* possible.

THEY CHANGED THE WORLD

200 ICONS WHO HAVE MADE A DIFFERENCE

JANE ADDAMS

1860-1935

BORN IN RURAL ILLINOIS the year before the start of the Civil War, American reformer Laura Jane Addams lived and worked through some of her young nation's most chaotic times. Fast on the heels of that bloody conflict came the repercussions of the industrial revolution—its sweatshops, child labor, appalling work conditions, and desperate poverty—and the crush of European immigrants into poor urban centers. World War I ensued, followed by the Great Depression. Addams, one of five surviving daughters of wealthy German-English parents, struggled with her last breath to ease the problems created by these events. Headquartered in Chicago, she baked bread for the hungry, lobbied for fair work laws, organized support for women's rights, and brought the friendly persuasion of her family's Quaker beliefs to the international treaty process. Charming and diplomatic, she nevertheless managed—with her marches, magazine articles and her meddling in "the affairs of men"—to incur the wrath of presidents and the ridicule of the press. Addams's moral integrity sustained her, however, and her unstoppable energy enabled her to further almost every cause she supported.

Except for the sudden death in 1881 of her father, a wealthy Republican senator who had been a friend of Lincoln's, Laura Jane Addams's early years were tranquil. Prepared for missionary work at the Rockford Female Seminary, she enrolled in medical school in Philadelphia but dropped out when her health failed. On a two-year tour of Europe that began in 1883, she was introduced to Toynbee Hall, a British settlement house, which inspired her life-long work. She soon began plans with her life-long friend Ellen Gates Starr for a similar establishment back home.

The two young women moved into a dilapidated mansion in a run-down slum on Chicago's West Side. Naming it Hull House, they made it the base for Addams's wide-ranging progressivism. There, starting from nothing in 1889, the twenty-nine-year-old enlisted the talents of a corps of middle-class women and college students to build a thriving community center that, in addition to providing such basics as food, clothing, and shelter, served as a cultural hub. It was also a center where its largely foreign-born neighbors could go for job counseling, medical exams, and advice. Addams believed that alleviating the symptoms of social problems was not enough; finding the causes of crime and poverty were equally important. By the end of the settlement house's first decade, she published *Hull-House Maps and Papers*, a pioneering study of the locale's major social problems, which marked the beginning of sociology as a distinct profession. By 1907 the institution had grown into a thirteen-building compound with an expanded social and political mission. Kept solvent through the generosity of local philanthropists, Addams stepped up her campaign to defuse the mounting hostility of second-generation immigrants to the newer arrivals and to insure equal justice for all under the law.

During her years at Hull House, Addams was also involved with the suffragist cause. In sisterhood with Lucretia Mott, Julia Ward Howe, Susan B. Anthony, and Carrie Chapman Catt, she called for the involvement of women in civic affairs, maintaining that women's ethical sensitivity and benevolent tendencies made them especially effective in addressing humanitarian concerns. To this end, she worked both regionally and nationally, serving from 1911 to 1914 as vice president of the National American Women Suffrage Association. During World War I Addams linked her feminist political agenda with her pacifism, serving in 1915 as chairperson of the International Congress of Women held at The Hague. Harassed in their home countries by pro-war factions and generally mocked for their naïveté, the assembly members sought unsuccessfully to convince neutral parties to serve as mediators between the warring factions without taking up arms themselves. To this end, a delegation of leaders from the Emergency Peace Foundation, including Addams, arranged for a meeting with President Wilson, who remained unconvinced by the pacifist arguments.

So, in fact, did much of America, and many of Addams's old cohorts swallowed hard and embraced Wilson's Fourteen Points. It was a harrowing time for Addams, who was assailed as a traitor for her stand against the draft, her objection to the persecution of aliens and foreign radicals, and her attempts to bring food to the German war victims. Her patriotism publicly doubted, she lost credibility with many financial backers and lost face with her fellow social reformers. Scorned by Theodore Roosevelt, whom she had helped elect, she was denounced by her own government as the "most dangerous woman in America." Plagued by a host of serious illnesses, she nevertheless pressed on, becoming president in 1919 of the Women's International League for Peace and Freedom. Formed when it appeared that the League of Nations would be powerless to offset the harsh provisions of the peace treaty, it was stamped as a Communist-front organization.

Though the receipt of the 1931 Nobel Peace Prize rehabilitated "Saint Jane," as her admirers called her, Addams was too ill to make the arduous trip to Stockholm to accept in person. But her work and her spirit had redefined community in America's cities.

ALI

MUHAMMAD

AT A TIME WHEN most of his peers were casting about for something to do with their lives, Cassius Clay had a lock on his. No one, he told whomever would listen, had been as great a fighter as he would become. Because of his sense of humor, most people thought he was joking. But Clay—who later renamed himself Muhammad Ali—would prove his prediction true, by becoming not only the world's three-time heavyweight champion but its most filmed and recognizable face.

It was a pretty face—a "beee-ooo-ti-ful" face, Ali loved to brag—and one the clever self-promoter was fast enough to protect from major damage during his two decades in the ring. Quick, enormously powerful, and as light on his feet as a leaf in a spring breeze, he started perfecting what would become known as the "Ali shuffle" at the tender age of twelve when his brand-new bicycle was stolen. When he told patrolman Joe Martin, who trained amateur fighters, that he would beat up the thief if he ever caught him, Martin suggested that the angry boy had better learn to defend himself first. Young Cassius took his advice, eventually taking on a grueling daily routine of sparring and shadowboxing, skipping rope, and hitting at the punching bag.

But Clay's victories in the ring weren't based just on sheer power. He was a disciplined boxer who, as early as his days at Louisville's Central High, maintained a Spartan lifestyle that excluded drinking, swearing, and womanizing and included drinking lots of garlic water, reading the Gospel, and going to bed early. Adopting the sweetness of his mother, Odessa, and shunning Cassius senior's roustabout reputation, he vowed to "be a clean and sparkling champion," and America's youth—black and white, but especially black—admired the fighter for his message.

Clay was a master of style and finesse, a thinking man's boxer who spent as much time developing his subtlety of movement as he did the deadly jabs and combinations that led him to an Olympic gold medal at age eighteen. He also excelled at unearthing his opponents' weaknesses, both pugilistic and personal. Unlike other boxers who only mouthed off during fights, the Louisville Lip wisecracked before, during, and after his matches, publicly teasing and trying to humiliate his opponents. The sport's most flamboyant showman loved to pinpoint the exact moment of his adversary's defeat. "They all must fall in the round I call" became his battle cry.

Clay's bravado and talent would earn him sixty million dollars in his lifetime and fill arenas with crowds that would have impressed P. T. Barnum. For his first big 1964 championship bout in Miami against Sonny Liston, he took home six hundred thousand dollars. It was a considerable sum for a twenty-two-year-old, a ninth-ranked contender, who had earned his chance to fight the reigning heavyweight champ by following Liston around the country in a battered old bus, calling him "the ugly bear." "I want Liston," Clay taunted his opponent in the press, claiming famously that he would "float like a butterfly, sting like a bee" once in the ring with him. He did just that, and Liston failed to answer the bell for round seven. The new champ soon had another surprise for the sporting world; inspired by black-rights activist Malcolm X, he had adopted the Muslim faith, exchanging his "slave name" for Muhammad Ali, or "Beloved of Allah."

In 1967, Ali's new beliefs made him a conscientious objector, and he publicly voiced his objection to the Vietnam War. A storm of protest followed, culminating in both a prison sentence and the nullification of his heavyweight title by the World Boxing Association that year. Deprived of his prime boxing years and millions of dollars in income, Ali nonetheless stood his ground. Surviving, but ultimately losing, his first attempt to regain the heavyweight title—his ferocious fifteen-round "Fight of the Century" against Joe Frazier in 1971—he came back to regain the title from Frazier in 1974.

Ali prevailed in other ways that have transcended the sport he so uniquely revived. Most importantly, maintained Thomas Hauser in his biography of the great boxer, "he reflected and shaped the social and political currents of the age in which he reigned." The Ali of the sixties "stood for the proposition that principles mattered, that equality among people was just and proper, that the war in Vietnam was wrong." Although he had experienced his share of racism— he was denied service in a Louisville diner right after his Olympic victory homecoming because he was "colored"—his brave idealism, his humanitarian work, and the strength of his personality earned him a hero's stature all over the globe.

With age, Ali's health was compromised by Parkinson's disease, which may have been brought on by "punch drunk" syndrome, the chronic encephalopathy frequently suffered by boxers. But the symptoms, including slowness of movement, poor balance, and a facial paralysis that slurred his speech, could not diminish the strength of his character. In 1996 Ali made a stunning appearance at the Summer Olympics, lighting the giant torch with a shaking hand before a television audience of over 3.5 billion. His spirituality deepened, the champion continued his devotion to Islam and to visiting children in hospital wards everywhere. His mission, something beyond the goal of victory at any cost, became preaching the lesson of love to a world that still adored him. As he said long ago, it is a lesson that has no color.

WOODY ALLEN

LIKE GERSHWIN OR ELLINGTON or his beloved Marx Brothers, Woody Allen is an American original. A comic, writer, playwright, director, actor and even jazz clarinetist, Allen's intelligence and wit animate all of his work. His mature movies, filmed under wraps and untitled until their release, are always stimulating and, when they are on the mark, masterpieces of ensemble acting and direction. Fiercely independent, he has long insisted on absolute control over any film he makes; neither big-budgeted nor star-powered, his work is a league apart from the majority of American movies produced in the last thirty years. His creation of an on-screen persona—a crafted pastiche of what would appear to be bits and pieces of the real Woody Allen—and his habit of casting his love interests as his leading ladies (among them, his ex-wife Louise Lasser, Diane Keaton, and Mia Farrow) gave him the latitude to produce a body of work which seems both intensely personal and, yet, at the same time, familiar and meaningful to his audiences. Ironically, this deliberate confusion of Allen the man and Allen on film, which he manipulated with great artistic success, damaged his career when, in the mid-1990s, his personal life came under intense scrutiny.

Unlike his on-screen persona—whose triumphs are always tempered by an equal number of failures—Woody Allen has always been, in his chosen fields, a prodigy. Born Allen Konigsberg in Brooklyn to Orthodox Jewish parents, he was a boy who very early on took refuge in the movie theater and found pleasure in music and magic. By the time he was a teenager, he was ghostwriting jokes for the celebrated program *Your Show of Shows* for such comics as Imogene Coca, Sid Caesar, Howard Morris, and Carl Reiner. After leaving college in 1953—at his parents' insistence, he had enrolled but was expelled from both New York University and the City College of New York for his academic performance—he joined Sid Caesar's staff.

By 1961, Allen, then only 26, was earning several thousand dollars a week writing comedy for television. Next, he turned to stand-up, becoming one of the top performers in clubs all over the country. Allen's persona seemed to mirror the insecurities of the sixties perfectly. As a writer, he began to flourish, writing for *The New Yorker* magazine, as his idol, S.J. Perleman had, producing books of short humor (*Getting Even, Without Feathers,* and *Side Effects*), and a hit play, "Don't Drink the Water" (1966).

His sense of comedy and timing revealed itself in a series of movies which pushed Allen in other directions; *What's New Pussycat?* (1965) showed him to be a master of slapstick (he both wrote and starred), while in *What's Up Tigerlily?* (1966) he dubbed manic dialogue over an inept Japanese spy thriller. By 1969, he was writer, director, and star of *Take the Money and Run.* Into the early 1970s, Allen continued to expand his satirical world view in films that combined parody, lighting-speed wit, and zinging one-liners: *Everything You Always Wanted to Know about Sex* (1972), *Sleeper* (1973), and *Love and Death* (1975).

Annie Hall (1977), perhaps his most popular film and arguably his best, showed audiences the serious side of his comedy. From its opening monologue—with Allen's Alvy Singer paying tribute to Groucho Marx, Sigmund Freud, and Annie Hall, the lost love of his life—to the voice-overs and subtitles which comment on the action of the movie itself, Allen created, within the framework of a romantic comedy, a picture about how the past and present connect. In the title role, Diane Keaton with her quirky WASP demeanor is the perfect foil to Allen's neurotic, Jewish intellectual.

Relationships—and the impossibility of sustaining them—continued to be the focus of Allen's art, from *Interiors* (1978) to *Manhattan* (1979), Allen's valentine to the city he lives in and adores. The stirring images of the city itself—its skyline and bridges set against the strains of Gershwin's "Rhapsody in Blue"—co-exist with the complicated and messy relationships of the people who live there. Allen's ability to direct what seems to be a seamless ensemble of actors—himself, Diane Keaton, Michael Murphy, Meryl Streep, and Mariel Hemingway—shines through this bittersweet portrait of love and intellect.

In the 1980s, Allen produced a string of highly personal films, among them *Stardust Memories* (1980), *A Midsummer Night's Sex Comedy* (1982), and *Zelig* (1983). His ability to create compelling women characters, already in evidence in *Annie Hall* and *Manhattan*, seemed to grow steadily with his new real life leading lady, actress Mia Farrow, who shone as the gum-chewing dreamer in *Broadway Danny Rose* (1984). In *Hannah and Her Sisters* (1984) and *Husbands and Wives* (1992), both starring Farrow, his focus on human relationships abandoned the protective aspects of humor. When Allen took up with Farrow's adopted daughter, whom he later married, the much publicized custody and other legal battles threatened to swamp his reputation and his career.

Allen has continued to make well-reviewed films such as *Bullets over Broadway* (1994), *Mighty Aphrodite* (1995), and *Deconstructing Harry* (1997) despite falling attendance at the theaters. In the end, though, it is Allen's work that prevails—his own singular and original vision of film, his unforgettable takes on sex, death, and therapy, filled with memorable dialogue, characters, and imagery. And then, of course, there is Allen's New York—its streets filled with people who are smart—talking and uncomprehending, driven and floundering, cynical and romantic by turns—which is as much a part of his legacy as anything else.

YASIR ARAFAT

UNTIL THE PEACE INITIATIVE of 1993, to Israel and the West, Palestinian leader Yasir Arafat was a terrorist whose defeat was devoutly desired. To his own people he promised to be a white knight of liberation, the shining soul of their dream for a restored homeland. Arafat has struggled in the service of an extremely difficult goal—the creation of a Palestinian state. From his terrorist beginnings to his rehabilitation as a statesman and spokesman for fellow Palestinians, Arafat has demonstrated his ability to change course in order to achieve that goal.

His activism began in 1948, when, as a student, he ran guns into Jerusalem from Egypt, arming Arabs who were fighting against the British army and Israeli defense force. It has been said that Arafat's businessman father moved his family to Cairo from Gaza after being accused of engaging in commerce with Zionists. Others believe Arafat was born in Cairo, where, after fighting against the triumphant Israelis, he would return in 1949 to study engineering. After a brief trip to Europe, he was not content simply to champion the Palestinian cause, and plotted against King Faisal in a conspiracy that exiled him from Egypt. In 1956 he co-founded an insurgent group he dubbed al-Fatah, "the conquest."

Despite its majestic name, al-Fatah was a small operation in an Arab war against the new state of Israel. Arafat, however, who had shown superior organizational talents training commandoes in Kuwait, now displayed a genius for maneuvering in tight quarters. While engaging in hit-and-run attacks against the Israelis, al-Fatah spent almost as much time ducking the angry soldiers of its host countries, who did not wish to be sucked into a war with the formidable Israeli defense force. Arafat was considered a loose cannon by the Palestinian Liberation Organization (PLO), which was created in 1964 to pull together Palestinian groups, but was really intended to be a tool of a confederation of Arab governments. Convinced of his own righteousness, he maneuvered for greater power while the Israelis mowed down his Fatah fighters, and fickle Arab sponsors played politics with his people.

In 1969 Arafat's plans bore their first fruit. He was elected chairman of the PLO and immediately mounted raids against Israel from neighboring Jordan. But he misjudged his own strength. In the fall of 1970, under pressure from Israel, King Hussein of Jordan moved against the PLO (in what was called the Black September purge), driving its commandos from Jordanian territory. Beleaguered by Israeli animosity, Arab perfidy, and the sense that the world was indifferent to its struggle, the PLO fragmented into splinter groups, which continued the campaign of terror. Arafat and the less visible chiefs of other PLO groups were blamed for introducing a horrified world to airline hijackings, attacks on schoolchildren, and the slaughter of Olympic athletes. The image of Arafat in his trademark *kaffujeh* began to instill fear and animosity in Western hearts.

Over the years, Arafat's confrontational style invited political disaster. At the United Nations, a uniformed Arafat appeared wearing a pistol holster. In 1982 PLO commandos at West Beirut, pushed to the sea by the Israelis, were evacuated under supervision of United Nations forces in a "victory" that celebrated little more than their survival of a nine-week siege. During the Gulf War of 1991 Arafat backed Saddam Hussein and then watched as Western and Arab armies quickly rolled over the hapless Iraqis. By 1993, with its Soviet sponsors gone and its Arab allies cool, the PLO was bankrupt, friendless, and unable to control the *intifada* that had wracked the occupied territories for five years.

Yet, at his career's nadir, Arafat somehow triumphed. The Islamic fundamentalism spreading in the Palestinian ranks made Arafat look relatively moderate to the Israeli leadership. The Israelis finally negotiated with Arafat. Soon he was at the White House shaking the hand of Yitzhak Rabin—with whom he would share the 1994 Nobel Peace Prize. The ancient city of Jericho became the center of an embryonic Palestinian state, and Arafat was photographed weeping at his homecoming in Gaza. The world, it seemed, believed that the peace process could succeed and that the promise of a Palestinian homeland could become a reality.

In 1995 Rabin was assassinated—not by an Arab extremist or PLO gunman, but by a right-wing Israeli, and the subsequent election fell to the right-wing group Likud and its Americanized leader, Benyamin Netanyahu. The new prime minister immediately put the brakes on the peace process, leaving Arafat to govern a legally and politically ambiguous region filled with angry, disappointed Palestinians. Governance proved to be even more difficult than armed rebellion. Intensely corrupt, the Palestine Authority demonstrated little ability to manage civic projects or anything else. Many Palestinians see their new government as a melancholy reprise of traditional Arab strongman politics, destining Palestine to a future as a Middle East dictatorship. Meanwhile, the rest of the world looks on, hoping to see the peace process which was initiated in 1993 realized.

HANNAH ARENDT

ONE OF THE TWENTIETH century's most brilliant, original, and controversial political thinkers, and a refugee from Hitler's Germany, Hannah Arendt is most widely remembered for her concept, "the banality of evil." Reporting for *The New Yorker* in 1961 on the trial of Nazi Adolph Eichmann, she argued that while it would be comforting to believe that Eichmann was a monster, in fact he was "terrifyingly normal," a typical bureaucrat pursuing fulfillment in his career, who carried out his duties with vigor and commitment and without any particular hatred for Jews. He was no demon and no psychopath, but rather an ordinary man "unable to tell right from wrong." In the same account (later published as a book, *Eichmann in Jerusalem: A Report on the Banality of Evil*), she enraged her fellow Jews by saying that European Jews "collaborated" in their own destruction by registering and handing over other Jews to the Nazis instead of organizing for resistance.

Born in Hanover, Germany, to prosperous, nonpracticing Jews of East Prussian ancestry, Arendt's childhood was marked by the glorification of German culture amid growing anti-Semitism. Intensely private and precocious, the beautiful teenager entered Marburg University in 1924. There she promptly succumbed to the spell of the teacher who became her great love: Martin Heidegger, the famed existentialist philosopher. She carried on a clandestine and passionate affair with the married professor for four years. Though she apparently severed the relationship, her correspondence makes clear that when the war was over she resumed her friendship with the man she called her "hidden king," and promoted his work in spite of the fact that he had supported Hitler in the beginning years of the Third Reich. The ethical ramifications of her relationship with Heidegger—what Arendt herself called their "star-crossed" love—have been a scholarly concern.

Later, at the University of Heidelberg, under the tutelage of Karl Jaspers—a philosopher and psychiatrist who served as friend and father figure, and whom Arendt called "the conscience of Germany"—she wrote her doctoral dissertation on love as conceived by St. Augustine, the most prominent of the church fathers. It was an unconventional subject for a young scholar intent on defining the extent of her Jewishness, but then Arendt's thoughts and actions were never bound by convention.

In 1929, Arendt entered a brief marriage with Gunther Stern, a fellow student. When Hitler assumed power in 1933, they fled with her mother via Czechoslovakia to Paris, where Arendt continued her writing and performed social work for Jewish organizations. She and Stern divorced in 1936, when she met Heinrich Blucher, a Marxist critic of working-class origins. After six weeks of internment in a camp in the south of France,

Arendt—who had never before considered emigration—escaped in 1941 with her mother and Blucher to New York. To help support them all, she wrote articles for such prestigious journals as *The Nation, The New York Review of Books,* and *Partisan Review* and taught part-time at Brooklyn College. It was during this period that she began her enormously influential book *The Origins of Totalitarianism* (1951), a three-part work exploring the link between the imperialism and anti-Semitism of the nineteenth century and the two most dominant twentieth-century forms of totalitarianism, National Socialism and Communism. For Arendt, Hitler and Stalin personified the crisis of the modern age, leaders who rose to power by exploiting the "organized loneliness" of mass society. This societal alienation and fragmentation had left the common man extremely vulnerable to the ideologies of modern tyrants. The physical expression of these tyrannies, which, she observed, had no precedent in classical despotism, was the concentration camp, a novel and "radical" evil. Her stature increased with the publication of *The Human Condition* (1958), lauded by many as a masterpiece of political philosophy.

Arendt became the first female appointed to a full professorship at Princeton in 1959, and a visiting professor at Columbia University the following year. In the 1960s, she taught at the University of Chicago and the New School for Social Research. During this time, she edited the English version of Karl Jaspers's two-volume work *The Great Philosophers,* and lectured widely, visiting with Heidegger and Jaspers when tours took her to Europe. Though she wanted nothing more than to return to her philosophical inquiries—especially the book she was working on called *The Life of the Mind,* a companion to *The Human Condition*—Arendt found herself writing political commentary on the turbulent events of the seventies. Her mind defied categorization; her writings could never be neatly classified as either conservative or liberal. Equally, she was drawn to Zionism but repulsed by Israel's militant chauvinism. For her part, Arendt lived the life of what she called the "politically conscious pariah."

In 1975, heart failure cut short Arendt's work on the second volume of *The Life of the Mind,* silencing one of the modern era's most learned and passionate voices. One of the century's most active intellectuals, her presence in the era's public forum elevated the level of discourse. Her writings on the Holocaust and totalitarianism established Arendt as a great political thinker; her views, while often controversial, were always stimulating. Few other twentieth-century philosophers possessed the intellect, the integrity, and the moral stature to stand as her equal.

LOUIS ARMSTRONG

LIKE A FIERY BRASS SUN, Louis "Satchmo" Armstrong's trumpet playing burned at the core of American music. His innovative solos, improvised like hip conversations, revolutionized the way jazz sounded and were the signposts for every great experimental horn player from Dizzy Gillespie to Miles Davis. With his wide grin and husky warble, as warm as the lullaby of a doting father, he was the epitome of the great entertainer who is also a great artist.

Armstrong was born on August 4, 1901, to a father who worked in a turpentine factory and a mother who lived for a time in New Orleans's notorious Storyville district. His quest for independence—a quintessential American one—started in a back-alley neighborhood filled with honky-tonks, knife fights, and the sounds of an emerging musical phenomenon: a hybrid of African rhythms, European tonalities, and American folk elements called jazz. Indeed, the word is thought to have originated in the steamy streets of Armstrong's hometown as slang for sex.

By 1912, the roly-poly eleven-year-old was strolling in this nighttown as one voice in a barbershop quartet. When he wasn't singing, he indulged in enough juvenile delinquency to land himself in a reform school known as the Colored Waifs Home. There, a couple of sympathetic teachers taught him drums, bugle, and cornet. Armstrong took to the horn immediately. He practiced diligently and was soon befriended by the jazz cornetist and composer Joe "King" Oliver, who tutored and encouraged the young player. In 1918, thanks to Oliver's recommendation, he joined the great trombonist Kid Ory's jazz band. Armstrong's power, range, and subtle syncopation drew packed audiences in the boîtes of the Vieux Carré. When King Oliver summoned Armstrong to Chicago in the early twenties to play second cornet in his Creole Jazz Band, the ambitious youth raced upriver and made the first of thousands of records, among them 1927's raunchy "Potato Head Blues" and 1928's sweetly charged "I Can't Give You Anything but Love."

Though he later became world famous for his raspy renditions of such popular show tunes as "Hello Dolly!," the younger Armstrong was no less inventive as a singer than as a horn man. He created the wordless improvisational singing technique known as scat (widely used in the later bebop era) when he dropped the lyric sheet during a recording session and had to fill in with nonsense syllables. Jazz writers also credit Armstrong's delivery with influencing singers from Bing Crosby to Ella Fitzgerald. But it was as a horn player par excellence that he changed music, blowing legato phrases in clever rhythm when other horn players were still playing the staccato style whose rat-a-tat phrasing derived from the military bugle. Armstrong twisted and stretched the melodic line like taffy, adding upper notes that were only suggested by the chord changes and some that weren't in the song at all. His discoveries were often imitated, never surpassed, and no less an authority than Miles Davis commented that no trumpet player could ever play anything Louis Armstrong hadn't already played. But whatever innovations he introduced were guided by his sense of taste and balance.

In 1924 Armstrong left Oliver to join Fletcher Henderson's big band in New York, recording "How Come You Do Me Like You Do?" and "Alabamy Bound," among others. For years he was a major force in American jazz. His work took him to Europe, where a British music critic whose ears could not decode Armstrong's Southern accent rendered the trumpet player's nickname, "Satchelmouth," as "Satchmo." He was on the top of his world, but it eventually proved too small for him. His need to entertain as many people as possible led him to dismay jazz aficionados as he embraced the show business and popular music that were always at the root of his art. He triumphed in Hollywood, where he was featured in such films as 1936's *Pennies from Heaven*, 1951's *The Strip*, 1954's *The Glenn Miller Story*, and 1956's *High Society*. When he was asked by the U.S. State Department to tour the world as "goodwill ambassador" in the fifties and sixties, Armstrong soon found himself playing in such diverse venues as a concert for one hundred thousand jazz fans in Ghana, where he greeted the country's monarch with a friendly "Whattaya say, King!"

His evident joy in making other people happy was so great that later in his career blacks with short memories and tin ears derided him as an Uncle Tom. But Armstrong was no accommodationist. Starting in 1956, for almost a decade he refused to play in New Orleans, where Louisiana law forbade racially mixed groups from performing together. The vicious beatings of civil rights marchers in Alabama moved him to observe angrily, "They'd beat Jesus if he was black and marching."

Perhaps what his enemies resented was his lack of resentment. But no one as connected as he was to the Great Cornucopia could be unhappy. If Armstrong wasn't a wealthy man, it was partly because, to the despair of his managers, he insisted on giving away thousands to anyone who asked. "He was born poor, he died rich, and he never hurt anyone along the way," remarked his fellow jazz giant Duke Ellington when Satchmo died. And if he was a bit of a hypochondriac, salving himself with mysterious potions before going onstage, none of his friends ever minded: He cured the world of some of the weariness that ailed it.

NEIL ARMSTRONG

IT MAY BE ONE of the supreme ironies of the twentieth century that the greatest achievement in the peaceful exploration of the cosmos—America's 1969 landing on the moon—came as the result of a cold war between the United States and the Soviet Union, in which even space loomed as a potential battlefield. Heeding President John F. Kennedy's call to make a lunar expedition an urgent national goal, America chose a civilian pilot to be the first human being to set foot on the moon. And in doing so, Neil Armstrong became an Everyman pioneer who stood for all humankind in its ongoing effort to understand the universe.

The road that led Neil Armstrong to the moon's Sea of Tranquillity began in the Ohio town of Wapakoneta, where his father had settled after roaming the state in a variety of public-service positions. From his early youth Armstrong was fascinated by flight; he took his first ride on an airplane at age six, in his teens he saved money from his after-school job to pay for flying lessons. Quiet and serious, he dreamed about flying, built model airplanes, and devoted himself to flight the way other boys devoted themselves to baseball.

In 1947, pilot's license in hand, Armstrong attended Indiana's Purdue University as a naval air cadet. Two years later he was called to active duty in Korea, where, as a fighter pilot, he was shot down and won three Air Medals. After his tour of duty, he returned to Purdue to teach, and played horn in a jazz band to make ends meet; but when he earned his bachelor's degree in 1955, Armstrong quit to become a civilian research pilot for the National Advisory Committee for Aeronautics (NACA), first in Ohio and then at Edwards Air Force Base in California. While NACA evolved into NASA—the National Aeronautics and Space Administration—Armstrong flew the super-fast aircraft that were being developed for both military use and space exploration. As pilot for the X-15 rocket plane, he reached an altitude of forty miles above the surface of the earth. But for Armstrong, forty miles wasn't high enough.

Seven years after becoming a test pilot, Armstrong applied for the astronaut-training program and was accepted. He piloted the *Gemini VIII* mission in 1966, and that March he performed the first manual docking maneuver in space. When a module malfunction sent his spacecraft, locked to a large rocket, into a potentially fatal spin, Armstrong manually unlocked the two components and righted his ship. He piloted it to an emergency crash splashdown in the ocean, showing considerable cool throughout the adventure. In 1968 he parachuted safely from only two hundred feet above the ground when a moon-landing training craft he had been flying crashed.

It was such grace under pressure that recommended Armstrong for the dangerous and difficult task of flying to the moon. The allure of a trip to the silver sphere had seduced the ancients and inspired writers through the centuries to imagine how such a trip might be accomplished. When the fantasy became reality, NASA sent the moon mission aloft using a huge *Saturn V* rocket. The American team figured out how to link and unlink the command module *Columbia* with the lunar landing module *Eagle,* how to land *Eagle* on the moon and get it back again, and how to slingshot the whole elaborate machine to the moon using the momentum of the earth's own rotation. After working out every detail, there was still one thing that worried the scientists: No one knew whether the surface of the moon was solid or a mile-deep layer of soft, dry quicksand that would swallow the astronauts and their craft in one horrifying gulp.

On July 16, 1969, *Apollo 11,* carrying commander Armstrong and colleagues Edwin "Buzz" Aldrin and Michael Collins, broke free of Earth's embrace. Even traveling at seven miles per second, it took three days for the Americans to reach the moon. Collins piloted the command module while mission commander Armstrong and copilot Aldrin descended to the surface in the *Eagle.* When the computer landing program threatened to deposit the module in a huge crater circled by boulders, Armstrong manually piloted the craft to safe harbor on a plain near the Sea of Tranquillity. Only seconds' worth of fuel remained before they reached the mission's mandatory abort limit. On July 20, 1969, Armstrong—who as senior officer had the honor of being the first person to set foot upon the moon—hopped from the module's ladder to the planet's cold, rock-strewn surface. Few will ever forget his simple, moving declaration: "One small step for man, one giant leap for mankind."

After Aldrin also descended, the two bounced along in the eerie light, looking, to more than 600 million television viewers, like two overgrown children in huge white snowsuits. Their boots made visible footprints in the chalky moondust.

Years later, after he had returned to Earth and to a new role as college professor, Armstrong let his accomplishments speak for themselves, shunning interviews and discouraging lionization. But the images of him and Aldrin, buoyant in gravity one-sixth that of the earth, remain in our minds. In a final gesture, he planted an American flag on the lunar surface, an act some called jingoistic. But Armstrong, such critics may have forgotten, also left behind a plaque. It read WE CAME IN PEACE FOR ALL MANKIND.

FRED ASTAIRE

AS ELEGANT AND COOL AS CHAMPAGNE, Fred Astaire was the most accomplished popular dancer of the century. Debonair and blessed with an agile grace unmatched by even the most talented of his contemporaries, Astaire came to epitomize an era in film in which music, dress, and movement were one charming, sophisticated swirl.

He was born Frederick Austerlitz to a former Austrian army officer who had moved with his vivacious wife to Omaha, Nebraska. The stage-struck senior Austerlitz soon decreed that little Fred and his older sister, Adele, should decamp with their mother to New York City to study dance. By the time the boy was seven, Fred and Adele—who adopted the professional name Astaire—were touring the grueling vaudeville circuit with their dance routine. Years of cheap hotels and rattly trains finally paid off in 1917, when the pair made their Broadway debut in *Over the Top*. The following year, they had their first hit, *The Passing Show of 1918*. Within five years, they were international stars, equally at home in New York or London. With *Lady, Be Good!* (1924), *Smiles* (1930), and the smash hit *The Band Wagon* (1931), they were elevated to show business royalty. Embraced by high society, Adele, the more frivolous Astaire, met and married Lord Charles Canvendish in 1932, leaving the stage forever. Her brother was shaken by her defection, but soldiered on, making a screen test that resulted in the now-famous assessment by a Goldwyn studio executive: "Can't act. Can't sing. Slightly bald. Can dance a little." Despite this dismissive appraisal, Astaire was cast with Joan Crawford in his first movie, *Dancing Lady* (1933). That same year he married Phyllis Livingston Potter.

The lithe, razor-thin Astaire was first paired with the sparkling blonde Ginger Rogers in a featured role in *Flying Down to Rio* (1933); the following year, in *The Gay Divorcée*, they received star billing. The duo appeared together in ten films over seventeen years, their on-screen chemistry and seemingly effortless dance routines—including such Hollywood classics as "Night and Day" (from *The Gay Divorcée)* and "Cheek to Cheek (from 1934's *Top Hat)*—obscuring a drearier reality of relentless rehearsal and personal friction. But they were box-office magic. "He gave her class," claimed actress Katharine Hepburn, "and she gave him sex."

Astaire's impeccable timing was perfect for carrying light comedy, as was his urbane body language and expressive face. He amazed audiences with his faultless carriage during even the most athletic numbers and his command of every form of popular dance from tap to ballroom. His extraordinary choreography sprang from his conviction that dance was not merely a series of steps, but the expression of one single, unifying idea or story. The result, in the view of many critics, was high

art, a subtlety of expression on a par with that of ballet master Rudolf Nureyev.

When not dancing, and sometimes while dancing, Astaire sang in a pleasant, weak tenor that was well suited for the featherlike material it was asked to carry. The great songwriter Irving Berlin, in fact, once remarked that he would rather have Fred Astaire introduce his songs than anyone else. Astaire's own composition, "I'm Building Up to an Awful Letdown" made "America's Hit Parade" in 1938.

After *The Story of Vernon and Irene Castle* (1939), Rogers left to pursue drama, and Astaire went on to make a series of films with less romantically engaging partners. The post-Rogers period did, however, include memorable routines with Rita Hayworth in *You'll Never Get Rich* (1941) and *You Were Never Lovelier* (1942), and an extraordinary pairing with crooner Bing Crosby in *Holiday Inn* (1942).

In 1946, with no new dance partners and the more muscular rival Gene Kelly coming on strong, Astaire retired from film. Two years later, responding to a petition circulated by disappointed fans, he made a comeback when he replaced the injured Kelly in *Easter Parade* with Judy Garland. In 1949, he received a special Academy Award for his contribution to film, the same year he was slated to make *The Barkleys of Broadway* with Garland. When the erratic singer fell ill, her surprise replacement turned out to be Ginger Rogers—a reunion that assured a hit. Two years later, in *Royal Wedding*, Astaire filmed one of the cinema's most astonishing dance numbers, in which camera illusions made him appear to dance on the ceiling.

In 1953, as his wife battled cancer, he paired with the lithesome Cyd Charisse in the film version of *The Band Wagon*. When the mother of his two children finally died, Astaire embarked on nearly thirty years of widowhood. Less a dancer than an actor now, he gave terpsichore one last go as a thoroughly roguish Irishman in *Finian's Rainbow* (1968). It was his final dance on film.

In 1974 he was nominated for an Academy Award for best supporting actor in *The Towering Inferno*. That same year, the television showing of the film *That's Entertainment* sparked a revival of the Astaire-Rogers films, with Astaire himself co-narrating the sequel. In 1981 he was given the American Film Institute's Life Achievement Award.

By then, the publicity-shy, intensely private Astaire was eighty-two. The previous year, he had married again. His bride, jockey Robyn Smith, was forty-six years his junior and shared his passion for horses. Astaire seemed not to notice the age difference, and in any case he was happy. He died that way in 1987, a strong contender for the title "Entertainer of the Century."

JOSEPHINE BAKER

PART PEACOCK, PART NIGHTINGALE, the exotically plumed Josephine Baker strutted the world's stages with an exuberant sensuality that helped give the twenties and thirties such a lurid reputation. The leggy nineteen-year-old dancer, who would become one of the century's most successful entertainers, hit Paris like a bolt of lightning. In her earliest theatrical incarnation, *La Revue Nègre* (1925), Baker epitomized the comedienne as tease. A consummate mimic who could mug as well as wiggle, she danced a boisterous Charleston and shimmied topless in one of the most famous flimsy costumes of all time—a G-string decorated with a fringe of bananas. Later, as she toured Europe and America with a coterie of suitors and trunkfuls of Diors, her naughtiness was shaped into an integral part of an erotic stage persona.

Her wild reputation was fueled by Baker's cheerful promiscuity and her penchant for jungle themes in her act. But the creator of the scandalous "La Danse de Sauvage," who strolled down the Champs-Elysées with a live leopard on a leash, reacted with clenched teeth when confronted with the era's clichés regarding black female entertainers. When asked why she performed so little in her native country, she commented that Americans would make her "sing mammy songs." She lived her opposition to racism by adopting a family of twelve mixed-race orphans and by fighting Nazism as a member of the French Resistance; deeply committed to her beliefs, she involved herself in the American Civil Rights Movement in the sixties, standing proudly beside Martin Luther King in the historic March on Washington.

Baker's chameleonlike public personality was a product of a background so fragmented and traumatic that the entertainer herself turned out five contradictory autobiographies. What is undeviating in all her accounts, however, is that her childhood in Saint Louis was an acid bath of poverty, abuse, and discrimination. Abandoned by an unknown father and ignored by a mother who favored her younger children, Josephine was sent to work as a live-in maid for wealthy white families when she was only seven. Her first employer scalded her hands as punishment for an innocent mistake, and the second tried to molest her. At eleven, the rebellious child witnessed the famous 1917 race riots in her hometown of East Saint Louis, in which thirty-nine African-Americans were killed trying to run across a bridge to safety. She told an interviewer many years later, "I have been running ever since."

Baker started dancing, she once joked, "to keep warm." Married to the first of five husbands at thirteen, she got her big break when she took the place of an ailing chorus girl in a touring vaudeville group called the DixieSteppers. She clowned outrageously and stole the show. After traveling with a 1924 production of *The Chocolate Dandies* and dancing in New York revues, she was sent to Paris by a wealthy female impresario who was financing an all-black show for European audiences. When the producers of *La Revue Nègre* asked her to perform nude, all of Paris came to see the notorious queen of *le jazz hot*. She received marriage offers by the hundreds and the adoration of the city's intelligentsia and beau monde. Picasso rhapsodized about the new star of the Folies-Bergère, calling her "the Nefertiti of now"; Georges Simenon courted her; Pirandello designed for her. A flashy style setter, she induced many of the era's fashionable women to wear her perfume and to use Le Bakerfix to set their new helmetlike coiffures.

"The Black Venus" quickly adapted to her newfound celebrity, aided by her manager and second husband, Pepito Abatino, who found a tutor to coach her in the necessary social skills for her new role as sophisticated hostess to the international set. A recording contract was followed by movie appearances, first in *Zou-Zou* (1934) and, a year later, in *Princesse Tam-Tam*. But Baker's appeal to European audiences could not be duplicated in America; when she returned in 1936 to star in the Ziegfeld Follies, the cultural antagonism toward "uppity" black entertainers—not to mention the daily racism in hotels and restaurants—sent her packing.

During World War II Baker distinguished herself as a spy for the Deuxième Bureau (her husband, a French Jew, and she, as an African-American, were both vulnerable to Nazi roundups) and as a tireless entertainer of Allied troops. Moving back to Paris after four years in Morocco, the Bird of Paradise's life became increasingly difficult. Famously inept with money, she staged endless farewell performances and comebacks to support her costly adopted family, then retreated moodily into herself. When she and her "Rainbow Tribe" were finally evicted from her château, another American expatriate, Princess Grace of Monaco, came to her aid, financing a villa near Monaco to house Baker and her brood. She continued to perform off and on, despite a heart attack in 1964. Her final resurrection at age sixty-nine was in a 1975 music-hall revue entitled *Josephine*, a pastiche of set pieces from Baker's eventful life. Days after her last performance, she died.

America, which had treated Baker so shabbily, largely ignored her passing. But the French, who had awarded her the Médaille de la Résistance and the Croix de Guerre, and had made her a Chevalier of the Légion d'honneur, poured into the streets surrounding the Church of the Madeleine. She had shared her colorful fantasies with a war-weary nation starved for gaiety. Her adopted country returned the gift by bidding farewell with an honor guard and a twenty-one-gun salute.

LUCILLE BALL

THE TITLE OF HER smash hit television series, *I Love Lucy* — and the show's heart-shaped logo—summed it all up. Everyone adored Lucy. Irrepressible and energetic, America's scatter-brained housewife kept the country laughing with her exaggerated mugging and no-way-out adventures. And everyone was no less crazy about Lucille Ball, the vivacious redhead who played her. In fact, the two were sometimes hard to separate. Ball's on-screen husband, a Cuban bandleader named Ricky Ricardo, was in real life her husband, a Cuban bandleader named Desi Arnaz, and the content of the show often veered close to their own lives. When Lucille Ball was pregnant, Lucy was, too. In one of TV's most watched episodes, the actress gave birth to her son Desiderio in a Los Angeles hospital while Lucy was delivering "Little Ricky" in prime time. The Hollywood couple's volatile marriage, with its frequent separations and reconciliations, was also reflected—in a much sanitized version—in Lucy and Ricky's on-screen quarrels.

A good cast of characters, great comic timing, and the heroine's naïveté and vulnerability, accounted for much of *I Love Lucy's* tremendous appeal. Many of Lucy's escapades—whether playing a confused Santa, a peasant grape squasher, or an inexperienced worker dipping chocolates in a candy factory—centered on the character's indomitable desire to break into show business, a goal Ball set for herself when she was a fifteen-year-old drama school student. *I Love Lucy* ended its original broadcasts on May 6, 1957, after 179 episodes, and Lucy was successively reincarnated in *The Lucy Show* and *Here's Lucy*. According to *TV Guide*, the longevity made possible by the phenomena of reruns and worldwide syndication insured that Ball had been seen "by more people, more often, than the face of any human being who ever lived."

Her success was a triumph for the stage-struck hopeful from Jamestown, New York, whom theatrical pros initially dismissed as an attractive no-talent. Ball ignored their assessment and persisted, though she faced a wall of rejection on Broadway. Supporting herself by working at a soda fountain and as a model for Hattie Carnegie—briefly calling herself Diane Belmont—she finally got a break in 1933, when she was chosen as one of the Goldwyn Girls in *Roman Scandals*. Eventually, after endless walk-ons, Ball found a secure, if uninspired, home at RKO, where she became "Queen of the Bs."

A stunning blonde with a voluptuous body, Ball began to be offered more and more comedic roles. Achieving real visibility for the first time in *Stage Door*, a 1937 release in which she co-starred with Katharine Hepburn, she shone as the comic lead in three films the following year: *Go Chase Yourself, The Affairs of Annabel,* and *Annabel Takes the Tour*. In 1938 she also got the chance to work with the Marx Brothers in *Room Service*, the first of her many instructive experiences with such legendary laugh-makers as Buster Keaton, Bert Lahr, Red Skelton, and Bob Hope, her co-star in later films like *Sorrowful Jones* (1949) and *Fancy Pants* (1950). From these masters of slapstick, Ball learned doubletakes, pratfalls, and perfect timing, as well as a repertoire of goofy expressions and a hilarious physicality she would later adapt so inimitably to the small screen.

In 1940, while portraying a pampered heiress in *Too Many Girls,* Ball fell instantly for the handsome musician playing the part of a football star hired to protect her. Some six years older than he, she married Desi Arnaz, that same year. They bought a ranch in Chatsworth, California, which reminded Arnaz of the *ranchos* of Cuba, and raised two children. The union was rocky from the start, but it led to entertainment history. Ball had been lobbying CBS to let Desi star with her in a TV show, but they didn't think his Cuban accent would play to the heartland. So the couple formed their own production company and hit the road to prove that Mr. and Mrs. America would accept the offbeat comedy duo. America did, and CBS financed a pilot. Desperate for material for the early episodes, the two cannibalized Ball's successful forties radio show, *My Favorite Husband,* doctoring the scripts as necessary to fit the new medium. Gambling the show might only last a season, the network granted Lucy and Desi all revenue from repeat broadcasts; it was a costly miscalculation, making Desilu Productions one of the most profitable entities in the history of television—and Lucille Ball its first powerful female executive. The couple also made technical history by filming the show using three cameras simultaneously, which allowed much more flexibility than the usual one-camera technique. During the heyday of *I Love Lucy,* Ball, like many entertainers of the fifties, was called before the House Un-American Activities Committee, to answer charges that she had registered to vote in 1936 as a member of the Communist Party. She explained that she had done so to make her socialist grandfather happy, and remarkably, HUAC cleared her name immediately.

Ball divorced Desi in 1960 and married comedian Gary Morton. A few years later, she bought out Arnaz's interest in Desilu, going on to produce both the original *Star Trek* and *Mission Impossible* television series. She sold the company in 1967 to Gulf & Western for seventeen million dollars. It was a typically shrewd move for the actress-cum-businesswoman, though a bank account was never what the career-driven comedienne was all about. She missed Lucy, she told *Rolling Stone* magazine a few years before her death. Looking back over her career, Ball also insisted that she was never funny. "What I am," she said, "is brave."

ROGER BANNISTER

IN 1954, THE WORLD record for the men's one mile was four minutes and one and four-tenths seconds, set nine years before by Swedish miler Gunder Haegg. (The previous record, nine seconds slower, had been set twenty-two years prior to that.) At the time, many believed that anything under four minutes was physically impossible. And because it was imagined to be so, it was.

Of all the amateur track stars of the day who were trying to breach that seemingly insurmountable psychological barrier, that final invisible wall, none was more determined than a young British doctor named Roger Bannister. Tall, pale, diffident, the skinny Oxonian with an upper-class accent seemed at first glance an unlikely candidate. In marked contrast to his colleagues on the cinders, Bannister did not like to run more than five races a year, and he was loath to practice close to a race day. But he imagined the possibility of triumph more clearly than anyone else, and that—plus an intense will to win and an enormous amount of intelligent hard work—made possible a giant leap forward in the psychology of sports.

Roger Bannister was born at Harrow on the Hill, England, to a treasury official and his wife. Fear of rejection at the City of Bath Boys' School led him to take up athletics as a way of belonging. He won his first race at age thirteen, and when he went on to University College School in London, he found in himself what one commentator later called a talent for "sudden and abnormal athletic effort." Bannister's own recollection was simpler and more telling: "Nobody could have wanted to run more than I did."

In 1946, while commencing medical studies at Exeter College, Oxford, he pursued his interest in track and field, securing a lowly spot on the university squad. In his first meet, he ran the mile in a leisurely 4:30.8, almost half a minute off Haegg's mark, in a sport where half a second is a lifetime. His career after that race would be one steady, implacable assault on the clock.

Two years later, Bannister, now captain of a joint Oxford-Cambridge team, raced against Princeton and Cornell in the United States, this time finishing in 4:11.01. The next year he shaved almost two seconds off that mark, posting a 4:09.9. In Philadelphia in 1951—still carrying a full load as a medical student at London's St. Mary's Hospital—he knocked it down to 4:08.3. During this period, Bannister studied his own body's limits scientifically, running himself to exhaustion on a treadmill every day while hooked up to a device that measured the buildup of lactic acid in the muscles. But his methods may have amounted to overtraining; his disappointing fourth-place finish in the 1500 meters at the 1952 Olympic Games led him to shun racing for a year while he built up his endurance through special exercises.

In 1953 he returned to competition with a 4:03.6 mile at Iffley Road, breaking the British national record. In June of that year he took an invitational race at Motspur Park, Surrey, with a time of 4:02.0—then the third-fastest time recorded anywhere, six-tenths of a second shy of Haegg's feat, but still two long seconds short of the shining goal. But the Amateur Athletic Association sniffed that Motspur was not a real meet and declined to recognize his accomplishment. Bannister went into intensified training with runners Chris Chataway and Chris Brasher, who had volunteered to pace the young doctor in his next attempt at the record. He rested for a full five days before the event, and on May 6, 1954, the day chosen for attempting the feat, he went to work at the hospital as usual, sharpening his running spikes on a grindstone in the laboratory.

That afternoon, he waited as long as he could for the wind to die down at Iffley Road track before the gun sent him on his way. With Chataway and Brasher setting a blistering pace, Bannister scorched the track in 3:59.4, including a whippet-fast 0:58.9 time in the last quarter-mile. His strong finishing kick had prevailed over the restraining hand of time. The great barrier of the four-minute mile was shattered at last.

Bannister would go on to do even better, running 3:58.08 against Australian archrival John Landy at the British Empire and Commonwealth Games in Vancouver that same year. He later remarked that breaking the four-minute mile was nothing compared to the pleasure of beating Landy. In 1955 he received a knighthood, and that same year became house surgeon at Radcliffe Infirmary at Oxford. He later moved to Hammersmith Hospital in London.

A neurologist and sports physiologist of renown, Sir Roger made headlines and deliberately stirred debate when he suggested in 1995 that blacks had physiological advantages that predisposed them to being good athletes. Far from considering this a racist remark, Sir Roger simply thought he was approaching the issue in the same way he solved the problems of running fast—objectively.

As 1997 closed, the last best time in the mile was 3:44.39, which was posted in 1993. Forty-four years had elapsed, with all its attendant improvements in equipment, training and running surfaces—not to mention the bodies of runners—and still only fifteen seconds lay between Bannister, with his primitive shoes, and the most recent champion. Fifteen seconds is, of course, a long time in track. Nevertheless, with typical optimism, Roger Bannister predicts that in the twenty-first century, the record to be shattered will be 3:30.0.

BARDOT

BRIGITTE

IN 1956, IN THE FILM *Et Dieu créa la femme (And God Created Woman)*, the twentieth century met the sex kitten. Part guileless innocent, part mature seductress, Brigitte Bardot helped define the era's sexuality—especially its male fantasies—with her on-and off-screen portrayal of a liberated child of nature, reveling in her sensuality and her exquisitely proportioned body. When the risqué film debuted internationally, women everywhere struggled to achieve the Bardot look: the petulant frosted-pink lips, the heavy false eyelashes, the skimpy ingénue clothing, and the morning-after tumble of wild blonde hair. The nearly vacant but come-hither stare was essential, too. The opposite of mere availability and vapidity, it was meant to telegraph an erotic acquiescence usually encountered only in dreams.

By midcareer, sculpted busts of Brigitte Bardot wearing the Phrygian hat of Marianne, the traditional symbol of the French Republic, were appearing in official *bureaux* throughout France. Radical party leader Jean-Jacques Servan Schreiber, echoing Bardot's popularity among the nation's intelligentsia, urged his countrymen to "be proud of her, of Roquefort cheese, and of Bordeaux wine" because of the triumvirate's immense export value. Culture maven Jean Cocteau called her "a pouting sphinx but with perfect curves."

Bardolatry lasted for decades, while the memorable nymphet made numerous forgettable films and vied only with the American star Marilyn Monroe for the title of international sex goddess. The lightweight French blonde was well suited for the role, escapading her life away in the sunny Côte d'Azur tourist haven of Saint-Tropez—and never driving herself, like her rival Monroe, with ambitions of being a great actress.

This is not to say that Bardot did not torture herself. From her initial appearance in 1950 at the age of fifteen on the cover of French *Elle,* she was obsessed with a fear of disfigurement. As she aged, she developed a morbid fascination with death, which she temporarily escaped with frequent bouts of drinking. Excruciatingly aware that she was losing the ripe allure that was responsible for the attention she got from men, "B.B." approached her forties, then her fifties, with a deepening dread. "It's the decomposition that gets me," she complained in a 1983 documentary aired on French television. "You spend your whole life looking after your body. And then you rot away, like that!" Her despondency led to many suicide attempts, one of the most notable occurring nine months after the birth of her son, Nicolas; another, tellingly, was on the evening of her forty-ninth birthday. But every birthday, her first husband Roger Vadim once remarked, was "a test for her, and it's usually a desperate time."

Vadim knew the private Bardot perhaps better than anyone. The French director had invented the public Bardot himself,

coaching the prim and properly raised schoolgirl in the coquettish mannerisms that would become her trademark, and creating a role for her that would raise exhibitionism to an art form. *And God Created Woman* was a light confection, a silly but sizzling story about a sex-crazed, guiltless gamine set against the warm lushness of the Riviera. The twenty-two-year-old beauty acted out a series of shockingly explicit—for the time—but brilliantly directed love scenes that exploited her physical charms in the most sophisticated manner possible. Bardot had already been in some sixteen minor films, but it took Vadim to see her potential as a symbol for a new kind of sexual permissiveness and then to package what he saw. For its release in the United States, softened versions of the film's daring episodes were prepared, problems with the censors were played up, and the press just happened to learn that not much acting was involved in her love scenes with screenmate Jean-Louis Trintignant.

The year after she made her English-language debut in the 1956 film *Helen of Troy,* she divorced Vadim. In 1959 she married Jacques Charrier, her leading man in *Babette Goes to War,* a comedy in which she made an unsuccessful attempt to change her image. It was at this time that Bardot's egotism and neediness began to sabotage her life. When her son Nicolas was born in 1960, she gave him to her in-laws to raise, a questionable move for a woman so desperate for public approval. Later she lamely explained that she "couldn't possibly have looked after a baby—*I* needed a mother." In spite of her need for stability and nurturing, the quick turnover in her capricious love life continued, while Bardot began to devote ever more of her time to the animal rights movement. The gentleness and honesty of animals reassured her, Vadim remarked in 1990, but as Bardot's household menagerie had increased, her human friendships declined. The faithful few who remained with her worried publicly about the star's increasingly eccentric and self-destructive behavior, especially a flirtation with the ultra-right-wing National Front Party of Jean-Marie Le Pen and a verbal attack on Muslims in 1996 for the slaughter of goats. The latter drew criticism as racism couched in the language of an ostensibly pro-animal statement.

Thirty years earlier, Marguerite Duras had brooded over Bardot's behavior from an artistic perspective. Writing in a *Vogue* essay about the sad lack of an aesthetic "conflagration" in Bardot's splashy but essentially bland career, Duras deplored the fact that "some great, strong wind, some force unknown to her" had not "swept its way through her life." Perhaps this, reflected in Bardot's splendid but frivolous idleness, is what lay at the core of her inner torment.

BARNARD

DR. CHRISTIAAN

ON DECEMBER 3, 1967, a fifty-five-year-old grocer named Louis Washkansky was wheeled into a surgery in Groote Schuur Hospital in Capetown, South Africa, where the heart of a twenty-five-year-old accident victim named Denise Darvall was transplanted from her dead body to his live one. Upon awakening after surgery, Washkansky told a nurse, "I am the new Frankenstein." The comment was apt: the doctor who had saved Washkansky's life in this revolutionary way was already under severe attack by critics as a man who had transgressed nature. By the time his patient died eighteen days later of complications arising from the procedure, Dr. Christiàan Barnard was world famous and heart transplants were the subject of a heated global debate.

Christiàan Neethling Barnard was born to near-poverty in the remote hamlet of Beaufort West, son of a minister of the rock-ribbed Dutch Reformed Church. The youngster grew up wearing his two brothers' hand-me-downs and having no better entertainment than pumping the bellows of the organ at his father's church. After graduation from high school, he went off to the University of Cape Town Medical School, where he earned his medical degree in 1953. After a brief and contentious career as a general practitioner in the town of Ceres, he joined the surgical research staff of the Cape Town Medical School. There, under unsophisticated conditions, he developed his skills with a scalpel by operating on dogs. He also met and married a pretty nurse named Aletta Louw.

Hungry for more advanced studies, Barnard traveled in 1955 to the University of Minnesota Medical School, supporting himself with odd jobs before he received a grant. It was there that he performed his first heart surgery. After three years of study, he returned to assume the post of director of surgical research at Cape Town. In 1960 he garnered some measure of attention from his international peers by transplanting the head of a dog.

By 1967, after conducting numerous heart surgeries, including the use of some of the first artificial heart valves, Barnard was ready to attempt a transplant, in his view the only viable option for a patient with an irreversibly diseased organ. A technique for transplanting a heart from one person to another had already been developed in America by Doctors Norman Shumway and Michael DeBakey, but the opportunity had not yet arisen to try it. Barnard thought he had the perfect candidate in Louis Washkansky, whose heart was a choked mass of fibrous tissue.

Barnard had to wait about a month before the unfortunate Denise Duvall was fatally struck by an automobile, causing irreparable brain damage. After determining that Duvall's blood type matched Washkansky's, lessening the possibility of his body rejecting her heart, Barnard removed her heart, attached it to a heart-lung machine, removed Washkansky's diseased heart, and replaced it with Duvall's healthy one. The entire operation, in which he was assisted by his brother, Dr. Marius Barnard, took five hours. At the crucial moment—when Duvall's heart began to beat in Washkansky's body—Barnard muttered in Afrikaans, "Christ, dit gaan werke" (Christ, it's going to work). Unfortunately, the drug regime that followed, designed to fight the body's natural rejection mechanism, disarmed Washkansky of the ability to fight infection. Pneumonia set in and was fatal.

Facing both plaudits and censure, Barnard was seen everywhere, meeting with the president of the United States, partying with what was then termed the "jet set," and dating attractive young women, the most notable being Italian actress Gina Lollob-rigida. His professional peers, some of whom were jealous of the South African interloper, called him a publicity hound. Many physicians were also disturbed—as were certain scientific and religious groups—by the moral implications of taking a still-beating heart from a "dead" person. Who had the right to determine that the donor was indeed dead? And wasn't there a conflict between the cardiac surgeon who needed a healthy heart in a hurry and the Hippocratic imperative to do everything to save the donor's life? A moratorium on heart transplants was suggested within the medical community in hopes that these deeply significant questions could be resolved before mistakes were made.

But Barnard was made of more decisive stuff. On January 2, 1968, he carried out a second heart transplant, this one on a fifty-eight-year-old retired dentist named Philip Blaiberg. The donor was a twenty-four-year-old stroke victim named Clive Haupt, who was in a coma. Haupt was designated "colored" under the South African race laws, a fact which intrigued the South African public.

As the handsome and gregarious doctor's notoriety grew, his philandering reached such proportions that his distraught wife divorced in him 1969. She was not the only one to find life with Barnard difficult. A high-strung perfectionist who was acerbic in his criticisms, he insisted upon the highest standards in the operating room, a trait which the unready found nerve-wracking. As the years passed, he suffered from advancing rheumatoid arthritis, a condition which gradually crippled his hands and forced an end to his surgery. Relying on teaching and writing for income, Barnard also forayed into cosmetics; his 1986 endorsement of a facial cream brought a wave of accusations charging him with debased commercialism.

By 1997 Barnard had retired from medicine to become a novelist and rancher in the Karoo region of his native land. Publicly, one of the few things he admitted to regretting was taking a lukewarm stand against South Africa's apartheid regime. He seemed to have left his momentous career quietly behind him, not unaware of, but no longer intrigued by, the thorny ethical problems he had created with his own hands over three decades earlier.

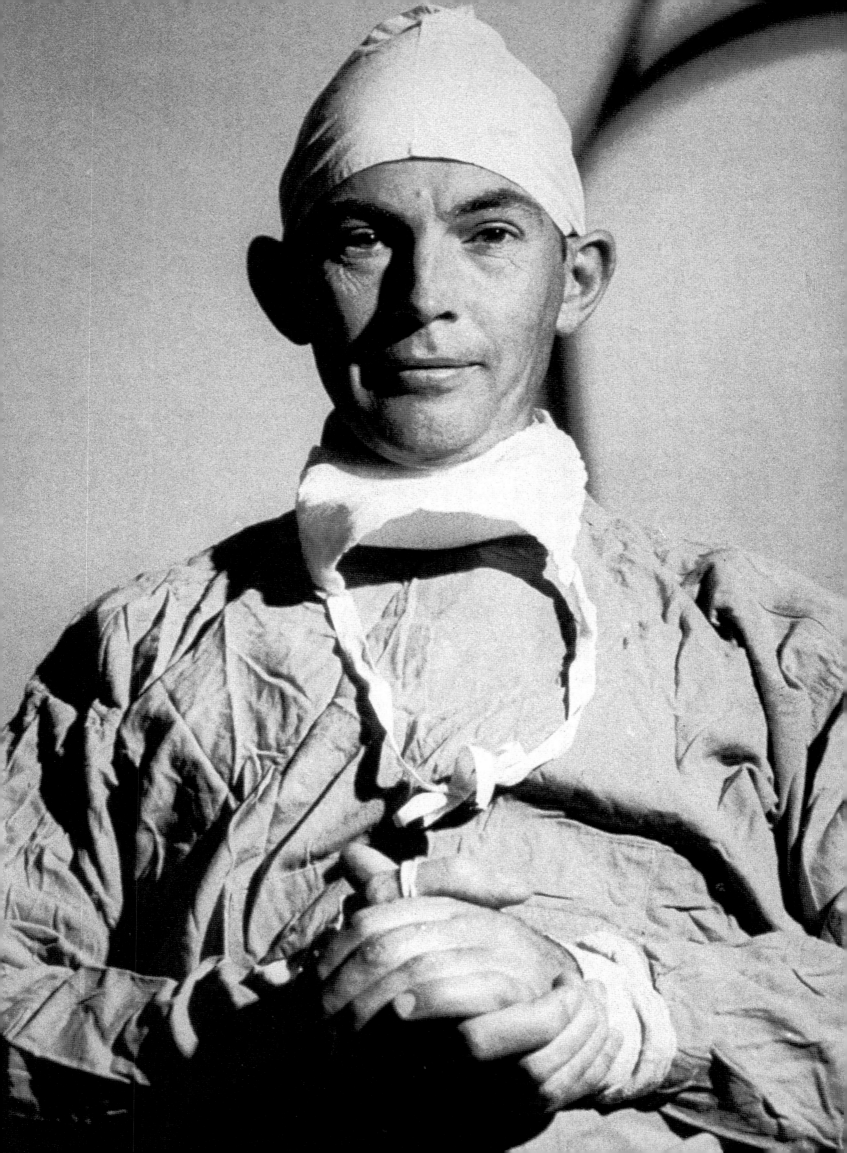

THE BEATLES

THE BEATLES WERE SIMPLY the most influential band of the century. Pioneering the concept of the leaderless group whose members write their own material, they asserted the primacy of the quartet first and foremost. Though millions would recite their names like a mantra—John, Paul, George, and Ringo—their individual personalities were less important than that of the whole. The Beatles were one with many parts, and always the Beatles.

In 1957, when he met Paul McCartney in the tough seaport town of Liverpool, the moody and rebellious John Lennon recognized the talent of the slick and charming left-handed guitarist. The boys had similar backgrounds—middle-class, brick-row "naffs,"— and their musical partnership was cemented when John asked Paul to join his "skiffle" band, the Quarrymen. Soon they invited the taciturn George Harrison to join them as well. When McCartney showed Lennon a song he'd written, he aroused his friend's competitive instinct, and Lennon quickly produced one of his own. This artistic rivalry would set the tone of their entire history together.

With bassist Stu Sutcliffe and drummer Pete Best, the group now called the Silver Beatles—named with Lennon's intentional misspelling, after Buddy Holly's Crickets—played gigs at the Star, a notorious club in Hamburg, Germany, over several years. They hammered out six sets of R&B a night for tough sailors and slumming students, meeting with mixed success. Drawing heavily on American influences such as Little Richard, Chuck Berry, and numerous "girl groups" such as the Chiffons, the Liverpudlians began to develop their own recognizable sound.

With their teddy-boy curls now combed into the bangs that were then the rage among European youth, the four returned to their hometown in 1961 without Sutcliffe, who married in Hamburg (and, tragically, died the next spring). They soon became the star attraction at the Cavern Club, a basement dive elevated by the group to rock-and-roll legend. Despite their growing popularity, however, the Beatles were still raw uplanders, unable to interest London record companies. Then ex-actor Brian Epstein stepped in as their manager, tossing out their jeans and black leather jackets in exchange for nattier, neo-Edwardian suits and ties. Epstein also dumped drummer Pete Best for the head-bobbing Ringo Starr, who was then the percussionist for Rory Storm and the Hurricanes. (In private the group called him Richie; when the Beatles met Elvis, the King kept calling him Bingo.) Though Starr's beat was uncertain, he would develop into a singular stylist much imitated throughout the Beatles' heyday. He was also their touchstone of reality; when the group traveled to the Indian ashram of the Maharishi Mahesh Yogi in February 1968, it was Starr who was concerned that the Maharishi was after their money—and who after several days, caught the first plane back to London.

Epstein talked the great EMI Records producer George Martin into giving the Beatles a contract, which they signed in the summer of 1962. That same year the band broke into the British charts with the bouncy "Love Me Do," and later "Please Please Me" in 1963. Then, in a rush, came the release of the classics "She Loves You" and "I Want to Hold Your Hand," and an appearance on the top American TV program "The Ed Sullivan Show." The latter transformed them overnight into an international phenomenon. Never as "nice" as their carefully constructed image, their appeal was all the greater because their fans could divine the suggestive subtext beneath the innocent lyrics. With Beatle wigs, Beatle boots, Beatle movies, and even a Beatles cartoon show featuring their latest hits, Beatlemania soon became a worldwide phenomenon.

The secret of the group's immense and long-lasting popularity with a multigenerational audience was that all of them except Starr were brilliant, innovative songwriters whose individual specialties combined a finely balanced repertoire. McCartney's fondness for English music-hall songs, Lennon's acid word plays, and Harrison's fascination with Hindu melodies drove the Beatles beyond their pop roots and into uncharted territory. Under Martin's guiding hand, they became the cleverest acoustic stylists, using at one time or another everything from Indian sitars and music played backward to string quartets and symphony orchestras in the creation of a sound that was unmistakably their own.

Like other great collaborations, the Beatles had distinct periods. Their middle period, when they abandoned the rigors of touring for the limitless possibilities of the studio, drew upon McCartney's lyricism and Lennon's passionate surrealism, resulting in tour-de-force albums such as *Sgt. Pepper's Lonely Hearts Club Band* (1967) and *The Beatles* (aka "The White Album," 1968), both filled with clever commenatry on modern life that would make the singular artistry of the group evident. The Beatles, it seemed, could do anything—rock, ballads, reggae, rhythm and blues— and often better than anyone else. At their height, Lennon unguardedly claimed they were "bigger than Jesus," a boast that caused outrage and controversy in many quarters.

It had to end, however, and when it did, the finish was as rude as the ascent had been intoxicating, involving a jostling clutch of lawyers, accountants, toadies, and ex-mates. When the Beatles unraveled, so did the spell they had cast over the world. Both John Lenon and Paul McCartney continued to compose and perform, each evolving his own style. Both were profoundly influenced by their respective wives and partners, Yoko Ono and Linda McCartney. Harrison and Starr retired to far less public lives. In 1980, when Lennon was shot dead at the age of forty outside his New York apartment, their old fans' wistful dream that the Beatles would reunite was ended forever.

BEN-GURION

DAVID

AS A LATTER-DAY MOSES who led the Jews back to the promised land, David Ben-Gurion—Zionist leader, guerrilla fighter, and statesman—was the father of his country, the new state of Israel. A mixture of cunning and obduracy, he achieved the leadership of his people only after years of toil in the corridors of Zionist politics. But as the first prime minister, from 1948 to 1953, and then again from 1961 to 1963, his commitment, vision, and sense of destiny shaped both his people and the politics of the Middle East.

Born David Grün in Plonsk, Poland, a *shtetl* thirty-five miles from Warsaw, Ben-Gurion was the son of a locally influential, though unlicensed, legal counsel. Never conventionally religious, he was nonetheless passionately and unequivocally committed to his identity as a Jew. Under the aegis of his father and grandfather—the former was active in the Love of Zion movement and the latter taught Hebrew to young David—Grün was a committed Zionist early in life. By age fourteen, he was secretary of a society promoting emigration to Palestine. By 1905, the young man was equally committed to both the ethnic and theocratic tenets of Zionism and Marxist economic theory.

In 1906 Grün himself emigrated to Palestine, where the forceful twenty-year-old quickly became head of the nationalist faction of the socialist Workers of Zion. As a union organizer he routinely ran up against risks ranging from malaria to suspicions of the indigenous Palestinians. Hoping to advance the Zionist cause by becoming part of the ruling Ottoman Turkish government, the multilingual Grün, who had begun using the pen name Ben-Gurion when writing for the Zionist publication *Achdut (Unity),* traveled to Constantinople to study law at the university and to lobby the elite on behalf of Zionism. Nearly starving on the meager stipend his father was able to provide, he returned to Palestine in 1914 to resume his work as a union organizer.

With the outbreak of World War I, Ben-Gurion was deported by the Turks, who were allied with Germany. He arrived first in Egypt, then proceeded to New York, where he unsuccessfully promoted settlement in Eretz, Israel. Perhaps his greatest achievement in America was his 1917 marriage to Paula Munweis, a nurse who bore him three sons and remained intensely devoted to her husband until her death in 1968.

The following year, 1918, Ben-Gurion joined the Jewish Battalion of the Royal Fusiliers and was sent to Palestine to fight under General Allenby against the Turks. The Turks lost the conflict in the Middle East, and in the division of the old Ottoman Empire that followed World War I, the League of Nations awarded Great Britain the mandate to rule Palestine. By this time, however, the power Great Britain held over its colonies was growing ever-smaller. For the next fifteen years Ben-Gurion worked as a secretary of the powerful labor federation Histadrut, overseeing administration, immigration, and a growing underground militia—in effect, building the appurtenances of a nation right under Britain's nose. He had long ago discarded Marxism as a viable political or economic philosophy. Ben-Gurion was seeking the right moment to make a nation, and World War II gave him that chance.

Taking advantage of British control, he used England's resources to increase Israel's military capacity. The accelerating rate of Jewish flight from a Europe darkening with anti-Semitism swelled Palestine's Jewish population. In 1939 Great Britain attempted to stanch this flow by issuing the notorious MacDonald White Paper, which, in addition to calling for the establishment of a binational Arab-Jewish state in Palestine within the decade, established strict immigration quotas for Israel—for the first five years, a total of only seventy-five thousand Jews would be allowed to settle in Palestine—and imposed restrictions on Jewish land purchases there. After World War II ended Ben-Gurion led the political struggle against the British from 1947 to 1948. The British, wary of the ever-escalating political and economic costs of trying to police Palestine, issued another paper advocating the establishment of a binational Jewish-Arab state. It then turned the matter over to the United Nations. With the UN partitioning of Palestine into two independent Jewish and Arab states— and with the Arabs' rejection of it and commitment to resistance—Ben-Gurion's goal was finally realized. On May 14, 1948, he declared the Republic of Israel. The next day the armies of the Arab League—Lebanon, Syria, Jordan, Egypt and Iraq—enraged by the partition, invaded Israel, but Ben-Gurion and his new country stood firm, claiming victory in the first Arab-Israeli war.

A wise and irascible prime minister who personified Israel for the rest of the world, Ben-Gurion established a strong economy but sometimes tested the limits of international goodwill. His greatest successes came in building, not running, the country. When, in the early sixties, his country no longer needed a father to help it walk, Ben-Gurion resigned as prime minister, retiring to a kibbutz in the Negev Desert. Politically active to the end, he had lived to see a dream come true.

INGEMAR BERGMAN

1918-

FOR THE GENERATION COMING of age in midcentury, Ingmar Bergman's bleak philosophical films loomed large. Squinting at subtitles in darkened art houses, aspiring young cineastes throughout Europe and the United States struggled to untangle the enigmatic Swede's grave symbolism, metaphysical questions, and black-and-white explorations of the psyche. After a Bergman film, heated conversations about humanity's alienation in the world of a silent God took precedence over sleep long into the night. Next to the raw anxieties of Bergman's obsessively reflective characters and the stark images of his innovative techniques, Hollywood's big-budget extravaganzas, with their less-than-cosmic concerns, suddenly seemed frivolous. Neurotic and egotistical, the somber Scandinavian quickly became the international intelligentsia's reigning auteur, a writer and director whose heavily autobiographical movies were forever destined to be referred to as "cinema." Yet Bergman himself never dismissed Hollywood, acknowledging the influence on his work of such master directors as Billy Wilder, George Cukor, and Ernst Lubitsch.

As a child in Uppsala, Sweden, Bergman used the magic of theater and film to escape what he has described alternatingly as an oppressive, unhappy childhood and a beautiful, gloriously contented one. Whatever the case, it is known that his Lutheran minister father and equally strict mother instilled in their son—along with an appreciation of music—a deep fear of both punishment and humiliation. When he was bad, there was the cane, and when he wet his bed, as often happened, he was forced to wear a red skirt in front of the family. A daydreamer, he found solace in building a puppet theater in his nursery and playing with his favorite toy, a crude paraffin-lamp projector for which he scavenged bits of film, spliced together with glue. When, at age six, he first saw *Black Beauty,* the experience so excited him that he was put to bed with a high fever for three days. He gained more detachment as he matured, but retained his ardor for films, sometimes watching two or three a day during his teenage years.

As a young adult, Bergman became professionally involved in theater at the Royal Opera House in Stockholm, where he took a menial job after quitting his art and literature studies at the University of Stockholm. His assistantship paid nothing, but it enabled him to find work in 1942 as a script doctor at Svensk Filmindustri. After several less than successful projects, he began to hit his stride with his 1955 *Smiles of a Summer Night.* But the international Bergman cult was not launched until *The Seventh Seal,* an allegorical declamation of humanity's struggle with God and the inevitability of mortality which won a special jury prize at Cannes in 1957.

Wild Strawberries (1957), *The Magician* (1958), *The Virgin Spring* (1960), *Through a Glass Darkly* (1961), *Winter Light* (1962), and *The Silence* (1963) solidified Bergman's reputation for genius and for certain themes and patterns that would guide the rhythm, content, and tone of his films for decades to come. In addition to sounding the depths of masculine anomie and despair, he also explored the interior landscapes of women in his films, drawing insight and inspiration from his five marriages and other personal liaisons. He surrounded himself with a coterie of talented actors—Ingrid Thulin, Bibi Andersson, Harriet Andersson, Max von Sydow, Gunnar Björn-strand, and Liv Ullmann, with whom he had one of his eight children. This loyal band was rounded out by the brilliant cinematographer and Bergman's frequent collaborator Sven Nykvist, who gave the often explosive director a surfeit of creative comfort. The consistency of his favorite performers and the excellence of his technical staff, as well as Bergman's shooting style—with its low budgets and well-prepared, tight schedules—gave him an enviable professional edge: total creative control.

Bergman lost his emotional control on January 30, 1976, when investigators from the Swedish government interrupted his rehearsal at the Royal Dramatic Theater and dragged him off for questioning on charges of tax fraud. Although he was eventually exonerated, the fifty-eight-year-old director sank into a suicidal depression. When his mood lifted, he left Sweden for a three-year self-imposed exile in Munich where he worked with the Rezidenz Theatre and directed his first film outside his native Sweden. Unlike the majority of his extremely personal films, *The Serpent's Egg* (1978), which starred Liv Ulmann and the American actor David Carradine, dealt with the public issue of how Naziism originated. His next movie, *Autumn Sonata* (1978), won considerable acclaim and when the director eventually returned to his homeland, a string of made-for-television productions, including *Fanny and Alexander* (1983), earned him kudos both on the small screen and later as theatrical releases.

With age, Bergman has involved himself more frequently in stage production, his first love and a less physically taxing medium for him than film. As he nears his eightieth birthday, he also professes to have become more compassionate. But he remains an enigmatic loner, spending much of his time on Fårö, a remote and barren Baltic island only one hundred miles from the Russian coast. His roots, Bergman says, are there, and he has everything he needs for his work, from cutting tables to a screening room. Forlorn and gray, it is the ideal habitat for a man who has tried to capture on celluloid the desolate dialogue between humankind and a taciturn Supreme Being.

INGRID BERGMAN

"OF ALL THE GIN JOINTS in all the towns in all the world, she walks into mine," growls Humphrey Bogart as the owner of Rick's Café Américain in the enduring classic *Casablanca.* Since the film's release in 1942, several million males no doubt would have loved to own *any* gin joint that Ingrid Bergman walked into. No adjective has ever been able to accurately define her exotic, earthy beauty or capture its on-screen effect. Perfection was not her allure: Her nose was a little large, her frame more robust than most movie stars of her time, her eyes a rather unremarkable blue. But there was a depth and directness about her that made her extremely appealing—to women as well as to men—and equally convincing as an actress. Offscreen she was equally compelling; interviewing the gracious Bergman, one journalist recalled poetically, was like speaking "with an intelligent orchid."

Bergman was the product of a tranquil middle-class upbringing tinged by early sadness: Her mother died when she was two, her father when she was eleven. An only child, she went to live with an uncle and aunt and their five children. Extremely shy and self-conscious because of her height, she retreated into a world of comforting fantasy through playacting. Gradually conquering her shyness, Bergman entered the school of the Royal Dramatic Theater and, after only a year of study, was put under contract by Svensk Filmindustri in 1934. In 1936 the promising young actress won the starring role in Gustaf Molander's *Intermezzo,* and in 1937 she married Petter Lindstrom, a dentist who eventually became a brain surgeon, with whom she had her first child, Pia. After signing with David O. Selznick and moving to America in 1939, Bergman was soon loaned out to Warner Brothers to play a woman in German-occupied North Africa who is torn between allegiance to her anti-Nazi activist husband and her rekindled passion for the café owner—played by Humphrey Bogart—who is reluctant to help her. Or to love her again. Under the superb direction of Michael Curtiz, *Casablanca,* with its evocative mood and tightly drawn characters mirrored the emotional climate of the time, becoming one of those rare films that grows in stature with age.

When the young Swedish actress first came to America in 1939 to make Selznick's English-language version of the Swedish sentimental romance *Intermezzo,* she swiftly and resolutely rebuffed Selznick's orders to cut her hair, pluck her eyebrows, and feminize her low-register voice. Instead of capping her teeth, she clenched them, refusing even to avail herself of such normal Hollywood necessities as makeup. When American audiences finally got a glimpse of this *au naturel* beauty, cosmetics sales plummeted. After her performance in *Casablanca* launched her cinematic winning streak, she starred in 1943 with Gary Cooper in *For Whom the Bell Tolls* and the following year made *Gaslight* with Charles Boyer. Portraying the unhinged victim of her husband's sinister attempts to drive her insane, Bergman won her first Oscar. The leads in two of Alfred Hitchcock's psychological thrillers, *Spellbound* (1945) with Gregory Peck and *Notorious* (1946), opposite Cary Grant, fixed her as an actress of international stature. She often played pure-of-heart characters—such as the engaging, tubercular nun in *The Bells of St. Mary's* (1945) and the virginal heroine of *Joan of Arc* (1948)—but even when she was forced on-screen to compromise her morality for patriotism in *Notorious* the public connected with the warmth and impeccable integrity of the actor behind the role.

This affectionate bond was struck a blow when Bergman failed to live up to the image the public had identified with her. In 1948 Bergman saw Roberto Rossellini's *Open City,* his neorealistic classic about the Nazi occupation of Rome. She fell in love with the film and then with the director himself. The affair became the scandal of the century, a media frenzy that peaked when Rome's riot police had to encircle the hospital where Bergman was delivering their son. When the world learned of the birth of Bergman's illegitimate child, the industry and her fans denounced and then abandoned her. Leaving her daughter Pia behind, she lived in exile, later giving birth to twins. Her marriage to Rossellini, though, would founder in the wake of a string of artistic disasters, among them *Europa '51* (1951). After seven long years, she returned in quiet triumph, a woman who had ignored society's sexual double standard and had become a symbol of defiance against the fallen-woman stereotype. The public would once again embrace its wayward saint.

Bergman's second Oscar, for her role in *Anastasia* (1956)—the tale of a woman posing as the youngest daughter of Russia's last czar—signaled to the world that her excommunication had been rescinded. Although she continued to act and in 1974 won yet another Oscar for her performance in *Murder on the Orient Express,* the woman who could not imagine life without acting—on stage or screen—never fully regained her earlier stature. Ingmar Bergman's *Autumn Sonata* in 1978 brought the sixty-three-year-old actress as close as she would get to redemption. Playing a guilt-ridden concert pianist who has chosen career over family, Bergman, who had experienced the pain of abandoning her real-life daughter and the joy of reunion with her, seemed to undergo those emotions all over again, ultimately transcending them through art.

Ingrid Bergman died after a silent seven-year battle with cancer. A radiant star, she had played the errant angel to a fascinated public who forgave all. At the end, she said she regretted nothing she had done—only the things she hadn't.

BOGART

HUMPHREY

HUMPHREY BOGART WAS THE screen embodiment of the mythic American tough guy, classic and classless. Unlike his screen persona, he grew up as the well-educated son of a well-to-do Manhattan physician and his wife, a well-known artist. Prepped for medical school at Phillips Academy in Andover, Massachusetts, he would have gone on to Yale had he not been expelled for disciplinary reasons. Impulsively, he volunteered for the U.S. Navy at the end of World War I, an experience that left him with his trademark scarred lip and snarling lisp. One of several conflicting anecdotes has it that an escaping German prisoner smashed Bogart in the mouth with his handcuffs, whereupon, the tale goes, Bogey brought down the assailant with one shot from a .45. In all likelihood, the injury stemmed from a mishap during the shelling of his ship, *Leviathan*.

Whatever its source, the lisp was hardly an asset when, at loose ends after the war, Bogart decided to try his luck in the theater, first as a gofer in a New York movie studio and later as a player of callow youths given to bounding into drawing rooms decked out in white flannels and swinging a tennis racket. Indeed, it was in such a role that Bogart became the first actor to utter the deathless line, "Tennis anyone?" Apart from that minor embarrassment, however, his theatrical career was deservedly obscure. In the beginning, he had no respect for the profession, and other actors of the time, like James Cagney, resented Humphrey DeForest Bogart's rich-kid connections. Finally, after years of study and a series of second-lead film roles, Bogart's big break came in 1936 when the English actor Leslie Howard—impressed with Bogart's interpretation of the shaved-headed killer Duke Mantee in Robert Sherwood's 1935 play *The Petrified Forest*—insisted that Bogart reprise the role in the film version. A grateful Bogart later named his daughter Leslie as a tribute to Howard.

His film career was finally on track, but moving like a slow freight train rather than a locomotive. For several unrewarding years, Bogart mumbled through a series of B-grade gangster epics, usually playing a sneering bad guy who dies like a rat in the last reel. Then came the second big break: Bogart was cast as Rick Blaine in *Casablanca* (1943), and a legend was born. As the broken-hearted fugitive soldier of fortune who wins—and selflessly sacrifices—the love of Ingrid Bergman, the tragic-eyed Bogart was the very incarnation of the shrewd, tough, but fair-minded American whose unsentimental appraisal of the world's evils cannot overcome his idealistic need to combat them. His roles as Dashiell Hammett's perversely upright private eye Sam Spade in John Huston's *The Maltese Falcon* (1941) and Raymond Chandler's detective

Philip Marlowe in Howard Hawks's *The Big Sleep* (1946) defined the genre—and even provided a model of behavior for real private eyes. Bogart's portrayals of *Casablanca's* Rick Blaine and Harry (Steve) Morgan, the Free French—sympathizing fishing boat captain in *To Have and Have Not* (1945), gave the world the lone wolf Yankee—an idealized persona that both reflected Americans' view of themselves and instructed the rest of the world what to think of them.

But in real life Bogart wasn't quite the leathery, case-hardened guy he portrayed on-screen. His sole sparring partner in Hollywood was no crook or Nazi, but his third wife, Mayo Methot, a struggling actress who shared her husband's love of argument and liquor. The couple were so combative—and so public in their displays of hostility—that the press dubbed them "the Battling Bogarts." Apart from their rows, Bogart was unfailingly well-spoken and polite, except when he would deliberately deflate the occasional bumptious ego with the vocabulary of a cavalry sergeant. No brawler, he loved to needle men to the brink of fisticuffs, then grandly buy them a drink; upon meeting John Steinbeck, Bogart began with: "Hemingway tells me you're not a good writer." His screen persona as a brooding, often sardonic lady-killer was belied by his three disastrous marriages, a pattern that was broken rather spectacularly in his final union to his twenty-year-old leading lady in *To Have and Have Not*, the sensuous Lauren Bacall, with whom he also starred in *The Big Sleep*, *Dark Passage* (1947), and *Key Largo* (1948). Bacall gave Bogey children, put up with his drinking and solitary sailing trips, and watched him die.

Making the transition from soulful heavy to mature character actor was no more difficult for Bogart than his earlier leap from gunsel to guardian angel. His portrayal of the boastful and greedy Fred C. Dobbs in John Huston's *The Treasure of the Sierra Madre* (1948) fairly limned the sin of avarice for the audience, and his twitching, strawberry-loving Captain Queeg in *The Caine Mutiny* (1954) was a masterpiece of paranoia. But the crowning achievement of his later career was his wry portrayal of riverboat captain Charlie Allnut opposite Katharine Hepburn's starchy spinster in *The African Queen* (1951) also directed by Huston. This role, in one of the screen's greatest (and most unlikely) love stories, earned him his only Academy Award, capping a career that Bogart, with a characteristic lack of arrogance, assessed as modest. He was wrong. His tenure as a star was briefer than that of most other movie legends, yet even when throat cancer cut him down at the age of fifty-seven, cinema's most romantic antihero stood alone and above them all.

MARLON

BRANDO

THERE IS ONLY ONE Brando, an undeniable truth that the masterful, high-voltage actor has spent decades trying both to sustain and to smother. In his riveting 1947 performance as Stanley Kowalski in Tennessee Williams's A *Streetcar Named Desire*, Brando seemed to set the stage on fire with his prowling, sexually charged portrayal, improvising his way toward a wholly new definition of acting. After playing that part, Brando—intuitive, naturalistic, and always stretching for more elbow room—struggled against being type cast. Choosing his movies carefully, his roles revealed his prodigious talent. Disaffection, ambivalence, and mystery were at the root of such powerhouse performances as the leather-jacketed Johnny in *The Wild One* (1953), the psychically bruised ex-prizefighter Terry Malloy in *On the Waterfront* (1954), and the shockingly erotic omnivore Paul in *Last Tango in Paris* (1972). But while these qualities may have honed Brando's exciting edginess as an artist, they also sabotaged his desperate quest to find a more meaningful role in life than that of the rebel prince of pop mythology.

In the early years of his career, Brando's Roman-coin handsomeness and physique had instantly established both his acting ability and his sexual magnetism—at once menacing and vulnerable—and therefore all the more exciting. But there was another side to him. In the 1960s, Brando took a leave from what he considered the perniciousness and banal commercialism of Hollywood and moved to the primitive island oasis of Tetiaroa in Tahiti. His life was reclusive and his once chiseled face grew ravaged in midlife and roughly etched. Only the set of his magnificent jaw and his searing eyes hinted at his earlier self; he lived sequestered with his Micronesian wife, two children, and a ham radio in a thatched hut near a sleepy blue lagoon. Weighing some three hundred pounds, he dressed in native garb, a frangipani blossom sometimes tucked behind his ear.

Brando's rise from drama student to star was swift. Born in Omaha, Nebraska, to an alcoholic semiprofessional actress and a tyrannical, hard-living feed manufacturer, "Bud" was raised on a farm in Libertyville, Illinois. Devastated at age seven by the departure of his beloved governess, the troubled, neglected teenager was sent to military school, but he soon channeled his rebelliousness into the theater when his father, whom he hated for constantly berating him, offered him financial help. Following in his sisters' footsteps, Brando studied in New York and played summer stock, eventually landing the role of Nels, the sympathetic Norwegian son, in the 1944 Broadway hit *I Remember Mama*. The show's success enabled him to enroll in Stella Adler's famous dramatic workshop at the New School for Social Research, where he absorbed her Stanislavsky-based Method. He would study later with the influential Lee Strasberg.

Soon he landed a part in the 1946 revival of Shaw's *Candida*, opposite Katherine Cornell. As with an effort earlier that year in Maxwell Anderson's *Truckline Café*, critics found little to get excited about. But after *Streetcar*—under the inspired direction of fellow Method advocate Elia Kazan—Brando's career immediately went west; in 1950 he made Stanley Kramer's *The Men*, followed by *Viva Zapata!* (1952), in which he played the Mexican rebel, and *Julius Caesar* (1953). His work was finally recognized with an Academy Award for his role in *On the Waterfront* (1954), a classic that revealed new layers of pathos and pain in his quirky characterizations.

The Wild One enthroned Brando, all sexuality and seething aggression, as both a teenage idol and a role model for generations of rebels and Brando wanna-bes. He was dark, he was doomed, he was dangerous. He scorched the earth, fellow actor Jack Nicholson would later comment, "for two hundred miles in any direction." All that was left for Nicholson, and the Pacinos and De Niros that followed was to accommodate themselves to the arid terrain.

The sixties led the star in other directions. His directorial debut in *One-Eyed Jacks* (1961) was drowned in cost overruns, and his off-screen antics during the filming of *Mutiny on the Bounty* (1962) quashed any hopes that the picture would come in anywhere near budget. Brando, meanwhile, had all but given up on acting, calling it "an empty and useless profession" at which he dabbled now and then only to finance his many ambitious—and always abandoned—Utopian causes, from the American Indian Movement to conservationist schemes for his island retreat.

With a brillant "comeback" performance as the Mafia patriarch Don Corleone in Francis Ford Coppola's *The Godfather* (1972), which garnered him a second Oscar, the prodigal son returned to Hollywood and all was forgiven. His disquieting presence in Bernardo Bertolucci's *Last Tango in Paris* (1972), in which he portrayed a middle-aged man exploring emotional catharsis through loveless sex, and in Coppola's haunting *Apocalypse Now* (1979) seemed to offer further proof that time had not quenched the fire in his gut.

Yet something would. Always given to philandering and self-destruction, Brando was now waging too many bitter internecine dramas between wives, ex-wives, and mistresses. Certainly the 1990 conviction of his son, Christian, for killing his sister Cheyenne's boyfriend, and Cheyenne's subsequent suicide, left their marks. "The messenger of misery," Brando announced after his son's trial, "has come to my house."

BRECHT

BERTOLT

THE MOST INFLUENTIAL GERMAN poet and playwright of this century, Bertolt Brecht was the ultimate intellectual roughneck. Coldly analytical and outrageously self-assured, he cast a contemptuous eye on modern society—especially the "rotten," materialistic West. On the cusp of middle age, he chose *Das Kapital* as his bible and Marx's proletarian man as his antihero. Brecht even dressed as a worker, wearing a shabby cap cocked at an angle; although, later on, it would be discovered that his unkempt clothes were tailored for that precise effect. He also left his irregularly cut hair unwashed, as he himself usually was, much to the distress of his companions. His ideologically correct appearance aside, what mattered most to him was the staging of disturbingly realistic political "parables" that addressed what he viewed as the individual's hopeless struggle against the cruelty of contemporary society. This idealistic pursuit was counterbalanced by a host of carefully camouflaged nonsocialist desires: a surfeit of sexually pliable women, a plentiful supply of Virginia cigars, a fame to equal that of fellow exile Kurt Weill, and a certified Broadway hit.

Brecht introduced the colorful language of the street into the stilted formality of German letters. Even more important, his highly original concept of "epic theater" transformed contemporary drama. Eschewing such conventions as suspension of disbelief, the Brechtian stage emphasized the theatricality of what was going on, letting the audience see the bare klieg lights and scene changes. The actors, surrounded by abstract sets and bathed in operating-room brightness, were never typecast or made to "act" in the traditional naturalistic way. Trained not to identify with their roles, Brechtian players further distanced themselves (and the audience) from the characters they played by relying on narration, gestures, and simple but obvious asides. By thus denying the illusion of theater, Brecht affirmed the Marxist dogma that human nature is not constant, but a response to the economic conditions of a particular historical moment.

Brecht's own Bavarian childhood was far from the gritty world he evoked on stage, where life, interpreted as a bitter battle between combatants, offered few tender moments. Like many avant-gardists of this era, his family was middle class, his early years more than financially secure, and his education fairly thorough. He even attended medical school for a while, later serving as an orderly in the army. Nurtured by a mother who thought him exceptional—and whose attention intensified after her frail son suffered a heart attack at age twelve—Brecht was a highly capable but stubborn child who seemed unusually expert at manipulating those around him.

After staging his first play, the grim, semiautobiographical *Baal*, in Munich in 1918, Brecht established himself critically with his next production, *Drums in the Night*. Primed for success, he moved to Berlin in 1924, where two important influences on his work coalesced: He began collaborating with the anti-romantic experimental composer Kurt Weill and reading Karl Marx. The dialectic of Marxism tempered Brecht's anarchism and gave him a model for the dynamic conflict of opposites. From his union with Marx and Weill (another leftist with a taste for moralizing), came the 1928 anti-capitalist classic *The Threepenny Opera,* a melodramatic but satirical musical that proved to be Brecht's single financial success and the instrument of his fame.

But with Hitler's ascent to power in 1933, Brecht—whose name was fifth on the Nazis' list of enemies of the state—was forced to flee, first to Denmark, Sweden, and Finland, then, in 1941, to the United States. From his exile came such lyrically powerful and didactic plays as *The Good Woman of Setzuan, Galileo,* and the oft-performed and searing *Mother Courage.* From the bleak Hollywood years that followed came *The Caucasian Chalk Circle* and a partnership with Fritz Lang on the film script for *Hangmen Also Die* (1943). Many in Hollywood considered Brecht an obnoxious "subversive" with a reputation as a contentious director who held almost everything the industry stood for in rancorous contempt. Chafing at the triumphs of other European refugee artists, Brecht was annoyed that the clubby capital of the entertainment business provided little work for him. In an ironic footnote to his West Coast sojourn, Brecht was one of the "unfriendlies" subpoenaed by the House Un-American Activities Committee in 1947. Immediately after testifying, he left the country hastily, settling finally in East Berlin.

There he established the celebrated Berliner Ensemble with his actress wife and partner, Helene Weigel. The company was beset by friction between Brecht's downbeat theater pieces and the Communist Party's upbeat propaganda. Although the repressive acts of the German Democratic Republic in the early 1950s—not to mention those of Stalin during the same period—must surely have given pause to this truculent opponent of imperialism, he did not speak publicly of any disillusionment.

Recently, Brecht scholars have had to confront their own disillusionment. In his 1994 book *Brecht and Company: Sex, Politics and the Making of the Modern Drama,* the American scholar John Fuegi, founder of the International Brecht Society, charged that eighty percent of *The Threepenny Opera,* which is based on John Gay's *The Beggar's Opera* (1728), was written by Elisabeth Hauptman, one of Brecht's mistresses. Citing the incident as part of a pattern of plagiarism and hypocrisy (Brecht may also have bilked colleagues out of royalties, and he lived in much greater comfort than his fellow East Germans), Fuegi raises serious questions that have yet to be satisfactorily refuted. But whether or not the works are best attributed to "Brecht and Company" or to the nihilist genius himself, the poetic and directorial achievements they represent will forever be known as "Brechtian."

1922- BROWN

HELEN GURLEY

A SELF-DESCRIBED "MOUSEBURGER" of a woman, timid yet possessed of a passionate nature, Helen Gurley Brown triumphed over an unhappy childhood in repressive pre-war Arkansas to become America's chief proponent of sexual liberation for single women. Before her, unmarried women were expected to adhere to a strict code of chastity: Then Brown declared boldly that the empress had no clothes, especially after five o'clock. Since single women were engaged in expressing their healthy animal instincts as actively as their married sisters, she reasoned, why not celebrate that fact? Indeed, why not encourage them? It was in taking that most unladylike of steps, both in her books and in the frothy pages of *Cosmopolitan* magazine, that writer-editor Brown made her lasting contribution to modern culture.

Her dithyrambs on sex were directed to the "femocracy"—the filing clerks, secretaries, and other forgotten women with whom she identified. Though expressed in a breathlessly italicized writing style reminiscent of high school yearbook inscriptions, her compassion came honestly. As a ten-year-old in Little Rock, Helen Gurley was devastated when her father, a teacher, was killed in a bizarre elevator accident. The deep and lasting pain of her loss was intensified a few years later when her sister Mary was stricken with polio. Gurley nursed her sister while attending high school in Los Angeles, and the little family slid perilously close to poverty as their meager savings were depleted by medical bills. Forced to work, Helen had held eighteen different lowly clerical posts by the time she was twenty-five. She managed during that time to attend only one semester of college in Texas and a business school in Los Angeles, graduating in 1942, and to hold posts at the Music Corporation of America, the William Morris Agency, and the Los Angeles *Daily News*. Her existence was unfulfilling in those grim days—with the exception of a love life that would have made Don Juan sick with envy.

In 1948 Gurley became secretary to advertising executive Don Belding, of Foote, Cone & Belding, advancing in a few years to the position of copywriter. She left the firm ten years later when a rival doubled her salary, only to find that in spite of winning several awards and being the highest paid ad copywriter on the West Coast, she had grown dissatisfied with advertising. In 1959 her new husband, movie producer David Brown, encouraged her to write a book describing her philosophy—which was, as the world was soon to learn, liberal to the point of libertinism. *Sex and the Single Girl,* written evenings and weekends while she continued her work in advertising, became a national cause célèbre when it was published in 1962. It was a veritable manual on how to

fascinate, manipulate, and ultimately bed, though not necessarily wed, a man. More than a middle-class *Kama Sutra*, however, *Sex* was a guide to success in life for legions of "mouse-burgers" who were not blessed with beauty, genius, money, or status. Earnest advice on grooming, perfume, couture, language, flirtation—in short, everything that could turn a man into a tower of Jell-O and a "girl" into a high achiever—poured forth in her sequels, *Sex and the Office* (1964) and *Helen Gurley Brown's Outrageous Opinions* (1966). In order to answer the flood of mail that came from readers after *Sex and the Single Girl,* Brown started writing a column called "Woman Alone," which was syndicated in more than fifty newspapers.

While women hungry for both ecstasy and expense accounts took notes, feminists raised a firestorm of protest about Brown's philosophy, accusing her of turning women into sex objects. She was stung by the harsh criticism, but hit back by pointing out that she was only writing what women really wanted to know about, not to mention that she regarded a good career as a moral obligation. And in 1965 she found hers: Assuming the editorship of the foundering *Cosmopolitan* magazine, the ebullient Brown turned a frumpy journal for young ladies into a eye-popping font of sex tips, diet plans, mantrap schemes, orgasmic seismog-raphy, and rampant cleavage and, above all, a pulpit for her gleeful gospel of sexual liberation. Derided for coining neologisms like "cupcakable" in describing feminine erotic attributes, Brown nevertheless was tremendously influential in flinging open the bedroom—and the boardroom—doors for ambitious women. She demystified and humanized female sexual desire by insisting on its parity with male lust and, in a clever twist, managed to turn men into the type of sex objects she was said to have made of women. And through it all, she always maintained that work, not relationships, is the thing that always gives back what you invest in it.

Brown wrote two more books: *Having It All,* in 1982, on how a "mouseburger" can have both a fabulous career and fabulous men, and *The Late Show,* in 1993, a manifesto of survival tips—that is, the *Cosmo* message—for the over-fifty woman. Her downplaying of the AIDS threat for all those *Cosmo* girls evoked the biggest storm of criticism yet, and it was probably this that made her inevitable retirement a reality. After thirty-two years as the editor of *Cosmopolitan*, she was finally eased out of her perch; her final issue was March 1997. But she remains busy and energetic, having reigned into her seventies as her era's most visible proponent of female sexual conquest.

MARIA CALLAS

MARIA CALLAS WAS THE *prima donna assoluta* of the twentieth century. "A great singing shark," as playwright Terrence McNally once described her, she did not sing her dramatic soprano roles as much as devour them, chewing up her rivals in the process. Her rich voice, which she commanded with astounding ease, was highlighted by a remarkable virtuosity and inspired musical phrasing. Though somewhat flawed by a reedy-sounding middle range and a wobbly high register, these imperfections vanished in performance. When the exotic beauty took the stage, the small details disappeared amid the drama and there was only Callas.

One of the earliest appearances of Maria Kalageropoulos was in 1937 on one of the first broadcasts of "The Major Bowes Amateur Hour." The thirteen year old reputedly used another name so her father, Giovanni, who frowned on his wife's ambitious career plans for their daughter, would not find out. Later that same year, her mother took Maria from her native New York to Greece where she felt she could afford to give her daughter the kind of musical training she needed. Arriving in the land of her ancestors, Maria was transformed. "My blood is pure Greek," she was to say over and over again, "I feel totally Greek." Taking up her vocation in earnest, she studied at the Royal Conservatory in Athens with Elvira de Hidalgo, a nurturing woman who became very close to her. As Callas's soprano developed, it revealed a raw character, the tone thinning and transmuting from register to register up the scale. Later, overburdened by the demands placed upon it, her voice acquired a tendency to waver on high notes—when it could hit them at all. Its assets, however, were smoke and flames, molten overflowings of feeling that sometimes threatened to overcome the score.

After debuting in The Royal Opera's production of *Tosca*, Callas returned to New York in 1945, and auditioned for the Metropolitan Opera. She did not receive an offer for a contract, a setback which ultimately proved fortunate. Instead of an undistinguished debut in an inauspicious role at the Met, which could have ruined her professionally, she had her first great triumph at the age of twenty-four in the 1947 Verona production of *La Gio-conda,* under the sympathetic baton of the great conductor—and her mentor—Tullio Serafin. In 1949, the year before she joined La Scala Opera, she married the much older millionaire Italian businessman Giovanni Meneghini, whose love and considerable fortune were lavished on an early career spent singing such heavy operas as *Tristan and Isolde* and *Turandot.* The real turning point for her career came when she got the chance to show her true talents, which were ideal for *bel canto* opera. Callas had just finished the role of Brunnhilde in *Die Walkure* at La Fenice, when the soprano for the next opera in the repertory, Bellini's *I Puritani,* became ill; Serafin convinced management to let Callas take the part of Elvira, in which

she triumphed. Thereafter, she gradually put aside the works of Wagner and the rest of the heavy repertoire for the older, lighter *bel canto* operas of Bellini, Rossini, and Donizetti, many of whose works had been ignored until she turned her attention to them.

Callas also shed sixty pounds—some say to the detriment of her voice—emerging as sleek and intriguing as Queen Nefertiti. (After several years of marriage, she also shed the companionship of Meneghini, preferring the luxurious protection of shipping magnate Aristotle Onassis, who, portentously, hated opera as much as he was drawn to celebrity.) For the next thirty tempestuous years, this difficult, magnificent talent dominated the world's great operatic stages, breathing the life force into heroines like Lucia di Lammermoor—and breathing down the necks of opera house managers who usually wilted before her demands. Having been painstakingly schooled in stagecraft by her friend the Italian film director Luchino Visconti, who had directed her at La Scala, Callas held audiences hostage with her theatrical wiles. She was, moreover, willing to use her voice as a general uses infantry, to sacrifice it, if necessary, in the service of epiphany.

Increasingly volatile, Callas sent her voice into battle in *Medea* and *Macbeth,* She walked out during performances when she felt she was not in good form, even before the president of Italy in 1958. In another famous episode that same year, she directed an insulting fascist salute toward the superintendent of La Scala, who was observing her performance in *Il Pirata.* In revenge, he forced the curtain down on her while she was taking her bows accompanied by a standing ovation, which nearly started a riot among her adoring fans. The year continued to be difficult. After a running battle with Metropolitan Opera director Rudolph Bing, she was finally fired for refusing to sing both *Macbeth* and *La Traviata* in one week.

When her voice began to burn out, and she lost the top of her range and much of her agility, people begged Callas to begin a second career singing mezzo-soprano roles. But the prima donna refused, probably out of wounded pride. Addicted to pills, and pregnant by Onassis, who demanded an abortion, she was ultimately abandoned by him in 1968. In spite of her tearful demands for marriage and a family, he coldly told her that he was marrying Jacqueline Kennedy, the widow of the American president.

Most believe Onassis broke her heart, but perhaps it was the loss of her divine gift that signaled the end. After he left, she went on a 13-month farewell tour, giving joint recitals with the tenor Guiseppe di Stefano, her third husband. Both of their voices were in such bad shape that one critic said they sounded like "dogs who barked at one other." Callas died in Paris at the age of fifty-three, unable to sing, unwanted in love, but survived by her artistic legacy—the numerous recordings of the immortal voice that continue to thrill the world.

AL CAPONE

BY THE TIME AL "SCARFACE" CAPONE, a hefty bouncer from Brooklyn, hit Chicago in 1919, the city was already the most corrupt place in America. A cesspool of crime and vice, it was a safe house for sleazy politicians, on-the-take policemen, and two-bit punks who profited from mutual cooperation in keeping the city's thousands of saloons, gambling parlors, dance halls, and brothels open for business. After Big Al was through taking control, the town could add bootlegging, big-time racketeering, bombings, motorcade ambushes, and hundreds of grisly homicides to its already seamy reputation. For years, Capone's private army of gun-toting, sharply dressed lieutenants enforced the rule of his multimillion-dollar-a-year empire. By the end of his reign, the short, overweight hoodlum with a taste for expensive checkered suits, silk underwear, and diamond-studded belts had become a legend. And despite his well-documented viciousness—he once clubbed two disloyal henchmen to death with a baseball bat—and his famous cowardice, his legend was somehow sympathetic and quirkily romantic. Part cold-eyed organizational genius, part hot-tempered gang leader, Capone also enjoyed playing the philanthropist. He ran depression-era soup kitchens, leaned on public officials to ensure that school children got fresh milk daily, and received fan mail for his generosity. These good deeds did not, however, make him a racketeer with a heart of gold. With each fresh tale of his mobster-style audacity, the nation, nourishing its hearty appetite for sensationalism, veered between revulsion and admiration.

The man who subdued a nest of feuding gangs to lay the groundwork for the modern Mafia was born in the slums of Brooklyn, New York, to Neapolitan immigrants. In this environment, Alphonse Capone rapidly fell into a life of petty crime. By his teens he was a pimp, having acquired his signature facial scar—so one of several stories goes—from a Sicilian barber who slashed the youngster's left cheek when Capone demanded a mafioso-style haircut the barber felt he had no right to wear. With a résumé that included armed robbery and murder, the cocky young hustler left his bartender-and-bouncer job to work in a South Side Chicago brothel owned by Johnny Torrio, whose cousin by marriage, "Big Jim" Colosimo, controlled illicit dealings in the city's third ward. When Big Jim was reluctant to expand the business, Capone brought Frankie Yale, his first boss in Brooklyn and a specialist in murder-for-hire, out from Coney Island to "take care" of him. In short order, Big Jim was found in the hallway of a café with a bullet in his head. Soon Capone and Torrio were partners, capitalizing on the biggest windfall ever to enter an American criminal's life: the 1919 Volstead Act, which outlawed the manufacture, sale, and transport of alcoholic beverages. Enacted to bring temperance to the nation, Prohibition also put the gin mill and the bootlegger in business. With the hip flask its token, a boozy, libertine spirit infiltrated America, and Al Capone became its undisputed symbol.

When Torrio himself was the target of an attempted murder in 1925, he wisely retired, leaving everything to his chief field general, Big Al. Now Capone was the uncontested ruler of Chicago's underworld, his fists thrust into every area of the city's life, from labor racketeering and big-business scams to municipal, state, and, eventually, national politics. Capone cruised his fiefdom in a sixteen-cylinder, seven-ton armored limousine equipped with automatic weapons and bulletproof glass. He also wore a bulletproof vest under his double-breasted suit and was protected by a corps of personal bodyguards, three to four men deep. As to his social life, he was an iron butterfly who hosted huge banquets, bought up whole blocks of seats at major sporting events, and, in general, reveled in his garrulous humor and his role as the town's ultimate problem solver.

To solidify his power, Capone, who had bribed his way into immunity from criminal prosecution, waged running wars with various competitors. His chief nemesis was a North Side florist named Dion O'Banion, whose special hobby was designing showy floral displays for mobster funerals. In 1924, after Capone arranged to have his rival murdered, the O'Banion gang was taken over by Hymie Weiss. When Capone tried to hit Weiss in 1926, Weiss retaliated by spraying Capone's favorite lunch spot with a hail of automatic-weapon fire from a ten-car cavalcade. This rivalry soon ended with Weiss's murder. The climax of the mob violence in Prohibition Chicago occurred when Capone attacked the "Bugs" Moran gang, which was brazenly hijacking some of Capone's carriage-trade whiskey during the infamous Saint Valentine's Day Massacre of February 14, 1929. Capone's men—two of whom were dressed in police uniforms—machine-gunned Moran's gang in a downtown garage. This last bloodbath generated so much public furor that the federal government, under direct orders from President Hoover, went into a full-court press to put Capone behind bars.

Unlike his hapless fellow mobsters, whose careers usually ended quickly and savagely, Capone slid slowly into his grave. The FBI finally nailed him in 1931, not for one of his violent crimes, but for tax evasion. When he was released from Alca-traz, after serving seven and a half years of his eleven-year sentence, he was suffering from paresis due to syphilis. By then, according to Jack Guzik, one of Capone's prison-term business managers, Capone was as "nutty as a cuckoo." The archetypal American gangster—whose unsavory lifestyle Hollywood's mobster movies would glorify to an international audience—died eight years later on his island estate.

RACHEL CARSON

IN HER GROUND-BREAKING book *Silent Spring*, published in 1962 near the end of her life, Rachel Carson paints a picture of a world without birdsong, where the forests have died off, where human beings die of mysterious ailments and the sky rains poison. The world she describes is not the stuff of science fiction, but the one in which we live. All the horrors she catalogues have already happened on a small scale, and are a wake-up call to humanity that nature is not indestructible. Her finely crafted book made the death of nature, if the massive and indiscriminate spraying of pesticides were to continue, vivid and imaginable. *Silent Spring* was an instant best-seller, and with Carson's voice crying in the wilderness, the environmental movement was born.

She was born in Springdale, Pennsylvania, to a Scottish-American father and mother who encouraged her to write. Even as a young girl, Carson was serious and matter-of-fact and passionate about nature. She had always wanted to be a writer, and before she reached her teens, she had sold her first story to *Saint Nicholas,* a magazine for children—an achievement that was not to be repeated for many years. While attending the Pennsylvania College for Women, where she discovered her talent for science, Carson submitted poems to various periodicals, but without success. Graduating in 1928, she entered Johns Hopkins University, where she earned a master's degree in zoology in 1932. After a stint of college teaching, she supplemented her education at the Marine Biological Laboratory at Woods Hole, Massachusetts. When the responsibility of raising two children fell to her and her mother after her sister's death (her father had died the previous year), she needed a serious job; in 1936, she became a marine biologist for the U.S. Bureau of Fisheries, which later became the Fish and Wildlife Service. She rose to become editor-in-chief of service publications in 1949 and worked there until her resignation in 1952.

Carson, though, had never stopped writing, and eventually, the lyric voice of her unpublished poetry found its natural place in her prose. In 1941 she expanded an *Atlantic Monthly* essay called "Undersea" into a book, *Under the Sea-Wind,* detailing the wonders of the oceans. It was only a modest success, but with it she had found her métier. By 1955 she had completed her oceanic trilogy with *The Sea Around Us* and *The Edge of the Sea.* These clear and beautifully written works, full of feeling, struck a chord in the reading public, and it was a letter from one of her many correspondents decrying the heavy spraying of pesticides within a bird sanctuary that inspired her to investigate the effects of DDT. Her research laid the foundation for *Silent Spring.* A lover of birds and a longtime member of the Audubon Society, Carson was appalled at the wholesale damage being caused by farmers, ranchers, the U.S. Department of Agriculture, and the chemical companies, all for the "progressive" notion of crops without insects. The research and writing of the book took four years, during which she endured arthritis, ulcers, the death of her mother, and finally the knowledge that she had cancer.

Carson understood as no one else had that these poorly tested chlorinated hydrocarbons, of which DDT was one, were undifferentiating killers that attacked not only the intended targets but also birds, fish and animals. When chemicals rained onto fields from crop dusters, nothing that swam, crawled, or flew below was immune. More alarming was the discovery that humans exposed to insecticides stored these poisons in the fat cells of their bodies. While the poisons could remain dormant for years, they could also lead to cancer and other life-threatening illnesses. In a style as plainly beautiful as a Shaker table Carson taught America that everything in nature was connected, and to disturb one part of it was to change it all, at a horrifying cost.

Though today's science has since embraced this view as conventional wisdom, yesterday's science heaped scorn upon the idea and its modest originator. "Not a scientist!" they said about this woman with the zoology degree. The chemical companies, their profits severely threatened by the rapid spread of Carson's novel ideas, counter-attacked with smears and vitriol. Even *Time* magazine, after some patronizing praise for her love of wildlife, deprecated the book as "one-sided and hysterically over-emphatic." But, in this case at least, the truth won out. Five years later the Environmental Defense Fund was born to "establish a citizen's right to a clean environment"; three years after that the Environmental Protection Agency was established, and finally, in 1972 DDT was banned in the United States. Unfortunately, Carson did not live to see what *Silent Spring* had accomplished: Two years after the book's publication, she died of cancer, returning to the physical world from which all things spring. "It is good to know," she had written, "that I shall live on ... largely through association with things that are beautiful and lovely."

HENRI CARTIER-BRESSON

WITH HIS 35-MM LEICA always within reach, Henri Cartier-Bresson roamed the globe as a documentarian of "the scars of the world." A stalker of fleeting reality ever since he bought his first camera, he has succeeded in capturing those exceptional moments when meaning bursts through the scrim of mere appearance, and irony or sympathy or joy touch the soul. If photography needed justification as an art—assuming its beauty were not enough—the work of this unpretentious cameraman provided it. To view a Cartier-Bresson photograph is to *be* there, to participate in that revelatory instant. One of the fathers of photojournalism, he brought his camera with him like a loyal friend to witness the savageries of the Spanish Civil War, and later, the pomp of George VI's coronation in 1937. A few years afterward, he was in Germany recording the liberation of the concentration camps, in China chronicling the revolutionary struggle between Mao Zedong and the Nationalist Kuomintang, and in India—where on January 30, 1948—he took portraits of Gandhi only minutes before the pacifist was assassinated. In the late forties, he dashed across America, assembling an unforgettable album of the nation's more downbeat side. Some twenty years later he photographed the 1968 student-worker demonstrations in Paris.

On assignment at various times for all the important magazines and newspapers since the early thirties, Cartier-Bresson seemed to be everywhere news was happening. But he "was out to ambush scenes that would stand on their own merits," wrote Dan Hofstadter about Cartier-Bresson in *The New Yorker,* "rather than furnish illustration to the text of history." This was only natural for an artist whose passion for geometry had given him an unerring sense of spatial relationships and an appreciation for "uncomposed" pictures. Highly strung, Cartier-Bresson also had an unerring sense of how to get under the skin of those who gave him work, and his verbal outbursts tried the most devoted of companions.

A painter first, Cartier-Bresson has had a more profound effect on photography than perhaps anyone else who practiced the craft. His famous images—the nuns encountering Matisse's dancing nudes, a picnicking couple on the banks of the Marne, the Frenchwoman accusing a Nazi collaborator—are often intensely private yet capture the spirit of their time. Shot in black-and-white and uncropped, his thousands of unforgettable pictures show his regard for the dignity of his subjects. Never condescending or maudlin, he has always been aware of the power of photography. And despite his prickly personality and left-wing allegiances in the thirties and forties, his work has no ideology. His photographs have generally focused on people, catching them in that unposed instant when they are most themselves and yet communicate something more to the viewer.

Although Cartier-Bresson was born the scion of a prominent textile family, his parents were so frugal that he grew up thinking he was poor. Raised near Paris, he began his dedication to canvas and brush in 1927, studying with Cubist painter André Lhote. After a year at Cambridge and Le Bourget, France's prestigious military academy, Henri took his first dangerous journey in 1931, on a freighter to Douala in the French Cameroon. He spent twelve months on the Ivory Coast, where he almost died of blackwater fever, followed by two years of travel across eastern Europe, Mexico, Germany, and Italy on freelance assignments.

Initially inspired to take up photography by the now well-known Martin Munkacsi image of three African children frolicking in the shallows of Lake Tanganyika, Cartier-Bresson quickly garnered prominence with several international gallery exhibitions. In World War II, after serving as an assistant director for Jean Renoir during the making of *La Régle du jeu* and producing his own documentary, the thirty-one-year-old photographer reenlisted in the French army, serving in its Film and Photo Unit. Captured by the Wehrmacht on the very day of the French Armistice in 1940, he was imprisoned for three years in the worst labor camps the Germans had to offer. After several failed escape attempts, he at last made it back to France, where he joined the Résistance.

In 1947, along with Robert Capa, David (Chim) Seymour, and George Rodger, Cartier-Bresson founded the Magnum Photos agency, a boon to independent-minded photojournalists who wanted to retain their autonomy, but needed a central association to shepherd their own individual commercial interests. Six years later, a book of photographs aptly titled *The Decisive Moment* appeared, the first of his many influential published works. In 1970 after divorcing his Javanese dancer wife, Ratna Mohini, Cartier-Bresson wed Martine Franck, a talented photographer who bore him his first son. On the heels of this event, the sexagenarian resumed painting.

His own words fell short of explaining his visual genius, even after decades of work. He had always compared his efforts to Herrigel's *Zen and the Art of Archery,* meaning that, like the archer, Cartier-Bresson could never discern a specific technique to learn. For the student, he believed, there is only the continual trying and then, one day, the sudden arrival of intuition. In the meantime, he offered a few less cerebral dicta. Abandon all gimmicks, travel light, look for the "basic connections." And walk, don't run.

FIDEL CASTRO

CUBAN REVOLUTIONARY FIDEL CASTRO was thirty-three years old when the guerrilla campaign he led toppled the corrupt regime of Fulgencio Batista on January 1, 1959. Possessed of magnetism and political vision, Castro was a persuasive and mesmerizing speaker, and garnered the full support of his countrymen. As Premier and then as President of the Council of State and Council of Ministers, he was revered as a symbol of true revolution and the fight against social injustice and as a hero for his promise to bring democracy to Cuba. However, instead of building a democracy, he named himself president without holding an election, while jailing, exiling, and executing those opposed to him.

The confident son of a modestly successful sugarcane farmer, Castro received a rigorous Jesuit education. In his teens, his heroes were Napoleon, Caesar, and the courageous Latin liberators José Martí and Simón Bolívar. Enrolling in the University of Havana's law program in 1945, Fidel Castro Ruz increasingly involved himself in left-wing politics and jostled for seniority among the student gangs warring for control of the university. Known as El Loco, he reputedly shot one of his rivals, severely wounding him in the chest. His use of violence and his forceful personality became the means by which he would control his tiny Caribbean nation.

Castro's battle against the Batista regime began inauspiciously. After an unsuccessful raid on the Moncada army post in Santiago on July 26, 1953, Castro and his brother Raúl were imprisoned until 1955, when they were released under a general amnesty. From Mexico, the brothers and their "July 26" movement planned the landing in the Oriente province, the failure of which was a shining example of Castro's hubris. According to biographer Tad Szulc, Castro, surrounded by Battista's troops, was suffering from hunger and blistering thirst, at one point hiding under the shadow of sugarcane leaves alongside two fellow soldiers. The man who would build the first Communist state in the Western Hemisphere whispered excitedly to his comrades: "We are winning! Victory is ours!" Their defeat at Oriente forced them to take refuge in the Sierra Maestra, the mountain range in south-east Cuba, from which they organized a more successful campaign, forcing Batista to flee.

As the revolution's acknowledged leader, Castro moved quickly to consolidate his power, executing hundreds. In the first year of his regime, Castro took over foreign industry, disenfranchised the propertied classes (most of whom fled the country), and collectivized agriculture. In December of 1961, he declared himself a Marxist-Leninist, and aligned the goals of his Cuban revolution with those of the Soviet Union, eventually bringing in billions of dollars of aid for Cuba and giving the Soviets a foothold in the Western hemisphere only a stone's throw away from the United States. For a time, at least, he fulfilled his promises of a better life for Cubans with Soviet money—he instituted national health care and practically wiped out illiteracy—but the price Cubans paid for these reforms was nothing short of a police state.

Castro became a major figure in the Cold War because of Cuba's financial dependence on the Soviet Union. In April of 1961, the failure of the CIA-backed invasion of anti-Castro exiles at the Bay of Pigs was as much a victory for Castro as it was an embarrassment to the United States president, John F. Kennedy. Relations between Cuba and the United States deteriorated even further, culminating in 1962 with the Cuban missile crisis which followed the discovery that Castro was housing Soviet nuclear missiles in Cuba.

For one week in October, the world waited to see if the crisis would set off a nuclear war between the two superpowers. Castro was, in the end, humiliated as Premier Nikita Khruschev and President Kennedy came to terms without him, and the missiles were removed. Castro's vision of himself as a world leader and of revolution as a goal remained, however, unaltered.

As part of his program to bring revolution to other countries, Castro sent Cuban soldiers to Angola (1975–1989) and Ethiopia; he also intervened in Panama, Nicaragua, and Bolivia, where his success faltered when his friend and colleague Che Guevara was captured and killed in 1967. With the dismantling of the Soviet Union and the evaporation of its monetary support in 1991, Cuba's standard of living plummeted, but Castro—despite the economic crisis—refused internal reform and instead imposed severe austerity measures.

In the midnineties, as unemployment and food shortages increased, the dictator prepared his troops for public unrest. He continued to live, as he had for the last twenty years, with Dalia Soto de Valle, the mother of his five sons, in a private world of his own design. Outfitted in his familiar *olivos verdes* and a new bulletproof vest, Castro still was a *comandante*, but beleaguered. He faced the "dollarization" of the Cuban economy, a flourishing black market, and the effects of the United States' thirty-five year embargo. With the Cuban economy in a free fall, he responded by liberalizing it to attract new investment, a move which brought a new wave of visitors to Havana's sunny beaches. Tourism soon replaced sugar production as the nation's largest source of hard currency.

During the previous decade, Castro published *Fidel and Religion,* an interview he had given to a Dominican friar. In the book the militant atheist displayed a surprising spiritual bent, stating that "Karl Marx would have subscribed to the Sermon on the Mount." He surprised the entire world in 1998 when he welcomed Pope John Paul II, who, for humanitarian reasons, called for an end to the U.S. embargo. The aging revolutionary had called an earlier meeting with the pontiff "a miracle." As he waited out the century's end, his ailing nation sorely needed one of its own.

CHANEL

GABRIELLE "COCO"

CHALLENGING HER PROFESSION'S SACRED credo of change for change's sake, Coco Chanel offered a tradition of timeless elegance. Instead of endless innovation, Chanel created innovative classics—wardrobe standards such as turtle-neck sweaters, pleated skirts, the jumper, trousers and blazers for women, costume jewelry, the trench coat, the strapless dress, and, most famous of all, the Chanel suit, which remains even today the benchmark of elegance and style. This revolutionary designer stripped away superfluities and insisted upon the simplest of lines: no frills, no pretentiousness, no ostentation, no witty historical references to other designers and other eras. Instead of condemning last year's clothes to fashion hell, she emphasized the concept of a total image, a wardrobe that a woman could add to her whole life. Freeing women from the confines of their whale-bone corsets, from outlandish hats and voluminous long skirts in the early twenties, Chanel created clothes that were casual and comfortable but still smart. Yet neither comfort nor smartness was the secret of Chanel's endurance; her clothes started from the premise that one need not be young or beautiful to look great.

Perhaps Chanel's abhorrence of frills came from her early days of penury. The doyenne of twentieth-century fashion began her life in 1883, in Saumur, western France, the illegitimate daughter of itinerant peddlers. Upon her mother's death, the twelve-year-old Gabrielle and her sister, Julie, were abandoned by their father and eventually placed for six years in an Aubazine orphanage run by Catholic nuns. Beyond this, little is known of her early life. Chanel herself encouraged the mystery, often adding her own embellishments. What is known is that she attempted a singing career in Moulins—hence her nickname, it is said, from a song she often sang, "Qui Qu'a Vu Coco"—and that her dark-eyed good looks attracted numerous wealthy lovers who not only introduced her to high living, but helped finance her early business ventures. They contributed their clothing as well—she loved wearing men's clothes, and she adapted her lovers' ties, coats, and jackets to her own constantly evolving style. In 1913 she opened a millinery shop in Deauville. When the hardships of the war left her *haut monde* customers without their boas and brocades, she supplied them with copies of items from her own serviceable wardrobe of middy blouses and long, straight skirts that brushed just below the ankle.

Around 1914, bankrolled by one of her admirers, she opened a boutique on Paris's rue Cambon with a few hats and only one dress—but "a tasteful dress," as Chanel said.

By the twenties, the Chanel look was fully realized: the pared-down and comfortably chic suit highlighted by ropes of pearls and faux jewels, the flirtatious little hats which hid half the face, the slim and softly clinging evening frocks, the sling-back heels in neutral tones. All bore her signature of elegance and confident sexuality. To accent everything, there was her very own perfume, Chanel No. 5. Named after her lucky number—she always previewed her new collections on the fifth of the month—it quickly became the world's most famous fragrance. As the reigning queen of Paris *mode*, she also introduced bell-bottom trousers—single-handedly starting the pants revolution—short hair, and, of course, the famous "little black dress," previously the uniform of Paris shop girls. To widen her customer base and her creative clout, she allied herself with the newly elite artistic vanguard, designing costumes for playwright Jean Cocteau and ballet impresario Sergey Diaghilev and socializing with Pablo Picasso, Colette, and Igor Stravinsky, among others. In the late thirties, weary from a fierce ten-year competition with Elsa Schiaparelli, and with World War II in the wind, a disillusioned Chanel suddenly closed her couture houses. Her self-imposed retreat, divided between the Ritz Hotel in Paris, Vichy, and Switzerland, is a nettlesome chapter in her life, involving as it did a liaison with Walter Schellenberg, an aide to the infamous SS head Heinrich Himmler.

Whatever her sins, however, she was soon forgiven. Chanel made a comeback in 1954, at the age of seventy, disturbed by what she saw as the undermining of Paris couture by male designers such as Dior, Balmain, and Balenciaga. Her show fizzled in the press because, according to the fashion journalists, it failed to deliver anything new. That, of course, was what Chanel was all about. In any event, the brusque but coquettish tycoon ultimately prevailed, because not only did women buy the collection, but all Paris began turning out Chanel-style clothes.

The woman whom Picasso dubbed "the most sensible in the world" was also a devoted romantic who had always made time for *l'amour* though she had never married. Not that she had not been asked. When the duke of Westminster requested her hand, she turned him down with typical candor: "There are a lot of duchesses but only one Coco Chanel." It was her work after all that really mattered to her. When Chanel died the next year, alone in her single room at the Ritz (across the street from her lavishly decorated apartment above the House of Chanel), she had three outfits hanging in her closet. But her empire was grossing over $160 million a year, and women of all ages and classes had adopted that unmistakable Chanel look.

CHAPLIN

CHARLIE

THE FILM FOR WHICH Charlie Chaplin most wanted to be remembered was the 1925 classic *The Gold Rush*. In one of its best-known scenes, the Little Tramp—Chaplin's trademark character—boils an old shoe for dinner, then eats it with the delicate relish of an epicure. Such moments, achieved through a subtle blending of tragedy and comedy, elevate the movie—and much of Chaplin's other work—to the level of lyricism. Happily for him, this lyricism was also highly commercial.

A universally recognized and beloved creation, Chaplin's tramp evoked admiration, identification, and empathy from moviegoers around the world. Tattered but dandified, the mustachioed vagabond became cinema's Everyman; armed with only a cane, a battered bowler hat, and a cheery gumption, he shuffled gamely through personal pain and adversity. In Chaplin's later career, the public adoration of his character and his endearing antics was tempered by political criticism. Conservatives waxed increasingly indignant at the star's avoidance of military service in World War I, even though he was medically unfit; at his failure to become a citizen after four decades of tax-free living in the United States; and at his "Communist leanings" in the 1940s, a charge he formally and vehemently denied when he was summoned to testify before the House Un-American Activities Committee.

Though disavowing leftist beliefs, Chaplin had good reason to cast his sympathies with the downtrodden. The son of an alcoholic father and a mentally unstable mother who both worked in vaudeville, Charles and his half brother, Sydney, endured a squalid childhood in the slums of London. The experience imbued Chaplin with a profound identification with outcasts of all stripes, as well as a lifelong terror of poverty.

After dancing on street corners for spare change, the child performer launched his stage career at the age of eight with a clog-dancing group called the Eight Lancashire Lads. As a teenager he toured with the Fred Karno slapstick troupe, honing his comedic craft and the sleight-of-hand tricks that lent so much charm and surprise to his later roles. By the time he was twenty-one, Chaplin was already a head-liner in London's music halls. Mack Sennett, one of silent comedy's most brilliant pioneers, spotted him on tour and in 1913 brought him to Hollywood to work at the newly formed Keystone studio for $150 a week. In a single year, the multitalented Chaplin appeared in some thirty-five shorts for Keystone, many of which he wrote and directed, all the while perfecting the costume, personality, and mannerisms

of his lovable, baggy-pants underdog. In 1915 he signed with the Essanay Film Company, which later that year released his first major work, *The Tramp*, featuring Chaplin's inspired screen persona at its most sublime. In 1919, with Mary Pickford, D. W. Griffith, and Douglas Fairbanks, Chaplin helped form the United Artists Corporation, the film industry's first independent production company. Four years later he produced its first film, *A Woman of Paris*. When talkies arrived in the late twenties, Chaplin held out for as long as he could. "If I talked," he explained, "I would become like any other comedian."

It wasn't until 1940 that Chaplin actually spoke on screen in *The Great Dictator*, playing two roles—a Hitler-like ruler, pirouetting with a huge prop globe of the world, and a Jewish barber. Chaplin's films became increasingly didactic—notably the pacifistic *Monsieur Verdoux* (1947), which incited a movement to have Chaplin deported from the United States—and less enthusiastically received. His popular appeal waned, too, as fans found it difficult to reconcile the image of the tattered but plucky tramp of *City Lights* with that of the real-life multimillionaire who led an unsavory private life that included serious tax problems, highly publicized divorces, a penchant for teenage girls, and an unseemly paternity suit. In 1952, while crossing the Atlantic to attend the London premiere of *Limelight*, Chaplin learned that he would be subject to a character review upon his return. He vowed not to return to the United States—a promise he kept until 1972, when he accepted an honorary Academy Award for lifetime achievement.

The combination of scandal, politics, and his own difficult temperament finally eroded the world-wide popularity Chaplin had once enjoyed. At the end of his life, he lived largely in seclusion with his beloved wife, Oona. But, with the passage of time, Chaplin's extraordinary contribution to the cinematic art is clear; the importance of his work was recognized not only by the knighthood bestowed upon him by Queen Elizabeth in 1972 but also the many subsequent critical appraisals of his work. A polymath in his field—he wrote, produced, directed, edited, starred, and even composed the scores of his films—Chaplin's singular and stubborn genius is still evident in the extraordinary and moving pantomime of *City Lights*, the social empathy of *Modern Times*, and in his own favorite, *The Gold Rush*. Films like these have made this diminutive master of pantomime one of the most influential entertainers in show business history.

AGATHA CHRISTIE

THE MOST POPULAR MYSTERY writer and the most commercially successful woman writer of all time, Agatha Christie enjoyed a long and prolific life. Born in a seaside village in Devon to an English mother and an American father who died when she was a child, Agatha Mary Clarissa Miller had little or no formal schooling. After lessons at home with her mother, she liked to roll her hoop down the shaded lanes, imagining scenarios in far-off, fantastic places. In her mature years the celebrated but reticent Englishwoman continued to indulge her unassuming tastes, which included leisurely train rides, long naps in the sun, and hot soaks in the bathtub, where she would munch on apples while plotting her mysteries. Dame Agatha—she was made a Dame Commander of the British Empire in 1971—could certainly have afforded plusher pleasures. Her prodigious output—some 94 books, 17 plays, and more than 130 short stories—resulted in a lifetime and posthumous income generously estimated to be in the billions of dollars. Not an outrageous sum in view of the billion or so copies of her books in print in English alone (exact figures are impossible to come by), in addition to earnings from foreign-language editions and film, theater, and television adaptations. Christie, in her most productive years between the two World Wars, wrote at least a volume a year; of her productivity, she once said, "I'm an incredible sausage machine." Her loyal and voracious fans came to count on "A Christie for Christmas" every year and were contentedly spoiled along with her publishers.

Speculation on the phenomenal appeal of the Duchess of Death rarely revolves around her writing abilities. Critics have uniformly considered her literary style workmanlike—spare, easily read, strong on dialogue, skimpy on description and characterization. Christie's strong suit is plot—circuitous trails, sprinkled liberally with red herrings, wily false leads that always resolve themselves plausibly. She never strains her readers' credulity, and she gives them the added comfort of a milieu in which they feel at home. Serene and conventional, the English settings of her fictional crimes couldn't be cozier. Amid genteel surroundings—lushly carpeted libraries, cheerful kitchens, and snug vicarages—Christie plants her corpses with consummate cunning. Murders, whether by bludgeon, gunshot, or her favorite, poison, are never random, senseless, or excessively bloody affairs. Though dastardly, the misdeeds are defined by strong psychological motives, usually of the seven-deadly-sins sort. Crimes are fatal, but they are ever so discreet, and always solvable.

Christie's mother encouraged her to write stories as a child, and later her older sister challenged her to write a detective novel that might surpass the banalities of the genre they themselves enjoyed reading. Christie picked up the gauntlet in 1916 when she was married to Archibald Christie, a junior officer in the Royal Flying Corps, and working as a hospital dispensing pharmacist among war casualties. There she would pick up much of the knowledge of poisons that would prove so useful to her writing.

The Mysterious Affair at Styles, not published until 1920, introduced the redoubtable and dapper Hercule Poirot, a retired detective who relied on his "little grey cells" to get the job done. Christie considered Poirot "an egocentric creep" and would have been content if his first case had been his last, but his constituency adored his fussy demeanor and observational genius and clamored for more. So great was Poirot's hold on the public that when, after his appearance in some twenty-five novels, Christie finally killed him off in *Curtain* (1975). *The New York Times* ran his obituary on the front page. Poirot's English counterpart, the dotty but indomitable Miss Jane Marple, appeared in 1930. The ever-so-proper spinster snoop of the charming little hamlet of St. Mary Mead debuted in *Murder at the Vicarage.* In 1926 one of Christie's innovations created something of a publishing sensation: At the end of *The Murder of Roger Ackroyd,* the narrator is discovered to be the murderer.

Shortly after the publication of *Roger Ackroyd,* Christie suffered two serious shocks: the death of her beloved mother and her husband's request for a divorce to marry another woman. She behaved as one of her characters might have done—she vanished mysteriously. Rivers were dragged and hounds scoured the woods. After eleven headline-filled days, Christie was discovered at a Yorkshire hotel where, apparently suffering from amnesia, she had registered as Tessa Neele, the name of her husband's mistress. Cynics suggested it was all a publicity stunt, and perhaps Miss Marple wouldn't have accepted such an alibi, but Christie herself refused ever to speak of the incident.

Serene and fruitful years followed. After divorcing Archibald, Christie visited friends at an Iraqi dig, where she met archaeologist Sir Max Mallowan, fourteen years her junior. They went back to England on the Orient Express and eventually married, thereafter traveling together, with Christie helping out on Mallowan's digs. From their rail journeys came, inevitably, *Murder on the Orient Express.*

Agatha Christie liked thinking of her detective stories and plotting them out, but the writing itself was grueling to her—perhaps because she felt inadequate to the task, fretting that she couldn't write like Muriel Spark or Graham Greene. She worried needlessly. As a mystery writer she was unsurpassed. She didn't offer literary depth, but a down-to-earth good read and an entertaining glimpse of a gentler life, now as quaint and remote as an English country cottage.

CHURCHILL

WINSTON

IT WAS GREAT BRITAIN'S blackest hour, and yet its finest. In those harrowing first years of solitary struggle against Hitler, fortune chose Winston Churchill, an experienced soldier and a brilliant strategist, to take the helm of his embattled nation. And throughout World War II, the indomitable statesman-scholar showed prodigious zeal, bravery, and tactical prowess. (Churchill insisted on accompanying the British naval forces to Normandy on D-Day, and was persuaded to remain ashore only by the personal pleas of King George VI.) Although he begged a recalcitrant United States to join the just fight against the Nazis, the pugnacious commander was determined in the summer of 1940 that England would fight on, albeit alone. Uniting his beleaguered people with elo-quent oratory, he steadied them against the mighty armies of the Führer, "a maniac of ferocious genius," who was "the repository and expression of the most virulent hatreds that have ever corroded the human breast." The phrases were vin-tage Churchill—poetic, emphatic, and eminently quotable. When Japan's bombing of Pearl Harbor eventually forced the United States into the war, he was both relieved and elated. "I went to bed," the no-longer-lonely warrior wrote, "and slept the sleep of the saved and thankful."

A leader who found time to cultivate his talents as a painter and gardener, Winston Spencer Churchill sprang from the Victorian aristocracy. As the elder son of Lord Randolph Churchill, he carried the genes of the Dukes of Marlborough and traces of Iroquois blood through his American mother, the beautiful Jennie Jerome. It was only natural that, having been born and raised in Blenheim Palace among the many ghosts of his heroic forebears, he should attend the Royal Military College at Sandhurst. He did not, however, need prodding: He was by birth and inclination passionate about soldiering.

In 1894, after graduating with honors, the young caval-ry officer served with the Fourth Hussars and in a variety of colonial posts, including India. After a year in Sudan, he became a member of the Nile Expeditionary Force in 1898 and saw action in the famous victorious charge at Omdurman. Combining the professions of soldier and journalist, Churchill served next as a war correspondent in South Africa, where his capture by the Boers—and his subsequent escape—helped him gain public prominence and, ultimately, in 1900, a Conservative seat in Parliament. He was just twenty-six.

Churchill's distinguished public service spanned six monarchies. Beginning in 1906, he occupied several cabinet positions, and in 1911 he was made first lord of the admiral-ty, where he presided over the mobilization of the British Navy in preparation for World War I. When his personally backed Dardanelles Campaign to isolate the Turks ended in heavy losses, Churchill was demoted and returned to active duty with the Sixth Royal Scots Fusiliers. Back in office in 1917, he became minister of munitions, pushing forward the final development of the tank, the weapon that would finally stop Germany. Afterward he served as colonial secretary, secretary of state for war and for air, and chancellor of the exchequer, in which capacity he returned England to the gold standard. The General Strike of 1926, a response to growing unem-ployment, was broken by Churchill and alientated the labor movement. By 1929, he was out of office.

Forced to the sidelines, Churchill would bide his time well, writing his acclaimed volumes of history and reminis-cences and making sure his expertise in military hardware didn't grow rusty. He especially kept his eyes on the east, warning in the House of Commons of Britain's unpreparedness in the face of Hitler's growing menace. When Poland fell in September 1939, public pressure forced Prime Minister Neville Chamberlain to bring the "gallant mariner" back on board, again as first lord of the admiralty. But this time, remembering earlier battles, he would demand of his German foes total and unconditional surrender. He was sixty-five years old.

Elected prime minister himself the following year, he proclaimed his goal: "Victory—victory at all costs, victory in spite of all terrors; victory however long and hard the road may be." Offering only "blood, toil, tears and sweat," Churchill achieved his objective. And through it all, whether lamenting the victories of Rommel's Afrika Korps, rejoicing over the Wer-macht's defeat in the Russian snows, or forging strategies and postwar realities with Roosevelt and Stalin, he was the lodestar of the Allied cause.

Like all great men, the doughty and durable Churchill was not without his critics, who viewed his opposition to the self-government of the British colonies as reactionary. Other detractors cited his concessions at Yalta in 1945—by which he and FDR allowed Stalin to carve out a sphere of influence in Eastern Europe—and his postwar elevation of American interests over those of his homeland. But his legacy to the cen-tury was enormous: his stoic composure in wartime and his leadership in peace, 1951 to 1955; his enlightening and best-selling works, such as the six-volume *The Second World War*, which won him the Nobel Prize for literature in 1953; his courageous sense of adventure; and his gifts of phrasing and laguage. On becoming prime minister in 1940, Churchill wrote that he felt as if he were walking with destiny, that all his life "had been but a preparation for this hour and for this trial, and I was sure I should not fail."

COLETTE

A CHILD OF THE *Belle Epoque*, the young Sidonie Gabrielle Colette grew up surrounded by the beauty of her family's farm in Burgundy. Her mother urged her to observe everything in detail—from the shimmering last rays of a sunset to the distant warbling of a rare songbird. And her ability to capture the essence of life around her served her well; as a writer, she would tenderly evoke the lost world of childhood. But eventually she turned her attention from bucolic joys to bedroom ecstasies, using the elaborate texture of her own life to explore the mysteries of love and sex. There was much to draw from: During Colette's eighty-one years this self-styled pagan married three times, seduced her stepson, bore a child at the age of forty, and danced half-nude in bawdy Parisian revues. An inveterate sybarite, Colette was capable of swooning over the most delicate of smells or the subtlest of colors. In her seventies, though crippled by arthritis, she would rush into her garden at first light just to see what had changed during her brief sleep.

Throughout her tumultuous life, Colette enjoyed tremendous success as both a popular and a serious writer. A much lionized personality, her work reflected a unique blend of her carefully acquired Parisian sophistication, her demimonde experiences, her lusty temperament and her lyrical vision of romance and betrayal. Her fans loved her unencumbered sensuality, the breathless play of satin against flesh, without the slightest suggestion of moral judgment or opprobrium. Colette's private worlds never hint of a larger, more politically complex universe.

While her themes and subject matter were shocking to many of her time, Colette held her work to the most demanding literary standards. Whether she was writing a memoir or a libretto (she wrote one for Ravel's *L'Enfants et les Sortilèges*), a cooking column, theatrical review, or fashion piece for *Vogue*—always on her favorite blue paper—she focused her attention on *le mot juste*. Disciplined to write three hours each afternoon, Colette developed a strong authoritative voice, vibrant characters, and natural dialogue. If not the deepest or most metaphysical of the great French writers, she was among the most evocative and entertaining, and perhaps the most self-revealing. Certainly, she was the most quintessentially French.

Colette's talents were discovered and developed by her first husband, a lecher-about-town named Henri Gauthier-Villars, known as Willy, who maintained a bevy of ghostwriters he exploited to further his own writing career. After marrying the beautiful twenty-year-old country girl, he suggested that she put some of her schoolgirl memories to paper and spice them up with some invented naughtiness. Each day Colette was locked in her garret until she completed her page quota. In 1900 she wrote the first of the Claudine novels, *Claudine at School*, which was an instant success. The credit, of course, went solely to her husband. To fuel the fad, Henri forced Colette to wear the wide-collared Claudine dress whenever they went out in public.

In 1905, after twelve years and four Claudine books, Colette left the marriage, tired of her literary duties and Henri's blatant infidelities. Temporarily disenchanted with heterosexual relationships, she gravitated to a circle of lesbian friends, eventually taking up with the famous transvestite entertainer "Missy" Mathilde de Morny, the marquise de Belboeuf, with whom she performed a scandalous love scene at the Moulin Rouge in 1907. Her reputation as a libertine grew during the years of her new career as a dancer and mime in Parisian vaudeville, and she used her risqué experiences to great advantage in *Music-Hall Sidelights* (1913) and *Mitsou* (1919). Colette's style and voice matured after her second marriage, to Henri de Jouvenel des Ursins, an editor of *Le Matin,* and the birth six months later of her only child, whom she named after herself. In 1920 she wrote *Chéri,* a story of passion between an older woman and an extraordinarily handsome, pampered, much younger man. That same year she was made a Chevalier of the Légion d'honneur for extraordinary service during World War I, when she converted her family home into a hospital for the wounded.

Years passed on, and the vivid, enticing woman evolved into a more matronly but eternally coquettish Colette, her cheeks heavily rouged, her apricot-colored hair styled into a halo of tightly frizzed curls. She divorced Jouvenel in 1925, the marriage having foundered after her affair with his son by another woman. She continued writing into her sixties, devising a new fiction genre in a combination of essay and autobiography, and was honored as the first woman to be elected to the Académie Goncourt, eventually becoming its president. In 1944 she wrote *Gigi.* (When she later met the young Audrey Hepburn, she insisted that Hepburn play the role of the French sprite in Anita Loos's Broadway adaptation.) Her third try at marriage was a charm; Maurice Goudeket, sixteen years her junior, faithfully nursed her though a last decade of suffering. Bedridden, Colette wrote enthusiastically through the long evenings, close to a window looking out onto a Paris that inspired memories of more pleasure-filled days. She remained glamorous, mysterious, unconventional— like the heroine of *Claudine and Annie,* she was "the woman traveling alone."

LE CORBUSIER

HIS CONTEMPORARIES NICKNAMED HIM *Corbu*—French slang for "crow." But Le Corbusier was not his real name either, just a professional pseudonym that Parisian architect Charles-Edouard Jeanneret borrowed from his maternal grandfather in the early twenties. If changing one's name, as well as dropping one's surname, usually signals a break with the past, then the twentieth century's most influential architect was true to form. Le Corbusier became a doctrinaire visionary who seized his tradition-bound craft by its overstarched collar and made it look into the future.

Before Le Corbusier, architecture had become mostly quaint, with regionally or ethnically inspired single-family homes at one end of the spectrum and ponderous, historically informed public buildings at the other. Both styles were plentiful in urban areas whose growth was increasingly being defined more by real estate speculation and the automobile than by thoughtful planning. After Le Corbusier published his influential 1923 book *Vers une architecture (Toward a New Architecture)*—in which he famously declared that "a house is a machine for living in"—"function" came to the forefront. With their design informed by utility, geometrical principles, and economy of shape, houses, he suggested, could be scaled precisely to human proportions by using a system of mathematical measurement he called the "modulator." Le Corbusier's unadorned dwellings experimented with sheer mass, unusual new materials such as steel, concrete, and glass bricks, and such pioneering innovations as "pilotis," or stilts, to liberate buildings from the ground. "Free plans" for interior space were intended to give structures a feeling of expansiveness, non-load-bearing walls to invite the use of temporary partitions, and variations in ceiling and floor heights to create a sense of freedom and surprise. His only exterior flourishes were elongated ribbon windows and stationary louvers of concrete.

Such shocking inventions came to exemplify the International Style in architecture. Le Corbusier's manifestos, which enjoined architects everywhere to look beyond the aesthetics of construction to a concept of cities as entire, organized entities, anticipated the urbanism of today. This bold new discipline soon became the rule, as more and more cities abandoned the uninspired grid layout for design that took into account their physical environment as well as the needs and ambitions of their inhabitants. In 1935, the father of modern architecture published *La ville radieuse* (*The City of Radiant Joy*). Taking cues from Sir Ebenezer Howard's garden city ideal, which envisioned cities of limited size surrounded by lush greenbelts, Le Corbusier's book called both for the efficient use of land, and for maximizing sunlight and green open spaces. It also advocated the expression of exuberance in a technological age that he dreamed would boast of skyscrapers, modular-unit apartment buildings set above ground on huge concrete piles, and traffic zooming along elevated expressways. This imaginary civic blueprint was soon realized, changing the face of the city forever.

The original scale and sweep of Le Corbusier's mind very early outgrew the provincial confines of La Chaux-de-Fonds, the French-speaking Swiss community where he was born. The family watchmaking tradition held little interest for the artistic and musically talented youngster, who enrolled at a local arts and crafts school. In 1905, at the age of eighteen, Le Corbusier set out for Italy, where his creative sensibilities were fueled by the beauties of medieval art. After studying in the Secession tradition with Joseph Hoffman in his Viennese studio, Le Corbusier moved on to Paris and Berlin, apprenticing first under the architect Auguste Perret and then with the industrial-space designer Peter Behrens.

If Le Corbusier practiced his craft with integrity and an admirable ferocity, he was also abrasive to his associates, condescending to his clients, and, despite his growing success, frustrated in his ambitions as an artist. Having settled in Paris in 1917, he established his revolutionary fervor in architectural circles with *L'Esprit Nouveau,* a journal of contemporary thought that he founded in 1920 with fellow artist Amédée Ozenfant. The two also collaborated in originating "purism," a tame offshoot of cubism that stressed carefully defined contours and clarity of color. Although sales of Le Corbusier's artwork were negligible, he never doubted his own brilliance, devoting every single morning to his painting. Meanwhile, architectural commissions multiplied. His 1914 "Domino" project, a mass-housing experiment (never built) that employed prefabrication, and the Citrohan housing project of 1919–20 had both been highly publicized; by the thirties, Le Corbusier's new firm had advanced to consulting with large cities poised for complete restructuring.

Slight of build, bespectacled and vainly precise in clothing and manner—he rarely appeared in public without a bow tie—Le Corbusier prescribed sweeping changes over the next few decades for Antwerp, Barcelona, Stockholm, Algiers, and his own Paris (he proposed gutting its entire center). His work for both the Vichy government and victorious France in researching wide-ranging physical and social alternatives for postwar reconstruction was respectfully received, as was his consultancy in the planning of Brazil's futuristic interior capital, Brasilia. He was also part of the ten-man team that designed the United Nations headquarters in New York.

Despite Le Corbusier's undeniable impact, his architecture, which looked cheerful and streamlined on the drawing board, turned out sterile and hermetic when realized. No doubt the artist in him wished that more of his buildings soared, like his wing-roofed church at Ronchamp. But his somber spirit tethered him, securely, to earth.

JACQUES COUSTEAU

IF THE SEA IS A woman, as some myths imagine, she has beckoned to underwater explorer Jacques Cousteau many times during his peripatetic life. The first time was in his childhood at summer camp near his hometown of St. André-de-Cubzac, France. Having fallen in love with swimming, the ten-year-old determined to become a naval officer. He honed his aquatic skills as a teenager, experimenting with all manner of diving equipment, and fulfilled his boyhood dream two decades later when he was admitted into the Ecole Navale in Brest. Cousteau had purchased one of the first movie cameras sold in France, and already an enthusiast of documentary film making, cruised around the world while still a student teaching himself the craft. A few years later the sea summoned Cousteau again, this time on the shores of the Mediterranean; now a Navy flier, he had been sent there to recover from a near-fatal car crash. As he explored the clear warm waters wearing special goggles, he was transfixed by the wonders he saw: a crystalline "jungle," he called it, alive with colorful creatures and fantastic plants. "Sometimes we are lucky enough to know that our lives have been changed," Cousteau wrote in *The Silent World* (1953), "to discard the old, embrace the new." Since that time, the man in the famous black wet suit who was been called "the conscience of the sea" dedicated his life to its preservation, inviting millions to share in its mystery and possibilities.

Jacques Cousteau made his first great contribution to the science of hydrospace during World War II, when he and his friend Emile Gagnan tested their revolutionary new Aqua-Lung, a diving apparatus with an automatic gas-feeder valve. In 1943, Cousteau made his first historic dive with the portable self-contained underwater breathing apparatus—or SCUBA. This bold innovation not only opened the boundless deep to anyone ready to take a sporting plunge, but also to military and commercial exploitation. Ironically, the reservoirs of oil in the Persian Gulf—the spills of which would later become his bête noire—were discovered by Cousteau himself.

In the fifties, Cousteau designed deep-penetrating one-and two-man submarines at the Centre d'Etudes Marines Avancées he had founded at Marseilles. Later he initiated projects in long-term underwater communal living, notably Conshelf I (Marseilles) and II (the Red Sea), by using bathyspheres to descend thousands of meters. The results of this saturation diving were recorded by underwater television cameras Cousteau himself had developed.

Few of Cousteau's countless admirers knew about his espionage work in the French Résistance, particularly his daring mission to secretly photograph the Italian navy code-book, which earned him the Légion d'honneur and the Croix de Guerre. In fact, except for the parts of his career in which he actively promoted himself, Cousteau preserved his privacy. The tragic death in a plane crash of his heir-apparent, Philippe, made headlines, and a recent unauthorized biography by Richard Munson revealed that Cousteau's brother, Pierre, had been imprisoned for Nazi collaboration and felt that Jacques's efforts to smuggle him off to South America before trial had been inadequate. Munson also described Cousteau's privileged Parisian upbringing and his father's occupation as traveling companion and legal adviser to wealthy American businessmen. Despite his four children and the help of his wife Simone, Cousteau sought not the image of devoted family man, but of seafaring wanderer, filmed frequently on the prow of his famed *Calypso*. He bought the converted minesweeper in 1949, and his tales of its travels and discoveries—in his numerous best-selling books, award-winning feature films, and popular television shows, such as the long-running series *The Undersea World of Jacques Cousteau*—made him a legend.

In his sixties, still plying every waterway imaginable from the Arctic to the Amazon, Cousteau became a one-man conglomerate. Already the winner of several Emmys and Oscars, he founded The Cousteau Society in 1973 as a nonprofit, member-supported organization dedicated to educational entertainment and underwater research. In the mid-eighties, the society financed the launching of the world's first turbosail ship, the *Alcyone*, which featured two cylindrical and incredibly wind-efficient aluminum sails. Cousteau also established the Paris-based Foundation Cousteau, which has acted as a clearinghouse for marine preservation data, and the multimillion-dollar enterprise Aqua Lung International. During his eighties, having groomed his son Jean-Michel to take over, Cousteau quickened the already frenetic pace of his lobbying efforts for stricter international control of nuclear arms, toxic waste, and fishing, and promoted a global effort to tackle the catastrophic problems of world hunger, population control, and the destruction of marine habitats.

In 1993, Cousteau ousted his son and made his second wife, Francine, head of The Cousteau Society. The family rift deepened into a lawsuit when Jean-Michel named his new diving hotel venture the Cousteau Fiji Islands Resort. But Jacques, never one to look back, made plans to raise forty million dollars to replace the famous *Calypso*, which sank in Singapore harbor after being hit by a barge.

Right up to his death, he continued to focus on the world's ecosystem and its diminishing supply of water. Wherever governments would listen, "Captain Planet," as he was known, warned of the dangers of destroying its fragility. And always he spoke of the sea, her beauty, her delicate contract with humanity, and of the sustenance she gave him since he first answered her call.

MARIE CURIE

GROWING UP IN RUSSIAN-DOMINATED Poland at the turn of the century, Marie Curie was well-prepared for another kind of suppression, the severely circumscribed role of a woman in the scientific community of her day. The first female recipient of the Nobel Prize and the first woman professor in France, she discovered radium, the luminous secret of matter itself. With this breakthrough—made in partnership with her husband, Pierre—Madame Curie secured the immortality of fame for herself. Ironically, the find would slowly kill her.

The daughter of two teachers, Wladyslaw and Brom-slawa Sklodow-ska, Manya, as she was then called, was raised above the school her mother maintained in the family home in Warsaw. She intended to follow in her parents' foot-steps, but her immense aptitude in science and mathematics took her career in other directions. In spite of her enormous talent—and the example of her sister Bronia, a Sorbonne M.D.—it was not an easy journey. At the time, it was illegal for women to pursue higher education, but after a notable high school career, Manya continued to study scientific technology and social reform in the Floating University, a clandestine—and mostly female—free enterprise run by like-minded youths. After working as a governess while studying at the local Museum of Industry and Agriculture, she finally entered the University of Paris in 1891.

In Paris the twenty-four-year-old student lived with her sister and her sister's husband, a Polish doctor in exile. Though her life took on new dimensions—on arrival in this foreign city she changed her name to Marie—she still intended to return to Warsaw when her education was finished and succeed her father in teaching. After two years she obtained her *licence és sciences,* in physics, ranking in first place; the next year brought a degree in mathematics. Determined and energetic, the young scholar used her education to investigate magnet-ism, a subject that fascinated her. When she decided to work for her doctorate, an unheard-of presumption by a woman in those days, fate drew her to the laboratory of Pierre Curie at the Paris Municipal School of Physics and Chemistry. Like Marie, he was interested only in pure research, and together they launched an investigation into magnetism.

They were married in 1895, the same year the German scientist Wilhelm Roentgen discovered X-rays. The excitement this finding produced was so enormous that few paid attention to a similar discovery by Antoine Henri Becquerel of the equally mys-terious "uranic rays" produced by uranium compounds—until Marie Curie chose this subject for her doctoral thesis. While sep-arating uranium from tons of pitchblende (the residue left in the ore after the uranium is extracted), she found that the pitchblende emitted more "radioactivity"—a term she coined in 1898—*with-out* the uranium. Investigating the source of this phenomenon, that same year she and Pierre—who had left his research to join in Marie's backbreaking work—found an element they named polo-nium, after her birthplace. But Curie was not yet satisfied. Clearly, since three elements produced these uranic rays, there had to be something more powerful than uranium or polonium remaining in the ore. She found what she was looking for in a sample of bari-um: the element the Curies named radium.

Curie was not an immediate star because the discovery of any new element was—and still is—always greeted with a certain amount of skepticism. Years of analysis and careful col-lation followed, until in 1903 the Nobel in physics went to her and her husband, with Antoine Becquerel. Awarded her doc-torate that same year, the high-minded Curie refused to patent the processes she and her husband had developed for the extraction of radium—which would have made them extremely rich—believing that other researchers should have full access to them. Meanwhile, she proceeded to teach and do research and even found time to have two daughters, Ìrene and Ève. (Both would receive their own Nobels in 1935.) In 1906 Pierre was killed in a street accident by a wayward cart horse. Despite her grief, Marie persevered in her exploration of the properties of radium, for which great things were predicted, especially in curing cancer—Pierre's last paper had discussed radium's usefulness in treating ulcers and skin cancer. Marie was given his post at the Sorbonne, writing in her diary the fol-lowing day: "To do it in your place, my Pierre, could one dream of a thing more cruel." A second Nobel, this time in chemistry, came in 1911. But the prize could not sweeten the vilification and shame that arose from the publication of her tender corre-spondence with a handsome—and married—French physician. (She would have her revenge, albeit posthumously, when her ashes—and those of Pierre—were placed in France's Panthéon in 1955.) During World War I she coordinated the use of diag-nostic X-rays in field hospitals, returning after the war to pure research at her Radium Institute. Despite her diffidence, she was now, next to Einstein, the most famous scientist in the world.

But the thing Curie had unleashed from its material prison, once heralded as a universal panacea, finally bit back. Early in their work, Marie and Pierre had realized that radium was capable of causing burns; however, ignorant of how truly destructive the element could be, they had worked with it for years virtually unprotected. (Even today her notebooks are too contaminated to handle.) Inevitably, Marie grew ill. Blind, but working to the end, she died from leukemia in 1934, the result of overexposure to her own shining discovery.

DALAI LAMA

AS A REINCARNATION OF CHENREZI, the Buddha of compassion, Jetsun Jamphel Ngawang Lobsang Yeshe Tenzin Gyatso, fourteenth Dalai Lama, is hailed by the Tibetan Mahayanan Buddhist faithful as "Holy Lord, Gentle Glory, Eloquent, Compassionate, Learned Defender of the Faith." His title Dalai Lama means "Ocean of Wisdom." As such, he is also the holy king of the ancient theocratic society of Tibet, a country he has not seen since he was twenty-four years old; for as suzerain of his nation, he is censured and exiled, as reviled by his political enemies, the Chinese Communists, as he is revered by the rest of the world.

In 1937, the monks and oracles at Lhasa, temple-capital of the mysterious "Roof of the World," began their search for the successor to the thirteenth Dalai Lama. In a trance, one of them saw a temple with a jade and gold roof and a peasant's house nearby. Recognizing the significance of the vision, and interpreting the sudden appearance of strange clouds and rainbows, the high monks sent emissaries throughout the kingdom. In the village of Takster, they found a little boy who carried all eight bodily marks of the reincarnated Chenrezi and who passed the tests that proved he was their reincarnated leader. Taken away to Lhasa, the four-year-old Dalai Lama lived in the Potala, the thousand-chamber palace that was Tibet's Vatican, where he slept in the unheated, mice-infested bedroom of the deceased Great Fifth Dalai Lama and was trained in religion and metaphysics. In time he obtained a doctorate in Buddhist studies, which included logic, Tibetan art, Sanskrit, medieval and Buddhist philosophy, poetry, music, drama, astrology, and—perhaps most important to his future role as a political leader—dialectics. He became proficient in debate with *tsenshaps,* experts trained in logic and rhetoric. As a fun-loving adolescent, the Dalai Lama often dismayed his mentors with a taste for old automobiles, which included a Dodge and two 1927 British Austins. He fixed up one of the latter and promptly ran it into a post. When he wasn't studying, holding court, or wrecking cars, he played with tame animals in the gardens of the Potala.

In 1949 the young man's hermetic world was shattered when the Chinese Communists, under Mao Zedong, conquered Chiang Kai-shek's hopelessly corrupt Nationalists and immediately set their eyes on the little theocracy to the west. The following year, the Chinese invaded Tibet, citing "imperialist aggression" as a pretext. Pressured by advisers and the populace, the Dalai Lama fled to India, only to return when his enemies promised full political and religious freedom. For the next nine years he struggled to negotiate continued autonomy for Tibet with Mao and to stem steady Chinese encroachment. He became Mao's friend and confidant, though he could

never accept his military approach to politics. But Buddhist adherence to the principles of nonviolence and truth was, in the short run, no match for the crude propaganda of the People's Liberation Army. Nor was the Dalai Lama's pacifism sufficient to deter some of his own people from mounting a guerrilla rebellion, funded by the Khampa of eastern Tibet and supplied by the American CIA. The insurrection elicited predictably vicious responses from the Chinese occupation forces. In 1959 the Chinese invited the Dalai Lama to a theatrical performance with the proviso that he leave behind his bodyguard. Aware that earlier Tibetan leaders had gone off to such fetes and never returned, thousands of people surrounded his summer residence to prevent him from going. The Chinese military moved into position around the palace but, disguised as a soldier, the Dalai Lama snuck out on the night of March 17. By March 20, when the Chinese attacked, crushing the Tibetan rebellion and killing thousands, he had fled his land for good, followed by more than one hundred thousand destitute Tibetan refugees. He eventually emerged in India, where the friendly government defied the Chinese by helping him set up a government in exile. The Dalai Lama felt confident enough to ignore official warnings not to engage in politics, possibly because he had added Indian prime minister Nehru to his list of intimates. With the Chinese violently purging the Tibetan religious community and populace, the Dalai Lama patiently lobbied the world for recognition of Tibet's rights as a nation.

People who came to the Dalai Lama, especially from the western democracies, found him avuncular, inquisitive and fascinated by things scientific. He once suggested playfully that if the Buddha's words did not conform with science, they must be rejected, yet he retained a very unscientific belief in such things as oracles. Despite the atrocities committed against his subjects, he maintained his pacifist views. He negotiated with the United Nations in 1965, visited the United States in 1979, and on both occasions he refused to condemn his tormentors, commenting that they were his spiritual teachers, and even acknowledged that they had done some good for Tibet. In 1989, thumbing its prestigious nose at the Chinese government, the Norwegian Nobel Committee awarded the Peace Prize to the Dalai Lama. In accepting it, he said, "I am a simple Buddhist monk—no more, no less." The Chinese showed their displeasure by rejecting his choice for a Panchen Lama in Tibet, installing one of their own tame Tibetans in the office. The Dalai Lama responded with a typically serene dissent, again going over Chinese heads to appeal to global opinion. As the century closes and Buddha's teachings speed their move westward, the world waits to see whether this monk's selfless devotion will deter an empire.

DALI

SALVADOR

INITIALLY HAILED AS A Surrealist master, subsequently derided as a promoter of kitsch, Spanish painter Salvador Dali was the prototype of the modern self-exalting artist whose greatest creation is himself. In his calculated assaults on propriety and his tireless pursuit of publicity, Dali was the spiritual father of such latter-day art-world celebrities as Andy Warhol and Jeff Koons. But in his prime, he was also an acknowledged leader of the revolutionary Surrealist movement and its most famous exponent in the United States. In the fifties and sixties there was probably not a dormitory in America that did not display somewhere on its walls a print of Dali's masterpiece, *The Persistence of Memory* (1931), with its eerie depiction of watches melting in a barren landscape. As the liquid timepieces and other hallucinatory images from Dali's oeuvre became part of the world's psychic and artistic vocabulary, their creator sank into sideshow sensationalism, eventually becoming as bizarre as his art.

Salvador Felipe Jacinto Dalí y Domènech was born in Fiqueras, Spain, in Upper Catolonia to supportive and well-to-do parents who loved to paint and draw. They were also in perpetual mourning over the untimely death of Salvador's older sibling, also named Salvador. All his eccentricities, the painter later claimed, grew from his childhood desire to emerge from the shadow cast by his dead brother. Typical of his need to shock, Dali claimed to have derived "delirious joy" from violent childhood acts such as pushing another little boy off a suspension bridge and kicking his younger sister in the head. But apart from the nervousness and theatricality that would last throughout his life, his childhood was superficially normal.

He exhibited his first paintings at age fourteen, and at seventeen he enrolled in the Escuela Nacional de Bellas Artes de San Feruanda in Madrid, where he produced workmanlike paintings first in the classical mode and later in the "metaphysical" style of the Italians Georgio de Chirico and Carlo Carrà, important precursors to the Dadaists and Surrealists. As Dali discovered the bizarre world of Dada, his sartorial and behavioral excesses brought him into conflict with school authorities, who suspended him for causing a small riot. Upon his return, the caped dandy refused to be examined by professors he deemed his inferiors. He was summarily expelled in 1926. In 1927, he produced *Blood Is Sweeter Than Honey,* which proved to be a harbinger of his later morbid and hallucinatory work.

In 1928 Dali grandly traveled by taxicab from Madrid to Paris, where he was introduced to the still-infant Surrealists by their "pope," the French poet André Breton. The meeting inspired the Catalonian to produce a series of dreamscapes of the unconscious, which with a keen ear for a sound bite, he dubbed his "critical-paranoiac" style. This method consisted of looking at one image and seeing another within it, a process influenced by his reading of Sigmund Freud, the Surrealist movement's Aquinas. Dali's future excesses are in evidence in *The Lugubrious Game* (1929), for example, a picture whose onanistic imagery disturbed even the shock-happy Breton.

That same year Dali, also a prolific writer, collaborated with fellow Iberian Luis Buñuel to produce *Un Chien Andalou* (*An Andalusian Dog*). With its grisly image of a woman's eyeball being slashed with a razor, this seventeen-minute silent film still has a nightmarish power. By the time Dali painted *The Persistence of Memory* in 1931, his relationship with the other Surrealists had been soured by his yearning for commercial success and a fascistic political bent that the Surrealists—who were enamored of Communism—found repellent. Breton took to calling him "Avida Dollars," a nasty anagram of the painter's name.

During World War II Dali broke with Breton and left for America, where he and his Russian-born wife, Gala—who'd been involved with a number of other Surrealists—exploited the movement's exoticism to the hilt. Fashion-design projects, such as the "shoe hats" and "lobster dresses" he designed for couturier Elsa Schiaparelli and other commercial ventures, combined with innumerable photo sessions and public antics to make the artist his most important product. Dali would also collaborate with Alfred Hitchcock on the dream sequences of the director's 1945 film *Spellbound*. As his fame grew, however, his art suffered.

Dali's rather baffling reconversion to Catholicism after the war resulted in a series of slick, shallow images like the almost photo-realistic *The Madonna of Port-Lligat* (1950), which he immodestly proclaimed as the painted banner of a new renaissance and gave to the Pope. He was still capable of producing oddly powerful works, such as *Leda Atomica* (1949) and *The Last Supper* (1955), but these were shrewd displays of virtuosity rather than windows on a new artistic reality. Dali was swiftly becoming a factory of weirdness with an enviable profit margin. By 1964 his commercial corruption was complete: he signed hundreds, possibly thousands, of blank sheets of paper—to be stamped later with the inscription "limited numbered print"—that were then peddled to naïve collectors from Honolulu to The Hague for a total price tag of over $625 million.

As his art dissolved into schlock and deception, Dali's appearance grew ever more fanciful, his shoulder-length black hair and waxed, exclamation-point mustachio as recognizable a trademark as the snails, erotic pianos, and fiery giraffes that graced his paintings. When Gala, his muse and protector of 48 years, died in 1982, Dali oscillated between despair and the old defiant hucksterism. But the flame had gone out, and in 1989 the artist himself passed into the void from which his best images had emerged.

BETTE DAVIS

NO ACTRESS IN THE history of movies, costume designer Edith Head once noted, dropped a mink like Bette Davis. That chic yet casual gesture in *All About Eve* (1950) is every bit as telling as her character's famous line warning everyone in the room to fasten their seat belts for the "bumpy night" ahead. A virtuoso of stage business, Davis often used the most unobtrusive of movements to convey meaning: the impatient, staccato pumping of her bejeweled wrist as the imperious queen in *The Private Lives of Elizabeth and Essex* (1939) or the haughty carriage of Regina Giddens in *The Little Foxes* (1941). And who could smoke a cigarette more eloquently: at times taking quick, hungry drags, at others just letting the smoke curl languidly past her magnificent unblinking eyes? She could use the naughty vice to sensual ends, too, as in the unforgettable scene from *Now, Voyager*, when Paul Henreid provocatively lights two cigarettes in his mouth and Davis, her smoldering gaze fixed on his, accepts one with calculated matter-of-factness.

No other actress has even vaguely looked or sounded like the not-quite-beautiful peroxide blonde from Lowell, Massachusetts, whom one movie executive derided as a woman no man would want to go to bed with at the end of a picture. Broad of brow, with a flawless complexion and a slightly dispirited mouth, Davis lacked the sex-goddess quotient that sparks overnight sensations. Her diction, crisp as a New England autumn and timed to a nanosecond for effect, was particularly distinctive. So was her voice, which she used as an accomplished singer would, changing tones and octaves for subtle emotional effect. She could fling words out like grenades or lob them with a velvet-gloved delicacy. Strong-minded, nervy, and doggedly ambitious, she chose, in her later, more successful years, scripts more tailored to her personality. Challenging herself as no actress ever had, Bette Davis played with unmatched mastery everything from classy dames and clip-joint chippies to decorous governesses and long-suffering wives.

Davis's career, initially hindered by bad screenplays, finally took off in 1934 with her portrayal of the slovenly cockney waitress in Somerset Maugham's *Of Human Bondage*. After this role she was rewarded with some of the most memorable scripts ever written and would prove her genius for portraying the emancipated woman, the more subtle but no less rebellious sister of the classic wisecracking "bitch on wheels." "Women's films," as they were patronizingly called, became her forte, a genre she ennobled with her intelligence, wit, and unyielding spirit.

Bette was born Ruth Elizabeth Davis on April 5, 1908, to a law-student father whom she could never please and a forceful mother who, upon her divorce when Bette was seven, turned her photography hobby into a career to support herself and her two children. "There was no such word as *can't* for my mother," said Davis, and Bette went to the right schools, even though she had to help with the expenses by waiting on tables. As a teenager, she nurtured her dream of acting by performing in amateur productions, and after drama school and considerable experience in summer stock, she debuted on Broadway in the 1929 comedy *Broken Dishes*. In 1930 Davis botched a screen test for the Paramount Studios in Astoria, New York, but in 1931, while in Hollywood, the discouraged starlet was tapped by George Arliss to star opposite him in the Warner Bros. film *The Man Who Played God*. Warner Brothers was so impressed that it put Davis under contract for several years, but they never formulated a plan to utilize her talents.

After completing six films annually for four grinding years, Davis finally rebelled. Fuming over the low salaries she was paid for such embarrassments as *20,000 Years in Sing Sing* and refusing yet another weak screenplay, she fled to England and was promptly sued by the studio in 1936 for breach of contract. Warner Bros. won the case, but since Davis's action came to be viewed as a symbolic challenge to the oppressive contract system, the gains were hers. Henceforth, she got better roles, a bigger salary, and longer vacations, not to mention improved status among her peers. Davis had already won an Academy Award as the dipsomaniac actress in *Dangerous* (1935), a performance in which she stunned audiences by making herself as unglamorous as possible. Three years later *Jezebel* gave her a second statuette, which Hollywood historians claim she named "Oscar" for the middle name of her then husband. Flings with Howard Hughes and William Wyler, among others, followed along with the mysterious death of her second husband.

Talented though she was, the thrice-divorced Davis was unable to pull off the tricky combination of marriage and career. Her last years, however, were brave and busy, highlighted by her riveting performance in *Whatever Happened to Baby Jane?* (1961) and marred by the physical hardships imposed by serious surgeries and a stroke. Even more painful was the publication of a vitriolic tell-all book penned by her daughter, B. D. Hyman. Irascible and bossy, and never one to give in, the mordantly humorous actress—she hung a black wreath on her door to celebrate her seventieth birthday—was working on her last film just weeks before her death. "Old age is no place for sissies," the indomitable Davis loved to quip. Dead at eighty-one, Hollywood's toughest cookie had lived out her favorite slogan in spades.

JAMES DEAN

JAMES DEAN ENDURES IN our memories perhaps because we have so few memories of him. His legend rests on just three films—all made during an eighteen-month period. In 1954 he appeared as Cal, the confused Cain-like son in Elia Kazan's movie version of John Steinbeck's novel *East of Eden*. The following year, he exuded even more raw sex appeal playing the title role in Nicholas Ray's famous drama of teenage delinquency, *Rebel Without a Cause*. A few months after that, he made *Giant*, George Stevens's sprawling epic of Texas life, costarring Rock Hudson and Elizabeth Taylor. As the slouching, defiant ranch hand Jett Rink, Dean ages from a callow youth infatuated with the boss's wife (Taylor) to a grizzled fifty-year-old who attempts to seduce her daughter. In life, Dean failed to see twenty-five.

This icon of troubled American youth—for some, of homosexual angst—started out as an Indiana farm boy. His parents, Winton and Mildred Dean, named him James Byron after the Romantic poet whose tormented spirit he would echo in his own life. When he was two, his family moved to the Hoosier farm village of Fairmount; just two years later, his father, a dental technician, was transferred to a hospital in Santa Monica, California. If there was a primary cause for the pain James Dean displayed to the world, it was his mother's death from cancer when he was only nine years old. His anguish was compounded when his father sent him back to Indiana, accompanied by his mother's body. In Fairmount once more, living with a kindly Quaker aunt and uncle, the sensitive adolescent had what in many ways was an idyllic existence, though he missed his father. But providence sent him the mentor he was lacking in the form of his high school drama teacher, Adeline Nall. In between 4-H club meetings and winning basketball games for the Fairmount Quakers, Dean—under Nall's tutelage—appeared in the school plays, competed in debates, and won the state prize in recitation. In 1950, he returned to California to attend college, later claiming that he'd long been eager to leave Indiana, but didn't want to hurt anyone's feelings.

Dean was cast in a UCLA production of *Macbeth,* but college exerted no great hold over him. Television, oddly enough, did: It was where he honed his craft. Most of his professional life, in fact, was spent playing small parts and large in such small-screen productions as *Father Peyton's TV Theatre, U.S. Steel Hour,* and *Treasury Men in Action.* Observing classes at the celebrated Actors Studio in New York, Dean developed the brooding style which was to become his trademark. What he didn't learn there, Dean acquired by sizing up other people and getting them "down."

An inveterate mimic, he often made his friends nervous with his skillful impersonations of them. In 1954, while appearing in a Broadway production of André Gide's *The Immoralist,* he was signed to a Hollywood contract.

To watch Dean's soaring performance as Jim Stark in *Rebel,* surely his signature role, is to understand what made Dean, despite a career cut short, into a cult figure for the century. His powerful portrayal single-handedly sustains a vehicle that would otherwise be a typical B melodrama. Even the other actors seem to watch in awe as the blue-jeaned, delinquent mutters, screws up his face, cajoles, and bellows, looking by turns sweeter than light and cooler than an assassin. With bravado masking vulnerability, Dean captures perfectly the torment of a sullen young man in search of truth.

Off screen, he flirted with danger. Dean's fascination with speed was the despair of his producers. His film success meant he could afford better and faster sports cars, and with the seriousness of an athlete, he competed in a succession of races, defeating professionals as well as amateurs. He announced that he preferred driving to acting, and would continue to race, regardless of the risks it posed to his career. He was not kidding. On September 30, 1955, only three days after finishing *Giant*—and two weeks after filming a safety commercial for the National Highway Committee—Dean climbed into his brand-new Porsche Spyder 550, a mean machine that had been custom-painted with the words "Little Bastard," and took off for a race in Salinas. At 3:30 P.M., somewhere near Bakersfield, he was ticketed for driving sixty in a forty-mile-per-hour zone; two hours and fifteen minutes later, at the intersection of Routes 466 and 41 near Paso Robles, Dean—cruising at a speed variously estimated to be anywhere from seventy-five to one hundred miles per hour—collided head-on with a Ford driven by a college student. The boy survived; Dean, hardly more than a boy himself, died instantly. Photographs of the aftermath show a twist of metal surrounded by grim-faced, crew-cut deputies.

Rebel premiered four weeks after the crash, followed by *Giant* a few months later. The studio's boss, Jack Warner, cynically predicted that no one would turn out to watch a corpse. But they did—and they haven't stopped since. Among teenagers the world over, Dean became an instant idol, paving the way for later examples of adolescent rebellion as diverse as Elvis Presley and Bob Dylan. Among actors, he became an archetype, a mythic model that both invited and defied emulation. Scores of articles and books have been written in an attempt to explain his phenomenal, and undying, appeal.

SIMONE DE BEAUVOIR

FRENCH PHILOSOPHER AND AUTHOR Simone de Beauvoir came of age intellectually during the Nazi occupation of Paris, a tumultuous era in which contrasting "isms" dominated all cultural debates. A fiercely dedicated writer who set about her craft at age seven, by the early 1940s she began to deplore her early political naïveté and found herself gravitating toward socialism and existentialism, often shaping her philosophical vision at the Café Flore, a pen in one hand, a cigarette in the other. Usually at her side was her lifelong partner, Jean-Paul Sartre, the man who would function variously, until his death in 1980, as de Beauvoir's lover, friend, role model, mentor, antagonist, co-conspirator, and "dream companion." Their much publicized life together—almost fifty years of intensely shared experience—would become one of the century's most fascinating relationships, an alliance that involved such prodigious devotion and deception that it is almost impossible to speak of one partner without alluding to the other.

The two met while attending the Sorbonne's Ecole normale supérieure in 1929. They were both in their early twenties, both studying for their doctorates in philosophy, and planning to be teachers. The frisson between them was immediate, and Sartre almost instantly proposed—not marriage, exactly, but an arrangement. In Sartre's words, "What we have is an *essential* love; but it is a good idea for us also to experience *contingent* love affairs." Both were to honor this open contract assiduously, Sartre with his liaisons (he always said he preferred croissants to sex, yet he managed to work a startling number of women into his life) and de Beauvoir with hers, many of which were conducted with Sartre's closest male friends or his mistresses. De Beauvoir was also romantically involved for many years with the American novelist Nelson Algren—she wore the ring he gave her upon their first meeting in 1947 for the rest of her life—and the filmmaker Claude Lanzmann, best known in America for *Shoah*. But what both Sartre and de Beauvoir seemed to enjoy more than these extracurricular intimacies was reporting them in detail to each other. Such behavior was far removed from the privileged bourgeois childhood de Beauvoir had spent in Mont-parnasse. But her mother's efforts to instill in her strict Catholic precepts failed almost from the beginning; the stubborn young schoolgirl declared herself an atheist at the age of fourteen.

Three years later, as she would recall in one of her five volumes of memoirs, de Beauvoir decided that she would become an author, based largely on the sense of meaninglessness that came with her loss of faith. By writing works that reflected her own life, she reasoned, she would recreate herself and thereby justify her existence. Thus, in the absence of divinity, she would provide meaning for her life and take responsibility for her own existence. At a very young age, not only was de Beauvoir committed to her life's work but also already living out the existentialist ethic that would become so large a part of her life. And indeed, this provocative writer's thoughts and experiences in later life proved to be as intertwined with her literary output as her numerous works were a reflection of her day-to-day reality.

After teaching posts in Marseilles and Rouen, where at Sartre's urging de Beauvoir applied herself to writing, she returned to Paris to stay. She wrote novels and plays, along with straightforwardly philosophical books, including *The Ethics of Ambiguity* (1947), a lucid defense of existentialism. But it was the publication of *The Second Sex* in 1949 that assured her reputation and caused a storm of controversy on both the right and the left. An exhilarating, scholarly, and passionate dissection of women's subordinate status in Western culture, *The Second Sex* placed the plight of women squarely at the door of culture, not biology. Her revolutionary statement, "One is not born a woman, one becomes one," became at once the manifesto and call to arms of the emerging international feminist movement. De Beauvoir arrived rather late in life at the feminist barricades but, once converted, saw the potential of uniting feminism with socialism as an engine of social change. In the seventies she became a formidable activist, signing the Manifesto of the 343, a statement signed by 343 women who admitted to having had an abortion, which was then illegal in France. She also helped organize a tribunal protesting crimes against women.

In her later years, de Beauvoir accelerated her radical activities, traveling extensively with Sartre to meet world leaders, protesting both French torture of Algerians and American involvement in Vietnam, and serving as president of the French League for Women's Rights. Always struggling against conventional propriety, she, at age sixty, and Sartre sold a banned Maoist newspaper on the streets of Paris, a gesture for which she was promptly arrested. She reconciled with her mother in 1963, which is touchingly recounted in her book *A Very Easy Death*, written the following year. In 1970, courageously facing her own declining years, de Beauvoir wrote *The Coming of Age*, another scathing indictment of society, this time for its treatment of the elderly. When Sartre died intestate in 1980, his young Algerian mistress, whom he had adopted in 1965, was in control of his estate, and consequently de Beauvoir could not even publish his letters to her without the mistress's permission. Finally, she simply published them illegally. Such act notwithstanding, de Beauvoir maintained her loyalty to Sartre's memory until her death six years later, her own intellectual stature intact and enduring.

DE GAULLE

CHARLES

THE REBELLIOUS YOUNG FRENCH general who had rejected the disgrace of surrender to the Germans in 1940 and four years later helped drive them from French soil was, ironically, forbidden by the Allies to land at Normandy on D-Day. He finally set foot on those bloodied beaches eight days later, and when he triumphantly entered the Hôtel de Ville in Paris on August 24, 1944, all of France gratefully surrendered its wounded heart to him. Arrogant, ruthless and brave, the brilliant soldier-statesman would dominate his nation's political passions until his death twenty-six years later, rebuilding France's tattered global image and holding sway with a grandeur normally reserved for monarchs.

De Gaulle's sense of grandeur was fostered by parents dedicated to both church and state. Born in Lille, he was educated by the Jesuits and raised by his professor father, a veteran of the Franco-Prussian War, to take pride in his role as a Roman Catholic born to the uniform. He was also taught to understand that his destiny was thus intertwined with that of his country. A graduate of the Ecole Militaire of Saint-Cyr, de Gaulle distinguished himself in World War I at the Battle of Verdun where he was wounded three times and captured at Douaumont in March 1916. During the next three years, as a prisoner of war, he wrote his first book, *La discorde chez l'ennemi* (1924), an examination of the relationship between the military and civil sectors in Germany. A gifted writer whose poetic touch was rivaled only by his skill at delivering eloquent yet seemingly impromptu speeches, de Gaulle produced numerous and lucid works on military strategy, most of which were ignored by his colleagues and opposed by France's left-wing leaders. Arguing for tactical mobility in his *Vers l'armée de métier* (1934), published as *The Army of the Future* in 1941, he correctly prophesied that professional mechanized armies would be the key to winning another war.

When the next world conflict began, de Gaulle found himself, appropriately, the commander of a tank brigade. In 1940 he was promoted by Premier Paul Reynaud to the cabinet post of undersecretary of state for defense and war; shortly thereafter, with the Wermacht occupying the northern quarter of France, he watched with interest as his old mentor—the famed hero of Verdun, Field Marshall Henri-Philippe Petain—assumed national leadership. When the young brigadier general heard of Petain's plans to negotiate with the Germans in order to create a collaborationist government at Vichy, he disagreed passionately and immediately flew to London. Within days, he named himself the leader of the French Resistance and, with Prime Minister Winston Churchill's permission, broadcast his appeals to his compatriots back home to resist surrender. Declaring that "the flame of French resistance must not and shall not go out," the soldier without an army proclaimed: "France is not alone.

She is not alone! She is not alone!" On August 2, 1940, two weeks after his first radio address, a French court martial tried him in absentia and sentenced him to death for treason.

A virtual nonentity in both England and his own country—and with no actual forces to back him up—de Gaulle gathered together what few supporters he already had and from 1942 on moved to consolidate his ties with the French colonies in West Africa and the underground Resistance movement. After the American and British landing in North Africa in November of that year, he saw his chance. He moved his offices to Algiers and with General Henri Giraud formed the French Committee of National Liberation which, in 1944, became the French republic's provisional government. Churchill, who tried to ignore the prickly general's nationalistic preoccupations, viewed him as a necessary evil. American President Franklin D. Roosevelt was less inclined to suffer de Gaulle's messianic stance. But by the time de Gaulle was elected the organization's president, he had succeeded through strained negotiations with Churchill and F.D.R. in ensuring that his nation would emerge from the war on an equal footing with the other Allies.

In 1946 de Gaulle retired, but returned to public life in 1958 and was elected President of France's Fifth Republic. As the architect of the Republic's constitution—which called for a nationally elected president and a weak parliament—he achieved what had eluded his country through 123 governments in the previous 83 years: political stability. He also imposed a foreign policy of decolonization, which included independence for Algeria, a controversial move that exposed France to potential civil war and de Gaulle to two assassination attempts. As a world figure, he championed the right of all nations—and certainly his own—to operate autonomously and managed to stand clear of the superpowers' struggle for world domination. Many of his international moves, such as his withdrawal from NATO in 1966, were interpreted as anti-American, just as his pursual of "desatellization" of eastern Europe was seen as Anti-Soviet.

The strikes and riots of May 1968 cast a shadow over de Gaulle, and when an insignificant referendum he had insisted on was defeated, he left Paris for his austere little house in Colombey-les-Deux-Églises. There he lived as he had always lived, without luxurious amenities, and largely without friends, except for his devoted wife Yvonne. When he died in 1970 and President Georges Pompidou declared "France is a widow," few remembered the protesters' cruel chants of "De Gaulle to the museum!" They recalled a man with a purpose much larger than himself, an obstinate dreamer who channeled his tremendous ego into the cause of his nation and, for over a quarter of a century, *was* France.

DIANA, PRINCESS OF WALES

WHEN DIANA, THE PRINCESS OF WALES, died suddenly in a car crash at the age of thirty-six, an otherwise fractious world seemed united in mourning. It was not just her celebrity that drew countless people from different nations to watch her funeral, to sign books of condolence, or to set up flower-laden shrines to her memory. Nor was it just the tragic ending of a young life which had seemed so full of promise and happiness when she married Prince Charles in a fairy tale wedding complete with horse-drawn carriages. It was not even the future she had been denied by death—the possibility of personal happiness and the fulfillment of seeing her sons grow up. People mourned Diana because they felt they knew her. The world had, after all, watched this most photographed woman of the century come of age.

Despite the very privileged circumstances in which Diana lived, her marital problems and her search for self-esteem were familiar to many. The way, too, in which happiness eluded this vibrant young woman struck a sympathetic chord in people's hearts. The relentless publicity—once she stepped into the spotlight, little she did was truly private—and the playing out of what became a rather tawdry royal soap opera did not diminish the public sense of Diana as a woman trying to give her life meaning. Her efforts to remake herself, her struggle to save a marriage that was probably destined to fail, and her attempt to keep the lives of her children normal amidst public scrutiny made Diana seem all the more like the people who adored her. Beneath the glamour, it seemed, was a person with heart, whose commitment to treating the less fortunate with humanity was sincere. Diana, Princess of Wales, became an icon of the century not for what she achieved but because of what she wanted to achieve.

Both Diana's life and the public's fascination with it were both an emblem and a result of the century's changing institutions, conventions, and technology. The century began with Queen Victoria's death in 1901, a monarch rarely seen and respectfully described in the press. She was succeeded by her son, Edward VII, whose romantic indiscretions were never publicly aired. By 1936, though, the world listened on radio as his son, Edward VIII, abdicated the throne to marry the woman he loved, an American divorcée. Royal life, once private, had become increasingly public. The new medium of television offered the royal family a powerful public relations tool they thought they understood. They used it to great advantage at the 1952 coronation of Queen Elizabeth II and at Diana's own 1981 wedding to Prince Charles, watched by one billion people all over the globe. But they miscalculated the control they had lost by putting the royal family in the public view. And after the royal wedding, as social mores continued to relax, what was considered newsworthy about the royal family's personal lives changed dramatically. There was now little about them that could truly remain private.

Diana had, at first, seemed the perfect choice to reinvigorate the monarchy's public image. Thirteen years younger than the man she was to marry, she was pretty and sweet. Born to an appropriate family—she was the daughter of the eighth earl of Spenser and Frances Roche—she could trace her bloodlines back to Charles II. Her parents divorced when she was seven, and Diana lived with her father, attending West Heath School and then a finishing school. Unaffected and direct, she had worked as a nanny, a governess, and a kindergarten teacher. Her fresh-faced openness and her virginal past made her, in royal eyes, the perfect match for the aging bachelor who had already garnered a reputation as an interiorized, rather unsociable man. Diana was a welcome addition to a royal family distinguished largely by its stiffness.

From the moment the engagement was announced, Diana was thrust into the limelight. Her wedding in July 1981 was the wedding every woman in the world had ever dreamed of, perfect down to the smallest detail. The announcement of her first pregnancy and then the births of her sons, William, the heir to the throne, and Harry, seemed the finishing touches to an ideal life. Over the years, in countless photographs, the world watched the shy young girl grow up into a slim, exquisitely dressed woman, whose love for her children was always in evidence. But what the constant presence of photographers also revealed was the growing distance between Diana and Charles; the deterioration of her marriage and the reasons for it were played out in full view.

By 1985, Diana was under severe strain; she was bingeing, purging, taking over-the-counter medication to stay awake, and engaging in self-mutilation. The clothes, the gems, the royal houses were not enough to assuage either her unhappiness or her profound sense of betrayal. In 1996, the marriage officially ended, and a distraught Diana was photographed leaving the courthouse in tears. The public's identification with both her plight as a woman deceived and her need for love and affection was profound.

Long before the end of the marriage became official, the public sided with the young woman who they saw as manipulated and hurt by the royal house. With the battle lines drawn between Diana and the House of Windsor, the royal family seemed only to stumble, bested by the telegenic woman they had once invited into their midst. When she was stripped of her title, her admirers bestowed their own: she was "the people's Princess." They watched with pride as Diana used her celebrity to attract attention to the causes she championed; they were moved when she embraced a patient dying of AIDS or stood in the middle of landmine-filled fields.

Diana's insistence on compassion, good works, and the value of love proved both the undoing and the reinvention of the British monarchy. Her untimely death meant, too, that Diana would always stay young, beautiful, and vibrant in the public's imagination.

MARLENE DIETRICH

STRUTTING IN AN IMPECCABLY tailored tuxedo and a man's fedora or floating through shadowed rooms in a gossamer gown, Marlene Dietrich was the epitome of androgynous allure in cinema's golden age. A ravishing and mysterious femme fatale, she brought to the films of the thirties and forties a smoldering, hard-edged sophistication that her fans and scores of lovers—from George Patton and Edward VIII to Edith Piaf and Gertrude Stein—found just threatening enough to be irresistible.

At the age of eighteen Maria Magdalena Dietrich von Losch, namesake of the penitent prostitute of the New Testament, had her career as a violinist ended by a damaged hand. Choosing instead to pursue acting, her other passion, she auditioned for drama school in Berlin at age twenty-one. The struggling young performer developed her talents through a number of insignificant roles while she supported herself working in a glove factory. At the same time, this respectable daughter of the Weimar bourgeoisie began to breathe in her city's wild, decadent air, absorbing the frankly erotic entertainment offered in the cabarets of pre–World War II Berlin. During this lively time she met and married Rudolf Sieber, a playboy casting director, with whom she had her only child, Maria. Though by 1928 theirs was a marriage in name only, the two never divorced, and they remained friends and confidants. It was in fact convenient for Dietrich to be able to say, when lovers became uncomfortably close, that she was, after all, a married woman.

When Austrian director Josef von Sternberg attended Dietrich's performance in the stage musical *Two Neckties* in 1929, he knew he had found the perfect actress to play the sultry show girl Lola Lola, who seduces and destroys a professor, in *The Blue Angel,* a film adaptation of Heinrich Mann's novel *Small Town Tyrant.* In preparation for her role, Sternberg forced the plump Dietrich to shed twenty pounds, then made her over—makeup, hairstyle, voice, wardrobe—to refine her rough edges. She emerged a screen goddess. Bathed in the director's dramatic lighting, which threw her sculpted profile into dramatic relief, she was a dangerous seductress, capable of great passion but also of cynical perfidy. *The Blue Angel* premiered to great acclaim, and Dietrich set sail for America that night, knowing she was going to be a star.

Paramount did not release *The Blue Angel* in America until late 1930, so that Dietrich could make her American debut in *Morocco,* the film that contained one of her most risqué and career-defining moments. As a singer dressed in white tie, top hat, and tails, she takes a flower from a woman's coiffure, kisses the woman on the lips in front of co-star Gary Cooper, and then, to accent the scene's bisexual sizzle, casually throws the bloom to Cooper. With this insolent gesture, the actress took Hollywood's breath away, and *La Dietrich* was launched. Sternberg's romantic obsession in the face of Dietrich's indifference lasted for several memorable films—*Dishonored* (1931), *Shanghai Express* (1932), *Blonde Venus* (1932), *The Scarlet Empress* (1934). Finally with *The Devil Is a Woman* (1935), said to portray the director's bitterness toward his unfaithful protégée, he unceremoniously ended their professional and personal relationship.

Dietrich had subordinated herself in a master-slave dynamic with Sternberg for their six-year partnership and swore that without him she was nothing. But this disciplined and resourceful woman quickly transcended her mentor's departure. Reunited with her daughter, Maria, she went on to soften her rather brittle image with such landmark roles as Frenchy, opposite James Stewart, in *Destry Rides Again* (1939), where she delivered her memorable whisky-voiced rendition of "See What the Boys in the Back Room Will Have." Still, though she moved away from the seductress roles that had been her stock-in-trade with Sternberg, she did not go on to play ingénues or happy housewives. When her career languished in the early forties, she joined the war effort—much to the dismay of Adolf Hitler, who is reported to have begged her to return to the fatherland to be his mistress. She reveled in her new patriotic role, entertaining Allied troops at the front with husky renditions of her famous standards "Falling in Love Again" and "Lili Marlene," calling it "the only important work I've ever done"; for her heroic efforts she was given the Medal of Freedom and named a Chevalier of the Légion d'honneur.

She worked with almost all the great directors—among them Alfred Hitchcock, Billy Wilder, Ernst Lubitsch, Fritz Lang, and Stanley Kramer. But after a second career lull there remained yet another reincarnation for Dietrich: She became in the sixties and early seventies the highest-paid nightclub entertainer in the world. Ernest Hemingway had long before written of her, "If she had nothing more than her voice, she could break your heart with it." Literally stitched into her fabulous costumes, the "Queen of the World" reigned until a series of onstage falls—possibly the result of her punishing garments—and the death of her husband sent her into relative seclusion. She emerged in 1978, to everyone's astonishment, in *Just a Gigolo* with David Bowie, then drew the curtain again. Despite her final pain-dulling dependence on drugs and alcohol, however, Dietrich preserved to the end the mystery that had made her, for more than sixty years, a distant, luminous myth.

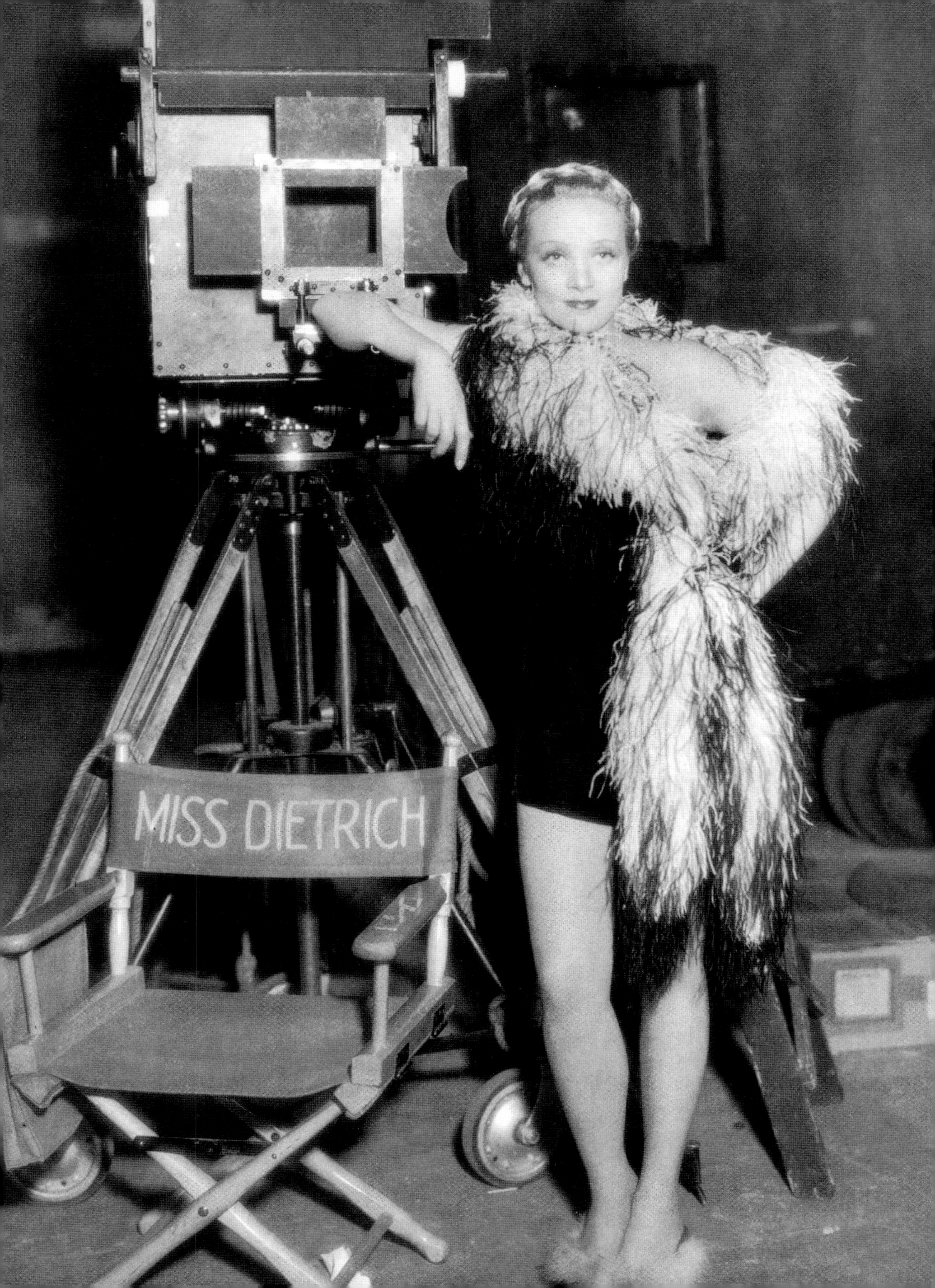
MISS DIETRICH

ISAK DINESEN

THE WOMAN THE WORLD came to know as Isak Dinesen was possessed of great courage, a rare independence, and steely determination—qualities which are very much in evidence in her evocative and stirring memoir of her years on a coffee plantation at the foot of the Ngong Hills in Kenya, *Out of Africa*. She was also an immensely gifted writer, and her achievement is all the more notable because the primary language, English, in which she wrote was not hers from birth. A sensitive storyteller, a creator of tales of the macabre, and an observer blessed with an eye for the telling detail, Dinesen's personal life was as dramatic and full of incident as her work. Unconventional and flamboyant, her love of mystery, intrigue, and romance marked not only the pages of the books she produced but the life she lived.

She was happiest when she was the center of attention, and then, when she went on to recreate the moment in words and images. Her life was shaped by a series of tragedies—her father's suicide, an unrequited love, the failure of her marriage and coffee plantation, and, finally, the syphilis she contracted from her husband—but in her art, the world was given spiritual meaning. "To love God truly," Dinesen once wrote, "you must love a joke." For most of her work—though, not all, for there were other pseudonyms—she called herself "Isak Dinesen," partly in homage to her father and because the name "Isak," she said, gave her imaginative freedom; it means "the one who laughs."

The death of Dinesen's father, a victim of syphilis who committed suicide when she was only ten, haunted her for life. She had been his favorite, and she identified with his adventurous spirit. An aristocratic soldier in the French army, he had lived in the wilds of Wisconsin and Nebraska among the Chippewa and the Pawnees before he settled down at thirty-five to have a family. For Dinesen's earliest gothic tales, published in Danish literary journals in 1907, she used the pseudonymn "Osceola," the name of a Seminole leader, a testament to her father's profound influence.

Born into a life of privilege on her family's isolated estate, Rungstedlund, where she was also to die after her father's passing. Karen Dinesen studied art in Paris and at the Royal Academy of Fine Arts in Copenhagen, and English at Oxford University. Her talent at both drawing and painting is clear from the works that survive. She returned to the quiet of the family estate, where she would remain until her marriage; her brother, Thomas, many years later in a memorial volume to his sister, would write,"… how desperately she longed for wings to carry her away." The years of her early adulthood were difficult; deeply in love with a Swedish cousin who did not return her affection, she married his twin brother, Baron Bror von Blixen-Finecke, instead in 1914. At the age of twenty-eight, marriage gave Karen Blixen the "wings" she had hoped for. The two purchased a coffee farm in Kenya, and set out for Nairobi, organizing extended safaris and holding elegant soirees for the local expatriate gentry. There she began the stream of correspondence to loved ones—posthumously published as *Letters from Africa*—describing her glorious days and nights at the foot of the blue-hazed Ngong Hills. When her marriage ended in 1921 (she had contracted syphilis in the first year of her marriage), she stayed on at the farm alone, and embarked on a great love affair with the Honorable Denys Finch-Hatton, a big game hunter. In addition to romance, Finch-Hatton gave Dinesen a rich intellectual life; he taught her Latin, and together they read the Bible and the Greek poets. The woman who had written poetry and stories since childhood became a storyteller on her long veranda, sometimes to tantalize Finch-Hatton into longer visits, sometimes to entrance the servants who called her narratives "talk like rain." In the evenings, too, she began to compose fairy tales and romances, which, she wrote, "would take my mind a long way off, to other countries and times."

In addition to her illness which grew ever more serious, Dinesen's life, by 1931, would be forever changed by a series of tragedies. Both her ex-husband, with whom she had remained friendly, and Finch-Hatton would die, and, with the plunge of the coffee market, her beloved farm would have to be auctioned off. Baroness Blixen, as she was still known, had no other choice but to return to Denmark and Rungstedlund, with nothing of her beloved Africa in hand, save her memories and a small box filled with soil from her farm. Ironically, it was bankruptcy that forced her to turn to her writing as a potential source of income.

Seven Gothic Tales, begun in the African wilderness to divert her attention from her failing coffee plantation, was published in 1934, to both critical and popular acclaim; like the legendary Arabian storyteller, Scherazade, to whom she often compared herself, Dinesen's tales were complex tapestries, rich in fantasy and full of intrigue. Once again, Dinesen's extraordinary energy and determination would yield fruits; *Seven Gothic Tales* was followed by *Out of Africa* in 1937, and *Winter's Tales* (1942), the latter completed despite the privations of war in occupied Denmark. Her health, though, during these years and those that followed, steadily declined. She managed to continue in her craft, producing, among other titles, *The Angelic Avengers* (1946), *Last Tales* (1957), and *Shadows on the Grass* (1960). Honored for her work by the Danish Critics' Prize, she was also inducted into the American Academy of Arts and Letters.

The feisty Dinesen died from emaciation, a result of her long illness. In sharing her fascination with Africa, her "heart's land," she produced some of the century's most evocative pastoral writing, as well as some of its best-known stories of the macabre. She was, even to the end, remarkable.

WALT DISNEY

MICKEY MOUSE, AS LEGEND HAS IT, was born in 1928 on a train ride from New York to the West Coast. His father was a twenty-seven-year-old animator who had just lost the rights to his cartoon creation Oswald the Rabbit and needed to revive his business. He remembered a field mouse that used to live in the wastebasket, near his drawing board and so, in what became famous as his can-do manner, Walt Disney created one of the world's most familiar and beloved characters by the time the train rolled into Los Angeles.

Mickey, whose squeaky voice was supplied by Disney himself, soon became a symbol of pluck for Depression-weary Americans. Launched in "Plane Crazy" (1928), the mischievous character rapidly boasted a number of international stage names: Michael Maus in Germany, Miguel Ratonocito in South America, Miki Kuchi in Japan. He then acquired a spin-off family, including characters like Minnie Mouse, Donald Duck, Goofy, and Pluto. Eventually, throughout the fertile years of the Disney Brothers Studios, a whole menagerie of whimsical creatures emerged, including flying circus elephants, learned toads, blushing bluebirds, and singing gargoyles.

The original Mickey, however, was not the congenial imp whose pie-eyed face has become ubiquitous around the globe. Dressed in red shorts and yellow shoes and sporting a tail, he was more naughty than nice when he made his sound debut in the musical short "Steamboat Willie" (1928). But under the guidance of Disney—and his chief animator, Ub Iwerks—Mickey slowly developed a more affable personality and a less rodent-like appearance.

Born in Chicago, Illinois, and the youngest of five children, Walter Elias Disney showed his remarkable imagination at the early age of ten. Having moved to a Missouri farm, he became fascinated with its animals and started selling sketches to the hometown barber in exchange for haircuts. After two years at the Kansas City Art Institute, he volunteered as a Red Cross ambulance driver in the last months of World War I. Ten years later, back in Kansas City, Disney was producing cartoon shorts with his life-long collaborator Iwerks. He soon concluded that Hollywood was the place to be, and in 1923, in partnership with his brother Roy, began his career writing and directing the "Alice" series, comedy shorts that mixed live-action and animation.

Emulating such top animation talents as Pat Sullivan ("Fritz the Cat") and Bill Nolan ("Krazy Kat"), Disney turned to such cinema greats as Charlie Chaplin, Laurel and Hardy, and Buster Keaton to hone his skills at constructing comic narrative. An experimenter, he wanted his creations to think, act and feel: "I want the characters," he said, "to *be* somebody." It took almost a decade of persistence in the face of brutal competition and bankruptcy, but eventually, Disney's precisionist approach launched what film critics now call the Golden Age of Animation. Children everywhere smiled at Cinderella's happy fate, cried when Bambi's mother died, and cowered in their theater seats as his films began exploring the darker sides of human behavior.

Disney viewed no detail as too small for his scrutiny. An intensely focused story editor, he pored obsessively for hours over lyrics, and special effects. The really big ideas percolated in his brain for years, and when they finally matured, he was their complete steward. Often he stayed late at the studio, convincing his wife Lilly to sleep on his office couch.

Disney's genius was evident in what his biographers consider to be the most significant decision he ever made after creating Mickey. When sound arrived in films in 1927, he immediately recognized its enormous potential and incorporated it into *Steamboat Willie*. Using a metronome to wed the film frames to the music's beat, he synchronized Mickey's actions with the tune "Turkey in the Straw," producing a commercial smash as well as a technological breakthrough. Disney's ability to anthropomorphize anything his artists could draw acquired an entirely new dimension in 1937 with the first feature-length cartoon, *Snow White and the Seven Dwarfs*. Taking three years to complete and costing $1,600,000, "Disney's folly," as industry insiders called it, grossed $8,000,000 in record time and was hailed as a milestone in personality animation. It was followed closely by two other successes, *Pinocchio* (1939) and *Fantasia* (1940).

When television arrived in America's living rooms, "Uncle Walt" himself became a star, hosting *The Wonderful World of Disney* for twenty-nine years. A lifelong smoker, he died of lung cancer in 1966, but his enchanted kingdom continues to reach for ever bluer financial skies with expanded retail ventures, more vastly-scaled theme parks at home and abroad, planned communities, and its own cable television channel. In the eighties and nineties, feature-length animated films, such as *The Little Mermaid* (1989), *Beauty and the Beast* (1991), *Aladdin* (1992), *The Lion King* (1994), *Pocahontas* (1995), and *Hercules* (1997) joined the long list of Disney hits, with the studio continuing to lead the way in animated family entertainment.

DUNCAN

ISADORA

USUALLY BAREFOOT AND SCANTILY clad in diaphanous costumes of her own design, Isadora Duncan, the American founder of modern dance, advanced a wholly new rationale of movement that, unlike the stylized rituals of classical ballet, rose directly from the soul. Rejecting pure technique and "pretty movements," Duncan saw her work as an expression of life, a natural art form in which she could synthesize all other art—music, literature, painting, and drama—into one noble vision of truth. Freedom, to her, was paramount, not only in the creative act but also in daily life as well, and she spent most of her short frenetic existence flouting every Victorian convention her ardently independent temperament encountered (In Paris, during World War I, she triumphed in a dance she set to the "Marseillaise"; as German guns were shelling Verdun, she outfitted herself entirely in red and at the refrain exposed a breast, becoming Marianne, the symbol of France.). An advocate of free love during a sexually repressive era, the attractive dancer turned innumerable European intellectuals and noblemen into worshipful beaux, using to her advantage her flowing persimmon hair, a lithe but voluptuous body, and a libertine forthrightness.

Duncan's native land was originally less than entranced with this blithe spirit, but audiences in London raved over her interpretations of Brahms, Wagner, and Gluck. In Berlin she was hailed as "godlike Isadora" and enthusiastic university students pulled her carriage through the streets. At the height of the Imperial Ballet's influence, the incomparable Anna Pavlova herself came to see Isadora's 1904–1905 recitals in Saint Petersburg, along with the formidable director-producer Constantin Stanislavsky and Ballets Russes impresario Sergey Diaghilev. They adored her, as did many others. Russian-born dancer and choreographer Michel Fokine, one of the creators of modern ballet, considered Duncan "the foundation of all his creation" and "the greatest American gift to the art of the dance."

The violet-eyed diva came to her unconventional ideas as a girl growing up in Oakland, California. The youngest of four children, Angela, as she was christened, began dancing spontaneously and creatively as a mere toddler. Her mother—who had been abandoned by her speculator-turned-chiseler husband—tried for a decade to provide a haven from poverty for her close-knit family by instilling in her children a love of literature and fine music. The self-assured Angela was a vital part of the family's amateur cultural aspirations, giving dance lessons to neighborhood children and later teaching social dancing with her older sisters. Isadora—now her stage name—joined the theatrical troupe of New York producer Augustin Daly, who tried in vain to interest his headstrong starlet in ballet. In 1899, after the family lost everything in a hotel fire, the Duncans boarded a cattle boat and sailed for what they hoped would be a sunny reception across the Atlantic.

The desperate move paid off. With the patronage of the distinguished actress Mrs. Patrick Campbell, the winsomely expressive dancer was soon on the engagement books of London's leading hostesses, escorted by painter Charles Halle, who introduced her to the best social and intellectual circles. Within months Duncan was working her ethereal and sensuous magic in presentations at the New Gallery, the city's *dernier cri* of highbrow refinement. She was an unqualified sensation, performing to Mendelssohn's *Welcome to Spring* as well as illustrating passages from ancient Homeric poems in dance. She became the first dancer ever to interpret a complete symphonic work, Beethoven's Seventh Symphony. There were critics, of course, who questioned whether the young Duncan, who had begun her sensational career performing atop a Chicago billiard table, could really dance. Was all that Grecian-urn posing in skimpy tunics a valid artistic discipline or simply the compelling experiments of a somewhat lightheaded artiste? If the Balanchines of the world didn't think Isadora could dance well, she certainly thought she could, and it was this pure, full-blooded conviction of her own uniqueness that made her electrifying and influential.

In Germany she met and fell deeply in love with Gordon Craig, an actor-cum-stage designer (and son of the famous actress Ellen Terry) who fathered the first of her two children in 1906 and added considerably to the profligate Isadora's mountain of debt. She survived the attachment, however, and eventually became enamored of millionaire sewing-machine heir Paris Singer, who, though already married and with four children of his own, fathered her second child. For the duration of their turbulent affair, she was able to relax somewhat from the frantic tour schedule that supported her free-dance school in the Grunewald district of Berlin. Then, most tragically, Duncan's two young children and their governess were drowned when their car rolled backward into the Seine. Stricken, Duncan traveled manically the next few months, eventually alienating many of her fans with her escapades. In a downward spiral, she married a man many years her junior, Russian imagist poet Sergei Aleksandrovich Yesenin—a violently jealous and abusive man—and while on tour in the United States in 1922 to fund her Russian school, she was wrongfully accused of being a Bolshevik agent. Shortly thereafter, the unhinged Yesenin committed suicide, but not before writing his wife a suicide note in his own blood. Isadora's demise was equally calamitous—and theatrical. Rather dispirited in her Côte d'Azur retirement, she set off one bright fall day in 1927 for an automobile ride. *"Adieu, mes amis, je vais la gloire,"* she announced gaily as she drove off. The scarf she had flung around her neck caught fast in the spokes of one of the wheels of her car and broke her neck instantly.

BOB DYLAN

1941-

A GENUINE HOMEGROWN genius, Bob Dylan lived in constant fear that people would discover he was a fraud, which may have been why he constantly reinvented himself. Born Robert Zimmerman in Duluth, Minnesota, he grew up listening to country radio and learning to play guitar and piano. In high school, after having discovered Little Richard, he played in several rock bands. At an eleventh-grade talent show, shy Robert stood up at the piano and screamed his songs at his astonished classmates. The next day, according to his English teacher, he appeared in his seat as usual, silent but "smirking." It wasn't until his days at the University of Minnesota—where he was immersed in the local Beat scene and the blues-folk hybrid of his idol, Woody Guthrie—that he changed his name to Dylan, and started writing folk songs. The effect his music would have on a generation of Americans would be profound and wide-ranging.

Dropping out of the college in 1961, Dylan left Minnesota to visit the bedside of an ailing Woody Guthrie, and soon after relocated to Manhattan. There, he quickly became the darling of the Greenwich Village scene, performing sets that combined blues/folk covers and original compositions. Young as he was, he had already mastered folk and blues, something he demonstrated convincingly on his debut album, *Bob Dylan* (1962). His name was made, however, with his second album, *The Freewheelin' Bob Dylan* (1963). With such anthems as "Blowin' in the Wind" and "A Hard Rain's A Gonna Fall," the album marked the beginning of Dylan's brief but enormously influential protest period, the peak of which would the classic *The Times They Are-A Changin'* (1964). A child of his time, Dylan wrote rallying cries for the youth of his era, an embittered time marked by anti-government protest, civil rights agitation, drugs, and cultural disaffection. In the matter of a couple of years, he transformed folk music.

Dylan quickly outgrew his political songs, though, and found new inspiration in the verses of the Symbolist poets, the jazz-inflected chants of Beat poets like Lawrence Ferlinghetti and Allen Ginsberg, and the guitar riffs of Chuck Berry. In 1965—the same year he "went electric" at the Newport Folk Festival—he released his groundbreaking album, *Bringing It All Back Home*. Despite the outrage from folk purists both performance and album wrought, songs like "Subterranean Homesick Blues" became as emblematic of their time as anything he'd done previously. In the following two years, he released two more albums—*Highway 61 Revisited* (1965), and *Blonde on Blonde* (1966)—that continued his exploration of new form and content, and contained some of the best pop music ever recorded. Songs as diverse as "Mr. Tambourine Man," "Like A Rolling Stone," "Rainy Day Women #12 & 35," and "Just Like a Woman" proved the astonishing range of Dylan's art, and marked the most productive and creative period of his career. His world tours in 1965 and 1966 attracted countless new fans, one of whom, D.A. Pennebaker, filmed Dylan on and off stage for his documentary, *Don't Look Back* (1965). The classic opening sequence—with Dylan feeding the lyrics of "Subterranean Homesick Blues" to the camera on a series of cue cards, as Allen Ginsberg lurks quietly in the background—both heralded the hig-mark of cinema verité and anticipated the age of music videos.

The same year *Blonde on Blonde* was released, Dylan's period of intense creativity was involuntarily ended by a near-fatal motorcycle accident. After the crash, he retreated for a period of two years to his home in Woodstock, New York, with his wife, Sara Lowndes, whom he had married in 1965. He recorded only occasionally, jamming with his friend Robbie Robertson and The Band in the basement of the group's home, Big Pink, the sessions of which were eventually recorded and released as *The Basement Tapes* (1975). A different Dylan emerged from his self-imposed seclusion, with a new country-rock sound and an album called *John Wesley Harding* (1968). Where the old Dylan might have used an image from Breton, the new one utilized the Old Testament to write songs like "All Along the Watchtower" or old Leadbelly material for "I'll Be Your Baby Tonight."

Throughout the seventies and eighties Dylan kept playing and evolving, though the playing became a little more subdued and the changes more radical. After years of sporadic live appearances, he launched a world tour with The Band in 1974—and released a live album named *Before the Flood*—that proved both a commercial and critical success. His chameleon persona spilled over into the very music he performed, as he recreated and recast his classic songs, a practice he would continue throughout his career. On the heels of that tour, and in response to his own failing marriage, Dylan recorded and released another masterpiece, *Blood on the Tracks* (1975), which added songs like "Tangled Up in Blue" and "Shelter from the Storm" to an already astonishing and increasingly personal body of work.

By the end of the decade, Dylan had taken a turn with *Slow Train Coming* (1979), the first of three overtly Christian albums, followed in the early eighties by a renewed interest in Judaism. The eighties were marked by a series of disappointing albums—with exceptions like *Infidels* (1983) and *Oh, Mercy* (1989), Dylan's first work with producer Daniel Lanois—and an increasing risk of irrelevance. It could not have mattered less to Dylan, though, as he moved restlessly across the land with the so-called Never Ending Tour, with various bands backing him up (Tom Petty and the Heart-breakers) or co-headlining (The Grateful Dead).

It would be in 1997—the same year he performed for Pope John XXIII in Bologna—that Dylan would release his next masterpiece. Teaming up again with producer Lanois, he recorded *Time Out of Mind*, a blues-laden, mordant reflection on his own mortality that won him a Grammy for Album of the Year. The album perfectly suited a fifty-six-year-old artist who had raised four children, divorced painfully, survived serious illness, and yet had no intention of relinquishing his role as poet-prophet. "My burden is heavy," he once said, "My dreams are out of control."

AMELIA EARHART

MOMENTS BEFORE HER WEDDING ceremony, world-famous aviatrix Amelia Earhart gave her future husband a letter politely outlining the conditions of their marriage. She wished to continue to lead her own life, wrote the woman who would take her place beside Charles Lindbergh as one of the early heroes of aviation history, and the petty confinements of a "medieval code of faithfulness," as she called it, were not the means to such freedom. If in a year they had not found happiness as a couple, Earhart further stipulated, they should go their separate ways.

The letter was pure Earhart, reflecting her cool objectivity and her boldness in defying convention. Most significantly, it revealed the attractive young midwesterner's strong streak of self-determination. That quality, combined with her unyielding nerve and high-spirited sense of adventure, led her to excel in a new and extremely perilous field of human endeavor. Challenging the unknown skies in much the same way astronauts would later take on the chasm of space, Earhart captured the world's admiration with an impressive lineup of aviation firsts. She was the first woman to fly nonstop across America, the first woman to cross the Atlantic solo and the first person to do so twice. She also was the first person to fly solo across the Pacific from Hawaii to California and the first woman to receive the Distinguished Flying Cross. When she vanished in 1937 while attempting the first round-the-world flight, mystery was added to her legend's already considerable luster.

Tall, tousle-haired, and quietly witty, Earhart spent her early childhood in Kansas, where money problems, as a result of her attorney father's heavy drinking, loomed large. In her early life she puttered around the edges of several professions, serving in World War I as a nurse's aide and studying medicine briefly at Columbia University. At the age of twenty-three, AE—as she was later known to her fellow pilots—caught the flying bug at an air show in California when she went up in a plane with a barnstormer "for the fun of it." She knew that she had found her calling. It was in 1928, while she was doing social work in Boston, however, that her hobby took an unexpected and dramatic turn. That year she was chosen to be the first woman passenger on a transatlantic flight. Her presence was more for publicity than anything else, but Earhart was game and later honest enough to give her two male pilots all the credit. She had been just "baggage," she modestly told waiting reporters when the trimotor *Friendship* landed with several bumps at Burry Port, Wales. But the world perceived otherwise.

One of the men who had invited her to make the trip was her husband-to-be, George Palmer Putnam, grandson of the publisher G. P. Putnam and publicist-promoter extraordinaire. As the detail man behind Charles Lindbergh's legendary transatlantic solo flight in 1927, Putnam saw the same heroic quality and—more to the point—marketing potential in Earhart. An astute, abrasive, and ceaseless public relations machine, Putnam carefully crafted his wife's image, billing her as "Lady Lindy"—an appellation she despised—arranging product endorsements, and lining up record-setting stunts and the sponsors to pay for them. Early biographers believed that Earhart's marriage to Putnam was simply a commercial partnership, but more recent opinions suggest that the union was based on genuine affection. They also speculate, however, that Putnam's ceaseless hustling may have contributed to the aviatrix's final disaster by forcing her to set out without proper preparations on the journey's dangerous last leg in order to fulfill publicity appearances he had booked. Earhart's personal involvement in the causes of international peace and women's rights, as well as her efforts to expand women's roles in aviation, have saved her from being regarded as a mere opportunist. Whatever she did in the way of pursuing fame she did for the purpose of continuing her exploits, for the sheer love of flying.

On July 2, 1937, a harried Earhart took off from Lae, New Guinea, for the most hazardous leg of her round-the-world journey, leaving behind the Morse code key, the parachute, and the life raft, among other things. She was accompanied by Fred Noonan, a crack navigator who had formerly worked for Pan American Airways but was well-known for his drinking. They were headed for Howland Island, a minuscule dot of coral 2,556 miles away over the open sea. One of Earhart's final radio messages conveyed that she could not see land and that she had little fuel left. Unfortunately, she failed to give her position, and the Coast Guard couldn't locate her because she had not adjusted her radio to the cutter *Itasca*'s frequency. When the greatest naval expedition ever organized to search for a single plane set out to find her Lockheed Electra, that missing piece of information made the four-million-dollar search hopeless from the start.

Speculation about Earhart's mysterious disappearance continues. Some recent books lend credence to the theory that Earhart simply crashed into the ocean, while others argue that she was on a secret government spying mission and was captured by the Japanese. There is no speculation, however, about why her fame has continued decades after her disappearance. She had moxie, as people would have said in her day, and she has inspired generations of women with her confidence, her fierce commitment to individual freedom, and, above all, her courage. "My life has really been very happy," the fearless flyer wrote in a letter to her mother on the eve of her first transatlantic flight, "and I don't mind contemplating its end in the midst of it."

EDISON

THOMAS ALVA

CONTRARY TO POPULAR BELIEF, Thomas Alva Edison was not a scientist: He was the rarest of those rare birds that America has produced in flocks, an inventor. Holder of 1,093 patents, the most ever issued to an individual, Edison was an eccentric and tireless self-promoter, a cantankerous misanthrope who worked by trial and error, and a technological magician who, quite simply, invented the twentieth century.

The sheer number and magnitude of his innovations dwarf the accomplishments of other geniuses: the incandescent electric light bulb, the electrical system, the phonograph, and a movie camera to name a few. Each discovery spawned a new industry— and more discoveries. Though Edison's talent often lay in improving an existing invention or building upon the visions of others, his imaginative creativity, his persistence, and his drive for success make him unique in the annals of inspired tinkering.

Born in Ohio to a family that had sided with the defeated in two revolutions (his great-grandfather had been a loyalist during the American Revolution, and his Canadian-born father fought with the forces of the failed Mackenzie Rebellion), Edison was destined to become a successful one-man industrial revolution. A series of ailments left the boy partially deaf, and his sporadic infirmities and restless mind made him a poor student, though he excelled in chemistry. When Alva, as he was called by his family, was twelve, his exasperated father, an eccentric who considered his son an idiot, allowed the boy to take a job hawking newspapers on a train. From 1863 to 1868, Edison moved from town to town, working as a telegraph operator for telegraph companies and railways, never forgetting to keep his chemical laboratory nearby. It was his experience as a telegrapher that led the penniless youth to his first practical invention in 1868, a telegraph capable of sending dual messages simultaneously. He next invented a stock ticker that telegraphically spewed out stock prices; and in 1870 the Western Union Company, then one of the primary supporters of industrial research in America, paid Edison forty thousand dollars for the instrument. He used the money to set up a laboratory in Newark, New Jersey.

Throughout his long life he was disdainful of pure scientists, whom he dismissed as "the bulge-domed fraternity." Edison was practical, antisocial, and ethically dubious, a man who directed his cleverness solely to the making of money, working for those who could pay the most. He invented the "quadruplex," a four-message telegraph transmitter, for his sponsor, Western Union; but when financier Jay Gould swooped in and paid Edison one hundred thousand dollars for the machine, the inventor blithely took the money and fought a lawsuit initiated by an outraged Western Union. In 1876, saddled with an unhappy wife and severe financial troubles,

thanks to his chronic fiscal bumbling, Edison moved his operation to Menlo Park, New Jersey. There, in 1877, he developed the carbon-button transmitter for Alexander Graham Bell's telephone, an innovation that led to the phone's mass use and which is still integral to the instrument today.

That same year he realized what some believe was his greatest achievement: the phonograph. Like many great discoveries, this one was an accident. While trying to figure out a way to convert sound to writing by moving a stylus across a paper cylinder, Edison was astounded to hear vague sounds issuing from the machine. Working his typically arduous twenty-one-hour days to exploit the breakthrough, refusing to bathe, eating nothing but pie and coffee, he presented an improved tinfoil-cylinder phonograph in December 1877. The recording was of his own voice reciting "Mary Had a Little Lamb." An astonished world proclaimed him "the Wizard of Menlo Park," despite the denunciation of a French scientist who insisted the mechanism was a ventriloquist's fake. The phonograph was real, however, and its creator reveled in the publicity he inspired, announcing that he would put a phonograph in the head of the Statue of Liberty.

Having turned silence into sound, Edison now rushed to turn night into day. His devouring energy focused on that bête noire of contemporary science, the light bulb. Replacing the preferred low-resistance filament with one of high resistance, he produced in 1879 a bulb with a carbonized thread filament that burned brighter and longer than any before. He then devised the basis for our modern electrical system, illuminating a small section of Manhattan in 1882. Unfortunately, even Edison had his blind spots. His stubborn and deceptive campaign against former assistant Nikola Tesla's alternating current system delayed the widespread use of electricity. In 1888 he made better use of his energy and created the kinetoscope. When this peephole creation was replaced by the Lumière brothers' screen projections as the preferred moving picture device, Edison called upon his promotional acumen: He acquired the rights to another man's projector and touted it as "Edison's latest marvel, the Vitascope."

An indifferent husband and father, Edison rarely slept at home, preferring the floor of his laboratory to his bed. By the turn of the century, he was more interested in organizing the myriad companies his contrivances had spawned than in creating new ones, though in World War I he worked on a number of defense projects. He lived out his years honored by an awestruck planet, never wavering in his belief that there was nothing he could not do. Edison was almost right. Yet even he could not create a machine that would allow one to live forever. If he had, he might have invented the twenty-first century as well.

ALBERT

EINSTEIN

WHEN THE GREATEST SCIENTIFIC mind of the last hundred years died quietly in his sleep at age seventy-six, his passing was mourned around the globe. Not because Albert Einstein's discoveries concerning the complex relationships between matter and the forces of nature had dramatically changed the human condition—though, of course, they had—but because his unwavering integrity in the pursuit of truth had transformed him into a kind of secular saint. "Suddenly," wrote C. P. Snow in *Variety of Men*, "he sprang into the public consciousness, all over the world, as the symbol science, the master of the twentieth-century intellect." Weary of war and spiritually drained by the evils of Nazism, people everywhere looked at the disheveled, grandfatherly professor and saw the spokesperson for a new age of human hope.

Born to nonreligious Jewish parents on March 14, 1879, in Ulm, Germany, Albert Einstein entered the world with an abnormally large head. His parents, in fact, suspected that he might be retarded, and his nurse found him so slow that she nicknamed him "Father Bore." Albert's education was further thwarted by his own intellectual rebelliousness. Fortunately, an uncle improvised a diversion to interest his lazy nephew in mathematics. It involved transforming algebra's elusive x into a tiny animal, which Albert was encouraged to track down. Deficiency in math, however, continued to plague him, and after the picky learner had begun to focus on theoretical physics, he was forced to take the entrance exam at the Federal Polytechnic in Zurich twice. Postgraduate employment was a problem, and Einstein needed money to marry his fellow student Mileva Martisch. The couple's poverty became so severe, in fact, that they were forced to give up their first child for adoption when she was a year and a half old, a situation which might have been avoided had Einstein not lost a choice teaching post. In 1902, he finally secured a patent office appointment in Bern, where he advertised his tutorial services in physics and math in a local newspaper. Mileva eventually gave birth to two sons, and Albert used free mornings and evenings to develop his scientific theories.

The fruits of Einstein's deeply meditative mind burst forth in 1905, in what science historians refer to as his *annus mirabilis,* his "year of miracles." During this period, the prestigious journal *Annalen der Physik* published three of his papers, a display of theoretical diversity that included his groundbreaking Photoelectric Effect and his Special Theory of Relativity. It was from the former, which suggested that light is constituted of minuscule packets of energy called quanta,

or photons, that future physicists would develop the Quantum Theory, a cornerstone of twentieth-century physics. Einstein's General Theory of Relativity, his 1916 revolutionary description of gravity, was equally profound in its impact, turning the world, as both scientists and laypersons understood it, upside down. Time and space, Einstein proposed, were relative entities, not the absolutes of everyday perception. Time, in fact, was not simply an extraneous factor in a three-dimensional universe, but part of a fourth space-time dimension. His Special Theory had shown the speed of light to be absolute, but as he now announced, light itself could be bent.

In 1919, Einstein achieved international acclaim when his General Theory was confirmed by independent experiment. He was awarded the Nobel Prize in 1921, not, ironically, for his pioneering work in relativity, but for his discoveries in quantum physics. It seems the Nobel committee was unconvinced that his relativity theorem constituted a real discovery. His famous formula, $E=mc^2$, had nevertheless cracked the code of nuclear transformation, and would eventually earn him the dubious title of Father of the Atomic Bomb. It was an abhorrent appellation for a man who held a strong spiritual reverence for what he believed to be the ultimate coherence of nature. In the end though, it was the lesser of two evils: In 1939 Einstein wrote to President Franklin D. Roosevelt urging him to develop the destructive device before Germany did.

By the thirties, he was deprived of his property and stripped of his German citizenship. Forced to flee to the United States (he became a citizen in 1940), the grim reality of Hitler's Final Solution soon reshaped his pacifist beliefs. After the war, at the Institute for Advanced Study in Princeton, New Jersey, the distinguished academician took part in formulating an international agreement to control nuclear energy. He also sought to further the cause of Zionism and was offered the presidency of Israel, which he declined.

Albert Einstein's legacy, in addition to tiny miracles like transistors and photoelectric cells, and larger wonders like modern cosmology and atom smashers, was his magnificent brain, which struggled till the very end to formulate a Grand Unifying Theory. Now preserved in a laboratory, it is still in search of a final resting place. Einstein did not believe that the God of theology would necessarily provide his soul such a home, but "the Old One," as he called the presence of a superior intelligence revealed in the incomprehensible universe, had given him "a holy curiosity" in life. That Force had driven Einstein's life and for him had been marvel enough.

EISENHOWER

DWIGHT DAVID

ANYONE WHO HAS PONDERED how greatness is thrust upon those who are not born great might consider the life of Dwight David Eisenhower. The supreme Allied commander of the European theater in World War II and the thirty-fourth president of the United States, Eisenhower was born to a hard-luck dairy worker and his long-suffering wife in the nowhere town of Denison, Texas. The family soon moved to Abilene, Kansas, where young Dwight was forced to work as an errand boy, ditchdigger, and cowboy to help the family financially.

Unable to afford even a state college, Eisenhower took the exams for the military academies at both Annapolis and West Point. Too old for the navy, he was accepted by the army, "passing out" of West Point in 1915. The following year, while stationed in San Antonio, Texas, he met and married Mamie Geneva Doud, the daughter of a wealthy Denver meatpacker. As she was less than an expert housekeeper, at the start Ike, as he was called by his classmates, did the cooking and cleaning. During World War I, Ike was given several training assignments, but after the war his temporary rank of lieutenant colonel was reduced to captain. His army career threatened to mire him in backwater anonymity as an army-post football coach until two events dramatically changed his fortunes: his young son's death of scarlet fever in 1921 and, his acceptance of an invitation from General Fox Conner to go to Panama as an executive officer to get away from melancholy associations.

Galvanized by both grief and opportunity, Ike, with Conner's pull, entered the Command and General Staff School, graduating first in his class. Now a major, he then worked for the brilliant, egotistical chief of staff, General Douglas MacArthur, who took him on assignment to Manila in 1935.

Ike was still a major in 1939, but after a succession of promotions during the next three years, Army Chief of Staff George Marshall summoned the highly capable but field-inexperienced soldier to his office to ask one simple question: What should be our general line of action in the Pacific? Eisenhower replied: draw the line at the Philippines, even though it will fall—because Asia will watch what we do—then reinforce Australia before it, too, succumbs. The subtle blend of psychology and strategy pleased Marshall, and Eisenhower quickly received another promotion. When Ike was given command of Europe in 1942, he was an unbloodied fifty-two-year-old with the rank of major general.

Dogged, diplomatic, by turns charming and ruthless, sure-footedly treading political and public-relations minefields, the man who was trusted by every friend and feared by every enemy brought all the harsh lessons of his humble upbringing to bear on winning the war. Organizing the movements of millions of troops fighting under a dozen flags, he mobilized vast fleets and phalanxes of airplanes, planning strategy on a map of half the world. Coordinating mutually suspicious services, he mediated the squabbles of jealous Allied commanders, administered captured territory, and dealt with the egos and talents of an extraordinary group: George Patton, Bernard Montgomery, Charles de Gaulle.

A consummate poker player, the normally cautious Kansan called nature's bluff on D-Day, June 6, 1944, when, in spite of threatening weather, he ordered the invasion of Normandy. The vast Allied Expeditionary Force, some two and a half million strong, crouched alert and nervous in England, miles away from the quiet French beaches. "You are about to embark upon the Great Crusade," Eisenhower told them, in bidding good-bye. "The eyes of the world are upon you." After saluting sorties of paratroopers from the U.S. 101st Airborne Division, many of whom he knew would not complete their missions, he turned back to the business at hand with tears in his eyes. As with his most controversial decisions—trafficking with the Vichy French in North Africa and slowing Patton's advance on Berlin—Operation Overlord had but one purpose, and that was to win the war as quickly as possible. The battle lasted fifty days, and win it he did. Also responsible for the liberation of Italy and North Africa, he personally accepted Germany's surrender on May 7, 1945.

After the war, he became president of Columbia University, rejecting offers to be a Presidential nominee. He succumbed by 1952, however, when he won the first of two national elections. As President, he extricated America from its Korean entanglement, as he promised he would, and sidestepped the tiger trap of Vietnam by refusing to commit troops. His cautious stewardship was marred by his lack of action on civil rights—though in 1957 he sent the 82nd Airborne to enforce court-ordered school desegregation in Little Rock, Arkansas—and by a hands-off foreign policy that fed the Cold War concerns of his secretary of state, John Foster Dulles. Presciently, he warned of a growing "military-industrial complex."

Eisenhower was not universally liked, still less universally respected, as visions of battlefields faded into presidential putting greens. But his solid qualities of common sense, diligence, and faith in himself and God enabled him to chart the course of an immense and savage conflict that was the defining event of the twentieth century. These simple virtues were what made him truly great at a time in history when anything less would have meant disaster.

SERGEI EISENSTEIN

THE PRECISELY STYLED, HEROICALLY scaled, and often disturbingly cruel images of the great Soviet director Sergei Eisenstein's magnificent films haunt the viewer long after they have worked their initial magic: expressionless soldiers in the 1925 classic *The Battleship Potemkin,* goose-stepping down those famous long steps, their marching intercut with footage of a motherless baby carriage careening toward a fearful fate; vast frozen tundras in *Alexander Nevsky* (1938), littered with fallen troops and swarming with lantern-carrying loved ones searching for their dead among a shifting gray sea of stiffening bodies; the portentous arch of a shaggy eyebrow in close-up and shadowy corridors menaced by malevolent *boyars,* both from the riveting 1945 and 1946 masterpieces, *Ivan the Terrible,* Parts I and II.

Yet Eisenstein—a film theorist, an intellectual, and a skilled propagandist for the Soviet Communist Party—was dedicated to the visual experience not as a primary goal but as a tool for political and social change, and as an aesthetic form capable of evoking a totally new and unexpected emotional response. Such personal transformation was possible, Eisenstein believed, because of cinema's superior capability to express the Marxist theory of dialectical materialism. He conceived of art as conflict, and used his montage technique—in which two images collide to form a third image in the beholder's mind—to create one film shot as the thesis, the next as the antithesis. The resulting synthesis would, he hoped, produce a politically meaningful insight on the viewer's part.

All this was light years away from the Hollywood way of thinking, though Eisenstein revered D.W. Griffith. And despite the vicious chastisement of jealous rivals within the party and the destructive effects of the unfathomable Soviet dictator Stalin, whom he could never seem to please, Eisenstein never wavered in his beliefs. The masses remained both the audience and the heroes (he preferred to use real people as actors) of his experimental, yet always realistic, art.

Born in Riga, Latvia, to a Russian mother and a German-Jewish father, Sergei Mikhailovich Eisenstein was educated as a Christian and grew up in a cultured atmosphere that fueled his precocious talents. By the time he was ten, he spoke Russian, German, French, and English fluently; later, he learned Japanese. At seventeen, following in his engineer father's footsteps, he was studying civil engineering and architecture in Saint Petersburg. But the Revolution intervened, precipitating a cataclysmic breach between father, who joined the White Army, and son, who joined the Red.

After the war, during which he worked as an agitprop poster artist in the army's psychological division, Eisenstein formed his own amateur theater group in Moscow. Thus commenced a comet-like career in the vibrant world of Russian avant-garde theater—a milieu in which every tenet of classical theory was guilty until proven innocent. As writer, director, set and costume designer, he was, at 25, the city's premier theatrical realist-in-residence.

But the intensity of conflict and transformation that Eisenstein envisioned through his use of rapid image changes could only be fully realized, he decided, through the medium of film. Bringing to his new craft a visual acuity complemented by drafting, engineering, and architectural skills, he immersed himself in every aspect of the cinematic process, working with the same breadth of intelligence, energy, and inventiveness he would have expected from his lifelong hero, Leonardo da Vinci. The movie *Strike* came first in 1924, followed the next year by *Potemkin,* which instantly established his worldwide reputation. Using the simple story of a mutinous crew to symbolize the failed revolution of 1905, he created an exhilarating piece of cinema that would become one of the most influential and critically acclaimed films of all time.

After he was forced by the party to cut large sections of *October* (or *Ten Days That Shook the World*), Eisenstein found himself in Hollywood. Arriving in 1930 to work for Paramount, he was unable to win approval for any of his projects, and was also publicly harassed for his political beliefs. On the advice of Charlie Chaplin, he wound up approaching American leftist writer Upton Sinclair to underwrite a film about Mexico. *Que Viva Mexico!* exhausted Sinclair's patience and when U.S. customs officials discovered homoerotic drawings in Eisenstein's belongings, Stalin summoned the errant director home to Moscow, where he endured heightened criticism from both fellow filmmakers and the government for his failure to adhere to the principles of Socialist Realism in his art. When the ever-dutiful director was finally allowed to begin his first sound feature, *Bezhin Meadow,* he was stopped in his tracks after months of preparation by his chief enemy, the Director of the Soviet Cinema. Even after the critical success of *Ivan the Terrible,* Part I, he was accused of portraying the barbarous dictator in Part II as too weak and indecisive, and the film was banned.

Eisenstein died of a heart attack in 1948, ending a life marked by aesthetic success coupled with immense creative disappointment. He had always been submissive to Stalin's erratic demands and had never once openly complained about the various campaigns of harassment against him. In allowing his works to be mutilated in the name of doctrinaire correctness, he has been labeled by film purists as an opportunist whose compromises are hard to forgive. Could he have chosen another path? Cinematographer Nestor Almendros, invoking Sartre, noted that a man is always free to choose imprisonment. "Eisenstein simply should not have made any of the films he did, or at least," observed Almendros, "he should not have made them so well."

ELIOT

1888-1965

THOMAS STEARNS ELIOT FELT himself to be trapped in the twentieth century. Circumscribed by his flinty New England antecedents, his bourgeois midwestern upbringing, and the stultifying propriety of his everyday life, Eliot sabotaged all by describing all. His perfect career at Harvard University and his utterly proper job as a bank clerk at Lloyd's of London were, paradoxically, both a surrender to his tight-lipped past and his liberation. Knowing as he did in his shrewd way that he could not escape his own character, Eliot submitted to it in order to free himself to write. The result was discerning, disturbing poetry that, giving weight to the plaints of a man raised in comfort, helped to shape modern verse.

As a boy Eliot felt somehow alienated by American life and oppressed by his family's careful culture. Born to a mother who could not permit him to swim in a pond without interrogating him about its cleanliness, young Thomas defied parental convention by frequenting the underside of his native Saint Louis, wandering through neighborhoods in which no Eliot would ever have set foot. Eventually even his Harvard education seemed to collude by introducing him to symbolist poetry. The polite but disaffected young man soon left the States and went to study philosophy, first in France and then in England. To his family's horror, he insisted upon staying in Europe to write poetry rather than return to the States to finish his graduate dissertation.

Eliot's initial reputation was made on the strength of one poem: "The Love Song of J. Alfred Prufrock," first published in 1915 in a Chicago magazine called *Poetry.* "Prufrock," became the very model of a modern poem, and its protagonist the epitome of the contemporary "gray little man." Eliot quickly became the protégé of Virginia and Leonard Woolf, who published his verse, and the American poet Ezra Pound, his champion and editor. By 1925 Eliot was working at the publishing house that eventually became Faber and Faber, where he would later rise to a directorship.

The Waste Land appeared in 1922, its five movements distilling the alienation of a world recovering from war—a civilization, Eliot felt, that had lost vision, faith, and possibly its soul. In this masterpiece, he imagined a spiritually deserted landscape, a place of "dry sterile thunder without rain," where life was death and death life, and good indistinct from evil. Based on stories about the Holy Grail, with its image of the wounded Fisher King, the poem owed its inspiration to Sir James Frazer's *The Golden Bough* and Jessie Weston's *From Ritual to Romance.* Its varied style is a tribute to Eliot's encyclopedic knowledge of the French symbolist poets, the Upanishads, various medieval writings, and the English metaphysical poets—in short, to everything he had read and loved. In drawing upon the past, he conjured something perfectly modern—his parting image of a man shoring fragments "against ruins" became the quintessence of our modern condition.

Moved by a profound distaste for the culture around him, Eliot embraced the traditional comforts of the Anglican church, British citizenship, and the concept of royalty. Unlike the poets of the eras he admired, he was neither romantic nor bohemian; his inclinations were strongly academic and he looked every inch the sober—albeit pinstriped—scholar. His nature was essentially ascetic and it revealed itself in the classicism of his literary tastes, as well as in the world-rejecting Brahmanical Hinduism he wove throughout his densely cerebral poetry.

Even in such a well-regulated life, however, there were eddies of chaos. Eliot sometimes sank into bigotry, condemning his native America for polluting itself with "foreign races." Some of his contemporaries thought these outbursts had their source in his desperately unhappy marriage to the sickly ballerina Vivienne Haigh-Wood. Though he nursed her and sympathized with her professional failures, Eliot nevertheless schemed to leave her. When he did so at last, he retreated to an Anglican parish house inhabited by celibate priests, where, perhaps guilty about this chilly treatment of his wife as she descended into madness, he lived six years in abject self-denial. This retreat seemed a suitable choice, since suffering was the stuff of which his poems were made, and since he believed not only in examining what he felt, but in feeling it as completely as possible.

Eliot was a prolific writer, and his art was varied. He produced criticism and essays and, beginning in the 1930s, neo-classic dramas such as the blank-verse *Murder in the Cathedral. The Family Reunion,* a play that derived its moral vision from Greek tragedy and medieval miracle plays, was both a critical and commercial success when it debuted in 1939. Unlike many of his great literary contemporaries, Eliot actually developed a notable popular following, which was quite an achievement for a poet and playwright whose lifestyle was so patrician. However, he was never a stranger to controversy, even posthumously: To this day there rages a literary debate over the anti-Semitism that many descry in his verse.

In 1948 Eliot was awarded the Nobel Prize for literature, his triumph making the story of the anxiety-plagued, unremarkable twentieth-century man suddenly a fashionable subject. After he died in 1965 his ashes were brought to the little village of East Coker, in Somerset, England, from which his ancestor Andrew Eliot had emigrated nearly three centuries before. For Eliot, the pessimistic Anglican who embraced the Hindu concept of cyclical time, it was the perfect coda.

QUEEN MOTHER

QUEEN ELIZABETH

TO ADOLF HITLER, THE home-front encouragement of Great Britain's queen, the former Elizabeth Bowes-Lyon, made her "the most dangerous woman in Europe." To her admiring subjects, in understandable contrast, Her Majesty's pluck during World War II made her the most beloved woman in England. Unifying symbol of a besieged nation, the Queen Mum, as she came to be affectionately known, seemed to be everywhere during the Blitz, comforting stunned subjects in the ruins of their former homes and visiting the wounded in hospital. While other royalty went into hiding or fled their countries, she and her husband, King George VI, remained with their people, displaying a loyalty and courage that would never be forgotten. For his identification with his subjects, George became known as the People's King—and Elizabeth as, most certainly, the power behind the throne.

An unlikely savior, with her rather plump form and outlandish-hats, Queen Elizabeth had come to the aid of her nation once before, in 1936, when the abdication of King Edward VIII seriously threatened the monarchy and brought her shy, stammering husband to the throne. Armed with an extroverted personality softened by a radiant charm, she bolstered the reluctant prince and lovingly groomed him into a respectable monarch. Under her watchful guidance, the royal household became a welcoming hearth where the nation could warm its heart.

Born on August 4, 1900, the delicately attractive noblewoman who married Prince Albert, duke of York, on April 26, 1923, came from St. Paul's Walden Bury in Hertfordshire, Scotland. The ninth of ten children born to the earl and countess of Strathmore, Lady Elizabeth Angela Marguerite Bowes-Lyon was raised behind the formidable walls of Glamis Castle. Educated by her mother in the proprieties of that fastidiously proper era—the indomitable Queen Victoria had only just recently died—Lady Elizabeth lived rather quietly until she caught the eye of the prince.

The manner of Albert's and Elizabeth's betrothal reveals much about their characters. Smitten but painfully reserved, the prince did not have the gumption to ask for his intended's hand in person but sent a friend on his behalf. Elizabeth, politely declining, said that Albert would have to propose himself, and when he did, she accepted for an unexpected reason: "It was my duty to marry him," she admitted later, "and I fell in love with Bertie afterwards."

The 1923 announcement of their engagement caused a stir for several reasons, not the least of which was Elizabeth's birthright: She could boast of noble British heritage dating back centuries, but she could not claim one drop of royal blood. As a result, the proposed marriage between commoner and crown—the first in more than 250 years—required the king's consent. George V willingly gave it, calling his bashful son a "lucky fellow." Lady Elizabeth was only twenty-three when the bells of Westminster Abbey pealed in honor of her wedding, the first royal union in more than five centuries to be held under its historic vaulted ceiling.

After her daughters, Elizabeth and Margaret, were born, Lady Elizabeth, now duchess of York, continued the physically draining "home duties" that touched every facet of English political and cultural life. Ever the flawless, sociable performer, she filled just over a decade with dedications of orphanages, Girl Guide functions, and other chores appropriate to a collateral royal. But the abdication crisis would change her life overnight. With uncharacteristic mettle, Lady Elizabeth saw to it that Edward and his mistress, Wallis Simpson, were forbidden to ever set foot on English soil. Politically astute, she recognized the handsome and sociable couple as a threat to the task at hand, which was to steady the reeling monarchy. On December 10, 1936, the same day her brother-in-law gave up the throne, her husband ascended it, giving Lady Elizabeth little time to prepare for her new role. Five months later, George VI gave his wife the title of Lady of the Most Noble Order of the Garter, and they were crowned soon afterward.

World War II found Queen Elizabeth operating as commandant in chief of Britain's women's services, dashing about London in an armored car as she looked after the needs of the homeless and dispossessed and often filling in for her traveling husband. The uncommon commoner, however, was always regal, insisting on wearing civilian clothes rather than a drab uniform throughout the conflict, as she felt that feminine attire would perk people up. She endeared herself to her war-beleaguered subjects forever when she refused to take her daughters to Canada for safety: "The Princesses cannot go without me," she declared. "I shall not go without the King. The King will not go under any circumstances."

With the death of her husband in 1952, the grieving queen accepted a new role as her eldest daughter ascended the throne. Now a more ordinary royal, the Queen Mother found a second calling, adding to the stuffy palace profile what *The London Times* called "a streak of raffishness" with her enthusiasm for horses, salmon fishing, and a partiality for gin. Living at the elegant Clarence House, the Queen Mother became a fountainhead of stability and counsel to a family whose image she had worked so hard to dignify and humanize during her reign. The decline of the once cozy tribe often jokingly referred to as "the firm," in the last decade of the century made faithful dynasty watchers yearn for the days when Windsors kept their quarrels and peccadilloes to themselves, and sovereigns such as the Queen Mother's own husband conducted their morning shave to the stirring strains of a tartanned piper pacing solemnly in the courtyard below.

ELIZABETH II

QUEEN

HER MOST EXCELLENT MAJESTY, Elizabeth II, queen of the Britons, symbolized tradition in a century that grew impatient for change. Self-composed and strong-willed, she has spent a lifetime in service to the crown, only to see its solemnity and prestige challenged by the scandalous behavior of her own kin. Her son and heir Charles, the prince of Wales, and her new daughters-in-law, the duchess of York and the princess of Wales, represented in less than flattering terms, have lived under the public scrutiny of tabloid newspapers and tell-all books. Queen Elizabeth watched as Diana, once divorced from the faithless Charles, became a kind of shadow sovereign, far more popular than she herself. After the Princess's tragic death in a car accident, approval of Elizabeth—and of the monarchy itself—declined precipitously. Rumors that her grandson was being groomed to unseat his own father no longer circulated, but suggestions that the Windsors might begin preparing themselves for gainful employment appeared in many headlines. This was not the world Elizabeth imagined when, as a self-assured twenty-six-year-old, she was crowned in 1953.

Elizabeth Alexandra Mary Windsor was born to the duke of York and his wife, Elizabeth Bowes-Lyon, at 17 Bruton Street, London. Her father, Prince Albert, as the second son of George VI, was never groomed to be monarch. Elizabeth, along with her younger sister Margaret, was nevertheless trained in the routine disciplines of royalty by her grandmother, Queen Mary. She enjoyed private tutoring and the run of the stables and seemed foreordained to be one of those royal ancillaries who christen ships and cut ribbons at hospitals. Her uncle's shocking abdication to marry an American divorcée placed the burden of monarchy on ten-year-old Elizabeth's father amid the politics which would end in World War II.

Though Elizabeth was eager to join one of the wartime services, her father would not consent until 1945; volunteering for the Auxiliary Territorial Service, young Elizabeth learned to drive a truck and fix a tire. But however grease-stained she got, she did not lose sight of the fact that, as the eldest child, she was now heir presumptive (not heir apparent, in case there should still be a male child). Her father, who by his own admission had never even seen a state paper before he ascended to the throne, vowed that his daughter would be better equipped to wield the scepter and coached her accordingly. During his reign, in 1947, she married her third cousin, Lieutenant Philip Mountbatten, and the next year she bore him a son named Charles. Other children followed: Anne in 1950, Andrew in 1960, and Edward in 1964.

When George VI died in 1952, destiny summoned the young princess home from a tour of the Commonwealth countries. Her coronation, on June 2, 1953, was televised, a historic first. Elizabeth declared her prince "first gentleman of the realms" and decreed that she and her children be known as the "House of Windsor," thereby continuing the family's attempts to distance their German lineage.

What followed was a life spent fulfilling royal duties—attending the state opening of Parliament, honoring the charitable celebration of Maundy Thursday, composing the honors list—practices paced in tradition-honored fashion like sacraments, season by season, year by year, as befits the heritage they honor. By the unwritten constitution of the land, Elizabeth was deemed to have no real power—she reigned, rather than ruled. Her presence, and that of the monarchy itself, was always intended as a splendid emblem of stability, an embodiment of the virtues of duty, loyalty, and selflessness. Her own unruly family changed all that.

When her son Charles married the beautiful twenty-year-old Lady Diana Spencer in spectacular fashion in 1981, the Windsors' stock had never been higher. Twelve years later the British were seriously discussing the abolition of the monarchy. The deluge of complaints reached its height in 1992, when Sarah Ferguson, who married Prince Andrew, was photographed poolside with an amorous Texan. Charles and Diana then divorced in the wake of tawdry stories of neglect, cruelty, anorexia, bulimia, and adultery. The metaphorical fire raging through the Windsor family then turned literal: a blaze tore through Windsor Castle, destroying priceless art objects and necessitating at least $100 million in repairs. The citizenry grumbled at being asked to pay for the damages, claiming that the Windsors were one of the richest families on earth (the queen's personal fortune is estimated at $11 billion) and that it was ridiculous that the castle had not been insured against fire. At that point the queen made a large donation to the restoration fund and offered to pay taxes on her $12 million annual salary. It was no wonder Her Majesty, in remarks to Parliament, described the year as an *annus horribilis*.

The palace spokesmen were helpless in the face of continuing revelations in the popular press. There was nothing Queen Elizabeth could do but endure her discomfort and offer her standard reply: "We could not possibly comment." There was open and continuing speculation about the future of the monarchy itself. Toward the century's end, however, the monarchy appears secure, largely because Elizabeth II, who had "never set a wrong foot forward," holds it together by the sheer force of her personality. But what will happen, her subjects wonder, when their beleaguered queen leaves them?

DUKE ELLINGTON

THE GREATEST AND MOST prolific jazz composer of the century often took umbrage when critics referred to his music as "jazz." For Duke Ellington, the versatile master who could write richly textured tonal pieces, Broadway shows, and memorable film scores like *Anatomy of a Murder*—not to mention scribble out a complex piece of orchestration while jouncing along in the backseat of a taxi—the word was simply too confining. From the fierce energy of his early "jungle beat" performances, beginning in the late twenties at Harlem's legendary Cotton Club, to the polish of his suave but sensuous blues, as well as the dignity of his deeply moving liturgical works, Ellington's musical range was too vast to be compartmentalized, his musical vision too panoramic for a single label.

On the swells of this immense sea, as one critic rhapsodized, rose the Duke Ellington Orchestra, a sleek, luxurious liner refined enough to play La Scala and large enough to accommodate some of the era's most brilliant instrumentalists—dazzlers like saxophonists Johnny Hodges and Harry Carney, bassist Jimmy Blanton, trom-bonist Lawrence Brown, clarinetists Barney Bigard and Joe "Tricky Sam" Nanton, and trumpet player Cootie Williams.

Holding together through some fifty-six years of wars, a devastating depression, and nearly 365 one-night stands a year, Ellington's big band navigated through bebop, Dixieland, rock and roll, and Ellington classics—like "Mood Indigo," "Solitude," "Don't Get Around Much Anymore," and "Satin Doll"—leaving in its wake some of the most beautiful and intelligent music ever made. The band's sound, often described as lush, was as precise as it was powerful, a distinctive blending of Ellington's warm, pulsating, and often witty compositions accompanied by a kind of rumbling joyousness that originated in the rambunctious interplay between the group's blanket-timbred saxophone section and its bellowing brass. Functioning as melodist, arranger, master conductor, and mentor to his often rowdy brood of virtuosos, the urbane and versatile Ellington wrote to fit the "tonal personalities" of his individual instrumentalists, and created a complicated yet cohesive harmonic language that was impossible for others to duplicate. As for his own instrument, he played not only the piano, but his entire orchestra. It was the steadfast vehicle of his nimble genius, and its recognizable sound and "feel" was part of the rich legacy he would leave behind, along with more than a thousand compositions.

Like his music, the tall, dapper performer was smooth in every way, except perhaps in his tendency to hypochondria. Sartorially resplendent—he bought at least one new suit a week and had his pants tailored with four-inch cuffs—he had a well-mannered, modulated way with women and was rarely without their companionship. He married his high school sweetheart at nineteen, but when the marriage ended, he became a rather solitary figure—friendly and entertaining, but always somewhat aloof with his fellow musicians. The exception was Billy "Swee' Pea" Strayhorn, his co-composer and creative shadow, who collaborated with the Governor (as Ellington was known to band members) usually until dawn, producing such classics as "Take the A Train" and the band's later theme, "Lush Life." Such was their closeness that Ellington answered a question about whether Strayhorn was his alter ego by saying, "Pea is only my right arm, left foot, eyes, stomach, ears, and soul, not my ego."

As a small child, Edward Kennedy Ellington learned the basics of what others called jazz by fingering tunes on his family's player piano. His parents, he wrote in his autobiography, "raised him in the palm of the hand and gave him everything they thought he wanted." His deeply religious mother took him to *two* churches on Sunday. At seven, Ellington began taking lessons, later picking up intricate harmonies and rhythm structure by watching the ragtime antics of Oliver "Doc" Perry, among others, in the poolrooms and clubs around Washington, D.C., his birthplace. A talented watercolorist, he later turned down an NAACP art scholarship to New York's Pratt Institute in favor of organizing bands. Soon his orchestra was touring the country in two special Pullman cars.

The Washingtonians, now renamed Duke Ellington and His Orchestra, burst into the spotlight in 1927 at the Cotton Club, the famous nightspot that was the symbol of the Harlem Renaissance. National fame brought the band to the CBS airwaves and European cities and, in the late thirties and early forties—the zenith of Ellington's creativity—to Hollywood, where the band appeared in such films as *She Got Her Man* (1935) and *The Hit Parade* (1937).

In the thirties, Ellington experimented with longer tone poems, mood pieces, and concerti. In 1943, he debuted at Carnegie Hall with his *Black, Brown, and Beige* suite, a dense and moving meditation on the African-American experience, a recurring theme he explored in other works such as "Black Beauty." Eternally young—only the pouches under his eyes, which he called "an accumulation of virtue," betrayed his years—the Ellington of the fifties and sixties refused to wind down. His only extravagance was hearing his orchestra play whatever he wrote almost immediately.

A teetotaler who read his Bible daily, Ellington considered devotional music one of his toughest artistic challenges. It was a challenge he began to confront in 1969, with the performance of his "In the Beginning, God" at San Francisco's Grace Cathedral. He felt another obligation as well: to convey to international audiences the emotional depth of African-American culture. In successfully responding to both these personal imperatives, Ellington grew even more majestic in his final years, an evergreen connoisseur who told the story of his people through his music—a music, he always said, that was theirs and theirs alone.

FEDERICO

FELLINI

WHILE MOST FILMMAKERS OF his era clung to narratives with discernible beginnings and endings, Federico Fellini wove seamless dreams. Fellini's landscapes are peopled by visitors from the unconscious—jovial sybarites, big-breasted earth mothers, and leering grotesques who alternately seduce and repel the viewer. Megaphone in hand, black Stetson tilted rakishly, il maestro played ringmaster to a cinematic circus of his own invention. From his earliest efforts, such as the auto-biographical I vitelloni (1953), a tragicomic remembrance of the lives of five directionless youths, to his international hit La dolce vita (1960), a satiric tale of promiscuity in modern-day Rome, Fellini was most successful when he plumbed his personal obsessions on film. Fortunately, his exuberant humor and sense of parody were as highly developed as his fascination with spiritual crises. With these-balances in place, his private reveries were able to strike a universal chord.

While critics and film historians dissected Fellini's neorealism and erotic musings, the director seemed insistent that his films speak for themselves. His anti-intellectual stance belied a sophistication far removed from the provincialism of his birthplace, the small Adriatic port of Rimini. Film, Fellini declared, was a woman—the mythical, mysterious spirit whose presence haunted every creative process. Influenced by Jung, the introspective director searched for the feminine within—the connection through which he could reach his subconscious.

A retired pharmacist named Anna Giovannini has claimed that her voluptuous type of beauty inspired Fellini in both his lovemaking and in his choice of leading ladies. But il maestro's official muse was Giulietta Masina, his wife, confidante, and radiant star of many of his films. He first heard her voice reciting one of his radio scripts in 1943; they were married eight months later. At that time, he had already tried his hand at writing short stories and reporting on crime and the law. Earlier, at nineteen, he had joined a traveling vaudeville troupe—an unforgettable experience that exposed him to the gritty realities of one of his work's recurring symbols, the circus. In interviews, he liked to exaggerate the date, telling reporters that he had run away from home at age six. In fact, his childhood was happy and middle-class, marred only by the physical punishments meted out by the friars who ran the private boarding school he attended.

After successfully avoiding military service during World War II, Fellini and a few friends opened the profitable Funny Face Shop, which created voice recordings and souvenir caricatures for the GI's then occupying Rome to mail to loved ones back home. He mined his own wartime experiences with the novice director Roberto Rossellini, with whom he collaborated on the screenplay for the neorealist classic Open City (1945). Three years later Rossellini used a Fellini story in Il miracolo (The Miracle). In it, Fellini himself, handsome as any movie star, made his screen debut as a fast-talking tramp who impregnates a guileless peasant woman, played by Anna Magnani, who thinks he is Saint Joseph. After some minor failures came the critical success of I vitelloni. Then, in 1954, Fellini began work on La strada, the grim fable of a cruel circus strongman, masterfully acted by Anthony Quinn, whose hard-heartedness eventually crushes the vulnerable spirit of his simpleminded assistant, played to perfection by Masina. La strada won Fellini the first of his four Oscars for best foreign-language film.

After The Nights of Cabiria, a 1956 comedy that again featured Masina in a moving performance as a simple-minded Roman prostitute whose good cheer and faith in the future remain unsullied by the bad luck she encounters, Fellini's art gained momentum in the sixties. His first extravaganza, the vibrant and satirical La dolce vita, starred Marcello Mastroianni, the actor who would become the filmmaker's alter ego, as a down-on-his-luck journalist caught up in the soulless culture of nighttime Rome. His anti-religious imagery—not to mention the notorious scene featuring a voluptuous Anita Ekberg cavorting in a fountain—brought condemnation from the Vatican but enormous success at the box office. Fellini's art reached its height in 1963, with 8½, named for the number of films he had made up to this point. Starring Mastroianni, the film records the farcical epiphany of a blocked film director who summons up a colorful jumble of people and images from his past to come to grips with his misfiring creativity. The movie's unforgettable closing scene, featuring the beleaguered director-hero using a megaphone to guide his quarrelsome comrades around a harmonizing circus ring, became the visual metaphor for an astonishingly fertile career.

Among the most notable of the films that followed 8½ were the surrealistic epic Fellini's Satyricon (1969), which chronicles the adventures of a band of young men in a pre-Christian world devoid of original sin, and the charmingly nostalgic Amarcord (1974), a self-referential, look at the director's own provincial boyhood in the 1930s. Fellini's tender-comic storytelling style and unforgettable imagery continue to touch millions, especially the beloved countrymen from whom he drew his inspiration and artistic collaboration. When he died the day after his fiftieth wedding anniversary, his nation mourned a man whose trademark extravagance was the perfect complement to an equally expansive heart.

ENRICO FERMI

IN 1939, WHEN FATE required a genius to unlock the mystery of matter, it found Enrico Fermi. A unique combination of physicist, mathematician, and engineer, the father of the nuclear chain reaction was an indispensable part of the creation of the atomic bomb. The culmination of his life's work, it ensured the triumph of democracy and, paradoxically, ushered in a new age of fear.

The grandson of a minor functionary of the dukes of Parma, the Roman-born Fermi was destined early to be a prince among scientists. While just a boy, he showed an unmistakable brilliance in mathematics and science and scoured bookstalls for Latin treatises on physics. By the age of ten, he had already grasped complex mathematical functions, and by the end of high school, his largely self-acquired scientific education equaled that of a university graduate student. While attending the Reale scuola normale superiore, the trim, self-possessed seventeen-year-old lectured his own professors on the revolutionary theory of quanta. But to become fully versed in the most avant-garde concepts and techniques of a rapidly evolving modern physics, he needed further study, which he obtained through fellowships at Göttingen in Germany and Leiden in the Netherlands.

Fermi began lecturing at the University of Florence in 1924. Within two years, he discovered a new kind of statistics that, by showing why it was impossible for more than one electron at a time to occupy an orbit defined by its quantum number, solved the problem of Wolfgang Pauli's exclusion principle. In 1927 he joined the faculty of the Physics Institute of the University of Rome, cradle of the new Italian physics. Eventually, his work in the most arcane reaches of atomic research led to his appointment to the Academia d'Italia by the newly installed dictator Benito Mussolini. Sensing that atomic theoretical physics was stagnating, however, Fermi, one of few scientists to have exhibited a deep facility in both theory and experiment, switched disciplines to experimental nuclear physics. Shortly, Fermi postulated a new constant in nature, the Fermi constant, also known as G. It described the significance of beta decay in the nucleus and was a major theoretical breakthrough in nuclear research. Following the Curies' discovery of some of the properties of radioactivity, Fermi next experimented with various elements, bombarding them with neutrons. Although he himself failed to recognize fission in his strafing of uranium and thorium, his experiment led directly to its discovery in 1938. Amazingly, all of his work on neutrons, which had reached its apex in 1936, was done with the simplest of technical means and cost the low sum of one thousand American dollars.

As World War II loomed nearer, work became impossible for Fermi and he worried about his family's survival. In 1928 he had married Laura Capon, the daughter of a Jewish admiral in the Italian navy. Mussolini, having bowed to Nazi pressure, had begun a systematic harassment of Jews, which culminated in the anti-Semitic edicts of 1938. Fearful for his wife, and by his very nature secretive, Fermi found it impossible to publicly protest. Unable to issue anti-Fascist manifestos he quietly let it be known to Columbia University that he would be willing to relocate. When he was awarded the Nobel Prize in Physics in Stockholm in 1938, he proceeded directly from Sweden to New York without ever returning to Italy.

Upon his arrival in the United States in January 1939, Fermi attended a conference of theoretical physicists in Washington, D.C., at which his friend, the great Danish physicist Niels Bohr, informed his audience that the uranium atom, when split, could produce a power millions of times greater than the world had ever seen. When Fermi asked for further explanation—Bohr had mumbled through his speech—the auditorium gasped in astonishment. The discovery of fission electrified Fermi, who immediately grasped the possibility of chain reaction and began intensive experimentation on this problem, already aware that his talents would be recruited for the coming conflict. The Americans, eyes on the prize of an atomic weapon, gave him what he needed to do his work. In a squash court under the football stadium at the University of Chicago, he built the first atomic reactor, a pile of uranium layered with graphite and "moderated" by rods of boron and cadmium.

Soon Fermi was living in the dry arroyos of Los Alamos, New Mexico, where the U.S. government sent him as part of the Manhattan Project, the top-secret undertaking President Franklin Roosevelt had funded with some two billion dollars. There he liberated the awesome power of nature by harnessing the atom. It wasn't until 1945, when Hiroshima and Nagasaki were destroyed by the power of the atomic bomb, that most Americans became aware of Fermi's incredible discovery. The agnostic scientist tried to remain intellectually detached from the events surrounding "Fat Man" and "Little Boy," the names given to the two bombs. But ultimately, his brilliant discovery was overshadowed by its devastating effects.

HENRY FORD

ON A RAINY SUMMER morning in 1896, with his wife watching expectantly, a thirty-three-year-old engineer for the Edison Illuminating Company in Detroit, Michigan, took his preposterous-looking "quadricycle" for its maiden spin. In a gesture characteristic of the impatience Henry Ford would exhibit throughout his career, the farmboy turned inventor knocked down the bricks surrounding his shop's narrow entrance when he realized that the door was too small for his new horseless carriage. Using the same principles of this four-cylinder, brakeless box on wheels—constructed in his spare time—Ford went on to create, twelve years later, the first full-size car designed for the masses, the Model T. The Ford Motor Company, which Ford founded in 1903 with twenty-eight thousand dollars from a local coal dealer, devoted itself to turning out this incredibly sturdy, inexpensive, and reliable vehicle after abandoning several less profitable models. It was to be—in the mind of this dedicated entrepreneur—"a car for the great multitude," one that "no man making a good salary will be unable to afford." Within a year of its introduction, there were some ten thousand Model Ts on the roads. By 1920, with one out of every two cars in the world a Ford, he had succeeded far beyond his wildest dreams.

Only a few years after the legendary black "Tin Lizzie," as the model T was nicknamed, first rolled out of Ford's factory in Highland Park, Michigan, the company was producing one car every three minutes. Improved production methods soon reduced the Model T's original price of slightly under nine hundred dollars to around five hundred dollars. The inventor became a billionaire and his "universal cheap car" began to transform the physical, social, and economic fabric of American life. Available for a mere $290 by 1924, the Model T quickly transformed rural America, bringing the newspaper, prosperity, and the world to the farmer's formerly distant doorstep and effectively ending rural isolation. It vastly expanded the farmer's market by creating the country's first national commercial network, and it carried the city dweller into the countryside. In a few decades a complex web of highways created cities and sprawling bedroom communities where there had once been pasture. The automobile changed the land, and how Americans worked and played.

Ford's most important contribution to the twentieth century was his introduction of the assembly line in 1913. With this innovation—inspired by a device for moving cows' carcasses used by packing houses—Ford ushered in the age of full-scale mass production, complete with moving conveyer belts and standard design and parts, all operating with the support of an efficient mass distribution and spare parts system. While none of these individual elements was uniquely Ford's, he alone combined them. The assembly line's speed, economy, and technological precision came to symbolize America's industrial preeminence in the world. Ford represented the ultimate American success story: The poor farm boy repairing watches in his humble room became a powerful tycoon who could take part in his own government—or choose to challenge it. Ford did both, running unsuccessfully for United States senator from his home state of Michigan in 1918 and facing down Franklin D. Roosevelt in 1933 by refusing to abide by the president's National Recovery Act auto industry code.

Ford remained popular even when, in his naïveté, this ardent pacifist chartered an ocean liner known popularly as "the peace ship" and sailed to Europe in 1915 to try to stop World War I. (Ford's slogan for the endeavor was "Out of the trenches and back to their homes by Christmas.") His hero's stature with the public survived his failed senate race and his million-dollar libel suit against the *Chicago Tribune*, which called him an anarchist. His court testimony revealed a man so woefully ignorant of widely known historical facts that a rumor spread that he could neither read nor write. The public even absolved him when his newspaper, the *Dearborn Independent*, printed anti-Semitic material, which he tried to excuse by professing ignorance of the paper's contents. When Ford strongly resisted unionization, the public forgave him that, too. But after the so-called 1937 Battle of the Overpass, in which labor organizer Walter Reuther and three other strikers were brutally beaten, and the United Automobile Workers strike of 1941, Ford was finally forced to capitulate to the union.

Ford could even claim a bit of glamour: To interest financial backers in his automobile research, he broke speed records driving his own racing cars. He spoke engagingly of the machine's role in liberating both the worker and farmer from lives of drudgery, emphasizing his own crucial part in this noble venture. When Ford raised his employees' minimum wage to an unprecedented five dollars a day—almost twice the going rate—reduced their workday, and gave them Saturdays off, fellow industrialists gasped in dismay, while workers cheered. But Ford was merely demonstrating his shrewdness: He recognized that mass production could not succeed unless there was also mass consumption. By giving average workers the means to pay for the cars they built and the leisure time in which to enjoy them, Ford created a mass market, which in turn fed the need for greater production. Ford's invention changed nothing short of everything in American life.

FRANCO

FRANCISCO

IN THE ANNALS OF twentieth-century dictatorships, Francisco Franco's fascist tyranny in Spain ranks as the longest running. During his cruel and oppressive regime, which began in 1939 and was thereafter perennially rumored to be on the verge of collapse, the petulant despot presided over thirty-six years of violent turmoil, suffering a humiliating international rejection that would have broken a less ruthless man.

The generalissimo's grasp on his ill-gotten office was so tenacious that long after his death in 1975, at age eighty-three, many observers, including his countrymen, feigned amazement that Franco was "still dead." But such black humor only hints at the Spanish people's complex view of the distant leader they both revered and feared, a man who could piously receive the Holy Eucharist at morning Mass, then later that day coldly order scores of executions. Recent international assessments of Franco are less ambiguous. Where once he might have been credited with bringing social calm and a modernized economic prosperity to a laggard but anarchic country, most historians now paint him as a power-mad vole whose harsh rule actually prevented Spain from achieving a higher cultural and political status within the western European community.

It was his leadership in the hard fought Spanish Civil War, however, that earned Franco his prominent place in modern history. Determined and methodical, he rose from lowly foot soldier to generalissimo of the rebel Nationalist forces as deviously as he would carry out his insurgent campaign against the Popular Front in 1936. Born in the small Galician town of El Ferrol and descended from a middle-class family with a tradition of naval service, fifteen-year-old Francisco Paulino Hermemegildo Teódulo Franco Bahamonde entered Toledo's Academia Militar de Infantería in 1907. Between 1912 and 1927, he distinguished himself in several campaigns in the Spanish protectorate of Morocco, finally subduing the rebellious Riff chieftain, Abd-el Krim. During this time, the thirty-three-year-old had earned the rank of brigadier general, making him the youngest general in Europe since Napoleon. In 1927, he and his wealthy Austrian wife of four years moved to Saragossa, a city on the Ebro in the northeastern part of the country, where he headed up the Academia General Militar. In 1931, when the Second Republic ousted King Alfonso XIII, pro-royalists—including Franco, King Alfonso's favorite general—were dispatched to semi-exile in the Balearic Islands off Spain's eastern coast.

Upon his return to the Spanish mainland two years later, the new center-right government assigned the favored commander to suppress a miners' strike in Asturias province; Franco performed the job so zealously and with such stunning brutality that he earned the nickname "Butcher"—and the eternal disdain of the leftists. With the Fascist Falange on the march and the Communists biting at his heels, the prudent Franco finally joined a coalition of rightists, monarchists, and fellow officers in plotting a coup against the Popular Front, a coalition of liberals and leftists that had won a plurality in the national elections of 1936. Launching the Civil War from Morocco in July of that year, Franco airlifted troops to the mainland with the help of Nazi Germany and Fascist Italy. The human and ideological consequences of the ensuing conflict were as devastating as the fighting was savage. Over half a million Spaniards, many of them civilians, died in the gruesome thirty-month struggle. Having had their first glimpse of a type of warfare that showed no mercy for noncombatants, an alliance of idealists, adventurers, artists, and intellectuals from all over the globe—including Franco's hated Bolsheviks—rallied to the Republican side. As Mussolini's troops shelled homes and churches and German pilots experimented with saturation bombing, the conflict between democracy and fascism gripped the world. It was in Spain, Albert Camus would write, where foreigners fought foreigners, that his generation learned the bitter lesson "that one can be right and yet be beaten."

When the Spanish Civil War ended in March 1939, Franco, with the support of the military and the Catholic Church, acted quickly. Under his Movimiento Nacional, the secret police murderously eliminated all opposition and subjected all aspects of Spanish life to *El Caudillo's* pathological need for total obedience. But suddenly, in the barely organized chaos, he was forced to focus his energies on Hitler's greedy quest for *Lebensraum*. Initially, it seemed inconceivable that given German and Italian support during the civil war, Franco could avoid joining the Axis. With his stubborn and skillful diplomacy, however, he did just that, using every declaration of "vigilant neutrality" to appease the Allies, every contact with the Führer to trade Spain's entry into the hostilities for postwar territorial concessions in Gibraltar and French Morocco. For the duration, Franco played his waiting game, hoping to land on the winning side and trying to mask his pro-Nazi feelings. But when the Germans invaded Russia, and he allowed recruitment of Spanish citizens for the "Blue Division" destined for the eastern front, his secret was finally out. Spain remained officially neutral throughout the war, however.

Gradually, the world seemed to forgive Franco. Ambassadors called again at El Pardo Palace and in December 1955, Spain's ostracism ended with its acceptance into the United Nations. As his country advanced materially, the octogenarian autocrat relaxed his hold on its throat. In July 1969, bowing to pressure, he designated his political heir: Spain would have its king again and Prince Juan Carlos would have the title that the now enfeebled generalissimo had surely coveted all along.

ANNE FRANK

SHE WAS A WINSOME, intelligent, and idealistic girl, a fugitive, with her family, from Hitler's anti-Jewish laws, who wrote her renowned diary in an Amsterdam attic. Anne Frank had always dreamed of being a famous writer; her diary made her immortal.

In 1933 the Franks fled Germany and reached Amsterdam, driven to emigrate by the gathering forces of nazism in their native land. Paterfamilias Otto Frank, lovingly christened "Pim" in the diary, was a well-to-do pectin manufacturer who had become sufficiently successful to arrange shelter for his family in the old quarter of town. When the Nazis, triumphant in their invasion of the Netherlands and relentless in their suppression of the Jews, issued a peremptory order for Anne's older sister, Margot, to be sent to work in the "East," a slave labor camp, the rooms above the warehouse at 263 Prinsengracht, became the alarmed family's sanctuary. They were shared with the Van Pels and their fifteen-year-old son, Peter, and a dentist named Fritz Pfeffer. (In the diary the Van Pels were called the Van Danns, the dentist, Albert Dussel.)

For the next two years it was Anne's home, and into that fearful, undependable hiding place she took a diary her father had given her. Romantically optimistic and occasionally ironic, possessed of great wit and warmth, she recorded the rich daily life of a young girl's coming of age in these extraordinary circumstances. A powerful and sensitive writer, her preoccupations have the immediacy of any young girl's, though described in an artistically mature voice. Her themes were love, growing up, and her relationship with her family, especially with her adored Pim.

The book known to millions as *The Diary of a Young Girl* was actually an edited version. Frank maintained two separate diaries—one for her daily entries and a second, edited diary written with hopes of publication as a book. When her father decided to carry out his daughter's wish and publish her diary, he pieced together a combination of the two, editing out all aspects of the growing adolescent's sexuality—including any mention of menstruation or her teenage crush on young Peter.

Anne wanted to live like any other teenager, but fate had other plans for her. As the news that reached her from the increasingly agonized world outside grew more horrific, she could still write with the generosity of a pure and intelligent spirit. Her humor and her seriousness shine from every page, whether she admits her enduring affection for her father or her abiding impatience with her mother within the close quarters of their hiding place. Her memorable sentiment, "In spite of everything, I still believe people are good at heart," proves that *she* was, though most would find it difficult if not impossible to assert the same of her enemies.

It is painful to read Frank's entries for June and July of 1944, infused as they are with joy and hope as news of D day reaches them on the contraband radio. For weeks she chronicles the fall of each important city. Then, on August 1, 1944, two years after she went into hiding, her writings stop, like a breath held before disaster. An anonymous informant (a warehouseman was suspected) had betrayed the occupants of the "Secret Annexe" to the dreaded SD, the Nazi security police. Three days later the Nazis raided the warehouse and hauled the terrified occupants off to Auschwitz in a cattle car. Separated from the others, Margot and Anne ended up at Bergen-Belsen, where first her elder sister and then Anne died in a typhus epidemic a few short weeks before the British army liberated the camp in April 1945.

Friends of the family found the diary where it was dropped during the arrest and after the war gave it to the only family member who survived the nightmare, Otto Frank. Publication began in 1947, with immediate and dramatic effect. Hailed by admirers as a literary revelation, denounced by enemies as a fraud or a propaganda trick of the victorious and vengeful Allies, the diary was a bestseller first in Europe and then in America, where its stage adaptation left audiences dumbstruck and weeping. In 1991 a second edition of the diary appeared, containing almost 30 percent more material than the original. *The Diary of a Young Girl: The Definitive Edition* presents a more acerbic, defiant, and smoldering Anne, an adolescent sometimes envious of her sister and often fuming at her mother. In addition, this longer version brings into even sharper focus the fraught atmosphere of the Franks' cramped safe haven. In 1997, a new version of the play was staged.

The influence of Anne Frank's writing continues to be enormous. Her diary put a human face on the Holocaust but her singular experience became a symbol of the resilience and nobility of the human spirit. Mature beyond her years, she herself expressed it best: "I can feel the suffering of millions and yet, if I look up into the heavens, I think that it will all come right, that this cruelty too will end, and that peace and tranquillity will return again."

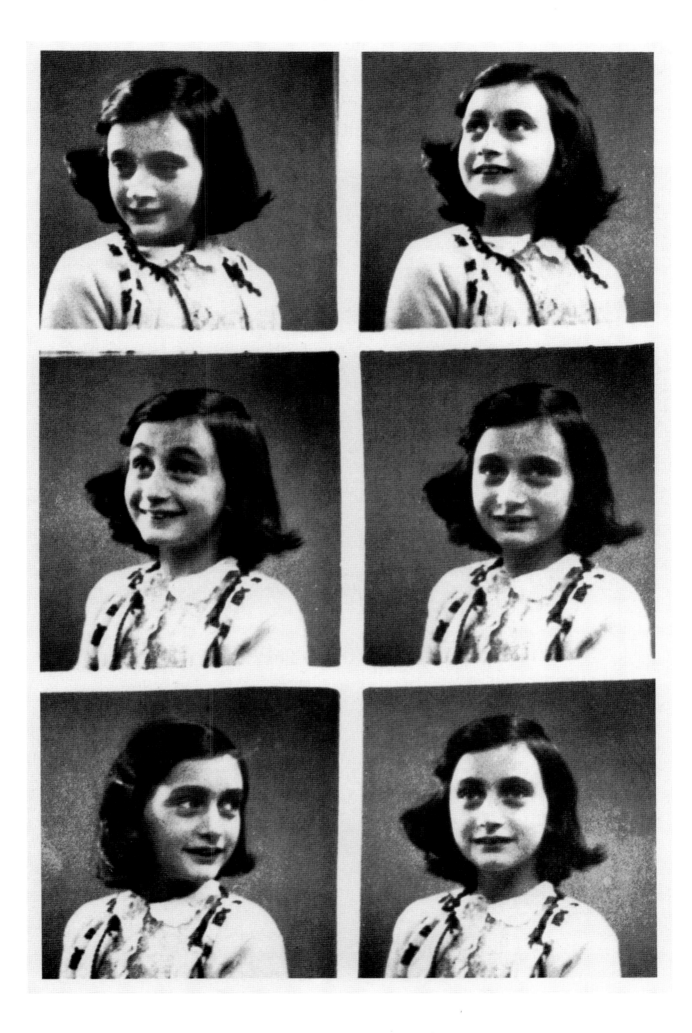

ARETHA FRANKLIN

THE QUEEN OF SOUL was born in Memphis, Tennessee, the daughter of the leading Baptist minister of the day, the Reverend Clarence Franklin, and grew up in Detroit, virtually at the knee of the greatest gospel singer America ever produced, Mahalia Jackson. As a child, Aretha was a soloist with her father's New Bethel Baptist Church choir, singing, as she put it, "all day, every day." At fourteen she made her first album for the Chess label and while in high school was a professional singer of religious songs. Encouragement came from her aunt, gospel singer Clara Ward; the example of such worldly soul and blues singers as Sam Cooke, Dinah Washington, and B. B. King, all of whom were regular visitors to the Franklin household, moved her to try pop. Traveling to New York when she was eighteen, Franklin auditioned her rich, fluid voice for John Hammond, who signed her to a Columbia Records recording contract. Unfortunately, the legendary producer's famous touch failed him when it came to Franklin: Every style to which he applied her voice—whether jazz, blues, pop standards, or show tunes—served only to stifle her gift as a soaring improviser and resulted in a series of dull, wishy-washy offerings which sold miserably.

Franklin left Columbia when her contract lapsed in 1966 and signed with the more flexible, more creative, and far funkier Atlantic Records, whose chief brains, Jerry Wexler and Ahmet Ertegun, were only too happy to give their new charge her wings. Recording with the house band at the studio in Muscle Shoals, Alabama, Franklin came up with the lean, gritty soul monster "I Never Loved a Man (The Way I Love You)" in her breakout year, 1967. It sold over a million copies and began an amazing run of hits: "Do Right Woman—Do Right Man," "Respect" (her signature song), and the hardly less well-known "A Natural Woman," along with "Chain of Fools" and "Since You've Been Gone." Between 1967 and 1974 she won ten Grammy awards.

Then, suddenly, the torrent of Grammies ceased. In the midseventies, disco and other styles completely eclipsed Franklin's melodic approach to material and her brand of hard-soul rock, which could not always be danced to. She also struggled with illness. She had disappeared so completely that a Steely Dan song of the early eighties bewailed the fact that a nineteen-year-old "don't remember the Queen of Soul." But Franklin signed with Clive Davis's Arista Records in 1980, and through the early and middle years of that decade found new life with 1982's *Jump to It,* produced by singer Luther Vandross, and the subsequent hits "Get It Right," "Freeway of Love," and "Who's Zoomin' Who?"

Triumph followed triumph. In 1985 Michigan declared her voice one of the state's natural resources, and in 1986 Franklin appeared in her own television special, *Aretha!* In 1987 she became the first woman inducted into the Rock and Roll Hall of Fame, and scored another number-one record pairing with George Michael in "I Knew You Were Waiting (For Me)."

But there was personal turmoil along with success. Franklin's first marriage, to manager Ted White, had shattered in the late sixties. A second marriage, to actor Glynn Turman in 1978, lasted until 1984, roughly coinciding with the decline and death of Franklin's father, who had been comatose since being shot by burglars in 1979. Devoted to her father and devastated by his passing—she had spent five years commuting between Detroit and her home in California to supervise his care—she sank even deeper into depression after her sister Carolyn died of cancer in 1988. The following year Arista issued her first gospel album in sixteen years, *One Lord, One Faith, One Baptism.* A moving tribute to her father that critics compared favorably with her 1972 gospel album *Amazing Grace,* it also featured Franklin's two sisters, Erma and Carolyn, her brother, the Reverend Cecil Franklin, and the Reverend Jesse Jackson. Despite the album's favorable reception, her habitual timidity and aversion to offstage publicity became all but absolute.

Franklin's career seemed to rise and fall with the joys and fears of her great heart. She emerged from seclusion after a long hiatus marked by a fear of flying, a phobia which developed after a frighteningly close call in a small aircraft and which precluded lucrative foreign concert tours. In 1993 she sang at President Bill Clinton's inaugural ball at the request of the president and the First Lady, both of whom were among her millions of baby boomer fans. Two years later Franklin was honored at the Kennedy Center for the Arts for her accomplishments in music, the youngest person to be given this distinction. Always struggling with a weight problem, she succeeded in giving up smoking, which, in return, gave her back some of her vocal range. Her protective cocoon a thing of the past, the long frustrated autobiographer announced in 1997, "It's time for a book," promising to finally share her private story. That spring she also brought a group of gospel singers to New York's Lincoln Center for a show called Aretha's Crusade Against Aids and made a surprise appearance at the Grammies. As the nineties closed, she rarely sat at the piano during concerts as she once had, her hefty playing style a close second to her rich, impassioned voice. But Franklin, the great soul sister who introduced the world to the rumbling joy of black American church singing, never needed accompaniment. It took only her to bring it all back home.

ONE LORD
ONE FAITH ONE BAPTISM

FREUD

SIGMUND

CARVED AND SCULPTED FIGURES from ancient civilizations stood on the polished top of Sigmund Freud's desk in both his Vienna and London studies. Cherished selections from his museum-worthy collection of primitive artifacts, these totems from a mythic past bore witness to Freud's ardent quest, as the father of psychoanalysis, to illuminate the deepest and most ancient recesses of the human psyche. What the self-professed archaeologist of the mind found buried there was a picture of human nature that was at once startling and revolutionary. His exploration—centered in his painstaking analysis of himself and his patients—revealed to twentieth-century mankind an alien and unrecognizable self, possessed of hidden motives, strange guilts, repressed hatreds, and shadowy sexual urges.

Freud's probing of the unconscious and his insistence on its power in influencing human behavior earned him the scorn of fellow professionals and perhaps the most controversial reputation in the history of modern thought. In his own estimation, however, he was a "conquistador," setting out grandly "to agitate the sleep of mankind." Many called him a charlatan and crank and even now, the conflict surrounding his theories—especially, though not exclusively, the sexual basis of neurosis, infantile sexuality, and the related Oedipus complex—continues. But at the same time, Freud's ideas and the terms he introduced to describe them have so permeated our culture and language that there seems no way back to a time when childhood represented innocence, and the basest of human emotions were attributable to others only.

Born in Freiberg, Moravia, to Jakob and Amalie Freud, Sigmund was his mother's firstborn and her favorite of ten children. He was a bright student from the beginning, but his natural inquisitiveness caused him to delay his main focus of study at the University of Vienna for several years. Although his first love was politics, his prospects as a Viennese Jew were not promising, and so he settled on medicine.

Freud's exploration of the psyche began after a highly productive research career in which he made important contributions to both the theory of evolution and the foundations of modern neurology. By the time his *Studies in Hysteria* (co-authored with Josef Breuer) was published in 1895, he was interpreting his patients' tangled personal histories through the technique of "free association," in which the analysand would talk spontaneously about whatever came to mind. A few years later, Freud himself slipped into psychoneurosis, fighting its debilitation by rigorously dissecting his anxious and perplexing dreams. The result of this courageous process was *The Interpretation of Dreams*, which, when it appeared in 1900, precipitated a torrent of scorn. Probing the nature and significance of dreams and the functioning of the unconscious, the work described this underworld as infantile in origin and teeming with thoughts and feelings that the conscious mind finds unacceptable and tries at all costs to ignore. The publication in 1905 of *Three Essays on the Theory of Sexuality* also provoked outrage. Its most unsettling aspects dealt with the heretofore hidden sexuality of childhood, a tumultuous period of development which Freud characterized as rife with strong, inescapable erotic attachments to parents—and an equal complement of hostile feelings as well.

It was a shocking view that drew vituperative reaction from all quarters, but then, new ideas often make new enemies. Freud had alienated his fellow Jews by writing in *Moses and Monotheism* that the great Hebrew leader was really an Egyptian. Eleven years earlier, he had created another storm with *The Future of an Illusion*, in which he stated that religious beliefs spring from mankind's need to create a supernatural being out of fear of death and the desire for immortality.

Freud's contemporaries resented being dictated to about their sexuality and other behaviors by someone who was a self-admitted study in guilt, recklessness, and neuroses. His biographers, for example, now suspect him of carrying on an affair with his wife Martha's younger sister, Minna Bernays, perhaps for the duration of his marriage. (In fact, Carl Jung, an early disciple, claimed that, the first time he visited Freud in 1907, Minna herself drew him aside and admitted that her relationship with her brother-in-law was "very intimate.") Freud admitted to having "unruly homosexual feeling[s]" for his dearest friend and most important confidant, Dr. Wilhelm Fliess, whose theory of a universal bisexual impulse Freud would later adopt as his own. He also offered phobia cures when he himself had an overwhelming fear of train travel, and though he coined the phrases "oral gratification" and "death instinct," he smoked twenty cigars a day and dabbled in cocaine for much of his life. (The drug was useful in coping with the considerable pain from some thirty-three surgeries for jaw cancer.) His ultimate folly—an original sin that remains largely unforgiven—was his psychoanalysis of his own daughter, Anna Freud, despite his own published prohibitions against such conduct.

Extremely closed about his own personal matters, Freud threw away large caches of his files and notes more than once in his lifetime, perhaps intending to defeat posterity's curiosity. He had "little faith in the biographical enterprise," one of his recent biographers, Peter Gay, asserted, but Freud must have also expected that he would be as misunderstood by future generations as he had been by his own. Despite ongoing assaults, however, Freudian analysis continues its erratic survival. This fact is perhaps the most telling tribute to the great confessionalist who, by extinguishing people's illusions about themselves, forced them into the often painful search for self-knowledge.

BETTY FRIEDAN

"I AM NOT THAT far from Everywoman," feminist leader and thinker Betty Friedan once said. What might be closer to the truth is that Friedan—housewife and mother of three—created the very idea of Everywoman from her own personal pain and compassionate outrage. Before Friedan's classic book, *The Feminine Mystique*, women were defined largely by their roles as helpmates, sexual partners, and mothers. It was Friedan's genius to change the status of her sex by transforming how the culture perceived it—in the minds of men and women alike. It was also part of her originality to apply the current theories concerning the meaninglessness of middle-class existence—formerly applied only to men—to women's lives. After the publication of *The Feminine Mystique* in 1963 no one thought of women in quite the same way. Through Friedan's decades of writing and politicking, women have moved toward social equality with men as well as the freedom to pursue self-knowledge.

Friedan possessed a curiously bourgeois vision, and, like many great reformers, she tended to idealize the underclass she was trying to free. In the beginning of her career, the lumpen proletariat were housewives Friedan wanted to turn into professionals. In Friedan's "gynotopia" there were women judges but no women murderers who were not themselves victims, women bankers but none who foreclosed on poor women, women political leaders but never any who were misguided. Yet, "the pope of women"—as she referred to herself in jest—never demonized men (unlike the radical feminists she was later to break ranks with), considering them allies in the fight for a decent human society.

Betty Naomi Goldstein was born in Peoria, Illinois, the daughter of a jeweler whose anxiety over her scholarly ways led him to limit her to borrowing five library books at a time. Being Jewish in a small midwestern town, the lonely, shy Friedan was acutely attuned to discrimination. Her innate sensitivity led her to study psychology at Smith College, where she helped to create the school's literary magazine. Graduating summa cum laude in 1942, Friedan was awarded a fellowship by the University of California, a rare honor for a woman in those days. She spent a year studying psychology at Berkeley, but when the school offered her a second fellowship in 1943, the jealousy of a young male physicist she was dating led her to turn it down.

Thereafter Friedan left Berkeley—and the physicist— and returned to New York City. Working as a journalist, she led a life of genteel bohemianism in New York's Greenwich Village until, in 1947, she married Carl Friedan, a summer-stock theatrical producer who later turned to advertising. Her life now dutifully followed the blueprint for middle-class marrieds in the 1950s. A move to Queens was followed in 1956 by an exodus to suburban Rockland County after Friedan had been fired from her job for asking for a second maternity leave. Later she was outraged by that dismissal, but at the time she was relieved: "I had begun to feel so guilty working." It was with a sense of reprieve that Friedan set up house with her husband and children in a Victorian house overlooking the Hudson River.

There she felt suspended in a kind of limbo of laundry, kids, and cocktails with the same drab people. She continued to write for women's magazines, discovering that anything that did not contribute to the image of the happy housewife was blithely excised from the articles she turned in. The trained psychologist then prepared a questionnaire for Smith alumnae on the occasion of their fifteenth reunion and found by the response that "the problem that has no name" was more pervasive than she had ever imagined. Emboldened by her discovery and by a growing sense of purpose, in 1960 she wrote an article for *Good Housekeeping* magazine entitled "Women Are People Too!" Reader response was so overwhelming and united in opinion that Friedan expanded her findings into a book.

The appearance in 1963 of *The Feminine Mystique* has had, in the minds of some, more impact on modern society than even the works of Freud. It was an instant best-seller, and its effect—a radical realignment of women's attitudes toward themselves and men's attitudes toward women—is still being felt more than thirty years later. The simple theory Friedan expounded—that to be complete human beings women must have full equality with men, and that equality was an absolute right—proved complex in practice: Not everyone agreed, and the political backlash led Friedan to form the National Organization for Women (NOW) in 1966.

As she strove to advance the cause, writing, lecturing, and traveling to demonstrations, the women's movement claimed her marriage and divided her family. For Friedan, these were hard and ironic blows. A believer in strong familial values, she never attacked marriage, finding herself at odds on this point with the more radical members within her own group. Yet she carried on, arguing, marching, and giving hope to women, always with the idea of widening their circle of opportunity.

In her later years, she turned her attention to the problems of older women, taking up their standard with great purpose. In 1993, after ten years' research, she published *The Fountain of Age*, designed to dispel the myth that aging is strictly a process of debilitation. Her feminism expanded, Friedan the humanist exulted in her travels through this uncharted territory. As always, however, her focus was the essential quality of the individual life. Everywoman may have grown older, but she was still busy fashioning a new world.

YURI GAGARIN

ON APRIL 12, 1961 at exactly 9:07 A.M. Moscow time the pioneer cosmonaut Yuri Gagarin left the earth in *Vostok I* to blaze a trail where the gods were once thought to dwell. He would sail weightlessly across the heavens for only 108-minutes in the nearly five-ton craft flying faster (18,000 m.p.h.) and higher (188 miles) than anyone had before. A courageous patriot, when he returned home from his around-the-globe odyssey, the world which welcomed him would never be the same.

Fittingly enough for the Era of the Common Man, this first human in space was a former foundry worker, although as a Communist Party member he was careful to append the word "Soviet" to his self-description of "ordinary man." A regular guy of extraordinary achievement, Yuri Alekseyevich Gagarin was born in Klushino, a village 100 miles west of Moscow near a town now named in his honor. Contrary to claims that the astronaut was a noble descended from Czarist Prince Gagarin, his father has been variously described as a collective farmer and a carpenter; his mother was a milkmaid. In 1941, with his village occupied by the invading Nazis, the seven-year-old Gagarin witnessed an act of selfless bravery that was both inspiration for his life's work and an eerie foreshadowing of his doom: a Soviet fighter pilot, his wounded plane spewing oily black smoke into the skies above Gagarin's head, emptied his machine guns at a German column before sacrificing himself in a dive into the enemy soldiers.

The war over, in 1950 Gagarin resumed his interrupted education by enrolling in the Lyubertsy foundryman's school near Moscow, seemingly destined to become the very model of the New Soviet Citizen—a worker bee in heavy industry. But Lyubertsy also boasted of an airplane factory where Gagarin chatted with the pilots and keenly followed their test flights. The following year, he entered Saratov Industrial College, and when he found himself near a flying school and aerodome, he began taking courses in aviation. Such is the official history, at any rate; but Saratov was also one of several Soviet "secret cities" devoted to highly confidential projects, including the exploration of space. Gagarin's presence there may not have been a coincidence.

Studying flight theory and aviation at night, Gagarin made his first parachute jump and was rewarded with his first flight in a fighter plane. At that moment, he later recounted, his life focused in diamantine clarity. In 1955 he earned both his foundryman's diploma and his flying papers, spending the summer learning to operate fighter planes. That fall he enrolled in the Orenburg Flying School, graduating in 1957 and joining the Soviet Air Force as a fighter pilot. At five-foot-two inches tall he was so short that his superiors would not allow him to march in the front ranks of parades, and he had to sit on a pillow to fly the MiG planes in which he trained. Later, this compactness

of frame would stand him in good stead in the cramped quarters of a space capsule. In 1957 he married a nursing student, and was promoted to Lieutenant. Two years later he heard about the top secret Soviet space program and volunteered—although there is just as much reason to believe he was being groomed for it all along. Frank and sincere, he was self-confident, fearless, and curious—excellent requisites for doing something exceedingly dangerous that no else had ever done before. Physically fit and intellectually vigorous, he exercised daily and neither drank nor smoked. As a military pilot who might be called upon to steer what was essentially a speeding cannonball, he was the perfect candidate for cosmonaut.

Nothing in his three years of intensive training, however, had done more than merely approximate the crushing G-force of rocket acceleration, the disorientation of weightlessness, and the rigors of re-entry. When on that fateful day Major Gagarin bid goodbye to his family with a cryptic explanation of "vital service" and prepared to leave the planet, there was still enormous uncertainty: no one knew precisely what would happen to a human being in space. How would the body react to the extreme changes in temperature? How would the mind deal with the psychological strain? With a technical failure, Gagarin could be burned to cinders or left out there in the hazy firmament to die a long, lonely death.

Only Gagarin was calm as he climbed into the capsule which was perched like a pebble atop a volatile rocket capable of 80,000 tons of thrust. After a few flashes of acceleration, it flung him and his little machine into circumnavigations which would take less than two hours. In one triumph, the Russian shattered all flight records and any American hope of getting in space first and placed his nation in the lead of the superpower race begun in 1957 by the Soviet's unmanned orbiter *Sputnik*. As *Vostok I* reentered the atmosphere, the tense Gagarin—singing *The Motherland Hears, the Motherland Knows*—watched flames streak past his porthole.

But he landed safely on solid land, in an unplowed field of a collective farm, Lenin's Way. Given a hero's welcome—as well as eventually the Order of Lenin and the title Hero of the Soviet Union—Gagarin was magnanimous in victory, announcing that there was enough room among the stars for everyone. But in conversation with Soviet Premier Kruschev, Gagarin allowed himself a tiny gloat over beating the capitalists. After a bathroom fall in which he damaged his inner ear, he was permanently grounded from cosmonautics. Then on March 27, 1968, while on a routine training flight in a MiG jet, he crashed and died, much as that anonymous Soviet flyer had done before the youthful Gagarin's eyes almost thirty years before. Anonymity, however, would certainly not be Gagarin's fate.

INDIRA GANDHI

TO HER NEARLY HALF a billion subjects, Indira Gandhi—first woman prime minister of a major country and heir to one of India's great political dynasties—was known as *Amma* ("Mother") or sometimes simply "She." For the predominantly Hindu population, the maternal image is a powerful one, freighted with allusions to their mighty goddesses. During her long career, Gandhi was sometimes Durga, goddess of fertility, whose bounty is bestowed upon all, and sometimes Kali, goddess of destruction. When the hour of her assassination arrived, Indira had earned at one time or another both the love and the enmity of her people.

Born Indira Priyadarshini Nehru in Brahmin splendor in the northern Indian state of Uttar Pradesh to the future leader Jawaharlal Nehru and his teenage wife Kamala, Indira grew up steeped in the turmoil of the Indian nationalist movement, witnessing or participating in every dramatic moment of India's march to independence. As a child, she watched the trial of her father and her grandfather Motilal Nehru for disobedience to the crown. When the younger Nehru was judged guilty of picketing shops that sold foreign products, the fiercely nationalistic Nehrus consigned their European velvets and chiffons to a bonfire and vowed to wear homespun.

With her father often away from home on protests or languishing in a British prison, the young Indira spent much time alone. Shunted from English to Indian school and back again as her father and grandfather bickered over the political symbolism of her education, Indira learned to rely upon herself first. Much of her erudition came not from school but from a series of letters from her father in jail, which amounted to a course in world history. Lonely and melancholic, she later maintained that her early emotional suffering gave her character. With a strong tomboy streak, she became aggressive and idealistic, identifying herself with Joan of Arc. In 1926, she attended school in Switzerland, where her ailing mother was being treated for tuberculosis. She returned to India in 1927, and in 1929—inspired by the nonviolent methods of Mohandas Gandhi, a close friend of her father—the twelve-year-old organized the Monkey Brigade, a group of nationalist children who smuggled messages for the Indian National Congress, the prime movers for nationhood.

Following the death of her mother in 1936, Indira left for Somerville College, Oxford, where she studied modern history and developed a relationship with Feroze Gandhi (no relation to Mohandas), a student at the London School of Economics, who was active in politics. Her Oxford years were interrupted by frequent tours with her father, drumming up support for Indian independence. As World War II approached, and the British viceroy committed an outraged India to the fray on the side of the Empire, Indira decided to marry Feroze. The union took place in 1942 against the strenuous objection of the aristocratic Nehrus, because Feroze was a Parsi whose parents owned a store. But when the Mahatma blessed the union, Jawaharlal capitulated. Meanwhile, the civil disobedience campaign saw Nehru jailed for the ninth time and Feroze Gandhi on the run. Indira was arrested at a public meeting in Allahabad and sent to the foul Naini Prison, where she taught illiterate prisoners for thirteen months. After her release, she rejoined her husband, giving birth to a son, Rajiv, in 1944. Two years later, unable to hold on to the Empire, the British offered independence. That same year her second son, Sanjay, was born. With her father named prime minister of a new India, Indira Gandhi saw the birth of the nation on August 15, 1947, amid the bloodshed of angry Muslim-Hindu street brawls as the country was divided into India and Pakistan. A year later, the Nehrus' dear friend Mohandas Gandhi was assassinated.

Indira Gandhi became her father's hostess and confidante, taking from him her belief in nonalignment and her determination to strengthen India's economy. In 1955 she decided to apply these principles, becoming a powerful figure in the ruling Congress Party. When Nehru died in 1964, the grief-stricken Gandhi agreed to become a minor minister in the government of new prime minister Lai Bahadur Shastri. Two years later Shastri died and Gandhi, a symbol of national unity as Nehru's daughter, was elected prime minister. The inexperienced Gandhi stumbled at first as she faced the toll of a disastrous Sino-Indian border war and a terrible drought. But she quickly learned to deal effectively with such troubles as inflation and Punjabi riots. She began a sweeping birth control program, and worked to increase food production in an ambitious scheme of moderate socialism designed to industrialize India and abolish poverty. Under her rule, India ascended to leader of the nonaligned nations.

Her time in office was never peaceful. She was accused more than once of corruption, and in 1975 she gave herself dictatorial powers to sidestep a court order banning her from politics for six years because of election abuses in 1971. The struggle against her political enemies occupied her remaining years, with dark intrigues and public betrayals. In 1977 she lost the election and was imprisoned briefly on charges of corruption; 1980 saw her back in office, a triumph marred by the death of Sanjay, her political heir apparent, in a flying accident. In 1984, after ordering the Indian army to storm the Golden Temple, the sacred locus of the Sikh religion where armed Sikhs had holed up, Gandhi ignored advice to purge Sikhs from her security force. On October 31,1984, two of them shot her dead in her garden, touching off the worst civil violence since the 1947 partition. Kali, the goddess of destruction, had prevailed in the end, taking India's mother to her bosom.

GANDHI

MOHANDAS

THE UNIFORM OF ONE of the century's great revolutionaries was as symbolic as it was purposeful: a simple loincloth of undyed, handwoven material. His weapons—prayer, fasting, and nonviolent resistance—were equally unorthodox, wielding a power far more persuasive than the guns and tanks of other freedom fighters. Itinerant saint, martyr to India's struggle for independence, antimodernist crusader who urged his compatriots to reject the values of materialism in favor of a simple, spiritually centered life, Mohandas Karamchand Gandhi—known to his legions of admirers as Mahatma (Sanskrit for "great-souled")—dedicated the majority of his almost eighty years to the proposition that all life was sacred and must be respected at any cost.

Born in the small fishing port of Porbandar, on India's west coast, Gandhi passed his childhood in pleasant, even coddled, circumstances. Members of the Vaishnavite sect of Hinduism, his merchant-class family enjoyed an average ranking in the rigid Hindu caste system and a comfortable number of "untouchable" servants to perform the household's ritually unclean tasks. In 1891 Gandhi was ostracized by his caste community of the Modh Banias for staying three years in the "polluting" environment of London to study law—a portentous event for the young scholar.

While abroad, Gandhi, characteristically self-critical and pragmatic, walked a fine line between familiar traditions and the unexplored mores of British sophistication. Having been partially assimilated as a "Brown Briton" in his native India, the newcomer to London was soon sporting a top hat and walking stick and taking lessons in dancing and elocution. But to his disappointment, his sartorial splendor and impeccable etiquette proved no hedge against cultural and racial snobbery. As his finances dwindled, Gandhi immersed himself in study, drawing on the steely determination that would later sustain him through numerous jail terms and countless campaigns of organized nonviolent resistance against the British raj.

In London, the frail, bespectacled, and shy young man was influenced by exposure to different philosophies, religions, and codes of conduct from Christianity and vegetarianism to theosophy and a host of utopian systems. Introduced as a child to the principles of Jainist nonviolence, he now discovered the related themes of loving compassion and self-abnegation in both the New Testament and the *Bhagavad Gita*, which he later memorized. In the works of Thoreau he found the idea of civil disobedience; in those of Tolstoy, the evils of the modern state; and in Ruskin's essays, the salvation of work. After returning to India to work as a barrister in

Bombay, Gandhi left home again two years later, this time for a low-paying job as counsel for a Muslim business firm in South Africa. It was there that the commanding yet humble leader first put into practice the program of enlightened, passive resistance that would later change the destiny of the Indian subcontinent.

Thrown off the first-class section of a train he'd boarded from Durban to Pretoria, then beaten by a coach driver for refusing to vacate his seat for a European, Gandhi quickly abandoned his assimilationist views. He spent the next twenty-one years organizing South African Indians to pressure the British for their civil rights. He soon came to realize that, to devote himself to the welfare of the public, he needed to sacrifice his own family's status by renouncing wealth and the claims of the flesh. Sexual control had been a source of turmoil ever since his father had died while young Gandhi was in bed with his own wife, Kasturba. To suppress sexual desire, this father of four sons took a vow of abstinence in 1906—a pledge he frequently tested in his later years by lying down at night next to female followers.

Upon his return to India in 1915, Gandhi soon organized nonviolent resistance to all forms of social injustice, whether from without or within; he campaigned against both colonial oppression and orthodox Hinduism's unconscionable practice of untouchability. Teaching his followers to take responsibility for the consequences of their civil disobedience, he joined the Indian National Congress and gradually molded its reformist stance into an all-out independence movement. In this determined advocate of rural village life, the British raj faced a tough adversary. "He is a dangerous and uncomfortable enemy," said one observer, "because his body, which you can always conquer, gives you so little purchase upon his soul." Against the moral force of Gandhi's long fasts and much publicized symbolic protests—such as his dramatic two-hundred-mile march to the sea in 1930 in defiance of a newly levied tax on salt—the colonial powers could muster few effective strategies.

Critics would accuse Gandhi of naïveté for his dismay at being unable to stanch the bloodshed that often flowed from his peaceful demonstrations. Compatriots like Jawaharlal Nehru winced at Gandhi's glorification of privation, while the poet Sarojini Naidu pointed out the high monetary cost of keeping "Gandhiji" in poverty. With independence, in 1947, came the partition of India into two separate states, Muslim and Hindu—for Gandhi, a tragic "vivisection" of his homeland to which he only reluctantly agreed. But his sudden death a year later—assassinated by a Hindu fanatic—sent shock waves throughout the world. Millions followed his corpse to the sacred river Jumna, wailing in concert.

GRETA GARBO

THAT FACE. EXQUISITELY BEAUTIFUL, yet possessed of an undefinable, haunting sadness. Languidly indifferent, yet capable of projecting immense passion. No screen actress has survived the camera's scrutiny with such detachment or exploited its mythmaking powers so effectively. And no face save Garbo's has communicated deep emotion with the same contradictory mix of intensity and calm.

When Greta Garbo—born Greta Lovisa Gustafsson—was fourteen, her father, a Stockholm landscapist, passed away. The subsequent death of her sister increased Garbo's sense of abandonment, making her hypersensitive and wary of both commitment and betrayal. Her arrival in Hollywood from her native Sweden in 1925 was almost an afterthought; Louis B. Mayer was humoring the talent he was really after—Garbo's mentor and lover, director Mauritz Stiller. A Polish immigrant who had found his protégée studying at the Royal Dramatic Academy in Stockholm, Stiller perceived a shimmering butterfly in the frumpy seventeen-year-old Garbo and cast her as the second lead in the four-hour silent *Gösta Bering's Saga* (1924). The movie immediately conferred starlet status upon Garbo, a fact that had much to do with Stiller's insistence that his ingenue lose twenty pounds and have her teeth capped. Even so, MGM—who had accepted Stiller's rather unremarkable companion as part of a package deal—could find no marketable image for her until her own taciturn manner with the press created her "Swedish Sphinx" persona.

In 1925 Garbo began shooting her first MGM film, *The Torrent*, Vicente Blasco-Ibáñez's story of a Spanish aristocrat whose mother prevents his marriage to a poor young girl living on their estate. In spite of the pedestrian script, the rushes were breathtaking, revealing to the studio's executives the exciting phenomenon Stiller had insisted was there all along. Garbo was incandescent. The camera loved her from any angle, and she projected an intoxicating eroticism. Stiller, on the other hand, was finished; MGM replaced him on *The Temptress,* his first film with Garbo, and he returned to Sweden, where he died two years later.

Paired with John Gilbert in *Flesh and the Devil* in 1927, and almost immediately afterward in *Love,* an adaptation of *Anna Karenina,* Garbo soon developed a more assured screen presence, though she relied to a great extent on Gilbert's personal direction. The two stars were probably romantically involved—a fact that seemed obvious to titillated audiences—but Garbo ended the affair the year the silent-film star spoke her first line in the 1930 blockbuster *Anna Christie.* By then she was MGM's darling, and nothing was too good for their number-one box-office attraction—except perhaps well-written movies. In truth, it was one of Garbo's triumphs that she seemed capable of redeeming any screenplay, which she often had to. Of the twenty-four movies she made for

MGM, the scripts were uniformly mediocre, the great exception, of course, being Ernst Lubitsch's delightful *Ninotchka* (1939). But the rest of the trappings were first-rate: Expensive sets, extravagant costumes, talented directors, and brilliant cameramen were all mustered to contribute to the Garbo aura. In return, she gave MGM her best. An untrained actress well aware of her shortcomings, she reached the accomplished level of her performances through intense concentration, gut-level intuition, and a professional pliability her gifted directors used to their advantage.

Garbo worked hard at her craft, but at the end of the day her personal curtain of privacy would always ring down. Director Clarence Brown remarked that "when she was done, she was through." A maid would walk onto the set and hand Garbo a glass of water, and the actress would say good night and leave. The more reclusive the actress became, the more her public wanted to know about Garbo's presumably exciting private life. But the actress was unyielding about her right to privacy; she both needed to perform and to withdraw. Defying Hollywood convention, the movie star refused to sign autographs or grant interviews—or to attend her own premieres. Even her own studio failed to obtain her telephone number. In later years she argued that she had never meant to give such a frosty impression, but it seems evident that when the mainly celibate Garbo uttered the line "I want to be alone" in *Grand Hotel* (1932), she really meant it. That she also had a sense of humor about these hide-and-seek games is clear, too, from the charming scene in *Ninotchka* when she is asked, "Do you want to be alone, comrade?" In response, the dour Bolshevik roars, "No!"

Garbo loved to disguise herself—"Miss Harriet Brown" was one of her favorite alternative identities. She was unconventional in even more provocative ways as well. If her whereabouts were a puzzle, her sexual orientation was a flat-out mystery. Of course, Garbo herself may have deliberately fed the rumors by juxtaposing torrid affairs with her leading men with whispered liaisons involving beauties of her own gender. Whatever her intentions, this elusive, ambiguous sensuality was perfect grist for MGM's publicity mill.

Her status secure with successes such as *Queen Christina* (1933), *Anna Karenina* (1935), and *Camille* (1936), Garbo made salary demands that soon turned her into something of a fiscal millstone for MGM. After *Two-Faced Woman* (1941), an ill-fated attempt to transform her into a comedienne, Garbo, at the young age of thirty-six, went into temporary retirement to wait out World War II. But as hostilities dragged on, the famous recluse eventually withdrew more and more completely—the camera, after all, was no longer so kind, and one needed little imagination to foresee the fate of an aging siren. Her preemptive exit left her sublime beauty intact and her legend indelible.

MÁRQUEZ

GABRIEL GARCÍA

PERHAPS ONLY THE SOUTH American rain forest, with its exotic fauna and flora, could have produced novelist Gabriel García Márquez. In his highly popular work, which includes the masterpiece *One Hundred Years of Solitude*, he has created a distinct landscape as miraculous as any ever created and populated it with imaginative and offbeat characters. The century's foremost practitioner of the magical realism school of literature and the foremost of a whole wave of Latin American writers, García Márquez brought the unique sensibilities of his culture to the world's attention.

García Márquez was born in northern Colombia, in Aracataca, the sleepy town that was to become the legendary Kingdom of Macondo in his *ficciones*. His father, a telegraph operator, was too poor to support him, and sent the boy to be raised by his grandparents in a huge and spooky mansion. There, García Márquez's grandfather regaled the boy with improbable yarns of bygone days in the village—a former banana boomtown—and of his own adventures as a soldier. Not to be outdone, García Márquez's grandmother spun macabre stories of ghosts and the troubled spirits of ancestors. This dual heritage of tales, both swashbuckling and bizarre, is evident in the novelist's mature style.

In 1946, he entered the school of law at the University of Bogotá, where he stayed five years, developing such an antipathy for the subject that he declined to take a degree. While in school, the magazine *El Espectador* published his early stories, which were more obscure than mysterious. When civil strife known as *La violencia* closed the university, a newly politicized García Márquez continued his studies in Cartagena and began a career as a left-wing journalist. This new passion took him to the city of Barranquilla, where he was a poorly paid columnist for *El Heraldo*. Living above a brothel, he read the works of the great international writers— Joyce, Hemingway, Faulkner, Woolf, and, above all, Kafka. The latter's *The Metamorphosis* was a revelation and inspiration. Dissatisfied with his own work, *La Casa* (1951), he put fiction aside to concentrate on film criticism and political journalism.

In 1955, after much reworking, *La Casa* was published as *La Hojarasca* (*The Leaf Storm*). It leaned heavily toward a Faulknerian gothic atmosphere, and its publication was appreciated by the writers in the cafés García Márquez frequented, but not much farther. Meanwhile, García Márquez was sent to Paris as a foreign correspondent for *El Heraldo*, and in 1955 was stranded there when the paper finally enraged the *Jefe* in Colombia enough to shut it down. Starving, struggling so desperately that he had to trade in bottles to eat, García Márquez began his second book in a cold Parisian garret. But despite his bitter circumstances, he was confident enough in his abilities to contemplate two separate books when his main character refused to be contained in a single volume. *No One Writes to the Colonel* was finished in 1957, the year García Márquez left Paris and went to live in Venezuela. In 1961, the novel and its twin, *The Evil Hour*, were published in Bogotá, where *No One Writes* was hailed as the best Colombian fiction in almost forty years.

From 1961 to 1965, García Márquez continued with his journalism and screenwriting. In the several short stories written before his magnum opus, he finally found his voice in the lush and fantastic legacy his grandparents had bequeathed him. Amid a landscape of magic and humor, García Márquez explored the themes of solitude and love. As if it had been dictated to him, the opening of *One Hundred Years of Solitude* came to him whole. He then shut himself in a room in Mexico City, writing eight hours a day for eighteen months. When he emerged, he was a thousand dollars in debt for every month he'd been sequestered, but he had a manuscript of tremendous value and power.

Translated into more than thirty languages, *One Hundred Years of Solitude* has sold over fifteen million copies worldwide, and García Márquez's name is now as renowned as the authors who once inspired him. In 1975, he wrote *The Autumn of the Patriarch* and in 1982 was awarded the Nobel Prize for Literature, *love in the Time of Cholera* (1985) and *Of Love and Other Demons* (1994) followed. In later years he has turned his attention to writing for the cinema, and lecturing at the Foundation for New Latin American Cinema, which he inaugurated in Cuba in 1985. He even wroted a journalistic account of Pablo Escobar's plan to avoid extradition to the U.S. by having ten prominent Columbians kidnapped, a book published in 1997 as *News of a Kidnapping*. His long friendship with Cuban dictator Fidel Castro has been a subject for controversy, but García Márquez has been resolute in the face of criticism, remaining loyal to Castro while pursuing his craft with characteristic dedication. Writing so slowly that five good lines a day is a victory, García Márquez is untroubled by the pace. He is confident that there are as many stories in the sad and beautiful land he writes about as there are butterflies in Macondo.

JUDY GARLAND

THE SURPRISE ABOUT JUDY GARLAND, noted *Life* magazine after her death, "was that she even lived to be forty-seven." Born Frances Gumm in Grand Rapids, Minnesota, Garland was a gawky seventeen-year-old when the world fell in love with her as Dorothy, the wistful-eyed but spunky Kansas girl who searched for her heart's desire in *The Wizard of Oz*. A bruising thirty years later, after too many drinks and too many pills, the woman who could cast spells on an audience with her heartbreaking voice was a burnt-out torch singer whose performances were almost too painful to watch. Garland's punishing insecurities started while touring the vaudeville circuit as "Baby Gumm" with her parents and two sisters. From her debut at two, she was pushed by an undemonstrative mother who sometimes disciplined her daughter by locking her in their hotel room alone for hours at a time. Three months after the twelve-year-old Frances was signed to a contract with Metro-Goldwyn-Mayer, her father died, and whatever remained of her childhood was promptly appropriated by MGM. Raised, for all practical purposes, on the movie lot, she was under the thumb of the studio, whose physicians prescribed drugs to help her lose weight, others to help her sleep, and yet others to wake her up. The medications, Judy claimed, took their toll on her youthful nervous system. Though she made millions for MGM starring in *Broadway Melody of 1938; Love Finds Andy Hardy; Everybody Sing; Listen, Darling*; and the evergreen *Oz*, by the age of twenty, she was facing divorce from her first husband, and had already had her first nervous breakdown.

For Judy Garland's fans, who were and are legion—thanks to the preservation of her prodigious talent in film, television, and recordings—it was her emotional vulnerability that made her one of the greatest American entertainers of the century. There seemed to be no personal problem Garland hadn't endured firsthand or couldn't understand. Her loyal public responded with an intensity of feeling that bordered on veneration. And the feeling was mutual: Garland adored her audiences, and when she closed personal appearances with her signature song, "Over the Rainbow," the bonding was complete. Her tenderness absolved her of every sin—the monstrous tantrums, the canceled engagements, and, at the end, the sight of a frail idol coaxing her fragile voice to reach notes it would have soared over in happier times.

Even at her professional peak, however, Garland's halcyon days were few. MGM, which kept its valuable property in constant use, schooled her on the set and even provided female "pals" who could tattle if Garland cheated on her chicken-soup diet. Her one true friend was fellow child actor

Mickey Rooney, who worked with her in the enormously popular Andy Hardy films. Known as the fastest study in the business, her talent was truly natural—she never had a singing or dancing lesson and couldn't even read music, yet she would offer a perfect rendition of a song after hearing it only once. The year of her first collapse, she won superb reviews co-starring with Gene Kelly in *For Me and My Gal*, her first adult role. A few years later, after hits like *Meet Me in St. Louis* (1944) and *The Harvey Girls* (1946), she teamed up with Kelly again for *The Pirate* (1948), adding Cole Porter's "Be a Clown" to her repertoire. That same year, she was paired with the inimitable Fred Astaire in Irving Berlin's *Easter Parade*, in which she gave one of her most popular performances as a hobo in "A Couple of Swells."

By the late forties, now married to director Vincent Minnelli and mother to their daughter Liza, the star's mental and physical disintegration were obvious. Often late on the set, Garland tried repeatedly to take time off from her grueling schedule to recuperate, but the studio was unyielding. Failing one morning to show up for work on *Royal Wedding*, she was suspended for breach of contract; MGM finally let her go in 1950. Later, the star who had worked forty-five of her forty-seven years would note wryly that for someone who was "undependable," she had "certainly made a lot of pictures."

In the fifties, though beset by more breakdowns, numerous lawsuits, and several publicized suicide attempts, this show business legend created a second career through her concerts, notably at London's Palladium and New York's Palace Theater. Managed by her third husband, Sid Luft—with whom she had a second daughter, Lorna—and signed to a generous RCA Victor recording contract, Garland's television popularity and earnings took off. When she returned to the screen in *A Star Is Born* (1954), opposite James Mason, her moving portrayal of an actress shattered by love earned her an Oscar nomination.

In the early sixties, however, Garland lost whatever sense of purpose had been holding her together. Dependent on massive doses of Ritalin to get her through engagements, she was usually broke and often without a permanent home. In 1969, the Yellow Brick Road came abruptly to an end, not in the land of Oz—or wherever it was that dreams were supposed to come true—but at home in London with her fifth husband. There, on the morning of June 22, she was found dead of an accidental overdose of sleeping pills. She'd led a tumultuous life, but she left behind a legacy of ageless music that only grows more poignant with time. As Bing Crosby said of Garland, "There was never anything that gal couldn't do—except look after herself."

BILL GATES

IN THE LATE TWENTIETH century, approximately 90 percent of the IBM-type personal computers in the United States are operated using Microsoft Windows. A utilitarian software program, it was developed by Microsoft, the multibillion-dollar conglomerate controlled by William Henry Gates III—a postindustrial visionary. Along with its older sister program MS-DOS, Windows has become an indispensable part of American life, and, in the process, made Bill Gates one of the richest people on the planet and one of the most influential entrepreneurs in history. Microsoft's dominance in operating software has also led to accusations of monopolistic practices: In October 1997, the Justice Department filed suit against Microsoft alleging that it was violating a 1995 consent degree by forcing personal computer manufacturers to load its Internet Explorer Browser as a condition of licensing the Windows 95 operating system. To all charges of market abuse, Gates pled innocent. His legal battles, projected to be lengthy, were seen by communications experts as part of an ongoing test of whether 19th-century laws against monopoly were indeed relevant or perhaps even potentially harmful to the development of twenty-first century technology.

The engagingly boyish Gates' profound understanding of computer technology was matched by his shrewd grasp of the marketplace, his energy and commitment, and his fine sense of timing. Gates came by his confidence and his business acumen honestly. His father was a successful and prominent corporate attorney in Seattle, and his mother a college regent and leading charity executive. A brilliant student who was especially gifted at math, Gates got his first introduction to computers—on an extremely primitive ASR 33 teletype—and to the computer language BASIC in his early teens at the exclusive private school he attended. He also formed a close friendship with a boy two years older, Paul Allen, who shared both Gates' passion for computers and his business drive. By the time Gates was sixteen, he, Allen, and some other friends had formed their first company, Traf-O-Data. Gates entered Harvard in 1973 but an article Paul Allen spotted in 1975 would change his and Gates' lives. The article, about the MTS Altair 8800, one of the first affordable personal computers, convinced both Gates and Allen that the future lay in software, not hardware. Part of their genius was their understanding that the software had to be easy to use and to learn.

The two formed Microsoft in 1975. Their first work was to create software for the MTS Altair, which they then licensed to MTS. Since personal computers had been largely used by hobbyists, who created their own software and shared it with their friends, Gates' move to make money on his software was a radical one. His tough stance on software piracy, too, would also shape the future of the industry. By 1977, Gates had dropped out of Harvard and Allen had come to work at Microsoft full-time.

Gates worked on pitching Microsoft's services to potential customers. That year, the Tandy Corporation—owners of the Radio Shack stores—licensed Gates' and Allen's version of BASIC, and Microsoft was on its way. The turning point, though, came in 1980 when IBM approached Microsoft for help: the giant corporation needed both software and an operating system for its new, still highly secret, personal computer which was scheduled to be shipped in a year. The tight deadline for developing both parts worried Gates and Allen, but they found a solution by licensing an existing operating system from Seattle Computers. The operating system they licensed was the basis for MS-DOS.

With the expansion of the computer industry in the eighties, Microsoft grew exponentially, not in small part due to Gates' skillful negotiating and his demanding perfectionism. Not only did IBM pay Microsoft a royalty on every machine it sold with MS-DOS installed, but in addition, the licensing agreement was non-exclusive. Microsoft was free to sell to IBM's competitors—manufacturers of so-called IBM "clones"—and it did. The pace of development at Microsoft was frenetic with successful new products released each year, among them the Word program for MS-DOS, the Microsoft Mouse, and Windows 3.0.

Gates' innovative business vision led to other ventures. He launched MSN, an online entertainment cite, MSNBC, a cable channel in partnership with NBC, and acquired a digital image bank, the Corbis Archive, that was growing at a pace of 40,000 images a day. In the nineties, Gates turned to the future beyond the Internet: the much-heralded convergence of computing and cable television in what Microsoft called "televisionspace." Delivering data 100 times faster than most modems and servicing 68 million homes (compared to the 20 million equipped with PCs), cable could be the wave of the future. In April 1997, Gates purchased WebTV for $425 million, a service which delivered the Internet to television; two months later, he paid $1 billion for 11.5 percent of Comcast, America's fourth-largest cable operator, which also gave him an interest in television production and the direct-broadcast-satellite business. In 1998, Gates announced a milestone deal with Telecommunications Inc. by which Windows CE—the new Microsoft operating software design to drive everything from tiny computers to digital phones—would run on the new computer/cable boxes of the future.

Brilliant and driven, Bill Gates will only be forty-five years old when this century comes to a close. He has much in common with the other technological trailblazers of this century, Thomas Edison and Henry Ford among them. The future of technology is still unfolding, and it seems sure that Bill Gates will be there at the forefront, helping discover it for all of us.

ALLEN GINSBERG

ALLEN GINSBERG WAS THE most notorious American versifier of the century. A poet *maudit,* he was condemned at first by "the establishment," which repelled and fascinated him and was later only too happy to lift the curse. A literary outlaw, he hijacked poetry from the hushed halls of academe and celebrated it in jazz clubs, in the streets, and in the arms of innumerable lovers. It was his voice—a monotone filtered through a bristling black beard—that dominated the countercultural sixties with its chants for peace, love, and the exploration of human experience.

Ginsberg was born in Newark, New Jersey, to Louis Ginsberg, a high school English teacher and conventionally-minded poet, and Naomi, a communist and nudist afflicted with paranoia and schizophrenia. As a boy he was often required to stay home from school to mind his disturbed mother as she paced through the house declaiming her theories of the conspiracy between her husband and Benito Mussolini, while her unhappy son tried to read. Awarded a scholarship to Columbia in 1943, Ginsberg originally intended to become a lawyer, but his exposure there to the teaching of Mark Van Doren and Lionel Trilling inspired him to turn to literature. Composing traditional poetry at college, he came under the influence of the "spontaneous" scribe Jack Kerouac, a former Columbia football player who would turn American belles-lettres upside down with his stream-of-consciousness novel, *On the Road.* Kerouac introduced the fledgling writer to such hipsters as William Burroughs and Neal Cassady. Experimentation with drugs, sex, and writing techniques were the *sine qua non* of the quartet, which became the matrix of the defining literary movement of the fifties, the Beats. (They were dubbed so by Kerouac because the word neatly combined the concepts of "beaten down" and "beatitude.")

In 1945, Ginsberg found himself in trouble when he was innocently drawn into the aftermath of a murder committed by Lucien Carr (a lesser member of the group) and when the college discovered him in his dormitory bed with Kerouac. Suspended for a year, he worked as a dishwasher, merchant seaman and reporter before returning to take his bachelor's degree in 1949. That same year he experienced a mystical vision while reading the poems of William Blake. It was the portal to further adventures.

Still fascinated by the noir lifestyle, he took up digs with occasional bard and full-time sneak thief Herbert Huncke, a junkie whose habit of stashing his swag in their apartment led to Ginsberg's second confrontation with the state. To extricate himself, Ginsberg pled diminished psychological capacity and was sentenced to eight months in the Columbia-Presbyterian Psychiatric Institute. There he had his serendipitous meeting with Carl Solomon, the "lunatic saint" who introduced him to the work of the Surrealists and impressed him with the political and prophetic power of verse.

Upon Ginsberg's release and return to his father's home in Paterson, New Jersey, a very different kind of poet, William Carlos Williams, trained him in the vitality of everyday life and language. Brilliantly, Ginsberg was able to synthesize the influences of Williams, Kerouac, and Cassady in a new colloquial style he called "speedworthy," in reference both to the full-out, non-reflective style of the composition and his use of amphetamines. Zooming across the country in 1953 in amorous pursuit of Cassady, he ended up in San Francisco, where, in an amazing volte-face, he took a well-paying job as a market researcher and settled in With a girlfriend in a Nob Hill apartment. After a year, however, with the blessings of his psychotherapist, he jettisoned job, flat, and woman for the bohemian life with Peter Orlovsky, whose dharma seemed to be keeping as much of the world as clean as possible.

In August 1955 Ginsberg sat down at the typewriter and in one long agonized breath of rage wrote "Howl," his "Melvillian-biblical" assault on "Moloch," the all-consuming evil genius of American power. Published in San Francisco in 1956 by Lawrence Ferlinghetti's City Lights Books, the poem landed Ferlinghetti in court—for publishing and distributing an obscene book—and Ginsberg in the not unwelcome glare of national fame. Now a regular on the poetry-reading circuit, Ginsberg championed not only his own work but that of Kerouac and Burroughs; "kindness" had become this Jewish Buddhist's watchword. With Timothy Leary's guidance, he started using LSD to stimulate his creative muse. In 1961, under the influence of morphine and amphetamines, he wrote "Kaddish," a mournful farewell to his mother who had died five years earlier in a madhouse. His champions placed it right next to "Howl" on the pyramid of his achievements, while his critics accused him of technical slovenliness, moral perversity and intellectual vacuity.

Ginsberg's response to all the attention was to escape it by traveling in India for a year. When he returned he had foresworn hard drugs and embraced meditation and yoga, although he testified before Congress that LSD was one path to universal love. Inventor of the phrase "flower power," he was the animating principal behind the first hippie "Be-In" in Golden Gate Park in January 1967. The following year, he famously squatted in Chicago's Lincoln Park, chanting "Om" while police and anti-war demonstrators rioted around him, and took part in the Yippie "levitation" of the Pentagon.

As guru to the sixties generation, Ginsberg promulgated a philosophy of personal freedom that, although skirting to the extreme, had an enormous and lasting influence. As poet laureate of counterculture, he inspired such great troubadours as Bob Dylan and the Beatles. He died in 1997, outspoken and controversial to the last, not to be forgotten by acolyte or enemy.

JANE GOODALL

"WHEN I FIRST WENT to Gombe," says Jane Goodall of her initial foray into Tanzania to investigate chimpanzee behavior, "reporters would ask me such questions as did I expect to see Tarzan." Sly insults notwithstanding, the untested twenty-six-year-old scientist ventured into the dense bush in 1960, intent on discovering the degree to which chimpanzees are like human beings. She found out, instead, how much we are like them. One of the great naturalists of all time, Goodall broke new ground with her unprecedented involvement with her subjects. She lived among them, ate and played with them, and earned their trust by simply observing how they lived. Before Goodall, most expeditions that had been mounted to study our closest biological cousins were so intrusive that they had frightened the chimps back into their rain forest sanctuaries. As a result, very little was actually learned about them. Goodall, who insisted on going into the bush alone for prolonged periods of time, amassed more information about apes than all her predecessors put together.

Born in London to a novelist and an engineer with a penchant for motor racing, Goodall inherited their daring and imagination—qualities that, along with her curiosity, would serve her well in her future occupation. She was mesmerized at age seven by the stories of Dr. Dolittle, the eccentric scientist who could talk to animals, and with her stuffed toy chimpanzee, Jubilee, by her side, the young girl spent hours studying worms in the garden, hens in the henhouse, and insects everywhere. Even when, after high school graduation in 1952, Goodall was working as a secretary at Oxford University, she knew she wanted to live in Africa. Fate was congenial: In 1957 she was invited to Kenya to visit a friend, and a few months later she set sail on an old freighter. While in Africa she met the world-renowned anthropologist Louis S. B. Leakey, who, impressed with Goodall's enthusiasm, hired her as an assistant. She soon found herself digging beside him in the Olduvai Gorge, searching for the remains of early humans. Leakey, knowing of Goodall's interest in apes, recommended her for a two-year research project studying chimpanzees under the vast leafy canopy of the Gombe.

It was a controversial decision, to send a mere slip of a woman—and one with neither a college degree nor scientific training—on such an arduous and demanding endeavor. Leakey had implicit trust in Goodall, but his colleagues loftily predicted the young novice would never lay eyes on a chimp. Goodall proved them wrong. After a few months' study and preparation in England, Goodall returned, with her mother as assistant, to set up her wilderness camp in Tanzania. When she trekked into the bush and promptly found her first tribe of chimpanzees, they didn't actually threaten her, but they ran away every time they saw her. Forced to discard the normal tactic of simply trailing her quarry, she perched with binoculars in hand on a promontory from which she could observe the tribe's movements and habits, and where they, in turn, could observe her. The ploy worked, and eventually the chimps grew to take "this peculiar white-skinned ape" for granted.

From this vantage point, Goodall made a number of startling discoveries. Chimpanzees fashioned and used tools to dig edible ants and termites out of their hills and mounds; they were hunters and carnivores; they enjoyed hugging, kissing and holding hands; and, perhaps most amazing of all, they were capable of love. Goodall's realization that chimpanzees experience a wide range of emotions quite familiar to humans, including anger and grief, was a significant breakthrough. Abandoning the dry rubrics of traditional scientific study, she began to confer colorful names on her subjects, and the world soon knew the stories of the matriarch Flo, the intrepid David Graybeard, the murderous Pom, and the seductress Gigi.

Goodall's naming of the apes was derided by the scientific establishment, but it proved advantageous in gaining support for her efforts. Their names, too, emphasized her conviction that the chimps were singular beings with defined personalities, more like people than unlike them. This kinship was the tirelessly reiterated theme of all her influential works: *My Friends the Wild Chimpanzees* (1967), the famous *In the Shadow of Man* (1971), and *Innocent Killers* (1971). These, along with her numerous films, television specials, and articles, made her one of the best-known scientists of the century.

In 1965 Goodall became the eighth person in the history of Cambridge University to be awarded a Ph.D. without first having earned a baccalaureate. Marriage to nature photographer Hugo van Lawick a year earlier produced a son, but the union failed. After divorcing him in 1974, she married Derek Bryceson, a member of the Tanzanian parliament, whose death from cancer in 1980 was a great blow to her.

In the nineties Goodall was a tireless agitator for the preservation of the chimpanzee habitat and, in a high-tech corollary, a precise archivist of chimpanzee behavior, using CD-ROM's and videotape. Her efforts at saving the often maltreated primates, however, were not always rewarded by their intended beneficiaries. In 1994, one of their caged brethren failed to recognize the benefactress of his species and bit off her thumb. The act was in stark contrast to a much earlier contact when another chimpanzee, overcoming his shyness and mistrust of a young Goodall out in the bush, touchingly accepted a banana from her hairless hand.

GORBACHEV

1931-

MIKHAIL

HE PRESIDED OVER THE last moments of a drama which began on December 20, 1922 and ended seventy-nine years and eleven days later, when the flags of the USSR were lowered for the last time. Mikhail Gorbachev, was the last president of the Soviet Union, the architect of glasnost ("Openness") and perestroika ("Restructuring"), and the reluctant dismantler of Communism in Russia.

Gorbachev descended from freedom-loving Cossacks who farmed on the outer fringes of the Soviet empire. His moderately prosperous grandfather was denounced by envious neighbors and imprisoned by Stalin's secret police, a whispered fact young Gorbachev learned, along with peasant songs, on his grandmother's knee. Working as a farm laborer, he earned the Order of the Red Banner of Labor when he was eighteen, and entered the Communist party in 1952. He studied law at Moscow University where he met and married a beautiful philosophy student named Raisa Titorenko, a forceful woman who inspired his scholarly pursuits, helped him to learn English, and later guided his policies. He depended on her as few Russian leaders have depended on their spouses. He returned to his birthplace, Stavropol, in the North Caucasus, and in the 1950s and 1960s moved up in the leadership ranks of the local Communist party. In 1970, he was elected to the Supreme Soviet of the USSR, and later became agricultural secretary of the Secretariat. In 1980, he joined the Politburo as Yuri Andropov's protegée.

When Gorbachev was made general secretary of the Communist party, it was clear that both the organization and the nation were in desperate straits. With reform as his goal, Gorbachev forced older conservative members of the Politburo into retirement, and replaced them with younger members who shared his vision. The reality that the party system was unable to provide for even the simplest daily needs of the people was finally faced.

The thoughtful, practical Gorbachev found himself having to play a dual and contradictory role. As both party leader and party reformer, he was forced to pit himself against the entrenched and inept bureaucracy upon which he depended for his influence. Shrewdly, he began his work in the West, moving diplomatically from the outside in. With the firm but genial Raisa at his side, he charmed prime ministers and presidents alike in global tours and meetings. In the Soviet sphere, Poland achieved independence in 1989, with Hungary and Czechoslovakia soon following suit. But what began as a trickle quickly became a flood. The Baltic states and the outlying republics all began agitating for independence, and the more they protested, the more the Soviet bureaucracy resisted.

Ever dedicated to communism as an ideal, Gorbachev had intended to reform, not eradicate, the party; but the economic crisis, compounded by the situation in Eastern Europe, governed the sequence of events. In 1989—three years after the Chernobyl nuclear disaster and the U.S. rejection of his proposed ten-year moratorium on most of President Reagan's Star Wars testing plan—he saw the Red Army retreat from Afghanistan and the Berlin Wall fall.

The economy continued to worsen. The loss of Soviet dominance in Eastern Europe, the demands for independence by the Baltic States and Georgia, and a miners' strike inspired an attempted coup to oust Gorbachev, instigated by members of the Politburo and the heads of the KGB and Interior Ministry. Opposition was led by Boris Yeltsin, to whom the power now passed, even as Gorbachev retained his office. Yeltsin moved quickly: later in the month, he banned the Communist party, seized its assets, and recognized the Baltic States and the Ukraine as independent. In September, the USSR was formally voted out of existence and, by December, replaced by the Commonwealth of Independent States. Gorbachev denounced this new political entity, though, ironically, his actions had brought it about.

In the West, the man who ended the Cold War remained a statesman-hero. His memoirs sold well to foreign readers, who compared him enthusiastically to Churchill; his speeches garnered as much as $100,000 apiece; and his institute in San Francisco remained a center for political inquiry. At home, however, crippled by criticism that his reforms had been halfhearted, and therefore the chief cause of the Soviet Union's destruction, he was largely ignored. Russian journalists spoke of "the tragedy of Gorbachev"—when they weren't vilifying him. "My greatest misfortune and my deepest sorrow," he said in 1995, "is that it was not possible to keep the country in one piece."

Gorbachev did try to reclaim what was left of it in 1996, by running for president against Boris Yeltsin. The attempt was futile in the extreme: Only approximately 1 percent of the Russian electorate was in favor of a new Gorbachev administration. The old hard-liners hated him, the intelligentsia—whom he had freed from police domination—had consigned him to the archives, and the rank and file in the new Russia—strangers to freedom and unaccustomed to its responsibilities—blamed him for almost everything that had happened in the country since glasnost. Still Gorbachev soldiered on, determined to be remembered as something more than the man who lost the Soviet Union.

BILLY GRAHAM

SINCE HE FIRST PREACHED on the "sawdust trail" in the late forties, Billy Graham seemed fated to reign as the unifying figure behind evangelical Christianity. No one was more energetic and wholesome, no one more staggeringly handsome and charismatic. "God can use that voice of yours," the famous Christian educator Bob Jones told him early on. "He can use it mightily." Graham listened and, beginning humbly as an itinerant preacher, his crusade audiences filled stadiums; by his late seventies he had proselytized in person to more people than anyone else in history, prompting more than 100,000,000 men and women to "accept Jesus Christ" as their "personal savior." (According to his staff's records, 2,874,082 have responded to his urgent call; there are no statistics kept on recidivism.) At century's end, having long abandoned the white bucks and pastel leisure suits he favored as a brash young minister, Graham looked more at eighty like an elder statesman who had once played college football than a minister. His celebrity status—from decades spent sharing National Prayer Breakfast podiums and golf carts with presidents—became him more than ever, and his aura of moral rectitude still shone. "I don't eat with beautiful women alone," he explained to Hillary Rodham Clinton, who asked him to lunch during his Little Rock, Arkansas, crusade.

The last of the old-time Protestant revivalists, he traced his fundamentalist roots back to Jonathan Edwards, the stern Calvinist theologian whose pyrotechnic orations paved the way for America's Great Awakening in the early 1740s. Graham's orchestrated spiritual spectacles—at once stirring and carnival-like—took their cues from the tent-top tradition of theatrical preachers such as D.L. Moody, Billy Sunday, and Aimee Semple McPherson. It was Graham's splashy "Canvas Cathedral" campaign of 1949 with its hundreds of "decisions for Christ," that caught the attention of newspaper magnate William Randolph Hearst, who helped launch the Bible-quoting young Baptist minister as evangelism's electrifying new star.

Graham made his own commitment to Christ at the age of sixteen when he was converted at a 1934 revival meeting. Born of Reformed Presbyterian parents near Charlotte, North Carolina, the lanky, less-than-studious adolescent had been lukewarm about religion until then, though his mother had read devotional books to her four children. Abandoning his ambition to emulate his hero, baseball star Babe Ruth, Graham worked for a time as a Fuller Brush salesman. He felt his call to the ministry at eighteen and, after baptism by immersion in a Florida lake on December 4, 1928, was ordained the following year. He finished his education at fundamentalist Wheaton College, where he met his wife-to-be, a devout young woman named Ruth McCue Gall, the daughter of a missionary surgeon. He practiced his fiery sermons in his room, in grassy fields—or

outside saloons—and was soon the main attraction at Youth for Christ rallies all over the country.

Becoming a showman of salvation, Graham exhibited not only magnetism and generous charm but also an extraordinary flair for organization. Each year his Billy Graham Evangelistic Association conducted several of his famous prayer crusades worldwide. The organization also managed a wide variety of publishing and promotional businesses, including a film production company, a weekly radio program, and a satellite-beamed television broadcast reaching a huge international audience. To give one example of his impressive reach, Graham's 1990 Hong Kong crusade was seen live by more than 100,000,000.

Bursting with vitality, the good-looking country boy, whom legendary Hollywood producer Cecil B. DeMille was determined to screen-test, reached his peak in the fifties. Backed by a huge choir and teams of personal counselors ready to advise the newly converted, Graham spoke with an intimate urgency to audiences spiritually exhausted by World War II and fearful of the Cold War's new uncertainties. His message was simple: because people are innately sinful, they have been separated from God; but because Christ died for mankind's sins, they can be forgiven if they repent, receive Christ as savior, and work for Him in His church.

Though lionized as one of the century's most beloved religious leaders—and as a fiscal purist for funneling all monies from his fund-raising into charities and the work of his organization— Graham has had his critics. Many theologians scoff at his watered-down gospel and his sentimental view of humanity's relationship to God. In his heyday, criticism was also directed at his perceived hunger to be near the heartbeat of power. Graham always professed a strong aversion to combining religion and politics—even though his conservative convictions ran deep—but his detractors found tantalizing proof in his disastrous support of Richard Nixon. As the president's unofficial chaplain, Graham was more than a little disillusioned by Nixon's impeachment. "He was a stranger to me," Graham stated, but he continued seeing his old friend.

The nineties Graham was, in some ways, a stranger to his earlier self. Ideologically, he distanced himself from his ultra-conservativestance of the past, (he once likened paradise to a place without labor leaders) and he adopted a more ecumenical, and socially progressive stance. Somewhat limited by Parkinson's, "America's pastor"—as President George Bush called him— refused to slow down any more than his disease dictated. Numerous televangelists stepped forward to accept Graham's mantle, but none exhibited the authority, or the sense of divine mission that filled his life. He never knew why God graced him with such a prodigious sense of purpose. He would ask Him, Graham once said, "when I get to heaven."

GRAHAM

MARTHA

FOR MARTHA GRAHAM, THE intense theatrical doyenne of modern dance, movement—not beauty—was the embodiment of truth. Movement could never lie, her doting father had told her when she was a child growing up in Allegheny, Pennsylvania, and through some sixty years of influential performance she focused all her energy and talent in giving expression to this simple dictum. What bloomed—or rather exploded—from her creative stance was a revolutionary approach to dance that rejected the codified forms of classical ballet for an earthier, more emotionally charged choreography.

"I did not dance the way that people danced," was the understated explanation Graham gave in her 1991 autobiography, *Blood Memory,* published twenty-two years after she had grudgingly left the stage. She danced, instead, like one anointed—indeed, she always insisted that she did not choose to dance but rather that she was chosen. As an explorer of the psyche, she created a starkly new kinetic language to express the secrets and yearnings of the human soul, using movement not for its own sake but to illustrate psychological states. Graham taught her students how to contract the solar plexus so that releasing it would send them spiraling into the air, how to use tautly controlled gestures to express primal feelings. She also introduced starkly sexual movements into dance and claimed that her bold, theatrical approach—spectacular backfalls, pendulum-like leg swings, great upward thrusts of the torso—flowed through her from the past, expressing timeless, universal truths. Critics often scoffed at her stylistic audacity and her decidedly abstract approach, but contemporary audiences all over the world were awestruck. Their seduction was complete after witnessing such compelling solo works as *Lamentations,* in which Graham, imprisoned in a huge wrapping of fabric, portrayed the anguished search for release from a self-inflicted inner torment through violent movement.

Martha Graham entered dance as a career almost too late for one with serious professional ambitions. She was a slightly chubby seventeen-year-old when her father—a doctor whose childhood influence on Martha deeply affected her long, tempestuous life—took her to see the graceful and exotic Ruth St. Denis, the former vaudevillian who created a new kind of movement based on non-Western dance. Graham, whose work would later take a wildly different direction, was beguiled by the free-wheeling, vaguely oriental performance. She began studying in 1916, when she was twenty-two years old, with St. Denis herself, debuting in vaudeville in 1920 as an Aztec dancing girl. Creative differences, however, caused her to leave the Denishawn Institute in 1924 to perform in what, retrospectively, seems an odd career choice, the *Greenwich Village Follies.*

By 1927, aided by her lover and musical mentor, Louis Horst, Graham formed her own company in New York City. Immediately she began commissioning original music for her group, a practice that fostered the creation of many of her most memorable works, including the landmark *Appalachian Spring,* composed by Aaron Copland.

Although Graham herself was always the focus of her highly individual pieces—and her grueling classes were as notorious for their brutal discipline as for their length—luring dedicated dancers to her side was no problem. Soon her all-female group began to command critical attention, and by 1930, she was soloing brilliantly as the Chosen One in Leonide Massine's lyrical choreography of *The Rite of Spring.* Graham was now a fiery, independent stylist and a force of radiant artistry.

Prey to a volcanic temper that she considered a source of strength, obsessed with the tragic heroines of classic literature and myth, and no stranger to the power struggle between men and women, Graham staged many of her most celebrated creations around such tormented figures as Medea, Jocasta, and Clytemnestra. Her portrayals of murderous women earned her the reputation of a man-hater, but she defended these roles: "All the things I do are in every woman," she said. "Every woman is a Medea. Every woman is a Jocasta." In 1936 wealthy American dance enthusiast Lincoln Kirstein introduced Graham to dancer Erick Hawkins, who became the first male member of her dance company. Critics noted that once she was paired with Hawkins both romantically and professionally, Graham's work became more sexual and rhapsodic. The forties were a time of inspiration for Graham, when many critics feel she created her richest and most complex works. She broke with Hawkins in 1950, and though the fifties closed with the powerful *Clytemnestra,* which many believe to be her greatest work, she began a long decline that lasted through the sixties. Graham was terrified by her body's aging—she had several face lifts—compounded by the onset of painful and restricting arthritis. What had started as "a daily dose of Irish whiskey," according to her biographer, choreographer Agnes de Mille, became full-fledged alcoholism. By the late sixties, she could no longer dance.

But in 1973, "Martha rose from the dead," as de Mille says. Ever forceful, Graham simply decided that she would stop drinking, leave her sickbed, and work again. She did so, choreographing until she was in her mid-nineties, though the last pieces lack the genius of her prime. Her reclamation of herself was as heroic as her stage roles, a gutsy renaissance that proved once again that no obstacle could ever restrain her spirit.

CARY GRANT

AT THE CORE OF Cary Grant's cinematic legend are stunning good looks and a youthfulness that eluded his aging peers. After a three-decade reign as the leading man in Hollywood, he was awarded a special Oscar in 1970 for lifetime achievement—and he looked as good as when he had played Marlene Dietrich's ardent tempter in Josef von Sternberg's *Blonde Venus* (1932). Throughout his career, the perennially suntanned actor maintained the kind of appeal that all ages and most cultures found irresistible. The nonchalant, hands-in-pockets aplomb, the mellowed Cockney speech: the whole charming package made him irresistible. His romantic aura, however, was counterbalanced by a deft comedic intelligence, making his female fans dream not so much about a heavy affair as perhaps a flirtatious escapade.

This epitome of savoir faire began life as Archibald Leach, in bitter poverty. Born in Bristol, England, to divorced parents, Leach joined up in his teens with a troupe of acrobats. When the troupe toured the United States in 1920, the singing juggler stayed on when the others returned home. He survived by selling painted ties and working as a lifeguard before going on to vaudeville with a mind-reading act. He returned to England in 1923 and began acting on the London stage, where he was discoverd by Arthur Hammerstein. Hammerstein hired Leach for his brother Oscar's Broadway musical *Golden Dawn*. But the actor had bigger aspirations and made his way to Hollywood. Soon after arriving, he was retained by Paramount to feed lines to a young woman being screen tested; she lost the part, but Grant (the name by which he was now known) ended up with a five-year contract. His first film, a musical titled *This is the Night* (1932), was followed by several supporting roles and the studio's growing enthusiasm for him.

After being paired with Dietrich in *Blonde Venus,* and with Mae West in *She Done Him Wrong* and *I'm No Angel* (both 1933), Grant was lent out to RKO to star with the spirited young Katharine Hepburn in George Cukor's *Sylvia Scarlett* (1936). Before the film hit the box office, Grant became a free agent, soon negotiating a unique nonexclusive contract with both RKO and Columbia that guaranteed him script approval. In the years to come, he would exhibit an almost unerring instinct for choosing vehicles that showed his particular brand of easy-going heroism to its best advantage.

He was fortunate as well to team up with some of the cinema's most talented directors. Following the advice of the British ambassador, he remained in Hollywood while Britain endured Hitler's Blitz. George Stevens chose him for the part of a feisty but amiable British soldier in the adventure *Gunga Din* (1939), based on the famous poem by Rudyard Kipling. That same year, Howard Hawks tapped him to star as a cold-hearted man made human by the death of his best friend in *Only Angels Have Wings*. With Hawks and Cukor, Grant refined the popular "screwball comedy," starring in the former's *Bringing up Baby* (1938), *His Girl Friday* (1940) and *I Was A Male War Bride* (1949), and in the latter's *Holiday* (1938) and *The Philadelphia Story* (1940), both opposite Hepburn.

It was with *Suspicion* (1941)—in which Grant is an embezzling cad whose wife, played by Joan Fontaine, suspects he's going to murder her—that he began to be credible as a dramatic actor. Although the original ending was changed to conform with the production code, Alfred Hitchcock's superb direction redeemed the movie. Not only was it a hit, it helped turn Grant into a more multi-dimensional film presence.

In 1941, as the Japanese bombed Pearl Harbor, Frank Capra was shooting his hilarious send-up of family loyalty, *Arsenic and Old Lace,* in which Grant plays a devoted nephew undecided about turning in his two zany aunts for murder. A year later in a very private ceremony at Lake Arrowhead, California, one of Hollywood's most sought-after stars married one of the world's richest women. When the union ended three years later, Grant (whose previous marriage to actress Virginia Cherrill had also ended in divorce) was just as much in demand, and Barbara Hutton was no less rich; he had signed a pre-nuptial agreement foregoing any monetary settlement in the event of a split.

In 1946 Grant was reunited with Hitchcock in *Notorious,* a masterpiece of action and mystery in which he portrays an American agent who falls for the woman he is assigned to work with to entrap Nazis in South America. In one of the most tantalizing love scenes ever filmed, the two kiss each other's lips and face while talking absent-mindedly about their upcoming meal. In 1955, again with Hitchcock, Grant and Grace Kelly lit up the screen in the romantic caper *To Catch a Thief,* in which the still agile Grant is a retired cat burglar. Two years later, while filming *The Pride and The Passion* in Spain, he fell passionately in love with his co-star, Italian actress Sophia Loren. After the two shot *Houseboat* (1958), Grant worked with Hitchcock one last time in the spy thriller *North By Northwest.* In one of his (and cinema's) most famous scenes, Grant is chased across an open field by a menacing crop duster plane.

In 1966, wife number four, actress Dyan Cannon, presented the 62-year-old with his first (and only) child, a daughter. Two years later in divorce proceedings, Cannon accused Grant of domestic violence and of taking LSD, which he had indeed dabbled in during his third marriage to actress Betsy Drake his co-star in *Every Girl Should Be Married* (1948). But his public image never suffered, and after leaving acting, he took a directorship with the cosmetics firm, Rayett-Fabergé. Some time after he retired, he appeared at a fundraiser, apologizing that he had forgotten his ticket. When he told the woman at the entrance who he was, she told him that it was impossible: "You don't look like Cary Grant." Smiling, he responded with characteristic wit: "Who does?"

GRIFFITH

D. W.

CINEMA'S ORIGINAL AUTEUR, D. W. Griffith was a fiercely independent and frenetic autocrat who brooked no interference, hesitation, or mediocrity. Physically, he played to type as well, shadowboxing or spouting Shakespearean sonnets with hammy flair on his film sets between takes, a jaunty fedora perched atop his head. Yet Griffith was a serious artist, committed and determined to guide film in its rapid transition from a nickelodeon craze to the dominant art form of the twentieth century. With a sure hand, this inspired storyteller of the silent screen created an immense body of work—between 1908 and 1913 alone he made some five hundred one-and two-reelers—and along with it, a technical vocabulary for film that, despite refinements through the years, remains essentially unchanged.

In Griffith's hands, the camera had a vitality all its own. It rushed forward atop speeding trains, shifted perspectives within scenes (an unheard-of practice), swept leisurely across majestic landscapes, and lingered in novel and revealing close-ups. After shooting, Griffith would sequester himself in a projection room to view the raw footage over and over, experimenting with his evolving methods of crosscutting, dissolving, and sequencing shots. These innovations fractured the linear conventions of theater, making way for psychological reality and, through his fiddling with rhythm and tempo, the enormously significant breakthrough of "film time."

This genius, to whom all subsequent film greats would pay homage, initially looked upon "the flickers" with contempt. Such scorn was typical in the theatrical world where Griffith had started his career as a bit player in a stock company, but his southern heritage only deepened the disdain. A sentimental Victorian of inflexible moral outlook, he had spent his childhood on a Kentucky farm in diminished circumstances. He clung, however, to the genteel culture his father (a Civil War hero) had risked his life to protect. Contempt could not put bread on the table, however, and when success as an actor and playwright eluded him, Griffith took his story ideas to Edwin S. Porter, who had made the first truly "cinematic" film—*The Great Train Robbery* (1903). Porter rejected Griffith's stories, offering him instead a part in an upcoming cliff-hanger, *Rescued From an Eagle's Nest* (1907). Griffith accepted the role but continued to peddle his plots. His efforts finally paid off in 1908, when he was hired by Manhattan's American Mutoscope and Biograph Company as an actor and writer.

Almost immediately, he was assigned to direct a one-reeler called *The Adventures of Dollie* (1908), which, like almost all of Griffith's films, had no script and was based on the merest wisp of a concept. The titles of the hundreds of shorts he wrote and/or directed at Biograph—at a clip of three to four a week—testify to his preoccupation with melodramatic struggles between good and evil: *The Honor of Thieves* (1909), *The Sorrows of the Unfaithful* (1910), and *The Lily of the Tenements* (1911). These assembly-line potboilers, zestful little one-act morality plays involving stalwart heroes, cruel villains, and fluttery heroines in need of last-minute rescue, also showcased his ability to spot talent and to wring the very best performances from it. His stable of actors included the young Gish sisters, Lillian and Dorothy; Mary Pickford; and Lionel Barrymore. All of them were subjected to Griffith's imperious fathering and grueling on-location conditions; all were incredibly loyal. During the making of *Way Down East* (1920), for example, Lillian Gish nearly froze to death while lying for hours on a drifting ice floe.

In 1914, aware that he had made Biograph a fortune, Griffith insisted on total control and profit participation in all future films. Astonished at such unprecedented demands, the studio's executives promptly fired him. Almost immediately, the director began putting together the financing for a film adaptation of *The Clansman,* writer Thomas Dixon's novel about America's bloody Civil War. Renamed *The Birth of a Nation* and released in 1915, the three-hour film was cinema's first blockbuster, a dramatic and technical tour de force that cost $110,000, was twelve reels long, and had, uniquely at that time, its own musical score.

Aesthetically triumphant, the film was, however, politically disastrous. Its negative characterizations of blacks gave rise to accusations of racism. Such charges puzzled Griffith, who, in his naïveté, found nothing insulting in his exaggerated portrayals of plantation slaves—played by white actors in blackface—as either miscreants or Uncle Toms. To silence his censors, he made the monumental 1916 epic *Intolerance,* which attempted to depict the wages of bigotry. The catastrophically costly film lived up to Griffith's vision but failed to find the kind of commercial success that the wildly profitable *Birth* had enjoyed. The millionaire filmmaker was left in financial ruin.

In 1919, Griffith, along with Charlie Chaplin, Douglas Fairbanks, and Mary Pickford, founded United Artists. But with the advent of sound, Griffith had lost touch. The man whom Charlie Chaplin credited with inventing Hollywood, was unable to find a niche in what had become a sophisticated, studio-dominated industry. Griffith spent his last eight years alone, often drunk, and understandably bitter. This tragic conclusion to a brilliant career was a portent of what would become one of moviemaking's most operative clichés, that one is only as good as one's last picture—or, in Griffith's case, one's last masterpiece.

CHE GUEVARA

"THE TRUE REVOLUTIONARY IS motivated by feelings of love." So wrote Ernesto Guevara, known to the world as "Che." The sentiment might surprise those who knew the comandante's ruthlessness first hand, but not those who understood the radical's inherent compassion. That both qualities resided in a man willing both to kill and to die for socialism, is a paradox that sums up the short, violent life of one the most universally recognized insurgents.

Like Lenin, Che was to the manor born, the eldest son of somewhat reduced Irish-Spanish aristos firmly established in Argentine high society. His mother, Celia de la Serna, was a descendant of Spanish nobility. His father, Ernesto Guevara Lynch, had noble antecedents both in Spain and Ireland. Moderately indulged while growing up, Che overcame a sickly constitution through athletics and sheer force of will. He also displayed a distinctly reckless macho streak in matters sexual, once surreptitiously dallying with the maid behind the back of a favorite aunt. The one ailment he could never quite overcome was chronic asthma—but in the end even that would add to his legend.

From 1945 until 1951 he studied medicine at the University of Buenos Aires, taking off the following year to vagabond around the northwest of the South American continent. He was in every way an annoyingly self-righteous proto-hippie, refusing to bathe and shunning material comfort while dunning his parents to send him money; as he edged toward Marxism, he lectured them about the poverty of the continent. In 1953 he returned to Argentina to receive his medical degree, but almost immediately took off again on his peregrinations. It was his visit to Guatemala, where the leftist government of Jacobo Arbenz had been elected, that galvanized the nascent rebel's philosophy. Witnessing at first hand the American CIA's bloody machinations in the 1954 overthrow of the Arbenz regime, Che concluded that only armed struggle could secure the rights of the poor. The fate to which this conviction would lead him was described by a mysterious stranger whose eerie prophecy was reproduced in Che's diary: "You will die with the fist clenched and jaw tense . . . the spirit of the beehive speaks through your mouth and moves in your actions."

Forced to flee as a known leftist, he secured a position at the Central Hospital in Mexico City, which was then a simmering cauldron of rival intelligence operations. In 1955 Che met one of the most notorious of the new seditionists, Fidel Castro, whose attempt to topple the Batista tyranny in Cuba had ended in failure and exile. Recognizing Fidel as a man with a revolutionary future, Che signed on with Castro's tiny military cadre. The following year Che left his new wife and daughter and joined the group's expedition to Cuba. They hoped to destroy a regime that had mired the peasants in poverty and mortgaged the country to land barons, American investors, and gangsters who had turned Havana into a combination casino and brothel.

Battling the batistianos and their own inexperience, the guerrilla force of around one hundred was reduced to less than twenty-four men before withdrawing to the fastness of the Sierra Maestra. By 1957 their fortunes had improved enough to allow Fidel to name Che commander of a second column. The next year Che led the counteroffensive that captured the strategically important town of Santa Clara. On January 1, 1959, Batista fled and soon thereafter the rebels liberated Havana.

After presiding over the drumhead trials of batistiano "war criminals," the young Argentinian found himself in the unlikely role of minister, heading first the Institute of Agrarian Reform, and then the National Bank. Working twenty-hour days, he often left his desk to cut sugar cane, in an effort to embody the new socialist man motivated by morality, not money. At the same time, he pushed for closer ties to the Soviet Union and China, which he saw as an alternative to the hated United States. When in 1962 the Cubans allowed the Russians to place missiles in Cuba, Che advocated a first strike against the Americans. Cooler heads prevailed.

By 1965 his restless and adventuring nature—and his absolute faith in the armed liberation of the masses—led him back to fomenting revolt, this time in the Congo. There his expedition in aid of the self-indulgent Laurent Kabila ended in failure. The following year he gave a famous address before the leftist Tricontinental Conference in which he called for "two, three, many Vietnams"; his own ambition lay in creating as many of them as he could in his own hemisphere. To that end, he infiltrated Bolivia in 1966, but within a few months his little band became isolated from the peasants, scorned by urban radicals, and hunted by their enemies, including the CIA. Hungry, harried, and subject to uncontrollable rages, Che led his now minuscule group on a zigzag path to doom. On October 8, 1967, after a battle in a ravine near the little town of La Higuera, he was captured. The next day he was summarily executed, his hands cut off for proof and his body buried in a secret grave.

In South America the poor erected shrines to the self-described knight errant, in the Third World they put up posters, and rallied to his name. But a different kind of tribute was bestowed by pop culture and capitalism, which used Che's romantic image to sell everything from t-shirts to motorcycles. The latter legacy would have appalled him. His own view of himself was expressed in a letter to his parents on the eve of his Congo campaign: "Once more I feel under my heels the ribs of Rosinante. Many will call me an adventurer, and I am, but of a different type, of those who put their lives on the line to demonstrate their truths."

HAWKING

STEPHEN

HAILED AS THE PERSON most likely to bring Albert Einstein's dream of a unified field to reality—a "theory of everything" that would explain all phenomena in space and time—English cosmologist Stephen Hawking defied a crippling disease and his own despair to formulate one of the century's most stunning theories on the origin and fate of the universe. An incandescent mind in a withered body, his genius is matched only by his iron will as he pursues the question of how existence itself came to exist.

Born the oldest of four in Oxford, England, to a research biologist and his ebullient wife, Hawking was filled with curiosity as a boy. Physically active and gregarious, his career at St. Albins School was barely distinguished enough to gain him entrance to Oxford in 1959. A party-loving coxswain for the rowing crew, Hawking was possessed of so agile a mind that he was able to survive academically with only an hour or so a day devoted to the study of math and physics. Or so he imagined. This cavalier attitude came back to haunt him when his written exams left him on the border between first-and second-class honors and he was forced to undergo an oral examination to determine whether he could enter the Ph. D. program. Hawking's examiners realized immediately that his was a prodigious intellect and unhesitatingly gave him a first.

Hawking went on to graduate school in 1962 at Cambridge University, where he could give full play to his fascination for theoretical astronomy and cosmology. He intended to be the man who finally answered the question "Where did the universe come from?" Not long after his arrival, however, he began to experience episodes of clumsiness. These were the first signs of the onset of amyotrophic lateral sclerosis, an incurable malady known as "Lou Gehrig's Disease," that disables skeletal muscles and ends in a fatal atrophying of the chest muscles. Given only a few years to live, he saw little reason to pursue his doctorate and began to drink. But then Hawking fell in love with language student Jane Wilde, and their 1965 marriage gave him reason to go on. The disease eventually stabilized, though it left him wheelchair-bound and unable to care for himself.

He was, nevertheless, still able to think. Possessed of extraordinary determination, he collaborated with Roger Penrose to propound a theory of "singularities," which was the subject of his doctoral dissertation. Einstein's equations had predicted that when a massive star consumes all of its thermonuclear fuel, it collapses upon itself, producing a singularity—an infinitely dense point with an irresistible gravitational field. The surrounding region becomes a "black hole" because the gravitational force is so intense that not even light can escape, and surrounding objects—such as planets—are sucked into it. Despite indirect evidence for the existence of black holes, scientists did not know how to deal with singularites, because the laws of science broke down at this point. Enter Hawking and Penrose, who in 1965 proved mathematically that if Einstein's theory of relativity is correct, singularities must exist; in fact, if they do not exist, general relativity is refuted. Furthermore, they argued, a singularity must be the point of origin of the universe.

The work in progress on singularities, coupled with Hawking's reputation in Cambridge academic circles, earned him a research fellowship at Gonville and Caius College. As a fellow there he demonstrated—using quantum theory instead of general relativity, because relativity does not accurately describe the random subatomic world—that the force of the Big Bang must have created numerous mini black holes, which do emit particles after all. This assertion created shock waves of disbelief, but has since come to be accepted; these emissions are now known as Hawking's radiation.

The career of the often irascible scientist advanced resolutely in spite of his inability to work out complex equations, a deficiency he circumvented by translating them into geometry problems, which he could picture in his mind. In 1978 he won the coveted Albert Einstein Award, and the following year he was made Lucasian Professor of Mathematics at Cambridge, a post once held by Isaac Newton.

After a tracheotomy following pneumonia in 1985, Hawking's speech was all but gone, and he began relying on a speech synthesizer operated by the solitary finger he was still able to move. He depended upon the help of his wife or an aide for the simplest of functions. But in that time he completed A Brief History of Time: From the Big Bang to Black Holes, a huge bestseller which popularized his complex and brilliant ideas in understandable terms.

If Hawking's scientific approach owed much to his intuitive, contrarian nature, it relied in equal amount on the ideas of philosopher Karl Popper, who turned the classical scientific order of observation, hypothesis and experiment on its head. In Popper's—and, by adoption, Hawking's—method, the scientist proposes a solution to a problem, then conducts experiments to refute his own theory and in the process come up with a better one. It was this kind of unconventional thinking that led Hawking to his discoveries about mini black holes. It also led him to propose the notion that if the universe ever began to contract, events would occur all over again, in reverse—a theory he later recanted. In 1990, this ardently romantic thinker—who kept a poster of Marilyn Monroe on his office wall—left his wife of twenty-five years for his private nurse, Elaine Mason.

The irony of Hawking's massive achievements is that they function only in the realm of the possible: No one has ever observed a singularity or a black-hole implosion. In the ultimate paradox, this driven atheist is confident he will be able to penetrate another invisibility—the mind of God.

HEARST

WILLIAM RANDOLPH

HE DID NOT INVENT yellow journalism, but William Randolph Hearst became its mightiest and most ruthless practitioner. And while not the first to found a newspaper chain, he created one more formidable than any before it. Ostentatiousy wealthy and a sybarite, he rivaled royalty in sheer grandiosity, building a California pleasure dome that contained some of Europe's most magnificent art. Media baron and social media tycoon, lionized by friend and foe alike, William Randolph Hearst intended to be more than rich and famous. His greatest ambition was to be president of the United States.

Born to a gold miner whose shrewd mining investments had made him a fortune, Hearst was a lumbering, pampered adolescent who attended St. Paul's School and later Harvard, before a tasteless prank in his junior year of 1885 led to his expulsion. His college career was distinguished only by his adroit management of the Harvard *Lampoon*, which showed a profit for the first time in its history under his direction. Returning to San Francisco and his indulgent parents, he fed his newly acquired journalistic passion by begging his father to give him the *San Francisco Examiner,* a money-guzzling paper the elder Hearst had purchased to advance his political ambitions in California. When his father reluctantly acquiesced, Hearst served a two-year apprenticeship with Joseph Pulitzer's *New York World*—noted for its heated headlines and overdeveloped taste for blood, sex, and scandal—and proved himself a keen student of Pulitzer's sensationalist style. By 1897, Hearst had absorbed all he needed to know to turn the *Examiner* into a West Coast version of the *World*. His strategy, which involved coupling lurid stories with pretentiously high-minded crusades against corruption, hiring the best talent he could at triple the going salary, and dropping the price to boost circulation, eventuallly resulted in a profit.

Emboldened by the *Examiner's* success and by several million dollars of his mother's money, Hearst mounted another journalistic coup. He bought the *New York Journal* and challenged his old mentor Pulitzer by raiding his pool of reporters, among other tactics. The two fought in a ruthless newsstand war, stealing each other's features and manufacturing stories where none existed. The latter was a black art that reached its nadir in 1898, with Hearst's brazen trumpetings for the United States to go to war with Spain over Cuba. His highly inflammatory account of the explosion of the *Maine,* which blamed Spanish agents for the ship's sinking, eventually stirred so much public outcry that President McKinley was goaded that year into the Spanish-American War.

Yet every standard Hearst raised in mock idealism—his anti-British ravings, his pro-labor stand, his attacks on McKinley as a puppet of the monopolies—was calculated to serve one end: his burning desire to hold the country's highest office. In 1901 an editorial lauding political assassination, widely interpreted as a direct attack upon McKinley, was followed five months later by the president's death at the hands of an anarchist. Hearst, however, never succeeded McKinley, or anyone else, to the White House. His service in Congress from 1903 to 1907 was intended as a springboard to national prominence, as were his unsuccessful bids for mayor of New York in 1905 and 1909, and for governor of New York in 1906. He also made a good run at the Democratic presidential nomination in 1904. It was the last time Hearst would even come close to realizing his dream, but it took him years to abandon it. In the late twenties and early thirties, he went on a fevered buying spree of newspapers which was designed to provide him with personal propaganda vehicles in important cities. By 1935 he owned twenty-eight newspapers, thirteen magazines, eight radio stations, and two movie companies. The last was intended as an outlet of sorts for his mistress, the sweet but barely talented Marion Davies, a comedienne turned movie actress whom Hearst had first seen in a music hall in 1917 and "kept," despite the fact that he had married Millicent Willson, herself a dancer, in 1903. His wife refused to divorce him, so Davies, whom Hearst loved, remained on the sidelines until the end of his life.

But if his marriage stood fast, his empire and his political career were on shaky ground. His bittersweet political triumph of swinging the 1932 California Democratic delegation to Franklin Roosevelt only underscored the party's rejection of candidate Hearst. Dispirited, he retreated to California to supervise the construction of his outrageously grand San Simeon home, complete with castle, wild African fauna, and more marble than a Medici villa. The thirty-million-dollar Xanadu became an exclusive playground for Hollywood, with its amiable hosts—Hearst and the faithful Marion—transporting their celebrity friends to lavish weekend house parties via a special train. Drained by this profligacy, his news empire tottered in 1937, and Hearst had to take a humiliating and highly public pay cut. Fittingly for the hawkish tycoon, only the prosperity of World War II could bail him out, and at its end he was back in the black. But his day had passed: His presidential ambitions unrealized, he was now distrusted as a self-serving megalomaniac—an image forever defined by Orson Welles's magnificent 1941 classic film *Citizen Kane*. Hearst spent his declining years with Davies, at whose home he died in 1951. Not surprisingly, he was eulogized most warmly in death principally by those he had paid well in life.

HUGH HEFNER

HUGH HEFNER TOOK SEX out of the bedroom and the motel and put it on the magazine rack at the local news-stand. The shy, self-absorbed son of a repressed Chicago Methodist couple, who grew up in a household marked by severe emotional reserve, he turned his loveless childhood into a new suburban philosophy that both heralded and abetted the sexual revolution. Communicating their sexual reserve to a resentful and affection-starved son, Hefner's mother and accountant father had led him, unsurprisingly, to believe as an adult that prudery was the root of all social evil. Hugh was a lackluster student but when his mother had him examined by psychologists, they informed her that her underachieving son had an IQ of 152. The doctors advised Mrs. Hefner to show him more physical tenderness; her response was to grudgingly allow him to post racy pinups of Vargas girls on his bedroom wall.

Although he overcame his timidity, as a young man Hefner felt uncomfortable putting his arm around a woman, and all through a dreary hitch in the army beginning in 1944, and GI Bill studies at the University of Illinois two years later, he brooded on his *idée fixe:* the puritanical suppression of sexuality in America. His student reading of the famous Kinsey Report on the nation's sexual mores disturbed him, not with its clinical depiction of sex, but in its implicit portrait of national hypocrisy. In sexual matters as in so many others, Americans' public and private behaviors differed drastically. Ending sexual hypocrisy was Hefner's mission, and *Playboy* magazine his mouthpiece.

Hugh married Millie Williams, his college sweetheart, in 1949. The two divorced in 1959, and Hefner would not show an appetite for monogamy and matrimony for many years. He then worked unhappily in various copywriting jobs, feeling more and more stultified at home and at work until *Esquire* magazine, for whom he was writing promotional material, offered him a job in New York at eighty dollars a week in 1952. When Hefner demanded an additional five dollars and *Esquire* refused, Hefner quit and, in his new found spirit of liberation, gave free rein at last to his "mission," as he saw it: "to publish a magazine that would thumb its nose at all the restrictions" that had bound him. With six hundred dollars of his own money and contributions from investors, he made his dream come true. He began producing a magazine for men that embodied what its creator had evolved in his nighttime musings as "The Playboy Philosophy."

Playboy premiered in December 1953, featuring the famous nude calendar photograph of Marilyn Monroe, for which Hefner had paid two hundred dollars. With its curious blend of the highbrow (fiction and articles by leading writers) and the lowbrow (naked women idealized to the point of angelicism by Hefner's obsession with the perfect girl-next-door look), *Playboy* and its creator became an instant success. The magazine illustrated Hefner's shrewd judgment of the postwar cultural shift that could make such a magazine popular, as well as the truth of the dictum that any strong idea will triumph when wedded to high social purpose. Unlike the common pornographer, the motive for this son of right-thinking Methodists was not only a hunger for financial success, but a missionary zeal to change a repressive sexual code.

Much of the country agreed that *Playboy was* right for its time, and the magazine's circulation chart soon rocketed, reaching at its peak more than seven million readers. Hefner became a Pepsi-swigging, night-owl executive of a colorful empire that included exotic magazines, Bunny-filled key clubs, casinos, recording labels, and television production companies. Jetting around the country in his own customized black DC–9, he could be found at all hours of the day or night padding in his trademark pajamas through the halls of the cavernous Playboy Mansions in Chicago and later Los Angeles. Of course, the most striking accoutrements at both locations were the women: gorgeous, young, and usually available at the beck-and-call of the reclusive philosopher, who lounged in his huge, round bed.

Hefner's dislike for sexual hypocrisy, however, was hardly evenhanded. Men were usually required to bring women to the "Mansions," but women, on the other hand, were discouraged from bringing dates. Nor did Hefner allow his fondness for sexual variety, a cornerstone of his philosophy, to be reflected in the tastes of his chosen, who were expected to be as faithful to him as his mother must have been to his father. For thirty years Hefner personified the *Playboy* philosophy; then, in 1989, he married Kimberly Conrad, the Playmate of that year, and fathered two sons. With his signature sense of timing, his late-life second marriage and parenthood marked a graceful step back from his ostentatious public life.

If his empire declined during the 1980s, losing magazines, key clubs, and the London casino like so many outlying provinces; and if the government attempted to blame *Playboy* for at least some of society's ills, it does not diminish his revolutionary effect on twentieth-century morals. For almost three decades *Playboy* and Hefner made their distinctive mark on America, the visions of a single man feeding the fantasies of millions.

HEIFETZ

JASCHA

THE WORD "PRODIGY" CONJURES up images of a serious small child, an outsized instrument in hand, remarkable for his infant precocity; or of Mozart, burning too brightly before an early death. By that measure, violinist extraordinaire, Jascha Heifetz, was no prodigy at all, but a rare, fully mature talent from the age of three. His ascent as the century's foremost master of the violin was more dramatic, and, once achieved, more enduring than any before or since.

His father Rubin was a violinist in Vilna, Russia; he gave Heifetz his first lessons, before consigning the toddler to the tutelage of master Ilya Malkin. In less than two years, Heifetz could play a difficult Mendelssohn violin concerto with authority. In 1910, he traveled to St. Petersburg to study at the conservatory under the great teacher Leopold Auer, who was known for his work with *wunderkinder*. Despite the professor's enthusiams for the young genius, however, Jascha's plans were almost canceled when it was learned that the exemption given to the school's Jewish students to live in the city—Jews were forbidden by law in St. Petersburg—did not extend to their parents. By special arrangement Ruvin Heifetz was enrolled *in addition* to his son. In two years Heifetz, still hardly more than a child, debuted in Berlin to sensational acclaim, and in 1917, at age sixteen, he left Russia to tour the United States. His premiere performance at Carnegie Hall caused the renowned violinist Mischa Elman to mop his brow and mutter, "It's hot in here," to which pianist Leopold Godowsky famously replied: "Not for piano players." Elman was not alone; Fritz Kreisler, no slouch at strings himself, having heard Heifetz in Germany, had half-humorously suggested to his colleagues that they break their instruments across their knees—such was the precision and impact of Heifetz's playing. It was a power he showed to the world: in Australia in 1921, in Palestine in 1926 (he returned forty-four years later, but this time to Israel) and in a cathartic 1934 concert back in his homeland.

Like so many Russian émigrés, Heifetz gravitated to America, becoming a citizen in 1925, settling in Beverly Hills. In 1926 the French made him a Chevalier of the Légion d'honneur. Two years later, he married silent screen starlet Florence Vidor with whom he had two children. In 1939 he became a temporary movie star by making a film called "They Shall Have Music." During World War II, a fearless Heifetz—who spotted planes in the Civil Defense Corps—toured the front with USO shows to tremendous acclaim. But after the war, he cut down on his personal appearances; married now to Frances Spiegelberg, the father of three began teaching a class at the University of Southern California (USC), in an effort to preserve and pass on all he knew about violin playing.

Critics said Heifetz was cold, because his demeanor on stage was as undramatic as his playing was emotional. Standing at attention, he held his back straight as a bayonet, his elbow jutting out and his instrument held high in "the Russian style." A Heifetz performance did not rely on gestures or theatrical swoons to convey feeling to the audience. What it did convey was the whole spectrum of musical expression. Heifetz played notes that sung, stung, whispered, or fluttered; that galloped, whirled, or trumpeted, but he let the music alone move the audience. The intensity of his playing was such that he lost weight during his performances. As undemonstrative as he was, he was nevertheless the quintessentially Romantic musician, an artist whose abiding love was for music from Beethoven onward. Having little taste for the avant-garde, Heifetz conferred commissions only on modern composers whose conservatism matched his own. He sometimes included his own versions of popular pieces in concerts otherwise heavy with classics. Such habits annoyed his supporters and delighted his detractors, but they helped make Heifetz the highest-paid violinist of his time; his name and reputation were so golden that RCA Victor paid him a six-figure retainer even after he stopped recording.

Heifetz's transition from boy wonder to *eminence grise* was apparently painless; the experience of his USC students was less so. As a teacher, he was a task master; he emphasized the fundamentals, including the ceaseless practice of simple scales. When asked why no one had written a biography of such a famous musician, he said "Here is my biography: I played the violin at three and gave my first concert at seven. I have been playing ever since." Such taciturnity was typical. He had always been a private man, aloof from and suspicious of the adulation of public and press. Perhaps he had been influenced by George Bernard Shaw, who once told him, "Nothing may be perfect in this world, or else the gods become jealous and destroy it. So you should make a habit of playing one wrong note every night before you go to bed." Throughout his career, Heifetz was convinced that if 2,000 people came out to hear him play, 1,999 of them were waiting for that single wrong note.

On his eightieth birthday he vanished from his home, only to be tracked down by a persistent reporter who begged for an interview. When the reporter proposed that the maestro was twentieth century violin-playing incarnated, Heifetz replied: "I have nothing to say." He had said it all with his playing.

He could not, however, prevent stories of his personal eccentricities from spreading. One such anecdote illustrates his obsession with punctuality: Heifetz once threw a party at 4:00 p.m. and opened the gates of his grand home at that hour. He then shut them promptly at 4:01, barring all latecomers. His own appointment with the Hereafter was met punctually on December 10, 1987, when, hopefully, Heaven's gates swung open and welcomed him—upright, serene, and, as always, alone in his class.

ERNEST HEMINGWAY

ERNEST HEMINGWAY'S SIXTY-TWO YEARS were a tumultuous, headlong journey. "A sort of demi-god of American manhood," as the press release for *A Farewell to Arms* described him, the bronzed and burly writer spent all of his energy in a continuing effort to prove himself—as a sexual creature, a hunter of animals, and an artist in perfect control of his craft. The most influential and imitated voice in modern prose, Hemingway was committed to risk and physical action, courting the two wherever he could find them.

At nineteen, Hemingway was at the Italian front in the Great War, serving as a volunteer ambulance driver with the Red Cross. He was wounded badly and decorated twice for his bravery. Later, serving as a correspondent, he bunked with Loyalist soldiers during the Spanish Civil War, and when World War II started soon after, tagged along with a band of irregulars in France. Though he subsisted in Paris by catching pigeons in the park for his dinner, his life's travels would also take him to Hollywood, where Marlene Dietrich and Gary Cooper would become chums; to Key West, where he slummed in various harbor-side bars; and to Africa where he tracked buffalo on safari. A street brawler with a taste for fast company and gorgeous women, Hemingway survived four wives, three serious car wrecks, several combat rescues, a near court-martial, and two plane crashes—both within only two days of each other. His love of such hair-raising experiences often showed in the courageous characters of his fiction; tightly wound, vital men, who, like himself, were engaged in a two-fisted struggle with mortality.

His themes were forceful ones: stoicism, self-control, nobility in struggle, and bravery (especially its redemptiveness when summoned in the presence of doom). For Hemingway, death—particularly sudden death—was an ever-present specter stalking its unsuspecting human prey. To face it, a hero needed courage, or he would go unsaved—an impossibility in a Hemingway scenario.

Born in Oak Park, Illinois, to a prosperous family, Hemingway absorbed his passion for the outdoors, especially hunting and fishing, from his physician father Clarence. In 1928, his father ill and financially troubled, killed himself with a revolver, an incident that scarred his twenty-nine-year-old son. Beginning his writing career as a reporter in Kansas City and Toronto, Hemingway later accepted work as a foreign correspondent. In the early twenties he moved to Paris, where he became the emperor of the expatriates, keeping company with Gertrude Stein, Pablo Picasso, Ezra Pound, and James Joyce. There, poor and as yet unknown, he immersed himself in the painterly world of Cézanne, which amplified his appreciation for careful method and style in his own work.

Ruggedly handsome and charismatic, Hemingway seemed to take over a room just by walking into it; his energy and intensity generated an extraordinary magnetism. Similarly, he blasted his way into the world's literary scene with the publication in 1926 of *The Sun Also Rises,* a poignant novel of desire and loss set against the backdrop of the fiery Spanish fiesta and the grisly *corrida.* The bullfight, with its mixture of solemn ceremony and annihilation, fascinated Hemingway—though not nearly so much as war, which he saw as the ultimate ritual separating men from cowards. Almost immediately, he became the voice of his era, the alienated "lost generation" stranded between two World Wars. *A Farewell to Arms* (1929), a frankly erotic novel about an affair between an American ambulance driver and an English nurse, solidified his reputation, with critics marveling at his terse, understated style.

Hemingway's spare but muscular writing appeared easy to duplicate. However, as legions of writers since have discovered, it is often unimaginably hard to "write one true sentence" and make it "the truest sentence that you know"—which was Hemingway's counsel to himself in *A Moveable Feast,* his memoir. From the start, he did his best to "put down what really happened in action; what the actual things were which produced the emotion that you experienced." His efforts were deeply admired by a growing international audience, but when he stumbled in 1950 with his first postwar novel, *Across the River and Into the Trees,* the critics pounced. Characteristically—as he had often done when challengers picked fights with him—Hemingway came out swinging. In 1952 he produced *The Old Man and the Sea,* a powerful allegory whose message was as deceptively simple as its title. That year, he won the Nobel Prize for literature.

Throughout his churning, competitive life, Hemingway the writer was continually sabotaged by the appetites of Hemingway the celebrity. Art and fame were uneasy bedfellows in his life, and often the recognition that he had squandered precious time occasioned real remorse. His well-publicized antics shored up his detractors' arguments who cited them as proof of an essentially reckless attitude toward his writing. Paradoxically, though, for Hemingway, writing was everything, even if it did not appear to temper how he lived.

Gradually, "Papa," as he had become known, began a physical decline, and his arrogance often overshadowed his finer qualities. The man who had worked in mud-filled trenches—and who later, because of his many injuries, had to stand up to type—could now no longer write. On July 2, 1961, following bouts of severe depression, Hemingway shot himself at his home in Idaho. Perhaps choosing the hour and circumstances of his own death was his ultimate act of courage.

KATHARINE HEPBURN

THERE MUST HAVE BEEN a thousand East Coast ingénues with razor-sharp cheekbones and cut-glass voices in the thirties. Surely there were plenty of debutantes with coltish legs and snappy comebacks hanging around the New York theater scene, any one of whom could have taken Hollywood by storm. Now, however, it seems there could have been only one. Whether playing a wisecracking WASP or a doughty old spinster, Katharine Hepburn, the American actress who seems to embody independence and common sense remained one of the screen's most memorable presences for over sixty years.

The daughter of a prominent Hartford, Connecticut, urologist and his well-educated suffragette wife, Hepburn was raised in a large, liberal, and—according to the actress—conventionally happy household. Her protestations notwithstanding, the family had suffered the suicides of Kate's grandfather and two of her uncles, a fact they wanted to sweep under the rug. But nothing could erase the scene of death by hanging of her older brother Tom in 1921, which she was the first to come upon. Thereafter, she took his birthday as her own, and replaced Tom as her father's favorite. "Jimmy," as she called herself, shaved her head every summer until she reached fourteen.

While a student at Bryn Mawr, the headstrong young woman defied her father's prejudices and decided to pursue acting. Hepburn Senior may have supported a woman's right to a career, but he thought acting was a silly, vain pursuit dependent on youth and beauty. His freckled, auburn-haired daughter had plenty of both, but whether she had any talent was open to debate. When her screechy voice relegated her to the tiniest parts, she began speech lessons with Frances Robinson-Duff. Despite training, however, Hepburn was fired from her first big stage role in The Big Pond (1928), when she raced through her lines so fast that the audience missed most of them. That same year she married blue-blooded Ludlow Ogden Smith, whose adoration for her was matched only by her own self-regard. The marriage lasted six years, during which the assertive Hepburn found herself dismissed from a series of Broadway plays, Death Takes a Holiday (1929) among them. Critical response to her abilities may be summed up in Dorothy Parker's famous reivew of her in The Lake: "Miss Hepburn ran the emotional gamut from A to B."

Tough-minded and in growing command of her theatrical gifts, she began the year 1932 by being fired and rehired twice in The Warrior's Husband, somehow ending up making the production her star vehicle. Summoned to Hollywood, she found her true métier in the very different craft of film acting and received an Oscar almost immediately for Morning Glory (1933). Three years later, she worked with John Ford on Mary of Scotland and, though in mid-affair with her agent Leland Hayward, fell in love with the director, who ultimately could not leave his wife for her.

Once she reached the top, Hepburn fought with all her New England tenacity to stay there. RKO studios put her in so many bad movies that she developed a reputation as box office poison, but the 1940 film version of The Philadelphia Story, which had been written for her as a stage play in 1939, saved her career. Her romance with the dashing millionaire Howard Hughes, who had purchased the movie rights to the play and who taught her to fly, foundered soon after the play began. The failure of this relationship, however, set the stage for the appearance of the love of her life, Spencer Tracy. When the forty-one-year-old actor first met the thirty-three-year-old Hepburn just before filming Woman of the Year, in 1942, she was so aggressively forthright that he, misunderstanding her fierce self-determination, assumed the trousers-wearing actress was a lesbian. As for Hepburn, the gruff alcoholic became the first person whose interests she put before her own. This, she discovered in the fullness of their brusque but tender relationship, was the meaning of love. Unfortunately for her, Tracy, a guilt-ridden Irish Catholic, was and would remain married until his death. Their teasing combination of patrician lady and salt-of-the-earth Joe was nonetheless so potent a box-office draw that to this day it remains the standard against which screen twosomes are measured.

They were linked for the rest of Tracy's life, some thirty years, making nine movies together, including Adam's Rib in 1949. Hepburn went on to make The African Queen with Humphrey Bogart in 1951 and Pat and Mike with Tracy the following year. In 1967, she was awarded her second Oscar for Guess Who's Coming to Dinner, her last film with Tracy, who died that same year. The following spring she won another statuette for her role in The Lion in Winter, and in 1981 earned yet another for the sentimental On Golden Pond, in which she portrayed a lovable old woman opposite a cantankerous Henry Fonda. A few mostly forgettable roles have followed, but clearly, although she has never tried very hard to endear herself to the moviegoing public, she is revered as the grande dame of American film.

Though some of her screen roles seemed a compromise of her freethinking ideas, Hepburn has asserted that her life has been one of glorious liberation. She lives her later years as strong-willed as ever—alone, in her own house, fending for herself. And though she is out of the limelight, she is no less famous than she always wanted to be.

SIR EDMUND HILLARY & TENZING NORGAY

THEY CLIMBED THE WORLD'S highest and most forbidding mountain together, the New Zealand adventurer and the Sherpa guide. They were the first to reach Everest's austere summit, some 29,028 feet above sea level. Sir Edmund Hillary and Tenzing Norgay were showered with laurels on their return, but the mountain—which has claimed the lives of many before and since—is no smaller for it, nor any less deadly.

Edmund Hillary was born in 1919 in New Zealand and grew up in Tuakau, Auckland, the son of a beekeeper. He was lonely, bookish and easily moved to tears, a condition aggravated by a rather severe father and the attention of school bullies. Not surprisingly, the shy, gawky youth thought constantly of escape. As a teenager he took a school trip to Ruapehu, one of New Zealand's volcanoes, and was instantly smitten with the grandeur of the great natural edifices, the first mountains he had ever seen. He began climbing his country's peaks with energy.

Despite serious injuries incurred during World War II, Hillary resumed mountaineering; in 1951 he joined the New Zealand Alpine Club, presided over by Jim Rose, and pitted his skill against Europe's highest peaks. His first attempt to reach the summit of Mukut Parbat, in the Garwhal Himalayas of India, ended quite literally in cold feet and failure.

Though furious at the defeat of the expedition he had led, Hillary's ego was soothed when later that year he was invited to join a British reconnaissance team, led by the renowned Eric Shipton, to explore the west side of Mt. Everest, still terra incognito to mountaineers. The first outing ended in an avalanche which only just missed killing them all. Continuing to train on smaller Himalayan peaks, he anxiously and jealously followed the progress of the Swiss assault on Everest, led by Raymond Lambert and his Sherpa guide Tenzing Norgay; to his relief, Lambert and Norgay got only as far as the South Summit.

Norgay was the first of his ethnic group to achieve fame as a climber; the Sherpas had always believed that climbing Chomolungma—their name for Everest—was an act of blasphemy against Miyo Lungsungama, the goddess who resided there. Born in the Thamay region of Nepal, Tenzing was drawn as a young man to Darjeeling, then a center for mountaineering. He became an Indian resident and developed a reputation as a tough, intelligent expert on the often grim realities of the mountain.

In 1953, Norgay, along with Hillary, got another chance at Chomolungma as part of the British expedition funded by the Joint Himalayan Committee of the Alpine Club of Great Britain and the Royal Geographic Society. On March 27, the group began the assault from the Nepal side, a feat never tried before. Headed by Colonel John Hunt, the team was equipped with the controversial innovation of oxygen bottles.

Reality on Everest is always fluid. Its crevasses appear and disappear, its avalanches and trail-obliterating snowfalls continually change the landscape. Less than three hundred tantalizing feet from the summit, the first assault team was forced to turn back because of a malfunctioning oxygen apparatus. Given the go-ahead, Hillary and Tenzing, the second team, took on extra supplies and struggled to 28,200 feet. There, having pitched a tent on a precarious ledge of ice, they spent a miserable night.

The next morning, May 29, Hillary thawed his frozen boots over the stove and, in unusually fine weather, the two resumed their ascent. Five hours later they had conquered the final eight hundred feet; they stood, finally, where no one had before, at the top of the world. With the glittering vastness at their feet, the two climbers embraced.

They achieved instant fame. When the British made the New Zealander a Knight of the Realm—without his knowledge and against his wishes—Hillary was furious. In the midst of the celebration he slipped away to write letters to his beloved Louise, daughter of Jim Rose, whom he married when he got back to New Zealand. Five years later, the intrepid adventurers completed the first mechanized overland crossing of Antarctica.

It would be three years before anyone would duplicate the duo's achievement, and ten before an American team reached the summit of Chomolungma-Everest. Hillary's wife and their youngest daughter died tragically in a plane crash near Kathmandu in 1975, after which he devoted his life to improving the lot of the Sherpas, advancing the art of mountaineering and raising funds for environmental concerns.

Norgay, who ultimately died an alcoholic in 1986, became a much feuded-over hero in both Nepal and India, spending most of his life teaching at the Himalayan Mountaineering Institute. During this time, he dictated several books on scaling the frozen ranges of his birthplace; the peerless climber spoke seven languages, but had never learned to write. He once commented wryly that he had come a long way: from mountain coolie to bemedaled celebrity who worried about income taxes.

Hillary and Tenzing were among the last great explorers of the old school, those who, in an era when the earth was yielding up its last great challenges, became justly famous for one astounding feat of human will and daring. Time has not dimmed their achievement in any way. Although increasing numbers of people seek to best Everest with ever more sophisticated equipment, its merciless majesty continues to claim casualties. The goddess Miyo, deity of humanity and prosperity, bestowed her blessings on Edmund Hillary and Tenzing Norgay, exempting them from the ancient taboo.

EMPEROR

HIROHITO

HIROHITO, EMPEROR OF JAPAN, was at once God-man on the Chrysanthemum Throne of the Japanese Empire, lineal and spiritual descendant of the sun goddess Amaterasu Omikami, and chief priest of the Shinto religion. During his sixty-three-year reign—longer than that of any modern sovereign—his country was transformed from an insular island kingdom to a modern world power. He presided over the rise of Japanese influence in Asia in the 1930s, the slaughter and defeat of World War II, and the post-war resurgence of Japanese economic might. Denounced as a war criminal by the victorious Allies, he was spared by the ruler of his occupied land, the shrewd American, General Douglas MacArthur. Paradoxically a symbol of both virulent militarism and benevolent constitutional monarchy, the emperor remains an enigma to historians, who are divided over his personal role in Japan's reckless expansionism and, in particular, over the extent of his complicity in its war atrocities.

Born in 1901, Hirohito lived in a world more rarefied than even his majestic coevals in other countries could imagine. The firstborn son of Crown Prince Yoshihito and Princess Sadako—later Emperor Taisho and Empress Teimei—Hirohito was destined to be the emblematic ruler of a country that had survived the culture shock of Commodore Perry's 1853 visit and was rapidly mastering both the blessings and evils of the modern world. Raised in the rigor of palace life and imperial duty and educated with only five other students in the Peers' School, the young Hirohito was named crown prince in 1912. His studies drew him more to his beloved marine biology than to military science, and though trained in the philosophy of Bushido, the way of the warrior, he often clashed with his soldier-tutors over the primacy of war and the divine origins of his own family. Yet Hirohito accepted the fact that, as emperor, no one could look upon his face, speak his name, or address him from a height greater than his own.

The future ruler got his first taste of personal freedom in 1921, when he broke precedent and became the first Japanese prince to travel outside his country. He visited London, where a robed and slippered King George V slapped the shy twenty-year-old on the back and warmly enjoined him to ring for whatever he wanted. What he wanted was bacon and eggs, a dish he loved and ate virtually every morning from then on. Hirohito then passed through Paris, where he happily rode incognito on the Metro, keeping the ticket as a memento for the rest of his life.

When his father slipped into insanity, Hirohito returned to Tokyo to become prince regent in 1921, then emperor in 1926, assigning the name Showa, or "peace and enlightenment," to the era of his reign. It was an ironic title, for Japan's military elite, still flexing its muscles after victory in the Russo-Japanese War, was preparing to inaugurate the bloody excesses of the Greater East Asia Co-Prosperity Sphere, a delicate name for Japan's hyper-imperialism. Despite his avowed disinterest in military matters, Hirohito rapidly achieved the high military rank that seemed inevitably to devolve on nobility. But his various medals and orders did not embolden him to defy the generals who acted in his name—and some believe with his express approval—during the 1931 sacking of Manchuria and notorious rape of Nanking in 1937. He did, however, suppress a mutiny in 1936 and order its ringleaders executed, an act that was itself evidence of his power. But in 1941, when he was asked to consider a war with the United States of America, the Son of Heaven was content to recite a cryptic haiku on the wind and allow his commanders to make the decision.

The result, after four years of carnage, was the brutal crushing of Japan by what seemed, in the eyes of such an ancient and proud nation, to be an upstart democracy that did not hesitate to exact a terrible revenge for the empire's attack on Pearl Harbor. America's massive nuclear destruction in Japan must have shocked Hirohito to his senses. In 1945, after the Japanese War Council deadlocked between samurai who wanted to fight to the death and pragmatists who recognized that the war was lost, Hirohito rose to the occasion and broke the tie, announcing that Japan would have to "endure the unendurable" and surrender to the Americans.

In a traditional and certainly sincere gesture, Hirohito humbled himself before the victorious MacArthur and took personal responsibility for his nation's acts. Critics felt that in doing so the emperor was merely belaboring the obvious and called for his execution as a war criminal. MacArthur refused, maintaining that Hirohito could do more good alive than dead. Head spared, Hirohito bowed to American pressure, renounced his divine status, and consented to rule as monarch under a new constitution dictated by the victors.

Though he was so retiring that his usual comment to any statement was a laconic "Is that so?" he began to make more personal appearances and to allow the publication of his photograph and stories about his family. Periodically, he escaped from the discomfort of public life by writing scholarly works on marine biology. When Hirohito died, his passing was regarded by the world with the same ambiguous mixture of respect and disdain that had marked its view of his turbulent reign.

ALFRED HITCHCOCK

A PUCKISH FILM DIRECTOR who originated the thriller genre with such classics as *Notorious* (1946), *The Man Who Knew Too Much* (1934 and 1956), *Vertigo* (1958), and *Psycho* (1960), Alfred Hitchcock was himself afraid of everything: high places, Sundays, little children, closed spaces, crowds, the law, and public conflict. Born in London to a poultry dealer and educated by the Jesuits to be a staunch Catholic, he was also petrified of corporal punishment and the police—the former because of canings at school, the latter because of a few minutes spent in a jail cell—thanks to a father intent on scaring an errant son. Perhaps because of these fears, Hitchcock became adept at probing the depths of the unconscious mind. In his films—a chilling fusion of carefully calibrated suspense, wry humor, and often interwoven psychological motives and sexual passions—he mesmerized his viewers while wreaking havoc on their nervous systems.

For the master of suspense, there was no such thing as a simple sunny day at the beach, either in his quiet and obsessive routinized private life or in his movies. His view of an anarchic, evil-charged universe dictated that "normal life" was a contradiction in terms, that some unexpected violent disruption was inevitable. A Hitchcockian day at the beach would be incomplete without the presence of potential danger: a glittering shard of glass in the sand, perhaps unobserved by a pair of strolling lovers. Much of Hitchcock's genius lay in his knowing use of details which left his audiences white-knuckled in their seats.

No one who has seen a Hitchcock classic is likely to soon forget its haunting, stark images: Cary Grant in *Suspicion* (1941), climbing an unlit staircase and carrying an oddly glowing glass of milk (an effect produced by a tiny hidden light), which may or may not contain poison for his mistrustful wife; Joseph Cotten in *Shadow of a Doubt* (1943) struggling with his niece at the open door of a speeding train as he tries to push her out; and Grant again, this time in *North by Northwest* (1959), being chased across wide-open fields by a crop-dusting plane without a hiding place for miles. Undoubtedly the most famous of his finely crafted scenes occurs in *Psycho* when Janet Leigh is stabbed to death in the shower. Typical of Hitchcock's art, the editing is fast-paced and ingeniously orchestrated, the director having spliced together seventy-eight separate shots to create a brief but unforgettable forty-five seconds of film, panning finally to the victim's open eye. Hitchcock exulted in both the craft and shock value of his controversial work.

He learned his craft from the bottom up, starting in 1919 as a title-card illustrator at London's Famous Players-Lasky studios. During his apprenticeship there he met and, overcoming his innate shyness, married his lifelong love and professional partner, Alma Reville, a film editor. Soon afterward Hitchcock, who had never been attracted to directing, found himself in Munich working on an Anglo-German production. Here he encountered the artistry of German director F. W. Murnau, whose *Der Letzte Maun (The Last Laugh)* of 1924 would have a profound effect upon his imagination. With its exaggerated camera angles, somber shadows, and reliance on simple images to tell the tale, it was "almost the perfect film." Forever after he would concentrate, like the German Expressionists of the twenties had, on creating his own personal reality, favoring form and structure over content—which he once said held no interest for him whatsoever. Even the actual filming of a script would soon cease to entertain him, since he would compulsively map out every detail in advance through storyboarding.

After his English phase, during which he produced the acclaimed 1926 silent film *The Lodger* and then critical hits like *The Thirty-Nine Steps* (1935) and *The Lady Vanishes* (1938), Hitchcock's international success took him to Hollywood. There he turned out splendid thrillers, including *Rebecca,* which won an Oscar for Best Picture in 1940 and among whose makers was the legendary David O. Selznick, who had lured the rotund, business-suited director into the California world of glaring sunshine and big-budget productions. Gradually, Hitchcock—a decorous gentleman who nevertheless adored practical jokes and dirty little secrets—expressed more eroticism in his work, sensuality often melding with violence and irony. He explored such themes as homoeroticism, sexual guilt, fetishism, and tranvestism with subtlety—heady stuff for mainstream filmgoers of the 1940s.

In the fifties, films like *Strangers on a Train* (1951), *Dial M for Murder* (1954), and *To Catch a Thief* (1955) attracted the attention of French critics, who canonized Hitchcock in the influential film journal *Les cahiers du cinéma* for his role as auteur and artist. As critics jousted over whether the director whose name now appeared over his film's titles was driven by Christian precepts or box office receipts, audiences the world over voted with their feet. From the mid-fifties through the mid-sixties, Hitchcock had two very successful television series which increased his popularity and visibility. Hitchcock, attuned to the uneasy peace of the modern era, continued to give them what they wanted: not the Gothic horrors of a Baron Frankenstein whose mutant creature everyone expected to run amok, but nightmares of the common folk, horrifying tears in the mundane fabric of daily life, where ambiguity coexisted with certainty and where charming villains could put a sudden end to life.

ADOLF HITLER

WELL INTO THE TWENTY-FIRST century, the world will still be struggling to exorcise Adolf Hitler from its collective memory. Seducer of the German psyche, and initiator of several of the defining events of our century, the leader of the Third Reich bears the responsibility for over fifty million casualties, the near-extermination of the European Jews, and physical destruction that reduced untold numbers of people to refugees and cities to cinders.

The son of Alois Schicklgruber Hitler, a lower-middle-class Austrian customs official and a gentle woman who spoiled her child to compensate for her husband's obsessive discipline, young Adolf sang in the choir of a local monastery. In his biography, *Adolf Hitler,* historian John Toland mentions that on the boy's way to choir practice he would walk past a stone arch carved with the monastery's coat of arms. Its most prominent feature was an ancient version of the cross, a swastika.

Adolf spent his pre-adolescence engrossed in warrior fantasies and the Teutonic myths of Wagnerian opera, which he adored. After his mother died in 1908, he became a drifting loner with vague dreams of becoming an artist. Leaving the family home in Upper Austria to seek his fortune in Vienna, Hitler was shocked to find Jews in what he perceived as a "German" city. After his efforts to enter the Academy of Fine Arts were twice met with rejection, he lived in penury, earning a few coins by selling hand-painted postcards. Starting over in Munich failed to improve his lot, and when World War I broke out, Hitler volunteered in a Bavarian infantry regiment. He was decorated with the Iron Cross and in 1918 was temporarily blinded in a mustard-gas attack. A psychiatrist attending him at the time diagnosed him as a psychopath suffering from hysterical symptoms. But Hitler's war experiences toughened him; they gave the tense young man—who'd been unable to stop crying over his mother's death—a taste for violence that could never be slaked. Now a rabid nationalist, he joined the chauvinistic German Workers' party in 1919, renaming it the Nationalsozialistische Deutsche Arbeiterpartei (NSDAP)—or the Nazi party. Two years later, discovering his oratorical ability, he became its autocratic chairman.

A desperate Germany, plagued by a deep sense of humiliation over its defeat in World War I and ravaged economically by a worldwide depression, was ripe for Hitler's emotional message of national salvation. Increasingly prey to both his own paranoia and his sense of divine mission, he offered the country's hard-pressed masses an appealing platform. Not only would he refuse to pay some thirty billion dollars in crippling World War I reparations, but he would create an entirely revitalized Germany, one free of breadlines, debilitating partisan politics—and Jews. In "World Jewry," as well as the Bolshevik "menace," Hitler found convenient scapegoats for his country's turmoil. To offset his bloody pogroms, he offered splendiferous pageantry. These spectacles inspired a renewed sense of patriotic purpose that, as he crudely set forth in *Mein Kamp*—the book-length treatise he composed in prison following the failure of the his Beer Hall Putsch in 1923—would revolve around "Aryan purity," a popular autocracy, and the expansion of Germany's borders, or *Lebensraum.*

Cloaking himself with the trappings of law, Hitler rose swiftly to power. Roughly ten years after he failed to topple the Bavarian government in the Beer Hall Putsch, his hypnotic speeches became the voice of German nationalism. On January 30, 1933, three years after his party's electoral breakthrough, President Hindenburg, ill-advisedly appointed Hitler chancellor in a coalition government. Within months, elections—which Hitler snidely referred to as "passing a magnet over a dunghill"—would be a thing of the past. With Blackshirts in control of the streets, a totally dispirited Reichstag granted the führer dictatorial powers. On March 23, 1933, the Third Reich was born.

After Hitler's unopposed takeover of Czechoslovakia's Sudetenland and the Austrian *Anschluss*—which the West had tolerated with its disastrous policy of appeasement—he blitzkrieged into Poland on September 1, 1939, less than one month after signing a non-aggression pact with the Soviet Union. Two days later, Britain and France declared war on Germany, officially launching World War II. Norway, Denmark, the Netherlands, Belgium, and finally, in June 1940, France itself capitulated to the Wehrmacht's lightning might. But Hitler's invasion of Russia the following year, part of his vision of colonizing and exploiting the natural riches of his eastern neighbor, was an enormous tactical blunder that eventually prompted the Soviets to realign themselves with the Allies. When Hitler rashly declared war on the United States immediately following Japan's attack on Pearl Harbor, he virtually assured the Reich's eventual defeat.

On April 30, 1945, with Soviet army scouts a scant three hundred yards from his Berlin bunker, Hitler ended his own life in a suicide pact with his new bride, Eva Braun. The tyrant who had once referred to himself as "the hardest man there has ever been" had vowed, in the last of his ferocious rages, never to let the enemy "lead us to the slaughterhouse." It was an ironic choice of words from a man whose butchery was on a scale unprecedented in history. Whatever the theories brought forth to explain him—that he was a psychopath born of child abuse, a victim of sexual disfigurement or a cold-blooded true-believer who represented a new genus of evil, to state a few—our need to know is just as urgent today as it was over a half century ago when *Newsweek* reported his end. "Death for once brought a smile to men's lips, a glow to men's hearts."

HO CHI MINH

WHEN A GAUNT YOUNG Indo-Chinese nationalist named Ho Chi Minh approached members of the Versailles Peace Conference in 1919, to interest them in his petition for his country's greater political independence from France, neither he nor his well-crafted eight-point program were paid much heed. In the following years, as Ho's struggles against Japanese occupation and French rule transformed him into a global symbol of righteous anticolonialism, the shy, frail-looking revolutionary was frequently mocked by the Western press, not only for his communist ideals and scraggly goatee but also for his unpretentious and ascetic lifestyle. In the mid-sixties, long after he had become president of North Vietnam and his small country was digging underground tunnels to defend itself against American bombs, Ho became less mysterious. To the left, "Uncle Ho" was a stoic saint in rubber-tire sandals whose single-minded devotion to the liberation of his martyred land perhaps excused a certain ruthlessness, such as his elimination of some fifty thousand people during the agrarian reforms of the midfifties. To the mostly right-wing hawks, this Moscow-trained Bolshevik—who had helped found both the French and Indo-Chinese Communist parties—was a cynical and pitiless agent of an international communist conspiracy.

Born Nguyen That Thanh in 1890, in what was then a part of French Indo-China, Ho was raised in a moderately comfortable family already involved in anti-French resistance. Traditionally educated in the Sino-Vietnamese tradition, he learned the language of the oppressor at the urging of his father, an herbalist and itinerant scholar. In 1911, after some years of study, Ho shipped off to Europe as a kitchen boy on a French liner and in 1914 apprenticed for the great chef Auguste Escoffier at London's Carlton Hotel. When Russian Bolsheviks commenced the "ten days that shook the world" in 1917, Ho began to develop his impeccable Communist credentials. Around 1918, now in Paris, Ho became caught up in a swirl of left-wing activity that assimilated continental political thought and Western values. Fascinated by both the French and American revolutions, he would later model Vietnam's constitution after that of the United States.

In 1923, he went to Russia for indoctrination, schooling himself in revolutionary tactics at Moscow's University of the Toilers of the East. Shortly thereafter, he embarked upon a peripatetic twenty-year career as an organizer of Communist cells and guerrilla forces throughout China and Southeast Asia, training Vietnamese exiles to infiltrate their native land and organize massive strikes. Ho became a phantom sojourner, acquiring endless aliases with alter egos that ranged from a prosperous businessman to a shaven-headed Buddhist monk.

In 1929 his pro-nationalist activities became such a thorn to the French government in Vietnam that he was condemned to death in absentia. With much of Southeast Asia under Japanese control during World War II, Ho temporarily allied himself with Chiang Kai-shek's Chinese nationalists to drive the invaders out. Then in 1941 he united with Vo Nguyen Giap in south China to form the League for the Independence of Vietnam, a coalition of Vietnamese nationalists and Indo-Chinese Communists known as the Vietminh. During this period, Ho was an American partisan, providing information about Japanese activities to American intelligence and narrowly escaping death from a tropical disease, reputedly thanks to sulfa drugs administered by an OSS medic.

Ho's Vietminh forces succeeded in driving the Japanese from Vietnam in 1945. Immediately after proclaiming the formation of the Democratic Republic of Vietnam—quoting the U.S. Declaration of Independence as he did so—Ho was elected president. But the French, unlike other colonial powers in the area after Japan's defeat in World War II, were unwilling to abandon their former protectorate. Eight years of war and some one million casualties later, the French finally quit, after the guerrilla forces of General Giap laid siege to the French-held village of Dien Bien Phu in March 1954. Dien Bien Phu fell on May 7, and in July negotiators in Geneva divided Ho's fatherland at the seventeenth parallel into North and South Vietnam—a supposedly temporary arrangement that would last until elections could be held in 1956 to establish a leader for the whole country. Ho, the president of North Vietnam, was the popular favorite, but the election was called off by South Vietnam's President Ngo Dinh Diem, who enjoyed the strong backing of the United States, which viewed him as a bulwark against Communism in the region. By 1961, the fighters of the North Vietnamese-backed National Liberation Front, called the Vietcong, were waging a guerrilla war in the South, and the United States (which had financed most of France's military effort) began pumping ever more money and, eventually, hundreds of thousands of its own military forces into defeating the North and upholding a series of wobbly, corrupt regimes in the South.

When the United States finally agreed to withdraw its troops from Vietnam on January 27, 1973, Ho—the fragile phantom warrior who had never actually led soldiers into battle—had succeeded not only in toppling a superpower, but in inflaming the idealism of a new generation of American antiwar activists. Yet this dignified and patient revolutionary never witnessed his ravaged nation's final victory. He had died of a heart attack in 1969.

BILLIE HOLIDAY

THE VOICE OF THIS century's most influential popular singer could not be described as classically beautiful, but it *was* unforgettable. And it was so many other things: sometimes vibrant and sophisticated, with an assured, penetrating emotional force; sometimes slow and lazy, with a cool, relaxed, behind-the-beat feel. It could be light and sunny and lyrical or intoxicatingly sensual, and because Billie Holiday had experienced almost everything she sang about, it could express deep anguish and bitterness. Holiday was her most powerful in the intimacy of small supper clubs, where her songs about wanting love or missing it came alive in an intensely personal way. Numerous recordings have preserved her gift—"You've Changed," "Good Morning, Heartache," "Lover Man," and "God Bless the Child" are just a few of Holiday's timeless standards—but they can never re-create the magic of the live performances, with her intensely moving but restrained delivery and her satin-and-smoke allure. Behind her ear she wore "the lascivious gardenias," in the words of writer Elizabeth Hardwick, who went on to describe "the laugh, the marvelous teeth and the splendid head, archaic, as if washed up from the Aegean."

Holiday's early life in Baltimore was a grim one. Deprived of a basic education and a father's love and support—Clarence Holiday, a guitarist with Fletcher Henderson's orchestra, left soon after the baby girl was born—little Eleanora Fagan scrubbed the large marble steps of the city's better homes for nickels to help feed the family. She was six years old. While her mother Sadie sought work in other cities, the child was physically abused while staying with her cousin Ida, whose household included Ida's two children and her grandparents and great-grandmother. When, at age ten, Eleanora was raped, her attacker was given a five-year sentence—and she was put in a reformatory for, as the judge said, enticing him. Four years later, after she joined her mother in New York, she was briefly jailed for prostitution. Renaming herself Billie, after her favorite movie star, Billie Dove, she began running errands for a local brothel in exchange for the privilege of listening to the madame's parlor Victrola. Her favorite vocalists were Bessie Smith and Louis Armstrong. Later in her career she would comment that she had always yearned to capture "Bessie's sound and Pops's feeling."

At the age of fifteen Billie began singing professionally at Pod's and Jerry's Log Cabin, a noted jazz joint on West 133rd Street in Harlem. Her voice was untrained and she lacked poise, but her genius for evoking a mood was already evident when, so the story goes, her audition moved the patrons to tears. She was hired on the spot, and she took in a hundred dollars in tips her first night. In November 1933, she was discovered by the well-known talent scout and record producer John Hammond, who paired Holiday with Benny Goodman's band for her first recording dates. Hastily produced, these discs are less than first rate, but gathering the aristocracy of jazz—greats like Count Basie, Duke Ellington, Chick Webb, Buck Clayton, and Freddie Green—they form the first permanent treasury of Holiday's music. Hammond also supervised her subsequent studio sessions, under the direction of Holiday's arranger and bandleader, pianist Teddy Wilson, until 1942. One of the instrumentalists who made these recordings memorable was saxophonist Lester Young, with whom Holiday established an instant and serendipitous rapport that was to have a major impact on the development of jazz. Prez and Lady Day—Young had originally given this sobriquet to Billie's mother, but it was appropriated by Billie—became musical soul partners, reaching new creative heights together.

Chafing at racial affronts—once, with Count Basie in Detroit, she had been forced to wear dark greasepaint because she looked "too white"—Holiday became difficult, in later years acquiring a reputation for contentiousness and artistic arrogance. It was probably while touring with Artie Shaw in 1938 that some of the troubles started. Holiday, the first black vocalist to perform with a major white orchestra, was constantly harassed on the road. Refused service in restaurants and access to toilets throughout the South, the singer tired of cooperating and eventually had a falling out with Shaw. She was, she said, weary of breakfast, lunch, and dinner turning into "a major NAACP-type production." A haunting ballad about southern lynchings, "Strange Fruit," became Holiday's personal anthem of protest against racism.

Introduced to heroin by her first husband, by the mid-forties Holiday was a confirmed addict with a five-hundred-dollar-a-week habit. In the devastating period that followed, she fell into a pattern of self-destructiveness and abusive relationships, dulling the pain and further damaging her body with drink. Arrested for drug possession in 1947, she served a year at a federal facility in West Virginia, working in the kitchens and feeding the prison-farm pigs. Other arrests followed. She died in a hospital bed with police posted outside her door. Attendants found $750 taped to her leg, the extent of her estate.

Though drugs and alcohol changed Holiday's voice, they did not destroy it. Pointing to the matured sounds and slow renditions of her later work as those of a wounded but resilient artistic spirit, critics raise the possibility of enjoying and paying homage to two Billies: the older, wearier, and more valiant Holiday, pushing her faltering voice to the edge, and the younger, sexier-sounding Holiday, full of irony and wit. Both were unique, and devastating, in their expressiveness. Both were incomparably and profoundly hip.

VLADIMIR HOROWITZ

AUDIENCES WERE ENTHRALLED by his extraordinary technical skill, his interpretation of the music itself, and the emotion he coaxed from the keyboard. Vladimir Horowitz was the century's greatest and most popular virtuoso.

Born portentously on Music Street in Kiev, Horowitz was trained in the Ukraine by his amateur-musician mother and by the piano maestro Felix Blumenfeld at the Kiev Conservatory. The young keyboardist dreamed originally of becoming a composer, sleeping with the score of *Götterdämmerung* under his pillow. But in the 1917 Russian Revolution his bourgeois family's possessions were seized by the Bolsheviks and the teenager was forced to the concert stage. There, he quickly established himself as a prodigy. Given permission to leave Russia to study in Germany in 1925, young Horowitz stuffed his shoes with the equivalent of five thousand American dollars and prayed that the Soviet border guards wouldn't realize he was never coming back. Horowitz later said that the guards examined his papers and commented, "Do not please forget your motherland."

For the next two years, Horowitz dazzled audiences in the capitals of Europe with his pyrotechnic performances. In 1928, he made his American debut at Carnegie Hall, performing Tchaikovsky's B-flat Minor Concerto under the baton of Sir Thomas Beecham. So funereal was Beecham's beat that the volatile Horowitz, feeling the audience grow restless, took off in the finale with Beecham and the rest of the New York Philharmonic in astonished pursuit. Fingers flying at breakneck tempo, the headstrong virtuoso beat the orchestra to the finish line by several measures, playing, as he later said, "louder, faster, and more notes than Tchaikovsky wrote." The audience and the critics hailed him as a genius. Horowitz's new style of pianistic bravura was meant to delight the listener first and foremost.

Horowitz was not to everyone's taste; some thought him egomaniacal, bombastic, and wrongly indifferent to the music as written. In a calmly constructed appraisal that demolished Horowitz, the American composer and critic Virgil Thomson left no doubt that he found the musician self-indulgent. Despite these criticisms, Horowitz's style and interpretation were a model to generations of pianists who strove—often unsuccessfully—to play as Horowitz played. Like many artists, Horowitz himself was not quite sure how he managed to do what he did. Of his ability to play swiftly and with delicate gradations of volume, he said simply, "It was there from the beginning." He was regarded as the master of technique, but in fact his technique was highly idiosyncratic. He played with his hands held flat and his seat positioned low.

His personal life was no more conventional than his art. Throughout his stormy fifty-six-year marriage to Arturo Toscanini's daughter, Wanda, whom he married in 1933, Horowitz routinely betrayed her with other men. He was a man of habit: He favored natty bow ties, ate Dover sole virtually every day of his adult life, and insisted that he perform publicly only at four o'clock on Sunday afternoons. His first recording in 1928 was a hit on the pop charts, and he made music business history by establishing his right to stop a pressing of one of his records—a veto power the exacting artist exercised more than once. His career was marked by musical controversy, and by his prolonged retirement inspired either by severe emotional problems or by simple indolence, depending on whether one believes the master's biographers or the master.

Unlike his father-in-law, Toscanini, who was content primarily with the offerings of the late Romantics, Horowitz ventured into more modern realms. Never forsaking Liszt or Chopin, he added Scriabin, Prokofiev, Kabalevsky, and Schumann to his vast repertoire, which also included an excerpt from *Carmen* and even his own transcription of John Philip Sousa's *The Stars and Stripes Forever*—so grateful was Horowitz to be an American (he became a citizen in 1944). He managed to excel in everything he attempted, whether it was filling an auditorium (he never played to an unsold seat), or staging a triumphant comeback in 1965—when, after a twelve-year hiatus, he played (at four o'clock in the afternoon, to be sure) for a rapturous Carnegie Hall audience. There seemed to be no mountain left to climb for this creatively fearless but socially shy émigré.

Finally, in 1986, the glasnost initiated by Soviet general secretary Mikhail Gorbachev enabled the eighty-two-year-old pianist finally to heed the never forgotten plea of that anonymous Soviet guard and return to Mother Russia at long last. In the music-loving country of his birth, Horowitz was treated as royalty, his return triumphant. Many of the tearful concertgoers who attended his emotion-laden concert at the Moscow Conservatory's Great Hall or a second performance in Leningrad had waited all night to procure tickets; in Moscow, a small but cheerful scuffle ensued as some ticketless students desperately pushed their way into the hall. Horowitz's playing, as always, enthralled his listeners. "It was," wrote one critic, "a kind of religious experience."

Horowitz died three years later. He was buried in the Toscanini plot in Italy, a citizen of the piano—a country whose limits, he proved, were almost boundless.

IBARRURI

DOLORES

FOR HER NATIVE SPAIN, suffering through a brutal civil war, Dolores Ibarruri (aka La Pasionaria) was the incarnation of the anti-Franco, pro-Republican cause. Fiery heroine of the battle-field and hearth, Mother Courage to the downtrodden, Dolores Ibárruri inspired her beleaguered comrades with a fierce orato-ry matched by her bravery. Her famous 1936 call to arms on the radio station in Madrid, "It is better to die on your feet than to live on your knees!" was followed by what became the rally-ing cry of the anti-Franco forces: *"¡No pasarán!"* ("They shall not pass.") A dedicated Communist revolutionary, La Pasionaria was abhorred and vilified by her right-wing nationalist oppo-nents. Later her unwavering support of Stalin would earn her a reputation—and not only from the Fascists—as a vicious oppor-tunist. When the Fascists emerged victorious in 1939, she fled first to Paris, then to Moscow, where she remained as a model comrade-in-waiting to a succession of Soviet leaders until a much publicized homecoming in 1977.

A loyal apologist for international communism throughout her adult life, Ibárruri became radicalized at a very early age. Born in 1895 of Basque and Castilian heritage in the northern Spanish mining province of Vizcaya, Dolores Gómez Ibárruri was the eighth of eleven children (of whom only eight survived). The region's harsh economic realities, punctuated by frequent violent strikes, were mirrored in her family's starvation-level existence. Everyone in the household except Dolores worked in the extremely dangerous open-pit mines. The young girl stayed in school, sup-ported by her parents' desire to see her become a teacher. But the family's deepening poverty finally drove the frail teenager into work as a servant, seamstress, and fish vendor. At the age of twenty she married Julián Ruiz, a miner and activist in the underground social-ist movement, who gave her books on Marx and Lenin. Suddenly, she wrote later, she realized that, with socialism as her guide, life need not be "a swamp"—it could be "a battlefield," and she would be one of its dedicated soldiers. Her Catholic faith ebbing, Ibárruri needed all the idealism she could muster. Her husband, frequently jailed for his trade-union activities, was no breadwinner, and as a result of their poverty, she laid to rest four of her six children because they lacked money for medicine.

Not long after the Russian Revolution, Ibárruri became "La Pasionaria," a pen name she signed to an editorial in *El Minero Vizcaíno* during Passion Week. In 1920 she joined the Basque Communist party, and the following year she was a delegate to the national party's founding congress. Moving to Madrid in 1931, after the declaration of the republic, she became an edi-tor of the party newspaper, *Worker's World,* and took charge of women's activities for the Politburo. Ibárruri lived and breathed her radicalism, often suffering imprisonment. She sent her two children, who had had to live with her on the streets, to a spe-cial school in Moscow, a common practice for activists who lived outside Russia. Now, as a member of the Spanish Communist party's Central Committee and a deputy from Asturias in the Spanish parliament, she had formidable national influence. So powerful was she, some historians have argued, that her par-liamentary diatribes against the monarchist leader José Calvo Sotelo may have caused his assassination, an event that signaled the beginning of the Civil War.

During the ensuing conflict, La Pasionaria ascended to global, and ultimately historical, prominence. Her image was plastered on the walls of the capital, and her fever-pitched broadcasts helped to swell the ranks of the Republican army and galvanize mass patriotic rallies. She traveled throughout Europe begging for aid, and she hounded the Russians for increased assistance. During the extended Battle of Madrid, when the government relocated to Valencia, she dug trenches, organized a Communist militia, built barricades, and gathered more than 100,000 women to run food and medical facilities. La Pasionaria was also instrumental in encouraging the enlist-ment of some 40,000 foreigners into the International Brigades, cadres of volunteers who fought alongside her coun-trymen. She welcomed them as allies against the spread of worldwide fascism and its assault on democracy.

In 1939, just before the republic was crushed, La Pasionaria made her escape to Russia, where she spent World War II broadcasting pro-Soviet and anti-Franco propaganda. She stayed there almost forty years, becoming an often imper-iled spokeswoman for the Comintern while traveling abroad. Her efforts kept a "pure" Communist flame alive in a Fascist-ruled but greatly changing Spain. Throughout her exile, except for a protest over the 1968 Soviet invasion of Prague, La Pasionaria was a staunch defender of hard-line communism. Eternally grateful for Stalin's "unconditional aid" to the Republican side of the Civil War, she considered him the great-est Communist she had ever known, turning a blind eye to his excesses. Fellow exiles, meanwhile, embittered by the hard life they had endured, criticized "La Pensionaria" for the special treatment she enjoyed from her Russian hosts.

In 1977, two years after Generalissimo Franco died, how-ever, she returned to her native soil, where she was elected to Parliament. *"Sí, sí, sí, Dolores esta aquí,"* the welcoming throngs chanted when the eighty-two-year-old woman arrived. Black-clad, stooped by age, but still irrefutably imperious and charismatic, La Pasionaria brought to mind her own farewell to the International Brigades in Barcelona after they were withdrawn in November of 1938: "You are history. You are legend. We shall not forget you."

MICHAEL JACKSON

A CONSUMMATE SINGER and dancer, Michael Jackson has been performing since he was a mere five years old. He and his brothers made memorable contributions to the soul and dance music of the seventies. On his own, though, he quickly surpassed the achievements of the Jackson Five and managed with only a handful of solo recordings to more than earn his title as the King of Pop. Through his records and videos, he has affected the way we sing, the way we dance, and the very way we define popular music.

Jackson was born to a former musician who labored in the steel mills of Gary, Indiana, and had grand ambitions for his nine children, five of whom formed the Jackson Five. Raised in the life of the touring musician, and exposed early to the intricacies of the R & B music business, the musical group were discovered in 1968 by vocalist Gladys Knight at a talent contest at Harlem's famous Apollo Theater. That same year, they signed a Motown recording contract, left Indiana, and moved with their family to Encino, California. Their first single, "I Want You Back" (1969), was an instant sensation, and Michael became the group's involuntary star. They quickly followed up with such hits as "I'll Be There" and "ABC" in 1970.

In the later seventies, having outgrown a kiddie image that even resulted in their own cartoon show, the group maintained moderate popularity, while Michael began to venture out on his own. He recorded a few solo singles, most notably the theme song to the movie Ben in 1972. By the end of the decade, he was trying his hand at acting, appearing as the Scarecrow in The Wiz (1978), a black adaptation of The Wizard of Oz. On the set, Michael met and befriended legendary musician and producer Quincy Jones, who was arranging the score for the film. When he recorded his first solo album, Quincy took the role of producer. The result, Off the Wall (1979), was a critical and commercial success, with such hits as "Don't Stop 'til You Get Enough" and "Rock With You" reaching number one on the pop and R & B charts. A perfectionist, Jackson was still disappointed with the level of success the album achieved. His next project would not disappoint.

In 1982, Jackson released Thriller, which went on to earn eight Grammy's and sell over forty-eight million copies. Its staggering success was the result of pitch-perfect musicianship and shrewd global marketing. The chart topping singles the album produced—a string of hits that began with his duet with Paul McCartney, "The Girl Is Mine," in 1982 and wouldn't stop until two years later—are still model examples of the pop song form; but Jackson was also one of the few artists to fully realize the potential of music videos to increase his exposure. Instead of treating videos as strictly promotional tools for his records, he put his songs in service to them. The videos for "Billie Jean," "Beat It," and especially the title track—a twenty-minute piece that cost a then-astronomical sum of one million dollars to make—were mini-movies, the songs soundtracks to those movies, and his fans could not get enough of them. Jackson had single-handedly transformed the video business, making it a necessary—even vita—part of the music industry. Jackson added to his exposure by signing a lucrative endorsement deal with Pepsi-Cola and co-writing the song "We Are the World" (1985) to benefit U.S.A. for Africa. His rise in the charts and the world's estimation seemed endless.

The follow-up to Thriller, Bad (1987) produced another string of hits—four of them reaching number one—and sold twenty-five million copies, but even such incredible numbers seemed disappointing in light of its predecessor. The sensation seemed on the wane, and with the accompanying lull came public scrutiny. Although he published a successful autobiography in 1988—named Moonwalk, after the highly-stylized dance move he created—and signed a reported one-billion-dollar deal with Sony Records in 1991, the papers seemed more interested in his personal travails. He continued to record with a host of talented artists, but details concerning his numerous plastic surgeries, his sleeping habits, his unsuccessful attempt to buy the remains of the Elephant Man and his successful attempt to purchase the rights to the Beatles song catalog—a move that caused a rift between Jackson and Paul McCartney, who had also bid for them—took precedence over news of his musical ventures. His 1991 album, Dangerous, failed to sell as well as his previous efforts, despite such number one hits as "Black and White."

In 1993, Jackson came under intense fire from the press. Allegations surfaced that the entertainer had been seducing young boys, and a grand jury was impaneled to investigate him. Jackson emphatically denied the charges, and, in the midst of the investigation, embarked on a world tour that was plagued by illness. By 1994, one of the civil cases brought against him was settled out of court, but the effects of the accusations lingered for the singer.

Further into the nineties, the media's focus on Jackson's personal eccentricities remained steady. In 1994, he announced suddenly that he had wed Elvis Presley's daughter, Lisa Marie—a marriage that, despite claims of early happiness, ended only two years later, when Presley left him as he lay in a hospital bed, recovering from exhaustion between concerts. Jackson then married his dermatologist's nurse, Debbie Rowe, who was pregnant with his child.

By the late nineties, the tremendous energy and talent Michael Jackson had shared with his fans was in danger of being eclipsed by the focus on his public and private behavior—although, just as he taught us to sing and dance, he also seems to have taught us something about the very notion of celebrity at the end of this century. Regardless, the mark he has left on American popular music is indelible.

MICK JAGGER

HE WAS THE MAN for whom the phrase "sex, drugs, and rock 'n roll" might have been invented, a performer who has lived a life as outsized and hedonistic as his fans demanded. But in a business where a band's lifespan is usually a few years, Mick Jagger, with his group, the Rolling Stones, has been recording and performing music for well over three decades. As lead vocalist, Jagger has been the mouth of the Stones, both figuratively and literally (his tongue and famous full lips became the model for the band's logo), while leading the phenomenon of rock music to the jagged edge.

Michael Phillip Jagger was the elder of two sons born into a comfortable existence in Dartford, Kent, to physical education instructor Joe Jagger and his wife Eva. As a youngster, Jagger had a dominant personality and was an eager student, spending his evenings and weekends in the family garden listening to blues records and aping the vocals of Muddy Waters, Bo Diddley, and Chuck Berry as neighbors complained.

In 1962 he received a grant to attend the London School of Economics, but he retained his obsession with American music, still singing in "fab" underground clubs. Two years earlier, in 1960, he had had a fortuitous meeting with guitarist Keith Richard (later changed to Richards), an old grammar school mate who would become his life-long songwriting collaborator and emotional sparring partner. Joining forces with guitarist Brian Jones, bassist Bill Wyman, and drummer Charlie Watts, Jagger and Richard played around small venues for a year before breaking into the mainstream, performing sets that mixed original tunes with covers of their favorite R & B songs.

The band's earliest hits—many of them covers—were steeped in the R & B tradition that Jagger, Richards, and Jones adored, but the Jagger and Richards combination—like that of Lennon and McCartney for the Beatles—would soon provide the band with a wealth of hits, starting in 1965 with "(I Can't Get No) Satisfaction." In no time, the Stones evolved from one R & B quintet among many to a worldwide sensation, thrilling their fans and terrifying their fans' parents. Their intentions were clear: "The Beatles want to hold your hand," observed journalist Tom Wolfe, "the Stones want to burn your town."

The group's stature rose to astonishing heights through the rest of the sixties, as the ever-practical Jagger—he kept up his enrollment at the London School of Economics for two years while the Stones were being formed—guided the group's finances. Had the band stopped recording in 1970, the songs they released would have been enough to make them legendary: "Get Off My Cloud" and "19th Nervous Breakdown" in 1965; ""Paint It Black" and "Mother's Little Helper" in 1966; "Let's Spend the Night Together" in 1967; "Jumpin' Jack Flash" and "Street Fighting Man" in 1968; "Honky Tonk Women" in 1969. But of course they didn't stop.

They did, however, have their setbacks. In 1967, Jagger was arrested for drug possession. The ordeal enhanced his carefully cultivated "outlaw" image—police found his girlfriend, singer Marianne Faithfull, wrapped in a rug naked—but it took its toll nonetheless. As well, the band had its musical missteps, most notably the psychadelic *Their Satanic Majesties' Request* (1967). The end of the decade represented both the highest and the lowest for Jagger and the band. In 1969, they released their brilliant album *Let It Bleed,* but later that year the exiled Brian Jones was found dead in his swimming pool. He was replaced by Mick Taylor and the Stones' tour that year ended with a free concert in Altamont, California, during which a security guard (and member of the Hells Angels) stabbed a fan to death. The sixties ground to a symbolic halt.

Jagger's first foray outside the band followed soon after, with his dual-sexed film role in *Performance* (1970). However, he was soon fronting his band again, and the early seventies marked the release of their career-defining albums, the raw and vibrant *Sticky Fingers* (1971) and *Exile on Main Street* (1972), which many considered the band's masterpiece. Toward the end of the seventies, albums like *Some Girls,* which managed somehow to exhibit both punk and disco characteristics, proved that the Stones still had fire, and that Jagger was as dynamic as ever. And the tours started getting bigger: by the time Ron Wood replaced Mick Taylor in 1975, the band had already built a reputation for their extravagant, almost mythic world tours, a trend that would reach its most commercial heights with the tours supporting *Steel Wheels* in 1989 and *Bridges to Babylon* in 1997.

In the mid-eighties, Jagger released his first solo album, *She's the Boss* (1985). It was followed by the less successful *Primitive Cool* (1987) and *Wandering Spirit* (1993). While his solo efforts enjoyed modest success, and achieved moments of pop splendor, to fans, the voice just wasn't the same without the back-up of his legendary rhythm section (other Stones' solo projects have not fared much better).

Still, Jagger enjoyed the perks of rock stardom—the private jets, the innumerable girlfriends, the palatial homes and beautiful wives (the first, Bianca de Macias, whom he divorced in 1979; the second, Jerry Hall, the mother of four of his six children)—even if, at age 50, the dressing rooms that had once reeked of pot and patchouli, began, journalists joked, to smell instead of Ben-Gay. The albums the Stones released in the eighties and nineties weren't as noteworthy as their classic work from decades past, but it scarcely mattered. Crowds gladly paid exorbitant ticket prices to see the electrifying Jagger belt out old and new favorites in concert. It seemed a small price to pay to see the man and the band that virtually defined rock music.

JIANG QING

(MADAME MAO)

IF MAO ZEDONG WAS China's mythical dragon—a fierce and towering monster who blew away ancient feudal mists with his fiery blend of Marxism and nationalism—his last wife, the cruel and prodigiously clever Jiang Qing, was his perfect mate. Called Li Jin, she met Mao, twenty years her senior, in 1937, in his military camp at Yenan, where she had fled after the Japanese occupation of Shanghai. The isolated caves that served as headquarters for the Chinese Communist Party (CCP) were also the staging area for Mao's insurgent forces, which were temporarily allied with Chiang Kai-shek's Kuomintang against the invading Japanese. Mao was smitten with the actress-turned-activist, who sat in the front row at his lectures. In a move that infuriated the influential comrades who had accompanied him on the historic Long March of 1934–35, he rejected his third wife, a seasoned veteran of that grueling journey, and took up with the former "Jade girl" (the name for very attractive actresses) whom he renamed Jiang Qing, or River Azure, an allusion to a line of poetry. As part of the agreement by which the party allowed its leader to marry his now pregnant mistress, they stipulated that she be forbidden to participate in political activity, and that the two of them never appear in public as husband and wife—in essence, reducing her to concubine status.

Born Li Yu-Ho to a violent father and a mother whose position as a domestic servant amounted to little more than prostitution, Jiang Qing's childhood was chaotic. Leaving her stormy working-class home in Shandong province at age fifteen, she began classes at the Shandong Provincial Experimental Art Theater. Her studies in opera were followed by small stage roles, after which she broke into film, making small waves with her acting abilities. Aided by her sensual and flirtatious charm, Qing made even larger ones in the bohemian, leftist circles of glittering Shanghai. Her life began to take on the humorous aspects of a Moliére farce, as lovers and husbands came and went. If she had not been forced to leave when the Japanese invaded, the gossip provoked by her antics might well eventually have driven her out.

Qing kept her promise to stay out of politics for more than twenty-five years, though because of her theatrical background, she was involved in minor cultural works. In 1963, however, her husband gave her a liberating directive to reform the country's arts along more ideologically correct lines; her goal was to expunge "revisionist" thought and bourgeois romanticism from traditional Chinese plays, operas, and ballets in order to create an art form for the masses. Under her direction a new and startling kind of ballerina appeared in Beijing's theaters, a proletarian one wearing a uniform and carrying a gun. In the mid-sixties, however, she stepped from behind the curtain and made her grab for power in earnest. Appointed deputy chief of the Cultural Revolution Group, an autonomous organization that grew out of the party's Great Proletarian Cultural Revolution program and reported directly to the CCP, she now had access to the Red Guards, Mao's youthful thought police. In the decade to follow, a vengeful and hard-edged Qing used her authority to purge the party—and the nation—of all doctrinal impurity and, in the process, to persecute old enemies, especially those who had opposed her marriage to Mao. As one of the "Gang of Four"—as she and her cohorts came to be known—she supervised the infamous cultural revolution and, in so doing, was directly or indirectly responsible for the torture, starvation, banishment, suppression, and imprisonment of thousands of innocent people. For ten years Red Guards under her aegis roamed the land, reviling and terrorizing not only China's intellectual elite but also faithful revolutionaries and the many others who were unfortunate enough to wander into their path. Mao's goals—a more decentralized government, new blood for the party, and the transformation of rural China—were accomplished, but in one of the most destructive periods in modern Chinese history.

Less than four weeks after Mao's death, a bespectacled and gray Jiang Qing was arrested as an enemy of the state. She was accused of plotting with her secret clique to subvert the government while Mao lay dying and of causing the illegal execution of opponents too numerous to estimate. Qing's Gang of Four was also charged with exterminating more than thirty-four thousand victims and falsely accusing 700,000 more.

By turns petulant, balefully silent, and sarcastic, the arrogant sixty-six-year-old widow stood her ground, refusing to comply with the tradition of pleading guilty. "Deng Xiaoping is a traitor and a fascist!" she shouted, taking a stand against the most powerful of her enemies among the newly appointed party leaders. Rigidly defiant throughout her carefully orchestrated, highly visible trial, Jiang Qing emphasized that her "crimes" could not be separated from the policies of the man to whom she had dedicated her life. "I was Chairman Mao's dog," she insisted. "When he said bite, I bit." She remained in control until the end, when her death sentence was commuted to life imprisonment, successfully denying her adversaries the satisfaction of the punishment they were too intimidated to carry out. After years of incarceration, hunger strikes, continuing battles with cancer of the larynx and esophagus, and severe depression, Jiang Qing hanged herself from a prison bed frame. A friend to conspiracy during her trip up the party ladder, Qing eventually became the victim of the very people with whom she had colluded.

ELTON JOHN

AFTER ALMOST THIRTY YEARS in the limelight, British singer, pianist and composer Elton John still holds splendid sway over the camp wing of rock and' roll, having churned out hits like "Crocodile Rock" (1972), "Daniel" (1973), and "Don't Let the Sun Go Down on Me" (1974), as rapidly as he changed his goofy glasses. Rising above his faint-of-heart competitors with ever more outlandish costumes and an ever more excessive lifestyle, Captain Fantastic earned standing ovations in bad times and good. While sales from such albums as *Honky Chateau* (1972), *Goodbye Yellow Brick Road* (1973), and *Jump Up* (1982) soared in the seventies and early eighties, drug and alcohol addiction, rages, suicide attempts, and tabloid rumors of his involvement with male prostitutes brought him, in the late eighties, to a moment of choice. He chose to reform his life and, against all odds, Elton John orchestrated his own salvation, even becoming a knight of the realm in 1998.

His beginnings were suburban and, to hear him tell, rather sad. Born Reginald Kenneth Dwight in Pinner, Middlesex, to a squadron leader in the Royal Air Force and his wife, young Reg was terrified of his withholding father and, at two hundred pounds, seriously overweight. His mother, Sheila, was understanding and supportive of her prodigy son, who began playing the piano by ear at age four. It was she, in fact, who bought him his first rock and roll records. In 1958, two years after the King reached the top of the charts with "Heartbreak Hotel," she registered Reg for Saturday studies at the Royal Academy of Music. He was eleven.

In 1964, the seventeen-year-old left school, a full-time music career in mind. He knocked about for a time, working days as a messenger and evenings playing piano in a pub. Drifting in and out of several local bands, he took up permanently with Bluesology, a group which backed up Long John Baldry. (When he changed the name he so detested, he picked up "John" from blues singer Baldry and "Elton" from saxophonist Elton Dean.) In 1967 he met his longtime collaborator, Bernie Taupin, through a Liberty Records advertisement for musical talent, and the two cut a demo. In a modus operandi that the pair would carry on for many years, Elton provided the tunes and Taupin the lyrics.

Liberty passed on the duo, but Dick James, a music publishing impresario who had played a part in the Beatles phenomenon put them under contract. Their efforts to write middle-of-the-road pop fizzled, however, and the two were forced to concentrate on their individual strengths. For Taupin it was poetic sentiment, though it veered occasionally to the overwrought; for Elton, it was a strong, adaptable voice that occasionally incorporated too many different styles. But persistence was rewarded with the 1969 hit "Lady Samantha" and the low-budget album *Empty Sky*. The latter set the stage for the lavishly produced album, *Elton John*, which featured two winning singles—"Your Song" and "Border Song." Artfully composed, skillfully arranged and full of Elton's soon-to-be- signature crescendos, they received much attention on both sides of the Atlantic. While the album was enjoying considerable airplay, his promoters were begging their stage-phobic client to perform live. Grudgingly, he agreed. That summer—trimmed down, dressed in the most eccentric clothes he could get his hands on, and accompanied by his new band—he opened at the Troubador. After his leaping finale, the jaded Los Angeles club erupted in cheers.

The album *Tumbleweed Connection* followed *Elton John* up the charts and was, in turn, followed by another hit album, *Madman Across the Water*. Released at the end of 1971, it meant stardom for the singer-songwriter who had at last managed to define an experimental, but now recognizable, sound. In 1973, Elton brought his sound to new levels of success with the double album *Goodbye Yellow Brick Road,* which not only included the title track, but a string of other hits, including "Candle in the Wind." "Bennie and the Jets," and "Saturday Night's All Right for Fighting." It would prove a defining album of his career—alongside *Rock of the Westies* and *Caption Fantastic and the Brown Dirt Band* (both 1975)—helping to secure his staus as the quintessential pop performer of the decade. In 1976, three years after starting his own label, Rocket Records, Elton announced he was bisexual.

The eighties were not as kind to Elton, despite the fact that he continued to hit the charts with singles like "I'm Still Standing" (1983), "I Guess That's Why They Call It The Blues" (1984), and "I Don't Wanna Go On With You Like That" (1988). The British scandal sheets had a field day with his marriage in 1984 to his onetime recording engineer, Renate Blauel, and with allegations linking him to male hustlers. Although the so-called "rent-boy" scandal was resolved in Elton's favor—the offending newspaper agreed to pay him a million pound out-of-court settlement—the singer was headed on a downward spiral. Hard hit by violent mood swings, strung out on drugs and alcohol, and bulimic, he finally, at the behest of his lover, checked into a rehab facility. The intervention, he admitted, came not a moment too soon.

In the nineties, a rehabilitated Elton John refined his sound for hits like "Sacrifice" (1990) and "The Way You Look Tonight" (1997), while playing sellout stadium tours with fellow piano man Billy Joel and establishing his own AIDS foundation. The essence of Elton's new sound was his Grammy-Winning hit "Can You Feel the Love Tonight," the theme song for the 1994 Disney film *The Lion King*. The single sold an astonishing seven million copies, a feat topped in 1997 when he rerecorded his classic "Candle in the Wind" for the late Princess Diana. "It's hers," he said, and pledged all income from its sales—around fifty million dollars to date—to the Diana Princess of Wales Memorial Fund.

POPE JOHN XXIII

WHEN HIS SWISS GUARDS remonstrated with him about allowing common folk to watch him walking in the Vatican gardens, Angelo Roncalli, Pope John XXIII, gently replied, "Why? I am not doing anything scandalous." That was, and is, a matter of opinion. To many within and without the Catholic Church, John—who at age seventy-seven was elected by the College of Cardinals as a compromise candidate too old to enjoy a long reign and have a lasting effect on the course of Roman Catholicism—initiated the most sweeping reforms the church had seen since the Renaissance. The architect of an ecumenical movement seeking to unite all Christians and to reconcile them with the world's other great religions, he was the mastermind behind Vatican II, the 1962 convocation of the world's Catholic leaders that issued sixteen ecclesiastical reforms (including, most saliently, the ruling that the mass need not be performed entirely in Latin) before it ended in 1965. John answered the outcry from conservatives with characteristic forbearance and good humor. "Woe to you if all men speak well of you," he once told a colleague. Yet this was a man of whom most spoke only words of love and admiration.

Born in 1881 in the Italian village of Sotto il Monti, in the Bergamo region, Roncalli was the son of an impecunious farmer. "In Italy," the pope once reminisced, "there are three ways a man can be ruined: women, gambling, and farming. My father chose the most boring of the three." No Franciscan, Roncalli was a worldly priest who served as a military chaplain in World War I, and whose *joie de vivre* and Rabelaisian love of food earned him a reputation as *una buona forchetta*—"a good fork." Even as pope, he took time from a crushing schedule to carefully instruct the Vatican chefs in exactly which hills produced the best Parmesan cheese for the papal pasta. But the rotund and good-humored Roncalli was a shrewd politician. During World War II, as a papal diplomat in Turkey, he was instrumental in helping to save thousands of Jews fleeing Nazi persecution, including a shipload of children. After the war, as papal nuncio to France, he cleverly—and some thought cynically—parried Charles de Gaulle's righteous demand that the Vatican remove collaborationist bishops by laboriously studying individual cases until, in the coolness of time, only three of about thirty alleged Vichyites were purged.

Roncalli might simply have risen through the ranks like a good bureaucrat, relying on his fiscal and statesmanlike savvy to raise funds and avoid trouble until he ended his days in the comfortable ecclesiastical post of Cardinal Prince. But on October 28, 1958, at a critical time in church and human affairs, Angelo Cardinal Roncalli was elected pope and found himself in a unique position to abandon petty politics and exercise power in pursuit of his highest ideals. He did so forcefully, announcing the themes of his pontificate as "peace and unity" and calling for a great ecumenical council to include the "separated brethren" of the Anglican and Eastern Rite churches. In the estimation of his critics, John's vision, essentially one in which the brethren were again received into the Catholic fold, was flawed in that it included such coreligionists in the council as observers only, not participants. Conversely, in 1961, John sent Catholic observers for the first time to the general assembly of the World Council of Churches, and established the Secretariat for Promoting Christian Unity.

Pope John XXIII's encyclicals reflected his liberal views. In 1961, he issued *Mater et Magistra,* in which he endorsed labor unions, approved some aspects of the welfare state, and, perhaps recalling his struggling-farmer father, called for agricultural reform. In 1963, he authored the great encyclical *Pacem in Terris,* which, in demanding an end to the Cold War, was addressed not only to the Catholic faithful but to all humankind. It gave a tentative nod to socialism, but only because John desired a concordat with hostile governments that would allow the church to exercise more influence in the elevation of the individual and not the state.

The burden of bringing the church into line with the changing world was a heavy one. When he was alone at night, John often brooded upon a problem, wondering, "What would the pope do in such a case?"—only to realize that he *was* the pope. He may have joked like a simple man, but he was as wily as a fox. He once told the visiting editor of *Pravda,* "You say you are an atheist, but surely you will accept an old man's blessing for your children." Cultivating popular support for his innovations by whirlwind tours of hospitals, schools, and shrines, he earned the sobriquet "Johnnie Walker." Yet by May 1963, his punishing pace had caused the gourmand, now eighty-one years old, to suffer from a condition that made it impossible for him to eat. His iron constitution, however, kept the pontiff lucid through much of an agonizing decline. Brief in time but long in influence, his reign ended with his death on June 3, 1963. Leaving behind a a Vatican Council in progress and a whole world in mourning, John XXIII also inadvertently bequeathed the possibility of a religious schism before the end of the century, a rupture rooted in the deep divisions among his flock over the scope and pace of changes that had proved far more radical than perhaps even he had ever foreseen.

JORDAN

MICHAEL

FOR THE PAST TWO decades his face has been everywhere—on billboards, in magazines, in advertisements, and especially on television; his body, lean and sculpted, has most often been seen clad in scarlet and black, flying through the air toward a basketball hoop. Rich beyond dreams, adored by millions around the globe, Michael Jeffrey Jordan is the epitome of the successful athlete-entertainer. As a prodigiously gifted and charismatic player in a highly competitive profession, some might say that he is largely responsible for his sport's incredible growth in popularity around the world. His ability to soar high through the air and to appear to change direction in midflight earned him the nickname of "Air Jordan," but he was more than a basketball player. With his jump shots, adroit passes, gravity-defying dunks, defense, and, above all, his dedication to the team, Jordan raised the game of basketball to new heights. His Chicago Bulls, once a weak presence in the National Basketball Association, accomplished the miracle of winning three NBA championships in a row—something the teams of his chief rivals in the modern era, the Celtics of Larry Bird and the Lakers of Magic Johnson, never did. As a corporate spokesperson, the handsome, cheerful, and intelligent Jordan is a man for all seasons, a commercial phenomenon who has improved the fortunes and annual reports of such companies as Coca-Cola, Nike, and Hanes. The effect of a Jordan endorsement on a company's bottom line is so direct that the star's considerable team salary pales beside his annual fees for blessing products. From 1990 to the end of 1997, the highest paid athlete ever earned over $300 million.

Jordan was born in Wilmington, North Carolina, to a family whose members had no particular athletic abilities—no one was even especially tall. Attracted to sports when he was young, he worked extremely hard to achieve skill in both baseball and basketball. Unfortunately, he was too small to make the freshman basketball team at Laney High School and was summarily cut as under-talented from the sophomore squad. When he grew from 5'11" to 6'3" in the summer of his junior year, however, and improved his play, his coach wrangled a spot for Jordan at an all-star summer camp for big college prospects. He excelled at the camp and was recruited by Dean Smith, coach of the University of North Carolina powerhouse. His early play for the university showed his penchant for clutch performance; in the 1982 national championship against Georgetown University, Jordan sank a last-second jump shot to win the NCAA title. His blocking and scoring made him a top candidate for the Olympic team; he joined it and led the United States to the gold medal in 1984.

A college championship and an Olympic gold medal in themselves would constitute a glittering career, but the goal-oriented Jordan had his eye on the National Basketball Association. He wanted the fame and fortune of stardom. In 1984, he left the University of North Carolina to enter the professional draft and was picked third. Jordan's club, the Chicago Bulls, desperately needed to make the play-offs to increase their slumping box-office revenues. Their new star did not disappoint them: He finished the year as the league's third-leading scorer, was chosen Rookie of the Year, and made the All-Star team. The attendance at Bulls games almost doubled, and Chicago was instantly transformed into a big draw on the road.

With his twenty-eight-point scoring average Jordan could not be stopped on the court, but the Bulls could. In the 1985–86 play-offs, a doomed series against Larry Bird's championship-bound Celtics, Jordan scored sixty-three points in one game, inspiring Bird to remark that Jordan might be God in disguise. It was Bird, however, who went on to earn the prize. Jordan and the Bulls would spend another five years in exile, finally winning their first title in 1991 against Magic Johnson's Los Angeles Lakers. The next year they won the title again, and the following year—to the amazement of every basketball fan—they triumphed a third time.

In 1993, Jordan's father was murdered by two drifters. This random horror, coupled with rumors about the athlete's attitude and gambling habits, convinced Jordan that he had nothing left to prove. In a belated gesture to his father—who thought that Jordan might make a pretty good baseball player—the court legend became a minor-leaguer for the Chicago White Sox. Reports were that he couldn't hit a curve-ball. He couldn't. Then in a surprising change of heart, Jordan returned in good form to the Bulls late in the 1994–95 season, proving that no one could count him out.

Then he did something that no one had ever done before in basketball: he came out of retirement and won a championship. His 1995–96 Chicago Bulls not only won the crown, they trounced their opponents in the regular season, winning a record seventy-two games, while Jordan won the scoring title—again. The accomplishment led to a thirty-million-dollar contract that assured his place as the highest-paid player in the league. Not confining himself to earning money on the court, he made a movie, animation and live-action hybrid Space Jam (1996), and came out with an eponymous cologne. A new model of his Nike "Air Jordans" debuted the following year, causing long lines at shoe stores across the country. As the century draws to a close, Jordan's famous leaps hover closer to Earth, and he drives a bit less to the hoop. But he remains the sole possessor of the title The Greatest Basketball Player in History.

JAMES JOYCE

IF COMPLEXITY OF PERSONALITY nourishes creativity, then Dublin's most famous literary vagabond was a glutton at art's table. Coldly aloof, skeptical, and self-centered, James Joyce could also play the jovial fool, initiating impromptu songfests and spending money like a sailor on shore leave. Yet the Irish expatriate, whose breezy self-assurance about his place in literary history often put people off, worked like a demon for that honor, eventually reinventing the modern novel. During years of frustrating rejection and penury, Joyce persevered through countless revisions of his works, even as he endured agonizing recoveries from ten separate eye operations.

The author's childhood, shadowed by his family's diminishing fortunes and the tantrums of his extravagant father, seemed to have steeled him against adversity. A mitigating force was his handsome mother, Mary, a talented pianist who carefully schooled her ten surviving children in the precepts of her own devout Catholicism. Trained for the priesthood in Ireland's finest Jesuit schools, Joyce drifted away from the church as he grew older, though he once admonished a biographer to refer to him "as a Jesuit." More than thirteen years of training under the most didactic of religious orders, he pointed out, had taught him how "to arrange things in such a way that they become easy to survey and judge." Despite his railings against the church and the Irish culture whose folkloric romanticism he despised, Joyce retained an abiding respect not only for his parents, but for kinship in general. Later, living all over Europe with his carefree Galway wife, Nora Barnacle, and their two children, he was continually sustained by family. He also received lifelong support, both aesthetic and financial, from his brother Stanislaus and from a circle of benefactors who so believed in Joyce's superior talent that they felt honored to support the courtly-mannered writer. When money was lacking, Joyce was never too proud to ask for it; when he had it, he spent it freely on dinners out with Nora. And because there was never enough, he would scrimp through the years, taking teaching jobs whenever he could.

After graduation from Dublin's University College, where his intellectual acumen and fervent anti-nationalism made him a well-known campus figure, Joyce left Dublin and the countrymen he characterized as the most benighted race in Europe. Soon after his arrival in Paris in late 1902, he began studies in writing and medicine. His life would soon become a peripatetic one, as he and his family lived between Paris, Zurich, and Trieste. His first major literary effort was a series of short stories that were published together in 1914 as *Dubliners*, followed two years later by the first of his important works, *A Portrait of the Artist as a Young Man*. Written in Zurich, the novel had been published in serial form in the vanguard journal *The Egoist* by Ezra Pound, who had heard about the prickly Celt from fellow poet W. B. Yeats.

In 1922, after seven years of toil, the nearly blind Joyce finished his final draft of *Ulysses,* a work considered by many the finest piece of literature produced this century. Modelled after Homer's epic *The Odyssey,* and focusing on eighteen hours of a single day in Dublin—June 16, 1904, a date now celebrated as "Bloomsday"—*Ulysses* tells the story of Leopold Bloom, a free-thinking Jewish newspaper-advertising salesman with a troubled marriage to singer Molly Bloom. By turns bawdy and heartbreaking, Joyce's novel is an extraordinary achievement full of tragedy and caricature, obscurantism and horseplay, and enough puzzlements to employ an army of scholars. Such obfuscation, however, was just what Joyce, who had provided in advance an outline of the book's formal structure, had intended—not out of any sinister plan to destroy the novel as a form, but to radicalize it by opening it up to the unconscious. To this end, Joyce used such literary techniques as interior monologues rendered in a stream-of-consciousness style and hosts of subliminal images.

Published in parts as a work-in-progress, the complete novel found no publishers willing to take on the inevitable charges of obscenity. After much difficulty, Joyce's friend Sylvia Beach, proprietor of Paris's Shakespeare & Co. bookshop, published it privately. Despite the acclaim it won on the Continent, *Ulysses* was deemed obscene in England and the United States and was suppressed until a famous court opinion allowed its publication nine years later.

The reception of *Finnegans Wake* (1939), an experimental mix of symbols, philosophy, fantasies, and myth informed by a cyclical view of history, was eclipsed by World War II. Regarded by many as equal in brilliance to *Ulysses,* it proved even more troublesome to what had become an industry of Joycean scholarship. In *Finnegans Wake* the reader is forced to render external reality completely for the world of the sleeping mind. It is hard not to see a reflection of Joyce's own personal isolation and withdrawal—his increasing blindness, his pain, and his daughter's increasing madness—in *Finnegans Wake,* the writing of which occupied seventeen years of his life. Yet no matter how far he roamed or how many foreign tongues he mastered (Gaelic was never one of them), his dreamlike work always focused on his native land. In 1940, Joyce moved back to Zurich with Nora, broken by pain and exhausted by their daughter Lucia's drawn-out battle with mental illness. He died there the following year, an exile from the birthplace that took many years more to accept his genius.

CARL JUNG

IF HIS ERSTWHILE FRIEND and mentor Sigmund Freud was the cartographer of the individual psyche, Carl Gustav Jung was the explorer of an uncharted world, the "collective unconscious"—a term he coined, along with such now-common usages as "introvert" and "extravert [sic]," "anima" and "animus." Comparing the two pioneers' respective positions to that of pontiff and apostate, Jung was the faithful protégé moving ever more dramatically away from the master's dogma of psychoanalysis, in which all behavior is seen as rooted in sexuality, to a new credo he called "analytic psychology." In Jung's view, the personal unconscious was a gateway to the collective unconscious, an inborn cornucopia of universally shared "memories" that manifest themselves in dreams, fantasies, fairy tales, myths, and religions, and that cannot be explained solely in terms of an individual's experience. The psychological archetypes Jung described—primordial images such as hero, witch, earth mother, warrior, wise old man—remain influential in other fields as well.

Carl Gustav Jung was born in Switzerland to a theologically rigid Protestant clergyman, against whose autocracy he rebelled but whose deep religious faith he never questioned. Fascinated as a youth by both the humanities and the sciences, Carl inherited a family tradition of healing. To placate his father, he enrolled in medical school at the University of Basel, an institution where his grandfather had been a professor of medicine. But even in his academic pursuits, Jung was guided first and foremost by a quest for spiritual meaning and the need to forge a connection to something larger than the individual self. Years later he would write in his memoirs, "My whole being was seeking for something still unknown which might confer meaning upon the banality of life." His doctoral thesis dealt with the "Psychology and Pathology of So-Called Occult Phenomena," a topic that engaged his interest until his death and one that was a source of much professional derision—and affectionate teasing from Freud.

In 1900 Jung began working as an assistant physician at the Burghölzli Psychiatric Hospital in Zurich under the direction of Eugen Bleuler, the psychiatrist who pioneered the concept of schizophrenia. He spent the winter of 1902–1903 in Paris, studying under Pierre Janet, whose explorations of hysteria and schizophrenia had anticipated Freud's theories of the unconscious. (Also in 1903, Jung married Emma Rauschenbach, who became his collaborator and staunchest supporter.) It was at the Burghölzli that Jung began his experiments with word association as a therapeutic tool. Those findings are still being applied, as is his notion of a "complex," a term he coined to describe the intricate knot of traits and ideas entwined around an emotional nucleus. Had his achievements stopped there, Jung would be thought of today as an important if not revolutionary psychological innovator, a significant lieutenant to the great Freud. And indeed, he loyally performed that role for the first years of his career, even becoming the first president, in 1910, of the strongly Freudian International Psychoanalytical Association. But his inquiries took him further and further afield from Freud's strict sexual interpretations of neurosis, forcing him to make his own path. Eventually, the two men, who'd once enjoyed a bond not unlike that of father and son, fell out irrevocably. After Jung published his groundbreaking book *Psychology of the Unconscious* (1913), which drew startling analogies between primeval myths and psychotic fantasies, the two never spoke again.

Yet, as intellectually daring as he was, Jung was not wholly fearless in his private life, nor wholly unimpeachable. In spite of the pain it caused his wife, he carried on a near-forty-year extramarital relationship with a former patient, Antonia Wolff, who became a brilliant colleague. (Jung's view of the two women seems to correspond to his theory of opposites, as borne out by the archetypal identities he assigned to each of them: His wife, Emma, was the earth mother who raised their five children and reveled in domesticity, Wolff the fiery muse who inspired his creativity.) An earlier affair with another patient, Sabina Spielrein, was cut short by his fear that he would be hurt professionally if their relationship were to become known. Throughout his life he experienced bouts of anxiety and depression, even psychosis, much of which he embraced. During the six-year period that followed his break with Freud, he kept a secret diary called the "Red Book," in which he recorded his inner turmoil in both words and paintings. Only by surrendering himself to crisis, visions, and hallucinations, Jung maintained, could he truly understand largely inaccessible places in his patients' psyches.

Jung's unique contribution might be called the spiritualization of psychology. In later life he drew increasing criticism from the psychological establishment—then mired in Freudian orthodoxy—for his interest in the symbolism of the Catholic mass, in astrology and UFO's, and in alchemy, which for him mirrored the psychological process of personal transformation. Yet Jung's approach has truly come into its own at the tail end of the century—an era characterized by a popular fascination with mysticism and a search for spiritual and psychic wholeness—even as Freud's mechanistic view of human behavior has lost favor. Deeply intellectual and endlessly curious, Jung spent his own life in pursuit of such wholeness, traveling to the Pueblo Indian reservations in 1925 to study myth and later visiting Africa and India. Through it all he remained adamant about the existence of a transcendent being. When asked by a BBC interviewer whether he believed in God, Jung replied, "I don't have to believe—I know."

FRANZ KAFKA

THOUGH FRANZ KAFKA HAS been hailed as the prophet of the totalitarian nightmare, his vision was born in the personal. His formal and darkly comic tales, which have provided cues to several generations of modernist writers, appear to foreshadow the twentieth century's imminent existential and spiritual dislocation and warn of yet-unidentified political persecution. His ominous and anxiety-laden stories about the fear and humiliation of victimhood rang so true that Nazis and Marxists alike banned his work.

The sinister world Kafka saw through his huge black eyes began in Prague, capital of the old kingdom of Bohemia, where he was born to the blustering owner of a dry-goods store and his slightly more socially elevated wife. Although they were Jews in an anti-Semitic culture, the Kafkas were prosperous enough for Franz to be raised by governesses while they ran their business. Franz's lonely and loveless childhood was exacerbated by a paternal anger so deep that the young boy was once locked out of the house by his father for the crime of calling for a glass of water.

It is not surprising that such a boy—sensitive, melancholy, and plagued by a sense of inadequacy and impotence—should grow up viewing the world as a penal colony filled with impersonal malevolence, and the individual as the prey of nameless authoritarian power. The wonder was that his vision did not paralyze him. Instead, Kafka struggled through high school as a dreamer, emerging as a candidate, in 1901, for Ferdinand-Karls University, where he vacillated between studying science and law. As a speaker of German in a predominantly Czech-speaking country, Kafka entered cultural institutions that were usually barred to Jews, like the Hall of Lecture and Discourse for German Studies, which had been conceived as an anti-Semitic organization. It was not the last time he would feel isolated from his surroundings. Yet it was here that he mingled for the first time with other intellectuals, including Max Brod, a hunchback and fellow Jew who became his lifelong friend and literary executor. Shy, self-doubting, yet curious about the cafés and bordellos that bustled around him, Kafka stumbled carelessly through college, failing to distinguish himself academically, but eventually earning a law degree.

By 1905, his frail constitution, demanding studies, and stressful relations with his parents compelled the hypersensitive Kafka to retreat to a sanitarium, as he would several times during his life. There, where he experienced his first sexual encounter with a woman whose identity remains unknown, the alienation and despair of his timid existence combined with his ongoing readings of Dickens, Goethe, and Dostoyevsky to produce his first writings. When Brod, who was also a novelist and playwright, heard his friend read his strange story "Description of a Struggle," he knew he had encountered an original and important voice in German-language literature. Kafka, however, did not write to make a living. So when he took up law in 1906, drafting documents for a Prague lawyer, he embarked upon a curious double life. Still under the thumb of his ill-tempered father—Kafka's bedroom was located between his parents' bedroom and the parlor—he appeared an outwardly normal, even charming young man who motorcycled, sunbathed, and was socially active. But he was at the same time writing some of the most disturbing stories, diaries, and novels ever imagined, missives from the macabre that included a collection of eight short prose pieces he titled "Meditations" (1908). A burst of creativity in 1912 produced the famous story "The Judgment," which depicts a son horribly oppressed by an overbearing father, and "The Metamorphosis," an allegorical fantasy in which the protagonist awakens to discover that he has turned into an enormous insect. These extraordinary stories contrast to Kafka's solidly bourgeois rise in the royal Workmen's Accident Insurance Institute, another steadfastly anti-Semitic venue usually closed to Jews. During this period, on the eve of World War I, while his dark stories were being read and praised by such luminaries as the Austrian writer Robert Musil his sober and lucid reports of dangerous machinery in factories were earning him an imperial medal of commendation.

Kafka's feelings of dislocation, so fundamental to his nature, were heightened by deteriorating relations with his parents, his dutiful but resentful afternoon employment in the family's asbestos factory, and his manipulative, schizoid engagement to an executive secretary named Felice Bauer. Apprehensive about marriage and afraid of losing the solitude he deemed necessary to his writing, Kafka, like his characters, was almost pathologically needy, insecure, and alienated. In spite of this, he found the spirit to write *The Trial* in the summer of 1914. One of Kafka's most powerful works of fiction, this novel explores the nightmarish fate of a law-abiding banker, Joseph K, who finds himself under arrest for an unnamed crime. "In the Penal Colony," the story of a military officer who turns an instrument of torture that he has invented on himself, came later that year, followed two years later by "A Country Doctor." Sick with tuberculosis, filled with dread, still wooing the patient Felice, Kafka struggled to finish what would be his final novel, *The Castle* (1921), which goes even further than *The Trial* in its portrait of a nightmare world. Within three years, his voice and his lungs were gone. On his deathbed, Kafka instructed Brod to burn all his unpublished manuscripts and to make no effort to republish any that had already appeared in print. Brod, to literature's immense good fortune, disobeyed his friend's instructions.

FRIDA KAHLO

THE AUTOBIOGRAPHY OF MEXICO'S most celebrated female artist is written in her paintings. Only recently canonized as one of modern feminism's heroines, Frida Kahlo was her own favorite subject, her anguished life the wellspring of her deeply unsettling work. Striking in her bearing, earthy, and stone-faced, she stares directly at her viewer out of her self-portraits. Her stark, almost savage beauty, accented by thick, wing-like eyebrows and the suggestion of a mustache, is instantly compelling. Amid a profusion of symbols drawn from a rich national heritage, a rejected but pervasive Catholicism, and nature at its most fecund, Kahlo sits impassively among her massive jungle fronds, wildly colored flowers, and overripe fruits. There is a dark side to this abundance: disturbing images of vulnerable naked bodies, bleeding fetuses, and the gruesome paraphernalia of her medical history—wheelchairs, intravenous tubes, soiled bed linen—all of which Kahlo treated like so many sacred relics.

Kahlo, whose fame was postponed until some three decades after her passing in 1954, was preoccupied with her own mortality—even given Mexican culture's familiar fascination with death. She gave the grim reaper a pet name—*la pelona,* the bald one—and kept a skeleton atop the canopy of her bed. Kahlo's obsession with her own demise began in 1925, when a trolley-car accident left her with horrific injuries, among them a crushed pelvis, a spinal column fractured in several places, a smashed right foot, and internal injuries that made her incapable of bearing children. While recovering from the first of several series of corrective surgeries—she was to have thirty-five of them between the ages of eighteen and forty-seven—she began painting as a means of alleviating her agony and depression, though she said she could never paint the accident itself. In her brutal and poignant oil *The Broken Column,* Kahlo shows her naked, wounded torso laced into one of the innumerable steel corsets she wore throughout the years to support her deteriorating spine. As in all of Kahlo's pictures, the unifying element is pain.

Kahlo's other lifetime comrade—aside from pain—was her beloved, if wayward, husband. As a feisty, leather-jacketed teen, she had boasted to a friend that one day she would bear Diego Rivera's child; when she could walk again after her terrible mishap, she sought out the leftist painter whose panoramic homages to the recent Mexican revolution were attracting world attention. He was entranced by her work, and soon they began their highly fraught relationship. Though neither was a paragon of fidelity: Rivera's affair with Kahlo's sister was a particularly cruel blow. It prompted her painting *A Few Small Nips,* which depicts a woman stabbed to death by her lover. They divorced in 1939 but, unable to live without each other, remarried in 1940.

Diego Rivera and Frida Kahlo were two powerful and highly visible personalities, both in the political arena through their Communist affiliations and in the art world through their allegiance to a common cultural heritage. For Kahlo, who had an affair with Leon Trotsky during his exile in Mexico and who did several paintings extolling Stalin, her activism came through her art. The well-educated child of a Hungarian-Jewish photographer and a Roman Catholic mother of Indian and Spanish blood, Kahlo was also a daughter of Mexico. Stylistically, her formalized and often intense primitivism reflected her nation's folk art; thematically it looked to Indian peasant life and ancient Aztec tradition. In this spirit, Kahlo, a well-traveled cosmopolite, plaited her long hair with blossoms and strips of colored fabric and dressed in the long ruffled skirts of the Tehuana, often painting plain scenes on small pieces of tin—like the *retablos* painted by the thankful and hung in Mexican churches to commemorate miracles.

But Kahlo's peasant garb belied the content of her art; André Breton, who claimed her as a Surrealist, called her sophisticated-yet-naïve work "a ribbon around a bomb." But decades later the art world still disputes her place in it. Her stance of saintly misery troubles those who find her visual pleas for pity tiresome. For others who would make the artist into a feminist idol, her tendency to wallow in her anguish, despite her brave front, can be equally irritating. Kahlo's increasingly erratic behavior and violent mood swings, caused by addiction to painkillers, affected the quality of her paintings at the end and drove away her loved ones. Art critic Hayden Herrera, whose 1983 biography helped elevate Kahlo to her current status, suggests that the artist may have been a victim of the Munchausen syndrome, in which a person needs to be ill, an eternal patient. Kahlo seized upon suffering and brokenness as a metaphor and in her tortured, self-referential oeuvre, Herrera speculates, searched for salvation by mythologizing the tragic events of her life—most significantly her endless surgeries, her inability to conceive a child, and her volatile union with Diego Rivera. In *Self-Portrait with Cropped Hair,* for example, completed in 1940 after her discovery of yet another one of Rivera's women, a saddened Kahlo sits somberly, scissors in hand, dressed in what must be one of her husband's suits, her shorn hair lying all about her. But many of Kahlo's canvases, Herrera asserts, were less about grief than they were "acts of gratitude," serving a purpose similar to the *retablos* she both painted and collected. Like one of the faithful who has been saved from illness or catastrophe, she created her symbolic oils to venerate what was left of her physical well-being and to affirm the survival of her spirit.

KELLER

HELEN

THIS AMERICAN AUTHOR AND HUMANITARIAN—whose courageous triumph over her blind, deaf, and speechless childhood has inspired millions throughout the world—spoke often of her two birthdays. One was her actual birthdate, June 27, 1880; the other, her "soul's birthday," as she called it, took place seven years later on March 3, 1887. It was on this day that a lively, intelligent young woman named Anne Sullivan, partially blind herself, entered Helen Keller's tortured, tomb-like existence and almost immediately began to transform it into a joyful life of fearless adventure and fulfilling accomplishment.

The progress of this amazing transformation was told movingly by Keller herself in her classic 1903 autobiography, *The Story of My Life*. A simple but powerful narrative, it starts with the account of a strange, lingering fever that left Keller totally deaf and blind at the age of nineteen months—"a phantom," as she would call herself, "living in a no-world." Desperate to communicate, Keller devised a crude type of sign language and, equally without effect, attempted to move her lips as she felt others doing. Her intense frustration at her inability to make herself understood led to such violent temper tantrums—many of them directed at her doting mother and father—that her parents were finally forced to seek special schooling and a firm hand for the uncontrollable Helen. In 1886 her father took her to Washington, D.C., to ask the advice of Dr. Alexander Graham Bell, who, all but deaf himself, had invented the telephone mainly as an aid to the hearing-impaired. At his suggestion, the Kellers wrote the Perkins Institution for the Blind in Boston, requesting an instructor for their daughter.

The very day Anne Sullivan appeared on the doorstep of the family home in Tuscumbia, Alabama, Helen hurled herself, flailing and shrieking, at her new teacher. Undaunted, Sullivan promptly scooped the little girl into her arms and took her upstairs for their first lesson. In a matter of weeks Sullivan's sympathetic manner and patience had calmed the quick-minded seven-year-old. She began trying to teach Keller the manual alphabet and to make her understand that these finger signals meant something, that everything had a name. Once Keller grasped this, she learned at an amazing rate. In three short years Keller, a tireless perfectionist, would learn not only to communicate through the manual alphabet but also to read Braille and to write using a special typewriter. After studying speech at the Horace Mann School for the Deaf, where she learned to talk by using her fingers to feel the position of the tongue and lips of others, Keller was able to tell her mentor—whom she called simply Teacher—"I am not dumb now." From

then on Keller's progress seemed boundless. At eleven she was already raising money for the education of other handicapped children, and by her late teens she had a perfect reading knowledge of French, German, Latin, and Greek. At twenty, gentle-mannered but radiant with self-confidence, she was enrolled in Radcliffe College, her tuition paid for from a fund organized by her admiring friend Mark Twain. Sullivan sat with her through the lectures, reporting them to her with sign language.

Graduated with honors in 1904, by this time an international celebrity and role model for the handicapped everywhere, Keller turned her attention from the conquest of her physical limitations to addressing the social problems of her era. Her beloved Teacher's past—she had been abandoned as a child and raised in a squalid orphanage—doubtless influenced her. In addition, Sullivan's marriage to John Macy, who was deeply sympathetic to the workers' cause, brought to the household another person whose attention was focused on societal injustices. In 1909, after reading H. G. Wells's *New Worlds for Old*, with its vivid descriptions of the wretched living conditions of industrial workers, Keller became a socialist. For the next decade, she was a tireless speaker on behalf of the movement until 1924 when, though still devoted to socialism, she curtailed her public speaking on its behalf. In 1920 she added her name to the roster of the National Committee of the newly organized American Civil Liberties Union. Keller was also active on behalf of the Industrial Workers of the World (IWW) and campaigned as a pacifist in World War I and as an anti-Fascist before World War II. After 1924, raising funds for the American Foundation for the Blind became her chief cause, and her efforts helped end the abominable but common practice of placing the deaf in insane asylums. When her beloved Teacher died in 1936, she continued her efforts to triumph over ignorance and mistreatment of the handicapped, with Polly Thomson as her companion.

In assessing Keller's profound accomplishments as a social activist and inspiring symbol of self-transformation, one thinks back to the moment—made famous on both stage and screen—when her teacher placed one of Keller's hands under a squirting pump spout and in the other spelled out the word "water" over and over. Suddenly, Keller felt "a misty consciousness as of something forgotten—a thrill of returning thought." In that explosive instant she was aware that the letters represented the cool substance that was flowing over her hand. "That living word" awakened her soul and let the whole world stream in. In thanksgiving, Keller would return the favor, letting her own inner light of serenity and joy pour forth for others.

GRACE KELLY

HOW DO YOU TOP a brilliant career that in the space of just five years boasted eleven films, all of them remarkably good, and an Academy Award? Princess isn't a bad start. One day the slim, elegant Grace Kelly was a Hollywood star radiating a gentle finishing-school naughtiness, and the next she was aboard the U.S. *Constitution* heading for the principality of Monaco with a festive entourage and trunks full of ball gowns. There, in the Gothic cathedral of Saint Nicholas, Kelly wed the dashing Prince Rainier III. Press reports of the elaborate nuptials, which were televised all over the world, reveled in fairy-tale-come-true descriptions of the extravagant event. Grace Patricia Kelly, the properly raised daughter of a wealthy Philadelphia family, had met her prince briefly while attending the 1954 Cannes Film Festival, but she did not see him again until Christmas of 1955. From there on, things moved rapidly. Two weeks later their engagement was announced, and in April the young actress became Her Serene Royal Highness. She would live, media narratives gushed, surrounded by liveried servants in a 225-room pink-walled castle overlooking the gambling mecca of Monte Carlo and the sparkling Mediterranean. Princess Grace would also now be the Countess Grimaldi, and as such she would be counted upon to produce the distinguished family's dynastic heir. If she failed, Monaco—an independent sovereignty since the thirteenth century—would be absorbed by France, and the residents of the 368-acre domain would no longer be privileged with their highly prized tax-exempt status.

Ironically, shortly before her marriage, Kelly had shot *The Swan*, a 1956 film in which she portrays a young woman enamored of a crown prince. In real life, the new princess found all the fairy-tale analogies less appealing but nonetheless strove for the next twenty-six years to live up to the responsibilities thrust upon her. In 1958 she presented her prince with his anxiously awaited successor, Albert, who was their second child. He and his two lovely but headstrong sisters, Caroline and Stephanie, would eventually make sensational headlines of their own as they developed into high-profile jet-setters. Princess Grace gradually took up less ink as she settled into child rearing and charity work. Her husband tried to forbid her from working in films—a decision he had made after his postmarriage visit to the set of *High Society* in 1956—and although the princess never made another movie, she never totally cut her Hollywood ties either. After a short but spectacular stint in Hollywood, which included an Oscar in 1954 for *The Country Girl*, the self-made actress certainly had nothing to prove. Having reached a pinnacle of success, it was impossible for her to estrange herself completely from her profession.

Kelly's dramatic career began while she was a sickly child, inventing little tableaux for her dolls as she lay in bed.

Her mother, a fine-figured former sportswoman, encouraged the dramatic inclinations of her shy, nearsighted offspring. Kelly's gregarious Irish father, an Olympic gold medalist in sculling who had built his sizable construction business from bricklayer beginnings, was stingier in his support, cautioning his ambitious daughter that success would come at the cost of privacy. Despite her family's comfortable circumstances, Grace chose to make a living on her own, working as a model to pay for classes at the American Academy of Dramatic Arts in New York City. Her Broadway debut came in a 1949 revival of Strindberg's *The Father*, which starred Raymond Massey, and two years later she got her break with a small part in Twentieth Century–Fox's *Fourteen Hours*. After her supporting role as Gary Cooper's wife in the 1952 classic *High Noon*, Metro-Goldwyn-Mayer signed Kelly to a seven-year contract. The following year John Ford cast her in *Mogambo*, setting her cool allure against the strong sexuality of veteran Clark Gable and a steamy Ava Gardner.

Kelly, a stunning beauty who had proved herself capable of both subtle and strong emotion, had made it. It was her work with Alfred Hitchcock, though, that defined her image as a woman whose poise and aloofness masked a volcanic passion. Under Hitchcock's guidance, in *Dial M for Murder* (1954), *Rear Window* (1954), and *To Catch a Thief* (1955), her "sexual elegance," as the director termed it, was revealed and perfected, with Kelly emerging as a fire-and-ice creature who, when the situation warranted, could also be a deft comedienne. Though rumors flew of romances with almost all of her leading men, the "Ice Maiden" held Hollywood at a distance with a white-gloved propriety, remarkably retaining her virginal reputation.

When the princess died at fifty-two, the victim of an auto accident, the once-upon-a-time parallels were again impossible to ignore. Echoing a scene with co-star Cary Grant in *To Catch a Thief*, she had been negotiating the hairpin turns of the Moyenne Corniche, the route high above Monte Carlo where the 1955 movie was made. This time, however, the car plunged down a shady embankment into a farmer's garden, with daughter Stephanie in the passenger seat. Stephanie sustained only minor injuries, but Grace, much more seriously injured than was at first suspected, died some twenty-four hours after the crash. She had always downplayed the Cinderella aspects of her life, preferring to see herself as a sensible contemporary woman with all the problems of a wife and mother. But as her coffin was carried from the cathedral in which she had been married, her grieving subjects had few thoughts of Grace Kelly, the former actress and commoner. They—and the world—mourned a princess.

JOHN F. KENNEDY

MORE THAN THIRTY YEARS AFTER he was struck down by sniper bullets, history still cannot decide if John Fitzgerald Kennedy, thirty-fifth president of the United States, and at forty-three the youngest man ever elected to that office, was a great leader or a great image. This is only one of the many paradoxes that surround the twentieth century's most charismatic American president, who was simultaneously intellectual and rake, high-minded leader and crafty political infighter, droll celebrity and serious statesman.

Born in Brookline, Massachusetts, on May 29, 1917, John was the second of nine children of Joseph and Rose Fitzgerald Kennedy, wealthy Irish-Americans who began grooming their oldest son, Joseph Kennedy, Jr., to be president from the day he was born. When Joe junior was killed in World War II, the elder Kennedys automatically shifted their political aspirations to their second son. They bequeathed to him their personal attributes: from Joe senior, a certain appealing ruthlessness; from Rose, an implacable will and boundless faith. They also gave him that most essential commodity for a career in modern politics: a fortune.

Kennedy chose to attend Harvard, his father's alma mater, joining his brother Joe. Charming and popular, he was an indifferent student for the first two years. In 1938, however, when his father was U.S. ambassador to Britain, Kennedy served as secretary in the London embassy, enjoying a rare opportunity to travel, meet dignitaries, and learn the machinations of diplomacy. His expanded undergraduate thesis, on British foreign policy in the 1930s, was published to great success in 1940 as a book entitled *Why England Slept*. When World War II broke out and the army rejected him because of a chronic back condition caused by a high-school football injury, Kennedy pulled strings to be commissioned as a lieutenant junior-grade in the navy. Taking command of a PT boat, he became embroiled in a fracas that was to make him a war hero: when his patrol boat was sunk in the Solomon Islands by a Japanese destroyer, he dragged a wounded seaman three miles through hostile waters to a remote island where he successfully organized a rescue.

After the war, Kennedy dabbled in journalism—a profession in which he had little interest. Then, in 1946, this grandson of two Boston pols decided to run for James Michael Curley's seat in Massachusetts's Eleventh Congressional District. Relying on personal connections and his boyish charisma, he easily won. In 1952, the Irish Catholic Kennedy took on Back Bay aristocrat Henry Cabot Lodge, Jr., for a seat in the U.S. Senate, winning by a slim margin. The following year he married the beautiful and patrician Jacqueline Bouvier. By 1956—a year after he made a splash with his Pulitzer Prize—winning biography *Profiles in Courage*, which he wrote during convalescence from back surgery—he had decided to make a run for the presidency. Four years later, he achieved his family's goal, overcoming American prejudice against Catholics and pulling every trick in the election playbook to squeak past Eisenhower's vice president, Richard Nixon.

As leader of the world's most powerful democracy, Kennedy instantly came into direct conflict with the countervailing force: communism. Having inherited the plan for the Bay of Pigs invasion against Fidel Castro's Cuba from the Eisenhower administration, the new president allowed it to go forward, only to see it end in humiliating failure. Next, he confronted wily Soviet premier Nikita Khrushchev, who was openly contemptuous of the playboy president. In October 1962, with Russian missiles in Cuba pointed at the United States, Kennedy called Khrushchev's bluff and blockaded the Caribbean island. After thirteen days of nuclear brinkmanship—during which the entire world remained anxiously poised for war—the Russians capitulated and the missiles were removed. (In a clever ploy, Kennedy ignored the second formal Soviet communication which called for the removal of American missiles from Turkey and responded instead to the first communication which did not include this demand.) His greatest foreign-policy coup came in 1963, however, with the signing of the Nuclear Test-Ban Treaty.

Then came the nightmare of Vietnam. Some historians believe that Kennedy, after encouraging the overthrow of the corrupt Diem regime, was preparing to leave that embattled nation to its own devices. At home, his "New Frontier" agenda was moving with increasing speed and confidence toward comprehensive civil rights legislation. This was a direction that met considerable resistance in Congress—and deep enmity in certain other powerful quarters.

In between managing these crises, Kennedy found time to carry on an astonishing number of extramarital sexual liaisons—which the press at the time chose to ignore. But even the recent discussion of such high jinks has done little to diminish his stature. Indeed, they seem to have enhanced his reputation as a swashbuckling pragmatist who placed more faith in risk taking than in the routinized grind. He was certainly the wittiest president of the century, and his streak of romanticism gave him an appealingly sensitive veneer. His youth, his vigor, and his splendid wife brought to the White House an elevated cultural consciousness that would later be invoked with a word borrowed from a Lerner and Loewe musical: Camelot.

Kennedy's brief tenure ended abruptly with an assassin's bullet on November 22, 1963, as his motorcade slowly snaked through Dallas, Texas. In his inaugural address, he had exhorted the nation, "With a good conscience our only sure reward, with history the final judge of our deeds, let us go forth to lead the land we love." History has stayed its judgment on a presidency cut short. As a man, Kennedy remains an all-too-human leader who symbolized to many a hopeful people's enduring belief in their nation's founding principles.

KEVORKIAN

HE IS KNOWN AS "Doctor Death." A pathologist fascinated with the phenomenon of dying, he defied the ire of criminal courts and the taboos of American society by "assisting" with the suicides of desperate and afflicted patients, who chose to end their lives rather than continue suffering. In doing so, he set off a profound debate about a person's right to die, and the sanctity of life.

Jack Kevorkian was born in Pontiac, Michigan, to an auto-factory worker and his wife, Armenians whose families had been victims of the Turkish massacres during World War I. To some commentators the emotional impact this event had on the Kevorkian family's view of life left an indelible impression on the future physician. But perhaps what shaped him more was his mother's lingering, agonized death from cancer, an ordeal the young Kevorkian watched helplessly.

Kevorkian eventually rejected his Armenian Orthodox faith and, with the advent of World War II, taught himself German and Japanese. In 1945 he entered the University of Michigan, matriculating from its medical school seven years later. Embarking on an internship in pathology at a Detroit hospital, he encountered a woman with terminal cancer who seemed to him to be "pleading for help and death at the same time." It was then that Kevorkian decided that euthanasia and suicide were morally acceptable.

After obtaining his medical license in 1953, Kevorkian first served as an army doctor, then returned to Michigan hospitals to continue his work in pathology. Using his position to study the stages of dying, he began to make what he referred to with gallows humor as his "death rounds," photographing patients at the moment life ceased. His behavior led one colleague in 1956 to nickname the pathologist "Doctor Death."

Controversial proposals followed. In a medical journal he suggested a connection between the invisibility of the veins of the cornea at death and the proper diagnosis of coma. In 1958 he publicly called for scientific experiments to be performed on the bodies of unconscious criminals, later adding that the healthy organs of the executed convicts should be used in transplants. His highly fractious campaign for this program—which he never abandoned—led the University of Michigan to ask for his resignation. Moving to Pontiac General Hospital, Kevorkian muted his contentious statements and turned his attention to the transfusion of blood from the cadavers of accident victims to healthy patients.

For the next twenty-five years Kevorkian moved from job to job, from Michigan to California, failing at business, making an unreleased film on Handel's Messiah—and always, everywhere, studying and writing about death. Only a little-known German journal would publish his radical writings on euthanasia and suicide. Even the pro-suicide Hemlock Society shunned Kevorkian's vision of unconditional, uncontrolled death-on-demand as a "slippery slope." For his part, the doctor ignored his critics, pressed on with his work and invented a death-machine he originally called the Thanatron (later, more euphemistically, the "Mercitron") out of an electric clock motor and a pulley. His attempts to market and publicize his machine caught the attention of the media—and of his first patient.

On June 4, 1990, a fifty-four-year-old woman in the early stages of Alzheimer's lay down in the back of Kevorkian's old and battered Volkswagen van and flipped the switch on the Thanatron, sending a lethal dose of potassium chloride coursing through her veins. "Have a nice trip," Kevorkian told her. Her destination was unknown to him, since he held no belief in an afterlife.

The authorities moved in immediately, banning the use of the machine—but Kevorkian was undeterred. In 1991 he helped a second woman die, but the subsequent autopsy showed no sign of the disease of which she had complained. After the third suicide, the state revoked Kevorkian's license. He turned to the use of carbon monoxide, and ten more people died with his aid before Michigan banned assisted suicide in 1993. Reflecting society's confusion over this highly emotional issue, the law was both overturned and reinstated in a single year, and Kevorkian was again indicted for assisting in the suicide of a young man with Lou Gehrig's disease. Acquitted in 1994, he launched a petition drive for assisted suicide. He was once again jailed after "mercy mission" no. 17, whereupon he went on a hunger strike. Again a jury refused to convict.

Defiant and deliberately confrontational, Kevorkian garnered more criticism when he attempted to mount an exhibit of Adolf Hitler's paintings as a charity fund raiser to garner some good for all the horror Hitler caused. In 1994 he wrote a book, *Prescription: Medicide,* to explain his views. In it he described his vision of "Obitiatry," a new branch of medicine dedicated to the study of the process of dying and reaffirmed his idea of using criminals for medical experiments.

In 1996 he resumed his primary campaign, helping two women to die and calling for "absolute personal autonomy." Once more, despite grave ambiguities in the Michigan law, he was brought before the bar of justice, and once again released by the jury. The debate provoked by Kevorkian's physician-assisted voluntary suicides continues as the century comes to an end. Even while he has been denounced by his detractors, his activism has raised serious questions for American society about government interference, personal autonomy, and even the right of a human being to exert control over his or her destiny.

KING

BILLIE JEAN

JUST ABOUT THE TIME she was entering kindergarten in Long Beach, California, Billie Jean Moffitt decided that she was "going to do something wonderful" when she grew up. Later, at thirteen, her pastor, the former Olympic pole-vaulter Bob Richards, idly asked what she planned to do with her life. She responded confidently that she had decided to become the best tennis player in the world. By 1961, the five-foot four-inch brunette, true to her intentions, had made her way to Wimbledon, where she demolished top-seeded veteran Margaret Smith of Australia in the first round. The crowd that day was stunned at the upset, but Billie Jean, while perhaps not exactly cocky, was considerably less surprised. She had, after all, clearly set her sights on the goal, conditioned herself mentally and physically, and then slaved and sacrificed until she had achieved it.

At the start of her career King faced the daunting obstacles common to many women in sports. Media interest in women's athletic pursuits was limited, and there was no national organization to support women's efforts. But by the time Billie Jean retired, her drive and talent had earned her a whopping total of thirty-nine grand-slam singles, doubles, and mixed-doubles victories. Along the way, thanks to her unrelenting promotion of the sport, King practically invented women's professional tennis. She also gave women everywhere new role models. King believed, as well, that the clubby game of tennis wasn't "just for rich kids" and fought mightily to democratize this bastion of upper-class-male recreation by reaching out through special programs to children of all classes.

King owed much of her spunk to her parents—a fireman father who turned his softball-playing eleven-year-old on to tennis and a secretary mother who shared the family's passion for sports. Genetics provided her with split-second reflexes, power, and superb concentration, and her endurance, her mother explained, came from her part-Seminole heritage. Her competitive spirit and energy were all her own. In 1958, at fourteen, the untested teen beat all comers in her age bracket at the Southern California Championship. After some coaching by Frank Brennan and the formidable tennis player Alice Marble, she followed that win with her first Wimbledon victory, playing doubles with Karen Hantze in 1961. Two years later, although her spirits were sapped by a loss to Margaret Smith in the Wimbledon singles finals, encouragement from her fiancé, Larry King, convinced her to devote even more of her energy to tennis. Leaving Los Angeles State College—and Larry—Billie Jean went to Australia for top-flight training and conditioning. Under the sharp eye of Mervyn Rose, she worked on increasing her stamina and rounding out her game.

Back home, King began an accelerated climb to the top. She beat all her American opponents in 1965 but lost in the semifinals at Wimbledon, after which her familiar nemesis, Margaret Smith, routed her in the U.S. lawn-tennis championships at Forest Hills. King, however, was learning to rebound from defeat, focusing more on mental concentration, technical correction, and putting an edge on her game. Her public personality, in turn, became more ebullient, her boisterous body language and spirited grandstanding soon making her one of the biggest attractions in tennis history.

King's banner year was 1966. In her first full-time season, she charged her way through a string of international tournaments to finally win the much coveted Wimbledon trophy. Her career record would eventually soar to nineteen more Wimbledon titles. In 1971 King, in spite of her ongoing battle with a weight problem and the pain from numerous bilateral knee surgeries, achieved the distinction of becoming the first woman in the history of tennis to earn more than $100,000 in one year. She then turned her attention to the earnings of her fellow female players. Thanks to King, they already had their own protour, but the feminist—who hated to be labeled as such—started campaigning for more: since women had recently proven to be bigger draws than men, they should get equal prize money. To this end, she held regular meetings with her fellow players in a hotel room at Wimbledon in 1973 resulting in the formation of the Women's Tennis Association. That year, for the first time, women players at the U.S. Open finally achieved equal prize money.

Bobby Riggs, a former top-ranked international player, also thought that women players should get what they deserve—which he calculated to be about 25 percent of men's prize money. The "Battle of the Sexes," the resulting challenge match between the two—held on September 20, 1973, and broadcast live from the Houston Astrodome to more than thirty countries—ended in a humiliating defeat for the brashly overconfident Riggs. In 1981, with King by now a successful coach, a businesswoman promoting her own line of tennis equipment, and a publisher of the first sports magazine for women, the public facade of tennis's household name began to show tiny fissures. When King tried to oust Marilyn Barnett, her longtime secretary and companion, from their Malibu house, Barnett filed a palimony suit against her. The public, shocked but devoted, stuck by her, and King as a monument of tennis stood firm. She'd always held that the game, with its ups and downs, put life—and winning and losing—into perspective. "You're only Number One for a few moments. You've got to be resilient."

KING, JR.

MARTIN LUTHER

THREE DECADES AFTER his voice was silenced, the message of Martin Luther King's stirring oratory still animates the American landscape. His achievement was singular and monumental: he brought America's racial prejudices and legal inequities out of the shadows and gave the nation a vision of a united future. A charismatic and inspirational leader, King gained national prominence by calling for passive resistance to segregation. The father of the civil rights movement, later he became a spokesman for the poor as well as the oppressed, and a model for activists the world over.

Born into middle-class comfort in Atlanta, Georgia, in 1929, King was the son of a minister, Martin Luther King, Sr., and a schoolteacher. After entering Morehouse College in 1944, intent on studying medicine or the law, he was drawn to the church through the influence of the religious scholar Dr. Benjamin Mays. Joining the NAACP, he immersed himself in the work of Hegel, Thoreau, and, in particular, Mohandas Gandhi, and his writings on passive resistance. In 1947, he was ordained in his father's congregation, Atlanta's Ebenezer Baptist Church, becoming assistant pastor there. He eventually earned his doctorate in theology from Boston University.

After his marriage in 1953 to Coretta Scott, a voice student, King became pastor of Dexter Avenue Baptist Church in Montgomery, Alabama. There he encountered destiny in the diminutive form of a courageous black seamstress named Rosa Parks, who, weary after a day's work, refused to surrender her bus seat to a white, as a local ordinance required her to do. She was promptly arrested and ordered to appear for her trial on December 5, 1955. Seizing the moment, King organized a boycott of the Montgomery bus system—*75* percent of whose ridership was black—for that day. "If you will protest courageously and yet with dignity and Christian love," he told followers, "in future generations the historians will pause and say, 'There lived a great people—a black people—who injected new meaning and dignity into the veins of civilization.'"

The boycott, which lasted 382 days, was the first victory for King's synthesis of Christian principles, Thoreau's political agitation, and Gandhi's tactics of nonviolent confrontation. For King, who had the steady gaze and patient disposition of a professional fighter, confrontation was as inevitable as nonviolence was indispensable. It was a combination that worked, and King's tactics were a model for such disparate political undertakings as Caesar Chavez' boycotts supporting California's farm workers and the civil rights marches through the slums of Northern Ireland in the late sixties.

The Montgomery bus boycott attracted international attention, and King's somber visage soon became a familiar sight in the world's media as he visited such places as Ghana and India and founded the Southern Christian Leadership Conference to further desegregation back in his own country. His successful 1963 confrontation with Bull Connor, the racist sheriff of Birmingham, Alabama, resulted not only in his imprisonment, but in a literary manifesto, *Letter from a Birmingham Jail,* which is credited with speeding passage of the Civil Rights Act of 1964. King's success garnered him enemies as well, notably FBI director J. Edgar Hoover, who orchestrated a campaign to discredit him. To his supporters, King was a continuing inspiration. King and the movement itself reached its high point in August 1963 during the March on Washington, when a quarter of a million civil rights advocates of all colors and walks of life convened at the Lincoln Memorial to hear him deliver one of the greatest and most moving speeches ever made: "I Have a Dream." In both its content and its cadences, King's oratory blended formal rhetoric, with the rhythms of gospel-style preaching—the perfect expression of the intensely spiritual man who delivered it.

The following year, King, thirty-five, was awarded the Nobel Peace Prize, and for the next three years, he campaigned for civil rights throughout the United States. In 1967, despite severe criticism, he broadened his focus: He denounced the war in Vietnam as a moral evil, declared his own war on poverty, and began organizing a Poor People's March on Washington for 1968. He held to his gospel of nonviolent resistance even as other more militant activists of the day began to turn to violent confrontation as a means to end racial injustice. On the evening of April 4, 1968, King was gunned down by an assassin as he stood leaning over the balcony of the Lorraine Motel in Memphis, Tennessee where he had gone in support of a sanitation workers' strike. James Earl Ray was charged with the murder and pleaded guilty in March 1969 (though he later recanted his confession), and was later convicted. As news of King's death spread around the country, riots erupted in more than a hundred American cities.

The day before he was killed, King had assured his followers that he was unafraid of dying: He had reached the mountaintop, he told them, looked over it, and seen the Promised Land. And while he might not get there, *they* surely would. Over thirty years later, that destination sometimes seems as remote as ever. But in the hearts of those who struggle to keep King's legacy alive, the torch of faith still burns.

VAN BUREN

LANDERS &

THE TWIN SISTERS KNOWN to the world as Ann Landers and Abigail Van Buren began dispensing down-to-earth advice and commonsense guidance to all and sundry in their syndicated newspaper features in 1955. Competing with one another in column after column, the siblings answered the queries of the forlorn and the lovelorn, the bewitched, bothered, and bewildered of America. In a country where the power of church, family, and society to give moral guidance was dramatically declining and the veracity of every pundit and politician was being called into question, Ann and Abby provided their correspondents with gingham-checked good sense, delivered with compassion and often flippant wit. They dealt mainly with family problems and relationship issues, but the Misses Lonely-hearts were never afraid to address either the most taboo topics, or the hotly debated ones.

Born Esther Pauline Friedman—Eppie to her friends—and Pauline Esther Friedman on the Fourth of July, 1918, the sisters came honestly by their penchant for dispensing advice. Their father, a Sioux City, Iowa, theater owner who had immigrated to the States with his wife to escape Vladivostok's pogroms, freely donated his wisdom to friend and stranger alike. The twins grew up doing everything together—tennis, dating, school band—and after graduating from high school in 1936, attended Morningside College in their hometown. In 1939, at age twenty-one, the twins had a double wedding: Esther married an ambitious businessman named Jules Lederer, who would later start a successful car rental company, and Pauline wed Morton Phillips, also destined for wealth.

For seventeen years the sisters lived in various places as mothers and housewives, each participating in politics and philanthropy and making a host of influential friends. It was to these paragons that Ann (then still Esther) turned for help in 1955, when she applied to the *Chicago Sun-Times* as a replacement for Ruth Crowley, a nurse whose death had ended the words-to-the-wise column she had produced under the pen name "Ann Landers." Esther's snappy answers to sample letters provided by the paper—and the new gimmick of quoting experts, such as Bishop Sheen and Supreme Court Justice William O. Douglas—landed her the job over a score of competitors.

Her workload was so overwhelming that she quickly enlisted the aid of her sister Pauline to answer the thousands of letters coming in over the transom. Within a year, the number of papers carrying Esther's column had quadrupled. Her phenomenal success as the new Ann Landers was not lost on sister Pauline, writing anonymously from faraway Hillsborough, California. Jumping into a chauffeured car, she drove up to San Francisco and talked her way into a job writing the advice column for the *San Francisco Chronicle*. With blithe self-confidence, Pauline took the name Abigail from the Biblical prophetess, Van Buren from the U.S. president, and began churning out witty answers to her own army of supplicants. When a young woman wrote that she had imbibed too many cocktails on her twenty-first birthday, she finished by asking Van Buren if she'd done anything wrong. Van Buren's answer: "Probably."

When Esther heard what her sister had done, she stopped speaking to her and maintained silence for the next twenty years. (They have since made up.) But neither one could afford to stop talking to a country famished for advice about everything from adultery to whether to serve kreplach to the in-laws on Thanksgiving. Each sister had a staff of level-headed people to help answer the growing deluge of mail and, still competing, they both went on to write books. Among Ann's were *Since You Asked Me* (1964), *The Ann Landers Encyclopedia* (1978), *Ann Landers Talks to Teenagers About Sex* (1981), and *Wake Up and Smell the Coffee* (1996); Abigail's included *Dear Abby* (1958), *Dear Abby on Marriage* (1962), and *The Best of Dear Abby* (1989).

Unfortunately for Esther, a staunch conservative on the subject of divorce, her marriage to Lederer dissolved in 1975. Beyond insisting that she had no idea why it happened, she refused to discuss it. Not surprisingly, her views on the permanency of wedlock changed soon afterwards. Neither the divorce nor her about-face on the subject had any discernible negative effect on her readers or her readership, however, nor did it prevent her from sharing her views as confidently as ever.

It has been some four decades since Ann Landers opened her first bulging mail sack. Since then, together but apart, the twin columnists have commented in near lockstep on the downward march of Western civilization, pronouncing judgments and providing information on recreational drugs, AIDS, masturbation, sexless marriages, marriageless sex—as well as countless other issues, large and small. The sisters claim a combined readership of about 90 million in approximately 1,200 daily newspapers, each receiving as many as 7,000 to 10,000 letters a week. Just as Walter Winchell, Hedda Hopper, and Louella Parsons paved the way years earlier for the new generations of gossip columnists, so too Ann and Abby solidified a journalistic niche, a sympathetic take on the times that other "Dear Abbys" around the world would soon imitate. Like clockwork, their advice arrives at the front door each day with the newspaper, the best of bromides in sensible prose. Their fans have occasionally found them too tart-tongued and at other times too forgiving. But Ann and Abby have stood by, always willing to empathize, giving America not one, but two shoulders to cry on.

LENIN

VLADIMIR

TENSE WITH EXPECTATION, THE founder of Russian communism returned from exile to St. Petersburg on April 16, 1917, in a sealed railroad car supplied by his country's age-old enemy, Germany. The homeland, to which he returned was ravaged by war and starvation. Near collapse and anarchy, Russia was primed for Vladimir Ilyich Lenin's impassioned message: "The people need peace, the people need bread, the people need land.... We must fight for the social revolution!"

For the next seven years, Lenin gave his countrymen that revolution, one of the most pivotal events of the twentieth century. He also gave them chaos, longer bread lines, and a legacy of terror that, while reminiscent of earlier despots in his nation's history, was unique in its vast scale. A master strategist, he combined practicality and idealism to achieve his end, a new kind of utopianism which sacrificed community to coercion and forbade dissent. Lenin's single-party dictatorship would marry the intellect to the gun like no other before it, forever changing the global political order. By the time of Lenin's death, the bulwark of Soviet-style totalitarianism—mass executions, the secret police, intellectual repression, arbitrary violence, and concentration camps—stood firm.

Even as the son of a hereditary nobleman, Lenin's philosophy was molded leftward. Born on April 22, 1870, in the small provincial city of Simbirsk, Vladimir Ilyich Ulyanov was immersed as an adolescent in his family's dedication to bettering the lot of the common folk. Perhaps because his parents were teachers, he was also drawn to a life of the mind. He played the piano, and excelled at chess, being equally magnanimous in victory and defeat. "Volodya" as the family affectionately called him, was a brilliant student, but he could also be mocking and cold. While he studied law at the University of St. Petersburg—signing himself "Nobleman V. I. Ulyanov" in his application—his older brother Aleksandr was hanged for plotting to assassinate Czar Alexander III. By the time Lenin passed his final examination, he was already a convert to Marxist theory. As an international activist and a member of the radical Union of Struggle, he was arrested in 1895 and sent to Siberia, where he completed his first major theoretical work, *The Development of Capitalism in Russia.* It reflected his growing belief that some spark was needed to radicalize the consciousness of his nation's workers. Upon his release, Lenin spent the next seventeen years mostly in western Europe, editing socialist organs such as *Iskra* (The Spark) with fellow Marxist Georgy Plekhanov. In 1902, his influential tract, "What Is To Be Done?," appeared, postulating a secret vanguard of professional insurgents devoted to overturning Russian society through the rise of the proletariat. He involved himself in just such an insurrection three years later. It failed and, fleeing again, he maneuvered the Bolshevik wing of Russia's Social Democratic Labor Party against the more numerous Mencheviks, who were concerned about the despotic tendencies of his revolutionary elite.

When not writing, Lenin read, voraciously and in a wide variety of fields from economics and socio-political philosophy to the natural sciences; he haunted library reading rooms. He also loved ice skating, skiing and hunting. His political urgency was unmitigated by sympathy: "Hang," the scholar who loved singing once wrote, "hang without fail, so the people see no fewer than one hundred known kulaks, rich men, bloodsuckers...Do it in such away that for hundreds of [kilometers] around, the people will see, tremble, know, shout...."

Lenin campaigned feverishly against his nation's participation in the Great War and wished for socialists everywhere to oppose it. Sensing the time was at last ripe, he left Switzerland by train in April, 1917, in that special car provided by the Germans, who were only too eager to help the skillful agitator destabilize his country's military operations. When the July uprising faltered, Lenin left for Finland. Returning after a brief sojourn, he organized the Bolsheviks into Military Revolutionary Committees, and, in the wake of Czar Nicholas II's abdication, engineered—with his comrade Leon Trotsky—the relatively bloodless coup that finally toppled the provisional regime of Alexander Kerensky. The date was November 7, 1917, but the old-style calendar read October 25—hence the "October Revolution" of 1917.

Having signed the humbling Treaty of Brest-Litovsk with Germany in 1918 to exit the war, Lenin now faced a civil conflict made all the more dangerous by foreign incursion and Allied backing of the anti-Bolshevik "Whites." By the time the dissidents were subdued, Russia was mired in discontent. So bad were social conditions that Lenin himself was robbed near the Kremlin in 1919. Fearing uprisings and anxious for foreign trade, he inaugurated his New Economic Policy (NEP) in 1921, which allowed peasants more free use of their land. In that same year, with starvation fanning across Russia, he accepted American aid, all the while insisting that communism was still working.

What will history ultimately make of this harsh messiah whose brand of Marxism has been the model against which all revolutionaries measure their orthodoxy? Of a leader who claimed to speak for the people but put his faith in assassinations and purges? In matters of the heart, he had been faithful to those who were faithful to his cause: most especially, Nadezhda Konstantinova Krupskaya, his wife until he died, and Elisabeth d'Herbenville Armand (called Inessa), a Parisian-born activist who lived on and off with Lenin and Krupskaya. But he abandoned other sentimentalities like listening to Beethoven, which, he said, made him weak. Clearly, his fellow Russians are now free from decades of Lenin idolatry. The Anti-Czar's statues have been dismantled and as the century closed, the revolutionary empire that had spread its influence across the face of the planet and had sacrificed millions for a Great Idea, was as moribund as its founder.

LINDBERGH

CHARLES

"DAREDEVIL LINDBERGH" READ THE headlines on the handbills and posters dotting dozens of America's sleepy midwestern towns. And daredevil he was, this incredibly good-looking, boyish young man who stood on the wings of rickety stunt planes as they swooped low over gasping fairground crowds; or flew across the hazardous night skies to sprinkle fireworks through hazy summer evenings; or performed the heart-stopping stunt of double-para-chuting, a perilous process that involved yanking open a second chute while in free fall several moments after the first was cut loose.

Only in his twenties when he began his barnstorming days, Charles Augustus Lindbergh had the kind of guts it took not only to perform hair-raising aerial gymnastics but also, as he did on May 20, 1927, to step into a tiny twenty-eight-foot single-engine plane and become the first man to fly solo, nonstop, across the Atlantic Ocean. He accomplished this extraordinary feat with a minimum of forward visibility and without benefit of a radio and a parachute—both of which he jettisoned in favor of more fuel. And even though he could have used something to help keep him awake on his long journey, he even did without coffee, out of con-cern that it would alter his concentration. From the first shaky moments after takeoff at Roosevelt Field on Long Island, New York, the solitary pilot fought the fatigue and fear that had hung about this chancy venture since its inception. Earlier attempts had claimed the lives of six fliers. But when *The Spirit of St. Louis* land-ed thirty-three hours and thirty-two minutes later at Paris's Le Bourget airport, the world—and $25,000 in prize money—was his. For the moment, at least, it all seemed worth it.

The fame of the Lone Eagle was limitless. In an era without mass media, Lindbergh became an international phenomenon of unequaled proportions. Around the world, people were enthralled both by his accomplishments in this pioneer era of flight and by his easygoing self-possession and humility. Immediately after his historic flight, Lindbergh was showered with honors, among them France's cross of the Légion d'honneur. Eager to claim him for their own, Americans planned their own lavish homecoming, bringing the fair-haired hero stateside aboard a U.S. Navy cruiser. Lindbergh was presented with both the Distinguished Flying Cross and the United States Medal of Honor, and when he reached New York the city turned itself inside out with a storm of ticker tape to greet the fabulous Lucky Lindy.

Despising his new nickname—for he knew that his success owed little to mere luck—Lindbergh soon grew impatient with his new celebrity. The only son of a moody and somewhat snobbish mother who separated from her husband when their son was only five, young Charles attended a bewildering variety of schools. Because he had made no significant friendships, he tended to be a man apart. His new status as a hero perplexed him as much as the

invasive attention of the press annoyed him, and he desperately sought solitude as a relief from the traffic jams and frenzied free-for-alls that his presence occasioned.

In 1929 he married Anne Spencer Morrow, the shy daughter of U.S. ambassador Dwight W. Morrow. In his wife, Lindbergh finally found the kind of enduring companionship he had been lacking. Charting travel routes and flying around the globe together, the charming couple captured the public's imagination wherever they went. When their son, Charles junior, was born and Lindbergh secluded his family in the New Jersey countryside, the picture seemed perfect.

Then, hideously, Lindbergh's luck changed overnight, in 1932 his twenty-month-old baby was kidnapped, held for ran-som, and then murdered; the decomposing body was found nine weeks later, only a few hundred yards from the family home. The investigation, controlled personally by Lindbergh, was a disaster, and the press's behavior—not to mention the public's—turned an intensely private tragedy into a circus sideshow, with vendors selling purported locks of the infant's hair. When intruders managed to photograph the child's remains inside the morgue, the Lindberghs were so disgusted that they fled to England. In 1935, in what was dubbed "the trial of the century," a carpenter named Bruno Richard Haupt-mann was convicted of the crime. Although he professed his innocence until the end, Hauptmann was executed in 1936.

During the 1930s, Lindbergh carried on a strange flirtation with the Nazis. Invited by Hitler's deputy, Hermann Göring, to tour Germany's airplane factories, Lindbergh became an admirer of Nazi air superiority and was awarded the Service Cross of the German Eagle, signed by Hitler himself. Unfortunately, Lindbergh was also impressed with Nazi propaganda and media control— a reaction that was heightened by his own belief that the press was responsible in large part for his own family's misfortune. He began to air anti-semitic views about Jewish control of American newspapers and its influence in fomenting prowar sentiments. When the Japanese attacked Pearl Harbor and Lindbergh wanted to be reinstated in the Army Air Corps—from which he had petulantly resigned in 1941 because of his isolationist sentiments—President Franklin D. Roosevelt refused his request.

In 1954 President Eisenhower restored Lindbergh's com-mission in recognition of his combat flying in the Pacific, an assignment the frustrated pilot had finagled through his defense-contract consultations. But his hero's reputation never quite regained its original patina. Lindbergh had thrilled a genera-tion with his courage and élan during one of the most inspiring media events of the century. But blinded, perhaps, by hubris, the living symbol of aviation singed his own wings.

LOREN

SOPHIA

A CHILD OF THE Neapolitan slums, Sophia Loren rose from a sea of troubles to become one of the cinema's great sex symbols. In her, the world found an enticing, quintessentially European woman, who was also warm, earthy, even maternal. As her fellow Italians might say, she was *esuberante*, radiating enough enthusiasm to fill the Colosseum. But perhaps her greatest achievement has been the sheer longevity of this allure.

Sophia Loren was born Sofia Scicolone in a Roman charity ward to Romilda Villani, a poverty-stricken woman whose lover refused to marry her—although he later allowed Sophia and her younger sister Maria to use his last name. Branded by Italian society as illegitimate, the four-year-old Sophia moved with her mother to Pozzuoli, a rundown suburb of Naples, where Romilda played piano in seedy cafes to keep bread on the table. Work was not plentiful; Sophia was so skinny that her Catholic school classmates nicknamed her *Stuzzicadente,* the toothpick.

When the war and its deprivations came to Naples—the most frequently bombed city in Italy—Sophia lived a ragged existence that left indelible marks. There was never enough food, and when the bombs rained down, the family sought shelter in train tunnels. Death and ruin were all around. The absence of even such a scoundrel of a father as Riccardo Scicolone also left her vulnerable to the taunts of other children.

As her adolescence progressed, Sophia's waif-like form metamorphosed into traffic-stopping curves. Her tall, lush body and exotically beautiful face became her ticket out of penury, her escape from the nightmare. Those huge liquid eyes, that pillowy mouth and extravagant body, wrapped in a pink dress her mother had sewn from a window curtain, earned her second place in a beauty contest. Abandoning her teacher-training studies, the fifteen-year-old journeyed to Rome with Romilda, herself a frustrated actress, to try for a movie career. The two found minuscule parts in the 1951 epic *Quo Vadis,* but the thirty-three dollars they earned did not last very long. Denied a modeling job by the very attributes that would later make her an international star, Sophia turned to "acting" in the *fumetti*—photo magazines with comic-strip-style stories featuring soap-opera plots and balloon dialogue. Her character was most often that of a gypsy vamp, and her poses on one occasion earned her the attentions of the Italian police censor. Still attempting to break into more legitimate show business, Sophia placed as a runner-up in the 1950 Miss Italy contest. Later that year she took second place in the Miss Rome competition, but won a much bigger prize than the official one, for film producer Carlo Ponti was one of the judges. Instantly struck by her quirky beauty, he remained undaunted by her disastrous screen tests. He did suggest, however, that perhaps something might be done about her oversized nose and hips. But the supremely confident teen ignored him. "Everything I have," she later boasted playfully to the American press, "I owe to spaghetti."

As training for her new craft, Loren accepted a bit part as a scantily clad harem girl in Giorgio Bianchi's *It's Him, Yes! Yes!* (1951). It was not until 1952, however, that she became known as Sophia Loren, when a producer renamed her to disassociate her from her *fumetti* days. A series of small films followed before Ponti offered her a contract—and made her his mistress. Their romance was complicated by the fact that Ponti already had a wife and two children. As he agonized over the potential repercussions of divorce, Loren cranked out movies and engaged in a "battle of the bosoms" with rival screen temptress Gina Lollobrigida. The carefully orchestrated publicity Loren garnered, plus a role in Vittorio De Sica's *Gold Of Naples* (1954), landed her in Hollywood. In *Boy on a Dolphin* (1957), audiences were treated to a vision of her famous endowments in the mesmerizing scene in which she emerges from the ocean wearing a dress made transparent and ultra-clingy by the water. In *The Pride and the Passion* (1957), the new sensation teamed with a bewitched Cary Grant, who impulsively proposed matrimony. The crisis his ardor caused finally moved Ponti to the divorce courts in Mexico, where both the dissolution and his marriage to Loren were performed by proxy. The tactic was publicly denounced by the Vatican; not recognizing the Mexican divorce, they villified Ponti as a bigamist and his new wife as a concubine. Observers were amused by the coupling of the short, portly producer with the statuesque siren, but the bride herself was lucid in her analysis of the situation: "I needed a father. I needed a husband. I was adopted by Carlo and I married my father."

None of this affected Loren's burgeoning career. *Houseboat* (1958), with the abashed but still smitten Grant was a solid hit. Nor did she abandon Europe, making fifteen Italian onscreen romances with Marcello Mastroianni, most notably *Marriage Italian Style* (1964). She reached the zenith of her career with her performance in De Sica's 1961 Italian production *La Ciociara,* known in the States as *Two Women.* For her portrayal of a wartime rape victim, she earned an Academy Award.

After several miscarriages, the actress finally bore two sons, Edoardo and Carlo, Jr., and for some time she made only promotional appearances, for her perfume, Sophia, and her line of eyewear. Her subsequent movies, such as *The Cassandra Crossing* (1977), declined in quality, but she continued to attract attention. In 1982 she was back in the press when the Italian authorities forced her to serve nineteen days in prison for tax evasion. Upon her release, "La Simpatica" went back to work, making more TV movies. In 1994, she co-starred in *Pret a Porter*—her last comedy with old friend Mastroianni—and the next year, in *Grumpier Old Men.* Loren was as sexy in both as she had been in her first film, forty years earlier. She had explained her secret in 1990: "I still like me, inside and out. Not in a vain way—I just feel good in my skin."

ROSA LUXEMBURG

SOCIAL REVOLUTION BECAME THE doctrine of the twentieth century, and no social revolutionary was more tragically gifted than the legendary Rosa Luxemburg. As a champion of the international proletariat, she embodied the intellectual rigor, the romanticism, and the violence—if only rhetorical in her case—that have come to be linked with Communist theory and some of the most transforming events of our epoch. As a left-wing political thinker, Luxemburg was compared to Marx, and in her day, which was brief, her influence on the direction of international socialist agitation was profound. But as a lover of art, literature, and life, she had no taste for the asceticism that was the hallmark of her contemporary revolutionaries. She could never be a single-minded fanatic like her lover, Leo Jogiches, to whom she wrote, "When I open your letters and see six sheets covered with debates about the Polish Socialist Party and not a single word about ordinary life, I feel faint."

Growing up Jewish, female, and crippled in a Poland dominated by czarist Russia, it is no wonder Luxemburg longed for a world where people were not defined by race, religion, and sex. The daughter of cultured merchant parents who exposed her to literature and politics, she grew up with a somewhat remote and condescending view of the workers she was trying to liberate. She spent hours writing poems—having been barred from more physical pursuits by a disabling childhood disease—and later applied her fiery mind to the twin pursuits of scholarship and sedition. The fruits of both soon became evident: A high school gold medal for achievement was denied her for her radical activities and resistance to authority. At the age of eighteen, learning that the czarist police were preparing to arrest her, the youthful agitator fled to Switzerland, where she entered the University of Zurich. In 1897, after a stellar academic career, she was awarded a doctorate on the strength of a Marxist study of Polish industry. A true believer in applied theory, Luxemburg established the Polish Social Democratic Party of the Kingdom of Poland. Its cofounder was an exiled young seditionist named Leo Jogiches, rebellious scion of a rich family, whose sullen rejection of capitalism did not include the money his father gave him to live on. The two began a rocky love affair of many years' duration, and the conflicted heir watched and fretted as Luxemburg rose to prominence through her many theoretical writings.

By 1896 she was a leading figure in the international socialist movement, alienating her Polish compatriots with her puritanical insistence that nationalism was inimical to socialism. A year later she coolly married Berliner Gustav Lübeck to obtain German citizenship, then left Zurich, and Jogiches, to foment revolution in the more promising terrain of Germany. For seven years she wrote analysis and propaganda for organs like *Die Neue Zeit (The New Time)*, inhabiting a highbrow echelon that established her reputation but did not bring her any closer to understanding the real needs and aspirations of common men and women.

Drawn back to Poland in 1905 by the false hope of the Russian Revolution, she was arrested with Jogiches, who had remained her political ally, and flung into prison. After her family arranged her release, she traveled back to Germany by way of Finland, visiting Trotsky and Lenin en route and writing one of her most important works, *The Mass Strike*. But for all her bloody rhetoric—giving her nickname, Red Rosa, a double edge—actual violence disgusted and frightened Luxemburg: She could never be a Lenin, coldly organizing terror. In fact, she believed that his antidemocratic brand of Communism was worse than the ills it was intended to cure.

Luxemburg's 1913 speeches to the workers—about the coming conflict when they would be asked to take arms against their brethren—landed her in prison again in 1915, just after World War I broke out. By this time, she had finished what was to be her most famous work, *The Accumulation of Capital*. She spent the duration of the war behind bars, translating literature and writing political tracts and poetry. When her ally Lenin successfully engineered the Russian Revolution, prisoner Luxemburg celebrated, urging the Germans to follow suit. Yet Luxemburg and her dogmatically pristine Spartacist League faction—named for the rebellious Roman slave—had little power or influence over events and, in any case, ultimately failed to establish socialism in Germany. In 1919, however, with left-wing agitation against the new Weimar Republic churning, the Spartacist League was the basis for the German Communist Party.

In January of that year, she participated in what came to be called the Spartacist Rebellion, a foolish attempt to bring down the government by mass protest. Luxemburg's ivory-tower faith in the masses proved fatal. The masses were not interested in revolution, and the government was not going anywhere. On January 15, 1919, she was arrested by officers of the Guards Cavalry, interrogated, beaten, and shot; her tiny body was dumped unceremoniously into a canal.

Rosa Luxemburg's grim death underscored her strangely compelling life. She was a brilliant theorist who, impelled by faith in the religion of socialism, took to the barricades to make a better life for society's dispossessed, a class she never really comprehended. It was a peculiar feature of her faith that, while never abandoning the exercise of her mind, she also took up the cloak and dagger, the firebrand and the bomb. In a postmortem tribute, Lenin called her an eagle who had flown low— low enough so that predators could catch her in their claws.

MACARTHUR

GENERAL DOUGLAS

ONE OF AMERICA'S GREATEST and most flamboyant commanders, General Douglas MacArthur bore his burdens through the strength given him by three hallowed words: Duty. Honor. Country. He served in every military capacity, from presidential aide to five-star general to de facto viceroy of post-Armistice Japan. Few have been called upon to exercise such power so publicly and with such dramatic consequences to world history. Superbly trained and self-possessed, he never doubted he was the man for the job—and he was very likely right.

Douglas MacArthur was born into an American family steeped in the traditions of military and government service: His father was a highly-decorated veteran of both the Civil War and the Spanish-American War, his brother a brilliant naval captain and his grandfather governor of Wisconsin. It was a heritage MacArthur cited as the primary reason for his own success. But perhaps the greatest influence on the future war chief was his mother, Mary Pinkney "Pinky" Hardy, a beautiful and intelligent daughter of the gentry who sent inspirational poetry to her son in his moments of trial.

After an Army-brat childhood spent in one or another dusty outpost, MacArthur attended West Point, graduating at the top of his class in 1903. Like Robert E. Lee before him, he was commissioned into the Corps of Engineers rather than the infantry. It was as an aide to his father during a tour of Asia that he first experienced the seductiveness of the place that became the scene of his greatest triumph and his greatest defeat. Seasoned by service, he advanced to the role of aide to President Theodore Roosevelt. Promoted to colonel and transferred to the infantry shortly after the entrance of the U.S. into World War I, MacArthur was also named chief of staff of the 42nd (Rainbow) Division in 1917. He was so often found at the most violent battlefronts that his commander called him "the bloodiest fighting man in this Army." Wounded twice, he collected seven Silver Stars for courage under fire. By 1918, he was a brigadier general.

From 1919 to 1922, MacArthur served as Superintendent of the U.S. Military Academy, from which post he undertook radical reforms not usually associated with a militarist—specifically, raising academic standards. Leaving West Point after three years, he returned to the Philippines, spending the next eight years there while also serving in 1928 as chairman of the U.S. Olympic Committee. In 1930, he was appointed U.S. Army Chief of Staff; during his tenure there he tarnished his reputation by routing the jobless veterans who marched on Washington to demand bonuses due them. When he relinquished the post of Chief, the United States Army numbered 139,000 troops of all ranks and was woefully undersupplied. Calling for greater preparedness, MacArthur accepted an appointment as military advisor to the newly-created Philippine Commonwealth to help prepare them for independence and develop their defenses.

It was too late. On December 7, 1941, the Imperial forces destroyed half his air force in one assault and within weeks invaded Luzon. Forced to abandon his Corregidor headquarters in 1942, he escaped to Australia, where he made the memorable pledge that became the Allied motto in the Pacific: "I came through, and I shall return." MacArthur had been soundly defeated, yet he became an instant national hero and was awarded the Congressional Medal of Honor.

He kept his promise, returning as Commander of the Allied Forces in the Southwest Pacific to pursue a "leapfrog" campaign to drive out and isolate the Japanese forces. By the end of the war, MacArthur, now a five-star general, had retaken most of Luzon. His instantly recognizable image—the corncob pipe, aviator sunglasses, and insignia-encrusted cap—personified American resurgence.

Following victory in the Pacific, MacArthur was given the awesome task of reorganizing Japanese society. He purged the ruling elite of militarism, instituted land reforms, and gave women the right to vote. Wisely retaining the Emperor for symbolic purposes, MacArthur's new Japanese constitution vested power in the Parliament and renounced war and the use of armed forces.

When the Korean War erupted in 1950, MacArthur was picked to head the United Nations military force. When President Harry Truman ordered him to send aid to the South Koreans on the heels of the North Korean invasion, MacArthur took it one step further and bombed North Korean airfields without Truman's prior knowledge. He then turned back the Communist advance with an enormously risky amphibious landing at the port of Inchon, a maneuver which allowed UN forces to take Seoul. In September 1950, mistakenly believing that China would never aid the Communists, MacArthur advanced north of the 38th parallel, the boundary between the two Koreas, boasting that the troops would be "Home by Christmas." The Chinese People's Liberation Army smashed his divided forces in a humiliating defeat.

Complaining that the President was hamstringing him, MacArthur was eager to bomb bases inside China. Truman refused, and MacArthur made the dispute public. "There is no substitute for victory," he declared. In April 1951, an angry Truman relieved him of his command.

In MacArthur's address to Congress he insisted that victory in Korea was still possible and recalled a refrain from a barracks ballad: "Old soldiers never die, they just fade away." Eleven years later, in his eloquent acceptance of the Thayer Award at West Point, he spoke movingly of lengthening shadows and the witching calls of bugles, and bade his fellow soldiers farewell.

MADONNA

MADONNA'S CONTRIBUTIONS to music, film, and fashion have always been part of a carefully calculated package, an image so protean and so meticulously crafted that her greatest work of art has been herself. Hence everyone has a favorite Madonna, whether it be the early Boy Toy version, the Marilyn-wannabe Material Girl, the super-toned Gautier-clad techno-dominatrix, or the mature earth-mother of her latest musical efforts. But these various identities have never eclipsed the artist herself: fans have come to expect and anticipate each new Madonna project—whether it be a new album, a new film, or something like her Mylar-sealed, too-hot-to-handle photo book, *Sex* (1990)—and with it, each new intriguing persona.

Growing up in suburban Detroit, Madonna Louise Ciccone (named after her mother, who died of cancer when Madonna was six) aspired to be a dancer. She studied for a period at the University of Michigan, but soon dropped out, and in 1978 moved to New York, penniless and intent on becoming a star. The nineteen-year-old got by with earnings from nude modeling and the generosity of new found friends, occasionally reduced to digging through garbage cans for food. After a brief stint studying with Martha Graham alumna Pearl Lang, she eventually won a place in Lang's dance troupe, and later in the Alvin Ailey company. Dance alone, however, could not begin to fulfill the goals Madonna had set for herself. Moving into the music scene, she picked up a basic education in rock music from one of her early lovers, Dan Gilroy, learning percussion and guitar, and occasionally playing drums and singing with Gilroy's band, The Breakfast Club. Her big break, though, came when she met her manager Camille Barbone. One of the partners of Gotham Productions, she very quickly got her new client a contract, a salary, and an apartment in a posh neighborhood. With a new band, Madonna was soon a popular fixture in trendy downtown clubs of the Eighties. At her favorite, Danceteria, deejay Mark Kamins played her demo tape for the late-night crowd, which loved it. From Kamins, she finessed a crucial introduction to the president of Sire Records, Seymour Stein. Defecting from Barbone, Madonna launched herself on an upward trajectory.

Her first album for Sire, *Madonna*, did poorly on the charts at first, but the budding star with a genius for public relations used her telephone to promote airplay. Freddie DeMann, then Michael Jackson's manager, was wooed by the fearless self-promoter and promptly began organizing her publicity efforts. In the spring of 1984, the song "Borderline" reached number 10 on the singles' charts, and by early 1985 her second album, *Like A Virgin*—propelled by her outrageous performance at the MTV Video Music Awards, and the videos for the title track and "Material Girl"—had hit number one. Whether it was MTV who helped make Madonna, or the other way around, the two would be practically synonymous for many years.

Meanwhile, the reactions that Madonna and her music evoked became more intense. Teenage girls around the world worshipped her as an artist who created irresistible pop songs with a liberating message of sex-as-power. Other sectors of the public, angered by songs like "Papa Don't Preach" (1991), about a girl deciding to go through with her unplanned pregnancy, railed against her as a singer who preached hedonism and immorality to her many fans. This conservative cry reached its peak with the release of *Like a Prayer* in 1989. The video for the title track, a controversial piece in which Madonna experiences stigmata, among other things, was denounced as sacrilegious, and eventually resulted in her excommunication from the Catholic church. The controversy only seemed to increase her fan base, as well as her record sales.

Though her concerts were continually sold out and her albums went double platinum, Madonna had yet to fulfill her goal of becoming a movie star. There was praise for her scene-stealing turn as a scheming but likable Village hipster in *Desperately Seeking Susan* (1985), but critics and moviegoers alike ignored her next two projects, *Shanghai Surprise* (1986)—which co-starred her then-husband, Sean Penn—and *Who's That Girl* (1987). Her role five years later as Breathless Mahoney in *Dick Tracy* received more attention, but not as much as her off-screen relationship with Warren Beatty, the director and star of the film. The documentary about her, *Truth or Dare* (1991), was an over-the-top and revealing look at the work and life of the singer, and Penny Marshall's film, *A League of Their Own* (1992), was a bigger success, but not the vehicle needed to make Madonna a star. (It did, however, mark the beginning of her friendship with co-star Rosie O'Donnell.) It would be her role as Eva Peron, in Alan Parker's film adaptation of *Evita* (1996), that would begin to earn Madonna the recognition she was seeking in film. Her portrayal of the actress-turned-politician earned her a Golden Globe Award the following year for Best Actress in a comedy or musical.

Other venues for her ambition soon followed. Pregnant by her personal trainer, Madonna gave birth in 1996 to a baby girl she named Lourdes. Transformed yet again by the experience of motherhood, she abandoned her grueling daily workouts for the peace of yoga, released a new album, *Ray of Light* (1998), and continued her recently begun study of Kabbalah, the ancient, mystical, and suddenly trendy branch of Judaism. She continues to manage her own record company, Maverick, with the same level of drive, and she is always scanning the horizon for new talent. As a close friend of hers was quoted in *Vanity* Fair: "The Madonna Corporation does not go on vacation."

MALCOLM X

IN HIS BRIEF AND tumultuous life he was known by many names: a teenage petty hoodlum called "Detroit Red," a grim convict dubbed "Satan," a devout pilgrim to Mecca named El Hajj Malik El Shabazz. But he will be remembered by a name that was half name and half bitter denunciation of the slavery that extirpated black identity and made his people ciphers in their own country: Malcolm X. A revolutionary voice lashing out at white racist society, Malcolm X's most radical change took place within his own heart, as he evolved from racialist incendiary to a man who embraced the brotherhood of mankind.

He was born Malcolm Little in Omaha, Nebraska, to the Reverend Earl Little, a Baptist minister active in the black separatist Universal Negro Improvement Association, and Louise, the West Indian offspring of a black woman raped by a white man. Her son would always carry with him the shame and rage engendered by this crime. But the family's persecutions were not to end there. His father's political activities attracted the ire of the Ku Klux Klan, who attacked the Little home, smashing all the windows. In terror, the family fled to Milwaukee, then on to East Lansing, Michigan. In 1931 the Rev. Little was found bludgeoned to death on a railroad track.

Overburdened by caring for ten children in the midst of the Great Depression, Louise Little succumbed to mental illness and was committed to the state hospital. Malcolm, made a ward of the state, was soon expelled from school for acting out and sent to a detention home. Improving his behavior, he managed to finish junior high school and in 1941 he persuaded an aunt in Boston to gain custody of him.

Once there he quickly acclimated himself to the life of a ghetto hipster, acquiring a zootsuit, and the nickname "Red" after his rusty-hued complexion and hair. He straightened his hair, and learned to deal marijuana and to pimp for the local prostitutes. In 1942, after working as a railroad sandwich vendor, he moved to Harlem and a life of dope and armed robberies. Chased back to Boston by death threats from a rival, he pursued his life of crime until a broken watch tied him to a string of heists. In 1946 the twenty-year-old began serving a ten-year sentence.

Prison was his university. After a brief period in which he stayed high and defiant, the youthful convict began to exercise his considerable intellect. Influenced by a prison mate who urged him to educate himself, he took correspondence courses in English and Latin and became a frequent visitor to the prison library. He was also influenced by his own brothers, who were adherents of the Nation of Islam (NOI or "the Nation"), and became a follower, shunning drugs, tobacco, and pork. Founded by Elijah Muhammad, a traveling salesman formerly known as Wallace Ford, the Nation's singular brand of Islam held that black people were Allah's Chosen People. Muhammad also preached the virtues of hard work, self-reliance, and an upright life as a way to escape the persecutions of a racist society.

No message was more suited to Malcolm's life and temperament. Leaving prison in 1952, he immediately joined the Nation, adopting the now-famous "X" as a symbol of the original African name he would never know. Given command of the Detroit mosque, he was so successful that Muhammad moved him to New York. There he founded the organization's newspaper *Muhammad Speaks* and was key to the Nation's expansion. In 1958 he married Betty X, with whom he had six daughters. The next year he became highly visible when a biased television program featured his most rabble-rousing pronouncements. Attacked by the major media for hate-mongering, the uncowed Malcolm responded, "The white man is in no moral position to accuse anyone else of hate!"

Privately, however, Malcolm was beginning to entertain doubts about the Nation's insular views. Those doubts were solidified when he learned that Muhammad had fathered several illegitimate children. His former mentor moved swiftly to suspend him, ostensibly for an unwise remark Malcolm had made to the effect that the assassination of John F. Kennedy represented "the chickens coming home to roost." But Malcolm soon learned of conspiracies from within the Nation to assassinate him. In 1964 he left the Nation, announced the creation of Muslim Mosque, Inc., and, observing the religious obligation of every Muslim, made a pilgrimage to Mecca.

Seeing Muslims of all races joined in faith at their most sacred site transformed his thinking. Embracing the true Muslim religion, he was determined to return to America and assist in the Civil Rights Movement, and to find a philosophy that expressed his new internationalist outlook.

He found it in the "liberation" politics of the Third World. After a tour of some of the new post-colonial African states, he announced in New York that "You can't have capitalism without racism." Perceiving the need to make common cause with white radicals, he embarked on the final, most frustrating phase of his career, that of trying to convince America that "ignorance and greed" lay at the heart of the country's troubles, not the least of which was segregation.

In mid-February 1965, amid growing threats against his life from the NOI leadership and white racists, two Molotov cocktails shattered the windows of his Queens home as his family slept. One week later, on February 21, 1965, three men shot him as he rose to speak at the Audubon Ballroom. His entire family watched him fall, and with him, a little of the hope in all those seeking racial equality.

MANDELA

NELSON

HE BECAME THE SPIRITUAL LEADER of the revolutionary African National Congress, a liberation movement locked in mortal struggle with the forces of institutionalized racism in the Republic of South Africa. As a lawyer with a politically colorful student career behind him, Nelson Mandela claimed to be inspired by the nonviolent tactics of Mahatma Gandhi, another law practitioner who had fallen afoul of the Boer Republic. He was not himself a Marxist, but political prudence led him to befriend the Communists. This was a distinction lost on the Afrikaner's National party, the reactionary white-supremacist organization which was dominated by the Dutch South Africans who came to political power in 1948 and immediately fixed in law the cruelty of apartheid, or racial separation, that became the central feature of South African life.

When the Afrikaners introduced the Suppression of Communism Act, a bit of Orwellian legislation that defined all enemies of apartheid as Communists, it didn't take Mandela long to get on the wrong side of the act. By 1950, he was the president of the ANC Youth League, and in 1952 he was named volunteer-in-chief of the Defiance Campaign, a prolonged antistate agitation. Soon the state confined him to Johannesburg for six months, and the "banned" Mandela founded his law firm with fellow ANC agitator Oliver Tambo. The next year Mandela was sentenced to nine months in prison for his role in the Defiance Campaign and ordered to quit the ANC. Instead, he further stung the government by endorsing the Freedom Charter, which called for a nonracist South Africa and redistribution of the land. More than once, the Afrikaner government put him on trial for his support of such ideas, only to fail to convict him every time. Finally, in 1961, with the ANC agitation made illegal, the African rebel went underground as the leader of *Umkhonto we Sizwe*, or Spear of the Nation, the ANC's guerrilla wing, conducting industrial sabotage and preparing for war.

Mandela was dubbed the Black Pimpernel for his amazing ability to elude the Bureau of State Security force, but his luck ran out when he was recognized, while disguised as a chauffeur, by a sharp-eyed cop. At his trial for treason he described himself as a patriot and an admirer of constitutional democracy but received a verdict of guilty and a sentence of life imprisonment. For over twenty-seven years Mandela lived in prison, keeping fit by exercising and boxing, organizing schools of prisoners, and conducting his politics in a confinement the harshness of which gradually eased as a nervous government moved slowly toward liberalization. Finally, in 1990, Mandela was released to world acclaim. With his wife, Winnie, by his side, he faced the hard task of negotiating a future with his enemies. He found himself dealing with the foot-dragging and internal confusion of the National party government, with intractable Zulus who wanted their own homeland, and with right-wing Boer extremists who marched up and down in neo-Nazi costume and prepared for insurrection. Nor was his own house entirely clean. Winnie, whom he eventually divorced, was accused of ordering the fatal beating of a Soweto youth, and Mandela himself was compelled to admit that the ANC had mistreated suspected enemies during his incarceration. (Eventually the world recognized that Graca Machel, widow of Mozambican president Samora Machel, was the new object of Mandela's affection. However, as figures of enormous symbolic significance in their respective countries, the couple decided that they could never marry each another.)

In the meantime, Mandela continued to visit the world's capitals, being feted as a great statesman, addressing the United States Congress, and not too subtly sending the message back home that the future of his country depended on him. He emphasized the need for racial equality as a sine qua non for building a new South Africa. And in the kind of strange development that marks either the end of a war or the beginning of one, Mandela and his chief antagonist, South African president F. W. de Klerk, were jointly awarded the Nobel Peace Prize in 1993. The following year the tall, elegant, and almost completely gray Mandela became the first democratically elected president of the new South Africa, inheriting a hopeful but wretchedly unequal nation.

His task was enormous, and the reconciliation of the two ethnic groups was only part of it. He established a Truth and Reconciliation Commission to encourage war criminals and other political transgressors to come forward, but many did not, and rank-and-file blacks objected that the blanket amnesty amounted to a derogation of justice. Crime rose, and the police—long merely paramilitary guardians of apartheid—were ill equipped to deal with it. When not answering his growing legion of critics, Mandela found himself acting more often than not as a drummer for foreign investment into South Africa. He was not the first insurrectionary leader in the twentieth century to discover that winning the revolution is one thing, while running a country is quite another. With his powerful convictions still intact, however, he may yet prove himself as competent at the second as he has been at the first.

MAO ZEDONG

FOUNDER OF THE People's Republic of China, Mao Zedong was that rare combination, a man of action and a theoretician. He shaped the century not only as a leader of one-quarter of he globe's population but also as a writer, whose thoughts on communism, guerrilla warfare, and revolutionary struggle would be extremely influential, especially in the emerging Third World countries. However, he was also a ruthless visionary, committed to transforming Chinese society regardless of the human cost; this reformer and idealist presided over the suffering and death of literally millions of his countrymen.

Born into relative wealth, Mao Zedong's father was a grain merchant who had been born a poor peasant. Despite his improved social status, Mao's father was a practical man, with no formal education; Mao, in contrast, was a voracious reader, who was influenced by the Eastern tradition, from Chinese historical novels of renegade heroes to political philosophers as well as the Western works of Mill, Spenser, and Rousseau. Mao's determined rebellion against his father—he would reject both life on the family farm and the marriage his father had arranged—revealed an iron will. In 1911, Mao fought as a recruit in Sun Yat-sen's Republican army against the Manchu order, and went on to be a student at the First Normal School in Changsha, where his knowledge of philosophy and political theory, including Marxism, broadened as he studied ethics. In 1917, at the age of twenty-four, Mao published his first essay.

After helping to establish the Chinese Communist party in 1921, by twenty-seven, Mao organized peasant and industrial unions in his native Hunan, and, in 1926, directed the Kuomintang's Peasant Movement. As a result of his activities, he moved away from the Marxist faith in the urban proletariat and focused instead on the long-oppressed rural workers and their mobilization to affect social change. While he had cooperated with Chiang Kai-shek's Kuomintang during the 1920s, after the Kuomintang and Communist split in 1927, Mao led the "Autumn Harvest Uprising" which led to his ouster from the party's central committee. His second wife and sister were executed by Chiang's forces in 1930. From 1928 to 1931, Mao and others organized rural soviets, and built the Red Army. By 1931, Mao was elected chairman of the new Soviet Republic of China, and the battle lines between Mao and Chiang were drawn.

When Mao's base in the Jiangxi province was encircled by Chiang Kai-shek's armies in October of 1934, some 90,000 women and men marched westward, embarking on 6,000 mile journey, known as the "Long March." 370 days later, they had crossed eighteen mountain ranges and twenty-four rivers, and the Communist ranks were literally decimated. But, in Mao's own words, the Long March was both a victory and a "manifesto": "It has proclaimed to the world that the Red Army is an army of heroes." It also confirmed Mao's absolute leadership.

The civil war continued during and after the Sino-Japanese war until 1949, when the mainland of China fell to the Communists and Mao became chairman of the central government of the new People's Republic of China. Bringing China into the modern age was a brutal process, and Mao's regime was extremely repressive. In the early fifties, protection of private business ceased, foreigners were sent out of China, and a campaign against so-called counter-revolutionaries—the millions who had served Chiang in their youth—began. Thirty thousand people were executed. Mao instituted a Five Year Plan—based on the Soviet model, both anti-capitalist and anti-imperialist—and thousands of Soviet technical advisors streamed into China, to build factories, hydroelectric power, and heavy industry. At the same time, tens of thousands of Chinese intellectuals were "re-educated" at "revolutionary colleges"; by 1957, 300,000 had been consigned to prison camps, jail, or were summarily sent into rural exile. As Mao's China emerged, the nation's four-thousand-year-old culture was methodically destroyed—a precursor to the decade-long terror of the Cultural Revolution twenty years later. In 1958, Mao launched the Great Leap Forward, a plan to modernize and collectivize agriculture; the resulting food shortages caused the death of over 20 million people by starvation, many of them children. During this period, too, Mao broke with the Soviet Union which cut off both economic aid and political support.

Threatened by the massive failure of his program and the end of Soviet support, his cadre moved to shore up the vision of Mao as China's destined and irreplaceable leader. By 1963, *Quotations from Chairman Mao*—the "little red book"—was read and studied by millions of Chinese, raising reverence for Mao to a cult. What would finally quash any criticism of Mao, though, was the reign of terror known as the "Cultural Revolution" which began in 1966 and continued for a decade; it was meant to insure that the now seventy-three-year-old Mao would not be shunted aside for new leadership. Routing out "old customs, old habits, old culture, old thinking"—any thought or action remotely connected to the West or the old China—Red Guards enforced the Cultural Revolution's tenets. Over 700,000 Chinese were terrorized; over 35,000 died at their hands.

When Mao Zedong died in September of 1976, a week-long period of mourning was set. At the funeral, which was heard on radio as well as televised, all four leaders of the Cultural Revolution, including Mao's wife, Jiang Qing, were present. They were arrested less than a month later, re-christened "The Gang of Four," and put on trial. The eradication of Mao's cult had begun.

A revolutionary and visionary, a man who tried to forge a modern state out of a feudal society, in the end, it was Mao's single-minded brutality, not his contribution to political thought, that was remembered.

THE MARX BROTHERS

IN THEIR ASSAULT ON conventional cant, social niceties, and the tyranny of rationality, the Marx Brothers at their height had no rivals. As first a four-man and then a three-man team, the comedic commando squad combined surrealist imagery, vaudeville shtick, and slapstick farce in a crazy mix that was as intellectual as it was physical. Their trademarks—Groucho's painted moustache, caterpillar eyebrows, and ubiquitous cigar, Harpo's crumpled top-hat and curly wig, and Chico's goofy Tyrolean cap—were as instantly recognizable to people of every generation as their comedy was inimitable.

The Marx Brothers grew up in very hard circumstances in the Yorkville neighborhood on New York City's Upper East Side, an immigrant population animated by the onging friction between the different ethnic groups who jostled for living space there. The sons of a French-speaking tailor from Alsace named Sam ("Frenchie") Marx and his sweet and funny German-speaking wife Minna ("Minnie") Schoenberg, the brothers were easily spurred on in their mother's ambitious dreams of show business fortune and the example provided by an uncle, Al Shean, who was well-known in the vaudeville circuit of the day. All five brothers—in descending order of age, Chico (Leonard), Harpo (Adolph), Groucho (Julius Henry), Gummo (Milton), and Zeppo (Herbert)—were dragooned at one time or another into "Minnie's" scheme. Chico, for example, was given piano lessons by a teacher who was vague about the function of the left hand in playing that instrument; such were the family finances that the young pianist passed on this truncated wisdom to Harpo, who meanwhile had taught himself the harp. Guitar-playing Groucho and Gummo were teamed with a girl to sing as "The Three Nightingales"; when they added Harpo, the nightingales became four. "The Six Musical Mascots" were born when Groucho, Chico, Gummo, and Harpo joined mother "Minnie" and an aunt. It was Minnie who held the family together—no easy job since her boys were as rambunctious in real life as they were on stage—and the Marx boys adored her. (In her honor, they later gave all their daughters names that started with "M.")

In these various musical configurations the brothers struggled in the backwash of the old vaudeville circuits for years. Booked by their mother into grueling one-night stands, they eventually created, with the help of their Uncle Al, a complicated comic routine that over the years developed into the characters that made them famous: Groucho as a fast-talking anarchic huckster, Harpo as a lecherous mute with a penchant for kleptomania and contorting his face in a "Gookie" (named after a New York cigar-roller), Chico as a dishonest Italian hustler (using an accent he learned on the streets of New York), and Zeppo—who replaced Gummo in the comedy act—as nice guy and foil in the quartet's first five movies. Their new names had been conferred upon them by a fellow comedian in the style of a popular book of the day: Dyspeptic Julius became Groucho, skirt-chasing Leonard Chicko (later Chico), and harpist Adolph, Harpo. Gummo was named after soft-soled gumshoes and Zeppo after a monkey named "Zippo" in a vaudeville act (the name later evolved to a more flattering Zeppo).

With a full bag of comedic tricks—word plays, visual puns, sleight-of-hand, insults, and smarmy double-entendre—the brothers stormed Broadway in 1924 with a stage play, "I'll Say She Is," followed quickly by "The Cocoanuts" (1925) and "Animal Crackers" (1928). While still appearing in the latter, they shot The Cocoanuts—their first movie. It heralded their golden age; after the film version of "Crackers" (Animal Crackers, 1930), in rapid succession came Monkey Business (1931), Horsefeathers (1932), Duck Soup (1933), A Night at the Opera (1935), A Day at the Races (1937), Room Service (1938), and At the Circus (1939).

Unbelievably enough, Duck Soup was not a hit, leading Paramount Studios to drop the brothers and convincing Zeppo to become an agent. But MGM signed them, and Zeppo's departure left the stage to a greater foil, the eternally obtuse Margaret Dumont, a grande dame of the let-us-meet-in-the-yellow-drawing-room tradition. Such now-classic lines as "I'm defending your honor—which is more than you ever did" or "When we're married, we'll have to move. I don't like Junior crossing the tracks to go to school. . .come to think of it, I don't like Junior" were as integral to Groucho's style as Harpo's taxi horn and habit of snipping off men's ties and Chico's conniving double-talk were to theirs. A Night at the Opera, is one of the best examples of their comedic talent with some of their best routines, and a literally smashing finale.

By the beginning of the Second World War, the scripts were getting thinner, their relations with the studios more bitter, and the brothers older. Go West (1940) was disappointing, though The Big Store (1941) was a fittingly crazed swan-song. After Chico, Harpo, and Groucho had all turned fifty, they retired, returning for one last encore in A Night in Casablanca (1946).

Though Chico and Harpo would make cameo appearances from time to time, they mostly stayed out of the public eye; Chico whiled away his time with gambling, and Harpo devoted himself to being what a friend called "one of the sweetest human beings that ever was." Only Groucho went on to become as big a radio and television hit as he had been a movie star, hosting a hilarious quiz show called "You Bet Your Life." The quiz was the least of the show; the real attraction was still the sexagenarian's provocative wit. When a minister gushed that he wanted to thank Groucho for all the joy he put into the world, Marx shot back that he wanted to thank him for all the joy he had taken out of it. The minister had it right.

MATA HARI

THE STORY OF MATA HARI, the most famous female spy in history, is as embroidered as the gauzy costumes the scandalous young dancer wore in her performances on the stages and in the elegant private salons of pre–World War I Europe. In Paris, Vienna, Rome, and Berlin, she undulated through a repertoire of "authentic" sacred Oriental dances she claimed to have learned in an Indian shrine of the goddess Shiva. These entertainments, inevitably involving a slow shedding of veils, ended in almost total nudity, as her titillated audiences were thrilled to discover. However, the dark-haired seductress was not, as she mythologized, the Brahman daughter of a temple dancer who died giving birth to her. She was instead the child of a typical middle-class Dutch family, who cultivated an insatiable taste for glamour, wealth, and powerful men. As one of the most notorious courtesans of her era, she indulged herself until her own theatrical lies led her into a web of intrigue, disillusionment, and finally death.

Born Margaretha Geertruide Zelle in the canal-threaded town of Leeuwarden in northern Holland, the future spy encountered scandal while barely in her teens, when she was expelled for seducing her convent school's headmaster, a priest. She was sent to The Hague to live with a wealthy aunt. From there she attended a teacher's college in Leiden, but instead of looking for a school, she answered a matri-monial advertisement on a whim, hoping to escape the inevitable boredom of a small-town future through marriage. The resulting union, in 1895, with Campbell MacLeod, a Scottish captain in the Dutch colonial forces, was a disaster from the moment the couple sailed for his assignment in Java two years later. On that trip, not only was her husband unfaithful and physically abusive, but a servant poisoned both of her children, resulting in the death of her son. Upon their return to Holland in 1902, MacLeod kidnapped their remaining child, Jeanne, whom the distraught young mother would see only once more in her life.

Mata Hari, which means "Eye of Dawn" in Malay, was a persona invented by the hard-pressed and now divorced Margaretha. She set off for Paris where, after a failed attempt as an artists' model she embarked on her new career as a "Hindu" dancer. For ten years she moved through the bustle of European high society, attracting a string of prestigious and affluent lovers with her charm and guile, including the crown prince of Germany. But World War I brought penury to the aging beauty, and as her taste for liquor and the size of her waistline grew apace, she began to boast in public about her daring exploits as an undercover operative.

Were her extravagant tales true or merely the braggadocio of a broken and bitter woman? She certainly had both the contacts and the access; as a citizen of a neutral country, she was allowed to travel wherever she pleased, and indeed she meandered through the continent's capitals with curious frequency, consorting with high-level officials of all nations. The French, at any rate, believed her extravagant stories. More to the point, perhaps, they were faring badly in the war, morale was low, and they needed a scapegoat. Mata Hari fit the bill perfectly. In July 1917 they accused her of espionage, charging that her disclosures of Allied military intelligence had caused the deaths of some fifty thousand combatants. Despite her protestations of innocence, she was sentenced to death.

Had Mata Hari really been the German agent H21? The evidence is labyrinthine, and it is almost impossible to separate fact from fiction. It was alleged that she had been trained in techniques of surveillance in 1908 by the famous Dr. Elsbeth Schragmuller at the German espionage academy in Lorrach. She herself admitted at her interrogation that the Germans had paid her twenty thousand francs to spy on the French, but she maintained that she had never really intended to keep her part of the bargain, and in fact had not. Some sources attest that she actually did pass on information to the Germans but that it was merely gossip and tales from newspapers. Others have speculated that Mata Hari was a double agent for the French, who, in turn, double-crossed her. She herself testified that she had indeed been recruited by the head of the French Secret Service himself, a Captain Georges Ladoux. Had she accepted money from the Germans and then failed to mention this fact to the French? Russell Warren Howe, a journalist who in the 1980s examined the sealed records of Mata Hari's trial, concluded that both nations wished to get rid of her. The Germans may have framed her by sending her a message in a code they knew the French had already cracked, and at her secret trial the French blocked the testimony of two key witnesses who might have exonerated her.

Whatever Mata Hari's ultimate loyalties, it is clear that she had tried to play a dangerous game that she was neither clever nor knowledgeable enough to win. She did, however, know how to die. On October 15, 1917, Mata Hari, dressed elegantly and formally down to her gloves and hat, walked gracefully to her death. She refused a blindfold and, just before the barrage of gunfire cut her down, blew her executioners a dainty kiss.

HENRI MATISSE

THE ARC OF HENRI MATISSE'S long life, linking the nine-teenth and twentieth centuries, symbolizes his unique position in the history of art. Along with his friend and sometime rival Pablo Picasso, Matisse acted as a bridge between the com-forting aesthetics of realism and the unsettling revolutions of abstraction. Indeed, these two masters are so fundamental to modern art that they are sometimes jokingly referred to as "Ma Tisse and Pa Casso."

Unlike the famously licentious Spaniard, however, Matisse lived a carefully circumscribed, essentially bourgeois existence. An upright man who dressed like the law clerk he once was, only his work and its focus on the female form revealed his lib-ertine side. "She" is everywhere in his art, dancing on sunlit walls, sunning nude by the seashore, or, in his most famous can-vases, painted in the twenties and thirties, lounging *au naturel* or half-clothed in some lushly patterned seraglio. His passion for his models' bodies, however—despite his practice of sitting extremely close to them—appears to have been gone no further than his absorption in the creative process.

It was a process about which Matisse was extremely articulate. Grounded in the essentials (he was trained in the academic tradition), he could experiment with form and plane. His use of line and equation of emotion and color looked effort-less, but disguised a rigor that he spent a lifetime tyring to fulfill. The father of the Fauvists, those "wild beasts" who scrambled both color and perspective, he set the avant-garde on its ear with *The Woman with the Hat*. Exhibited at Paris's Salon d'Automne in 1905, the canvas was a kaleidoscopic portrait of his wife wearing a rather prosaic hat. Rendering oceans baby-bottom pink and green-leafed trees sparkling sapphire, his art expressed what the artist felt as he saw.

Matisse was late to discover his talent. Born in the unin-spiring environs of Le Cateau-Cambrésis in northern France, he was encouraged to pursue a legal career by his grain-merchant father. At the age of twenty-one he was miraculously—the word he later used to describe the event—stricken with an acute case of appendicitis that rendered him bedridden for months. To ease the monotony, his mother gave him a box of paints and an instruction book; they became the instruments of a spiritual and creative awakening. From that point on, every decision in Matisse's life was dictated by his need to make art. In 1892 he began studying with the great French Symbolist painter Gustave Moreau, who urged his protégé to learn from the mas-ters but to paint his own masterpiece. Moreau also helped cure Matisse of his obsession with murky tones—a dramatic change in palette that is richly evident in *La Desserte* (1908), which features large patches of pulsating, saturated color. In 1898,

Matisse married Amélie Parayre, a young woman from Toulouse; the couple adopted Marguerite, the artist's daughter from a previous liaison, and went on to have two sons of their own. Amélie, who spent most of her life as an invalid, immedi-ately devoted herself to serving the needs of her utterly self-absorbed husband.

After the 1905 Salon, Matisse began to attract the inter-est of such notable collectors as Gertrude Stein and her broth-ers in Paris and the Russian patron Sergei Shchukin, who in 1909 commissioned *Music* and *La Danse*. Two trips to North Africa left him entranced with the intricate motifs of Islamic art and the sexually tinged exoticism he encountered there. *The Piano Lesson* (1916) and *Moroccans at Prayer* (1916) both grew out of his stays in Morocco. (His well-known *Studio* [1915-16] and *Quai Saint-Michel* [1915-16] reveal interest in cubism as well.) Around 1917, he settled more or less perma-nently in Nice. The cyan sea of the Côte d'Azure shimmered outside his shuttered balcony window; inside, Matisse focused on the room, painting costumed odalisques against flattened, highly decorated planes. Far removed from his Fauvist and Cubist endeavors, these opulent harem fantasies, done mostly in the 1920s, increased his fame but incurred charges of "banal ornamentalism" from the art establishment. Yet hedonis-tic seduction could not have been more alien to Matisse's credo, which called for a pure and balanced art that eschewed "troubling or depressing subject matter."

Having endured World War II in Vichy France relatively unscathed, Matisse bade a farewell to painting with his mas-terful *Large Interior in Red* (1948). Increasingly infirm, he moved more and more into "the private garden," where he could be alone. Fortunately for art, he took along a pair of scis-sors. Sitting in his bed or wheelchair, hands no longer steady enough to wield a paintbrush, he applied this humble imple-ment to large sheets of paper covered with brilliantly hued gouache and began, simply, to "cut into color." The resulting semiabstract forms were used to illustrate *Jazz*, a 1947 book of his reflections on life and art. With these cutouts, which he later executed in mural size, Matisse believed he had perfected a medium that combined the spirit of drawing with the expres-siveness of color and the sensual contouring of sculpture.

Perhaps the most dramatic monument to this technique can be found in Chapelle du Rosaire, a tiny chapel in Vence, near Cannes, in the South of France which Matisse designed just seven years before his death. The church's tall stained-glass windows, alive with these bright, fluid shapes, exhibit the same lyrical free-dom and fervent simplification that animate all of the artist's work—and that enabled him to constantly reanimate modern painting.

MARGARET MEAD

IN A 1976 ISSUE of *Life* magazine honoring "Remarkable American Women," an intriguing black-and-white photograph shows a youthful Margaret Mead dressed in a loosely draped sarong and surrounded by lush tropical flora. Her neck, wrists, and close-cropped hair are adorned with island greenery, and her right arm is draped over the bare shoulders of a similarly clad and equally innocent-looking girl, a chieftain's daughter. It is 1925, the year the adventurous twenty-four-year-old anthropologist sailed to the balmy South Pacific—with several notebooks, one thousand dollars from her father, and the backing of the legendary Franz Boas, her mentor and the chairman of the department of anthropology at Barnard—to observe the behavior and attitudes of adolescent Samoan girls. Her nine-month solo expedition yielded a seminal book in her field, *Coming of Age in Samoa,* which compared the lives of Samoan adolescents with their Western counterparts. The ensuing international fame would permit this passionate scientist to disseminate her original and provocative ideas about everything from sibling rivalry, extraterrestrial life, and birth control to city planning, healthful diet, and equality between the sexes.

Mead's mind was encyclopedic and unique in perspective. It was keen and curious: a kaleidoscope in which knowledge was interrelated, constantly in flux, forming new patterns of insight. She wrote some two dozen books, and because she wrote with clarity and fluidity and without the jargon of social scientists, her ideas were readily grasped by the layperson. During her long career, she learned six languages, pioneered the development of semiotics—the study of how people communicate by gesture—and the use of photography in field research, and integrated numerous other fields such as psychology, psychoanalysis, and biology into her theoretical musings.

From an early age Mead was schooled in the techniques of social-science research by her sociologist mother and her grandmother, who had been a teacher. It seemed natural for this child to begin examining her environment, and one of her first projects, at the age of eight, was to keep a written record of her younger sisters' speech patterns. In her later years, Mead felt compelled to speak out on the human condition and the problems of the planet, but despite her flawless academic credentials and her longstanding curatorship at the prestigious American Museum of Natural History in New York, her ideas were not always popular. Disdainful critics called her a meddler and a dilettante for taking public stands on issues outside her purview. She became a heroine to alienated youth, however, by explaining the generation gap to their parents and by suggesting that primitive societies might have something to teach the West about child rearing. When she advocated the decriminalization of marijuana, Mead was branded a "dirty old woman," and the outraged attacks of society's moral watchdogs were equally vicious when she championed a more relaxed approach to sexuality. Undaunted, Mead resolutely guest-starred on television talk shows, led conferences on child rearing, cybernetics, and the women's movement, and presided over a host of influential organizations such as the American Association for the Advancement of Science, the World Federation of Mental Health, and the Scientists' Institute for Public Information.

Mead was a pioneer in the research of sex roles and male-female relationships—her book *Male and Female* appeared in 1949—and she brought the authority of her field studies to bear on many of the questions feminists were struggling with. She made headlines when she kept her maiden name after marriage, but she did not hesitate to incur the wrath of the women's movement by chastising working mothers who abandoned their babies to all-day nurseries. Married three times, Mead refused to characterize divorce as failure. She once explained that it wasn't that her marriages didn't work out, but that "they got used up."

Despite the universality of her interests, the unchanging focus of Mead's attention—almost everything she found personally and professionally rewarding—was rooted in her work among the peoples of the South Seas: the Manus, Arapesh, Iatmul, Tchambuli, and Mundugumor tribes. Looking at individual native societies, Mead took what she learned about maturation and socialization and applied it macrocosmically, viewing humanity as one vast tribe. Her aim in all cases was to fuse science with humanism. Contemporary society, she maintained, with its seemingly insoluble problems of worldwide hunger, overpopulation, mechanized warfare, and often frightening technological change, had much to learn from the primitive cultures whose relatively stable and idyllic ways of life she described with such empathy. Such cross-cultural lessons permeated Mead's later, more wide-ranging work as she taught at Yale, Vassar, Fordham, and New York University and continued to publish her scholarly studies. Her personal experiences—as wife, mother, and grandmother and through three divorces and several miscarriages—further deepened her wisdom and fortified her courage. In her later years, despite infirmities that forced her to walk with a cane, she strove to teach individuals, families, and governments not merely to cope with but also to embrace, "with human ingenuity, imagination, and faith in life," the radical new demands brought about by a changing world. Even in her twilight years she was possessed of awesome energy and kept a schedule that would have left most younger people gasping for breath. When she died in 1978, still a confirmed optimist, the media seemed at a loss as to how to label this protean humanist. Perhaps *Time* magazine captured her best when it called her the "fond grandmother of the global village."

GOLDA MEIR

GOLDA MEIR, A PIONEER in the founding of the state of Israel, was a woman of contradictions. Cunning and obdurate, she was an astute politician as well as a maternally protective presence for her struggling infant country. She ruled with a ruthless bravery, resolutely ordering thousands of young soldiers to Israel's defense, yet she brought to her leadership a very personal devotion. When as premier Meir would go to the airport to watch the arrival of a new group of immigrants, she was always moved to tears. She was a tireless fund-raiser for her new nation: On her first speech-making trip to America, she raised fifty million dollars, twice what David Ben-Gurion, then head of the Jewish Agency, had set as her goal. Later, when the battle for Israel's independence was won, Golda, as she was known by her compatriots, would dispense firm directives and homemade chicken soup in her kitchen to party allies, bodyguards, and cabinet ministers alike.

While this most ardent of revolutionaries had little stomach for bloodshed, she was as capable of orchestrating aggression as the most impassioned of her male comrades. Truly committed to peace, she nevertheless viewed readiness to fight as Israel's only tool for national survival, insisting candidly that "a nice, liberal, anti-militaristic, *dead* Israel" was a concept she could never sanction. Her childhood memories of Kiev and Pinsk—of her father's frantically boarding up the front door to protect his family from the pogroms, or the screams of men and women being beaten—were always with her. In the years following the Holocaust, she would summon up this experience to argue that the best defense against another Auschwitz was a militant offense. As she explained to Pope Paul VI many years later when he complained about Israel's fierceness, "When we were merciful and when we had no homeland and when we were weak, we were led to the gas chambers."

From her earliest years in Milwaukee, Wisconsin, where her family settled in 1906, Goldie Mabovich's young life was absorbed by activism. Studying to be a teacher, she was influenced by her sister Sheyna's example and became a socialist Zionist, organizing marches to protest the Jewish persecutions in Russia. In 1915 she joined the socialist Poale Zion (Labor Zionist party) and with her parents became involved in recruiting Jews to fight for the liberation of Palestine. Eventually, having "no taste for parlor Zionism," as she wrote in her autobiography, *My Life,* Meir became determined to make her own *aliyah,* or immigration, to the Promised Land. She managed to convince her new husband, Morris Meyerson, who was less enthusiastic than she, to emigrate with her in 1921. At the Kibbutz Merhavia, where at first their application was rejected because they didn't believe an American woman would be willing to put her heart into hard physical labor, Golda—who later Hebraized her name from Meyerson to Meir—fed the chickens and

organized the communal kitchen. Eventually, her husband's distaste for this primitive collective life took them to Tel Aviv, where their two children were born. They separated shortly after the birth of their second child.

Taking in washing to help make ends meet, Meir advanced her political career through tireless work with the Women's Labor Council of the Histadrut, the Jewish Labor Federation. When the Mapai (Labor party) was formed in 1930, she quickly rose to prominence, traveling on fund-raising missions abroad for both the Jewish Agency and the World Zionist Organization. In 1936 she took charge of the Histadrut's political wing and, as the hostilities with the British and the Arabs intensified, found herself at the hub of power in Palestine. In 1946, when the British arrested Ben-Gurion and other influential members of the ultranationalist Jewish Agency, Meir became chief executive of the agency's powerful Political Department. Throughout this whole period, she labored tirelessly for unlimited Jewish immigration and to keep Jewish immigrants out of British detention camps.

After the signing of Israel's Declaration of Independence on May 14, 1948, Meir was appointed ambassador to the Soviet Union, but in 1949 she returned to take up a post as minister of labor, continuing to help her country assimilate its hordes of new immigrants. Seven years later she became foreign minister under Ben-Gurion, who often relied upon Meir's skill as a negotiator, and in 1969 she became Israel's fourth prime minister. With her broad, angular face, low-heeled shoes, and simple hairdo, Meir was nevertheless a formidable presence as she fought for her nation's precarious existence with both passion and a deep sense of responsibility for the lives of her soldiers.

Meir's tenure was marked by the tumult of two major military conflicts—the 1967 Six-Day War, in which Israel gained the West Bank and Gaza territories, and the disastrous 1973 Yom Kippur War, in which an Egyptian-Syrian surprise attack left her reputation severely shaken. Her military and intelligence officers, who didn't believe the Arabs were about to attack, advised her not to order full mobilization of her forces. That decision cost her nation dearly, and she was never able to forgive herself. More than 2,500 Israelis died, and in 1974 Golda resigned. As for absolving her lifelong enemies, she was equally stern but not without compassion. "When peace comes," she had said in 1969, "we will perhaps be able to forgive the Arabs for killing our sons. But it will be harder for us to forgive them for having forced us to kill their sons."

Having suffered from cancer of the lymph glands for fifteen years—a fact she had kept secret—the "stalwart lioness" was laid to rest in 1978.

MONROE

MARILYN

IN *ALL ABOUT EVE* (1950), the Oscar-winning send-up of New York's high-powered theater world, Marilyn Monroe is introduced as a "graduate of the Copacabana school of dramatic art." It's a throwaway line, but the patronizing barb would haunt Monroe throughout her career despite her fame. Hollywood's offhand contempt for her talent only increased her desperate desire to be taken seriously as an artist, and her all-too-public neediness. The eternal ingenue, Monroe was doomed to play the consummate fantasy object, a "sweet angel of sex," as author Norman Mailer described her, whose titillating but still wholesome appeal challenged the repressiveness of the fifties. It was an image she once cultivated, then sought to escape.

Monroe's much-chronicled story began in illegitimacy, poverty, and cruel abandonment. Born in Los Angeles to Gladys Mortensen, a film cutter who had a family history of insanity, and a father who could have been any one of a number of beaux, Norma Jean Mortensen (later changed to Baker) spent her formative years in neglect. After her mother was hospitalized with paranoid schizophrenia, the seven-year-old brunette was passed from one foster home to another and placed in an orphanage for two years when she was nine. Such scarring experiences were responsible for her almost palpable vulnerability as well as her hunger for unconditional acceptance. Like a true child of Hollywood, Norma Jean—named after movie star Norma Talmadge—escaped the pitiful circumstances of her youth by immersing herself in cinematic illusions, imagining, for example, that her unknown father was Clark Gable. Dropping out of school after the eleventh grade, she entered into a brief marriage to a merchant seaman. When he went to sea during World War II, she worked at the Radioplane Company in Burbank. It was here that an army photographer, watching her spray varnish on fuselage fabric, took her picture for a *Yank* magazine story featuring women on the home front. The publicity led to a modeling career—and a change of hair color. Twentieth Century-Fox snapped up the blond with the radiant smile just before tycoon and actress collector Howard Hughes could sign her to his RKO studios. In 1948, after giving her a new name, the studio signed her to a contract, but released the starlet after she had made only two films. Her sixty-nine-year-old companion, Joseph M. Schenck, got Columbia Pictures to put her under contract, but president Harry Cohn let her go after *Ladies of the Chorus* (1949).

Monroe's film career began to spark interest with the 1950 release of *The Asphalt Jungle* and *All About Eve*. But it was the rapid-succession releases of *Niagara*, *Gentlemen Prefer Blondes*, and *How to Marry a Millionaire* in 1953—and

the publication of a nude calendar photograph she had posed for in 1949—that made her a star. The calendar, a potential career-wrecker in the fifties, was explained away by Monroe as an expedient way to pay the rent. Appreciating her sweet-but-direct daffiness, America forgave her. Even the movie critics mellowed, mentioning her deft comedic touch and her flair for bemused self-parody.

At the zenith of her fame, the voluptuous bombshell in *The Seven Year Itch* (1955), who had posed above the subway grating with her white dress billowing around her, began to tire of her beautiful-but-dumb stereotype. She had appeared in some two dozen films, but always as the bimbo—or even worse, as the unfaithful wife. "To put it bluntly," Monroe said, "I seem to be a whole superstructure without a foundation." Forming her own company, Monroe began producing films, first *Bus Stop* in 1956, then the less successful *The Prince and the Showgirl* (1958). By this time she had married and divorced baseball hero Joe DiMaggio and was wed to playwright Arthur Miller, whose intellect appealed to her. But the actress's fragile hold on reality began to slip. Following the 1959 smash *Some Like It Hot,* the box-office failure of *The Misfits* (1961), which costarred her idol Clark Gable, was a huge blow to her, and the role itself a terrible disappointment; Miller wrote it specifically for her, but Monroe's Roslyn came off as just another empty-headed beauty. She was also devastated by gossip that her chronic tardiness on the set had contributed to Gable's subsequent death from a massive coronary. Exhausted, in 1961 she checked herself into the Payne Whitney Psychiatric Clinic for alcohol and barbiturate abuse. To her horror, she was placed in a locked and padded room, reminding her of her mother's fate; DiMaggio got her moved to Columbia-Presbyterian Hospital. Weaned from the sleeping pills she was addicted to, she started work on *Something's Got to Give* (1962). But by mid-1962, trapped once again by depression, alcohol, and drugs, Monroe had been fired for persistent no-shows and jilted by both President John F. Kennedy and his brother Robert.

"What the hell is that girl's problem?" Gable had once wondered aloud, articulating a question the public has long sought to answer. Was Monroe suffering from a serious character disorder? Or was her suicide—if that's what it was—triggered by the two Kennedy rejections? Or was a life so fraught with contradictions simply too difficult to endure? Perhaps all these factors, combined with Monroe's own naïveté and all-consuming ambition, conspired to cut short her glamorous life. "I am not interested in money," she was quoted as saying. "I just want to be wonderful."

MARIA MONTESSORI

MARIA MONTESSORI FITS PERFECTLY the mold of the turn-of-the-century feminist. Self-motivated, starchily independent, and alert to unexplored social territory, the young woman from provincial Chiaravalle, Italy, made a name for herself in a number of male-dominated professions. A child math prodigy, she was the first woman in Italy to receive a doctorate in medicine, having had to obtain support from Pope Leo XIII to even gain admission to the University of Rome's medical school. But it was as a revolutionary in the field of children's learning that "La Dottoressa" really made her mark. As one of education's most original practitioners, she fought to make the child, not the teacher, the center of the learning process and, in so doing, forever changed not just traditional pedagogical theory and practice but the whole concept of primary education.

Montessori's schools were like none that had existed before. Instead of a rigidly structured classroom, with pupils stuck at their desks "like butterflies mounted on pins," Montessori wanted children in action, using their own individual and creative potential and progressing at their own developmental pace. She envisioned teachers not as purveyors of facts and supreme disciplinarians but as partners in a process, observers and guides who followed the pupil's lead in mastering his goals. Stressing correction without blame, Montessori saw learning not as an ordeal but as a self-directed game that could be as joyful as it was instructive.

To these ends, "Mammolina," as the reformer was called by her disciples, designed special tools and furniture for preschoolers. She created a pint-sized environment filled with little tables and chairs and low-level windows, cupboards, and shelves. One of her most famous innovations was the "didactic apparatus," materials designed to involve students in the learning process, according to her strict motto: Hands first, then brains. Montessori noted that children chose the work of "real life" over play; thus there were graduated beads to introduce students to mathematics, shoelaces to be tied, buttons to be buttoned, sandpaper letters for tiny fingers to trace, and smooth pieces of wood to aid left-to-right eye training for reading. To the astonishment of her educational colleagues, this revolutionary approach produced four-year-olds who could read their own nursery rhymes and five-year-olds who could solve algebraic equations.

Montessori's new methods of teaching were hatched during the young psychiatrist's two-year co-directorship of Rome's Scuola Magistrale Ortofrenica, a training center for teachers of mentally deficient children. Convinced by the works of Dr. Edouard Seguin that retardation was less a medical problem than a pedagogical one, the doctor began formulating the radical approach and simple materials that would soon bring the world to her door. She called it "psychopedagogy," and

her success with it was so extraordinary that some of her impaired eight-year-olds were able to pass regular grade-level examinations in literacy skills. At that moment, Montessori became an educator rather than a psychiatrist.

But it was in the Casa dei Bambini, a one-room day-care center that a building association in Rome had asked her to set up to keep the local tenement children from defacing the apartments, that the Montessori method came into full bloom. Eager to prove that her techniques could benefit children of normal intelligence, she took on the job, giving her word that the children wouldn't scratch the walls. Within weeks of her arrival she transformed the unruly two- to six-year-olds into happier, more cooperative young students. Montessori told the press that her young pupils had been naughty not because of their working-class background but because of mental starvation. Casa dei Bambini was soon followed by other progressive schools, and Montessori became the inspiration for a bustling worldwide movement that saw her system as the ultimate educational experience and the single path to self-actualization.

Montessori herself promoted her vision as the right one, brushing aside controversy and critics by pointing to her successes. Hadn't she turned squalling ruffians into studious bookworms? Wasn't her academic pedigree far superior to that of most of her detractors? She was, after all, a psychiatrist with expertise in psychology, physical anthropology, and educational philosophy and a bona fide crusader for the rights of children. And she had published trailblazing works on the pedagogical model that was almost immediately known simply as "the Montessori method."

But in the thirties, enthusiasm for the once wildly popular system waned rapidly. Many academics, and most especially followers of the eminent American educator and pragmatist John Dewey, disagreed with certain basic Montessori tenets—for example, that intelligence was not fixed, or that behavior was not always a carrot-and-stick phenomenon. On a more practical level, detractors interpreted her insistence on the primacy of schoolroom spontaneity as an invitation to chaos. Some others saw the reason for La Dottoressa's eclipse in her personal reputation: It had been discovered by the rather stuffy educational establishment that her adopted son and assistant was really her natural son born out of wedlock.

In the fifties, however, the Montessori method was revitalized, and she began franchising her schools across the continents from Japan to Venezuela. As open classrooms and readiness programs like America's Head Start became popular, even Montessori's skeptical academic fellows began to see the worth of many of her concepts. At eighty-one, on her deathbed, the leader of her own personal crusade for children's education told her son that she felt she had done her part: Her butterflies had been set free.

HENRY MOORE

IN BOTH PHYSIQUE AND sensibility, British artist Henry Moore was an equal match for the massive blocks of stone and wood which were his preferred "canvases." As strong in spirit as he was solid in stature, the most celebrated sculptor of our century created monumental works of great force and sensitivity, sentries of modernism that live on in public plazas and in countless private gardens around the world. With his broad shoulders and large, muscular hands, Moore loved the hard physical toil involved in carving, believing that the resistance of the material transferred to the carver a certain resilience and energy in return. He reflected these qualities in a prodigious oeuvre that was rooted in a deep love for nature and in a profound understanding of the beauty and communicativeness of the human form. In his heroic females, intertwined family groups, reclining figures, and huddled pairings in which larger figures appear to protect smaller ones, Moore articulated his respect for the composure and courage of women and the importance of both community and perseverance in sustaining life.

Born in Yorkshire's Castleford, the seventh of a coal miner's eight children, Moore lived his youth geographically and temperamentally far from any centers of art. The neophyte sculptor found much inspiration in literature, however, and credits massaging his mother's rheumatic back when he was a child with teaching him the basic concept of three-dimensionality. It was from her, in fact, that he inherited his exceptional physical stamina. As a teaching apprentice in the local elementary school, Henry's first real encouragement came from a dedicated art instructor named Alice Gostick, who helped him obtain a grant for furthering his art studies.

During World War I, just at the beginning of a teaching career, the eighteen-year-old Moore joined the army. He was gassed at the Battle of Cambrai and spent several months in recovery, then returned to attend Leeds School of Art on an ex-serviceman's grant. In 1921, he went to London on scholarship at the Royal College of art, and began what he came to consider his real aesthetic education—regular visits to the city's magnificent museums, especially the British Museum with its exhaustive collections of Etruscan, Egyptian, African, and Mexican sculpture. While perusing an art book during this period, Moore became particularly intrigued by the invincible-looking Chacmool, the Toltec-Mayan rain spirit, which later inspired one of his richest works, the Leeds' Reclining Figure (1929). His "museuming" also led him to the Museum of Natural History and Geological Museum, where he spent hours analyzing the structure, shape, color, and design of such natural objects as bones and shells.

After several study trips to Paris, in 1925 Moore won a traveling scholarship to Italy from the Royal College of Art. He lingered in Florence, where he reveled in the painted figures of Giovanni Masaccio, the sculptures of Pisano, and the great masterpieces of Michelangelo. The visual extravagance he encountered clashed with the earlier influences of his more primitive mentors, and for a while, he found himself at a creative impasse. But following his first one-man show, in London, he obtained his first commission in 1929. That same year he married a Russian woman, Irina Radetzsky, and settled in Kent, where he could sculpt during time off from his part-time teaching position at the Royal College. During the thirties, Moore produced some of his most memorable works, absorbing the irrational and darkly sensuous aspects of surrealism and continuing always to wed the abstract and the representational. Sculpted "holes"—what Moore himself referred to as "the form inside another form"—began appearing in his pieces, 1935's Reclining Figure (in Buffalo, New York) being an outstanding example . His reputation grew internationally during this decade, and art lovers proclaimed him an iconoclast, which of course served only to augment his popularity.

During World War II, while teaching at the Chelsea School of Art, Moore was appointed an Official War Artist. Drawn down into London's underground air raid shelters during the Blitz, he produced his famous Shelter Drawings of 1940–1941, somber sketches of the city's besieged populace that represent some of that era's most disturbing and enduring images. They led him to begin clustering and draping his figures—as shown in his Madonna and Child (1943–1944) for the Church of St. Matthews in Northampton—and to further humanize his vision. The birth of a daughter in 1946 had a similar impact.

The prolific forties, with its tender family groupings, was followed by two full decades of world-wide prestige. Showered with commissions, Moore proceeded to dot the globe with hauntingly powerful archetypes in stone and cast metal, among them the bronze Draped Reclining Figure of 1952–53 for Antwerp's sculpture museum; the sixteen-foot travertine marble reclining figure in 1957–58 for Paris' Unesco building; the white marble "walk-through," Square Form with Cut (1969–70) for a private client in Prato, Italy. He became the unofficial ambassador for British art, but most of his time was spent at home in his seventeenth century farmhouse working ten to twelve hours every day.

In his later years, despite the huge retrospectives, his expansive pieces slipped somewhat out of fashion. Art students who quipped that "Less is more, and Moore is a bore" forgot that the meditative and unpretentious artist had almost single-handedly forced his suspicious countrymen to accept and then champion modernist forms three decades earlier. Being young, they knew nothing about the test of time, about resilience and endurance as standards of a sculptor's work and about the power of a patient man who found the ancient, weathered ruins of Stonehenge a worthy inspiration.

EDWARD R. MURROW

THE VOICE OF THE twentieth century, which one critic described as sounding like "God's older brother," belonged to pioneer broadcaster Edward R. Murrow. Cool, reflective, intelligent, like the reporter himself, that voice became identified, first on radio and later on television, with the era's most important moments: Hitler's 1938 Anschluss, the fiery Battle of Britain, Pearl Harbor, the discovery of Buchenwald's horrors, and the beginnings of Soviet-American hostilities. Murrow was his generation's most insightful and peripatetic oral historian—a wily, often baleful-sounding witness whom audiences came to trust as much for his intense truthfulness in telling the tale as for his resourcefulness in seeking it out. He was, in the words of his wife, "a sufferer," a maverick newsman who fretted over his ethics—and those of others—as much as he "bled" over his copy. With legendary honesty and a touch of well-earned arrogance, he fought courageously for both independence and objectivity in his industry.

Murrow came to almost instant prominence during World War II, soon after CBS president William Paley sent the twenty-nine-year-old to London as the network's European director. Although he had no journalistic experience, Murrow enjoyed his first scoop at the microphone in March 1938; he had flown to Vienna on a tip—in a twenty-seven-seat Lufthansa transport plane he'd chartered for one thousand dollars—and arrived just in time to report the Nazis' occupation of the city. Murrow stayed with the story for an unprecedented ten days and in so doing established a new tradition of on-location reportage of breaking events. The face of American broadcasting abroad would be transformed forever.

His most remembered moments, however, were the brisk but soulful shortwave accounts of the London Blitz, aired live by CBS. While bombs rained and a terrified populace huddled underground for cover, Murrow stood on rooftops to describe the destruction. "This is London," he gravely intoned. "The windows in the West End were red with reflected fire, and the raindrops were like blood on the panes." Listeners back home were riveted, and before long his voice was as recognizable as Churchill's or Roosevelt's. It is not incidental that the United States soon joined the Allied effort.

The man who helped change the course of the war came from an extremely humble home in Greensboro, North Carolina. The third son of a poor tenant farmer, Egbert Murrow was raised on hard work and Biblical teachings. After graduating from Washington State College in 1930, he headed up the National Student Federation of America, moving on to become assistant director of the Institute of International Education, where he arranged student exchanges and relocated persecuted German academics in the States. His career with CBS, which

was to last over twenty-five years, began in 1935, when he was appointed to coordinate programs on current issues.

After his spectacular wartime debut, Murrow put in a brief and uncomfortable stint as a vice president at CBS, then tackled television. Working on-screen in the medium that would help shape the rest of the century, he quickly assumed the role of seasoned elder statesman. To his devotees, he became the rock-solid personification of high urbanity and authority; but beneath the suave, handsome mien was an edgy journalist who suffered from insomnia, bottomless depressions, and sweaty bouts of stage fright. He also chain-smoked four packs of unfiltered Camels a day—a habit that eventually resulted in the lung cancer that claimed his life. If he was never truly beloved by the millions of listeners and viewers who faithfully tuned in for his reports, the stone-faced broadcaster was nonetheless profoundly respected—an appraisal shared by his professional colleagues.

Debuting in 1951, his weekly television show, "See It Now," with its trenchant reports on everything from the abuse of migrant workers to Senator Joseph McCarthy's demagoguery, dramatically shaped the medium's documentary format. McCarthy's crusade to stamp out Communist "conspirators" in the highest levels of government was at its most intimidating, but Murrow exposed the senator for the mendacious bully that he was. Murrow's fearless attack helped bring McCarthy and his blacklist down, even as it added another layer of resilance to Murrow's potent public persona. But as entertainment shows—like his own awkward bit of fluff, "Person to Person"—began to proliferate, Murrow became increasingly disenchanted with television. In 1958 he even gave a speech urging television's executives to forego excessive profits and vacuous entertainment programming in favor of public service. He contributed notably to the latter with his 1960 *Harvest of Shame*, a documentary about the plight of migrant workers that survives as the most influential in TV history. The following year he resigned from CBS, taking President John F. Kennedy up on his offer to become director of the United States Information Agency.

Prestigious as Murrow's last job was, it does not represent the man we remember. The Murrow who endures is the courageous young reporter with a taste for danger and a need to be in the middle of the action, and later the brilliant veteran who exposed injustice and believed that information—the coin of a journalist's realm—was the last, best hope for effecting social change. A consummate communicator who was unafraid of authentic emotion—he once broke into sobs during a wartime report—Murrow was wise enough to know that the heart of his profession lay in restraint as much as realism. His art was to shed light, rather than heat, on the crucial issues of our time.

BENITO MUSSOLINI

FROM TEENAGE STREET BRAWLER to socialist agitator to international thug, Benito Mussolini goose-stepped his way to absolute power to the tune of a nationalist march. He had an ambitious, megalomaniacal dream: As the self-styled new Caesar of a people victorious in World War I but denied any of its spoils, he would restore confidence to his impoverished nation. Once rebuilt and burnished to an imperial shine, Italy, under his leadership, would reestablish its historic hegemony in the Mediterranean. Part earnest reformer and hardheaded revolutionary, part opportunistic bluffer and unscrupulous sociopath, "Il Duce" assembled his grandiose thoughts about the need for a unified proletariat and the state's imperative to use violence to maintain unity and labeled his beliefs "fascism." He promised relief from labor unrest and corruption and from radical agitation by Communist and socialist fringes.

Lulled by a glowing future painted in bombast, his infatuated countrymen embraced Mussolini's vision, as did many politicos and intellectuals abroad. Winston Churchill, among many, at first admired his aim to strengthen Italy's destabilized economy but later called the capricious leader a "jackal." No less an authority than Sigmund Freud found many of Mussolini's concepts, such as government by a national assembly in control of economic, industrial, and professional corporations, highly original. Other early admirers praised him for his virulent anti-Bolshevik stance as well as for his support of universal education and the creation of large-scale public works. But Mussolini's stature—both as demigod and demagogue—disintegrated as his nation underwent a humiliating drubbing during World War II.

The man who felt himself destined to be Italy's savior in the twentieth century came from the town of Dovia in the destitute area of northern Italy called the Romagna. His schoolteacher mother was a fervent Catholic; his father, an impoverished blacksmith, was anticlerical and a socialist who took a great interest in politicizing his firstborn son. Benito was a quick study, but despite keen intelligence, he proved untamable. At eighteen, he took a teaching job in the Alpine town of Tolmezzo, where he contracted syphilis—perhaps, it has been speculated, the cause of his megalomania. He married during World War I, and in the mid-1920s, at loose ends, he began traveling through Europe, taking up journalism and organizing trade unions. Soon a confirmed socialist, he tried to integrate what he had learned from Nietzsche, Kant, Spinoza, and Georges Sorel, the French theorist who viewed trade unions, or syndicates, and violence as the foolproof means to revolution.

Mussolini's rise in the Italian socialist party began in earnest in 1910 as he assumed an office in the local party in Forlì. Foreshadowing his later ideological somersaults, he went from an impassioned advocate of neutrality to an equally impassioned interventionist during the first months of World War I—though not before his pacifism landed him in jail. His newfound hawkishness was a scandal to both the party and its official journal, *Avanti,* of which he was editor. Forced to resign, an undeterred Mussolini founded his own newspaper, *Il Popolo d'Italia,* served in the war, then returned home to begin building his own personal socialist movement.

Mussolini moved swiftly. Rallying a disparate group of unemployed veterans and disenchanted youth to his ultrachauvinist, antiliberal cause, he also attracted more conservative elements who feared that the nation's poverty and violent labor unrest would turn into an all-out Marxist revolt. As near-anarchy reigned, he began forming his Fascist party in 1919, then made plans to seize power with his Blackshirts in the now famous march on Rome in 1922. Recognizing the threat, King Victor Emmanuel III invited the thirty-nine-year-old strongman to organize a government. As prime minister, the vulgar Mussolini, who required tutoring in proper manners and cleanliness, began to command the world's newsreels. Vain and macho—though he was never without his pocket-sized statue of Saint Anthony—he was photographed on horseback, reviewing Italian brigades as they set off to conquer Ethiopia in 1935. The following year he sent troops to support Franco in Spain's disastrous civil war.

Isolated from France and Great Britain by his expansionist adventures, and sizing up Hitler as the most powerful—though not necessarily the most desirable—ally, Mussolini formalized Italy's alliance with the Axis powers in 1939 through his military "pact of steel." He waited until the fall of France in June 1940, however, to actually enter the war. Alternately admiring and despising the German dictator, Mussolini was dismissive of the Nazi's racial theories, suspicious of his flattery, and increasingly irritated by his own humbling as "Hitler's taillight." The führer, in turn, had gleaned many useful ideas from his incompetent partner's mesmerizing oratory and modern talent for dominating the media.

Italy's ignominious defeats in Greece, North Africa, and Stalingrad, where Mussolini lost almost all his invading troops, and the Allied landing in Sicily in 1943 signaled the dictator's demise. The king had him arrested, but a daring German raid freed him from his Italian captors. He played out his final fantasies of a revived Fascist government at his Lake Garda headquarters, until finally Allied troops closed in. Mussolini and his mistress, Clara Petacci, were captured by Italian partisans and, after a summary trial, were shot, then strung up by their heels in Milan's Piazzale Loreto. In sharp contrast to the adulatory throngs to whom Il Duce had railed during two decades in power, the bloodthirsty rabble set upon the pair, pummeling their faces until their features were unrecognizable as human.

JOE NAMATH

AS A LONG-HAIRED, FLASHILY dressed, and much-ballyhooed quarterback coming out of the University of Alabama in 1965, Joe Willie Namath was the nation's first rock 'n' roll football player. At once athlete and entertainer, the charmingly candid party man became the forerunner of a new kind of media-savvy superstars—a commercial giant who transformed athletics from a scoreboard to a billboard phenomenon. Awarded a contract by the New York Jets, of the upstart American Football League (AFL), he became the most highly paid rookie in the annals of professional football.

Namath was born the youngest of five children in the small mill town of Beaver Falls, Pennsylvania. When he was five years old, his three older brothers drafted him for the quarterback slot in their pickup football games; the youngster grew so proficient at passing the ball that he could hit a tree stump forty yards away. It was a childhood filled with Huck Finn-like mischief and an endless variety of sports. Upon graduation from high school, the six-foot-two-inch student was recruited by more than fifty college football programs and offered baseball contracts by no less than six Major League teams. Acquiescing to his mother's wishes, however, he applied to the University of Maryland. Rejected because his SAT scores were too low, he was rescued from a life in the mills by a scholarship from University of Alabama coach Paul "Bear" Bryant.

His college career, capped by Alabama's 1963 National Championship and an impressive 29-4 record, was marred by two events: a suspension in his junior season for drinking, and the first of many debilitating knee injuries. The former made him determined to demand more of himself and to be a better leader; the latter would eventually end his career.

Namath was the type of player most pro teams coveted. The Jets and the St. Louis Cardinals tussled over him until New York owner Sonny Werblin, former president of MCA records, stepped in. He wanted Namath—who titled his autobiography *I Can't Wait for Tomorrow 'Cause I Get Better Looking Every Day*—as much for his blue-eyed crowd appeal as for his athletic ability. Namath signed with the Jets for a bid of $427,000 and a Lincoln Continental convertible.

Despite typical rookie problems in adjusting to the progame, the 1965 season wound up with Namath ranked third in passing—and first in print and television. His grinning, bent-nosed face was on so many magazine covers—and in so many fancy restaurants and clubs with so many gorgeous women that one of his teammates affectionately christened him "Broadway Joe." The nickname stuck, and as Werblin had hoped, Namath's combination of gridiron prowess, trendy lifestyle, and sex appeal brought fans into the stadium in droves. Despite a penchant for limousines and ladies, Namath never forgot the lessons learned from his college suspension; he never let his carousing interfere with his on-field performance.

His fans, the owner, and the star himself were all relieved the following year when the quarterback flunked his military draft physical. His wry reaction to the news was typically astute: "How can I win? If I say I'm glad about it, I'm a traitor. If I say I'm sorry, I'm a fool."

But the Army's loss was football history's gain. By the 1966–67 season, the AFL had become such a serious threat to the established NFL that the leagues had agreed to play an annual inter-league championship game, which in 1969 they named the "Super Bowl." Before the third such contest, Namath—still regarded as a smart-mouthed, dissolute hippie by football's old guard—confidently promised a Jets victory over the rival circuit's most dangerous team, the Baltimore Colts. He made his boast in public, and—even more infuriating to the opposing team—he reiterated it to some of them in person in one or another of the many bars he frequented. The supremely confident Namath went on to lead the Jets in a steamrolling offense that resulted in a 16-7 victory over Baltimore. It was one of the biggest upsets in sports history and one of the most exciting Super Bowls ever. The film footage of Namath leaving the field after the game, wagging his index finger in the gesture universally recognized as "We're Number One," is one of the most enduring images in sports iconography.

Increasingly plagued by knee problems, his mobility severely limited, he was never able to repeat that performance. In 1977 the Jets waived him, and he signed with the Los Angeles Rams. It would be his last season. But he had shrewdly diversified his interests from the outset of his career, investing in restaurants and clubs (including Bachelors III, which aroused the ire of football's very proper commissioner, Pete Rozelle) and making product endorsements. (One of his most famous had the grizzled veteran modeling a pair of women's pantyhose.) In retirement, Namath was as busy as ever, working as a sports commentator, acting, marrying in 1984 and starting a family. He gave up alcohol, had his knees surgically repaired, and concentrated on the care and upbringing of his two daughters. But despite his domestication, Super Joe remained a legend. If his fans couldn't see him in person, they sought him out in cyberspace, buying signed memorabilia and chatting with him on the Internet at the official Joe Namath Home Page. Decades after their hero carried football into prime time, they still wanted contact.

NASSER

GAMAL ABDEL

AS A CHAMPION OF Arab unity, social revolution, and post-World War II anticolonialism, Egyptian president Gamal Abdel Nasser was universally loved by the Arab world and just as fervently distrusted by Cold War America and the West, which suspected him of dangerously close relations with the Soviet Union. But Nasser, a patriot whose earliest political activity included a student demonstration against the British occupation of Egypt, was aligned with no empire but his own. His life was dedicated to the elevation of the common *fellahin*, or peasant, the confederation of all Arabs under Egyptian leadership, and the development of a true sense of nationhood among his countrymen. His means included the use of draconian measures, a socialist redistribution of wealth, and a charisma that earned him the title "El Rais" ("The Boss"). Like no other Arab leader in history, he had the power to inspire the masses—especially the *shaab*, "the forgotten ones."

Nasser was born in Alexandria to a minor postal official and his wife, the cosmopolitan daughter of a building contractor. As a British protectorate, Egypt was effectively part of an Empire that still dominated much of the world. English and French, not Arabic, were the daily languages of society's higher echelons; the country was nominally ruled by a corrupt monarch; and no son of a lower middle-class government functionary could expect to grow up to be an army officer. An insignificant "wog"—the derisive term used by Egypt's European masters—Gamel Abdel Nasser had dim prospects indeed.

His education began in the impoverished village of Khataba in the Nile delta. Fortunately, his father's brother, just released from a British jail, offered to have his nephew live with him in Cairo where the schools were substantially better than in Khataba. Lonely and unconstrained (particularly after his mother's premature death and his father's remarriage); young Gamal spent his time going to American movies and becoming involved in political organizing. As educational opportunities for Arabs began to open up, Nasser studied law for a few months before entering the Royal Military Academy at Cairo in 1937. He graduated the following year and, assigned to a rifle brigade, served in Upper Egypt. There he met several officers—among them another lieutenant also fated for greatness, Anwar el-Sadat—who would soon join him in scheming against the government. In 1941, Nasser was posted as an instructor at the Academy; later, he moved to the Army Staff War College, where he filed away for future use the lessons on how to defend the capital against attack.

Corrupt, lazy, and top-heavy with poor officers, the Egyptian Army reflected the nation's near-feudal society, with its deep cultural antagonisms and smug pashas living off the sweat of the "fellahin." Nasser, efficient and patriotic, determined to change both the Army and the country. He patiently researched and planned his insurgency for years, learning from all of his experiences. After he was wounded in the Arab–Israeli War of 1948, he even asked his enemy counterpart how his country got rid of the British. "Maybe we can learn from you," he commented. Later, the devout Muslim would read the Old Testament to gain insight into his Israeli foes. In 1952, after years of Machiavellian intrigue—one historian called it "a masterpiece of secrecy"—Nasser and his Free Officers Movement overthrew King Farouk I and sent him into exile.

At first Nasser operated through a front man, Major General Mohammed Najuib. But in 1954, annoyed with Najuib's advocacy of civilian parliamentary rule, he took the reins of government in his own hands, becoming prime minister. Dynamic and bursting with optimism, Nasser was hugely popular among the common people. But he was hardly a democrat: in 1956, as president, he abolished political parties and dissolved Parliament.

Focusing on land reform, he set limits on ownership and redistributed vast tracts to the peasants. His grand scheme to bring electricity to the rural poor through the construction of the Aswan High Dam ran into difficulty when the United States and Britain, peeved by Egypt's purchase of arms from the Soviet Union, withdrew their financial support from the project. In 1956, in retaliation, Nasser boldly seized the Suez Canal and its lucrative tolls from the British, goading Britain, France, and Israel into mounting an ill-conceived invasion. Although his own troops were badly outgunned, Nasser managed to turn the military disaster of the Suez Crisis into a personal triumph when the United Nations—led by the United States and the Soviet Union in a rare show of solidarity—denounced the invasion.

In the wake of the Suez Crisis Nasser's prestige in the Arab lands soared, as did his influence in the Third World. Yet as his stature increased, so did his suppression of Communists, Muslim fundamentalists, and most partisan debate within Egypt. His dream of a grand pan-Arab coalition, symbolized by the creation of an Egyptian-Syrian United Arab Republic in 1958, foundered when Syria withdrew in 1961. The economy lagged and Nasser's taste for intrigue earned him a disastrous war in Yemen (1962–67) and a humiliating defeat at the hands of the Israelis in 1967's Six-Day War. With Israel in command of the West Bank, the Gaza Strip, and the Golan Heights, Egypt's eminence was in ruins. Nasser resigned, but popular outcry—some of it orchestrated—brought him back.

From plotting, Nasser now turned to peacemaking. He helped end the Yemeni war, accepted the "land-for-peace" solution to the Palestinian issue, and mediated the armed dispute between Jordan and the Palestine Liberation Organization, a rising challenge to his primacy. On September 28, 1970, shortly after seeing Kuwait's Emir Sabah es Salem es Sabah to a plane, Nasser collapsed of a heart attack. An ardent Arab nationalist to the end, he would join Mao Zedong, Nehru, Castro, and Ho Chi Minh as a leading hero of anti-colonial revolution.

NIXON

RICHARD M.

FROM ITS INCEPTION, THE political career of the Richard M. Nixon was shadowed in controversy; as he ascended to higher office, the shadow grew, eventually obscuring the genuine good he achieved with many of his policies, some of them surprisingly liberal for a man so vilified by the left.

Born in Yorba Linda, California, Nixon was the second of five sons of Francis A. Nixon, a lemon farmer, and Hannah Milhous Nixon, a devout Quaker. The Nixons had little money—a fact that grated upon their socially awkward and introverted son. Long after becoming president, Nixon still recalled boyhood snubs from richer children. His anger at these slights was transformed into raw ambition. After he was denied entrance into the snooty Franklin Club at Whittier College, the expert debater formed the Orthogonians ("Square Shooters"), a group composed, as he put it, of "athletes and men who were working their way through school." Graduating in 1934, he won a scholarship to Duke University Law School, earning his degree in 1937. When he failed to find a position in a Wall Street firm, he returned to California.

Practicing law in the small town of La Habra, Nixon honed his courtroom skills as a contract prosecutor and began courting Thelma Patricia Catherine ("Pat") Ryan, a school teacher and amateur thespian whom he'd met through a community theater group. He later called their 1940 marriage "the best decision I ever made." In 1942, just eight months after the Japanese bombed Pearl Harbor, Nixon obtained a commission in the Navy. He spent the duration of World War II in the South Pacific, where his skill at poker netted him $10,000, which he used to finance his first congressional bid, in 1946. He won that campaign by accusing his New Dealer opponent, Jerry Voorhis, of being pro-Communist. Nixon's red-baiting ways continued after he got to Washington and was appointed to the House Un-American Activities Committee. His dogged pursuit of former State Department officer Alger Hiss brought Nixon to the attention of Republican Party leadership.

After two terms as a Congressman, Nixon ran for the Senate against liberal Democrat Helen Gahagan Douglas. In what is still regarded as one of the ugliest campaigns in American political history, Nixon used smear tactics to suggest that Douglas—whom he dubbed "the pink lady"—had Communist sympathies. That victory led Dwight D. Eisenhower, the war-hero-turned-politician, to name Nixon as his running mate in the 1952 presidential campaign.

Nixon's ascent to the White House was momentarily thwarted when it was revealed that he had accepted money from a special campaign fund set up by friends. Facing ruin, he defended himself on television, giving the famous "Checkers" speech, in which he denied accepting all gifts but one—the family dog, named Checkers. Voters backed him, and the Eisenhower–Nixon ticket went on to victory in November.

In the largely powerless office of vice president, Nixon shrewdly stayed in the public eye, most notably when he engaged Soviet Premier Nikita Khruschev in the angry Kitchen Debate (held in the model kitchen of a 1959 show of American culture in Moscow). In 1960 Nixon was chosen as his party's presidential candidate. His opponent was the wealthy, charismatic senator from Massachusetts, John F. Kennedy, who was everything Richard Nixon was not—a contrast that was vividly apparent in a series of televised debates. The telegenic JFK appeared fit and self-assured, while Nixon, sweating and ill at ease, came across as somewhat sinister. Embittered by Kennedy's paper-thin margin of victory, Nixon retreated to California, only to be defeated two years later in the state gubernatorial race.

By 1968 Nixon was again poised for another shot at the White House. This time his opponent was Vice-President Hubert Humphrey, who had the unenviable task of defending the Democrats' handling of the war in Vietnam. Asserting that he had a "secret plan" to end the conflict, Nixon defeated Humphrey by half a million popular votes. The war dragged on, but elsewhere Nixon demonstrated a sophisticated touch in foreign affairs: He boldly opened relations with China, cemented ties to Egypt in the fractious Middle East, and dealt deftly with the Soviet Union. Domestically, he launched a "war on cancer," established new anticrime laws, improved the lot of American Indians, and instituted environmental reforms. But he also began an ominously reactionary campaign for "law and order," pursuing a host of left-wing activists and personal political "enemies."

It was his fear and hatred of anyone who opposed him that led to the legal and moral quagmire that was Watergate. In June 1972, a few months before Nixon routed George McGovern in the national election, burglars were dispatched from the White House to break into the headquarters of the Democratic Party, housed in a Washington apartment complex called the Watergate. The burglars' discovery and arrest, and the subsequent cover-up by Nixon and his aides, led to the nation's most severe constitutional crisis since the Civil War, and to the establishment in 1973 of Congressional committees that voted the following year to impeach the man a federal grand jury had already named as an unindicted co-conspirator. Nixon declared publicly "I am not a crook," but the secretly recorded tapes of his conversations in the Oval Office, indicated otherwise. On August 9, 1974, all his options gone, Richard M. Nixon became the only president in U.S. history to resign.

In his later years, he attempted to fashion himself as an elder statesman, and in the eighties even enjoyed a brief resurgence of popularity, but nothing could erase the memory of his hubris. Vengeful, duplicitous and wracked by envy, Richard Nixon remained a citizen of the dark side of democracy.

NUREYEV

RUDOLPH

HE MOVED WITH A powerful and controlled animal grace, sometimes slinking pantherlike across the stage, other times bounding almost impossibly high into the air. Executing elegant leaps, with amazing athleticism, he could hover over his partner as if he would truly devour her with his ardor. Though cynical and often disdainful in person, Rudolf Nureyev never let down his adoring public—or the ticket scalpers who depended on the hysterical devotion of his fans. He lived and breathed dancing, and his blazing talent and beautifully proportioned physique brought a rare drama and incendiary excitement to the formal ambience of classical ballet.

When the celebrated young dancer made his Western debut in Paris in 1961, the year of his sensational defection from the Soviet Union, the audience's reaction was euphoric. So frenetic were the fans that they could not wait to stand and shout their hurrahs: They simply screamed in their seats.

In both heritage and heart, Nureyev was a Tartar, a peasant whose blood, he liked to say, ran hotter and faster than others'. As a dancer whose métier was lyric roles, he enjoyed recounting the circumstances of his birth, which he called the most romantic event of his life. Born on a train racing along the edge of Lake Baikal near Mongolia, Nureyev wrote in his 1963 autobiography that his entry into the world was symbolic of his destiny to be cosmopolitan and, by extension, an outsider whose life was marked by impermanence and statelessness.

There was certainly nothing romantic about his childhood. His hometown of Ufa was, in wartime, "like a ravenous wolf," according to Nureyev, with few resources to stave off the ever-present shadow of death by starvation. Within this "icy, dark and, above all, hungry world," however, young Rudolf encountered his salvation. When he was eight his mother took him to his first ballet, and at the sight of the spectacle the child was struck speechless with joy. Immediately, he recognized his calling. Eventually, through raw willpower and relentless practice, the penniless seventeen-year-old was accepted to the prestigious Leningrad Ballet School. It was a rather late age to start serious training, but with his obvious talent and personal magnetism, and with the legendary teacher Alexander Pushkin as his mentor, Nureyev advanced rapidly. Within three years he became a member of the Kirov company, having turned down the Bolshoi as too inflexible for his expressive taste.

Among Nureyev's youthful rebellions were a refusal to join the Communist Youth League, disobedience of curfew regulations, criticism of his troupe's policies, and friendship with foreigners. On June 17, 1961, while waiting at Paris's Le Bourget airport to board a plane for London, he carried out his most intrepid rebellion yet. Told just before boarding that his destination would be Moscow, not London, Nureyev feared the worst. Often criticized for insubordination, he suspected that, once he arrived back in the Soviet Union, his budding career would be destroyed. So "in the longest, most breath-taking leap" of his career, he literally jumped over an airport railing into the arms of two French inspectors, gasping, "I want to stay!" Given five minutes alone to contemplate his decision, Nureyev then walked calmly through the door to sanctuary—and almost instant worldwide acclaim.

For a time he toured with the International Ballet of the Marquis de Cuevas, but it was his pairing with Dame Margot Fonteyn, the prima ballerina of London's Royal Ballet, that spurred Nureyev's real ascendancy in the West. The untamed young dancer was just twenty-four, his partner forty-two, well past a dancer's usual retirement age, when they formed their unlikely partnership: Fonteyn's charm, disciplined grace, and femininity coupled with Nureyev's bold expressiveness, power, and narcissistic panache. The ballet world was set afire in a manner it had never before experienced—and has not again since.

Fonteyn's "young lion leaping" soon moved beyond the classical repertory he had mastered—works such as *Le Corsair, Swan Lake,* and *Sleeping Beauty*—into experimental works choreographed by such modern masters as George Balanchine and Martha Graham, who created *Lucifer* for him and Fonteyn in 1975. In all, he danced nearly one hundred roles. Still, his most fruitful associations were with the Royal Ballet and the paris Opéra Ballet, which he directed from 1983 to 1989. In addition to creating new roles and reviving others, he also staged several seasons of a Broadway show called *Nureyev and Friends* , which presented an eclectic menu of both modern and classical pieces.

Nureyev was just as rebellious and sexually charged offstage. Partying at discos and nightclubs, clad in his signature black leather outfits, he created a parallel image to that of devoted artist. A dancer whose virtuosity—and intensify—launched the revision of the male role in ballet, he was also a sensuous pop idol and an extremely rich and acquisitive megastar with retinues of male and female admirers and patrons, young and old.

But although the nightlife had its allure, it could never compete with the dance. A tireless performer, he fought his body's inevitable decline and insisted on performing long after his prime. Even after he was stricken with AIDS—a fact he never publicly acknowledged, even as he lay dying—he could not stop himself, no matter what the critics wrote. His work was sacred to him, and his appetite for it—like his lust for life—was as all—devouring as the "ravenous wolf" of his childhood.

GEORGIA O'KEEFFE

FOR THE LAST HALF of her ninety-eight years, every aspect of artist Georgia O'Keeffe's life—from her sternly pulled-back hair and long monochromatic kimonos to her sparsely furnished adobe house adorned with bleached bones and timeworn rocks—was pared down to a highly stylized and elegant aesthetic. And all was in visual harmony with her beloved New Mexico desert, its panoramic solitude providing inspiration for the poetic austerity of her art. O'Keeffe immersed herself in the stringent beauty of "that wild world," creating from its flinty landscape ghostly cattle skulls, solitary crosses, and countless portraits of the ever-changing Pedernal mountain. The blue-violet peak was hers, she once remarked: "God told me if I painted it enough I could have it."

O'Keeffe discovered the desert in her early twenties, driving recklessly through its dry flats in her old Model-A Ford. Learning the tonal hues and spectral vegetation, she quickly developed her own unmistakable style—pure, solemn shapes that wavered between abstraction and representation, clean, flowing lines, and a distinctive palette of umbers, deep oranges, blood reds, and purply browns, often surprised by pinks and yellows and bright blues. Bold and profoundly original, she is considered a pathfinder in the abstract idiom.

O'Keeffe was a proud child of the Wisconsin prairie, accustomed to spaciousness and the outdoors, and throughout her life, her physical surroundings would be immensely important to her personally and professionally. Her patrician Hungarian-American mother drove her and her sisters—she was one of seven children—by buggy into nearby Sun Prairie each Saturday for art lessons. By the age of twelve, Georgia had decided to become an artist, and Ida O'Keeffe wholly supported her self-possessed daughter's decision. In 1905 she sent Georgia to the Art Institute of Chicago and a few years later to the prestigious Art Students League in New York. Disenchanted by her art, the twenty-two-year-old abandoned painting for a time in 1908 to take up commercial illustration.

At this point, three men who would prove influential to her entered O'Keeffe's life. The first was Columbia's Alon Bement, a follower of Arthur Wesley Dow who encouraged students to create original artwork rather than copy others and who taught composition based on Japanese rather than Western models. Bement would become O'Keeffe's intellectual mentor; she would become his teaching assistant at the University of Virginia, after first teaching in public school, an experience which bolstered her confidence that she could be independent in the world. The second was Arthur Dow himself, a former student of French Postimpressionist Paul Gauguin who was teaching at Columbia. It was he who led O'Keeffe in 1915 to the pared-down forms and color refinements of Asian art, rekindling her creative ambitions. In 1916, after a friend had brought the results of O'Keeffe's efforts—several large charcoal abstracts—to the 291 Gallery in New York, O'Keeffe encountered

the third and most significant force in her career, Alfred Stieglitz, famed photographer, advocate of American modernism, and a passionate promoter of photography as an art form. With the much older Stieglitz as mentor and O'Keeffe as muse, the two eventually became one of modern art's most fascinating and mercurial couples.

O'Keeffe's work made such an impact on Stieglitz that he included her drawings in an exhibit that year, without telling the artist, who was then teaching in Amarillo, Texas. When she stormed back to New York, demanding that her work be withdrawn from the show, Stieglitz won her over. The following year, at O'Keeffe's first one-woman show at Gallery 291, her new love asked her to pose for him, thus beginning the famous fifteen-year series of more than five hundred photographs that would document the depth of their passion. When his wife of twenty-four years saw the baldly intimate photos and gave her husband an ultimatum, he promptly abandoned her for O'Keeffe. Plugged into the intellectual zeitgeist of the twenties and thirties, Stieglitz offered his protégé exposure both to the public and to his talented and erudite circle of friends. O'Keeffe never really acknowledged his help—nor that of any of her mentors—and her 1976 illustrated autobiography never even mentioned their marriage.

In 1924 the two were wed, when he was sixty and she was thirty-seven, but their rigid personalities and roving eyes made coexistence troublesome. Stieglitz was gregarious, obsessive, and controlling; O'Keeffe was an austere personality, a brooder who needed peace and privacy. After discovering he had had a serious affair, O'Keeffe experienced a breakdown and sought solace in her long annual trips to Taos, New Mexico, where she had first gone in 1929. There she was swept into the reckless bohemianism of rowdy heiress Mabel Dodge Luhan, making Stieglitz wild with jealousy. By now she had achieved a certain notoriety for her bold flower paintings, though she dismissed the Freudian interpretations of such canvases as *Black Iris* (1926) and *Two Calla Lilies on Pink* (1928), two of her most famous works.

Her art through the years continued to grow, from the giant floral canvases, the early paintings of New York's cityscape and her the iconic churches and crosses to more evocative images inspired by the panorama of the desert itself. Her work revealed not simply the nature of the landscape itself, but the feelings the land evoked. Her paintings of the red hills were fluid, warm, and maternal, as the curves of the land became the curves of the female body; in 1945, O'Keeffe would write,"I did a painting, just the arms of two red hills reaching to the sky and holding it."

After Stieglitz's death in 1949, she moved to New Mexico permanently. By the end of her life, she came to possess almost every natural and spiritual aspect of the domain she had made her refuge.

OLIVIER

SIR LAURENCE

THE FILM ACHIEVEMENTS FOR which he is remembered are nothing less than brilliant: his brooding Heathcliff in William Wyler's classic, *Wuthering Heights* (1939); his malevolent *Richard III* (1955); his poignant Archie Rice, the third-rate comedian of *The Entertainer* (1960); his *Othello* (1965), played with an unusually coarse passion and mindless rage. But the stage was his favorite milieu throughout a career that spanned almost seven decades; these performances are, of course, preserved only in the memories of those privileged enough to have witnessed his prodigious gifts as he brought Sophocles' Oedipus, for example, or Chekhov's Uncle Vanya or Eugene O'Neill's' James Tyrone from *Long Day's Journey into Night* to life on the stage, to name just a handful of his masterful characterizations. Not to have seen Olivier perform live is to have missed the English-speaking theatrical experience of the century.

Olivier was one of the greatest modern interpreters of Shakespearean drama on stage and in film. He did more than any other single person to familiarize contemporary audiences with the immortal Bard. In one legendary eight-month sojourn at London's Old Vic Company during 1937–38, he took on seven major Shakespearean roles. When his country needed inspiration during World War II, he was released from military duty to work on a Technicolor adaptation of *Henry V* (1945). Despite wartime austerities, Olivier pulled off a critical and popular success—as producer, director, and the soldier-king himself. This triple coup earned him a special Academy Award.

Born in the small English town of Dorking, in Surrey, to Gerard Olivier, an Anglican clergyman, and Agnes Crookenden Olivier, Sir Laurence's background of genteel poverty gave him, he later recalled, an added impetus to succeed. A move to London brought him under the influence of Geoffrey Heald, the priest in charge of student theatricals at the Church of All Saints, where he attended choir school. Encouraged by Heald, he was already playing Brutus and other Shakespearean roles at age ten. Olivier spent his youth being terrified of his father and adored by his mother. When she died unexpectedly of a brain tumor while Olivier was at St. Edward's, Oxford, the twelve-year-old was devastated.

This early abandonment, in addition to his inability to please the puritanical vicar, resulted in an intense conflict that seemed never to resolve itself. Theater critic and friend Kenneth Tynan once commented that throughout Olivier's life the actor maintained "a pipeline to a childhood pain we can only guess at."

Olivier progressed from brash adolescent prodigy to seasoned professional in just about a decade. He made his Broadway debut in 1929 with *Murder on the Second Floor* and enjoyed success the following year in Noel Coward's *Private Lives.* He was good enough to make his first Hollywood film, *The Yellow Ticket,* in 1931, but he was not good enough for Greta Garbo, who refused him as her co-star in *Queen Christina* (1933). The early thirties were a disappointment for Olivier on both stage and screen; to make matters worse, the career of his wife, the talented actress Jill Esmond, began to eclipse his own.

Enter the beautiful English actress Vivien Leigh. In 1937, the two costarred in the movie *Fire Over England* (1937), and when they appeared that same year in a repeat performance of Olivier's Old Vic *Hamlet*—which was actually staged in Elsinore's Kronborg Castle—the tortured Dane and perhaps the most fragile of all Ophelias fell in love for real. Each still married to someone else, they did not wed until after Olivier was launched in Hollywood with *Wuthering Heights* and Leigh had triumphed as Scarlett O'Hara in *Gone With the Wind,* both released in 1939.

These were the early days of World War II in England, and the now famous Oliviers, like many British artists, were struggling with the decision of whether to go back home. Olivier flew to Washington with Cary Grant and others to settle the matter. The British ambassador's advice was that if Englishmen were to be portrayed in combat movies, it would be better if those roles were played by the genuine article. Olivier returned to Los Angeles to finish up Alfred Hitchcock's *Rebecca* (1940) with Joan Fontaine and went on to star with Leigh in *That Hamilton Woman* (1941), the story of Lord Horatio Nelson, created to inspire the war effort. Olivier's next bit of cinematic patriotism, *Henry V,* was an amalgam of stagecraft and naturalism that owed much to his earlier experience on *Wuthering Heights.* A one-time snob in his attitude toward cinema, Olivier had learned from Wyler that film was not celluloid theater but a medium deserving of its own interpretive techniques. In 1948, he won acclaim again in his Oscar-winning screen adaptation of *Hamlet.*

His enormous achievements earned him first a knighthood, in 1947, and in 1970 he was made a peer of the realm, the first actor to have been so honored. As founding director of the National Theater of Great Britain, Olivier spent the decade between 1963 and 1973 focused on stage projects. He had divorced Leigh in 1960, and when she died in 1967 after a long struggle with manic-depression and tuberculosis, he himself was in the hospital, suffering from pneumonia. Now married to actress Joan Plowright, Olivier left his hospital bed and went to keep vigil alone with Leigh's body. He had always blamed himself for her misery.

Commanding and athletic, but never afraid to be impish or vulgar in his reach for artistic truth, he arrived at a point in his art where calamity could turn in an instant into comedy. His own end leaned toward tragedy, with Olivier suffering from numerous ailments, chief among them dermatomyositis, a condition which made his being touched incredibly painful. It was an ironic fate for a man who lived to reach out to others.

JACQUELINE KENNEDY ONASSIS

FOR A THOUSAND DAYS, she was the undisputed queen of a country that claims no royalty. Married to a charismatic American president—the youngest and most handsome ever to hold that office—Jacqueline Bouvier Kennedy was the perfect wife for what has been described as a mythical era. Well bred, elegant, and as glamorous as the movie stars she rivaled, Jackie, as she was known around the world, brought impeccable style to the White House and achieved role model status for a generation of women. Her shining moment came during one of the nation's darkest hours.

Jacqueline was born in Southampton, New York, on July 28, 1929, to a dashing Wall Street wheeler-dealer known as "Black Jack" Bouvier and his comely wife, Janet Lee. The depression stripped them of their wealth, and the struggle tore the family apart. Jacqueline grew up adoring horses and her charming, rakish father. But his parental possessiveness, his jealousy of his ex-wife's new husband (the enormously wealthy Hugh Auchincloss), and the never-ending bad blood between him and Janet eventually combined to invest his daughter with a deep insecurity, belied by her public poise.

Named debutante of the year following her 1947 Newport debut, Jacqueline attended Vassar, wended her way to Europe for study at the University of Grenoble and the Sorbonne, and finished her education at George Washington University in 1951. Launched on the path of a white-gloved socialite schooled for the good life, she obtained a suitable job as the inquiring photographer for the *Washington Times-Herald* and became engaged to a Wall Street broker from the cream of WASP society. Then, in 1952, at a Washington dinner party, Jackie met the irresistible John Fitzgerald Kennedy, a boyish congressman, war hero, and cocky politician with an eye on the White House—and the veritable reincarnation of her playboy father. Warned about his reputation as a philanderer, she replied, "All men are like that." With some nine hundred guests attending the nuptials and three thousand onlookers pressing against the police barricades outside, she joined the dynamic Kennedy clan on September 12, 1953. Black Jack Bouvier was not permitted to walk Jackie down the aisle for fear he would arrive intoxicated and embarrass the wedding party, but the ceremony—and his daughter's life—went on.

When Kennedy's presidential ambitions were realized eight years later, Jacqueline became first lady of the land. Her proudest legacy was her much-heralded restoration of the White House, a project that she insisted focus on authenticity. When the results were showcased on television—with Jackie herself the tour guide—the quality of her work silenced her critics. During an administration that has since taken on the aura of Camelot (thanks in no small part to Jackie's own efforts), she became a patroness of the arts unlike any presidential wife before her. The other Kennedy women may have faulted her breathy voice and genteel ways, but with her uncommon beauty and intelligent wide-set eyes, Jackie seemed a figure bred to more rarefied air. Her choice of couture became the nation's fashion mandate, while her extravagant spending habits were often a source of irritation to her extravagantly roguish spouse. Kennedy, however, respected his wife's popularity and power, once wryly introducing himself as "Jackie Kennedy's husband."

The marriage itself was far from a fairy tale. Jackie forced herself to turn a blind eye to Jack's affairs. When their first child was stillborn, in 1956, Jack was amusing himself with friends on a yacht in the Mediterranean. Jackie gave back a little of what she got when newspapers printed photos of her dancing barefoot on the yacht of Gianni Agnelli, the playboy Fiat heir who squired her around Italy. But emergencies seemed to bring them together: The Bay of Pigs fiasco and the Cuban missile crisis gave Jackie a chance to stand by her husband, and the death of their two-day-old son Patrick gave Jack the chance to show his support for his disconsolate wife.

But what forever endeared Jackie to the nation was her comportment in those anguished days after her husband's martyrdom. When the shots rang out on November 22, 1963, Jacqueline drew on her breeding, her training as a woman of refinement, and her immense courage, and held the country together with the dignity that had become her hallmark.

Choosing to leave what must have seemed a sinister America after the assassination of her brother-in-law Robert Kennedy in 1968, Jackie stunned the country by marrying Aristotle Onassis, a Greek shipping magnate. It was not the most popular decision she had ever made, and some believe Jackie was simply acting to protect her children. The tabloid-christened "Jackie O" spent only a few years with Onassis, his death leaving her with a large fortune. Using her literary talents to find work as a book editor, she managed a reasonably private existence, occasionally surfacing to stroll in Central Park or to attend a gala for one of her preservationist causes with her companion of over a decade, financier Maurice Templesman. Through it all, she did her best to shelter her two children, Caroline and John, from the celebrity-mad world.

On May 19, 1994, at sixty-four, she succumbed to lymphatic cancer. The street outside her Manhattan apartment was thronged with mourners paying tribute to the woman who had taught an entire country how to grieve. When a bereaved nation buried her with full honors next to President Kennedy in Arlington National Cemetery, it was reminded that the woman who had fashioned the mold for an era had, in dying, quietly broken it.

J. ROBERT OPPENHEIMER

WHAT WAS IT THAT drove American physicist J. Robert Oppenheimer to lead his country's effort to create the atomic bomb? Was it a deep belief that he must seize a moment doubly historic, in both scientific and political terms? Was it a desire to serve his country in a time of need? Or perhaps a conviction that the bomb would provide what Winston Churchill called "a miracle of deliverance" after so much bloodshed? A contradictory character, an enigma even to his closest friends—some of whom he would later betray—Oppenheimer may have had all of these motives.

Oppenheimer's early life was as academically idyllic as it was cloistered from care. Born in New York City to a rich textile importer and his artistic wife, Robert Oppenheimer (the "J" was added by his father for its touch of class) attended the liberal Ethical Culture School, where he studied Latin, Greek, and all the science he could absorb. In 1922, he attended Harvard, graduating summa cum laude after only three years, then moving on to study physics with Ernest Rutherford at Cambridge, where Oppenheimer quickly mastered the new theory of quantum mechanics. By the time he earned his doctorate in 1927 at German's University of Gottingen, he was so deeply immersed in theoretical physics that his doctoral examiner was afraid Oppenheimer was going to question him.

Returning to America in 1929 after two further years of study in Europe, he began teaching and conducting research at the University of California and at California Institute of Technology. They were halcyon days; vacationing in Corfu or at his ranch in New Mexico near a place called Los Alamos, Oppenheimer learned Italian so he could read poetry in the original, and mastered Sanskrit, language of the Hindu spiritual epic the *Bhagavad Gita*. He told friends that reading Proust in French was one of the most moving experiences in his life. Independently wealthy, Oppenheimer was sufficiently sheltered that he realized only in 1930 that the stock market had crashed the year before.

World War II changed his life forever. The United States, in a race to develop the ultimate secret weapon, recruited him in 1942 to form a team of the best and brightest to reach the goal first, despite the fact that it was well-known that Oppenheimer had flirted with Communist intellectuals. (Katherine Harrison, whom he married in 1940 and with whom he would have two children, was, in the era's political parlance, a "fellow traveler" when he first met her.) Forming a stellar band of scientists—Edward Teller and Enrico Fermi among them—into a project code-named "the Manhattan Project," he decamped with them to an abandoned boys' school in familiar Los Alamos. There "Oppie," as he was affectionately known, acted as interlocutor between the army and the strange new invisible gods of the atomic world. After nearly three years of exhaustive secret labor, during which the already rail-thin Oppenheimer dropped thirty pounds, the bomb was ready for testing. As the sinister mushroom cloud rose like a gigantic wraith above the sands of New Mexico, a terrified Oppenheimer quoted the *Gita:* "I am become Death, the shatterer of worlds."

Now that the bomb existed, discussions continued among President Truman, top advisors, and America's scientists: should the bomb be used as a warning to the Japanese, a demonstration of America's potential weaponry, or should it be used militarily to bring an end to the war? The scientists themselves were not unanimous, although Oppenheimer, writing for the scientific panel, finally concluded, "we see no acceptable alternates to direct military use."

With a new weapon of this power, prediction was uncertain; even Oppenheimer himself, who arguably knew more about the atomic bomb and its potential than anyone, estimated that 20,000 would die when it was dropped. What actually happened at Hiroshima and Nagasaki would change his views forever. Extremely agitated, Oppenheimer went to President Truman, saying he had blood on his hands; the pragmatic Truman replied, "The blood is on my hands. Let me worry about that."

But Oppenheimer couldn't let others do the worrying for him. Chairman of the U.S. Atomic Energy Commission from 1946 to 1952, and consultant to the American delegation on atomic energy to the United Nations, he was, nonetheless, vocal in his opposition to America's development of the hydrogen bomb, after the Soviets detonated an atomic bomb of their own, for both moral and technical reasons. He was an equally passionate proponent of civilian and international regulation of atomic power. His criticism of American atomic policy led, in 1953, to his suspension by the Atomic Energy Commission on the grounds that he was an alleged risk to security, a move that was enormously controversial. The secrets Robert Oppenheimer had helped to discover were now officially forbidden to him.

But Oppenheimer's genius had other venues. In 1947, he had been elected director of the Institute for Advanced Study at Princeton, and in 1954, he was unanimously re-elected. He was acknowledged as one of the great teachers of his era, leaving behind a legacy of research and education. Oppenheimer's influence on the century was tremendous, both in his contributions to theoretical physics and in the morality lesson his creation of the atomic bomb taught him and the world at large. The world Oppenheimer left behind him was a different one than the one into which he had been born.

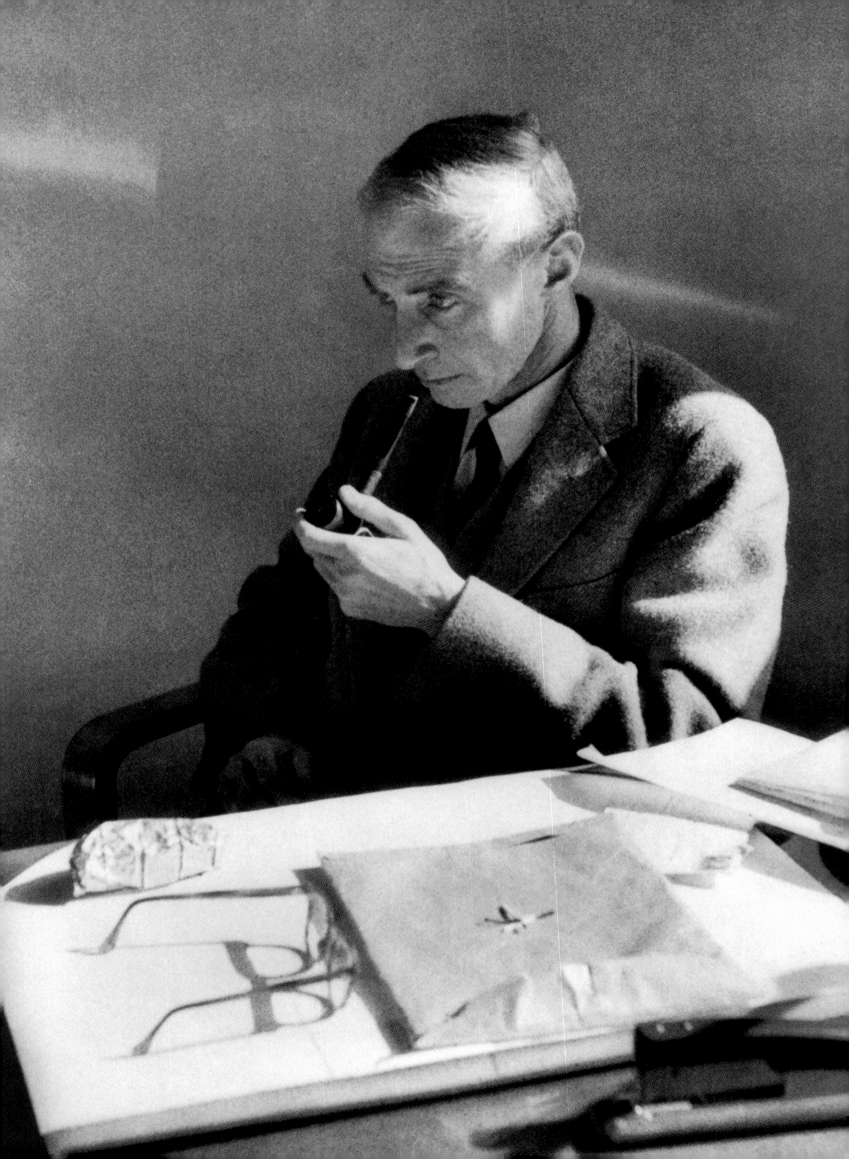

JESSE OWENS

"THE GOLDEN MOMENT." That's what athlete extraordinaire James Cleveland Owens, known as Jesse from the time he was nine, called his extraordinary triumph at the 1936 Berlin Olympics. Competing in the 100- and 200-meter runs, the long-jump, and the 400-meter relay, the twenty-two-year-old competitor garnered four gold medals for the United States, making Olympic history and in the process crushing Germany's crude trumpeting of Aryan superiority, which Adolf Hitler had counted on the Berlin events to demonstrate to the world. The victory of this African-American over time, gravity, his fellow sportsmen, and Nazi bigotry was as complete as any providence has ever allowed a competitor. Yet he was fully aware of its bittersweet irony: "When I got home to America, I had to ride in the back of the bus and use the back door," he said. "Now you tell me, what is the difference?" Only this: Under Hitler, Owens would have had no chance at all. In segregated 1930s America, he had a slim one—and, true to his optimistic and steel-willed character, the great sprinter took it and ran with it.

Born the seventh of eleven children of Henry and Emma Owens, poor sharecroppers in Danville, Alabama, Owens was a thin, sickly child who had trouble breathing. He attended a one-room schoolhouse that seemed to grow more and more primitive every time the adult Owens, an accomplished orator and raconteur, told the story. As he grew, he ran everywhere: to school, to the store, to the horizon. This was just the sort of solitary athletic pursuit at which a poor boy with big dreams could excel, and Owens had big dreams, starting with college. Shortly after World War I, the family moved to Cleveland, Ohio, where the slimly muscular teenager established himself as a high-school track star. When he informed his amazed parents that he wanted to attend Ohio State University, his father worried aloud about black men exceeding their place, but his incredulous mother pinched him with delight.

Despite his being a bona fide track phenomenon, Owens was not given an athletic scholarship by a school whose home state was then experiencing a resurgence of the Ku Klux Klan. He was forced to wait tables to pay for his tuition, but his cheerful determination raised him above insult—even those inflicted by his own body. In 1935, while competing in an Ohio State track meet, he broke three world records in forty-five minutes—in the long jump, the 220-yard dash, and the 220-yard low hurdles—while suffering from a painful muscle strain in his back. Performances like that earned him a place on the 1936 U.S. Olympic team, which was preparing for a showdown in Berlin's extravagant Kulturplatz.

The Nazi propaganda machine had gone into overdrive, mocking American racial hypocrisy with all-too-cogent slyness, and predicting the total victory of the formidable athletes Adolf Hitler had assembled. Also sitting in the stands with the Führer were all three of his primary henchmen: Hermann Goering, Joseph Goebbels, and Heinrich Himmler. But when Owens took the gold in the 100-meter dash, it was a bad omen for the Germans. The next day, he turned to the long-jump, in which a German dark horse named Luz Long battled him to the finish. On the last jump, however, Owens leapt 26 feet, 5½ inches, setting a new world record that would not be surpassed for twenty-five years. It was a feat that the consummate sportsman Luz—with whom Owens forged a genuine friendship—courageously acknowledged by throwing an admiring arm around Owens's shoulders and strolling with him past the official box of a smoldering Hitler. (This would be the last time Owens would see Long, who as a German soldier in World War II was killed in Sicily. But he returned to Germany after the war and met his friend's widow and son.) Amid roars of approval from the mostly German crowd, the man whom Goebbels had derided as "a black auxiliary for the Americans" next took the 200-meter race in record time. Then it was the Americans' turn to make a dramatic decision: At the last minute, the team's only two Jewish members were bumped from the relay race squad to make room for Owens and a second African-American, Ralph Metcalfe from Marquette University. The motive for this choice is still debated today, but the athletic results were unambiguous—a fourth gold medal and another world record as Owens, running lead-off, led the American team to victory. Throughout, a furious Hitler refused to acknowledge Owens's remarkable achievements, conspicuously leaving the stadium as Owens accepted his awards. Owens later acknowledged his own relief at being snubbed by Hitler: It spared him the disagreeable task of having to shake hands with someone he despised.

Owens had achieved almost more than was imaginable. Yet when he returned to America, he discovered that President Franklin D. Roosevelt was no more inclined to shake his hand than Hitler had been. Reduced over the years to exhibition racing against dogs, horses, and even automobiles to make ends meet, Owens became a kind of carnival attraction. He continued to race seriously, however, until he was thirty-five years old—ancient for a sprinter—and quit only when he could no longer run the 110-meter dash in 9.7 seconds or better. In later life, he overcame financial hardships to become a successful public relations executive in Chicago, and his speaking skills took him across America expounding on the topics of civil rights, race, and sports. His secret of running, he said, had been to hold his breath in the stretch. But, ironically, the pack-a-day cigarette habit he had indulged since boyhood led to lung cancer, which finally ended his life at age sixty-seven.

PANKHURST

EMMELINE

EMMELINE PANKHURST SET THE standards and methods of militant feminism from parliamentary maneuvering to street agitation. This driven, beautiful, and extremely proper Englishwoman, in devoting her life to the principle that women should have total equality with men, marshaled every known tactic of political disturbance: speeches, riots, newspaper broadsides, and even a few stones slung through the windows of 10 Downing Street, attracting an audience to what was, for Edwardian England, the greatest political show on earth.

She hailed from the northern industrial town of Manchester, where her father, in the utopian if rather schizoid spirit of the era's enlightened middle class, was both a capitalist and a radical protosocialist. It was a bipolar approach to life that his daughter, with her talent for defiance enunciated in wellbred tones, raised to the level of art. Educated in Manchester and at the Ecole normale in Paris, at the age of twenty-one she married another suffragist, a barrister named Richard Marsden Pankhurst. Emmeline Pankhurst's interest in public service and politics led her as an Independent Labour party (ILP) candidate in 1894 to the Chorlton Board of Guardians, a public charity committee, and six years later to the Manchester School Board. But her public philanthropy was as much a costume as the expensive gowns and hats she favored, cloaking a deep antipathy for society as it was constituted. This usually sweet, gracious and well-mannered woman had a public career as a true radical.

One of Pankhurst's first targets was Dame Lydia Becker, whose women's-suffrage group was far too tame for the combative Pankhurst. Becker asked for the franchise only for women of property, which would have excluded all married women. But nothing less than full rights would do for Pankhurst. Behind her passion to get the vote for women lay her knowledge, much of it gained from her experience as a poor-law guardian, of how poverty often drove women to desperate acts. She cofounded the Women's Franchise League with her husband in 1889 to carry out her ideals-after an eight-year stay in London to try to revive her husband's parliamentary career—but the organization folded for lack of funds after a few years.

If, perhaps, Pankhurst regarded men as morally inferior, it did not stop her from marrying and bearing five children. In 1898 Richard Pankhurst died, leaving Emmeline debt-bound and with four children to support (her oldest died of diphtheria in 1889). She sold her furniture to dissolve the debt and took employment as the local registrar of births and deaths—a position that brought her into even closer contact with the wretchedness of working-class life. Meanwhile, her support for the ILP evaporated when it proved too timid to support immediate women's suffrage.

It was Pankhurst's daughter Christabel who showed her the glories of militancy when she was arrested for disrupting a meeting of the Liberal party to demand the vote for women. Her daughter's example was exhilarating. "I *love* fighting!" Pankhurst was to say later. Certainly she did enough of it, becoming a committed scofflaw. Without ever abandoning her dignified mien, the firebrand in fine lace led demonstration after proscribed demonstration, brawling with the police, disrupting meetings of the opposition—which included every organized political party in Britain—and learning to use a slingshot so that she could whip a few flints past the head of a cowering Prime Minister Asquith. She was arrested countless times, even when protected by a phalanx of athletic working-class girls who acted as her bodyguard. With Pankhurst's assent, if not her active collaboration, her cohorts even attempted to kidnap a policeman who had been overly enthusiastic about arresting her. As it happened, they had the wrong man. But Pankhurst and the other suffragettes embarked on more distruptive acts, setting houses afire, destroying gardens, defacing works of art, and even planting a bomb in Lloyd George's new house (no one was injured). Pankhurst was sentenced to three years' penal servitude. In prison she launched several hunger-and-thirst strikes to embarrass the government. In spite of being a dedicated advocate of democracy, Pankhurst ran the suffrage movement like a dictator, issuing commands and edicts, elevating protégées, and banishing enemies when they would not do her bidding.

It took the upheaval of World War I to give Pankhurst her opportunity to make women's suffrage a reality. A patriot who was convinced of British national superiority, and the war's threat to English civilization she turned her considerable leadership skills and her suffragist organization to the war effort at hand. In 1918, the war over, Lloyd George was not eager to resume battle with the suffragettes, so he compromised: Women over thirty could have the vote.

Pankhurst barreled on, lecturing in America, opening an English tearoom on the French Riviera, and reinventing herself as a conservative grande dame, horrified by socialism, short skirts, and jazz. Her final decline came when daughter Sylvia, who had never subscribed to her mother's prim ideas on sex, produced a baby out of wedlock. Pankhurst went into a swoon of shame that led to her death in 1928. Her soul left her body at the very hour Parliament gave the vote to all women.

PARKER

CHARLIE

IF ANY ARTIST KNEW his creative destiny, it was Charlie Parker, the great popularizer of modern jazz. Pursuing his musical fate like a man half crazed, "Bird" lived high on a heady cocktail of talent, alcohol, and drugs. The latter two sapped his strength and his mind—and ultimately sabotaged his career—but his soun—a voluptuous, often sharp-edged miracle—still flowed with incomparable technical authority.

Choosing the alto saxophone—his favorite singer, Rudy Vallee, also played it—the teenaged Parker lied about his age so he could perform in the small, smoky clubs of Kansas City, Missouri. It was a city alive with jazz and the cocky young Parker, without any formal musical training, jammed every night with toughened musical road warriors, working out his free-flowing and highly personalized style gig by gig. Combining complex melodic lines, extended chord progressions, strong blues bedrock, wildly variant interweavings of pitch and rhythm, and the birdlike flights of soaring improvisations that were his signature, Parker's style evolved into something unique and revolutionary. As his talent developed, however, so did his taste for the vices that were part and parcel of the jazz club lifestyle. He was probably still an adolescent when he first acquired his narcotics and alcohol habits.

Bird was a restless soul, musically and otherwise. He toured for the first time with Jay McShann's band, and made his first recordings with them in Dallas in 1941. Then in the early forties, he joined up with Dizzy Gillespie in New York to form the core of Billy Eckstine's band. He stayed as close to his teenage idol, Buster Smith, as he could, and absorbed everything that virtuosos like Don Byas, Oran "Hot Lips" Page, and Charlie Shavers could teach him. He was an enormous fan of pianist Thelonious Monk and saxophonist Lester Young, and in his characteristic way of devouring anything that interested him, he also acknowledged, in his own music, the modernist messages of composers like Stravinsky, Schoenberg, and Hindemith.

Parker eventually became as much a prophet of modernism in his field as Stravinsky was in his. His particular form of avant-gardism was born out of juke joints, barrelhouse blues, and the marriage of African musical sensibilities to European instruments, with ears wide open to any and all influences. There were few rules in this evolving pop form and they were mostly honored in the breach. You were expected to make it up as you went along, and Parker was a bona fide genius at making things up.

By the time he hit his stride with his own group at the age of twenty-five, he and Dizzy had established themselves as the co-kings of a new tide in jazz called bebop, which was more acrobatic and technically demanding than the currently popular "swing." It was also pointedly less commercial, and critics were painfully slow in coming around. Many felt Parker and Gillespie had departed from the jazz tradition entirely, but Parker ignored his detractors and proceeded to explore outmoded forms. His harmonic complexities, his august command of his instrument, and his accelerated tempos continued to thrill his fans and challenge his fellow musicians. In May of 1945, the Parker—Gillespie combo recorded sleek renditions of "Shaw 'Nuff," "Hot House," and "Salt Peanuts," which became bebop anthems.

As it turned out, the bicoastal music scene didn't agree with Parker. Although his classic single "Lover Man" dates from his 1945 Hollywood visit, his major venue there was a stay at Camarillo State Hospital for a nervous breakdown related to his addictions. Back in his New York element—where he could score heroin much more easily—Parker formed a quintet with the up-and-coming trumpeter Miles Davis and, despite an extremely productive recording period, began a rapid downward spiral. In 1951, the New York narcotics squad forced the revocation of his cabaret license, which caused the debt-ridden musician even more financial trouble. Three years later, he twice tried to take his own life.

Parker's difficulties stemmed largely from his neurotic personality, alternatingly warm and abrasive, playful and stern, and often destructively aggressive. But then, his strange behavior was inextricably entwined with the toll of his addictions. Other contributing factors were his lifelong battle with racism and his skirmishes with the critics, whom, he felt, too often tried to diminish him by pigeonholing his gigantic talent. But probably Parker's greatest stumbling block was his chaotic personal life, ruled as it was by his lively appetite, especially for sex. By the time of his last public appearance—which took place, appropriately enough, at Birdland, the jazz club named in his honor—he had left a string of failed relationships, and several children, behind. Parker died at the age of thirty-four, watching television in the apartment of Baroness Nica de Koenigswarter. The doctor who made the postmortem examination guessed at his age, writing down "55." There were so many things wrong with Parker's body that the physician had his pick of causes of death; the official cause was listed as pneumonia.

Despite the adoration of his disciples, many of whom even crumpled their trousers to look like his, Parker never reached the level of fame he craved while he was alive. It was only after his death that Charlie Parker's stature as one of the most formidable jazz musicians—*ever*—was finally recognized, with his recorded performances—and compositions like "Ornithology," "Anthropology," and "Scrapple from the Apple"—becoming revered standards.

BORIS PASTERNAK

IN THE TWENTIETH CENTURY, filling the literary shoes of Leo Tolstoy, the peasant/nobleman master of the Russian novel, was Boris Pasternak's lot. Highly original and imagistic in his style, this most revered of all his nation's post-revolutionary poets blended his melodic and romantic sensibilities with the agonies inflicted by two civil wars and one world war to create his generation's most lyrical epic. Some forty years in the writing, the partly autobiographical *Dr. Zhivago* helped earn Pasternak the Nobel Prize for Literature in 1958, a laurel the Soviet government forced him to decline. When its love story of lonely wanderings and tender loyalties was captured on film by David Lean in 1965, the melancholy looking intellectual with the heavily shadowed eyes became an instant worldwide celebrity. The "Pasternak Affair," in turn, released a barrage of verbal missiles in an East-West cold war that was just heating up. In London, Paris and New York, the author was lionized for his unblinking courage in the face of a physically dangerous persecution that would have crushed a less principled man. In Moscow where the book was banned, Pasternak was excoriated as a traitor, a Philistine "pig" whose unjust account of the "glorious" October Revolution had slandered his fellow citizens. Soviet literary critics attacked him as a writer whose individualism made him an unlikely candidate for aesthetic transcendence, much less a suitable member of the Soviet Writers' Union, which ousted him after his Nobel nomination.

Criticism, however, had always been the least of Pasternak's concerns. Swept from his earliest years into the vortex of violence and uncertainly that was Russian daily life, throughout his life Pasternak explored the range and tonalities of his poetic voice, while coping with larger issues of artistic integrity in a repressive motherland. As a youth, he had been refined by his parent's culture—his father was a noted portrait painter, his mother a famous concert pianist—and embraced by their guests. One of them, Tolstoy himself, was to draw the young idealist into the aging genius' slipstream of pacifism. Another persuasive force, composer Alexander Scriabin, directed his admirer toward music, but Pasternak would turn instead to philosophy.

In its infancy, revolution as a concept of renewal had appealed to Pasternak; he wrote *Lyutenant Shmidt* (1926-27), an arduously produced poem about a mutinous naval officer of the 1905 revolution, in a struggle to interpret the meaning of the much more significant uprising twelve years later. Government-sanctioned Socialist Realism, however, was simply too far removed from Pasternak's own work and its intensely personal, spiritually colored themes. In the early Thirties, the poet who had achieved no little notoriety through the publication of *Sestra moya zhizn* (*My Sister, Life*) in 1922, and then the debut of his autobiography *Safe Conduct* in 1931, acquired the label "deviationist," and, unable to publish, worked on translations of classics instead. While the Russian intelligensia was decimated, miraculously Pasternak escaped Stalin's bloody purges, perhaps because he had translated several poets from the dictator's Georgian homeland.

It was during his subtle war of wits with the iron-handed dictator that the beleaguered poet fell in love with Olga Ivinskaya, a clerk at the literary journal *Novy Mir* which, ironically, would later refuse to publish *Dr. Zhivago*. Nothing could stand in the way of their mutual obsession—neither Pasternak's second wife nor Stalin's personal reproaches, which included the now famous phone call in which the leader snidely taunted the poet for failing to defend his recently jailed writer friend, Osip Mandelstam. Ivinskaya, Pasternak's fourteen-year partner, muse, secretary, and "golden sun," would be immortalized as Lara, the radiant love of the young physician Yuri Zhivago, the alter-ego of Pasternak, whose poems appear in the novel at various points. Ivinskaya would suffer dearly for her unwavering allegiance to her hero, enduring nine years of incarceration and psychological torture for her complicity with him. While Ivinskaya was pregnant with the writer's child, her jailers told her Pasternak had come to visit; when they took her to the prison morgue instead, she assumed him dead and suffered a miscarriage.

Pasternak's refusal to help shape the proletarian consciousness through literature-as-dogma has been deemed an act of faith in the freedom of the individual by the West—and recently and somewhat reluctantly by his own land. But it is perhaps too simplistic to view him as a warrior-saint who never wrestled with compromise and self-preservation. In sadness, Pasternak lived out his final days, wracked with the remorse of a survivor and shamed by his minor complicity with Olga in signing his infamous 1958 letter, which she had ghosted, begging Nikita Khrushchev to spare him exile.

But it is exactly this flawed grace that, in its wounded humanity, has made his life such an inspirational example. Even Stalin had been forced to acknowledge Pasternak's breadth of soul and spirit, when he cautioned his subordinates: "Do not touch this cloud-dweller."

PAVAROTTI

LUCIANO

COMPLEMENTING THE CULTURAL CONTRIBUTIONS of his magnificent operatic performances and recordings, Luciano Pavarotti has raised more money for the cause of music than any person in history. The twentieth century's greatest tenor has also surpassed all others in his efforts to transform the world of Verdi, Puccini, and Wagner from an insular bastion of haute culture into a multi-media spectacle with popular appeal. Well into the nineties almost everything Big Luciano—as his fellow Italians call him—did was for opera, from offering master classes and personal consultations to sponsoring competitions. His new cross-over audience, brought in by his pioneering move from smallish opera houses to enormous sports coliseums and the even larger venue of satellite television, gives considerable distress to the old guard. Highly cliquish and hypercritical, opera traditionalists have often taken offense at Pavarotti's recital of sentimental Neapolitan love songs and crowd-pleasing arias, like his 1993 concert in Central Park. Die-hard purists believe an almost devotional knowledge is required of an opera buff and have been perplexed by the singer's forays into product endorsement and his attractiveness to groupies who jet around the globe attending every performance of a Pavarotti season. And what was to be made of the much-marketed "Three Tenors" spectacles co-starring Pavarotti and opera greats Placido Domingo and José Carreras?

But for each voice of disapproval, there have been the millions who stomp and shout their praises and throw long-stemmed roses while the Italian singer pours out mellifluous notes. With uniform tone, subtlety of shading, and brightness of timbre, Pavarotti's clear; flawless voice has been compared to an earlier and equally thrilling performer, the great Enrico Caruso, whose powerful voice reigned during opera's Golden Age, just before World War I. Unlike the well-loved Caruso, however, this baker's son from the Po River valley could reach a high C. Indeed, he was one of the first tenors in the modern era to accomplish the heroic feat of singing the nine high C's in the first tenor aria of Donizetti's *La Fille du Régiment*. (His first attempt was the result of coaxing by soprano Joan Sutherland and her conductor husband, Richard Bonynge, during rehearsal for Pavarotti's 1966 Covent Garden performance as Tonio.) Such altitudes have put incredible stress on Pavarotti's essentially delicate tenor voice, but the high C's are what bring in the money. So, though he wishes to be recognized as "a tenor of line" and not a "tenor of the top"—and though the high-register notes terrify as much as exhilarate him—he has continued to make

the brutal effort to sing these *scassavocces,* or voice busters. At moments like these, he once commented, when the sonic boom of applause rolls across the footlights, he inhales it. It is oxygen to him, proof of his fans' devotion that both sustains and spurs him on. "Sold out," he once told his manager, are the only two words he is interested in hearing, and he always hears them, earning some twenty million dollars annually in the nineties.

But it is happiness, not money, that is most important to Pavarotti, who in midcareer still lived most of the year in his birthplace of Modena, Italy, and doted on his wife and three daughters as zestfully as he indulged his appetite for pasta, tennis, fast cars, and oil painting. For Pavarotti—unusually free of the crippling neuroses that often affect tenors—his family and his extended circle of friends, he insists, has meant the world. In fact it was closeness with his father, also a talented tenor, that prompted him to take up singing—that and winning a local competition in 1961. The prize, a debut in *La bohème* in a nearby town, led to his 1963 Covent Garden debut, in which he replaced his idol, Giuseppe di Stefano, as Rodolfo. His debut at the Met, made at age thirty-three, came only five years later.

As a teenager, Pavarotti's athleticism had developed his stamina and musculature; but it was putting his hands around the waist of the magnificent and robustly statured Sutherland, who had taken the rising singer under her wing, that taught him the ultimate technique of proper diaphragmatic breathing. Dame Sutherland's artistry profoundly influenced Big P, as she called him, and their lengthy partnership produced some of opera's most memorable recordings.

From his early *tenore lirico* roles, such as Nemorino in *L'Elsir d'amore*, Pavarotti adroitly paced his vocal development, moving slowly into the difficult *spinto* range and then into a heavier, more dramatic repertoire, including Manrico in Verdi's *Il trovatore* and Enzo in Ponchiello's *La gioconda*. As more than one critic has pointed out, he was wise to move slowly. Perhaps realizing this himself, as Pavarotti expanded his commercial enterprises he sold more and more videos and CD's featuring the lightest Italian fare.

Some of his massive income was surrendered to Adua, his wife of thirty-five years, when she divorced him for his affair with his twenty-six-year-old secretary, Nicolletta Mantovani. Fortunately for opera, neither amorous complications nor the loss of millions has hampered Pavarotti's singing in the slightest. When this *voce lungo* is gone, there will be no operatic voice to fill fans' hearts as he has, no singer worthy of being called the King of "issimo."

ANNA PAVLOVA

TO SAY THAT RUSSIAN ballerina Anna Pavlova was a dancer is like saying that Dante was a poet: It says everything and nothing at the same time. Pavlova was *the* première danseuse of the century, completely dominating her art. The ethereal lightness of her step, the elevation of her leaps, and the swanlike grace of her body epitomized ballet in its golden era. An artist of great emotional power, she was also one of select musical taste. As a result, during her long career she danced only a few carefully chosen choreographies, most of which were created expressly for her and centered on cultural themes or various flora or fauna: *Oriental Impressions, Dragon Fly, California Poppy.* Yet her highly approachable style, applauded by adoring crowds on her endless tours of music halls and grand theaters, made her a kind of missionary of ballet, popularizing classical dance as no one else had ever done.

Her St. Petersburg origins were so humble that it could be said that dance saved her life. Raised by her impoverished mother—her father died when she was two—Pavlova's early flair for dance led to her admission in 1892 to the School of the Imperial Ballet, now known as the Kirov. Trained by the greatest Russian dancers of her time, including the subtle and brilliant Preobrajenskaya, she graduated in 1899 to the Imperial Ballet, where it took her seven years to rise from supple *coryphée*—a dancer in a small group of three or four rather than merely the corps de ballet—to prima ballerina. Making the role of *Giselle* her own, Pavlova toured Europe with the principals of the Imperial, including the famous Nijinsky, from 1907 to 1910, and for a time fell under the spell of the émigré impresario Serge Diaghilev, with whose Ballets Russes she briefly performed. But Diaghilev's blend of avant-garde innovation and showmanship was not for her, as it placed the dancer in an almost subordinate role. Refusing the title role in Stravinsky's *Firebird* because the score did not seem to her like music for the ballet, she concluded, with the childlike simplicity that was her chief personality trait, that Diaghilev's troupe was dedicated not to dance, but to music. Music was secondary to Pavlova's approach; she tended to favor popular musical offerings to the symphonic masterworks, the better to highlight her dancing. She also believed that ballet should be pure romance, defining art as, "The steady elimination of everything which is ugly, and the substitution of true and lasting beauty."

Pavlova had another reason for rebuffing Diaghilev: She had an acute need for money. Her reputed husband—it is not certain whether she ever married him—the minor noble Victor Dandré, was languishing in a Russian prison.

Originally her protector and lover, he had proceeded to the combined role of provider and manager and eventually ruined himself in shady business dealings. (Whatever their relationship, it did not stop either of them from liaisons with others, though hers were more discreet than his.) To ransom him, Pavlova embarked upon an exhausting but financially rewarding tour of England, Ireland, and France, dancing her by-now-famous interpretations of *Giselle* and the other staple of her repertoire, *The Dying Swan,* which audiences insisted upon at every performance. Choreographed in 1905 by the Russian dance genius Michel Fokine and set to Saint-Saens's "Carnival of the Animals," *The Dying Swan* called upon all of Pavlova's remarkable acting abilities. Her performance of this piece was so moving that it invariably reduced her audience to tears.

Pavlova settled in London, buying a home that had once belonged to the painter Turner (one room of which is now a Pavlova museum), and from 1911 on, she toured the world with her own company, managed by Dandré. In the spirit of the music hall, she included dances from various countries, including those in the Spanish, Indian, and Russian folk traditions. Nervous, obsessive, tempestuous, she worked incessantly and demanded that everyone follow her example. Whether happy or angry, she spoke in a rapid-fire but rambling manner, stringing disparate and sometimes contradictory thoughts together. It frustrated her greatly that her inability to explain her art made it impossible for her to teach. Even though she toured revolutionary Mexico guarded by a company of soldiers, the scatterbrained Pavlova appeared not to notice the upheaval surrounding her. She was often verbally abusive toward Dandré, but she was also capable of generosity and kindness, providing her corps de ballet with medical benefits and leave and giving gifts to those she loved, which were many. She was also very superstitious: Once, admiring a rosebush in a friend's garden, the melodramatic Pavlova suddenly declared that she would die when the roses did.

With her intense schedule, which carried her year after year to far-flung places at an age far more advanced than that of most dancers, it was surprising that she did not succumb to illness sooner than she did. In January 1931, while her husband dallied with a dancer from the chorus, Pavlova hurried through bitter winter frost to a performance at The Hague. A slight cold developed with shocking speed into pleurisy, and Pavlova fell into a coma. Three days later, she awoke and spoke her last words, to her beloved maid, Manya: "Bring me my swan costume." At that moment, her friend later swore, the rosebush withered.

PELÉ

WHETHER HE IS CALLED "The Black Pearl," "The King of Soccer," or "La Tulipe Negro," Edson Arantes do Nascimento—better known as Pelé—was at one time the most famous athlete in the world. In his heyday, he was absolute ruler over a sport that claims the fanatic allegiance of the first, second, and third worlds, with the notable exception of the United States, where professional association football—soccer—has never been able to rival American football or baseball. But so global is his fame that Pelé is the only soccer player who is instantly recognizable even to most Americans.

His professional achievements were gargantuan: more than twelve hundred goals scored in his career, twice as many as his nearest rival. Leader and inspiration of a Brazilian team that won an unheard-of three World Cup championships, in 1958,-1962, and 1970, he scored almost a goal a game in official Brazilian competition. His professional club, Santos, won two world club championships and countless city championships. In all, his clubs won fifty-two titles. But more than that there was his style, a swift and gliding fluidity that combined, as no other ever has, extraordinary leaping, heading, passing—and scoring.

Pelé first learned the game in Três Corações, the small Brazilian town where his father, Dondinho, a minor league footballer, pursued an uneven career. When Donhinho moved to the city of Bauru to play for the team there, his son helped augment the modest family finances by shining shoes and apprenticing to a cobbler. Though cheerful and athletic, Pelé was an unenthusiastic student. Instead he honed his skills for hours in the slum streets of Bauru, kicking a makeshift ball made of socks. Initially coached by his father, at age ten he came under the tutelage of Waldemar de Brito, a famous player who was a family friend. By age fourteen he was one of the best on the Bauru team, and in 1956 de Brito took him to São Paulo, where the big-league players scorned him as a hick. The team belonging to the smaller city of Santos was less picky, and their famous coach Lula gave Pelé a chance.

Like so many great athletes, he didn't initially impress his new employers. But in his first game he scored a surprising four of the team's seven goals and within a year he was a star in Brazil. In 1958, the rest of the planet discovered him at the World Cup in Stockholm, Sweden, when Pelé made a spectacular winning goal against Wales, leading to a victory over Sweden and Pelé's first World Cup championship.

By then the athlete had already experienced the dubious distinctions of being the best. Wherever Pelé played, the opposing players tried to take him out of the game by kicking him or crashing into him. He was routinely "triple-teamed," a tactic that only inspired him to more astonishing athletic feats. In fact, one of his goals, in which he wove through nine opposing players on his way to score, was so exciting it was played over and over again every day for a month on Brazilian Television.

Pelé's vision was remarkable, enabling him to see all the field both before him and peripherally; his sense of what teammates and opponents would do several plays in advance allied him with the greatest chess grand masters. His well-developed legs, the product of hard training instituted by his father, allowed him to leap high for headers and to sprint one hundred yards in under ten seconds. There seemed to be nothing Pelé couldn't do, as he proved to his own and his teammates' satisfaction time and again. During the bloody Biafran conflict of the 1960s, the combatants called a cease-fire so that both sides could watch him play football; his incredible athleticism had stopped a war.

By age thirty-four, rich and married to a beautiful Brazilian woman, Pelé's energy for physical pyrotechnics was depleted. Tired of being mobbed wherever he went, either on the field by vicious and frustrated opponents, or on the street by deliriously adoring fans, he retired in 1974 to his investments, his family, and a burgeoning movie career. A coffee was named after him; endorsements brought in millions.

But in 1975, the New York Cosmos of the nascent North American Soccer League (NASL) gave Pelé the final challenge of his life, which was to colonize the recalcitrant United States for the world's favorite sport. With that gauntlet and almost five million dollars flung down before him, Pelé moved to New York, delighted to find that no one mobbed him in a city where he was just one of a host of famous athletes. For three years he labored with missionary zeal to get the Yanks excited about *futbol*. In his first game with the Cosmos, twenty-one thousand people saw him play; three years later, seventy-six thousand paid tribute to him at his last hurrah. Yet the NASL is no more and the Cosmos are a fading memory.

When Pelé became a television football commentator, America had a chance to savor another of his talents during the 1994 World Cup, which was held in the United States with surprisingly strong support from audiences. But if America still loved Pelé more than the game he played, in that at least they joined the rest of the world.

EVA PERÓN

THE LIFE OF EVA PERÓN, glamorous wife of Argentinean leader Juan Perón and one of the twentieth century's most powerful women, was a strange brew of ambition, charisma, and unerring political instinct. An actress turned stateswoman, she projected a complex personality that encompassed almost every major female archetype: whore, benevolent mother to the needy, self-sacrificing wife, and, finally, the goddess whose whims determined a political or physical death. Ironically, Evita was proclaimed a saint by her followers, who ignored her profligate spending on jewels, furs, and storerooms full of Paris frocks. They pointed instead to her lavish public charities and to a life dedicated to improving the lot of her beloved *descamisados*, "shirtless ones," the millions of workers who supported the Peróns' husband-and-wife cabal. Upon her death from cancer in 1952, loyal Perónistas cabled Pope Pius XII to request that he begin the beatification process, the Catholic Church's first step in canonization. They were rebuffed.

Born the illegitimate daughter of a cook somewhere in Los Toldos, a small, remote village in Buenos Aires province, in her early teens Eva Maria Duarte abandoned her childhood home—and her childhood—for an acting career in the big city of Buenos Aires. Striking but not beautiful and lacking education and social finesse, she struggled for almost a decade. After finally attaining a modest success, especially in radio soap operas, the still-ambitious twenty-four-year-old met her "heart"—the handsome widower Colonel Juan Domingo Perón—at a rally for earthquake victims soon after the military coup of June 4, 1943. Perón, then secretary of labor and welfare, set her up as his mistress in the elegant Calle Posados. Two years later, after Juan was arrested during one of many Argentinean power struggles, Evita organized a triumphant march of fifty thousand trade union supporters to engineer his release from prison. They were married four days later, and the flamboyant Evita, fanatically devoted to her spouse, became indispensable in creating the populist infrastructure of his single-party, quasi-Marxist regime.

As soon as her husband was elected president in 1946, and throughout his first six-year term, the first lady began solidifying the Perónista party's alliances with organized labor by purging the unions of unsympathetic leaders. Dismissed as a political dilettante, Evita soon proved her critics wrong. However new she was to the realm of political shadow alliances and back-stabbing, she was ardent in her hatred for her enemies, the oligarchy. (Evita loyalists trace this deep antagonism to her sexual assault as a teenager by two young landowners' sons.) The existence of the poor, she said, pained her "less than the knowledge that at the same time others are rich." Making the most of every moment of her eighteen-hour days, she set the hearts of her country's workers on fire and

transformed the nation's most influential labor alliance, the General Confederation of Labor, into a tool of Perónism. Evita also won the gratitude and respect of women, campaigning as she did for the legalization of divorce, for women's right to vote, and for the formation of the Perónista Feminist Party, which was crucial to her husband's reelection.

While Juan kept the military at bay and administered far-reaching land reforms, Evita acted as his hatchet person and pursued social betterment. When the aristocratic ladies of the Sociedad de Beneficiencia disdainfully refused her its honorary presidency—a post that traditionally belonged to the president's wife—Evita promptly destroyed the organization and set up her own Eva Duarte de Perón Social Aid Foundation. One of history's most wasteful welfare machines, it was also a personal slush fund for party patronage, funded by contributions from labor, business, and government to the tune of $100 million a year. The foundation, which aided in national disaster relief, built sumptuous housing for unwed mothers, a luxurious facility for the aged with hired butlers, and an entire children's village, complete with its own tiny houses and a tot-sized jail. A propaganda genius, Evita traveled throughout Argentina every day, dispensing medicines, food, and jobs—usually in the presence of photographers. Always elegantly dressed, she looked more like the movie star she had aspired to be than the redeemer her nation's despairing people had begun to venerate. Yet despite the Peróns' burgeoning Swiss bank accounts, privately the couple lived simply, rose early, and worked hard.

Evita Perón's first grab for official power, in the summer of 1951, coincided with her declining health. While she waited for her husband to ask her to run as his vice president during his second term, the military—appalled at the possibility of a female commander in chief—lobbied the president to force his wife to back down. Just prior to the election Evita underwent surgery for cancer and she died several months later, but not before her distraught husband had guaranteed his helpmate the grandeur of a full presidential burial by placing the ornately jeweled Collar of the Order of San Martin into her almost lifeless hands.

The public lamentation upon Evita's death was deep and long-lasting. For days, business and government simply ceased. As her glass-topped and silver-trimmed white coffin lay in state in the headquarters of the General Confederation of Labor, flowers piled up in colorful drifts against the surrounding buildings. After public viewing, Evita's emaciated but meticulously embalmed corpse lay on a laboratory slab for three years, eventually disappearing mysteriously. It would go on reappearing and disappearing for decades, until, after being exhumed in 1971 and returned to Perón, it finally came to rest in the family vault in Buenos Aires's Recoleta Cemetery. Or so it is said.

1915-1963
EDITH PIAF

THE "NIGHTINGALE OF PARIS," so small and frail looking in the glaring spotlight, seems touchingly awkward for the moment. Unadorned by jewelry or stage makeup and wearing her familiar short black dress—"It is my uniform. I am a soldier"—she plants her tiny feet wide apart, throws back her frizzy curls, and begins to sing in a prodigious voice, enthralling the audience with doleful tales of wrecked destinies and lost loves. It is a throaty, vibratoed voice, seasoned by street singing, refined in cabarets, assaulted by illness, accidents, drugs, and alcohol, and informed by the drama of her own achingly tragic experience.

Piaf's life reads like a Victorian novel. Born quite literally on the sidewalk, with two gendarmes in attendance, baby Edith Gassion was abandoned by her mother, a French-Algerian café singer, to the care of her maternal grandparents when she was two months old; her father, an itinerant acrobat, went off to fight in World War I. When he returned two years later to find her living in squalor, with wine added to the milk in her baby bottle to sedate her, he took her to be raised by his mother in Normandy. At age three, a severe case of conjunctivitis left her blind for four years. The blindness ended suddenly after her grandmother took her on a pilgrimage to the shrine of Saint Teresa of Lisieux. (Piaf would come to believe the event had been a miracle.) From that time on the child wore a medal bearing the saint's likeness. Later in life she would never be without her emerald-studded cross, a Christmas gift from Marlene Dietrich.

Now old enough to travel the circuit with her acrobat father, Piaf began singing in the fairs and small cafés of rural France and Belgium. In 1930, the fifteen-year-old struck out on her own in Paris, making her way as a street entertainer in the alleys of Montmartre. Five years later, she was discovered by Louis Leplée, owner of a famous cabaret on the Champs-Élysées, who not only gave her the courage to confront his polished clientele, but insisted that her waif-like persona be part of her image on stage. Even her name, *La Môme Piaf* or "the urchin sparrow," was Leplée's inspiration. He also helped the singer rework her quirky body of chansons into a sophisticated repertoire more worthy of the star he was helping to create. By the eve of World War II, Leplée's once scruffy little bird, who prepared for performances by gargling with coffee, was the toast of Paris nightlife.

The murder of the man Piaf had come to call Papa Leplée, some six months after her momentous 1935 debut,

had a devastating effect on the singer, who was detained by the French police as a material witness. Together with the recent death of her illegitimate daughter, Marcelle, when Piaf was nineteen, this traumatic event seemed to suggest that she was somehow cursed. Her life rapidly became a bruising sequence of drinking, exhaustion-induced breakdowns followed by triumphant comebacks, and eternal loves that always proved disconsolately finite. The latter were particularly difficult for Piaf, whose craving for affection was such that she could never—not even for one night—sleep alone.

During the Second World War, Piaf traveled to Germany many times to sing for French prisoners of war, who called her godmother. It was a generous gift that, for a time after the surrender, her countrymen interpreted as collaboration. But with the postwar disclosures of Piaf's efforts to save Jewish friends from capture and the danger she braved on these journeys during the height of Allied bombings, the rift evaporated. Piaf made some ten tours of the United States, though she hated nightclubs and was always afraid that American audiences would, through some gesture, shatter the mood she strove to create. Audiences all over the world were captured by the voice that, in Jean Cocteau's words, "unfolds itself like a wave of black velvet." By 1946, after starring in the film *Étoile sans lumière*, Piaf began touring with Les Compagnons de la Chanson, a vocal group whose "Les Trois Cloches" became an international hit for her in the late forties. In 1949 she was, once again, struck by misfortune when her great love, world champion boxer Marcel Cerdan, died in a plane crash in the Azores. Piaf, never self-pitying, stumbled on. She cheered her fans with the upbeat "Milord" in the sixties, her last hit, but audiences clung to their older favorites, like "Non, je ne regrette rien," "La Vie en rose," and "L'Accordéoniste," a vintage Piaf song about a *fille de joie* whose musician lover is killed in the war.

While Piaf's life was impulsive and chaotic, her art was not. Supremely conscious of her gifts and always in control, she created a stage persona that was at once completely contrived and totally authentic. Every gesture, every expression, was calculated to serve the creative whole. Every song was especially chosen and labored over with its composer, with Piaf herself often contributing lyrics. In the end, what she projected was searingly genuine because, through her art, the pale, woeful sparrow had taken on the pain of the lost and the forgotten as her own—as the tens of thousands of Parisians who filled the streets upon her death in 1963 attested.

PABLO PICASSO

TWO IMAGES SURFACE FROM the stream of anecdotes about the remarkable life of Pablo Picasso. In one, an intent nine-year-old, perhaps showing off for one of his father's friends in his hometown of Malaga, executes an impressive sketch of a horse in one fluid movement. In another, a considerably older Picasso is stretched out on the floor in front of his television with the sound off, intently drawing right onto the fluorescent screen. Neither of these vignettes is especially important historically, but together they reveal much about the master of modern twentieth-century art. Nothing, in fact, was more crucial to his genius than the energy of playful exploration. Until the very end of his ninety-one years—eighty of which were enormously productive—Picasso managed to sustain a spontaneity and inventiveness that, combined with his prodigious talent, made him perhaps the most important artist of the century.

When he was barely ten, Pablo Ruiz y Picasso began his formal training under his father, José Ruiz Blasco, a professor of drawing who eventually transferred his own ambitions to his more talented offspring. After study at the Barcelona Academy of Fine Arts, the ambitious sixteen-year-old settled in Madrid, where he reveled in his discovery of the Prado's masters. He absorbed the work of Goya, El Greco, and Velázquez, but rejected the career of academic painter that his family had hoped for, and in 1900 journeyed with his Catalan studio mate, Carlos Casagemas, to Paris. Briefly liberated by the art of Van Gogh, Toulouse-Lautrec, and Cézanne, Picasso soon plunged into a deep depression caused by Casagemas's suicide, an event that inspired several paintings and inaugurated his renowned Blue Period. The despondent figures of these years gave way in late 1904 to his Rose Period, characterized by more classical, clay-hued subjects and by the carnival's harlequins and *Saltimbanques*.

One of Picasso's most significant breaks with traditional art came in 1907, with his monumental painting *Les Demoiselles d'Avignon*. A stunning masterpiece featuring five heroicsized nudes whose aggressively posed bodies appear to break up into angular, shaded planes, it signaled the birth of analytical Cubism. This revolutionary movement, developed by Picasso and fellow painter Georges Braque, turned Renaissance perspective inside out—and Picasso into the rage of his adopted city. The varied sources that fed this extraordinary new vision—African sculpture, early Iberian art, Christian iconography—underscore Picasso's ability to borrow and transform older art in order to create something totally new. Picasso saw artistic form and content everywhere—in the works of his favorite painters and sculptors, including himself, and in the dusty accumulation of decades of hoarded objects. Picasso

ordered everything he had ever worn to be saved because, he believed, they retained a certain magic akin to saints' relics. Literature also fired his visual imagination, especially the works of Oscar Wilde and his friend, Guillaume Apollinaire.

Picasso was equally voracious in his amorous liaisons, chaotic affairs that included four wives and several long-term lovers, all of whom functioned as both partners and muses. At once obsessed with yet rejecting of his women, he often pitted them against each other and seemed to derive pleasure from the jealousy—often violent—that arose in the triangles he engineered. Yugoslavian photographer Dora Maar—who by the midthirties had usurped the roles of both Picasso's first wife, Russian ballerina Olga Kokhlova, and his mistress, Marie-Thérèse Walter—was finally driven to a nervous breakdown, while Walter eventually hanged herself. Françoise Gilot, much to Picasso's fury, simply left him, taking their two children, Claude and Paloma. His last wife, Jacqueline Roque, chose to end her days with a gun. Picasso's misogyny, and incidents such as his failure to help extricate his old friend, poet Max Jacob, from Nazi imprisonment, have created difficulties for biographers and critics alike as they attempt to unravel his powerful and manipulative personality.

Picasso's imagination seems to have been rooted in this irrational, often destructive aspect of his character: hence, the victim/aggressor who fathered the satiric couplings of his later works, and the Minotaur, the Aegean man/bull that symbolically communicated Picasso's fascination with the dualities of love and hate. But all was not negative emotion, as any admirer of his work will know. Picasso often tempered his self-indulgence and egocentrism with warmth and great gestures of magnanimity. Fueled by prodigious physical energy, he was adept at matching his quixotic moods spontaneously to all media, excelling in sculpture, lithography, set design, drawing, ceramics, and all types of construction. No found object, it was said, was safe in his presence.

From analytical Cubism, Picasso moved to collage and synthetic Cubism and then on to Surrealism's archetypes. Arguably his most famous canvas, 1937's wrenching *Guernica*—the passionate Loyalist's protest against the German bombing of the Basque capitol during the Spanish civil war—reflects these trends. Like everything in his oeuvre, it also recorded his sentiments. This stream-of-consciousness monologue was the very essence of Picasso's modernism, the method by which he could project his conflicting urges onto canvas. Toward the end of his life, it focused increasingly on death. While failing to staunch his prodigious output, Picasso's obsession with the impending loss of self left him lonely and embittered, but also perhaps more human.

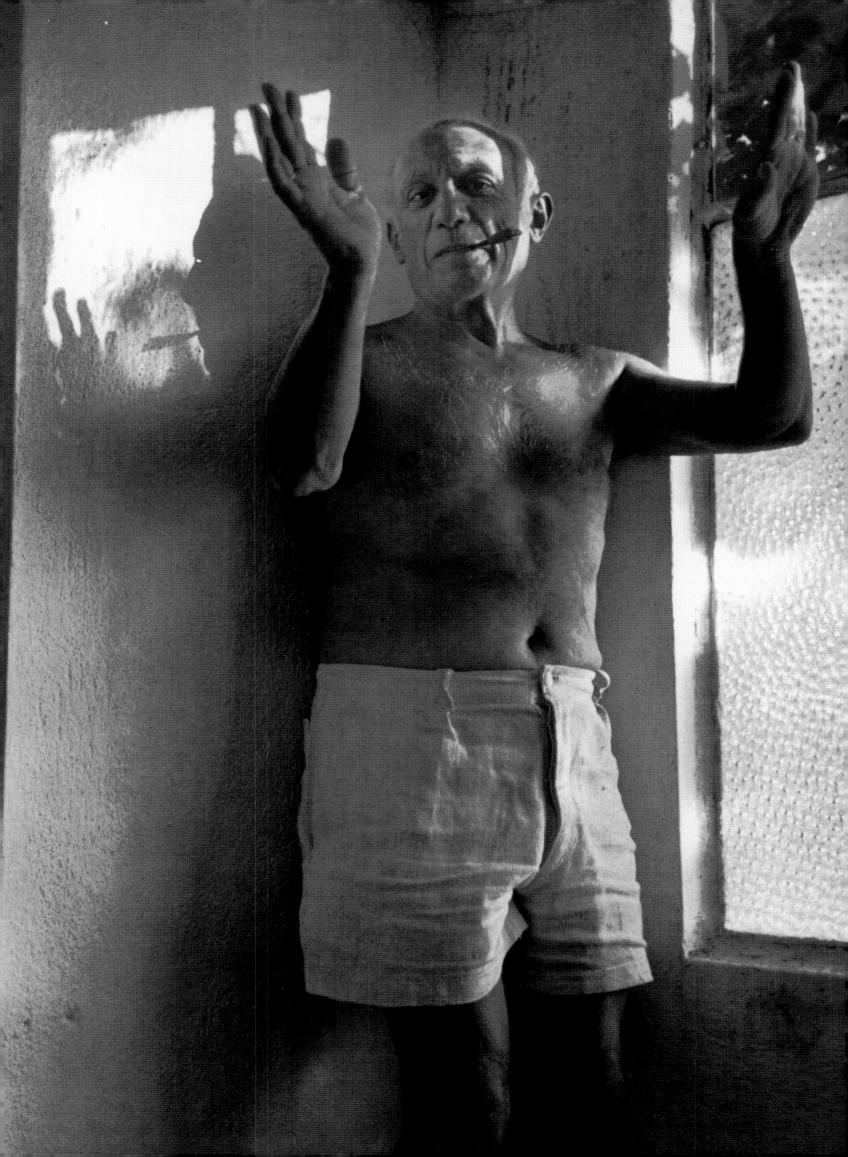

MARY PICKFORD

SHE WAS "THE WORLD'S SWEETHEART," the sparkling young girl with the golden ringlets who became not only the first bona fide movie star but also the most famous woman of her era. Despite her influential position as prime power broker in what all her colleagues were certain would become the century's most important medium, Pickford saw film as a transient phenomenon. She made it a point to buy up all her movies so that they couldn't be shown, planning to burn them all eventually. She was worried, too, that "Little Mary" might, in the end, be ridiculed. Fortunately, Lillian Gish, among others, deterred her and Pickford established a fund for the films' preservation and restoration. Thanks to her friend's persuasiveness, "Little Mary," as millions of admirers called her, can still be seen in such classics as *Rebecca of Sunnybrook Farm* (1917), *The Poor Little Rich Girl* (1917), and *Pollyanna* (1920).

Warm and refreshingly open, Pickford acted the role of maiden-in-distress as if she were born to it. Sadly for her, however, audiences never allowed her to break the mold. Refusing to let her grow up, they insisted that the comedically gifted actress play virtuous adolescents even as she approached forty. Although Pickford proved to be an astute image builder and a skilled movie producer, the typecasting that checked her acting ambitions plagued her to the end.

Born Gladys Mary Smith, Pickford began her career touring in stock companies with her Toronto-based "gypsy" family: mother Charlotte, a strong-minded widow who had taken small parts in stock companies to support Gladys, sister Lottie, and brother Jack. The wholesomeness of Baby Gladys Smith, as the child was soon dubbed, assured her early success and her family's survival from the start. In 1906, Mrs. Smith took a new stage name for her family of actors—Pickford, after the children's paternal grandmother. The next year, the veteran fourteen-year-old finessed her way into a meeting with Broadway producer David Belasco, winning a role in *The Warrens of Virginia*. Two years later, now performing as Mary Pickford, she sought work with film pioneer D. W. Griffith, who interviewed her and immediately hustled her onto the set of *Pippa Passes*. She responded to the director's offer of five dollars per day by asking for double. She got it, eventually collaborating with Griffith on some seventy-four films. The plots, maudlin in the main, were brightened by her spontaneity. Behind all those wronged virgins and grieving young mothers was an actress of subtle, persuasive talent whose warmth and buoyancy enabled her to rise effortlessly above the melodrama.

In a short time Pickford progressed technically far beyond her first movie, *The Violin Maker of Cremona* (1909). Marrying actor Owen Moore, she soon parlayed her identity as "The Biograph Girl with the Curls" into a profitable relationship with famed producer Adolph Zukor. The partnership was artistic magic, with Pickford becoming an immediate sensation in 1914's *Hearts Adrift* and *Tess of the Storm Country*. Zukor cut her an astonishing deal: an unheard of weekly salary of $10,000, a $250,000 guarantee per film, a $300,000 bonus, plus profit sharing and help in forming her own independent production company. In his 1923 autobiography, Zukor wrote: "It often took longer to make one of Mary's contracts than it did to make one of Mary's pictures." In her peak earning years—a time of minimal personal income taxes—Pickford enjoyed an annual take-home income of more than a million dollars, money that she providently invested in real estate. In 1919, Pickford joined Charlie Chaplin, D. W. Griffith, and Douglas Fairbanks in forming United Artists, a groundbreaking venture in the film industry and one the quartet hoped would guarantee them both creative independence and profits.

Pickford obtained a divorce from Moore and in 1920 and married the eternally boyish Fairbanks, athletic star of the costume spectacle. The dashing Fairbanks was just what the nation had in mind as the perfect match for its heroine, whom the public believed to be saddened by the failure of her first marriage. In reality Pickford had been carrying on an affair with Fairbanks for five years, abandoning her Catholicism in the process. On their European honeymoon, the couple was literally mobbed by hysterical crowds. When they finally came home, filmdom's king and queen settled into Pickfair, their rambling estate near Benedict Canyon. In 1929 Pickford won an Oscar for her first talkie, *Coquette*, and made a talkie version of *The Taming of the Shrew* with Fairbanks. It was a dismal failure. Tiring finally of her restless swashbuckler's indiscretions, she ended the marriage in 1936. Depressed by her divorce and several failed attempts to extend her career into talkies, she found solace the following year in marriage to Buddy Rogers. As her co-star in *My Best Girl* (1927), Rogers had given Mary her first screen kiss—at the age of thirty-four.

Pickford remained active in United Artists until 1956, when she sold her interests. A philanthropist, she retired to Pickfair in the 1970s, preferring the company of Buddy Rogers and a few old friends. The Academy of Motion Picture Arts and Sciences presented her with a special award in 1976. At eighty-three her intelligence and inner beauty still shone through.

JACKSON POLLOCK

SPLASH, SPATTER, DRIP—American Abstract Expressionist Jackson Pollock's mature artistic technique was like a force of nature. Tapping deep into his subconscious, his energy burst the boundaries not only of the canvas but of modern art itself. Of watching Pollock work, fellow painter Barnett Newman, remarked, "Forget the hand. It's the mind—not brain, but mind—soul, concentration, gut." But the mind that could create a canvas of incredible shimmering pattern, layer after layer of line and movement, was a troubled one. Throughout his adulthood, Pollock was subject to violent rages, alcoholic binging, blackouts, and creative blocks. Even during his most creative and successful years, keeping his private demons at bay became more and more difficult. In the end, Pollock and his art would be vanquished by them.

He was born in Wyoming, at home in the open spaces of the American West. The baby of the family, the last of five brothers, four of whom would become painters, Paul Jackson Pollock spent his early years on a sheep ranch in the town of Cody. The children had a rootless childhood, moving with their mother, a genteel and artistic matriarch, and their father, a tough-minded and unaffectionate surveyor who was often away. When the family finally settled in Los Angeles, Jack, as he was always known, enrolled in sculpture and painting classes at Manual Arts High School. His lack of facility at traditional exercises such as life drawing and tracing was a problem for him. At the age of sixteen, Pollock embraced Theosophy, under the tutelage of the Hindu poet and philosopher Khrisnamurti. It was the first of many times in his life that Pollock would seek spiritual and psychological guidance; later, he would embrace aspects of Native American culture and Jungian archetypes, during his many attempts at healing through psychoanalysis. Expelled from high school twice, he finally decided to try his hand in New York, going to study at the Art Students League under Thomas Hart Benton, one of the masters of American objective painting. The macho Benton—physically imposing, rebellious, and a legendary womanizer—was to influence Pollock profoundly; his student not only imitated Benton's artistic style but his personal one as well. While Pollock would, in time, become Benton's star pupil, the apprenticeship was not an easy one. Pollock's lack of facility, already evident at Manual Arts, was an embarrassment; he seemed, in Benton's appraisal, incapable of working in a logical progression. A fellow student later recalled "the continuous running battle" between Pollock and his tools.

During the Depression years, Pollock worked on several federally funded arts projects, painting one canvas which featured a horse bearing the stylistic stamp of both Benton and Chagall. Between the late thirties and early forties, Pollock produced a series of paintings inspired by Picasso and the Surrealists with mythic, sometimes, brutal themes. Soon after, he was introduced to the unconventional techniques such as spray-painting and stenciling by the Mexican David Alfaro Siqueiros.

The new techniques would change his artistic vision, while his relationship to Lee Krasner, an artist whom he would marry in 1945, would provide him with an environment which would nurture his creativity. Pollock and Krasner moved out of New York City to Springs, a town near Amagansett on Long Island, with a studio space which facilitated Pollock's new techniques. The next four years would be the happiest and most productive of his life. Pollock moved away from the representational and began to drip color—sometimes aluminum radiator paint—directly onto the l canvas. In swift succession, he renounced the easel and its ordered universe of up, down, left, and right by the simple act of nailing the canvas to the floor. Pollock would move around the canvas—sometimes across it—drizzling, flinging, darting pigment from different angles, producing thread after thread of color. Energy and line emerged from the work with dazzling clarity. Liberated from the traditional tools of art with which he had never felt totally comfortable, Pollock continued to experiment, working on different surfaces (canvas, composition board, metal, and cardboard) and using different ways of applying pigment to them. In order to further distance the images he created from content and representation, he numbered his works, rather than giving them titles. Pollock's reputation grew steadily. By 1948, when *Life* magazine featured him and his work—the headline asked "Is he the greatest living painter in the United States?"—he had become a celebrity. In 1949, eighteen out of twenty-seven of his paintings hung at a show sold to patrons of the arts, among them Mrs. John D. Rockefeller; at the age of thirty-seven, Pollock was a success.

But neither his success nor new-found artistic liberation freed him from violent outbursts of temper, alcoholic binging, or the periods when he was unable to work. If anything, success seemed only to create a window of opportunity for his self-destruction. His always volatile and abusive relationship with his wife grew more so, and each of them began to talk of divorce; friends and acquaintances alike were driven away by the rages induced by liquor. Unable to work, this once-handsome man was physically ravaged as well. By the midfifties, what Pollock did produce seemed to the critics to fall short of his earlier efforts. The year 1956 brought things to a crisis; Pollock turned his attentions to a younger woman, Ruth Kligman, and Lee Krasner took refuge in Europe. Then on August 12, 1956, after a night of drinking, Pollock, his mistress, and a friend, Edith Metzger got into his car. Only Ruth Kligman survived the crash. At the age of forty-four, the man who had brought American art to the cutting edge was dead. The legacy he left was enormous: the huge, luminous landscapes of the mind, *Simmering Substance* and *Blue Poles*, among them.

ELVIS PRESLEY

BLENDING RHYTHM AND BLUES, gospel, and country-and-western, Elvis Aron Presley blasted into the somnolent fifties with a backbeat that would jump-start an entire generation. A good old boy from Tupelo, Mississippi, the man who would become the undisputed "King of Rock and Roll" loved his mama, his church, and his guitar and, even when he was making millions, still dined on deep fried peanut butter and banana sandwiches. Surviving a stillborn twin brother, Elvis started out singing spirituals at revivals with his rural-poor parents. At ten, he won second prize for singing "Old Shep" at the Mississippi—Alabama Fair and Dairy Show and later thought about a career as a gospel singer. Before he reached twenty-five, however, Elvis had become the teen idol of a new rebel music, a still-influential global phenomenon.

Determined to become the next James Dean and obsessed with his appearance, he relied largely on instinct, defining his racy hybrid music as he went along. Elvis's performances—with his husky, hard-edged delivery and insinuating hip gyrations—were scorching. Truculent, aggressive, and cool, he wore peg-leg pants and a swirled-up pompadour, appearing vulnerable and dangerous at the same time. His look and sound created a cultural explosion, empowering teenagers with a novel and defiant way of dressing and behaving. Indignant over Elvis's bad influence, parents, the clergy, and other authority figures—often people who simply disapproved of "black music"—forbade children to even listen to him. But it was too late; the driving pulse of rock and roll had become the heartbeat of America's youth.

Sam Phillips, who ran Sun Records in Memphis, was the first music professional to respond to Elvis's unique sound—and originally he wasn't that impressed. Elvis, an eighteen-year-old truck driver at the time, had gone to the producer's studio to make a four-dollar 45 RPM recording for his doting mother, Gladys. Back home, he played the disc again and again, an activity his fans would later replicate countless times. When Phillips started looking around for white performers to sing "Negro" songs, he called Elvis back into the studio and, with 1954's "That's All Right (Mama)," made music history. Elvis, who always acknowledged his debt to the African-American musical tradition, continued to develop what he called his "goosed up" version while touring with the Blue Moon Boys. Eventually, he attracted the attention of Colonel Tom Parker, a colorful Dutch-born booking agent who would end up managing the rest of Elvis's career. With Parker in charge, Elvis set off on a rural tour as "The Hill Billy Cat."

It wasn't until the spring of 1956, however, that he got his major break. Under a thirty-five-thousand-dollar contract with RCA Victor, Elvis recorded a love-and-loneliness ballad called "Heartbreak Hotel." It sold two million copies, much to the surprise of Sam Phillips, who with millions of others would watch Elvis grow into a megastar with lifetime earnings of over a billion dollars. An extraordinary flow of top-ten hits followed—"Don't Be Cruel," "Hound Dog," "Blue Suede Shoes," and "Love Me Tender" among them. Later that year the Dorsey Brothers asked Elvis—who had already debuted, and bombed, on radio's Grand Ole Opry—to make his national television debut on their weekly Stage Show. But the real breakthrough came when Elvis performed on The Ed Sullivan Show, and Mr. Sunday Night assured fifty-four million Americans that this apparent threat to adolescent morality was actually "a real decent, fine boy." Sullivan had bolstered that claim—and taken no chances—by having Elvis shot only from the waist up.

Hollywood was next, and in 1956 Elvis signed a seven-year contract with movie producer Hal Wallis. His first movie, Love Me Tender, grossed almost six times its production cost. The critics, however, had little good to say about it, or about Elvis's thirty-two subsequent B-grade productions, which found a somewhat softer pop idol cast adrift in such unlikely roles as a tuna fisherman. Elvis, though seldom lacking female attention, never really settled into the Hollywood scene, choosing instead the company of his familiar down-home buddies. Paid hangers-on, the "Memphis Mafia" protected the genuinely shy and self-effacing star, carousing with him and catering to his expensive whims. No matter how flagrant his excesses, however, he remained deeply spiritual, continuing to view his talent as a gift from a God who could take it back as capriciously as it had been bestowed.

His formula-film period of the sixties followed Private Presley's much-publicized stint in the U.S. Army. He did not return to television or make personal appearances again until 1968, the same year he embarked upon a comeback career as a Las Vegas–style crooner. Now married to the former Priscilla Beaulieu, he sang to SRO crowds, who seemed not to care that he had been away—or that his spangled costumes failed to camouflage a physique grown bloated from years of abuse.

During the last of these strange, glitzy years—which reached their apogee in 1973, with a televised concert from Hawaii watched by a billion people—Elvis became even more reclusive than before. Divorced that same year, he retreated between concerts to his twenty-three-room mansion, Graceland. A consuming addiction to prescription drugs and other health problems led to his death on August 16, 1977. Adoring fans came by the thousands to the gates of Graceland that day, many to weep uncontrollably. Florist shops all around Memphis actually ran out of flowers. But no one ever ran out of hyperbole when speaking of Elvis Presley. As the Beatles' John Lennon put it simply, "Elvis was the thing."

MARCEL PROUST

A SEMIRECLUSE OF MOST unorthodox habits, the greatest French novelist of the twentieth century lived and wrote for much of his life in Paris in a small, cork-lined room littered with debris. Asthmatic, frail, and highly neurotic, the perennially-ill Marcel Proust was nonetheless able to complete a literary work so monumental, so complex in style, and so profound in its impact that many critics—and Proust himself—have likened his seven-part novel to a cathedral. Massive in scope yet baroquely detailed, *À la recherche du temps perdu (Remembrance of Things Past)* is an intricately planned work, which draws its readers into exploring every nuance of its structure until its grander architectural harmony and ultimate meaning can be fully appreciated.

Begun in the early 1900s, abandoned, then resumed several years later, *Remembrance,* with its vast array of characters and thematic overlays, stubbornly resists synopsis. As its title suggests, the novel concerns itself with time, that "invisible substance" that transforms as surely as it ticks away, and with memory, which for Proust existed in two forms, "voluntary" and "involuntary." The latter was to be preferred, its sudden shock of "illumination" bringing the kind of primal joy that rescues humankind, though only momentarily, from what he viewed as life's essential disillusionment.

Proust's semiautobiographical and allegorical tale begins with just such a surprise recollection, the legendary scene that opens the first volume, *Swann's Way,* which the author published himself in 1913 after it was rejected by every publisher who saw it: His narrator (named Marcel, like the author) savors a "petite madeleine" soaked in lime-flower tea, thereby unexpectedly releasing his recollections of an aunt who used to serve this treat to him. The incident begins one of the most sensual and intriguing stories ever told.

Set in the era of the Third Republic against a background of high-society elegance and base behavior, *Remembrance* is both the author/narrator's all-consuming search for his past and a depressing panorama of impermanence. Caught up in World War I and undergoing cultural and political flux, France was also in turmoil over the Dreyfus affair, a national debate in which Proust agitated on behalf of the Jewish army officer unjustly accused of treason in 1894. Parisian aristocracy, to which the devout social climber Proust was ambivalently attracted, had gone into eclipse. Through his descriptions of its demise—the subtle breaches of etiquette, lusty heterosexual and homosexual couplings, and disastrous fluctuations in status—the reader encounters the bleakest of worldviews. Passion is agonizing in its impermanence, Proust's characters show us over and over, and love is impossible, because we can never truly see "the other." When the circularly designed novel ends, the reader is stunned to find himself once again at the beginning. In the search for time lost, the narrator has discovered his vocation and decides to share his embitterment over his shattered beliefs by writing the novel the reader has just finished, a process in which time is recaptured.

The author was born in Auteuil, near Paris, to an eminent physician of Catholic background and his wife Jeanne. Diagnosed with asthma at nine, frequent illness kept Proust tied to his mother, a cultivated, sexually frigid woman who, along with her husband, pampered her highly sensitive son. The precocious young scholar found it difficult, however, to impose his desires on the indifferent world outside his privileged middle-class home. He was further frustrated by the repeated rejections of his adolescent sexual overtures to many male acquaintances. Armed with his mother's money—she was the daughter of a well-to-do Jewish stockbroker—and diplomas in philosophy and law from the Sorbonne, the erudite dandy, after a year of military service, took up company with a belles-lettres circle. Its bright young men, in turn, would introduce their fledgling writer friend into the Belle Epoque salons of their socially connected mothers. Soon Proust, the most calculating of climbers, was worming his way into the palm-and-plush parlors of the city's *haut monde,* an inbred universe in which time was idled away in glamorous pursuits.

From this elegant 1890s milieu, the romantic fabulist would bridge the gap between the highly personal and sentimental cosmos of the nineteenth century and the harsher ego-as-all twentieth. From the fading Victorian past came his reverence for language and nature. To the future he brought psychologically intoned dialogue; interrelated leitmotifs of symbol, theme, and image; and "prepared characters" whose nature changed as the narrator became more familiar with them. Beginning his journey into the unconscious with *Jean Santeuil* (1896–99)—an unfinished work found in the 1950s that foreshadowed *Remembrance*—and continuing with *Swann's Way* and *Within a Budding Grove* (1918), the second part of his masterpiece, which won him the prestigious Prix Goncourt, Proust moved through his "life" with amazing deliberation. He simultaneously reached the end of his life—and that of his extraordinary and influential fictional saga—in his oeuvre's last volume, *Le Temps retrouvé (Time Regained),* published posthumously in 1927.

Proust, the ceaseless ruminator, had wished to teach posterity to cherish "privileged moments," those bursts of spontaneous memory that surprise one with their gift of self-knowledge and intimations of a beyond. Exhausted by his self-neglect and his endless nights of writing, he died of a pulmonary infection on November 18, 1922, satisfied that his finely wrought message would not be soon forgotten.

AYN RAND

1905-1982

SELFLESSNESS, IN MOST OF the world's ethical and religious systems, has generally been considered a virtue—until best-selling author and self-proclaimed philosopher Ayn Rand introduced her beliefs in the early 1940s. The objectivist philosophy, as she called it, was "a morality of rational self-interest," a code of behavior discernible in objective reality in which altruism had no place. Bolstered by her own unrestrained egotism—she placed herself second only to Aristotle as a philosopher—the Russian émigré turned American patriot aimed to become the poster woman for both unrestrained individualism and its freewheeling cousin, capitalism. To this end, Rand wrote two phenomenally successful novels, *The Fountainhead* (1943) and *Atlas Shrugged* (1957), both of which candy-coated a tough-as-nails philosophy with romance and intrigue, prompting *Newsweek* to comment in 1961 that her values made "well-poisoning seem like one of the kindlier arts."

Rand the philosopher attracted a small but intensely loyal following. Her adherents proclaimed that a human's moral imperative was to seek his own happiness, with achievement as his goal and nothing but reason as his guide. Along with her philosophical proclamations, the rather humorless Rand articulated a host of intense likes and dislikes. On the approval list were laissez-faire government, free trade, atheism, solitude, overachievers, her signature dollar-shaped gold brooch, smoking, and what she described as romantic-realist fiction—which of course included her own. Her disapproval was reserved for things more numerous, among them altruists of any stripe—including, and perhaps especially, the religious—totalitarianism, conservatives *and* liberals, mediocrity, the impoverished ("the mob," whom she saw as undermining the American way), women's liberation ("a grotesque phenomenon"), collectivists (especially Communists), and anyone who disagreed with her.

Many years after her death, Rand's books continue to be a publishing marvel. Her almost fifteen million dollars in worldwide sales to date is a tribute to the compelling nature of her writing. She has generally not been critically well received, though *The New York Times Book Review's* discussion of *The Fountainhead* praised her "subtle and ingenious mind." There were few champions for the artistic merit of *Atlas Shrugged*. In any case, Rand the rationalist aimed from the start to mix her theories with throbbing emotion. Having learned to read and write at age six, Alice Rosenbaum, the studious daughter of a Jewish pharmacist, decided three years later to become a writer. At thirteen, she noted in her diary: "Today, I decided to be an atheist." In a godless universe, her art would provide something else to worship—ideal people of courage and principle, whose specialty was the impossible. She particularly admired the works of Fyodor Dostoyevsky and Victor Hugo and, to be sure, the *Übermensch* of Friedrich Nietzsche's *Also Sprach Zarathustra*.

Rand graduated with highest honors from the University of Petrograd in 1924, having survived the hardships of the Bolshevik Revolution, during which her father went bankrupt. Young Alice then went to visit distant cousins in Chicago and never returned. In 1926 she followed her dreams to Hollywood, where she perfected her English by writing film scripts. She chose her last name from the Remington-Rand typewriter she had brought from her homeland. Before and after working for Cecil B. DeMille, whom she met, literally, at the gates of his studio, Rand took odd jobs to finance her writing. Her struggle, ameliorated in 1929 by marriage to an actor named Charles Francis ("Frank") O'Connor, foreshadowed her up-by-the-bootstraps proselytizing: Whatever she learned, she later recalled, "I had to learn by myself and in my own way." Her efforts were rewarded by the sale of a screenplay in 1932 and, three years later, by the Broadway production of her first play under the title *Night of January 16th*.

Seven years after the publication of *We the Living* in 1936, a novel which deals with the ruination of three lives under the soulless oppression of a Communist regime, came Rand's blockbuster, *The Fountainhead*. Often presumed to be based on the life of Frank Lloyd Wright, the book is the story of genius architect Howard Roark and his quest to express his individuality in an increasingly collectivist society. Railing against a world perishing in "an orgy of self-sacrificing," the protagonist defines himself by blowing up a housing project he has created after bureaucrats alter his original designs.

After writing the script for the movie version of *The Fountainhead*, Rand wrote *Atlas Shrugged*. At well over one thousand pages, and filled with dialogue-as-objectivist-gospel, it solidified Rand's already formidable reputation as a maverick thinker with absolutely no fear of the intellectual establishment. Set in a futuristic America ruled by a complex network of repressive bureaucracies, *Atlas Shrugged* chronicles the efforts of John Galt to subvert a communal order that rewards freeloaders.

Rand wrote no more fiction after *Atlas Shrugged,* but she became a popular speaker. Nathaniel Branden, a staunch adherent she befriended in 1950, founded an institute to teach her philosophy; when he refused to recommence their open affair after a hiatus of several years, the sixty-two-year-old Rand fumed, cutting the thirty-eight-year-old apostle from her life. She maintained her popularity through the sixties and seventies, her concept of the hard-charging, self-made man perhaps in sync with the narcissistic fixations of the time. Rand died in 1982, still convinced that objectivism was a valid, self-contained system. A sharp-tongued rabble-rouser, she had indeed provoked a lively debate in social and political thought, but in the end objectivism was not as widespread a social philosophy as she had hoped.

REAGAN

RONALD

MANY CALLED HIM "The Great Communicator," though some, noting that the misconduct that marked his administration never seemed to stick to him, dubbed him "The Teflon President." He was Ronald Wilson Reagan, actor turned politician, one of the least likely and most popular occupants of the Oval Office. He came to Washington to dismantle Big Government, but government—sometimes in the form of his most trusted advisers—came very near to dismantling him.

Reagan was born in Tampico, Illinois, to a sweetly optimistic mother and a cynical, alcoholic father. In young Ronald, his mother's cheery gloss on a hard and penurious life took form in a talent for make-believe. As a young man, he was a good enough athlete to play football at Eureka College, where he was elected student body president and where his flair for drama earned him an acting prize. His straight-arrow good looks led to a Hollywood screen test, and in 1937 he signed a contract with Warner Brothers, going on to make a score of action features and light comedies. During World War II, he played an army officer in the movies and in training videos, but the nearsighted soldier never saw combat, despite later claims to the contrary. From 1947 to 1950, Reagan served as president of the Screen Actors Guild, but secretly he also testified for the FBI in its investigation of supposed Communist activity in the film industry. The new medium of television was perfect for him, but his fascination with politics, born during his SAG tenure, continued and he began to think seriously of the California governorship. Early on, Reagan's charisma was evident. But what his detractors failed to understand was the power of the few simple ideas he put forth: individual freedom, individual responsibility, and an insistence that government be subservient to its citizens, not the other way around. Religious fundamentalists, too, were drawn to his strong moralizing streak. In 1962, leaving the Democratic Party he had once admired, he became a Republican, and his keynote speech for presidential candidate Barry Goldwater in 1964 made him a leader of the party's conservative wing. Two years later, he thumped wily Democratic governor Pat Brown in the gubernatorial race in California, where his energetic reduction of spending led to tax relief and budget surpluses that swept him into a second term.

In 1976, Reagan challenged President Gerald Ford for party primacy, as he had Richard Nixon in 1968, but lost. In 1980, with Jimmy Carter the incumbent, the resilient candidate pounced and triumphed, shrewdly contrasting his own sunny outlook to the belt-tightening born-again Christian who opposed him. At sixty-nine, the man whose old-style pompadour was still a gleaming chestnut brown became the oldest man ever to occupy the White House. There followed eight years of one of the most scandal-ridden administrations since Ulysses S. Grant's, with Reagan overseeing the most remarkable economic resurgence in U.S. history unassociated with a major war. Storming the Beltway at the head of a brigade of right-wing lawyers, PR men, and ex-marines, Reagan froze federal hiring, slashed at regulation, cut taxes in accordance with the controversial "supply-side" economic theory, and loosed the dogs of unregulated capitalism. Some of them turned out to be jackals who devoured a large portion of the country's savings and loan system, necessitating just the sort of massive federal bailout Reagan said he loathed. Far from reducing federal spending, he ballooned the national deficit with massive increases in military spending. It was not just a cynical ploy: Reagan, who had narrowly escaped death by an assassin's bullet in 1981, firmly believed the Soviet Union was the "Evil Empire" and that his mission was to save his country from nuclear holocaust. In vain, Soviet premier Gorbachev tried to dissuade Reagan, at a 1985 summit, from pouring American dollars into the "Star Wars" project—an antinuclear defense system the bankrupt Russians despaired of matching. Reagan's resolve hastened the economic and political collapse of the entire Soviet bloc.

Beginning in 1985, the men he had trusted with the nation's security marched him right into the foreign policy mess known as "Iran-contra," a clandestine scheme to sell arms to Iranians in exchange for the release of hostages held by proxy, and then to use the proceeds to fund a terrorist war between contra rebels and the Nicaraguan Sandinista government. "What did the president know and when did he know it?" was the question on the minds of 250 million people; yet after years of investigation, though many of his underlings suffered disgrace and prison, Reagan himself was left unscathed by the whole sorry catastrophe.

When he left office in 1989, Reagan was almost eighty years old. During his eight-year tenure, his cheerful resiliency had made his nation feel full of itself again. His grand vision of smaller government, though, failed to materialize. Beset by Alzheimer's disease and nursed by his iron-willed first lady Nancy, Reagan took on the image of an enfeebled but beloved grandfather. The reality was that, for better or worse, he had left his mark on America.

LENI RIEFENSTAHL

IN 1934, WITH NAZISM rapidly gathering might, one of Germany's most gifted young filmmakers was summoned to Berlin to make a documentary of the Nuremberg party convention. Leni Riefenstahl demurred at first, but Hitler himself promised she would have complete control over the work. "Make it as an artist," he told her. The result, *Triumph of the Will,* was one of the most visually seductive pieces of propaganda ever made. The film apotheosized the führer, giving him a credibility in the world that the Nazi agitprop machine could never have achieved. But the cost to Riefenstahl was not just six days' work: In placing her genius in the service of Hitler, she forfeited her career and touched off an impassioned discussion of the moral responsibilities of the artist.

The businessman father of Berta Helene Amalie Riefenstahl initially denied his daughter's wishes to pursue a career in dance, insisting instead that she pursue commercial art. The strong-willed teenager took dance classes secretly and eventually ended up working for the great theatrical impresario Max Reinhardt. Her career hopes dashed by a knee injury in 1924, Riefenstahl chanced to see a film by director Arnold Fanck, a specialist in the uniquely German *bergefilm,* or "mountain film," which featured heroic athletic pursuits set against a backdrop of epic scenery. She arranged a meeting with Fanck, who gave her a starring role in a series of films that popularized the sports-minded beauty as a Garbo in climbing boots.

In 1931, the now famous actress mortgaged everything she owned to make her own film, a fairy tale called *The Blue Light.* Her innovative lighting and closeup techniques won her a gold medal at the 1932 Venice Film Festival. Having made a name as both actress and director, Riefenstahl was eager to meet the man whose mythic vision for her nation she so admired. Her fatal flirtation had begun.

To detractors, *Triumph of the Will,* her next film, is Riefenstahl's vilest outrage. In its opening scene, Hitler descends in his plane through the clouds to a soundtrack of Wagnerian majesty. Gradually, with the aid of flattering camera angles and innovative film techniques, Hitler is transformed—against the background of a torchlight parade through the medieval streets of Nuremberg—from a glowingly robust father figure into a magisterial idol. In spite of its being staged, the film stands as an important historical record; but as a political document it is even more revealing. And for Riefenstahl it is damning: Neither Hitler nor his aides ever saw footage from the film until the night of its premiere, which establishes that the film's enthusiasm for its subject is Riefenstahl's. As *Film Quarterly* pointed out, *Triumph* "could never have been made by anyone not fanatically at one with the events depicted."

Not long after, Riefenstahl was commissioned to make *Olympia,* the documentary of the 1936 Berlin Olympic Games that won first prize in the 1938 Venice Film Festival. The most ambitious of her works, it exquisitely and almost abstractly celebrates the grace and beauty of the human form. Some critics maintain the movie reflects nazism's obsession with perfection—though to be fair to her, the single most important athlete in the film is the African-American Jesse Owens, whose four-gold-medal triumph so infuriated Hitler that he walked out of the games. Furthermore, Riefenstahl's lyrical enthusiasm for the subject is hardly surprising in one who was both an athlete and a dancer.

After the war, the filmmaker spent three years in Allied prisons. She was finally cleared of all charges in 1952, after separate investigations by American, French, and West German courts, all of whom found that she had participated in "no political activity in support of the Nazi regime." Even so, she was ostracized by the film industry for her willing participation in fascism, and spent the rest of her life resolutely maintaining her innocence. Yes, she had been fascinated by Hitler, but no, she had never possessed any knowledge of his atrocities—and she had never been romantically involved with the führer as had been rumored. But that Riefenstahl counted on him as her friend and mentor is irrefutable. Besides the numerous photos of the two of them, there is the fact that the powerful Goebbels, Hitler's minister of propaganda, despised her and wished to destroy her. Clearly, without Hitler's patronage and protection, Goebbels would have done with her what he wished. And though not a Nazi, and not Hitler's mistress, she nevertheless served both the man and the cause inarguably well.

Riefenstahl was never given another film to direct. After half a dozen deals fell through, she found herself in Africa, where she went to live among the Nuba people in the Sudan, recording their daily life with her camera. These astounding photographs appeared in her 1973 book, *The Nuba,* highly praised for its ethnological insights and sheer beauty. At seventy, she took her photographic exploration under the sea, lying about her age in order to qualify for a diving certificate.

At ninety, Riefenstahl was still protesting her innocence. In spite of a recent movement to rehabilitate her reputation, the films of the woman who was arguably the best director of her day are rarely shown. By her rights, all she ever wanted to do was make great cinema—and the fact that she did is the reason she is both remembered and despised. Obsessed by her creativity, ruled by her ambition, Riefenstahl compromised herself as a human being by refusing to acknowledge any connection between art and morality. She spent a lifetime enduring the consequences of her repudiation.

JACKIE ROBINSON

AS THE FIRST AFRICAN-AMERICAN to play major-league baseball, Jackie Robinson had to be both a superlative athlete and a paragon of his race. That he triumphed in the face of every obstacle, from virulent bigotry to pitchers' beanballs, is a tribute to the immensity of his talent and courage. Playing for the Brooklyn Dodgers, Robinson succeeded alone and without the comfort of friendship, his every word and action scrutinized and his every failure magnified. The pathfinder for a legion of black ballplayers waiting to follow him, he knew that if he failed, it would be a long time before another ball club would attempt to breach the color barrier.

Jack Roosevelt Robinson was born in Cairo, Georgia. His father abandoned the family when Jackie was six months old, and Robinson's mother moved her five children to Pasadena, California, where she worked a host of domestic jobs to keep the family fed. As a student, Robinson seemed to use his considerable intelligence mostly to calculate the minimum grade average required to qualify for athletics. Baseball—the sport that would later make him world-famous—was his weakest game at John Muir Technical High School, where he earned letters in football, basketball, and track. Following in the footsteps of his adored brother Mack, a silver medalist in the 1936 Olympic Games, Robinson set a record for the running broad jump at Pasadena Junior College in 1937. Two years later, he earned an athletic scholarship to the University of California at Los Angeles. There he averaged a phenomenal twelve yards per carry as a running back and, in an era when low scores were the norm, led basketball's Pacific Coast Conference with an average of over twenty-five points per game. He stole five bases, including home plate, in his first college game, but he still regarded baseball as no more than a diversion. In 1940 he won the broad jump in the National Collegiate Athletic Association.

Drafted into the army in 1942, Robinson was kept from combat duty by "football ankles," but as morale officer, he fought other battles while serving his country. He was told that Negroes did not attend officer-candidate school, but Robinson applied anyway and emerged as a lieutenant. When he refused a bus driver's order to move to the back of an army bus, the incident led to an imbroglio and ultimately to charges of insubordination and a court-martial. Robinson was acquitted, but the experience soured him on army life, and he requested a release in 1944.

After a brief stint as a college basketball coach, he signed a contract with the Kansas City Monarchs of the Negro American Baseball League. At the time, black professionals were barred from all-white major leagues, and no

black had played in the majors since 1888. Unbeknownst to Robinson, the visionary general manager of the Brooklyn Dodgers, Branch Rickey, had concocted a plan to change baseball forever.

When the shrewd, eccentric Rickey summoned Robinson to his office in August of 1945, he opened Papini's *Life of Christ* and began to read from it out loud. The meaning behind this flamboyant gesture was clear: Rickey was challenging Robinson to "turn the other cheek" to the insults he would inevitably suffer playing for the Dodgers. Without such forbearance, Rickey warned, no major-league team would hire a black again for another twenty years. Robinson, who had never turned the other cheek to anyone, asked, "Do you want a ballplayer who's afraid to fight back?" Rickey bellowed, "I want a ballplayer with guts enough *not* to fight back!"

From the moment he signed his contract on April 10, 1947, Robinson was subjected to the vilest of insults from fans and opposing players alike, many of the latter southerners. One of his own teammates, Dixie Walker, balked at playing with him and was summarily traded away. In Saint Louis, the team's hotel refused to let him stay with the other Dodgers. In Cincinnati, he was taunted with racial epithets by the Reds pitcher, and in Atlanta, the Ku Klux Klan threatened to shoot him. The Dodgers' Kentuckian shortstop Pee Wee Reese felt comfortable enough to tell his teammate jokingly during warm-ups, "Jack, don't stand so close to me today."

Robinson responded to racist sentiment by stealing twice as many bases as anyone else in the National League and being voted Rookie of the Year. During his career he batted .311, stole home in a World Series game, and was voted 1949's Most Valuable Player. He could run, field, throw, bunt, hit, and think faster than anyone else on the field. With him, the Dodgers won the National League pennant six times and the World Championship once.

In 1956, ten years after they brought Robinson into the national spotlight, the Dodgers traded him—to, of all teams, the hated crosstown New York Giants. He immediately announced his retirement. Later in life, he wrote a newspaper column about civil rights issues and dabbled in politics as a "Rockefeller Republican," for which he was vilified as an Uncle Tom by members of his own race. As usual, Robinson ignored his defamers and held to his convictions. As an African-American, it had never been enough for him to be good. To truly succeed, he had to be great. With the help of the manager who believed in him, this quiet but fierce competitor had freed baseball from its crippling racism, greatly improving its moral caliber—and that of his country as well.

JOHN D. ROCKEFELLER

SELDOM IN THE ANNALS of capitalism has one man acquired so much wealth and attracted so much opprobrium as John Davison Rockefeller, founder of Standard Oil, father of the Trust, and grand-prize winner in the American pursuit of money, if not happiness. In his lifetime he was both hailed as philanthropist and cursed as heartless robber. He gave away his wealth to religious and educational institutions, ignoring the venom directed at him, bolstered by his adamant belief that Christian values were ever at work in his life.

He was born on a farm in Richford, New York, the son of Eliza Davison and William Rockefeller, who was in his own way an oil man—he sold snake oil. The elder Rockefeller traveled the United States billing himself as Dr. William Rockefeller, cancer specialist, purveying quack remedies, bedding farmer's daughters, and speculating in timber and livestock. William Rockefeller instilled in his son a superlative skill for acquisition and negotiation by systematically hornswoggling him every chance he got. Rockefeller's mother, on the other hand, was a Scottish Baptist who bestowed an intense Christian ethic of charity and forbearance upon him, once whipping young John D. for the sins he might commit in the future. The common theme of these lessons was that virtue and guile are rewarded equally with success. The lesson was underscored for the youngster when he made money charging interest on a fifty-dollar loan to a farmer.

With such training, it was not surprising that ruthless business tactics and high moral purpose were the twin foundations on which John D. Rockefeller began to build his fortune in 1855. He started in Cleveland, as a $3.50-a-week accounting clerk with the commercial merchants Hewett & Tuttle. In four years, rebuffed in his demand for a raise, the restless twenty-year-old was on his own, taking Englishman Maurice Clark as his partner in a hay and grocery business that boomed when the Civil War broke out in 1861. Neither military man nor abolitionist, Rockefeller's ideal was money, and his battlefields, he discovered at the height of the conflict, were the rich and turbulent oil fields of Pennsylvania. Rockefeller's unerring instinct for opportunity and his accountant's love of order told him that the chaos of the oil fields could be arranged to a man's profit, if that man controlled the valve at the oil refinery.

With the wartime expansion of railroads, Cleveland became the transportation and refinery nexus of the fledgling oil industry. In 1863, dragging a skeptical Clark with him, Rockefeller joined his coreligionist Samuel Andrews in the refining business. The partners soon dominated the Cleveland refinery scene, buying out the competition when possible, crushing them when necessary through the cutthroat practices of "rebates" and "drawbacks"—in essence, kickbacks from the railroads that penalized the smaller refiners. Rockefeller was a brilliant organizer and cost-cutter, introducing both meticulous accounting practices and vertical integration, a system of interlocking committees to which his successors at Standard Oil still adhere.

By 1875, he had ridden out a boycott of oil producers and expanded into Philadelphia and Pittsburgh through buyouts and mergers. A year later he was in New York, organizing everything from pipelines to drayage under the Standard banner, and conceiving the legal device of the Trust with his lieutenants, which would eventually hold all his far-flung properties in one locale. By 1878, Rockefeller stood alone atop the industry, overseeing a vast monopoly that controlled most of the oil refineries in the United States, affecting millions of lives, and made Rockefeller unimaginably rich.

The denunciation from government, his business enemies, and the public came the following year. Muckrackers delved into his business practices and published the results for a horrified citizenry. Assailed with lawsuits from the states and hammered by the Sherman Antitrust Act of 1890, Rockefeller fought the battle from his New York headquarters, the very portrait of the capitalist in his high silk hat and morning suit. In a financial civil war between the plurality and the monopoly, beleaguered Standard was ousted from state after state. In 1907, the craggy and formidable Judge Kenesaw Mountain Landis punished Standard Oil with "The Fine"—thirty million dollars for violating rebate laws. It took another four years for the courts to decree the dissolution of the holding company, which had replaced the trust in 1899.

Through it all, the eccentric Sunday school teacher, who had tithed even in the days when he had next to nothing, remained confident in his conviction that he was without sin, and bemused by his country's failure to appreciate that truth. As the cool, efficient winner in a nasty bar brawl of a business, he believed he was merely the victor upon whom nature and tradition should confer the spoils. He continued to share his gains, founding the University of Chicago with $35 million in 1889, and funding a hundred church projects—although a group of Congregational ministers, having first solicited his alms, rejected them as "tainted money." (Even vaudevillians got into the act with a new one-liner: "It's tainted, all right. 'Taint yours and 'taint mine.") Not incidentally, he also founded a dynasty which has boasted not only entrepreneurs, but also scientists, politicians, philanthropists, governors, and presidential hopefuls. When Rockefeller spent his cash on moving hills around to improve the view at Pocantico, his New York estate, playwright George S. Kaufman was prompted to quip that it just showed what God could do if He had money.

ELEANOR ROOSEVELT

IT WAS SAID OF Anna Eleanor Roosevelt that "no woman has ever so comforted the distressed or so distressed the comfortable." Her ability to console others, however, came at great cost. Eleanor herself, reflecting back on her amazingly productive and influential life, saw fear as the dominant emotion of her childhood. Introspective and rather homely, the shy young girl who would evolve into the world's most admired—and most ridiculed—woman learned from the cool rejection of her mother to avoid evoking disapproval in others. The lovely but insensitive Anna Rebecca Hall, who openly described her daughter as an ugly duckling, died of diphtheria when Eleanor was eight. Her beloved but unstable alcoholic father, Elliott, the linchpin of her tiny universe, died two years later. "Suddenly," she later wrote, "something locked me up." The solemn, self-effacing orphan was sent to live with her equally solemn maternal grandmother, under whose supervision she acquired the additional problems of insecurity and a deep hunger for affection. From this barren emotional earth sprang much of this crusading humanitarian's empathy for the poor and the oppressed.

A sojourn at England's exclusive Allenswood school for girls softened Eleanor's upper-crust smugness with freedoms and liberal ideas. She returned to New York to fulfill her social duties as a debutante, and a year later a more confident and thoughtful young woman began to address the imperatives of the privileged class by joining the Consumers' League, which sought health and safety legislation for garment workers and department store employees. Soon after Eleanor began her relationship with Franklin Delano Roosevelt, her fifth cousin once removed, she took him on a tour of the Lower East Side settlement house where she worked with disadvantaged children. The future president shared with Eleanor his deeper thoughts, among them a concern for bettering the lot of the underprivileged. Herein lay the bedrock of their personal commitment to each other, a tie that remained strong long after the romantic connection between them had been broken.

The society-page wedding, in which the president, Eleanor's uncle Teddy Roosevelt, gave the bride away, took place on March 17, 1905. In the ensuing years, Eleanor's civic involvements faded into the background as she bore six children in eleven years, one of whom died in infancy. Gradually, she overcame her despondency—and her overbearing mother-in-law, who had a way of insinuating herself into every corner of their existence—and, supporting FDR's ambitions, took up a zestful life in Albany in 1910 as the greatest political asset of New York State's dapper new senator. By 1913, with FDR assistant secretary of the navy, the popular and well-connected couple settled in Washington, D.C.

In the fall of 1918, FDR fell gravely ill with pneumonia. While sorting through his letters and personal effects, Eleanor learned of the liaison between FDR and her own personal secretary and friend, Lucy Page Mercer. Deeply wounded, Eleanor nevertheless felt that if her husband truly loved his mistress, he should be free to marry her. Franklin's mother, however, threatened to cut off her son without a cent if he left his wife. Prudently, FDR gave in to his mother's ultimatum and cast his lot with his wife. Three years later, when he was struck down with polio, the ever-loyal Eleanor shored up his self-confidence and stood firm against his mother, who wanted her son to come home to stay. Eleanor maintained his interest in world affairs and, under the tutelage of his trusted adviser, Louis Howe, consciously molded herself into an articulate and knowledgeable alter ego for her husband.

When FDR won the White House in 1933, Eleanor immediately began forging a controversial role for herself as first lady. In addition to serving as her husband's moral arbiter on many controversial issues, she wrote a syndicated newspaper column called "My Day," held press briefings for women journalists, and launched her own radio show. As her husband's traveling ambassador during the Depression, she strove to insure that his New Deal applied equally to women and men, and, gradually discovering the insidious effects of racism and anti-Semitism, she sought to eradicate these prejudices within herself before taking her crusade public. By this time ER, as her intimates knew her, had also managed to develop very intricate and intense emotional bonds with politically active women such as Lorena Hickock and Esther Lape.

With the onset of World War II, Eleanor lobbied with the NAACP, of which she was a member, to eliminate discrimination against African-Americans in the military and defense industries. She also pushed for expanded roles for women in wartime activities and visited U.S. troops wherever and whenever she could. When FDR died in 1945, however, Eleanor told reporters in her familiar wobbly voice that "the story was over." The indomitable ER would, in fact, continue her work for almost two decades more, acting as her nation's conscience in a world that seemed to have none. Devoting the remainder of her life to social justice, she served as a U.S. delegate to the United Nations, helping to draft and secure passage of the Universal Declaration of Human Rights in 1948.

Though remembered as "The First Lady of the World," Eleanor Roosevelt was not without enemies, especially in the South and among the political right. Critics spoke of her "bolshevism" and her meddling, even cruelly mocking her physical appearance. A few years after she was interred in the rose garden at the Roosevelt home in Hyde Park, Archibald MacLeish wrote that Eleanor had turned out not to be an ugly duckling after all, but rather a Sleeping Beauty of unstinting generosity and grace.

ROOSEVELT

FRANKLIN D.

THE TWENTIETH-CENTURY PRESIDENT with the most genuine connection to the underprivileged was, ironically, a member of the American upper class. Born in 1882 at his family's six-hundred-acre estate in Hyde Park, New York, Franklin Delano Roosevelt was the only son of James Roosevelt and Sara Delano Roosevelt, Mayflower-descended members of New York's Hudson River aristocracy. Pampered by an overcontrolling mother and tutored at home until age fourteen, the man who would shepherd his nation through the cataclysmic years of the Great Depression and World War II traveled extensively abroad before entering the elite prep school Groton, where he was the magnetic nucleus of his social set. His charm and élan were qualities he later put to good use in more serious jousts with such adversarial allies as the Republican Party and Joseph Stalin.

Graduating in 1904 from Harvard, where he was active in The Missionary Society, the handsome, athletic Franklin became engaged to a distant cousin, the brilliant Anna Eleanor Roosevelt. She shared his liberal views and blue-blood status, and her influence on his reformist inclinations would prove incalculable. Together they had six children, one of whom died in infancy.

After passing the bar and then practicing a few years with a Wall Street firm, Franklin was attracted by the progressivist career of his famous presidential uncle, Teddy Roosevelt. Nevertheless, FDR made his first political foray as a Democrat, winning the race for New York State senator from strongly Republican Hyde Park in 1910. He supported Woodrow Wilson for president at the 1912 Democratic Convention, and was awarded the post of assistant secretary of the navy, which he held from 1913 to 1920. His upward soar brought him the vice presidential nomination in 1920, but his party's ticket, buried by Harding and Coolidge, sent him into a shattered retreat.

In August of the following year, Roosevelt was stricken with poliomyelitis. He spent most of the decade in Warm Springs, Georgia, undergoing physical therapy in hopes that he would walk. Without braces, however, he would never take more than a few halting steps again. He suffered from depression during this period, but Eleanor's constant encouragement—despite her own lingering melancholy over his affair with her secretary five years earlier—did much to restore his cheerful combativeness.

In 1928, upon his election to the governorship of New York, Roosevelt became a figure of national prominence. Then, three years after the stock market crash of 1929, amid growing economic hopelessness, he won the presidency in a landslide election that promised a "New Deal" for the American people. Moving fast, with the jaunty confidence that endeared him to supporters and infuriated his foes, FDR inaugurated an alphabet soup of new federal agencies intended to alleviate the nation's suffering and

to curb abuses. Immediately, he closed all banks until the fiscal soundness of each could be established and set up the Federal Deposit Insurance Corporation (FDIC) to guarantee deposits. He then muscled through legislation creating the Federal Emergency Relief Administration (FERA), the Civilian Works Administration (CWA), the Public Works Administration (PWA), and the National Recovery Administration (NRA), all targeted to get the country back on its feet. One pundit commented that lawmakers did not so much debate his bills as "salute them as they went sailing by." Other enemies, considering him a "traitor to his class," predicted that the Social Security Act (1935), which provided pensions to the elderly and ill, and the Wagner Act (1935), which sanctioned collective bargaining, meant nothing less than the eventual end of capitalism and the start of a socialist welfare state.

But Roosevelt pressed on. Presenting himself up as a somewhat dandified father figure, his booming, cultured voice soothed a troubled America via radio with his shrewdly avuncular "fireside chats." He was everywhere—his measured statements in the press, his silvered eminence on the newsreels—encouraging, joking, bucking everyone up. Eventually, all anyone had to see was the confident tilt of their president's trademark cigarette holder to know that everything was going to be all right. When the Supreme Court began to rule against many of his programs, FDR responded by trying to pack the Court.

Ultimately, it was not Roosevelt's policies but World War II that pulled the country out of the economic mire. Coming late to active antifascism, he nevertheless signaled America's allies that aid would be forthcoming. The country's isolationist stance, however, could only be overcome with strong provocation—provided when Japan attacked Pearl Harbor on December 7, 1941, a date that Roosevelt told Congress "will live in infamy." Within a week the United States was engaged in a two-front war against the Axis in both Europe and Asia.

The duration and breadth of this conflict took a terrible toll on the world—and on Roosevelt's health. Although he was strong enough to win an unprecedented fourth term in 1944, opponents felt that his physical deterioration accounted for a far too conciliatory stance toward Stalin at the 1945 Yalta conference, which resulted, they charged, in the unnecessary ceding of Eastern Europe to the Russians and the start of the Cold War. Exhausted from the trip, Roosevelt retreated to Warm Springs. He died there on April 12, 1945, of a cerebral hemorrhage about a month before Germany surrendered. He is remembered as the patrician architect of social reform, the rock-steady commander in chief of imperiled world democracy, and the creator of Big Government—in short, one of the political pivots upon which the American century turned.

ROSENBERG

ETHEL & JULIUS

WERE THEY INNOCENT VICTIMS of a Cold War witch-hunt by the American government or Communist spies who went willingly to their deaths in an auto-da-fé intended to inspire the American working class?

FBI Director J. Edgar Hoover denounced the alleged post-war transmission of atomic secrets by the Rosenbergs as "the crime of the century." But Hoover's evidence that the couple had given the Russians anything of value was thin, depending as it did upon the testimony of informers and turncoats. Pawns in America's grim struggle against Communism, the Rosenbergs represented different things to different partisan groups. For Communists, Socialists, leftists—most of whom ignored the couple's life-and-death legal struggles—and some liberals, they were principled martyrs. For reactionaries, conservatives and other liberals they were traitors, sinister agents of an evil empire. Though at century's end more information had emerged pointing to Julius as a Soviet agent, the whole truth may never come out.

Esther Ethel Greenglass was born on New York's Lower East Side, to a cheerless mother who cared little for her daughter but doted on her son. Fascinated by theater and poetry in high school, after graduation she found a job at a shipping firm and managed to eke out money for singing lessons. She was talented enough to be admitted to the prestigious choral group Schola Cantorum in 1935. That same year she was fired from her job for recruiting for the shipping clerk's union. In 1936 she met a U.S. Signal Corps engineer named Julius Rosenberg. Also a New Yorker, Julius was a committed Communist who had rebuffed his father's wishes that he become a rabbi, embracing a quite different kind of faith. He and Ethel were married in 1939, eventually having two sons, Robby and Michael, who would later dedicate their lives to the vindication of their dead parents.

In 1943, according to some historians, Julius began to build an amateur spy network on his own initiative, recruiting college friends to engage in industrial espionage. This ring would later become the real focus of the FBI's hunt. That same year, the Rosenbergs, committed anti-Fascists, suddenly dropped out of the Communist Party, an ambiguous event that could have been an overture to "secret work."

As Julius' fate would have it, his wife's brother David Greenglass happened to work as an Army machinist at the top-secret Manhattan Project, where the American atomic bomb was being developed at Los Alamos, New Mexico. Julius enlisted an enthusiastic Greenglass into his ad hoc organization. Strangely, at the same time Julius was carrying on this highly dangerous work, neither he nor Ethel tried to hide their left-wing views; even after leaving the Party, Julius' politics cost him his job with the Signal Corps.

Their world collapsed in 1950, when Klaus Fuchs, a British nuclear scientist working at Los Alamos, was arrested by British Intelligence as a KGB spy. Fuchs named Philadelphia chemist Harry Gold as his courier, and Gold in turn implicated David Greenglass. Questioned by FBI men, Greenglass broke immediately, pointing to Julius Rosenberg as the ringleader. But he adamantly denied that Ethel had anything to do with espionage. On July 17, Julius was arrested and charged with giving the secret of the atomic bomb to the Russians—at the time a strange assertion, given the more sophisticated scientific activities of Fuchs. A month later, as part of a ploy by Hoover to pressure Julius, Ethel was arrested and charged. Hoover gambled that Ethel would not want to abandon her young sons, and that Julius would not want Ethel to spend life in prison or worse. The Rosenbergs, however, refused to break. In 1951, at the height of the Korean War and of the anti-left McCarthyite hysteria, they went on trial in New York. Though the evidence against Julius was strong, the case against Ethel was pathetically weak—until just ten days before the trial, when her brother suddenly remembered that she had typed the notes he had given to Julius.

Influenced by the national paranoia of the times, and naively supposing that the grotesquely grinning Greenglass could not be foul enough to tell a lie that would save his own neck while putting a noose around his sister's, the jury convicted both. Inexplicably, Judge Irving Kaufman—a man with ambitions for the U.S. Supreme Court and a fawning fan of J. Edgar Hoover—imposed the death penalty; the sentence went against the express wishes of both the Assistant Attorney General and Hoover himself, one of whose aides said, 'We didn't want them to die—we wanted them to talk."

But they would not. After two stubborn years in Sing Sing, on June 19, 1953, they were electrocuted, as an FBI counterintelligence team stood by to take the confession Julius would never make. As the news of the executions spread, riots exploded around the world, and Pope Pius XXII joined in the universal condemnation of the United States. The controversy over the Rosenberg's guilt or innocence raged for decades, with numerous committees formed to reopen the case. The Soviets themselves failed to illuminate the debate, although premier Nikita Krushchev in his memoirs averred that the couple's work "provided very significant help in accelerating the production of our atomic bomb." Yet Boris Brokhovich, one of the directors of the Soviet team, stated flatly in 1989: "We got nothing from the Rosenbergs."

In 1995, the American National Security Agency released partial transcripts of clandestine Soviet cables unscrambled by U.S. cryptographers working since 1944. This "Venona" material identified Julius by the code-name "Antenna" and later as "Liberal." Ethel was not mentioned, however, a fact that could not have surprised the FBI. For one of the questions the counter intelligence team waiting at Sing Sing intended to ask Julius read: "Was your wife cognizant of your activities?"

RUDOLPH

WILMA

THE ODDS SEEMED TO BE stacked against Wilma Glodean Rudolph from birth. The twentieth of twenty-two children born to Ed Rudolph (from two marriages), she was sickly from birth; a bout with polio at age four left her severely crippled in one leg. With this history, she would be lucky to walk, even with a limp. Thus it was nothing short of miraculous when, at twenty, Rudolph streaked her way to glory in the track and field competitions at the 1960 Rome Olympics, becoming not only the first American woman to win three gold medals in a single Olympics, but also the fastest woman in the world.

Rudolph's handsome six-foot form in all its flawless, floating splendor displayed remarkable agility and speed. As if surprised by the sound of the starting gun, she would spring into flight, gliding as she straightened into a powerful but seemingly effortless gait, her long legs slicing the air and her slim arms pumping in quick-time rhythm.

Rudolph's triumph, in conquering both her physical disabilities and the racism then a staple of organized sports to become one of the most celebrated female athletes in history, is a tale replete with unlikelihoods. Though proud and hardworking, Ed Rudolph, her railroad-porter father, and Blanche, her domestic-worker mother, had often been hard-pressed to feed their many children. With the additional hardship of Wilma's bad leg, their daily struggle assumed heroic proportions. Told by specialists at Nashville's Meharry Medical College that her daughter needed intensive physical therapy, Blanche Rudolph made the weekly two-hundred-mile round-trip to the clinic in Nashville for more than two years, traveling by bus on her only day off and carrying Wilma in her arms.

When doctors held out the promise that daily treatment might restore the muscles of the paralyzed left leg, Mrs. Rudolph asked them to teach her the restorative techniques involved so that she could work with the child at home. Wilma's recovery became a household project, with her mother and three of her siblings taking turns massaging the leg four times a day, and at the age of eight Wilma began walking with the help of a brace. Soon she was faking what she called "a no-limp walk," wearing an orthopedic shoe in place of the brace and shooting a basketball through a peach basket her brothers had rigged to a backyard pole. Despite her agility, the special shoe sometimes made her feel awkward and different, but as with other obstacles Wilma would encounter, it became a spur to the achievement of her goals.

Feeling optimistic about her recovery and urged by her father to compete, the willowy teenager went out for basketball at Burt High School. "Skeeter"—coach Clinton Gray's nickname for the youngster who was always buzzing around—shattered the girls' state basketball record with an amazing twenty-five-game seasonal total of 803 points. To keep in shape between basketball seasons, Wilma had joined the track team, and by this time she was winning every event she entered: the 50-, 75-, 100-, and 200-meter dashes. Her winning streak came to an abrupt halt during her first official track meet, at Alabama's Tuskegee Institute, where she failed to win even one race. It was a humbling experience for the breezily confident newcomer, one that taught her that talent alone was not enough.

To increase her stamina and discipline, Rudolph began working out with the Tigerbelles of Tennessee State University during the summers. Coach Ed Temple ran his crew twenty miles a day, five days a week, and the rigorous workouts brought results. In 1956, in Philadelphia, at the national Amateur Athletic Union (AAU) meet, Rudolph won every one of her races, and the Tigerbelles captured their first AAU championship. In 1956, at the age of sixteen, the high-chool junior qualified for the Melbourne Olympics, and, as the United States team's youngest member, won a bronze medal as part of the relay team. In her senior year, Rudolph fell in love with a football hero and became pregnant. Her family would not permit her to marry, and the baby was sent to live for a time with her grandmother. Two years later, Rudolph joined the 1960 Olympic squad, establishing a new world's record in the 200-meter dash.

At the Stadio Olimpico in Rome, Rudolph was primed for the apogee of her career. Catching catnaps between her races, she took her first gold medal in the 100-meter dash, unofficially breaking the world record and beating the pack by a three-yard lead. The second gold came in the 200-meter dash, and the third was won in the heart-stopping final leg of the relay in which she survived a botched baton pass and went on to an amazing last-stride victory. In the two years following that stunning sweep, she won numerous races and set a few world records, but she stopped racing in 1962: "I couldn't top what I did," she said, with wisdom beyond her years, "so I'll be remembered for when I was at my best."

Rudolph was inducted into the Black Athletes' Hall of Fame, the National Track and Field Hall of Fame, and the U.S. Olympic Hall of Fame. She died of a malignant brain tumor in 1994. She had raised four children, coached briefly, and devoted her life to developing athletic and educational programs for youth through her Wilma Rudolph Foundation. "If I have anything to leave," she said, "the foundation is my legacy." But Rudolph's three-medal victory in Rome remained the one glorious day she would savor above all others. "I love what the Olympics stand for," their lifelong spokeswoman stated. "They'll always be a part of me."

BERTRAND RUSSELL

AS A THINKER HE was compared to Voltaire, but as a man he was once denounced as a "lecherous, libidinous erotomaniac." For Bertrand Arthur William, reluctant third Earl Russell and Viscount Amberley, life was a maddening oscillation between brain and body, logic and lust. His childhood, spent under the puritanical thumb of his grandmother, perhaps set the tone for the entire ninety-seven years of Russell's life. Orphaned early and educated by private tutors, the lonely aristocrat had neither the tempering love of his parents nor the society of schoolmates. His escape from Lady Frances Russell's icy rectitude led him to the realm for which he was destined: mathematics. When his brother taught him geometry straight from Euclid—and little "Bertie" discovered that he could work out the difficult fifth proposition with ease—he fell in love with numbers.

Upon arriving at Trinity College, Cambridge, in 1890, Russell pursued a love of another sort—an American Quaker woman named Alys Pearsall Smith—with the painful obsession peculiar to first love. Wheedling her out of her doubts about him, he parried his family's objections to a marriage in 1894 whose passion would quickly cool. It would be the first of four marriages for Russell—in 1921, to Dora Black; in 1936, to Patricia (Peter) Helen Spence; and in 1952, to Edith Finch—and the beginning of his controversial views about marriage and sexual liberation.

His views on mathematics and philosophy, however, were already advancing rapidly by the time he was elected Fellow of the Royal Society in 1908. Five years previously, he had published his first great work, *Principles of Mathematics* (1903), in which he first attempted to apply his scientific temperament to the abstract field of mathematics. It was from 1910 to 1913, however, when he and Alfred North Whitehead published the three-volume opus *Principia Mathematica,* that Russell made his most lasting and ambitious contributions to modern philosophy. Considered a masterpiece of rationalist thought, it was Russell's work with Whitehead that fully enabled him to bring an analytic framework to bear on mathematics. It was a work so laden with the hieroglyphs of symbolic logic that the printers had to hand-fashion page after page of wordless text. In these efforts, Russell helped to create the field of analytic philosophy.

World War I, however, transformed Russell from an ivory-tower theorist to a social reformer who focused on the real world. This leap was perhaps hastened when he met Ludwig Wittgenstein while teaching at Cambridge. The great Austrian mathematical philosopher aimed his irascible brilliance at his mentor with disastrous results for Russell's self-esteem. But Russell's despairing conviction that his former pupil, not he, had the greater mind for philosophy did not deter him from commitment to social change.

In another sense, however, Russell's descent from pure reason to social reflection and activism was an echo of his childhood unhappiness. Except for a brief lapse in his pacifist attitude during World War II (in which he supported the anti-Nazi effort and urged the United States to fight the Soviets), he practiced what he preached, and took on the consequences. In 1911, he began a somewhat one-sided affair with Lady Ottoline Morrell, the wife of a friend of his, a clandestine liaison that lasted years, despite her claim that his sentimental attentions were suffocating.

But while Lady Ottoline—and his other loves—admired Russell's brain, the British government was less enthusiastic about his commitment to pacifism. He was thrown into prison for six months in 1918 for disseminating anti-British propaganda under the Defence of the Realm Act, and again, in 1961, for inciting civil disobedience. His writings on war, education, sex, and marriage and society in general were so controversial that George VI, conferring upon him the Order of Merit in 1949, felt moved to mention that not everyone should emulate him. Russell's writings on religion, such as *What I Believe* (1925) and *Why I Am Not a Christian* (1927), and his views on freedom of sexual expression in such books as *Marriage and Morals* (1929) sparked such controversy that a lawsuit was brought against him to prevent his taking a post at New York's City College in 1940. The judge had ruled the appointment a "chair of indecency" which would lead to "abduction and rape."

No such transgression occurred, however, during his successive appointments at the University of Chicago, UCLA, and Pennsylvania's Barnes Foundation. His dissection of the body politic during those years, including his famous *History of Western Philosophy* (1945), resulted in a Nobel Prize for Literature in 1950, in addition to a host of other honors. Not content to go gently, the indefatigable activist opposed nuclear armament, bringing the fire of his radical politics to a new generation when he organized a 1967 ad hoc War Crimes Tribunal, which judged America's war activities in Vietnam. He died three years later at ninety-seven, none the worse for his seven daily scotches. Having enriched the world by more than forty books and his memorable wit, Bertrand Russell helped us believe that Reason could solve all the world's problems.

"BABE" RUTH

GEORGE HERMAN

IF STATISTICS ARE A large part of the fun of America's national pastime, then Babe Ruth had the most fun of all: sixty home runs in one season (1927); 714 home runs in a twenty-two-year major league career; a lifetime .342 batting average; a lifetime .690 slugging average; strike-outs totaling 1,300; 2,056 bases on balls; and fifteen home runs in ten World Series. Like the six-foot-two, 215-pound athlete who earned them, the numbers are big and impressive. But do they make this barrel-bellied, pigeon-toed crowd pleaser the greatest baseball player who ever lived? Not by themselves. Still, while less incandescent stars have since hit more homers, they will never capture the imagination or the character of an age in quite the same way as "the Bambino" or the "Sultan of Swat." A man of huge appetites—both amorous and gustatory—Ruth was a genuine working-class hero, a cheerful hedo-nist who exemplified the nation's Jazz Age efforts to shed its puritan constraints.

After the scandal of the 1919 World Series, in which members of the favored Chicago White Sox were accused of deliberately losing the series, many sports historians cred-it Ruth with saving the sport. He filled stadiums almost as much for his devil-take-the-hindmost persona as for his leviathan hitting. No square-jawed Adonis who ate a hearty breakfast every morning after a good night's sleep, Ruth reportedly consumed so many hot dogs before one game that he was off the roster for weeks. A notorious rule-breaker, he was once punished for playing winter exhibition games—strictly forbidden in the majors—by being ordered to join his fellow Yankees six weeks after the season had begun. His visits to whorehouses and saloons were more frequent than his highly publicized ones to orphanages and hospitals. Nevertheless, this straightforward, unsophisticated man connected with the game and with its fans in a spectacular fashion, stoking the ambitions of millions of kids in sandlots everywhere.

Ruth's heart went out to the young and troubled, it is said, because of his own miserable childhood. One of five children born to a poor Baltimore saloon keeper and his wife, neither of whom had time for him, young George spent his early days on the streets. Fortunately, he was sent to St. Mary's Industrial School for Boys, where a Brother Matthias taught him the rudiments of the sport that would one day immortalize him. Though he eventually reconciled with his father, Babe's self-image was to remain tattered his whole life. "I guess I'm just too big and ugly for anyone to come to see me," he once confessed to another boy at

St. Mary's. But once he joined the majors, starting out in 1914 as a pitcher with the Boston Red Sox, there were enough cigars and cash and camel hair coats to satisfy any high roller. From the beginning, his amiable showmanship was a boon to ballpark attendance, his slugger's approach to the game redirecting its somewhat conservative "inside" strategy. More than any other player, the Babe enlivened baseball, making the home run its most thrilling play.

During his four years as a pitcher with the Red Sox, Ruth started building his phenomenal stats. Winning twenty-three games in two of those years, he helped his team cap-ture three American League pennants, the record of which he was proudest; in the 1916 and 1918 World Series, Ruth pitched twenty-nine and two-thirds consecutive scoreless innings. He also hit amazingly well, a fact that prodded then-manager Ed Barrow to put him in the outfield so that he could be in the line-up every game. Another record was set in 1920, when the Red Sox's cash-needy owner sold Ruth to the New York Yankees for an unprecedented $125,000. Ten years later, Babe became the league's highest-paid ballplayer.

During Ruth's fifteen-year stint with the Yankees, the club had to open a new stadium to handle the huge crowds. The press quickly dubbed Yankee Stadium "The House That Ruth Built;" the Yankees won on opening day as Ruth christened his new residence by hitting a home run with two men on base. Spectators were again on the edge of their seats when he hit his legendary homer at Chicago's Wrigley Field in the Yankee–Cub Series of 1932. One version of what happened has it that Babe, up at bat and having missed the first pitch, beamed at the stands and held up a finger. With the second strike, he held up two. The catcalls turned into wild cheering as he pointed to a spot deep in center field. When the Babe connected with the next pitch, he parked it right where he had indicated, and the stands erupted. The Yankees won the game, and the Series as well.

On May 25, 1935, the crowds went through the turn-stiles of Pittsburgh's Forbes Field with both anticipation and regret. It was the Big Guy's final game. True to form, he gave his fans one last exhibition of his thunderous batting, wallop-ing three homers into the bleachers. In 1948, he donned his familiar number-three uniform for a celebration that was as much his formal good-bye as it was a twenty-fifth birthday party for Yankee Stadium. Not long afterward, in August of the same year, some 115,000 fans came back again, this time to file quietly past his candlelit bier. It was their turn to say farewell.

MARGARET SANGER

AT THE BEGINNING OF her fifty-year crusade to promote contraception as an essential health service, Margaret Sanger brainstormed with several of her colleagues to find a phrase to describe her new movement. "Voluntary parenthood" was suggested, as were "preventception" and "conscious generation." The name the group eventually agreed on—"birth control"—sounded innocuous enough. But when Sanger began to use it in her magazine columns and public lectures, the phrase took on the characteristic of an opening salvo in a war.

In 1912, the year Sanger began her efforts among the working-class poor of New York's Lower East Side under the auspices of Lillian Wald's Visiting Nurses Association, contraception in the United States was not only unmentionable, but was considered "obscene." Even a doctor was forbidden by federal law to send information about it through the mail. Defiantly insisting that contraception was every woman's right, Sanger strove to liberate her sex from their repressive role as "brood animals." Her dream was to disseminate birth-control information until women were freed from their body's servitude, enabling them to enjoy a life of self-determination and unfettered sexual fulfillment.

Sanger's taste for controversy came from her father, Michael Hennessey Higgins, an apostate Roman Catholic who was well known in the local pubs of Corning, New York, for his political harangues. Because of her father's reputation as a free-thinker and the resulting difficulty he had in finding work—he was a stonemason, plying his trade mainly on churches— Margaret, as the oldest girl at home, had to help shore up the family's perilous finances. As a midwife's aide, Margaret became aware of the painful and far-reaching consequences of unplanned pregnancy, but her drive and devotion to the cause was no doubt a result of witnessing her own mother's suffering. After eighteen pregnancies and eleven births, Anne Higgins— whose tuberculosis worsened with each birth—was so physically debilitated that she could barely speak, much less get out of bed. Margaret became convinced that her mother's perpetually weakened condition, which led to her death at forty-eight, was caused quite simply by bearing and caring for too many children.

While studying nursing, the young radical met and married William Sanger, an architect, who like her was an ardent socialist. Sanger was inspired by the views of Emma Goldman, who—with Big Bill Haywood, John Reed, H. G. Wells, and other notables active during American radicalism's halcyon days—spent many an evening at the Sangers' Greenwich Village apartment, planning a more just and noble future for the working classes of the world. Like Goldman, Sanger believed that ending women's "sexual slavery" was the cornerstone of meaningful reform. Sanger also had many sobering experiences as an obstetrical nurse in tenement houses, a job she took to supplement the family income, especially dealing with the often grisly aftereffects of septic abortions. Such horrors made her determined to find a more humane alternative to unwanted pregnancy than the extremely dangerous five-dollar abortion— or even the more desperate methods women employed. But even as part of the medical community, Sanger lacked the practical facts that her poverty-stricken female patients often begged her for. She had previously written a series of articles called "What Every Girl Should Know" for the socialist daily *The Call,* which dealt frankly with the prevention of venereal disease. Specific birth-control information, however, was simply not available for common dissemination in America. Sanger visited medical libraries up and down the East Coast, finding nothing reliable, and physicians, refused to tell her. In 1913 she went to France, where she found that every housewife had access to the material she sought. A year later Sanger began using her new journal, *The Woman Rebel,* to help educate people about sex.

After a confrontation with Anthony Comstock, the head of the New York Society for the Suppression of Vice and the force behind the obscenity-related Comstock Laws, Sanger was charged with sending "obscene" birth control information through the mail. She fled to Europe to avoid prosecution, but as her fame grew, she returned to face a series of incarcerations. In 1915 she formed the National Birth Control League, the forerunner of the Planned Parenthood Federation of America, and in 1916 she opened her first birth control clinic in a storefront tenement in Brooklyn's Brownsville section.

Leaving her husband and three children to fend for themselves in 1921—she had always professed to find family life unfulfilling—Sanger took her campaign worldwide, lecturing and setting up clinics. She raised millions of dollars and kindled a lifelong enmity with the Roman Catholic church when she attempted to get governments and public health-care systems to support population control. Her determination and work would change the lives of countless women everywhere.

Today the battle lines in the birth control controversy remain drawn as they were over eighty years ago when this petite, redheaded firebrand handed out contraceptives in front of her clinic. In Margaret Sanger's life, the social activism which characterized much of the century took a unique form for she understood the dynamic between poverty and the size of the family. Her legacy is both profound and nettlesome. "I am the champion of women's right to control the consequences of their sexuality," she wrote confidently. And with those words she separated sexual pleasure from procreation and started a revolution.

JEAN-PAUL SARTRE

FRENCH PHILOSOPHER, PLAYWRIGHT, AND novelist, Jean-Paul Sartre was also the century's primary example of the engaged intellectual, a thinker who takes action in the world. His many political activities—often controversial and sometimes unpopular with even his most dedicated admirers—and his ever-evolving political thought were closely tied to his understanding of the universe in which humankind found itself adrift and alive. At the heart of his existential thought, based in a Godless and ultimately meaningless universe, is a formulation: If there is no God and therefore no master plan, then humanity is free to act, free to choose, and, by extension, ultimately responsible for its choices. From his involvement in the French Resistance during the Second World War to his pronouncements on the state of postwar Europe, to his support of revolutionaries all over the world, to his refusal of the Nobel Prize, Jean-Paul Sartre, again and again, showed himself free to choose and to be responsible for his choices. A contradictory and complicated man, both his passions—whether his total disavowal of capitalism, social injustice, colonialism—and his rectitude—his dedication to all the oppressed and his awareness of himself as a public figure whose actions had influence—were legion.

"Man must create his own essence," Sartre wrote in 1944, "it is in throwing himself into the world, suffering there, struggling there, that he gradually defines himself." Sartre became a voice of conscience for Europe as it emerged from war; from his late forties when Sartre first addressed the issue of anti-semitism in France to the last year of his life, when blind and sick, he went to the Elysée to plead with the French president for increased aid to the fleeing Vietnamese and Cambodian boat people, Sartre continued to define himself by throwing himself into the world.

An only child of a reserved Roman Catholic mother and a naval officer father who died when he was barely two, Sartre was raised in the Parisian household of his Lutheran grandparents. Crosseyed, small in stature, and resembling, as he himself once said, a bespectacled toad, the precocious boy learned to read when he was around four years old. Rejected by other children, he found solace in fantasy and writing. His stern but doting grandfather attempted to dissuade him from literary pursuits, but Jean-Paul rebelled by making words the center of his world: "By writing I was existing," he wrote in his acclaimed 1963 autobiography, *Les Mots [The Words, 1964]*.

After completing his lycée studies, Sartre pursued his interest in philosophy at the Ecole normale supérieure, where he met the woman with whom he was to share the rest of his life. Though they never married, Sartre and the brilliant feminist author Simone de Beauvoir became intellectual fellow travelers, helpmates, and lovers. In spite of numerous affairs and betrayals on both their parts, they remained at each other's sides and enjoyed a tumultuous relationship which continued until Sartre's death.

Throughout his life, Sartre's philosophy was inseparable from his art. Moving from Cartesian rationalism in the thirties, he came under the influence of Edmund Husserl's phenomenological methods, which favored description over deduction. In 1938, Sartre's own existentialist views, which owed much to Søren Kierkegaard and Martin Heidegger, were expounded in his first novel, *La Nausée* (1938; *Nausea*, 1949). In this self-referential work, the narrator, Roquentin, explicitly describes in his diary the revulsion he feels for his own corporeality, and resolves the dilemma of his physical humanity by planning to write a novel. A year after the book was published, Sartre, who had been teaching in various lycées, was drafted into the French army. Captured by the Germans, he returned after nine months to Occupied Paris where he joined the Résistance and risked further incarceration with his inflammatory writings, notably his play *Les Mouches [The Flies, 1943]*.

That same year, Sartre published *L'Être et le néant (Being and Nothingness, 1953)*, his first important philosophical work. In it he used what de Beauvoir termed his "opposition aesthetics" to argue that because consciousness is a non-thing, it escapes the causality to which the physical world is subject. Consciousness, and thus human beings, are therefore essentially free. In his four other major treatises, nine plays, and three remaining novels, Sartre continued to meditate on the nature of human existence, insisting on the need to take responsibility for one's choices. In an era demoralized by humanity's failure to respond to ethical imperatives, Sartre's call for defining life through self-determined action offered unusual solace.

Intent on wedding his existential beliefs to Marxism—and later, in his work on Gustave Flaubert, to psychoanalysis—Sartre was dedicated to those he identified as society's oppressed. He joined movements, organized rallies, and edited the review *Les Temps modernes*, which he founded in the 1940s. His political affiliations changed constantly over the years, and even his relationship to Communism, though he was never a party member, was complex and personal. In 1956, even though he reacted to the invasion of Hungary by declaring that his friendship with the Soviet Union had been replaced by "horror" at its actions, he nonetheless visited the USSR nine times in four years. At the same time, he was vocal about the abysmal state of human rights he found there.

In 1964, avowing he did not want to become a pawn in the Cold War, Sartre rejected the Nobel Prize. He focused increasingly on issues of social responsibility, and late in life, like many French intellectuals of his era, he found comfort in Maoism, which like Marxism, took its cues from the masses. One of the principal inspirations of the international student movement in the sixties, he felt that the Chinese Communists seemed to embody "engagement," the single quality Sartre admired most. It was the same characteristic that others, even his critics, found most admirable in him.

ALBERT SCHWEITZER

AT THE END OF a long day's work in his primitive jungle hospital at Lambaréné in French Equatorial Africa (now Gabon), Dr. Albert Schweitzer would practice organ compositions on his specially equipped pedal piano, a gift from the Paris Bach Society. It is a curious image: the white-haired Messiah of the Forest alone under the dim equatorial moon, the notes of his favorite composer hanging heavily in the hot evening air. This scene also summons up the Renaissance accomplishments of Schweitzer's varied, extraordinary life—a ninety-year span of scholarship and self-sacrifice that brought him fame as a physician, missionary, philosopher, theologian, musicologist, organist, and educator.

Nurtured in a Lutheran home in Alsace, Schweitzer acquired both his devotion to music and his compassion for the suffering of others through the efforts of his pastor father, who instructed him in piano from the age of five and filled his son's mind with stories of courageous missionaries in far-off Africa. While only a student of twenty-one, Schweitzer vowed to himself that nine years hence, after developing his talents, he would offer them to the world's poor in exchange for God's gift of his own humble but comfortable life. For years it had seemed "inconceivable" to him that he should be leading a happy life while so many around him were "struggling with sorrow." Such empathetic tendencies, in concert with Schweitzer's religious beliefs and deeply held conviction that actions were more spiritually eloquent than words, converged in his famous doctrine of "reverence for life," a moral imperative that held all existence sacred and demanded of everyone "that they should sacrifice a portion of their own lives for others."

At age thirty, Schweitzer did exactly that. By this time, he had already cut an impressive swath through academe, having studied in Paris at the Sorbonne and earned doctorates in both philosophy and music and a licentiateship in theology, all from the University of Strasbourg. He had also published the first of some forty-two books, *The Philosophy of Kant,* and written the pioneering *J. S. Bach,* a two-volume biography that dusted the romantic sentimentalism off his musical idol. In addition, he had begun his chef d'oeuvre, *The Quest of the Historical Jesus,* which argued against the separation of the scriptural Jesus from the historical one—a theological position that laid the groundwork for secular humanism.

An appeal for doctors in a missionary magazine prompted Schweitzer, then a minister and theological-college principal, to obtain a medical degree with a specialty in tropical diseases. In 1913 he left Strasbourg with his wife and longtime assistant, Hélène Bresslau, for the stifling, physically draining climate of Lambaréné. The ensuing years of tireless manual labor, constant exposure to exotic maladies, and complicated fund-raising would have daunted a less determined couple.

There, on the Ogooué River, living arrangements were harsh and medical assistants as fickle as the region's unexpected torrential downpours. Though his old European manner was a bit gruff and authoritarian, Schweitzer did his best to adapt his medical methods to the traditions of the region, which called for the entire family to participate in a patient's care. It was never a perfect fit, though, there at the "outpost of the kingdom of God," where electricity was nonexistent and animals meandered in and out of open buildings. Schweitzer's African patients appreciated his toil, however, even if later critics—charging egotism, paternalistic condescension, and unsanitary conditions—did not.

World War I brought its own special misfortune: Schweitzer was deemed an enemy in the French-controlled region because he had been born in Alsace, then in Germany's possession. So, in the fall of 1917, he and his wife were sent to France as prisoners of war. In 1924, after publication of his ethical treatise, *Philosophy of Civilization,* which fully explained his "reverence for life" theory, Schweitzer returned to Lambaréné. Finding mostly disrepair and rampant vegetation, he rebuilt his hospital on a slightly grander scale. Now in his fifth decade, he began visiting Europe regularly, lecturing, recording, and giving his memorable organ recitals to raise money for medical supplies for the new leper colony he was planning. His international profile had increased so dramatically by this point that, after World War II, which had further weakened his declining health by seriously interrupting supplies to the hospital, Schweitzer was able to declare his own war against the impending doom he felt had been ushered in by the Atomic Age. In 1952 he was awarded the Nobel Peace Prize; three years later he sounded the battle call with his "Declaration of Conscience," a radio address in which he begged the people of the world to force their governments to stop nuclear testing.

With the passage of time—and the recognition of the importance of racial and cultural self-determination—Schweitzer became an easy target for mockery, his deeds diminished by a "modern" interpretation imposed on a less progressive, bygone era. (In his rumpled white garb and explorer's pith helmet, he seemed the very embodiment of the white man carrying his nineteenth-century burden.) Yet he remains perhaps the most famous Christian of the first half of the century—a model of renunciation and good conscience. Standing on the muddy banks of the slow-moving Ogooué, frozen in photographic time, he is often shown waving a brotherly greeting, an eternal invitation, perhaps, to all who would join him in loving their neighbors by serving them.

SHAW

GEORGE BERNARD

A POLYMATH WHO WAS a master of the English language, George Bernard Shaw was a theatrical visionary who moved drama out of the Victorian age into the modern era. His was a theatre of ideas made powerful by wit, energy, character, and, always, a marvelous ear for language. Theatergoers were at once challenged and enriched, while Shaw's private circle enjoyed the warmth and generosity of his expansive friendship.

So long was his career and so unassailable his stature in the theater of ideas that, at the end, his admirers forgot how many years it took him to attain any success at all. Born into a Dublin family, the most quotable playwright of the twentieth century was the child of an alcoholic father who nevertheless displayed a wry comedic talent which his son clearly shared. As an adolescent, his contempt for his family's station deepened when his parents were forced by poverty to send him to Central Model Boys' School, an institution for lower-middle-class Catholic youth. School was inhospitable to George's quirky turn of mind, and at fifteen he ended his formal education to begin a wearying series of menial laboring jobs and clerkships. Office life, however, did not appeal to the Dubliner's burgeoning literary bent.

In 1876 Shaw left Ireland for London, where he began to write the first of five unpublished novels. A long twelve years later, he began to find steady journalistic work, which included writing a series of brilliant music columns for *The Star*. He overcame a lack of technical knowledge with a sharply honed aesthetic sense and a keenness for crossing swords with mediocrity. "My method," Shaw said, "is to take the utmost trouble to find the right thing to say, and then say it with the utmost levity." He moved on to the *World* in 1890 with a dedicated readership.

As a drama critic, Shaw made his reputation by savaging the unrealistic dialogue and empty forms of the "well-made play" then dominating the West End's stages. It was as theater critic for *The Saturday Review* from 1895 to 1898 that he developed his highly personal dramatic philosophy, rooted in his disdain for the false authority of social convention. Shaw believed the stage was an ideal vehicle for the communication of ideas if they were expressed in a naturalistic setting and with everyday language. The art of Ibsen, which Shaw wrote about exstensively, provided an example. But while Ibsen's focus was on the psychological motives of his characters, Shaw's characters mirrored their social—and therefore political—concerns. His growing fame as a literary iconoclast was

further enhanced when, in 1884, he helped to found the Fabian Society, a socialist group which preached the evolution of socialism as opposed to the Marxist vision of class struggle.

It was not until 1892 that Shaw wove his life's disparate skeins of ideology, drama, and critique into the play *Widowers' Houses*. Booed by a single patron as he bowed to applause at the end of its premiere, Shaw responded, "My friend, I quite agree—but what are we two against so many?" With that comment, the controversial critic donned a second cap as a playwright, trading barbs with his own judges. Financial stability did not come to him until *Candida* and *The Devil's Disciple* (1897). Shaw soon abandoned his career as a critic and married Irishwoman Charlotte Payne-Townshend. Although their marriage was sexless by agreement, his libido found an outlet in the "incorrigible philandering" he had always carried on with a bevy of admiring young women—not all of whom were his mistresses in the biblical sense. In fact Shaw's biographers have made more of his sex life than he ever did. He once told Ellen Terry, the famous actress whom he considered his Platonic soul mate, "My genius for hurting women is extraordinary, and I always do it with the best of intentions." As for his other friendships, he was gregarious by nature but had few intimates; Oscar Wilde seems to have summed up Shaw's social life with his famous quip: "He has no enemies, and none of his friends like him."

Unlike many great artists, Shaw achieved his loftiest triumphs rather late in life, with *Man and Superman* (1903), *You Never Can Tell* (1905), and *Androcles and the Lion* (1912). Two years after the 1923 debut of *Saint Joan*, he received the Nobel Prize for Literature. His *Pygmalion* (1913) survived in American hearts both as a play and in the decidedly un-Shavian costume of the Lerner and Loewe Broadway musical *My Fair Lady* (1956) and in George Cukor's 1964 film of the same name. Shaw continued to write essays throughout the Second World War, during which he provoked his readers by announcing that he did not find either Hitler or Stalin offensive. He also declared with awesome presumption that he did not want his plays taught in schools like Shakespeare—whom he had railed against in his drama-critic days, though mostly, he later admitted, to advertise himself. Yet his plays are as much studied today as they are performed, and they still provide not only entertainment but the "moral instruction" Shaw thought was the hallmark of good theater.

FRANK SINATRA

TO WATCH FRANK SINATRA evolve from boy crooner to tough-guy swinger to aging showman was to watch America grow. The big bands he started with are now faded memories, but as Sinatra and the world around him changed, one thing remained: his voice. When he was young, its mellow tones affectionately embraced the tenderest of love songs; toward the end, it swung to more worldly ballads, cool and relaxed as it soared over the heavily orchestrated arrangements he grew to favor.

Born in Hoboken, New Jersey, Francis Albert Sinatra moped through his education before dropping out of high school in his sophomore year. Not content with his job as truck loader for the local paper, he was inspired by a Bing Crosby concert to take up singing, much to the chagrin of his parents. His father, Marty, was a boxer-turned-saloonkeeper; his mother Dolly, a hefty and aggressive woman, kept her rowdy son in tow. "But my mother wasn't tough," Sinatra once commented, "the neighborhood was tough." By 1938, after being expelled from school, "Frankie Trent" was performing for tips at the Rustic Cabin, a New Jersey roadhouse. Skinny and intense, he sang at any radio station he could persuade to hear him, eventually landing an appearance on *Major Bowes' Amateur Hour* radio program. In 1939, trumpet virtuoso Harry James heard him on the air and offered him a one-year contract in his new band. Sinatra accepted, but left James after seven months to join trombonist Tommy Dorsey, whose musical phrasing and sophisticated breathing techniques Sinatra quickly absorbed. Mastering, too, the jazz inflections of singer Billie Holiday, he developed an approach to lyrics that was dramatically narrative and emotionally loaded. By 1942, a few years after marrying his first serious girlfriend Nancy Bar-bato, the singer had left Dorsey and become a romantic sensation among swooning "bobby-soxers" who reacted to him as their children would to Elvis Presley. Sinatra saw the frenzied phenomenon in the context of World War II's "great loneliness." "I was the boy in every corner drugstore, the boy who'd gone off to war."

When the soldiers came home, Sinatra traveled to Hollywood, where in 1943 he debuted in the film *Higher and Higher,* going on to make a series of equally light musicals such as *Anchors Aweigh* (1945) and *On the Town* (1949). But by 1947, like the boxer he had trained to become in his teens, Sinatra's career was taking devastating blows: a passionate defender of civil rights, he was linked to the Mafia and the Communist Party by both gossip columnists and the House Un-American Activities Committee (HUAC). He lost his velvety voice, aided in part by his disastrous marriage to

actress Ava Gardner and by his notorious appetite for "booze and broads." While his movie roles diminished and his record sales dropped, "the Chairman of the Board" was characteristically defiant, but also shrewdly conciliatory: he blasted HUAC in print, while bowing to anti-Communist pressure that he fire a blacklisted man from one of his films. Far from abandoning his turf, he successfully revived his stalled film career by lobbying for the part of feisty Angelo Maggio in *From Here to Eternity* (1953). The role earned him an Oscar. Then, while starring in a string of hit movies like *Guys and Dolls* (1955), *The Man with the Golden Arm* (1955), and *High Society* (1956), Sinatra turned with renewed interest to singing, finding in arranger Nelson Riddle's lush, jazzy orchestrations the perfect setting for the rough diamond his voice had become.

While providing theme music for the fifties, Sinatra and his "Rat Pack" cronies (Dean Martin, Sammy Davis Jr., Peter Lawford, and Joey Bishop) circulated between the leatherette lounges of Los Angeles and Las Vegas, keeping company with beautiful showgirls and wise guys like Sam Giancana. In 1960, Sinatra threw his support behind fellow New Frontiersman John F. Kennedy, and his 1959 hit "High Hopes," with new Sammy Cahn lyrics, became the presidential campaign's theme song. In 1966, at age fifty, he married actress Mia Farrow, who was twenty-one, but the union only lasted a little over a year. Ten years later he wed Barbara Marx, Zeppo Marx's ex-wife. Increasing his quiet and already generous philanthropy, Sinatra also became more conservative in his politics. Earnest pronouncements about the underdog and his fast-lane allegiances were replaced, after the president's 1963 assassination, by political leanings that led him to associations with Richard Nixon and Ronald Reagan.

Though he kept recording music and acting in films throughout the seventies and eighties, Sinatra did not take gracefully to aging. He sometimes took his "Sicillian temper" out on the press, attacking journalists who reported his decline. His new pals seemed not to notice—President Reagan awarded him the Medal of Freedom in 1986—and audiences didn't much care. Despite the fact that his voice was somewhat diminished in his later years, he continued to delight crowds with standards like "Moonlight in Vermont," "Fly Me to the Moon," "All or Nothing at All" and "My Way." To his fans, "Ol' Blue Eyes" was still the finger-snapping hipster whose love songs had convinced two generations that romance was the most important thing in life. Toward the end, watching his fighter's instinct prevail, fans and detractors alike had to admire his determination to go down singing.

SOLZHENITSYN

ALEKSANDR

THE SOVIET WRITER ALEKSANDR SOLZHENITSYN combines the clear eye and steady pen of a great novelist with the moral rectitude of an Old Testament prophet. Imprisoned for years in the old Soviet Union's system of forced labor camps, Solzhenitsyn rose to public consciousness during the final stages of the Communist state. He was soon honored around the world as heir to Tolstoy and Chekhov, a nineteenth-century Russian master reincarnated as a political prisoner.

Solzhenitsyn was born in 1918, one year after the Russian Revolution had consolidated the Communist Party's role as the new oligarchy. His father, an artillery officer in the Army, died six months before Aleksandr was born. His mother, a stenographer, raised the child in the city of Rostov-on-Don, helped by her sister-in-law Irina Shcherbak, who instilled in Aleksandr a love of books. Inspired to become a writer by the age of nine, by age ten he had devoured Tolstoy's War and Peace.

Though Solzhenitsyn was a committed Marxist, he never quite abandoned the ritual of the Russian Orthodox Church he had loved as a boy. Graduating in 1936 from the leading high school in Rostov, Solzhenitsyn attended the university there, where he met his first wife, Natalya Restetovskaya. He took a copy of Marx's Capital on his honeymoon.

Despite his love of writing, Solzhenitsyn earned his degree in mathematics in 1941, and began teaching the subject, as well as astronomy, in a local high school. When Nazi Germany invaded Russia, Solzhenitsyn was drafted into the Red Army. Like his father before him, he was made an artillery officer, and earned a medal in the Battle of Orel. He was promoted to captain in 1944.

The next year he was arrested by Russian counterintelligence agents for anti-Stalin remarks he had allegedly made in a letter. Dragged before a kangaroo court, he was charged with favoring the creation of a new, strictly Leninist political party, and duly sentenced to eight years in a labor camp. In 1947 the authorities sent Solzhenitsyn to Marfino Prison, a scientific research facility where he worked as a mathematician. Abandoning Marxism, he rebelled against the Marfino regime, refusing to participate in research projects. For criticizing his superiors he was transferred in 1950 to a hard-labor camp at Ekibastuz in Kazhakhstan. This became the scene for his first novel, One Day in the Life of Ivan Denisovich, which he wrote on tiny scraps of paper.

Solzhenitsyn was released from prison in 1953, on the very day his tormentor Stalin died. But the ghost of the dictator continued to haunt his life: he was sent into "perpetual exile" in Soviet central Asia, where he taught mathematics and physics. His banishment lasted only three years, however, and upon his release in 1956, his conviction was nullified.

Solzhenitsyn resumed writing but, afraid of the authorities, he kept his manuscripts secret from everyone except his second wife. Then in 1961, encouraged by the more liberal cultural pronouncements of the Communist Party's 22nd Congress, he submitted Ivan Denisovich to the journal Novy Mir ("New World"). Khrushchev approved its publication, and immediately, Solzhenitsyn became a celebrated author. After Khrushchev's swift removal from power in 1964, however, Solzhenitsyn's manuscript for The First Circle was confiscated by the reactionary government of Leonid Brezhnev, who viewed the writer with great wariness. Solzhenitsyn embarked upon a series of attacks against the Party and the Union of Soviet Writers, provoking his government's distrust.

His success in the wider world proved dangerous to Solzhenitsyn in his own country. He was awarded the 1970 Nobel Prize for Literature, which he was forced to decline by the government. The 1971 London publication of August 1914, with its apostate views of the Great War and the Revolution, further antagonized the authorities, but the publication of The Gulag Archipelago, with its unblinking depiction of the labor camps, finally brought the full weight of the State down upon him. The novel blamed not only Stalin, but the heretofore sacred Lenin, for the existence of the gulags, and held the Soviet people accountable for their leaders' crimes.

Goaded into reaction, the secret police arrested the author's typist, who revealed the location of the manuscript and promptly committed suicide. Solzhenitsyn, who had tried to protect his sources by delaying publication, ordered the book printed immediately. Volume one was smuggled out of Russia and appeared in Paris bookstores in December 1973. Two months later, Solzhenitsyn was expelled from the Soviet Union.

The writer decamped for the U.S., but once ensconced in a small Vermont freehold, he turned on his adopted country and attacked it for its lax morality. His champions were appalled to learn that his vision of good Russian government involved not democracy, but an authoritarian theocracy rooted in the precepts of the Russian Orthodox Church. Undaunted by criticism, Solzhenitsyn continued to write plays, essays, and stories, interspersing his literary efforts with gardening and long walks in the woods. His sallies against the decadence of Western culture were interrupted by an event he did not foresee: the collapse of the Soviet Union. In 1994, he returned to mother Russia, to host a television talk show which was canceled in the fall of 1995. Sadly, The Red Wheel, his enormous history of the Russian Revolution, was mostly ignored by the Russian public and intelligentsia. But the impact of his work on world literature will be felt well into the next century.

SPIELBERG

STEVEN

IN HIS SIGNATURE BASEBALL CAP and sneakers, Steven Spielberg does not look the part of the Western world's most famous living filmmaker. No one but Spielberg, however, has enticed such large audiences into theaters around the globe. (Though new releases keep changing the numbers, *Jaws* (1975), *Close Encounters of the Third Kind* (1977), *Raiders of the Lost Ark* (1981), *E.T., The Extra-Terrestrial* (1982) and *Jurassic Park* (1991) continue to hold their places among the highest-grossing movies ever.) And no one but Spielberg has so successfully blended the styles of so many cinema greats before him to produce such a unified body of work. Finally, no one but Spielberg has managed to combine the coolness of the technical wizardry with the emotional warmth of a storytelling that is at once adventurous and intensely personal.

The origins of the man George Lucas, the multitalented producer of the *Star Wars* series, calls "the T-Rex of directors" were anything but grand. The son of a computer expert, Arnold Spielberg, and his concert pianist wife, Leah Posner, Spielberg was born in Cincinnati, Ohio, and, after a time in New Jersey, raised in middle-class suburban ease in Phoenix, Arizona. Forbidden to watch movies and television programs that might upset him and his three siblings, he nevertheless managed to turn the family's TV set into a "third Parent." When he was six, his parents took him to see *Snow White and the Seven Dwarfs*, and the child, who as an adult would frighten millions with his gigantic dinosaurs and glowing UFOs, was so unnerved by the wicked witch that he had to spend the next few nights in his parents' room. Five years later, his father held up a transistor and announced, "This is the future." The giant-to-be of computer-graphic imaging and robotics solemnly took the transistor from his father's hand, and ate it. He made better use of his father's 8mm movie camera, chronicling his family's activities with the participation of his sisters and always-accommodating mother. (He once asked her to put cherries jubilee in the pressure cooker so the fruit would spatter and he could film the "blood.")

These early years were not always so amusing, however; Spielberg's parents fought, the family's frequent moves cast him over and over in the uncomfortable role of new boy in the neighborhood, and in high school he suffered anti-semitic taunts. His disgust with school was so intense that poor grades kept him from his first choice of colleges, the University of Southern California's film school, despite the fact that he had won a movie-making contest at thirteen. Attending his second-choice, California State University at Long Beach, as an English major, Spielberg watched films incessantly. His twenty-minute short *Amblin'*, which resulted in a seven-year contract with Universal–MCA, was followed in 1971 by the television movie called

Duel, now a cult classic. Its overseas success led to his first feature, 1974's *The Sugarland Express*. Though a box-office disappointment, its sophisticated technique inspired producers Richard Zanuck and David Brown to hire Spielberg to direct the pioneering shocker *Jaws* in 1975. The knuckle-biting blockbuster featuring a twenty-four foot-long polyurethane Great White made box-office history—and Spielberg's reputation.

He enhanced his new fame with 1977's *Close Encounters of the Third Kind*. A jolting tale of human contact with extraterrestrials, it reflected the writer-director's childhood preoccupation with science fiction and further developed his blend of compelling sentiment, fast-paced action, and dazzling special effects, often seen through the unblinking eyes of children. He repeated the formula with variations in his 1981 collaboration with George Lucas in *Raiders of the Lost Ark,* the first of three Indiana Jones films which drew their inspiration from the old serials. The series meant something even more valuable to Spielberg than its double-digit million dollar earnings: a marriage to actress Kate Capshaw, whom he met in 1983 when she auditioned for *The Temple of Doom*. But it was 1982's *E.T.* into which he poured the heart-tugging lessons of every Disney film he'd ever watched, that represented the director at his beguiling and—what detractors carp—his manipulative best. At the core of this and most all Spielberg movies is the family, a nest from which a heroic child might venture harmlessly to challenge the world—but one that was also vulnerable to the intrusions of evil.

While *E.T.*'s anthropomorphic spaceling star and his young friends captured America's hearts, in some Hollywood quarters, *E.T.*'s creator was not as enthusiastically embraced. The enormous numbers by which Hollywood usually measures genius were suddenly irrelevant when it came time to grant Spielberg an oscar. When *E.T.* relinquished its record as number-one box office grosser to its director's 1993 dinosaur spine-tingler *Jurassic Park,* critics sniped that the film was slick, shallow, and formulaic. The "excessively commercial" Spielberg then confounded his detractors with his Holocaust epic *Schindler's List* (1993), a wrenching portrayal of brutality and hope that won him, at long last, his Oscars for Best Director and Best Picture.

In 1994 Spielberg teamed with two other media titans, former Disney executive Jeffrey Katzenberg and record mogul David Geffen, to create DreamWorks, touted to be the next century's most influential entertainment entity. Three years later it released the Spielberg-directed slavery epic *Amistad*. He has also continued his work with Starbright World, a computer network that allows seriously ill children to communicate in cyberspace. Like all the other worlds Spielberg has created, it is a place for telling stories.

SPOCK

DR. BENJAMIN

HAILED BY MANY PARENTS as the savior of their young and denounced by others as the unwitting architect of the "permissive society," Dr. Benjamin McLane Spock helped raise three generations of America's children. His revolutionary guide to raising babies, the simply-named *Baby and Child Care,* made him famous when it appeared in 1946, the first year of the post-war baby boom. In it, the well-intentioned pediatrician broke with the regimented and sometimes quite eccentric child-rearing theories of the past and offered what he steadfastly believed was a more common- sense approach. Based on discipline and love, its quiet, good advice, he hoped, would contribute to a sane and compassionate society and parental peace of mind. In the winter of his years, however, he grew to despair of what he felt the human community had become. Many of his harshest critics shared his gloom but claimed he had no one to blame but himself.

Born in 1903 in New Haven, Connecticut, Spock was the oldest of six children. His quiet, self-effacing father was a lawyer descended from an American soldier in the Revolution. But it was his mother, the beautiful, intelligent, and coldly puritanical Mildred Stoughton, who most shaped his life. He described her as a "very moralistic, excessively controlling" woman who habitually grilled her offspring about their potentially vile daydreams and deeds. Many of this imperious woman's ideas of motherhood sprang from a book, Dr. Luther Emmett Holt's *The Care and Feeding of Children,* which identified well-being with proper diet; a zealous disciple, Mrs. Spock banned "dangerous" foods, like bananas, from her house, and also insisted her children spend the night—both summer and winter—outdoors on the sleeping-porch. Under such strictures, young Ben grew shy and insecure and possessed of a conscience he described in his autobiography as "more severe than was necessary or wise." But he also identified with his mother, owing his vocation to her casually efficient way of raising her children. She gave birth at home to all of them and, as Spock later reminisced, the fact "that a doctor came and delivered a baby at home at intervals throughout my childhood gave me a realistic view of where babies came from."

In 1919, Spock was sent to Phillips Academy in Andover, Massachusetts—sufficiently distant from his mother to give him a small measure of happiness. Yale came next, where the six-foot-four beanpole, yearning to be a "regular guy," pursued athletics. He joined the rowing team after a varsity crew chief challenged him to partake in a "real man's sport." In the 1924 Olympics in Paris, he rowed on the Gold Medal team. He was never a brilliant student, but, following his graduation in 1925, his "gentleman's C" average was adequate to gain him admission to medical school. He received his M.D. in 1929 after attending both the Yale and Columbia medical

schools. Two years earlier, while still a student, he had married Jane Davenport, with whom he would have two sons.

Spock devoted seventeen years to pediatric training and study before he emerged as a national figure. In order to concentrate on the new field of prevention of emotional problems in children, he enrolled at the New York Psychoanalytic Institute. There he underwent psychoanalysis with Sandor Rado, the institute's director, and encountered one of his early mentors, Caroline Zachry, a leader of the progressive education movement, who taught a seminar on personality development. Spock also taught at Cornell and was a consultant in pediatric psychiatry to the City of New York.

All this was a prelude to *Baby and Child Care,* written at the request of an editor at Pocket Books who realized that a worried young America sorely needed an alternative to the prevailing "scientific" theory that held parental affection to be unwholesome and stifling. Against the frosty advice that babies were to be fed according to a rigid schedule and were not to be picked up when they cried, Spock offered calm counsel: "Trust yourself," he wrote. "You know more than you think you do."

When *Baby and Child Care* appeared in 1946, priced at twenty-five cents, it was an immediate hit. Spock had hoped to sell 10,000 copies a year; it became one of the best-selling books of all time, with over 46 million copies in print in over 30 languages. Public response, however, was not all favorable. A common criticism was that Spock was too permissive, excusing all manners of misbehavior as somehow perfectly normal—he would even be blamed for the turbulence that would accompany the baby-boom generation's coming of age in the 1960s. Confounding his dissenters with his level-headedness and his penchant for debate, Spock spread his teachings at the Universities of Minnesota, Pittsburgh and Western Reserve and on the staffs of the Mayo Clinic and the Rochester Child Health Institute in Minnesota. Appearing on television, he reached millions with his pointers on teething and toilet training.

It was with the Vietnam War, though, that Dr. Spock met his greatest ethical challenge. Convinced that war was as great an evil to children as disease and malnutrition, he embarked on a campaign of principled non-violent opposition. His pacifism resulted in numerous arrests and a conviction in 1967 against the U.S. Universal Military Training and Service Act for advising draft evasion. In 1971, he ran for president on the People's Party ticket, and in 1986, still crusading, he climbed over a chain-link fence at Cape Canaveral to protest missile testing. A dedicated sailor into his nineties, Spock credited macrobiotics, meditation, and Mary Morgan, his attentive second wife, for his longevity. To the end, doing right by future generations still weighed heavily on his mind, a moral imperative he had learned at his mother's knee.

STALIN

JOSEPH

HE WAS THE INDOMITABLE RULER of the USSR from Lenin's death in 1924 until his own. In that time, Joseph Stalin's rule was one of terror, dedicated to the absolute control of information and bent on quashing any opposition to him or his policies. His purges were unparalleled in their violence and in the number of lives they affected, even in a country long accustomed to oppression. And yet, this most modern tyrant, who understood the cult of personality well and manipulated it throughout his career, was also a man of considerable military skill and diplomatic talent who won important concessions at the conference table from Franklin Delano Roosevelt and Winston Churchill to build a Soviet sphere of influence in Eastern Europe. Instigator of the Cold War, he was ready to challenge the West for control of the globe. After the Second World War, he was widely hailed in his own country as a heroic leader, the horrors of his purges seemingly forgiven by a grateful populace. At his funeral, while the eulogies of his comrades were notably muted, the crowds rushing into Red Square were so enormous that men, women, and children were trampled to death.

Born in the Georgian town of Gori on December 21,1879, Josif Vissarionovich Dzhugashvili was the son of an illiterate washerwoman and an alcoholic cobbler. Physically abused by his father, "Soso"—or "little Joe," as his mother called him—entered the Orthodox seminary in Tbilisi in 1894, four years after his father died in a fight. The priesthood, so it seemed to his devout mother, was the only chance for a sickly young man with a face scarred by smallpox and an arm withered by septicemia. Her ambitions for him were unfulfilled; he was expelled in 1899. Two years later he joined the Georgian Social Democratic Part and, taking the alias of "Koba" or "The Indomitable," the name of a famous Georgian outlaw, he started to build a reputation for himself.

In 1903, he joined the Bolshevik wing of the communists, thus aligning himself with Lenin, and began turning out revolutionary pamphlets on his clandestine press while engaging in robbery to support the cause. Between 1903 and 1913, he was arrested five times, managing to escape each time. He first met Lenin in Finland at the Bolsheviks' first national congress in 1905. The twenty-six-year-old was disappointed that his hero, whom he had imagined to be physically imposing, was simply an ordinary-looking man, but Lenin thought enough of the "wonderful Georgian" to select him seven years later.

In 1912, Stalin—as he now called himself, "the man of steel"—was made a member of the central committee by Lenin, and became one of the first editors of *Pravda (Truth)*. Stalin was arrested in 1913 and exiled to Siberia, where he would remain until 1917, when he was released under amnesty after the February Revolution. After the October Revolution, Stalin was part of the cabinet as the people's commissar for nationalities,

and during the civil war, proved himself an able administrator. By 1922, Stalin was the secretary general of the central committee.

When Lenin died suddenly of a stroke in 1922, Stalin became part of a *troika* leadership along with Lev Kamenev and Grigori Zinoviev to challenge Leon Trotsky's claim to leadership. In 1925 with Trotsky defeated and sent into exile in Mexico, Stalin realigned himself with Nikolai Bukharin against Kamenev and Zinoviev. With Kamenev and Zinoviev out of power and out of the party, Stalin then turned on Buhkarin, whom, like the others, he would later have executed. (Leon Trotsky fell to an assassin's bullet in Mexico in 1940.) In 1928, Stalin instituted the first of his five year plans, meant to industrialize the country as quickly as possible, and collectivize agriculture. The collectivization resulted in the execution and relocation of hundreds of thousands of *kulaks,* or middle-class farmers, and the death by starvation of countless more. Repression and terror were the tools by which Stalin forged his power, and in 1930s, he turned to the Bolshevik party, the Red Army, and even the Secret Police to weed out any potential enemies or opponents after the murder of one of his cadre, Kirov. Puppet trials of former Bolshevik colleagues ended in execution; countless ordinary citizens feared the knock on the door that signaled imprisonment or death. Stalin's second wife, Nadezhda, died mysteriously in 1932, reportedly a suicide in reaction to her husband's excesses. Stating that "with her have died my last warm feelings for all human beings," Stalin spent the next two decades transforming himself and his country into a world power.

With Hitler's invasion of June, 1941, a betrayal of Russia's 1939 non-aggression pact with Germany, Stalin, after some hesiation, spurred his nation on to victory. Defending borders that lay far to the east, he held the enemy at bay with brilliant strategies devised from the Kremlin, substantial help from the Allies, and the cooperation of the punishing Russian winter. The bravery of his people under fire was extraordinary and with an astounding eight million casualties, Stalin was determined to hang on to what the Russians had died for. In 1945, at Yalta, he proved a clever negotiator, convincing Churchill and Roosevelt to allow expansion of Soviet control into Eastern Europe, as well as half of a divided Germany. His two Allied partners, assuming global conflict had somehow sensitized him, expected Stalin to institute postwar reforms, but his boot remained firmly on Russia's neck.

In 1956, a scant four years after Stalin's internment next to Lenin, Nikita Krushchev and others denounced Stalin for his tyranny, his self-aggrandizement, and his falsifying of history. In 1961, his body was moved, and statues and portraits of the former leader removed from all over the country. Cities, streets, parks, and squares, named in his honor, were renamed. By 1991, the empire that Stalin had built was no more.

Возрастъ по изм ду 30-32

Ростъ 1 метр 69

1879 Декабр

GERTRUDE STEIN

CONSIDERED BY MANY THE unsung hero of modernism, Gertrude Stein spent a mere thirty minutes a day writing novels and plays that were idiosyncratic in the extreme—often without action, characterization, plot, and conventional grammar—and achieved a quite considerable body of work. With her close-cropped head, her Buddha-like body, and her cultivated talent for witty aphorism, literary savant was a part that Stein was more than happy to play. "I have been," she once announced, "the creative literary mind of the century."

Born in Allegheny, Pennsylvania, to Daniel and Amelia Stein, young Gertrude loathed her bullying, impatient businessman father and dismissed her mother as ineffectual. The family spent nearly three years in Europe soon after Gertrude was born, then settled in Oakland, California, a city Stein later neatly summed up with the terse judgment, "There's no there there." Meanwhile, she and her siblings (Gertrude was the youngest) watched unperturbed as first their mother died (in 1888) and then their father (in 1891). None of them much liked their parents, she said vaguely. Guardians were appointed, though eventually the eldest brother, Michael, took on that role.

Squabbling between themselves over who was the family prodigy, Gertrude and brother Leo, who was two years older, were very attached to each other. Both attended school in Cambridge, Massachusetts—Leo at Harvard, Gertrude at Radcliffe, where she studied psychology under William James. Subsequently, the two of them attended Johns Hopkins University, where Gertrude was enrolled in the medical school. After she failed four courses, in 1903 they left for Paris, where they settled in the famous flat at 27 rue de Fleurus. Leo painted and Gertrude wrote stories. Together they collected great paintings and great painters like Henri Matisse, Francis Picabia, Georges Braque, and Picasso, who painted a portrait of her. The sweet-tempered Alice B. Toklas moved in, and within a few years, Leo moved out. Paris's avant-garde came to pay court, and Stein and Toklas fed the Sunday guests with their sumptuous cuisine. After meals, Stein banished wives and girlfriends to be entertained by Toklas and surrounded herself with the men, holding forth at great length on the mysteries of life, death, and art, but always eventually bringing the conversation back to what for her was its proper focus: herself.

It was one of the greatest literary and artistic salons in history. In addition to impressionists, cubists, and surrealists, writers such as Jean Cocteau and Guillaume Apollinaire were her tablemates, as were most of the "lost generation" (her apt phrase) of American expatriates. Ernest Hemingway (who described the studio in *A Moveable Feast*), F. Scott Fitzgerald, Ford Madox Ford, and Ezra Pound all found their way to her door, though Pound was eventually banished because of his competitive nature and a tendency to smash things in the heat of argument. James Joyce was also unwelcome, not for obstreperous behavior but because Stein regarded him as her chief rival in modernist literature.

It was at rue de Fleurus that Stein produced *Three Lives* (1910), a psychological triptych still hailed as her best work; *Tender Buttons* (1914); *The Making of Americans* (1925), a family history; *How to Write* (1931); and the wryly titled *Autobiography of Alice B. Toklas* (1933), a paean to herself nominally penned by her patient and loyal friend. It was this last, written in a clear, comprehensible style and full of wickedly funny portraits of her circle, that made Stein a best-selling author in America and realized her not-too-secret dream of being famous. She was much gratified. "My little sentences," she said with satisfaction, "have gotten under their skins."

As a writer Stein's work was deliberately and self-consciously innovative. Her words were chosen for sound, not sense, and her texts deliberately abandoned progression. While her writing forged a path few were to follow, Stein nonetheless influenced Ernest Hemingway, William Burroughs, Sherwood Anderson, and Jack Kerouac, as well as thousands of less talented beat writers. Behind Stein's artfully spare style and verbal gymnastics, was an extraordinarily analytical mind. Celebrated and mocked for such pronouncements as "Rose is a rose is a rose is a rose" ("Sacred Emily") and "Pigeons on the grass alas," *(Four Saints in Three Acts)*, Stein was, in fact, rigorously logical. Among her confederates, who were busy experimenting with the power of the unconscious, she was probably the only one who firmly believed in the ability of reason to apprehend all of reality. Stein was firmly rooted in nineteenth-century rationalism. Despite her taste for revolutionary art and bohemian friends, she was a staunch Republican and very much a lady.

Though they were largely able to ignore the First World War, the Second frightened Stein and her companion to the safety of a Swiss village. When she returned to liberated Paris, she who had been indifferent to nationalism fell in love with the adoring GIs who flocked to her flat, even taking a jaunt with them in an American bomber. She was enigmatic to the end, which came in 1946, from cancer. On her deathbed, Stein turned to Toklas and whispered, "What is the answer?" When Toklas remained silent, the ever droll Stein asked, "In that case, what is the question?"

IGOR STRAVINSKY

BY TURNS A CZARIST subject, a Parisian, an exile in Switzerland, and an American citizen, Igor Stravinsky, this century's greatest musical pioneer, was ever a Russian. A cultivated student of his nation's ancient tradition, his art reflected his roots—Russia's literature, folktales, liturgy, emotions, and graphic arts—and his formalist genius. The result was no less than a musical revolution. Stravinsky's father was a leading basso at the Imperial Opera House in Saint Petersburg, but though he was allowed piano lessons, Stravinsky was discouraged by his parents from pursuing a musical career. As a child, he was fascinated by a mute red-haired peasant who clucked his tongue in syncopation and made strange rhythmic noises by placing his hand under his armpit and pumping his arm.

At Saint Petersburg University, the slight and bird-faced Igor studied the law, enjoying musical improvisation and composition largely as an escape from the environment of his home. While attending the university, he presented some of his first works to his father's friend, Nikolay Rimsky-Korsakov. Recognizing the depth of Stravinsky's talent, the composer took him on as a private pupil, advising him to steer clear of conventional conservatory training. His association with Rimsky-Korsakov exposed Stravinsky to harmonic dissonance and insured that his early compositions were given regular public performances.

In 1909, a few months after Rimsky-Korsakov's death, a concert featuring two of Stravinsky's orchestral pieces was attended by Sergey Diaghilev. The impresario immediately recognized his young compatriot's musical gifts and he invited him to compose some orchestral pieces for his Ballet Russes, the innovative new dance company. For the company's second season, Diaghilev commissioned Stravinsky to write the score for a full-length ballet, *The Firebird*. Traveling with his wife and two children to Paris for its premiere in 1910, Stravinsky embarked on a new life in the city of lights.

His second ballet, *Petrushka,* followed in a rush. Then, in 1913, came the revelation: the premiere of *Le Sacre du printemps (The Rite of Spring)*. Conceived in a daydream in which Stravinsky saw a pagan dancing girl being ritualistically sacrificed, the score—as well as its choreography by the legendary Ballets Russes dancer Vaslav Nijinsky—was shocking in its repudiation of the conventional, romantic characterization of the onset of spring. From the first eerie strains of a lone bassoon, there were mutterings in the audience, which soon escalated into loud boos. When the curtain lifted on the "Dance of the Adolescents," cries of *"Ta gueule!"*—"Shut up!"—echoed throughout the theater. A riot ensued, and Stravinsky, seated near the front of the theater, was forced to take refuge backstage. Within a year, however, the fiercely original composition—with its dissonances, irregular rhythms, and complex chordal construction—had been proclaimed a revolutionary masterpiece.

With the coming of World War I, and then the Russian Revolution of 1917, the bourgeois Stravinsky, as conservatively orthodox in religion as he was unorthodox in music, became a man without a country. He and his family spent the war years in Switzerland, their usual winter residence, then returned to France in 1920. While there, he conducted an open affair with the fashion designer Coco Chanel. Another long-term mistress, the artist Vera Sudeikina, became his second wife after Catherine's death in 1939. Finally, in 1940, he moved to America with Vera. A hypochondriac who claimed that strong odors interfered with his sense of hearing, Stravinsky drank while composing, favoring a different alcoholic beverage for every country. He sipped Neuchâtel during his Swiss sojourn, Bordeaux in France, and scotch in America—always to enhance the effectiveness of the medications he took constantly to ward off the colds and flus he expected at any moment.

In America, the couple settled in Hollywood, where many dislocated Europeans congregated during World War II. For the next thirty years Stravinsky struggled to make ends meet, surviving by virtue of his commissions, income from conducting and performing, and the generosity of his friends. Meanwhile, he composed such powerful works as *Symphony in Three Movements* (1945); *Mass* (1948); and *The Rake's Progress* (1951), his only full-length opera. His dedicated following was shocked, however, when at the age of seventy he performed an amazing artistic volte-face, embracing the austere atonalities of serialism, the principal compositional theory used by Arnold Schoenberg, his chief rival for primacy in modern music.

Fortunately, he never relinquished that which was uniquely his. Possessed of a vitriolic wit, he battled pompous critics who limped uncomprehendingly three steps behind his stylistic innovations, skewered conductors who were too shallow to attempt his music, and other less than adequate colleagues. He mocked conductor Leopold Stokowski for spending "an hour a day trying to find the perfect hairdo" and dryly observed that composer Samuel Barber "could be counted on not to divert publicity from the social event."

With age, hypochondriacal complaints became true ailments, and Stravinsky moved to New York to be near the doctors he now required. He died there at the age of eighty-nine and was buried, not in his Russian homeland or in either of his adopted countries, but in the Russian section of Venice's San Michele cemetery, near his great patron Diaghilev.

BARBRA STREISAND

IN THE EARLY SIXTIES, the singer who would become the single most powerful woman in late-century American entertainment was usually broke. Dressed in thrift-shop ensembles, Barbra Streisand earned almost nothing performing at Manhattan's hipper nightclubs and gay bars. She was always hungry and when patrons offered to buy her a drink, the Brooklyn-born pop singer would ask for a meal of potatoes instead. Streisand combined this savvy with here exotic beauty and tremendous singing talent to launch her career. That talent was her voice, a two-octave, velvety wonder that could be both quiet and musically intimate and, at full volume, positively electric. By the end of the sixties, having attained multimedia stardom, Streisand was no longer building her wardrobe around second-hand clothes. Having portrayed comedian Fanny Brice in the smash Broadway musical *Funny Girl*—and having won a special 1969 Tony Award for "Star of the Decade" in the process—she could boast of two Grammy awards for her first album, an Emmy for her first one-woman television special, *My Name Is Barbra,* and an Oscar for her reprise role in William Wyler's 1968 film version of *Funny Girl.* In the seventies she shifted her focus to moviemaking, and by the eighties, though her records continued to "go platinum," she had almost given up performing—in part because she had always considered herself primarily an actress but not least because of her paralyzing stage fright.

Having risked a remake of the classic *A Star Is Born* (1976), for which she garnered four Academy Award nominations, Streisand staked everything—as actor, producer, star, director, and cowriter—on the making of Isaac Bashevis Singer's tale *Yentl* (1983). The film, which tells the story of a clever young woman in turn-of-the-century Poland who disguises herself as a boy so she can study the Talmud, received five Academy Award nominations. But Streisand herself was passed over, most notably in the Best Director category. It was the ultimate snub from the industry. Nevertheless, with the success of *Yentl* came a rediscovery of her Jewish faith and the self-confidence to adapt Pat Conroy's novel about familial dysfunction, *The Prince of Tides,* onto the screen. The movie garnered a new kind of respect for Streisand, but again no Best Director nomination.

At the root of such blatant resentment—which she struggled for years to understand—was her ambition, interpreted as unusually naked even by industry standards. She was viewed for years by her creative peers as being too candid, too demanding, and too insistent on having her own way. Pleading guilty, director Streisand once explained: "It's my vision of the film, and therefore every costume, every piece of furniture, and every color is something that is part of this vision." Repeatedly she has also expressed anger about her profession's "sexist" double standard: "You don't ask a man, 'Do you want to be in control?'" she once commented. "Why would a woman be any different? How could anyone not want to be in control of their work?" But underneath all the chutzpah, she has insisted, was a frightened child who injured easily. She has always craved success, she admits, but she has never pursued it ruthlessly.

Having lost her English-teacher father when she was only fifteen months old, Barbara grew up lonely. Her embittered mother was less than accepting of her rather gawky daughter and the used-car salesman Diana Streisand wed in 1949 was even more distant. But Barbara—the second *a* had not yet been dropped—was brash and, despite her imperfect nose, filled with dreams of becoming an actress. So after graduation from high school (two years early, with honors), she moved to Manhattan and at sixteen was on her own. In 1962 she won the lead in the Broadway musical *I Can Get It for You Wholesale,* as well as the heart of actor Elliott Gould. They married and had a son, Jason. After the 1964 theatrical production of *Funny Girl,* she starred in the 1968 film version; two of the numbers from the Jule Styne score—"People" and "Don't Rain on My Parade"—became permanent fixtures of her repertoire. She added other Streisand standards to her SRO revues, among them "You're the Top" from *What's Up, Doc?* (1972), "The Way We Were," a big hit from the 1973 film costarring Robert Redford, and the Oscar-winning "Evergreen," which she cowrote and sang in *A Star Is Born* (1976). The latter was coproduced by Jon Peters, whom Streisand, by then divorced from Gould, had met two years earlier when he came to style a wig during the shooting of *For Pete's Sake* (1974).

A more politically committed Streisand emerged in the nineties, as she threw her considerable talent and clout into fund-raising concerts for presidential hopeful Bill Clinton and made large contributions to the Democratic party, which she had long supported. She established the Streisand Foundation, which was dedicated to environmental protection and both civil and women's rights and in 1994, after a twenty-two-year absence, stepped once more into the spotlight with a sellout concert tour. In 1996, lightening struck in the form of a blind date with James Brolin. The handsome actor became her husband, her substitute father, her "mitzvah." Later that year, her film, *The Mirror Has Two Faces,* featured a song apropos to her new life: "I Finally Found Someone."

TAYLOR

ELIZABETH

THERE NEVER SEEMS TO have been a time when the shockingly beautiful, violet-eyed Elizabeth Taylor—the woman whom everyone thinks of when hearing the words "movie star"—wasn't famous. Long after her most memorable films and her love affairs made headlines, her life continued to be sensational, a glittering and very public drama worthy of the quintessential leading lady. Yet Taylor did not achieve her star status merely through constant exposure. At her most captivating, she remained that rarest of exotica, an actress who gave credible performances.

Taylor's long career in film began when she was nine. Attracting admiring stares wherever she went and possessed of a remarkable stage presence, the British-born American beauty was taken by her parents to audition for Universal Pictures, which led to a minuscule part in There's One Born Every Minute (1942). After a screen test for Metro-Goldwyn-Mayer, the luminous eleven-year-old was signed to make Lassie Come Home (1943) and then loaned out to Twentieth Century–Fox for a small role in Jane Eyre (1944). Molded by a domineering mother, Elizabeth spent her childhood working under contract to MGM. The center of attention, this child star, like many others whose world was the studio backlot, grew up with both a skewed sense of self and a fear of losing her center-stage position.

Taylor's early training in horseback riding proved important to her budding career: She was a natural for the part of the plucky young jockey in National Velvet, and her charming performance made her an instant sensation. Three years later, the studio publicity machine revved into overdrive for her first screen kiss, in Cynthia. By 1950, she had graduated from high school and won the role of Spencer Tracy's daughter in Father of the Bride. The following year her developing allure was showcased in A Place in the Sun, opposite Montgomery Clift, who became a lifelong friend. Giant, however, made in 1956, found her playing third fiddle to Rock Hudson and teen idol James Dean, and the next year's Raintree County was met with a cool reception (though Taylor's portrayal of a mentally disturbed woman earned her an Academy Award nomination). But Taylor endured and eventually triumphed. In the 1958 film adaptation of Tennessee Williams's Cat on a Hot Tin Roof, she made her mark as the smoldering, silk-slipped Maggie the Cat. With that role she established herself as a screen actress who could demand enormous fees.

And she got them: For the infamous 1963 extravaganza Cleopatra, the miscast Taylor received the then-unheard-of sum of one million dollars. Adorned in lavish costumes, she appeared amidst massively expensive sets opposite the great Welsh actor Richard Burton. However, it wasn't their performance on-screen that riveted audiences, but the couple's explosive romance off the set. The married Taylor (thus far to hotel heir Nicky Hilton, actor Michael Wilding, and director Mike Todd, whose tragic death left her reeling) obligingly discarded husband number four—the pop singer Eddie Fisher, whose abandonment of Debbie Reynolds for Taylor in 1959 had rocked the press—to wed the brooding, hard-drinking Burton. On their engagement, he presented Taylor with a thirty-three-carat ring, the Krupp diamond.

Taylor and Burton's stormy romance ricocheted from high drama to low comedy, but their film collaboration yielded such gems as the adaptation of Edward Albee's Who's Afraid of Virginia Woolf? (1966). Playing the blowsy, boozy Martha against Burton's drunken George, she won her second Oscar—in a role that couldn't have been more different from that for which she won her first, as Laurence Harvey's lovely but lonely paramour in Butterfield 8. From 1966 through 1972, however, Taylor and Burton made a series of expensive bombs, while their marriage—they had twice taken formal vows—sizzled and ultimately flamed out in 1976. That same year Taylor married soon-to-be Virginia senator John Warner. Finding the role of politico wife lonely, she tried her hand at the stage, appearing in The Little Foxes in 1981 and reuniting with Burton in 1983 for a much heralded but nonetheless indifferent revival of Noël Coward's Private Lives. The following year, when Burton died suddenly of a stroke, Taylor was devastated.

Throughout the eighties, serious illnesses and a painful recurring back problem took their toll. But Taylor's survival of more than twenty operations and numerous unrelated hospitalizations, including two stints at the Betty Ford Clinic, made her acutely sympathetic to the pain of others. In 1985, following the death of dear friend Rock Hudson, Taylor took a public stand—the first great star to do so—in support of AIDS research, becoming a tireless advocate through the American Federation for AIDS Research (AmFar) and the Elizabeth Taylor AIDS Foundation.

In 1991 the fifty-nine-year-old Taylor married Larry Fortensky, a construction worker she had met while they were both recovering at Betty Ford. The $1.5 million nuptials, conducted at pop star Michael Jackson's Neverland estate, seemed to open a more stable chapter in the private life of a woman who once remarked that "trying to grow up" has been her most challenging role. Husband number eight, however, was swimming against the tide of Taylor's history, and the two separated in 1995. Two years later she underwent brain surgery for a benign tumor. Her fans, however, remained hopeful. Taylor has been no stranger to suffering over her career. Perhaps she put it best when she said: "I've been through it all, baby. I'm mother courage."

SHIRLEY TEMPLE

THE CHILD ACTRESS WITH the dazzling smile who began tap-dancing her way through films at age three, Shirley Temple was the darling of America's Great Depression. In those bleakest of breadline years, the nation needed something or someone to brighten its days. Little Miss Miracle, affectionately nicknamed for her role in the 1934 movie *Little Miss Marker,* filled the bill perfectly. With her halo of blond ringlets and her sweet voice, the ever cheery youngster gave legs to a dozen or so tired and treacly scripts, shoring up the sunken spirits of an entire population. Astonishingly, her finger-wagging moralisms—inevitably delivered with a pout—appealed to adults even more than to fans her own age. This held true despite the press reports that the remarkable child was earning what might have seemed—even in good times—the unconscionable salary of ten thousand dollars a week.

At the height of Shirley-mania, mothers dressed their daughters in Shirley Temple fashions and bought them Shirley Temple dolls. No one, it seemed, could get enough of the bouncy moppet's unspoiled innocence and affectionate nature or her high-spirited song-and-dance routines, which she performed as professionally as any grown-up. At the apex of her career in the late thirties, when she starred in such hits as *Heidi* (1937), *Wee Willie Winkie* (1937), *Rebecca of Sunnybrook Farm* (1938), and *Little Miss Broadway* (1938), ranking ahead of Clark Gable as the world's box office favorite, her costars could not have been more purple in their praise for Shirley's theatrical instincts, veteran perfectionism, and unflagging determination. She even received her very own miniature Oscar for "her outstanding contribution to screen entertainment during the year, 1934."

Her ability to steal any show, however, clearly annoyed many screen professionals, who found themselves at a distinct disadvantage when sharing the screen with "that Temple kid," as actor Adolphe Menjou half-jokingly referred to her. A few cynics in the business were so suspicious of Shirley's unusual aplomb, in fact, that they were convinced she was really a midget. Graham Greene, commenting in a British magazine about the coquettishness of her performance in *Wee Willie Winkie,* insinuated that she was an adult impersonating a child, an allegation resulting in costly litigation that bankrupted the journal.

Meanwhile, as ordinary fans mobbed the star and her bodyguards in the streets, her more notable fans—like General Pershing, H. G. Wells, and Eleanor Roosevelt, with whom Shirley would share hamburgers at Hyde Park—paid court in her bungalow-playhouse on the Twentieth Century-Fox lot. One of her biggest boosters was Bill "Bojangles" Robinson, her dancing partner in several movies. He was fifty-six and she was six when they began as film's first interracial dancing duo.

One of the world's most accomplished tap dancers, he never ceased to marvel at her instinctive ability and speed in mastering their complicated routines.

Temple, in fact, was known as One-Take Shirley, a reputation she acquired by rarely fluffing a note, a step, or a cue. This knack was, of course, a natural one, but it was shaped immeasurably by her doting mother, who helped her daughter rehearse her lines at night. From her seat on the set, Gertrude Temple—put on salary early in Shirley's career—was always ready to help the director with a "Sparkle, Shirley, sparkle!" From the very beginning, when Shirley mimicked Marlene Dietrich in one of a series of one-reel satirical comedies called *Baby Burlesks,* it was her mother who oversaw everything, from Shirley's between-meal snacks to the minutiae of exactly how she should cock her head in a particular close-up.

There seemed never to have been a better little girl. When the accounts were finally settled, however, there could have been better personal managers than her parents. After making almost sixty films in nineteen years, Shirley discovered that her financial-manager father had lost all but a few thousand of her millions in a string of inept investments, and neglected even to make regular deposits to her trust fund. But with characteristic grace and generosity, she forgave her parents everything.

Like many stars who excel as very young children, Shirley Temple did not continue her theatrical success into her teenage years. The world wanted its tiny Curly Top, and at twelve, though not gangly or unattractive, she was essentially through. Unlike other Hollywood wunderkinder, however, Shirley Temple built a productive second life, marrying a successful businessman (her second husband, Charles Black) in 1950, raising three children, and, after staging a profitable comeback on television in the fifties, running on the 1967 Republican ticket for Congress. The campaign was unsuccessful, but she proved herself a valuable Republican loyalist. Temple's 1969 appointment by President Richard Nixon as American ambassador to the United Nations raised some criticism, but her hard work overcame her diplomatic inexperience.

Braving yet another front, she held a news conference in 1972 at which she became the first celebrity to go public with information about her breast cancer. "I felt I could help my sisters," she remarked years later. After her recovery, Shirley Temple Black went on to serve as ambassador to Ghana from 1974 to 1976 and was appointed chief of protocol for the state department during the Ford administration. It was the perfect job for a star who had been born unflappable, a quality she still displayed when appearing at the 1998 Academy Awards ceremony.

MOTHER TERESA

ON A HOT AND DUSTY train ride to Darjeeling on September 10, 1946, Sister Teresa, then thirty-six years old, received her second divine call. The message was clear and insistent: She was to leave the serene and cloistered life of St. Mary's School for Girls in Calcutta, where as a sister of the Loreto Convent she had taught history and geography to middle-class girls for seventeen years, and serve the poor instead. But she was not just to supply them with food and other necessities, as she and her community of Irish nuns had been routinely doing in the nearby slums of Moti Jheel; she was to actually live among them. "It was a greater sacrifice," Mother Teresa recounted in her authorized biography by Navin Chawla," than to leave my family and country to enter religious life."

The pious but pragmatic girl who was to become known as the "Saint of the Gutters" was born in Skopje, Yugoslavia (then the Kingdom of Albania), to Nicholas Bojaxhiu, a successful building contractor, and his Venetian wife, Dranafile Bernai Bojaxhiu. Because she was pink-cheeked and plump, Agnes—as she was baptized—was called "Gonxha," or flower bud in Albanian. Her youth was a "joyful" time, though her father's death when she was six brought great sorrow and—because of his business partner's misappropriation of assets—financial hardship as well. She was extremely close to her mother, an intensely spiritual woman who, though she barely made ends meet by selling embroidered cloth, never turned away the needy. Called "Nana Loke," or mother soul, by her three children, she personified the compassion and sharing that would mark her daughter's lifetime ministry of caring for the sick and starving. The two said good-bye on September 26, 1928, when the earnest eighteen-year-old started out from Zagreb for the Loreto Abbey in Ireland. They would never meet again.

To found her new mission, she needed to get permission from the Catholic hierarchy to leave the cloister, which after two years was granted. The day she bade farewell to her mother superior, there were three white cotton saris (the sari is the dress of India's poorest women) laid out for her; her spiritual advisor, Father Celeste van Exem, blessed them, as they were to become her new religious habit. In August of 1948, Sister Teresa accepted the supervision of the archbishop of Calcutta, and she became "Mother Teresa." That same year, after three months of intensive medical training from the American Medical Missionary Sisters in northern India, she opened her first school for slum children in Calcutta. She learned Bengali and Hindi herself and conducted class outdoors, on the barren earth, where she scratched out words in the dirt with a wooden stick. Within two years Mother Teresa's new order, the Missionaries of Charity—numbering only twelve women—became an official religious community within the Archdiocese of Calcutta.

Starting off with an ambitious project, in 1954 she established the Home for Dying Destitutes, located in a former temple dedicated to Kali, the Hindu goddess who is both the giver and destroyer of life. Nirmal Hrida—the place of the pure heart—was the first of the order's over one hundred official hospices, all of which address both the physical and emotional needs of the dying. As her humble community grew, its work expanded to include a leper colony; begun in a clearing under a tree, it presently serves fifteen thousand patients a year. Eventually, her "family," as she called her fellow workers, began to care for AIDS victims, battered women, prisoners on death row, the aged, the handicapped and cast-off children and orphans.

In 1979, along with the Nobel Peace Prize, Mother Teresa acquired the burden of celebrity. She accepted the award in the name of the poor, commenting with a hint of political sagacity that "Poverty and hunger and distress also constitute a threat to peace." With her driving energy, non-stop travel and tough management style, by the mid-nineties the tiny, wizened nun represented an empire of good works. It included over 286 houses for the needy, over 140 schools, and almost 840 mobile medical clinics serving more than five million people each year. Her Missionaries of Charity embraced some 4,000 nuns and one hundred twenty thousand coworkers and fanned out over 120 countries. Ascetic though she certainly was, Mother Teresa's piety was of a muscular sort, a resilient force which somehow suited the needy intensity of the times. Never asking of her fellow sisters what she did not demand of herself, she maintained a demanding regimen of sixteen-hour days that began at four a.m. She herself always slept on the floor.

Despite her service to society's forgotten, Mother Teresa was never entirely safe from criticism: In a country where the effects of overpopulation are shockingly obvious, she was uncompromising in her Catholic position against abortion and contraception, a stance which especially infuriated feminists. Others sneered at the fact that her ministrations addressed only the symptoms of poverty and illness without affecting the root causes. But real poverty, Mother Teresa always maintained, could be spiritual as well as material. In her oblique fashion, she once referred to it simply as "the absence of love."

She continued on following her first heart attack in 1989, but after two more in 1996, she was finally forced to take seriously the disagreeable idea of retirement.

She died soon after in 1997, her simple coffin born through Calcutta's teeming streets in the same carriage that had carried Mahatma Gandhi to his funeral pyre. "Mother Teresa marked the history of our century, " Pope John XXIII stated while talk of her canonization circulated in the press. "She… served all human beings by promoting their dignity and respect, and made those who had been defeated by life feel the tenderness of God."

MOTHER TERESA

ON A HOT AND DUSTY train ride to Darjeeling on September 10, 1946, Sister Teresa, then thirty-six years old, received her second divine call. The message was clear and insistent: She was to leave the serene and cloistered life of St. Mary's School for Girls in Calcutta, where as a sister of the Loreto Convent she had taught history and geography to middle-class girls for seventeen years, and serve the poor instead. But she was not just to supply them with food and other necessities, as she and her community of Irish nuns had been routinely doing in the nearby slums of Moti Jheel; she was to actually live among them. "It was a greater sacrifice," Mother Teresa recounted in her authorized biography by Navin Chawla," than to leave my family and country to enter religious life."

The pious but pragmatic girl who was to become known as the "Saint of the Gutters" was born in Skopje, Yugoslavia (then the Kingdom of Albania), to Nicholas Bojaxhiu, a successful building contractor, and his Venetian wife, Dranafile Bernai Bojaxhiu. Because she was pink-cheeked and plump, Agnes—as she was baptized—was called "Gonxha," or flower bud in Albanian. Her youth was a "joyful" time, though her father's death when she was six brought great sorrow and—because of his business partner's misappropriation of assets—financial hardship as well. She was extremely close to her mother, an intensely spiritual woman who, though she barely made ends meet by selling embroidered cloth, never turned away the needy. Called "Nana Loke," or mother soul, by her three children, she personified the compassion and sharing that would mark her daughter's lifetime ministry of caring for the sick and starving. The two said good-bye on September 26, 1928, when the earnest eighteen-year-old started out from Zagreb for the Loreto Abbey in Ireland. They would never meet again.

To found her new mission, she needed to get permission from the Catholic hierarchy to leave the cloister, which after two years was granted. The day she bade farewell to her mother superior, there were three white cotton saris (the sari is the dress of India's poorest women) laid out for her; her spiritual advisor, Father Celeste van Exem, blessed them, as they were to become her new religious habit. In August of 1948, Sister Teresa accepted the supervision of the archbishop of Calcutta, and she became "Mother Teresa." That same year, after three months of intensive medical training from the American Medical Missionary Sisters in northern India, she opened her first school for slum children in Calcutta. She learned Bengali and Hindi herself and conducted class outdoors, on the barren earth, where she scratched out words in the dirt with a wooden stick. Within two years Mother Teresa's new order, the Missionaries of Charity—numbering only twelve women—became an official religious community within the Archdiocese of Calcutta.

Starting off with an ambitious project, in 1954 she established the Home for Dying Destitutes, located in a former temple dedicated to Kali, the Hindu goddess who is both the giver and destroyer of life. Nirmal Hrida—the place of the pure heart—was the first of the order's over one hundred official hospices, all of which address both the physical and emotional needs of the dying. As her humble community grew, its work expanded to include a leper colony; begun in a clearing under a tree, it presently serves fifteen thousand patients a year. Eventually, her "family," as she called her fellow workers, began to care for AIDS victims, battered women, prisoners on death row, the aged, the handicapped and cast-off children and orphans.

In 1979, along with the Nobel Peace Prize, Mother Teresa acquired the burden of celebrity. She accepted the award in the name of the poor, commenting with a hint of political sagacity that "Poverty and hunger and distress also constitute a threat to peace." With her driving energy, non-stop travel and tough management style, by the mid-nineties the tiny, wizened nun represented an empire of good works. It included over 286 houses for the needy, over 140 schools, and almost 840 mobile medical clinics serving more than five million people each year. Her Missionaries of Charity embraced some 4,000 nuns and one hundred twenty thousand coworkers and fanned out over 120 countries. Ascetic though she certainly was, Mother Teresa's piety was of a muscular sort, a resilient force which somehow suited the needy intensity of the times. Never asking of her fellow sisters what she did not demand of herself, she maintained a demanding regimen of sixteen-hour days that began at four a.m. She herself always slept on the floor.

Despite her service to society's forgotten, Mother Teresa was never entirely safe from criticism: In a country where the effects of overpopulation are shockingly obvious, she was uncompromising in her Catholic position against abortion and contraception, a stance which especially infuriated feminists. Others sneered at the fact that her ministrations addressed only the symptoms of poverty and illness without affecting the root causes. But real poverty, Mother Teresa always maintained, could be spiritual as well as material. In her oblique fashion, she once referred to it simply as "the absence of love."

She continued on following her first heart attack in 1989, but after two more in 1996, she was finally forced to take seriously the disagreeable idea of retirement.

She died soon after in 1997, her simple coffin born through Calcutta's teeming streets in the same carriage that had carried Mahatma Gandhi to his funeral pyre. "Mother Teresa marked the history of our century, " Pope John XXIII stated while talk of her canonization circulated in the press. "She... served all human beings by promoting their dignity and respect, and made those who had been defeated by life feel the tenderness of God."

THATCHER

MARGARET

THE FIRST WOMAN LEADER of a major industrial nation, she was dubbed Attila the Hen by men whose wills were not as strong as her own and whose ambitions not as keen. Soviet premier Mikhail Gorbachev hailed her as the "Iron Lady." And French president Francois Mitterrand sighed that she had "the lips of Marilyn Monroe, the eyes of Caligula." Bourgeois daughter of a dressmaker and a Grantham grocer with an interest in politics, Margaret Thatcher governed Great Britain for eleven tumultuous years, longer than any British prime minister in this century, wielding a mailed fist against her twin bugaboos, the welfare state and the upper-class incompetence she believed had turned Britain into a second-rate nation. A radical, if not a revolutionary, she ruled as a belli-cose Britannia, importing essentially American ideas of personal enterprise and responsibility into an English body politic that ultimately proved immune to them. In the process, she outfought and outthought every man who stood in her way.

"A populist politician who," according to the *Sunday Times,* "was never popular with the voters," Thatcher was an outsider. Not destined to be one of the club or part of the old-boy network, Margaret Hilda Roberts received a scholarship to Somerville College, Oxford, where she studied chemistry and cultivated an interest in politics. After graduation in 1947, she went to work as a research chemist, but in 1949 the local Tory party in Dartford, Kent, asked the twenty-four-year-old to run for Parliament. Defeated, she ran again and lost again the next year. These failures early in her political career galvanized her to greater effort. In 1950, she began to study law, and when in three years' time she was called to the bar, she had already made one of the most important decisions of her life—to marry businessman Denis Thatcher, whose loyal support and financial acumen freed his wife to pursue her ambitions. She practiced as a barrister for a few years, with a specialty in tax law, and in 1958 she ran as a conservative for Finchley, an upper-middle-class enclave north of London. This time she won.

In 1961, Thatcher was appointed parliamentary secretary to the ministry of pensions and national insurance. In 1964, as front-bench opposition spokesperson, she gave the Labour gov-ernment a regular taste of the rhetorical knout; three years later Prime Minister Heath made her shadow minister of power, then of education. Each post was a lesson in administration as well as in the subtleties of British politics, and Thatcher displayed a certain steeliness and a facility for generating controversy. Made secretary of state for education and science in 1970, and wish-ing to cut the budget in ways that would not affect education per se, she eliminated free milk for older primary school children, earning for herself the sobriquet "Thatcher the Milk Snatcher."

After Tory leader Edward Heath resigned as prime minister in 1974, Thatcher deposed him as party leader in 1975. Immediately, she undertook a total personal makeover—hair and dress, even diction, were whipped into the shape she felt necessary to run the nation, even though she was not yet in power. She showed the same ruthless efficiency in unhorsing Labour prime minister James Callaghan in 1979, engineering a no-confidence vote that precipitated an election campaign, during which Thatcher drummed the essence of Thatcherism—thrift, individual drive, self-reliance—into British ears weary of Labour's social democracy slogans. But Thatcher saved her real vitriol for the trade unions, at whose door she laid the blame for most, if not all, of the country's ills.

There followed the most dramatic class conflict modern Britain had seen. Under Thatcher, unemployment tripled and racial disturbances erupted in poor black neighborhoods. The prime minister's earliest innovations were in riot-control methods, while lectures on self-reliance to the unemployed (and perhaps unem-ployable) were her specialty. The howls her policies produced turned to cheers, though, when she successfully led Britain in a war with Argentina over the Falkland Islands. She was reelected in 1983, still loathed by the workers and the intelligentsia, still facing down the unions and chronic joblessness, and inaugurating an aggressive program to privatize moribund British industry.

In world affairs, Thatcher's shrewd assessment of Soviet leader Gorbachev as a man with whom Britain could do business made it easier for her American ally, President Ronald Reagan, to do so, and she trumpeted a message of free enterprise to a recep-tive Eastern bloc. Though she was developing a more positive global image—she was a staunch supporter of NATO—it was local politics that was her ultimate undoing. In 1988, she called for an across-the-board charge for local services, in place of a property tax. This notorious poll tax caused riots, and in 1990 Tory rebels, leery of defeat, launched a coup that saw Thatcher—who had axed many a minister—cast out of power by her own.

Thatcher's political choices had proved her undoing. Her quintessential conservatism had made it all too easy for her to turn her back on the poor, while leaving unscathed a fossilized class system that strangled personal initiative. As Life Peer Lady Thatcher, she became one of the titled cronies she detested, doomed to harangue nobles in the red-leathered comfort of the House of Lords. Finally, betrayed by her own party, battered by an electorate disenchanted with her policies, reproached even by the queen herself, Thatcher took reluctant leave of the world stage. Her brand of politics was shrewd and occasion-ally unabashed, but she never wavered in her belief that Britain's future would be great.

JIM THORPE

HE WAS THE CENTURY'S BEST all-around athlete: a football star of the first magnitude, a multitalented gold-medal track-and-field man, and an expert baseball player. Indeed, the Sac-and-Fox Indian from the plains of Oklahoma has no peer in the chronicles of sport. Yet for all his accomplishments, Jim Thorpe is most readily remembered for a humiliation: the day the International Olympic Committee coldly stripped him of his medals. If the experience taught Thorpe that while life was not a game, the politics of gamesmanship could be, he gave no sign. He continued playing for thirty more years before his slow, painful slide to oblivion.

Thorpe was born in what was then the Oklahoma Territory to a part-Indian, part-French mother and a part-Indian, part-Irish father. He later described himself as "an American Airedale." His Indian name was Wa-Tho-Huck ("Bright Path"), perhaps a harbinger of the swath he would later cut through opposing lines on the football field. As a boy, Thorpe ran like a deer and grew strong by wrangling horses. By 1904, he was a sinewy sixteen-year-old ready for Pennsylvania's Carlisle Indian Industrial School, an institution that was part high school, part trade school, with an assimilationist curriculum designed to extract the Indian from American Indians. Thorpe had a difficult time adjusting to his new surroundings and to the regimentation he found at the school. The young athlete may have lacked discipline, but he excelled at physical activity. He casually beat the school's best high jumper while wearing boots and overalls and refused to be tackled during football practice, knocking opponents right and left. Thorpe also often acted as Carlisle's entire track squad: Against Lafayette College's forty-seven-man team, he won eight first places. It was as a football player, however, that Thorpe really shone. He ran like a rocket, could both pass and catch, and could dropkick and punt a football well over sixty yards. In a 1911 contest against the great Harvard team, Carlisle relied on Thorpe to score all the points and win the game. He was named an All-American that year.

It was inevitable that such a prodigy would be part of the 1912 U.S. Olympic team training for the Stockholm games. In that competition, Thorpe captured the gold in both the decathlon and the pentathlon, inspiring the King of Sweden to remark, while conferring the medal upon him,: "You, sir, are the greatest athlete in the world."

But two years later, when the self-righteous patricians of the International Olympic Committee (IOC) learned that Thorpe, as a college student, had played semipro baseball during summers off from school, they stripped the young man of his victories on the spurious grounds that this activity violated the Olympic rule that only amateurs could compete. Thorpe was hardly a professional, and baseball was clearly not an Olympic event, yet this injustice was maintained for decades—notably by Avery Brundage, chairman of the IOC and, not incidentally, a runner Thorpe had left in the dust at Stockholm. Both second-place winners at Stockholm refused to accept Thorpe's awards; it was not until 1982 that a chastised IOC posthumously returned Thorpe's gold medals to him.

Hiding his bitterness, Thorpe began playing professional football with the Canton Bulldogs in 1915. Five years later, when the Bulldogs became a charter member of the new National Football League, Thorpe was made league president, his name lending luster to the nascent circuit. As a quadruple-threat superstar, he was unconcerned about the opposing team. Some critics charged that Thorpe, a moody man, could be lazy and indifferent in a game, but he also possessed a sharp sense of showmanship. When rookie lineman Knute Rockne, fresh out of Notre Dame, once tackled him too savagely, Thorpe chided, "Let the old Indian run, Rock—that's what the people paid to see." Rockne ignored this advice and hit Thorpe again on the next play. On the third try, Thorpe blasted Rockne so hard he knocked him out, then danced to a touchdown. As Rockne came to, he heard Thorpe's gentle voice say, "That's a good boy, Rock. You let old Jim run."

When Thorpe wasn't battering Bears, he batted baseballs for the New York Giants, the Cincinnati Reds, and the Boston Braves, in a career that lasted from 1913 to 1919. His lifetime batting average of .252 might have been even more impressive if he had decided to focus on baseball exclusively. As a natural athlete, Thorpe was not much given to practice. His tendency was to put out just enough effort to win, not always pushing himself to his greatest capacity, and he was often accused of not trying very hard. One can only imagine what he would have accomplished with proper training and motivation. As Thorpe grew older, his frequent recourse to the bottle might have slowed him down a bit, but it certainly didn't cut short his career. He played for four minor-league teams from 1920 until 1925, then made a comeback in 1929 with the Chicago Cardinals when he was forty-one years old. From 1933 to 1937, Thorpe resided in Hollywood, taking bit parts in B pictures and eventually trying his hand at careers as diverse as lecturer, Indian dance master, night watchman, and ditch digger. His great heart gave out in 1953, but by then he had fully demonstrated that a human being could achieve greatness just by having fun.

TOKYO ROSE

IN TRUTH, SHE NEVER existed: That insinuating feline voice that mocked and sweet-talked American GI's in hundreds of World War II radio broadcasts throughout the Pacific theater belonged not to one woman but to as many as fourteen. The name "Tokyo Rose," coined by perversely amused Yanks to refer to their invisible siren, was never uttered over Japanese radio at any time during the great conflict. But some of what "she" said would have been considered treason if spoken by any single American. In the fullness of the United States' postwar wrath, one lone Japanese-American was charged with treasonous broadcasting and thereby betraying her country. She was Iva Ikuko Toguri d'Aquino, a second-generation *nisei* stranded in wartime Japan, who had been dragooned into serving on Radio Tokyo, an act that branded her in history as Tokyo Rose.

The deep-voiced d'Aquino was quintessentially American. Born Iva Toguri on the Fourth of July in Los Angeles to hardworking and patriotic shopkeepers, she loved Jimmy Stewart and attended U.C.L.A., where she studied zoology and cheered for the football team. She spoke no foreign language, let alone Japanese, and in 1940, when she was old enough to vote, she registered Republican. This peaceful middle-class existence would be shattered when Japan and the United States went to war.

Toguri's father, doubting there would be war, asked his duty-bound daughter to travel to Japan to care for a sick relative. Reluctantly, she sailed from Los Angeles for Yokohama on July 1, 1941. Toguri found the language incomprehensible, the customs strange, and the food all but inedible. Miserable, lonely, and out of place, the young American longed for the day she could return home. Then came Pearl Harbor. Because of passport problems and the tangles of Japanese red tape, the last boat to America sailed without her. As a belligerent American national, Toguri was placed under surveillance by secret police, who urged her to renounce her American citizenship. She refused repeatedly throughout the war. She even demanded that she be interned as a hostile alien, but the Japanese scornfully declined. Unable to draw rations without government assent, d'Aquino lived under terrible psychological pressure. Desperate for work, she answered an advertisement offering part-time work for an English typist at Radio Tokyo. Here the story splits into intriguing and contradictory versions.

One version claims that Toguri was recruited for Radio Tokyo by a mysterious American POW—arguably a traitor himself. Another version has it that Toguri was assured by an Australian POW that the broadcasts she would be making were "straight entertainment" for American troops, a claim the naïve Toguri may actually have accepted at face value.

A third story is that the Japanese pressed her into service under threat of punishment. Whatever her motivation, she began broadcasting in 1943.

As her defense later pointed out, not one American monitoring or recording of the thousands of Japanese broadcasts during the war yielded a shred of evidence that Toguri herself had said anything remotely treasonous. While she did broadcast to U.S. troops from an enemy station whose larger purpose was to demoralize them, testimony at her trial established that Toguri had not written her own material, and witnesses deposed that she had smuggled medicines and food to Allied prisoners whenever she could.

Her behavior after the American invasion in 1945 was more ambiguous, though. When reporter Harry T. Brundidge used his prewar press contacts in Tokyo to arrange a meeting with her, d'Aquino—who had acquired her new surname after a wartime marriage to Portuguese national Felippe d'Aquino—swore that she was "the one and only Tokyo Rose," though she knew that was far from true. For a huge fee, she had sold Brundidge her exclusive story, a "confession" that he and a colleague memorialized in seventeen crucial pages of notes. The deal and the story fell through when *Cosmopolitan* refused to glorify a "traitor." Intelligence agents then arrested her but ultimately released her for lack of evidence.

Her status remained in limbo until the hotly contested election of 1948, when, stung by Republican gibes that he was soft on treason, President Harry S. Truman called upon Attorney General Tom Clark to prosecute d'Aquino. Her San Francisco trial was not a high-water mark in American jurisprudence. The prosecutors, aware that their case was a tissue of innuendo, proceeded only when ordered to do so, and the government, while flying prosecution witnesses to San Francisco from Japan in the most expensive federal trial up to this time, refused to do the same for witnesses who could have exonerated d'Aquino. The only count on which she was ultimately convicted—an alleged reference to a loss of American ships—was unsupported by any recording or witness who might have identified her as the speaker. Faced with so little evidence, the jury returned a conviction only when the judge virtually directed them to do so.

D'Aquino was sentenced to ten years in prison and a ten-thousand-dollar fine. After her early release in 1956, the United States attempted to deport her until it was pointed out that one could not be both a traitor and an undesirable alien. She retired to a quiet life in Chicago as a clerk in her father's shop. In 1976, perhaps in belated recognition of a grievous miscarriage of justice, President Gerald Ford granted "Tokyo Rose" a full pardon.

TOSCANINI

ARTURO

THE GREATEST AND MOST influential conductor of the first part of the twentieth century was a man who rejected the idea of the primacy of the conductor's interpretation. The music, Arturo Toscanini believed, rightly belonged to the composers; his own job was merely to do as they bade him. Yet he was renowned for his dramatic intensity, the absolute control he exerted over his orchestras, and his ability to inspire his musicians to strive for perfection. His readings of great classical scores set a standard for conducting, and were a marked contrast to the self-indulgence of Romantic-era conductors, who often departed altogether from a composer's written directions.

Born in Parma to a humble tailor who had fought with Garibaldi's revolutionary Redshirts, Toscanini showed an early interest in clothes design. But at the age of nine he entered the Parma Conservatory, graduating in 1885 with highest honors in cello and composition. He learned the Italian opera repertoire by heart, an achievement that served him well the following year when, as a young cellist on tour in Brazil, he was called in at the last moment to fill in as conductor. The audience jeered when Toscanini leapt to the podium, but his passionate yet disciplined interpretation of *Aida* so stirred them that few noticed that the pages of the conductor's score had never been turned. The electrifying performance assured his engagement for the balance of the season. Toscanini's astonishing gift of recall was a great boon in his later years, when failing eyesight made it necessary for him to conduct from memory.

His growing reputation led him to works with provincial opera companies in Italy. As a cellist, he met Verdi at the rehearsals for the 1887 world premiere of *Otello*, but the two men did not really come to know each other until 1896. In 1892 Toscanini, now a champion of the new operatic composers, conducted the world premiere of Leoncavallo's *I pagliacci* and, in 1896, the premiere of Puccini's *La bohème*. But his greatest admiration was reserved not for one of his countrymen but for Wagner, whom he called "the greatest composer of the [nineteenth] century."

In 1897 Toscanini married Carla de Martini, the daughter of a Milanese stockbroker. The couple had three children, euphonically named Walter, Wally, and Wanda; Wanda would later marry the great Russian pianist Vladimir Horowitz. In 1898 Toscanini was appointed chief conductor and artistic director of Milan's celebrated La Scala opera house, where he opened his first season with the Italian premiere of Wagner's *Die Meistersinger von Nürnberg*. He filled this position for five years but, ever rigorous, resigned in 1903 rather than allow an encore—a practice he deplored as much as the curious nineteenth-century tradition of including a ballet within an opera. After five years of touring in Europe and South America, Toscanini came to New York's Metropolitan Opera in 1908, where he demanded and won extra rehearsal time and imposed strict discipline on the orchestra.

The maestro's tantrums in rehearsal became the stuff of legend: He once summed up an orchestra's effort with a single word: "Assassins!" Yet he was also capable of great subtlety. At a loss to describe the gossamer effect he required in one passage (his English was poor), he drew a white silk handkerchief from his pocket and cast it into the air, watching with the orchestra as it floated dreamily to the floor. "There!" he said. "Play like that!" If working with Toscanini was tempestuous, Toscanini's musicians understood that he drove himself as hard as he did them. "I give blood—you must give blood, too!" he would exhort them as they labored over Brahms or Verdi. If the orchestra met Toscanini's demands, he would weep for joy. Once, when Toscanini himself made a rare mistake, he slapped his own face in front of the orchestra to show he would not spare even himself from punishment.

During World War I he forswore his own career to organize a military band that played at the Italian front during the assault of Monte Santo; later he conducted benefits for war victims. In the post–World War I era, he was initially attracted to the protofascist ideas of Benito Mussolini, but later was vociferously and consistently anti-fascist. In 1931 Toscanini was physically attacked in Bologna for refusing to play the fascist anthem and to protest Hitler's ban on Jewish musicians, he ended his long association with the prestigious Bayreuth and Salzburg festivals.

In 1937 the pioneering radio broadcaster David Sarnoff asked Toscanini, who had become head of the New York Philharmonic in 1928, to lead the NBC Symphony, a task he fulfilled happily for the next seventeen years. Later, his brilliant white hair, delicate, soulful features, and trim mustache became a familiar sight to the millions of Americans who learned about classical music under his precise and lively baton through the medium of television. At his last concert for NBC, on April 4, 1954, the eighty-seven-year-old maestro dropped his baton on the final chord of the *Die Meistersinger* prelude and strode from the podium into history, joining the company of the great composers whose works he had brought to life.

HARRY S. TRUMAN

IT FELL TO HARRY S. TRUMAN, America's thirty-third president, to make decisions which would shape decades of world politics. Feisty and scrupulous, "Give 'Em Hell Harry" thought with dispatch and acted with surety. Chosen as the seriously ailing Franklin D. Roosevelt's running mate in 1944, Truman would, after Roosevelt's death less than a year later, preside over the end of the Second World War and its political aftermath. A participant in the Potsdam Conference which dealt with postwar Germany and Europe, Truman also authorized the bombings of Hiroshima and Nagazaki to end the war on the Pacific front. While he personally confided to his diary on July 25 that "we have discovered the most terrible bomb in the history of the world," his judgment as president was to use it to save American and Japanese lives alike. In the postwar world, Truman saw nothing less than the survival of Western democracy at stake; he countered Soviet expansionism with his own policy of containment, thus playing a substantial role in dividing the world into two ideological and armed camps, and setting the stage for four decades of cold war. But if, as some critics have charged, a more conciliatory leader better educated in foreign policy might have averted the stand-off, it is still fair to say that Harry Truman, who found himself at a crossroads of history, chose with what he felt were his country's best interests in mind.

Truman came from a rural midwestern background. Born May 8, 1884, in Lamar, Missouri, the eldest of three children, Truman claimed to have had "the happiest childhood imaginable." But after the family moved to Independence, Missouri in 1889, his father's get-rich-quick schemes undermined the family's financial security. A studious boy who played the piano, Harry was unable to afford to go to college, while his poor eyesight kept him out of West Point. His father ordered him to help manage his maternal grandmother's farm, a job he performed for the next eleven years, gaining confidence in the process. Service during World War I as a captain in the 129th Field Artillery further fostered his confidence in his leadership abilities. Home from the war, he married Beth Wallace, whom he had been courting for almost a decade, against the wishes of her mother who disapproved of Truman's low social standing.

After the failure of his retail clothing business, Truman was recruited into politics by Kansas City political boss T.J. Pendergast. With the backing of the corrupt Pendergast, he was elected county judge in 1922. The well-oiled machine pushed him all the way to the Senate in 1934, where his relations with the Roosevelt administration remained cool because of Truman's unsavory connections to the political boss. In 1940, after Pendergast was convicted of tax evasion and his political machine dismantled, Truman won a hard-fought re-election campaign. Chairman of a Senate committee on war-time expenditures, Truman's tough-minded investigation of inefficiency and abuse gained him national prominence.

In the summer of 1944, when President Roosevelt's advisors became aware that their leader was dying, Truman was chosen as FDR's vice-presidential running mate. Acceptable to the New dealers, labor, and the more conservative Democrats, Truman initially did not want the job, saying," It is a very high office which consists entirely of honor, and I don't have any ambition to hold an office like that." Eventually he relented.

Truman succeeded to the nation's highest office without Roosevelt's ever having briefed him on background, plans, or even the process of the highest-level of decision-making. As a result, he found himself uninformed, unprepared, and frightened: he had no background or experience in foreign policy, no trusted advisors to call upon. He had no first-hand knowledge of the two leaders, Stalin and Churchill, with whom he would negotiate the settlement of war. He was at clear disadvantage too for having succeeded to the office after twelve years of the formidable Roosevelt. Important decisions faced him immediately: choices about German's unconditional surrender, the fate of Europe, an increasingly recalcitrant Soviet Union, and the hastening of Japan's defeat. To almost everyone's surprise except perhaps his own, Truman responded to the challenge with determination.

In the presidential election of 1948, Truman—now very much his own man—whistle-stopped his way across America, pulling off the most astounding upset in the national's electoral history, defeating Thomas Dewey by a tiny margin. Domestically, Truman strove to extend FDR's New Deal through his own Fair Deal, but was blocked by a largely Republican Congress; it is mainly as a foreign affairs president that he is remembered. To contain Soviet ambition, he articulated the multifaceted Truman Doctrine, beginning in 1947 with his plea to Congress for a $400 million aid package for Greece and Turkey to use against communist-led guerillas. The doctrine was further implemented by the creation of NATO; the launch of the Marshall Plan, which insured economic recovery for Western Europe; and the commitment of American troops in Korea, climaxed by his famous dismissal of General Douglas MacArthur. In 1952, he declined to run for the presidency again.

This famously plain-speaking American found himself in charge at a moment in history which would prove pivotal to the century and to the future of the world. While, in the five decades since the Second World War ended, the debate has continued over the morality of the use of atomic weaponry and Truman's handling of what he perceived as the Soviet threat, America's thirty-third president still holds a special place in the nation's heart, as a man who took charge, who could come from behind and tell his detractors, "If you can't stand the heat, get out of the kitchen."

TED TURNER

TWO TED TURNERS EMERGE in tracing the personal history of the man whose singular vision helped create what Marshall McLuhan once termed "the global village." First there is the "Captain Outrageous" Turner, the young tycoon who, at the age of twenty-four, rescued his family's failing billboard advertising firm, gambled its revenues to create the first cable TV superstation and, later, the first twenty-four-hour worldwide TV news service, Cable News Network. Universally respected as the world's most widely watched—and heeded—news channel, CNN transformed reporting into a watch-it-as-it-happens phenomenon that shaped world events and opinion even as it recorded them.

Along the way, the ruggedly handsome Turner acquired two sports franchises, baseball's Atlanta Braves and basketball's Hawks, and a reputation for antics both on and off the field. At the Brave's home games, "The Mouth of the South" would perch in his favorite seat behind the dugout, jumping into the stands to catch a foul ball or to provide occasional commentary for the fans over his personal public address system. The competitive outdoorsman took up sailing, winning more ocean races than anyone else in the history of the sport, and captured the America's Cup in 1977.

Turner inherited his drive and ambition from a hard-boiled alcoholic father, an angry and volatile man who was a salesman in Cincinnati, Ohio and was a millionaire by the time Robert Edward Turner III was born. Ed Turner was particularly hard on his son; by turns, his father was withdrawn, generous and filled with rages, beating his son to keep him in line. "Terrible Ted," as he became known at the McCallie military school in Chattanooga, set his sights on the U.S. Naval Academy, but his father forced him to study business at Brown University instead. When Ted was suspended for entertaining women in his dorm room, his father stepped in again and sent him off on a tour of duty with the Coast Guard. When Ted Turner joined the family business and his father decided to sell it, the hostility between them was open. When his father shot himself in 1963, Ted Turner was both devastated and determined.

Using clever fiscal maneuvering, Ted quickly put an end to the sale of Turner Advertising and began to rebuild his patrimony. In 1970, he bought Channel 17, a failing Atlanta television station that he soon built into Turner Communications Group's flagship station, WTCG, which he hoped to turn into a fourth network. In 1980, in the face

of amused heckling among his peers, Turner launched CNN. A few years later, with audiences all over the world watching rockets flash over Beirut and the Berlin wall come down, it would become clear that news, reporting, and television had been transformed. Turner purchased MGM's invaluable hoard of films in a one-and-a-half-billion-dollar deal, horrifying critics by colorizing many of the studio's black-and-white classics, and then launched the spectacularly successful TNT channel.

Over time, a mature and mellow Turner—the second Turner—became known as a committed reformer and philanthropist. Overcoming his severe bouts of depression, he turned his energies to political and social issues. A leader in telecommunications, he had both the means and opportunity to educate the world about overpopulation, racism, arms proliferation, hunger, pollution, and environmental catastrophe. In 1991, he married actress and fitness advocate Jane Fonda, a long-time and dedicated activist.

The older Turner retained some of yesterday's Ted. Still charming, sometimes tenacious and focused, his passion for his social causes had the same intensity as his youthful dedication to sailing. His love of the outdoors continued; Turner took pleasure in his vast ranch out west and concentrated on raising buffalo. He has continued to use CNN and his media outlets as a means of cultivating interest in his favorite crusades.

In 1996 he found himself forced by increasing competition to make a dramatic move. His response was a $7.5 billion merger with Time-Warner, a union which netted Turner $2.3 billion, but "demoted" him to No.2 under Time-Warner's Gerald Levin. Now he was not only not his own man, but his "owners" were cooperating in numerous ventures with his former rivals, most notably, Rupert Murdoch, the Australian-born owner of News Corp. Within the new structure, Turner's vision continues. CNN continues to expand into new markets. Original movies developed for the cable network have made Turner a familiar and formidable presence in Hollywood. And Turner's personal comitment to social change has grown as well.

In 1997, Turner announced that he would give $1 billion over the next ten years to the United Nations for its social programs, giving him yet another way of shaping the world. Asked by *The New York Times* why he gave to charity, the pragmatic progressive likened the process to an acquired skill: "I've been learning how to give."

VALENTINO

RUDOLPH

THE RAGS-TO-ROMANCE STORY of the cinema's greatest lover is equal to any melodrama Hollywood could create. Born Rodolpho Alfonzo Raffaelo Pierre Filibert Guglielmi di Valentina d'Antonguolla in Castellaneta, Italy, at the turn of the century, Rudolph Valentino began his life in trouble, lived it in sensationalism, and ended it in loneliness—but not before he had titillated the fantasies of millions of women all over the world.

He was a part-time taxi dancer when, in 1921, he was cast in the screen extravaganza *The Four Horsemen of the Apocalypse*. Appearing in just a few scenes as an Argentinian gaucho who radiates melancholy and forbidden lust, Valentino tangoed his way, literally, into the big time. The impact was instantaneous. There, up on the silent screen, was a square-jawed northern European leading man whose amorous intent could not be appeased with an innocent peck on the cheek. Clearly, Valentino's agenda was something else entirely. Despite such exotic affectations as jeweled turbans and oversized rings—or perhaps because of them—he made women swoon. It was almost entirely to women, in fact, that this smoldering new screen hero belonged. Men, in stark contrast, not only failed to identify with the "Latin Lover" but felt overtly threatened by him, often reacting with derision.

Valentino's youth was tinged with petty criminality. Even as a child, his wild escapades often kept him locked out of his own home. Later, after he was denied entrance to a naval academy, Valentino moved to Paris and found himself begging on the streets. A series of run-ins with the law followed his arrival in America at age eighteen. Well built and graceful, the darkly attractive young immigrant found work as a gardener's assistant, then turned to a career in dancing. Working first as a smooth-mannered gigolo in Broadway's dime-a-dance ballrooms, he soon graduated to exhibition dancing in New York cabarets—such as the famous Maxim's—where he performed the maxixe, the hesitation, and the Castle walk with a variety of partners. After his arrival in Hollywood in 1917 and a flurry of forgettable roles, his parts—if not his finances—gradually improved. To keep his spirits up and his rakish image intact, he would occasionally help out at a garage on Sunset Boulevard so that he could be seen cruising by local hangouts in a luxury car.

Valentino's disreputable past was soon swept under a deluge of press releases publicizing *The Four Horsemen*. The film was a huge success, grossing a staggering four and a half million dollars and forcing the studio to recall and alter the prints so that Valentino could be given star billing. After his requests for an increase in salary went unmet at Metro, the new star moved to the Famous Players–Lasky Company (later

Paramount), where he cemented his reputation as a suavely dangerous new leading man with *The Sheik* (1921). Instantly, sheik mania swept America and, much to the distress of his fans, one Natasha Rambova swept into Valentino's life. Their marriage would sabotage his career.

A former ballerina and cinematic art director, Rambova had well-defined aesthetic tastes and sought to use Valentino to develop them. Uncharacteristically—at least based on his screen roles—he gave in to his new wife on everything. Under her influence, he demanded a higher salary and a better choice of scripts, and he transformed his image in a way that confounded his normally adoring audiences. His screen persona, as in *Monsieur Beaucaire* (1924), became increasingly effeminate, as did his publicity shots, one of which featured him in 1925's *The Young Rajah* as an almost naked princeling clothed only in a headdress, loincloth, and strategically swagged strands of pearls. Rambova's interference in Valentino's day-to-day work became so disruptive that his contracts were altered to stipulate that she be barred from his sets. Eventually, the marriage ended, enabling Valentino to resurrect his failing career.

Weathering arrest on bigamy charges—he married the second Mrs. Valentino before his marriage to the first was officially dissolved—the dashing matinee idol went on to make *The Eagle* (1925) and *The Son of the Sheik* (1926). Proud and ambitious, the actor, who had always studied and emulated the lifestyles of the wealthy, became a collector of rare books, a talented linguist, and an accomplished horseman. But any pleasure he took in his recycled success was offset by press attacks on his manhood. One slanderous editorial in the *Chicago Tribune* called him a "painted pansy" and bemoaned his negative impact on American manliness. An outraged Valentino challenged the columnist to a duel.

When Valentino died suddenly of a perforated ulcer on August 23, 1926, women all over America mourned, and thousands streamed into the streets for his funeral. A worldwide cult was immediately born, with the so-called "Lady in Black" its acknowledged queen. For years this mysterious mourner brought roses to Valentino's grave on the anniversary of his death. In the 1950s she revealed both her identity (she was a musician named Ditra Flame) and the mutual vow she had made with the star, who had once visited her in the hospital when, at fourteen, she lay gravely ill. Valentino had assured Flame that should she die, he would place roses on her grave every day. If, on the other hand, he should die first, all the screen idol requested was that she remember that loneliness had been his own fear as well.

VON BRAUN

WERNHER

DEDICATED SCIENTIST, VISIONARY THEORETICIAN, and organizational wunderkind, Wernher von Braun was largely responsible for one of the twentieth century's defining moments: the landing of man on the moon. As the person behind the creation of the V-2 rockets that rained destruction on London and various other English cities during World War II, this most vocal of space enthusiasts has also been branded by his detractors as a whitewashed war criminal turned U.S. patriot and, as such, one of the most ethically suspect individuals ever elevated to high profile in American government.

In 1945, the United States recruited von Braun, a former Nazi party member and technical director of Germany's enormous rocket weapons program, along with hundreds of other top-notch German scientists as part of a top-secret operation to work on classified military projects. This questionable enterprise, unknown to most Americans until several decades later, paid off handsomely. On February 1, 1958, at 10:48 A.M., von Braun's army-sponsored team (which included most of the key experts who had been with him at Peenemünde, the German rocket facility on the Baltic coast) launched *Explorer I*. The 30.8-pound satellite, which achieved lift-off from Cape Canaverel, Florida thanks to a Jupiter-C rocket, enabled a temporarily stunned United States to recover from two humiliations: the Russians' launch of the world's first orbiting satellites, *Sputnik* I and II (the latter carrying a dog on board), in October and November 1957; and the explosion on the launch pad of the U.S. Navy's much-ballyhooed *Vanguard* rocket in December of the previous year.

The success of *Explorer I* was quickly followed up by two other triumphs in von Braun's master plan to "explore the mysterious universe." Three years later, America's first astronaut rocketed into space, and eight years after that, on July 20, 1969, *Apollo 11* carried three astronauts to the moon. One of them, pilot Neil A. Armstrong, was the first human to set foot on the lunar surface, taking, as he told millions of awed television viewers back on earth, "one small step for [a] man, one giant leap for mankind."

Growing up in Wirsitz, Germany, von Braun had dreamed at an early age of making that very leap. The second of three sons born to Baron Magnus von Braun, a member of the Weimar Republic cabinet, young Wernher was encouraged in his interest in astronomy by his amateur astronomer mother, Baroness Emmy von Quistorp. After his family moved to Berlin, the eight-year-old discovered the ballistic propulsion authority Hermann Oberth's mathematically complex book, *The Rocket into Interplanetary Space,* and made a rocket-powered wagon three years later. By then, the engineering prodigy was a student at the Berlin Institute of Technology, where he joined a small club of space enthusiasts who experimented with dangerous missile

launchings at an abandoned munitions dump in the Berlin suburbs. In 1932, the tall, broad-shouldered, and strikingly handsome young pioneer was discovered by Captain Walter Dornberger, a German army physicist who was searching for a long-range weapon not proscribed by the Versailles Treaty of 1919, which had severely limited Germany's military capacity. Impressed by von Braun's theoretical grasp of supersonic aerodynamics, Dornberger arranged for the doctoral student to head up the development of liquid-fuel rockets in Kummersdorf.

In 1936, von Braun, just twenty-four, became civilian technical director of the huge rocket research station at the dreary outpost of Peenemünde, where he produced the infamous V-2, which stood for "Vengeance Weapon Two." Almost driven to the point of resigning by short production schedules, he was briefly imprisoned in 1944 by the head of the Gestapo, Heinrich Himmler, because he refused to cede his program to SS control, as Himmler demanded. Dornberger intervened, convincing Hitler that the V-2 program would flounder without von Braun at the helm. Released by the Führer himself, he returned to Peenemünde and to the forging of a strategy that would place Germany at the vanguard of missile technology. At the time of von Braun's surrender to American troops in Austria on May 2, 1945—after an escape with Dornberger and others by rocket-fueled trucks that drove them into the Bavarian mountains—his team had begun speculating about work on a projectile that could target New York City.

Almost immediately, von Braun's group of crack German scientists was placed under contract to the U.S. Army in New Mexico. Prompted by the Korean War, the army sent von Braun and his crew to the Redstone Arsenal in Huntsville, Alabama, to construct an intercontinental guided missile with nuclear capability. Eventually becoming an American citizen and head of NASA's George C. Marshall Space Flight Center, America's top rocket scientist broadened his scope to include promotion of its infant space program. When the *Saturn 5* hurtled the Apollo craft to the moon, von Braun would finally realize his daring childhood imaginings.

The question of von Braun's Nazi past remains troubling. Donning the cloak of pure science, he calmly and assuredly justified his position in 1971 by proclaiming that it is not the discoverer of the invention whose hands are clean or dirty but the "sponsor" who actually controls its use. Yet he is on record as saying he was sorry for the blitz of V-2s that reduced much of London to rubble and killed thousands of British citizens. Like many of his fellow scientists, von Braun was a strong believer in God, insisting that any real scientist must eventually come to religion. When asked, however, in a 1951 *New Yorker* article, if he went to church at Peenemünde, he responded that, after a war begins, "it's really too late to go."

DIANA VREELAND

HER FRIENDS WERE THE "beautiful people"—a phrase she coined—and her world the glossy dreamscapes of fashion magazines. Into this ephemeral but highly competitive domain, Diana Vreeland interjected originality and elitism that brooked no mediocrity. "My dear," the ever quotable arbiter of modern style once told an assistant, "you must never fear being vulgar—just boring, middle-class, or dull." Having been spoiled in the European beau monde tradition, Vreeland was unabashed in her embrace of snobbery and of the kind of elegant flair attainable by either the impossibly rich or the very clever. And she had the eye—the uncompromising, idiosyncratic Vreeland eye—which could spot a major fashion message on the street as well as on any runway. In fact, "Dynamite D." was the first to acknowledge the importance of antifashion trends, featuring unconventional celebrities like Cher, Andy Warhol, and Mick Jagger in her layouts. She, of course, was touted for having created a few trends of her own, first at *Harper's Bazaar* and later at *Vogue*. The sixties look, with its boots and miniskirts, was her creation, as was the word *youthquake* to describe the impact of that generation. Trench coats, pants for women, and costume jewelry were also Vreeland favorites, along with transparent tops, outlandish wigs, and faux fabrics. Not beautiful herself, she discovered and molded many women who were, among them Penelope Tree, Twiggy, and the enduring Lauren Hutton. The photographers she chose to shoot them—talents like Richard Avedon, Irving Penn, and Cecil Beaton—also became stars.

The eldest of two daughters of Frederick Young Dalziel, a well-to-do stockbroker from Scotland, and his attractive American socialite wife Emily Hoffman Dalziel, Diana spent her childhood in a rarefied cultural milieu in Paris. She watched Vernon and Irene Castle dance the Castle walk in her own home, which exhibited a luxury that was not reflected by her parents' bank account. She met Sergey Diaghilev, Nijinsky, Isadora Duncan, and other greats of the dance world, and when in 1914 the family left their champagne-and-chauffeur life for a slightly more austere existence in New York, these memorable characters were succeeded by others, chief among them Michel Fokine, with whom she studied ballet, and "Buffalo" Bill Cody, with whom she backpacked in Wyoming. Her formal education was spotty during these years, and Vreeland was taken up largely with amusement and fluff. This included clothes, of course, from the great couture houses like Balenciaga and Dior. When she met Thomas Reed Vreeland, an exquisitely dressed gentleman straight from the Yale quad, she fell head over heels. Two sons later, the Vreelands were living it up in London, while Diana studied chorus dancing and went museum hopping.

When her husband was transferred to New York in 1936, where the cost of one's daily Dom Perignon was considerably higher than in London, Vreeland found it necessary to supplement his income. Providence soon provided the perfect position for this woman who claimed never to have been in an office. Spotted dancing at the St. Regis by *Harper's Bazaar* editor Carmel Snow, Vreeland landed a job in the magazine's fashion department, where her twenty-eight-year tenure as fashion editor redefined what it meant to be smartly dressed. Her career of oracular pronouncements for the à la modish began with her outrageous and quasi-facetious column, "Why don't you," which, while people cued up in Depression breadlines, advised readers to turn their old ermine coats into bathrobes. The sheer outrageousness of it all secured her status as an eccentric to be reckoned with. But while her influence continued to grow, her salary did not. From 1937 to 1962 her annual pay remained at exactly twenty thousand dollars—nowhere near supporting her extravagant "necessities," such as fresh flowers everywhere and crepe de chine bedsheets pressed daily by her maid.

In 1962 Vreeland left *Harper's* for its archrival, *Vogue*, and within a year she was Editor in Chief. She chucked the magazine's stuffy image, opting instead for visual flash and verbal flourish. Moving grandly at night between New York's Studio One crowd and the ritzier jet set, she was plugged into all the splintered-off Zeitgeists of the sixties and seventies, and her eclectic, breathtaking pages showed it. "Laying out a beautiful picture in a beautiful way is a bloody bore," she maintained. "You've got to make something of it."

Aside from her influence on *Vogue*, Vreeland's creative statements were herself and her interior decorating, especially her famous "red-red-red" living room. The embodiment of her own perfectionism, in person she was stunning to behold. With her ebony hair slicked back from a face that resembled a primitive Mayan sculpture, she would simply sweep into a room, projecting her aura of energetic authority.

After being fired from *Vogue* in 1971, Vreeland was not interested in fading into retirement. She found her perfect professional adieu at the Metropolitan Museum of Art, where, as special consultant to its Costume Institute, she staged lavish and critically acclaimed exhibitions. Her often impossible demands there and her high-handed treatment of her staff sometimes made the going rough, but Vreeland's modus operandi had always been more thunder than sunshine.

On her death, more than one writer contemplated what a woman of her considerable talents might have accomplished had she pursued a different career. Vreeland—who always said she was seeking "the suggestion of something I've never seen"—had no regrets about her occupation, however. What was really important to her was delighting the eye with "a certain amount of splendor" and making sure that "a great, great prettiness" went on.

LECH

WALESA

THE CROWNING IRONY OF the collapse of Communism in Poland was that it was brought about by a worker. All the security apparatus of the state—the soldiers, the secret police, the informers, the party functionaries—was, in the end, helpless before an electrician from the shipyards. Lech Walesa, who began adulthood as a common laborer, spent a great deal of it in struggle against the ruling Polish Communist Party; victorious, he then rose to the presidency of a new Poland. In his fight and in his triumph he gave hope not just to just his countrymen, but to democrats everywhere.

Walesa was born in the village of Popowo to a carpenter and contractor who, around the time of his son's birth, was arrested and imprisoned by the occupying Nazis. Though he was released after the war, his health was broken and he died less than two years after his return. Walesa's mother then married her dead husband's brother, an act which lead to friction between the four children and the older Walesas.

As a teenager, Lech was a good student at the region's vocational school, but he was marked down as a "troublemaker." Graduating from the school's agricultural mechanization division in 1961, he worked for two years as a technician for the state. Drafted, he spent an equal length of time in the army, emerging as a corporal. In 1967, after several years as a provincial state technician, he decided to try city life and left for the Baltic Coast. Abandoning his original goal of the port town of Gdynia, he settled in Gdansk, home of the enormous Lenin Shipyard and its thousands of employees. There Walesa found a position as a naval electrician.

In 1968, Polish students and workers protested across the country for greater freedom. For the students, it was a matter of intellectual liberty. For the workers, it was question of equality—their working conditions, food, and pay were equally ghastly, and they wanted redress. The government attempted to pit students against workers and vice-versa in a policy of *divisi et impera* that Walesa, for one, rejected. By 1970 the situation had deteriorated to such an extent that the workers called for a strike. Walesa, named a delegate to the strike committee, was unable to stop the workers from rioting against the police. But he learned how the authorities thought in a crisis.

For the next several years, as the government and the workers wrestled over economic policy, Walesa learned the work of agitation. In 1976 he made his first public speech, calling for the creation of an independent trade union. Fired for his impertinence, he secured another post and allied himself with various ad hoc worker's groups. He was fired again for his activities and in 1979 signed a charter demanding independent trade unions and the right to strike. He was arrested again and again by the police.

In 1980, when strikers seized the Lenin shipyards, Walesa became leader of the workers and voice of the opposition to the Communists. He led the negotiations for the union, which issued twenty-one demands, including—ominously for the government—the right to free speech and the right to strike. The power of the union, now called Solidarity, to speak for the entire Polish nation was underscored by the fact that, joined by intellectuals and dissidents, it represented a mass movement of 10,000,000. As Walesa pressed for the implementation of the accords amid rumors of a Soviet military invasion, Polish Prime Minister Wojcieck Jaruzelski declared martial law.

For the next three years Walesa carried on a non-violent political guerrilla campaign against the Communists, one that entailed his arrest and detention. In 1983 he was awarded the Nobel Peace Prize for his principled and peaceful efforts to bring democracy to Poland.

By 1987 the government was tottering, a referendum on its reforms boycotted by a great many Poles. Two years later, in the midst of increased unrest, it surrendered, inviting Solidarity, now more a party than a trade union, to help form a government. Walesa's victory was made complete in 1990, when he was elected President of Poland.

Walesa's tenure was not unmarked by controversy; he announced that Jews who ran for office in Poland should reveal their "nationality." Foreign criticism was swift. But there were many Poles, especially those in the academic community, who were also critical of him. As President, he was autocratic and impatient, and also drew accusations that he wanted power for its own sake. In 1994, after a series of petulant acts on his part, the Polish parliament passed a toothless resolution censuring him for being a danger to the state.

Undeterred by critics at home and abroad and convinced he was in touch with the temper of the people, Walesa ran for president again in 1995, asking the electorate to give him a mandate so that he could dramatically expand the powers of the presidency and rule by decree. Some among Polish voters recalled that one of his heroes was Marshall Jozef Pilsudski—who had led a military coup d'etat in 1926, becoming a virtual dictator for the next nine years—and Walesa was voted out of office in favor of a former Communist turned blow-dried Social Democrat.

Walesa's later mercurial career, his authoritarian bent, his estrangement from the very people who had propelled him to the heights, even the revelation that Solidarity had received secret funds from the CIA, Mossad and, weirdly, the KGB—none of this could obscure the value of his great achievement in bringing democracy to one of the keystones of the old Soviet Empire. His retirement was his last contribution to that democracy.

ANDY WARHOL

THE HUNGRY EGOS OF the modern age had no greater role model than the pop artist Andy Warhol, whose need for celebrity was reflected in the group of supplicants and hangers-on who invariably surrounded him. Shrewd in exploiting his era's obsession with fame, the pale androgyne in the silver-blond wig was himself the perfect practitioner of all that he preached. His artistic vocabulary was drawn from images of everyday life in America—from brillo boxes to the faces of movie stars. He was an avid merchant of his own brand of mass-produced art which, whether inspired by cynicism or guilelessness, nonetheless invigorated the art world. To his fans, he was a genius who combined photography, printing, and painting in a revolutionary way and who knew instinctively how to give a graphic image impact. To his harshest critics, his work testified to the demise of modern art.

Warhol was born Andrew Warhola in Pittsburgh to Catholic Czech immigrants who were staunchly working class. His father, a construction worker, died when Andy was fourteen. At an early age, he was stricken with Saint Vitus' dance, a rare disease reponsible for his blotchy skin and bouts of shakiness in his limbs. Warhol first became interested in drawing and fashion design when he took a summer job in a department store. In 1945, he enrolled himself at Carnegie-Mellon University, then known as Carnegie Tech, graduating in 1949. With a bachelor's degree in pictorial design, he ventured to New York City, the celebrated mecca of American fashion. Despite his secondhand clothes, chosen with the dreamy insouciance of someone whose mind was elsewhere, Warhol was no bohemian. In the magazine world in which he worked, he was as highly regarded for his professionalism and businesslike approach to art as he was for his talented advertising designs for shoes, liquor, clothes—anything he was commissioned to do, and in any style the client desired. But Warhol never relinquished his ambition of becoming a fine artist. It was his peculiar gift to realize that the commonplace and the commercial could become the basis for "serious" art.

The idea was not new. The dadaist Marcel Duchamp had, years before, with his contemporaries challenged the definition of what constitutes "art" by taking ordinary objects and simply declaring them "art." In America, Warhol's contemporaries Robert Rauschenberg and Roy Lichtenstein had followed in Duchamp's footsteps, creating art which deliberately drew on the vocabulary of the commonplace. In this view, even the lowly comic strip could provide the basis for creativity. Warhol's 1962 Campbell's soup cans, along with Rauschenberg's and Lichtenstein's work, gave the world what came to be known as pop art.

Warhol then abandoned painting and turned to silkscreening, which permitted him to reproduce the same image over and over with minor variations, from car crashes and Brillo pads to celebrities like Marilyn Monroe, Jackie Kennedy, and Elvis Presley. From his wittily named Factory, he transformed himself into a master of Pop Art, spending the sixties and seventies churning out silk screens (most of them executed by his assistants), a pop culture magazine, several non-fiction books, and a novel. In the midsixties, he retired from art for a time to devote himself to cinema, setting movie critics' teeth on edge with his intentionally vacuous 8-hour long *Empire*, which was essentially just one long shot of the Empire State Building. ("I like boring things," he said of his six-hour, 1964 movie *Sleep*, which features minimal movement.) That same decade he filmed *The Chelsea Girls, Poor Little Rich Girl,* and *International Velvet*, which were populated by instant "superstars" drawn from his intimate circle. In a manner that was simultaneously calculated and daffy, everything he did drew attention to Andy Warhol himself.

If Warhol's films deliberately lacked drama, his life did not. After being shot by a demented woman named Valerie Solanas in 1968, Warhol moved away from the netherworld of drag queens, druggies, and outcasts and to high society, where he became court painter to the rich and famous. In 1973, in addition to continuing to produce his now signature portraits, Warhol founded *Interview* magazine. Its focus was, not surprisingly, the cult of celebrity.

Warhol died unexpectedly in a New York hospital in 1987, of complications from a relatively routine gall bladder surgery. In death he became, if anything, even more notorious than in life. Collectors vied for his work, the Museum of Modern Art mounted a huge retrospective, his diaries from the 1970s were published as a bestselling book, and, on one heady afternoon in April 1988 at an auction of some of his possessions—Warhol was an inveterate collector of all manner of things—a pair of ordinary cookie jars he had bought at a flea market sold for the wildly inflated sum of $23,100. His oddly inexhaustible afterlife represented an irony the artist himself would have savored, defying as it did his own often quoted decree that "in the future everyone will be world-famous for fifteen minutes."

FRANCIS CRICK

JAMES WATSON &

WATSON AND CRICK CONVERGED on their shared destiny from somewhat similar backgrounds, if a continent apart. James Watson grew up poor on Chicago's tough South Side, but he inherited his parents' love of learning. As something of an intellectual prodigy, he was a "Quiz Kid" radio-show panelist who graduated from the University of Chicago's high school at the age of fifteen. He took a bachelor of science degree when he was nineteen, in 1947, before pursuing graduate studies in genetics at Indiana University.

Francis Crick was the son of a middle-class English shoe manufacturer from Northampton who was forced to shut down his factory after World War I. Crick showed an early fascination with science and, like Watson, received encouragement at home: "What a pity it's all been discovered already," he said to his mother as a small boy, and she assured him that a world of scientific mysteries remained to be solved. Fortunately, young Francis earned a scholarship to the Hill School, an all boys public school where, not surprisingly, he displayed an aptitude for science.

Crick earned his bachelor of science degree in physics from University College, London, in 1937, then labored enthusiastically as a wartime explosives expert at the British Admiralty before quitting to study molecular biology. He wanted to discover the material mysteries that constituted life and consciousness. When Watson learned at a 1951 scientific conference that genes—whose existence had been confirmed but whose structure remained mysterious— were able to crystallize and therefore had to have a regular structure that could be solved, he had found his direction. Serendipituously for science and human knowledge, Watson applied to Cambridge University's Cavendish Laboratory, a medical-research facility where Crick was already tracking the elusive "division between the living and the nonliving."

The two hit it off immediately, sharing not only an office, but all of their ideas and theories as they attempted to crack the code of creation. Crick felt strongly that two minds were better than one because "solitary thinkers cling to their ideas," while collaborators, he believed, would stimulate each other creatively by tackling the same problem from different points of view.

The shape of DNA was crucial; it was the first step to comprehending all of encoded life. Watson's intuition was that the shape would be "simple as well as pretty." They knew it was made of sugar, phosphates, and nitrogen, but they did not know how the ingredients were put together. Photographs of X-ray diffraction patterns suggested the pattern was helical, but was it one, two, three, or a thousand helixes? Aware that they were not the only ones searching for this knowledge, they worked quickly and constructed a triple-helix model out of their best data. It was so dead wrong that their superior, Sir Lawrence Bragg, alienated already by the team's arrogance, cracked down on them by taking the DNA project away. In a way, they were saved by Linus Pauling, who brought out his own triple-helical DNA model in 1952. It, too, was erroneous, but the prospect that Pauling might beat them to the finish line galvanized Watson and Crick into reentering the race.

The pair postulated any number of possible structures of DNA before the answer came. They knew they were close when they imagined the very inverse of the now-famous "twisted ladder." Watson thought DNA might be a single spiral from which the four nucleotides radiated outward. Crick suggested that he try building a model whose backbone would be on the outside. Watson thought that would be too simple, and Crick countered, "Then why don't *you* do it?"

One day in March 1953, following Crick's suggestion, Watson began to construct a double-helix model. In a burst of insight he discovered the serpentine winding of DNA, "the most golden molecule of all," and the Age of Biotechnology was born. Watson loved the elegance of the model he and Crick had made. "It's so beautiful, you see," he said once in an after-dinner speech, "so beautiful." Watson's candid 1968 best-seller about the discovery, *The Double Helix,* angered his scientific colleagues with its fractious criticism of them. Crick's 1981 offering, *Life Itself,* was more tempered, reflecting its author's personality.

Crick went on to become senior scientist at California's Salk Institute but had to step down because of ill health. Commenting on the Nobel Prize in Medicine and Physiology which he and Watson shared with M.H.F. Wilkins, he remarked that, while important, the award was really "a lottery" and should not be considered the zenith of scientific achievement. It did, however, make one feel "cozy." After being on the faculty at Harvard in the 1950's, Watson went on to shape the human genome project, an effort to decode all of human DNA, and to build Cold Spring Harbor laboratory. He has remained dedicated to the promotion of molecular biology. After forty years of feeling like "a giraffe in the corner," the ever-controversial scientist's assessment of his life was typically unsentimental: "Being famous is a lot better than not being famous."

JOHN WAYNE

PROUD, TOUGH AND HONEST, John Wayne, the "Duke," lived, like the men he portrayed, a self-reliant existence that was always true to his personal code of honor. His image as a leader of men, hero of the battlefield, and ardent if mono-syllabic lover was so compelling that it stands as one of the country's great cinematic achievements.

He was born Marion Michael Morrison in Winterset, Iowa, to an Irish-American mother and druggist father of Scottish antecedents. When Wayne was six, his consumptive father moved at doctor's orders to California, where he tried his hand at ranching and later abandoned it to run a phar-macy. Far from having the sort of Great Plains life depicted in his movies, young Morrison was a typical middle-class youth who stayed with his mother after his parents divorced when he was a freshman in college. A hard worker, he made extra money passing out handbills for movies, a job that enabled him to see films for free. A football scholarship allowed the six-foot-four athlete to attend the University of Southern California in Los Angeles. There, during the summers, he worked as a prop man on the Fox lot and eventually met John Ford, the director of some of the screen's greatest Westerns, with whom Wayne struck up a close friendship. Graduating to stunt man, then bit player, the accidental actor spent five years in the extras' ranks before he rose, on Ford's recommendation, to star billing in *The Big Trail* (1930). But the next eight years saw Morrison, now renamed John Wayne by director Raoul Walsh, cranking out some eighty low-budget westerns. Improbably enough since he couldn't sing, the rawboned actor even became the first singing cowboy, thanks to dubbing.

Ford rescued Wayne from B-movie obscurity by casting him as the Ringo Kid in *Stagecoach* (1939). His brooding por-trayal of the sentimental outlaw—made even more laconic by his rasping trademark drawl—showed an economy of emo-tional expression that seemed to have ridden full-blown out of the badlands. It was, however, the product of years of experi-ment. Many of his most famous mannerisms—his oddly broken cadences, his pigeon-toed, leaning walk, the grand sweeps of his arms—were practiced for hours in front of a mirror.

If the goal of the classical or method actor was expres-sion, for Wayne the idea was impression—and the impres-sion he wanted to create was that of a stoic exterior with a fundamentally good but potentially dangerous man lurking beneath it. This combination of moral rectitude and deadly action was Wayne's inimitable distillation of the American hero, whether the action was set on the plains of the old west or on a modern battlefield. He honed this character—what he termed in his self-depreciating way "the John Wayne thing"—through many different genres and fifty years of movie-making. On screen, the Wayne hero was tough but appealing; he was always one of a kind. He was above all, distinctly American.

So long is the list of Wayne's films that a precis must suffice: the 1940 adaptation of Eugene O'Neill's *The Long Voyage Home, Red River* (1948) (directed by Howard Hawks who, with John Ford, did most to create Wayne's legend), Ford's *Fort Apache* (1948), *She Wore a Yellow Ribbon* (1949) and *Rio Grande* (1950), in all of which Wayne played a dauntless cavalryman. In 1952, departing from westerns (as he had in 1950 for *Sands of Iwo Jima*), he played a troubled American boxer in Ford's affectionate trib-ute to pastoral Ireland, the classic homecoming film *The Quiet Man*. Eight years later, Wayne realized his dream of making *The Alamo*—starring, directing, and producing. Believing it captured the spirit of his nation, he sunk over a million dollars of his own money into the movie, which suffered a worse defeat than the Texans had.

The Green Berets, his 1969 pro-Vietnam War film from the pulp novel of the same name, secured Wayne's reputation as a "hawk" and a political reactionary. The latter had become evident during the McCarthy era when the conservative star, a friend of the notorious senator himself, helped organize The Motion Picture Alliance for the Preservation of American Ideals. As flawed as *Berets* was, his next effort, *True Grit*, a comically brilliant recreation of bygone dime novels and penny dreadfuls of the Old West, won Wayne an Oscar as Best Actor in 1969 for his knowing and hilariously self-referential depiction of sly, bibulous U.S. marshal Rooster Cogburn.

In 1993, fourteen years after his death, Wayne was voted second in a poll of America's favorite movie stars. The phenomenon was repeated the following year. In 1995, he was number one, beating out not only every living actor, but every movie star in history. Even critics began to reassess the art behind Wayne's performances, finding them more subtle and variegated than they had previously believed.

Though he went on to make several more films follow-ing *True Grit*, including the reprise *Rooster Cogburn* in 1975, his graceful swan song was *The Shootist* (1976), a dignified and unsentimental portrait of an old gunfighter dying of can-cer. As art, it was a brave gesture: Wayne himself was dying of the disease, which took him three years later. A husband of three Latinas, he could barely speak a word of Spanish, but said he wanted his epitaph to read *"Feo, Fuerte, y formal"*—"Ugly, strong, and dignified." Only the latter two adjectives were obviously true.

WELLES

ORSON

AS A THEATRICAL AND cinematic genius, Orson Welles was a combustible mixture of brains and adrenaline and hypersensitivity that eventually went up in smoke. Proclaimed a genius at eighteen months, he was self-confident almost to a fault, once boasting that he knew exactly what worked in every medium. But whether or not Welles was incapable of making a mistake, which he also asserted, he absolutely excelled in almost every field of the performing arts. As an actor, he used his rumbling, buttery voice with command, performing with bold originality and intelligence. As a director, producer, impresario, stage and costume designer, and screenwriter, he also delivered astonishing results.

George Orson Welles was born in Kenosha, Wisconsin, the son of a gifted inventor and a mother who encouraged his precocious creativity. Orphaned at nine, he started his professional career at age sixteen, making his way to Dublin with the aid of inherited money and bluffing his way—he said—into lead parts at the city's Gateway Theater. The American stage—beginning with Katharine Cornell—embraced Welles two years later. His colleagues found him to be brusque, unpredictable, and excessive in his lifestyle, but they were seldom bored in his presence. His role in The Third Man (1949) was one of his most powerful, introducing into movie myth the intriguing character of cryptic black-marketer Harry Lime.

However, it is not as a performer that Welles will be especially remembered. He proved his virtuosity beyond a doubt with the astounding directorial triumph of Citizen Kane (1941), which he also produced, cowrote, and starred in. Every American filmgoer knows of it, every film class discusses it, and every critic refers to it again and again. It has become a touchstone for aspiring moviemakers. But while audiences and critics thrilled to Welles's tensely wrought themes and expressionist camera angles, the industry itself cared less about his depth-of-focus technique than it did about the depths of its own pockets. Early on, and despite the success of Kane, it judged Welles to be out of sync with its commercial needs.

In assessing Welles's career, it is, therefore, paramount to remember this premature success. In 1940, the man who negotiated unheard-of creative concessions in his Citizen Kane contract was only twenty-five. Two years earlier, his Mercury Theatre of the Air adaptation of H. G. Wells' War of the Worlds had convinced a large segment of America—despite adequate warning—that the country was being invaded by Martians, and Time magazine put him on its cover. And two years before that, Welles's production of Macbeth, an electrifying all-black version performed in Harlem, had been staged as part of the New Deal's prestigious Federal Theater Project.

Welles liked to tell alternative versions of his early life, but it seems the boy wonder—when he was not poring over Nietzsche or playing the piano—acquired his interest in Shakespeare from hearing his mother read it aloud. His most popular theatrical and film endeavors, in fact, would be Shakespearean adaptations: his unforgettable Othello (1952) and his refashioned Henry IV in Chimes at Midnight (1967). Aptly, the fact that his favorite character was the boisterous Falstaff speaks volumes about the actor's love of trickery and wit, and his appetite for lustier pleasures.

It is Citizen Kane, however, not Welles's Shakespearean tours de force or his other critically successful films, that best represents his somewhat unfocused search for artistic fulfillment. It is the work that not only made him a legend, but compelled American cinema to abandon its tidy forms for more sophisticated and oblique narratives. Drawing on forgotten techniques from the past and his own inventiveness, Welles created a shockingly new—albeit romantic and somewhat Gothic—realism, replete with overlapping dialogue, circular plot development, fast-cut montages, and a play of light and shadow that has been compared with poetry. The tale of millionaire publisher Charles Foster Kane (a thinly-veiled William Randolph Hearst) was also a film of ideas, a boldly declared work that assailed the evils of power and technology and bespoke doom for a society trapped in technological progress and for those whose hearts were closed to love.

Citizen Kane proved an impossible act to follow. Films regarded as American classics now, like The Magnificent Ambersons (1942) and The Lady from Shanghai (1948) died at the box office. After Shanghai, his marriage to its star, Rita Hayworth, failed as well. Fortunately Welles was adroit at small-budget cinema, notably the twisted film noir Touch of Evil (1958), in which he starred as a seedy American detective. Poorly distributed in the United States and therefore unsuccessful, it has nevertheless attained cult status for its gritty but lyrical decadence.

The reasons for Welles's untimely creative finale continue to intrigue. Perhaps Welles was simply a victim of Hollywood, a system fueled by jealous rivalries and irritated beyond patience with his arrogance and capricious disdain for budgets and shooting schedules. Or perhaps he was a victim of his own making. His seeming impulsiveness—he often left major films such as Ambersons and Touch of Evil to be edited by others—may have been merely a mask for what his profession universally feared and derided as "flop-sweat." Whatever the causes, the curtain on his career came down much too early. He traveled throughout Europe for decades, playing bit parts to finance projects—such as his legendary and unfinished Don Quixote—that he would then toss aside like the stub of one of his big cigars. During this time many of Welles's brilliant film ideas died in embryo, making his one of the entertainment industry's saddest success stories.

MAE WEST

IN REAL LIFE, WHILE the personal ethic of Mae West—no drinking, no smoking, no married men—may not have made her the girl next door, it was certainly a contrast to the flamboyant and voluptuous screen image she created. Though she made only twelve full-length films in her sixty-year career, she was the best-known and most controversial performer of her era. In the thirties, at the apex of her fame, the sultry ex-vaudevillian and Broadway star brought a new kind of sex appeal to the screen, a witty, over-the-top eroticism that involved more word play than passion. In her lighthearted duels on what she referred to as "the linen battlefield," insinuating winks and racy wisecracks replaced the cinema's usual depiction of love and passion.

The anti-thesis of the flat-chested, androgynous flapper, West's womanly figure, suggestive walk, and signature décolletage, were the visual cues for her new brand of naughtiness. She took on the censors with her broad and open treatment of sex and boasted of having been the primary reason for the oppressive motion picture code: She claimed to have consistently outsmarted the enforcers of the Hays Office—the industry's self-regulatory agency—by writing so much blue material that, even after being censored, some of it was bound to be left intact.

As cheeky as her double entendres were, it was West's self-mockery and honky-tonk delivery—a hand on her hip or a pat on her white-blond, marcelled hair—that gave her ripostes their spicy bite. In one of her early movies, *She Done Him Wrong* (1933), a youthful Cary Grant (playing a Salvation Army cadet) asks West's gold-digger character: "Haven't you ever met a man who could make you happy?" "Sure," she answers with her signature knowing glance and her slightly patronizing smile, "lotsa times." West could even carry off this teasing innuendo opposite her frequent and unlikely romantic lead, W. C. Fields, whose business card she read aloud in *My Little Chickadee* (1940): "'Novelties and notions.' What kinda notions ya got?" West's eminently quotable one-liners, such as "I used to be Snow White, but I drifted," or "Is that a gun in your pocket, or are you just happy to see me?" were absorbed almost immediately into the national vocabulary.

Mae West began her career at a talent show in her hometown of Brooklyn. Singing and dancing in a swirl of ruffles, "Baby Mae" soon moved on to burlesque with the encouragement of her indulgent mother, Matilda. When she outgrew her vaudeville nickname, "The Baby Vamp," the nineteen-year-old West debuted on Broadway in a 1911 revue that included the sketches "A la Broadway" and

"Hello, Paris," but after several other shows, she returned to the circuit where she often appeared with her sister, Beverly. West shattered house records dancing her novel and seductive shimmy in the 1918 musical *Sometime,* and as her dolled-up, off-color persona bloomed, she began writing provocative lines to bring it to life. Her first effort was the outrageous *Sex*, a highly successful 1926 play about a Montreal prostitute, for which she served an eight-day jail sentence. After *The Drag,* a play that some critics observed was the first to deal seriously with homosexuality, West penned the 1928 stage sensation *Diamond Lil,* a Gay Nineties melodrama in which her flippant saloon singer provided the comic relief.

Diamond Lil, which turned the charming but salty performer into the toast of the international social set, became West's touchstone role, one she would reprise again and again as she moved from Broadway to Hollywood. Arriving on the West Coast in 1932, she teamed up with George Raft in *Night After Night* and then in 1933 with Cary Grant in *She Done Him Wrong* (the film adaptation of *Diamond Lil*), two of a string of Depression-era movies for Paramount that would rescue the studio from near bankruptcy. By 1935 she was the highest-paid woman in the world, a bona fide phenomenon, who dined with society's upper crust and made more in a year than many of her hosts made in a decade. In her honor, the pilots in the Royal Air Force named their inflatable life jackets "Mae Wests."

While West's on screen characters continued to charm audiences, in real life, she was tenacious in maintaining her unique identity, especially where men were concerned. She was determined, despite numerous liaisons, not "to stop being Mae West for any man," noting seriously and often that "sex and work" were all that really mattered. Her only marriage—to a song-and-dance man in 1911—ended in divorce nearly three decades later, only after her husband had sued for alimony.

In her declining years, after two awkward comeback films, *Myra Breckinridge* (1970) and *Sextette* (1978), and a nightclub tour featuring a retinue of musclemen, West retired to her Los Angeles apartment, a place that seemed to her infrequent visitors unchanged from when she had first moved in during the early thirties. She lived to the end on a strict fitness and health-food regimen supervised by a longtime male companion, pedaling her stationary bike faithfully even at age eighty-seven. But it was only her celluloid image, beckoning us "to come up and see me some tine" that was able to withstand the onslaught of time.

HANK WILLIAMS

WIDELY REGARDED AS THE leading country musician of the century, Hank William's simple but evocative lyrics continue to move and amaze almost fifty years after this death. He not only composed America's most brilliantly definitive country-and-western songs, but lived the quintessential country-and-western existence. Despite a life cut short—he was only twenty-nine when he died—in the four years before his death he wrote and performed twenty-seven top-ten hits.

Born in Lowndes County, Alabama, to Elonzo Huble Williams, a disabled veteran of World War I, and his shrewd and driven wife, Lillie Belle (née Skipper), Hiram "Hank" Williams grew up amid extreme poverty. With the advent of the Great Depression, his parents' fortunes sank even lower. Hank was only six when his father entered a VA hospital in Biloxi, Mississippi, never to be united with his family again. Lillie Belle embarked on a Southern odyssey, toting her children from town to town every few years in desperate search of work. In this uncertain and unhappy environment, Hank grew up fast. By age twelve he'd acquired his first guitar, drunk his first whiskey, and smoked his first cigarette, and was learning songs and patter from a street minstrel named Rufe "Tee Tot" Payne. He was thirteen, living with his family in Montgomery, Alabama, when he won a talent contest at The Empire Theatre, singing his own song "The WPA Blues." The bitter lyrics belied the age of the composer, but revealed his soulful understanding.

His knowledge came from life, not books; indeed, by 1942, at nineteen, he was still in the ninth grade. After flunking his draft physical, he dropped out of school and worked for a drydock company in Mobile while writing songs and dreaming of a big career. In 1944 he married an aspiring singer named Audrey Mae Sheppard and landed a job as a regular performer on radio station WSFA. With the station as his base, he toured honky-tonks and bars anywhere within broadcasting range. It was a hard way to earn a living, and he augmented his salary any way he could, even self-publishing a songbook that he sold for thirty-five cents.

In 1946, when Williams went to Nashville, Tennessee, to sign with the burgeoning Acuff-Rose music publishers, his career took off. That year he recorded two songs that epitomize the clash of the secular and the sacred in Williams's work: "Calling You," and "Wealth Won't Save Your Soul." It was an approach that stemmed as much from show business concerns as from conviction, and the following year it produced two more successes, "I Saw the Light" and the more earthy "Move It on Over," both for MGM. That same year he recorded "Honky Tonkin'," one of his all-time greatest hits,

and a year later released "The Lovesick Blues," which went on to become the top hit on the *Billboard* charts in 1949.

Already a fixture on the "Louisiana Hayride" live radio show, Williams graduated to the The Grand Ole Opry, performing six encores in his 1949 debut. When his son Hank, Jr., was born that year, Williams nicknamed the infant "Bocephus," after a puppet used on the show. That same year he composed and recorded another of his timeless songs, "I'm So Lonesome I Could Cry." But hard living and hard drinking were already beginning to take their toll; in the autumn of 1949, Williams entered Nashville's Madison Sanitarium ("the Hut") in an unsuccessful attempt to exorcise his demons. Yet this inner turmoil could not silence, or even slow, the steady stream of music he produced: "Cold, Cold, Heart" (1950) was recorded with a lush string arrangement by Tony Bennett, and became a national hit. Three other titles, "Why Don't You Love Me," "Long Gone Lonesome Blues," and "Moanin' the Blues," climbed the charts that year. Moanin' the blues was an apt description of Williams's art: His melancholy voice was the perfect vehicle for his musical expressions of regret, rage, and passion.

The next two years were equally tumultuous and productive. In 1951 he recorded another classic, "Hey, Good Lookin'." Along with "Cold, Cold, Heart" and "Crazy Heart," it made the charts, giving him another year with three hits; that same year, he again admitted himself to a sanitarium. In 1952 Audrey, who had already left him once, divorced him. Williams checked into a narcotics program; upon his release a month later, he made "Jambalaya" and the wryly prophetic "I'll Never Get Out of This World Alive."

Despite another number-one release, "Take These Chains From My Heart," he was fired from The Grand Ole Opry for his drunken behavior. He married a beautiful telephone operator named Billie Jean Eshliman, checked into yet another hospital, and upon his release went on the road. Sick, drunk, and dependent on pain killers, he received a vitamin injection from a doctor summoned to his hotel room on New Year's Eve 1952. Then he was loaded into the back seat of his baby-blue Cadillac, as his driver tried to make the next engagement in Ohio. Somewhere on a West Virginia highway, Williams was discovered dead in his car. He was pronounced dead on arrival at a West Virginia hospital on January 1, 1953. "Jambalaya" was currently in the number-three slot on the *Billboard* charts.

In the years since his passing, Williams has garnered fans around the world as the best of America's country-and-western singers. His voice, like those of the great blues singers, was authentic, born to misery and poetry. Poured straight from the bottle, it was rough and powerful—and heart-breaking.

WILLIAMS

1911-1983

TENNESSEE

IN THE HIGHLY ENERGIZED UNIVERSE of the American theater, Tennessee Williams was a talent who shone most brilliantly when reflecting the glow of critical acclaim. His world, a very private and quirky one, was populated with marginal beings who battled daily to keep possession of their dreams. Many of his characters were based on people who had played significant parts in his "purgatorial" past: His father, a combative alcoholic salesman "with a bad territory" who called his effeminate son "Nancy;" his mother, a delicate but indomitable soul known as "Miss Edwina;" his mentally disturbed and later lobotomized sister, Rose. His brother, Dakin, had Tennessee institutionalized when his neuroses—along with a combination of alcohol and various controlled substances—had rendered him fit for a padded cell. In Williams's provocative, darkly comic plays, these members from his idiosyncratic clan became the basis for some of the most memorable stage characters ever created. These include the painfully shy Laura (sister Rose) of his first real Broadway success, *The Glass Menagerie* in late 1944; the fading magnolia, Blanche DuBois (Mother Edwina), sparring gamely with that force of nature in a torn T-shirt, Stanley Kowalski, in the 1947 sensation *A Streetcar Named Desire;* and all the feisty members of Big Daddy's hot-blooded family in *Cat on a Hot Tin* Roof (1955).

In all of Williams's plays and stories his aberrant spawn are always compelled to melodrama, revealing a raw emotional hunger that commands the audience's sympathetic attention. However vibrant, they all seem slightly wilted by loss, a condition which the playwright considered to be one of life's universal experiences; and like Williams himself, they are studies in disrepair. From within his self-indulgent but profoundly affecting work, this little band of misfits assaulted the morally rigid code of postwar American theater with dashes of cannibalism, drug addiction, homosexuality, and incest. For two decades, beginning with *Menagerie* and continuing with *Streetcar* and *Cat*—both Pulitzer Prize winners—*The Rose Tattoo* (1951), *Suddenly Last Summer* (1958), *Summer and Smoke* (1948), and *Sweet Bird of Youth* (1959), he served up this spicy stew and made America gasp.

As his art testifies, Williams cared desperately about those living on the periphery. It was, in fact, his own sympathy for his creations that enabled audiences to accept them, however unconventional and even repellent their desires. Williams cared equally about his writing, which for him was an almost physical need. From the time his mother bought him his first typewriter at age eleven until his decline in the sixties and seventies, he struggled bravely against his famous "muses." "I fear if I lose my demons," Tennessee once explained, "I might lose my angels as well."

Williams's sensitivity to the critics' lash occasionally drove him to artistic accommodation; always it contributed to his madness, a recurring condition rooted in a childhood marked by the dominance of women who were scarcely paragons of stability themselves. His own diphtheria, and the kidney problems that damaged his eyesight and temporarily paralyzed his legs, had also radically destabilized his character. Born in Columbus, Missouri, in 1911, and cared for by his maternal grandparents, Tom Williams—who became Tennessee in 1938—moved at age eight to Saint Louis. There he and his "butterfly" of a mother both suffered from the squabbling and social ostracism that plagued their family, country mice who were lost in the big city. Tom took solace in his sister's companionship and his developing craft, and during this time stories and poems tumbled from his agitated mind. Then, while traveling with his Episcopalian pastor grandfather in Europe, he had a frightening psychic episode that convinced him he was gong insane. Years later, after the Broadway failure of *Orpheus Descending,* one of Williams's encounters with formal psychiatric counseling ended abruptly when "the man," Tennessee said, "began asking questions of a personal nature." The witticism was offered in lieu of the truth, which was that this particular therapist thought Tennessee should try giving up his homosexuality and raise a family and that he should take a lengthy hiatus from writing.

In Saint Louis, his sister, Rose, was becoming more and more withdrawn, and his father, it is suspected, was instrumental in breaking up the one heterosexual love affair Williams would ever have. These events, in addition to his emerging homosexuality and increasing discomfiture with the brassy rudeness of the "new" South, began increasingly to color his work. Williams cherished his Old South, especially the tumbledown city of New Orleans, where several of his plays are set. Drawn to the region's sensuality and its celebration of vice and temptation, he was respectful—in the spirit of Blanche DuBois— of its attempts to preserve illusion at whatever cost. Most of all, he loved the rambling lilt of its language, turning its lazy cadences into dialogue that was musically rich and real.

Southern critics largely loved him back, praising his frankness, his perceptive sense of place, and his charitable portrayal of a waning culture. Others, and not always "northerners," detested what they saw as bald sentimentality in what Williams himself referred to as his "cornpone melodrama," nor did they approve of his commercial preoccupation with sex and violence. Many preferred the powerful gloom of Eugene O'Neill or the sociopolitical ruminations of Arthur Miller, both contenders, along with Williams, for the century's top laurels. It was Williams, however, who most inspired playwrights-to-be and who kept America mesmerized with each bawdy new glimpse into the bedrooms— and souls—of his fragile, dissipated characters.

OF WINDSOR

DUKE & DUCHESS

THE LOVE STORY OF the century began as a favor between two friends. In January of 1934, Lady Thelma Furness, mistress of the Prince of Wales—who as the eldest son of Queen Mary and King George V was next in succession to the British throne—was leaving London on a trip. Lunching at the Ritz, she asked Wallis Simpson, a Baltimore-born divorceé married to a prosperous shipping magnate, to look after the dapper, party-loving Edward during her absence. "See that he does not get into any mischief," Lady Furness said. Her request turned into mischief itself. The prince fell in love with Simpson, and on December 11, 1936, only ten months after his coronation as Edward VIII, he abdicated, forsaking crown and scepter for the woman he loved.

The noble beau-about-town had been very ripe for the taking. Having spent World War II in the Royal Navy and the following decade making ceremonial rounds throughout the empire, he was extremely popular with the British people. The playboy prince was, however, the product of what he himself described as a "wretched childhood." Lacking the kind of familial love and companionship that ease the transition from youth to adulthood, he had never really grown mentally or emotionally much beyond late adolescence. His vulnerability was no match for the driving force that was Wallis Warfield Simpson.

But what exactly did this rather plain, thirty-nine-year-old daughter of the American South possess that could entice England's sovereign to reject family and monarchy and endure the censure of both church and parliament? It seems to have been a matter of charm and will. Far from beautiful, Bessie Wallis Warfield nevertheless projected an engaging vitality and boasted a fine figure, a translucent complexion, and large, violet eyes. She was born into financially diminished southern aristocracy and as such was never able to lose her nearly pathological fear of poverty. Revenge against the haughty relations who had looked down on her family was her driving force, but young Wallis seemed ill-prepared for upward mobility. No great intellect, she had limited cultural interests, as did Edward. (The height of her quotable wit was that "one can never be too rich or too thin.") After an unhappy marriage, she had wed wealthy, American-born Englishman Ernest Simpson who had access to the society she envied.

It was at one of those smart-set parties that the Simpsons were introduced to the future king. Very quickly, Ernest, the eager Wallis, and Edward became a staple trio of London's most exclusive clique. But soon, much to the distress of the royal family, rumors were afloat that accommodations for Mrs. Simpson but not her husband had been made at Fort Belvedere, the prince's country getaway. The King often had words with Edward about his unseemly alliance.

The father-son disagreement ended with the king's death in January 1936, but Edward's infatuation with his mistress did not.

When he took the throne and Mrs. Simpson filed for her second divorce, family fears that the new monarch had marriage on his mind were quickly confirmed. Prime Minister Stanley Baldwin, diametrically opposed to the idea, was against even a morganatic union, in which, according to tradition, the commoner Mrs. Simpson would not enjoy royal privileges. I told him I didn't want to be queen," she later recounted, speaking of Edward, "but he said he didn't want to be king without me. What could I do? What *could* I do?" More resolute than he would ever be again, the king made up his mind. In a determined voice, occasionally breaking with emotion, he informed his subjects in a radio broadcast that he had found it impossible "to discharge my duties as king as I would wish to do without the help and support of the woman I love."

Haunted by the bitterness he felt over the wedding present from his brother, George VI—a brief letter announcing that the duchess would not be accorded the status of royalty despite her marriage—the duke now slipped gracefully with his wife into a life of opulent vacuity. It was a glittery limbo, interrupted only by World War II, during which he served as governor of the Bahamas, and by ugly publicity over their pro-Nazi sentiments. (The threat to England's national security that possibly resulted from the duke's German contacts would only be examined extensively decades later.) Through it all, he tried to atone for his failure to give his difficult mate the ultimate social prize: If he could not make her a queen, she could at least live like one. Slavishly dedicated to her every need throughout their thirty-five-year marriage, he showered her with a dazzling array of expensive jewels. In return, she bullied him and ultimately, with her cold, authoritative strength, came to control his every move.

Ostracized by the royal family, the duke and duchess had promised never to return to England without permission from the reigning sovereign. They lived in Paris, for the most part, ensconcing themselves in a thirty-room mansion furnished almost rent-free by the city, where they held court among the *gratin* of high society.

Their exile came to an end in 1967 with Queen Elizabeth II's invitation to a centenary celebration of the birth of Queen Mary. Five years later the duke died, and the duchess's life declined into an even more superficial existence. Lonely, increasingly forgetful, and surrounded only by servants, Simpson maintained her opulent Bois de Boulogne residence for as long as she was physically able, going into her husband's room each evening to say good night to him. A particularly poignant memento, a gold-framed message from the duke, sat on her dressing-room table. It read:

My Friend, with thee to live alone
Methinks were better than to own
A crown, a scepter, and a throne.

OPRAH

1954-

WINFREY

IN A TIME AND place where the darkness of the confessional has been replaced by the unforgiving light of television, Oprah Winfrey has become at once medium and message. From a childhood marked by poverty, racism, and sexual abuse, she rose to become the reigning diva of daytime TV. Along the way, she never hesitated to reveal the lurid details of her own life, from teenage pregnancy to grown-up drug addiction. And the more she confessed, the more audiences loved her. Today she is the richest woman in America, one of the most powerful people in modern entertainment and, parenthetically, extremely influential.

Born in Kosciusko, Mississippi, to fourteen-year-old Vernita Lee, Oprah—her euphonious name is a mistaken rendering of the biblical Orpah—was shuttled as a child between her grandmother in the South and her irresponsible housemaid mother in Milwaukee. While in her mother's care she was sexually abused by several male relatives, experiences that not only scarred her but made her both wild and fearful as a young girl. A stint in juvenile detention was averted only because the facility was overcrowded; a year later, following in her mother's footsteps, Winfrey gave birth to an illegitimate child. (Born prematurely, the child died shortly after birth.) She was saved from further trauma by the intervention of her father, Vernon, a civic-minded barber in Nashville, with whom she went to live. Under his loving discipline, the adolescent blossomed into a star student and public speaker. While still in high school, she was hired as a part-time newscaster at radio station WVOL. She started attending Tennessee State University in 1972, where she eschewed the black power interests of many of her classmates and exercised iron discipline in her studies in rhetoric and drama.

In 1976, Winfrey landed a job as a newscaster at a small Baltimore television station, where the station management asked her to have her hair straightened. An indifferent anchor-woman, the former Miss Black Tennessee found her niche in the morning talk show, *People Are Talking.* Her questions were so empathetic and probing that by 1984 she was recruited by the much larger Chicago station, WLS-TV. Within two years, her time slot was pitted against that of talk-show king Phil Donahue. She used her first Chicago show to confess how fat and frightened she felt. Her candor was a total contrast to Donahue's middle-aged waffling and the effect on her audience was dramatic. Letters and telephone calls of support flooded WLS-TV. The message was always the same: we, too, are afraid, insecure, lonely, and uncertain, and we take comfort in the fact that you feel the way we do. Oprah had found her vocation.

From then on, her ascent was meteoric. *The Oprah Winfrey Show* beat the heretofore unbeatable *Donahue* in the Nielsen ratings, and she was soon syndicated in more than a hundred cities. On a parallel track, she was spotted by producer Steven Spielberg in 1985, and cast as Sofia in his film version of Alice Walker's novel about the transforming power of love, *The Color Purple,* a role that earned her an Academy Award nomination. Four years later, she starred in the television miniseries *The Women of Brewster Place.* It was through her television program, however, that she excelled, exposing the nation to a stream of life's walking wounded—alcoholics, teen gangsters, abandoned children—all of whom told their stories to her. She became so successful that she founded the twenty-million-dollar-grossing Harpo Productions (the name, of course, is Oprah spelled backwards), making American entertainment history as only the third woman—after Mary Pickford and Lucille Ball—to own her own production company.

Like a good general, Winfrey did not ask her guests or her audience to go where she would not go herself. Her yo-yoing weight—in 1992, as host of the Emmy Awards, she weighed in at 235—was a regular topic of discussion, and when she tearfully recounted the sexual abuse she had suffered as a child, the nation wept with her. When she admitted that she had smoked crack and become addicted to cocaine in the seventies, her audiences applauded her courageous recovery.

In 1994, standing beside President Bill Clinton, Oprah watched as he signed the bill she herself had proposed to Congress; it provided for the creation of a national database of convicted child abusers. That year she was also inducted into the Television Academy Hall of Fame. Despite her show's success, she promptly announced with her usual zeal that she was tired of tabloid TV. From now on, in spite of the ratings potential, her show—like her grand-scale philanthropy—would be about positive solutions. In the fall of 1996, hard on the success of *Make the Connection,* a fitness bible written by Oprah with her personal trainer, she switched to a multiple topic format, and instituted a monthly book club, complete with author appearances and literary analysis, extending Ophrah's influence on America's culture.

In 1997 she renewed her commitment to *The Oprah Winfrey Show* through the end of the decade. Her deal with King World Productions was perhaps the final step in making Winfrey America's first black billionaire.

WOOLF

VIRGINIA

WHEN VIRGINIA WOOLF FILLED her pockets with rocks and stepped into the river near her house in Sussex, she ended a life that had oscillated between debilitating madness and a creative power that produced some of the century's finest works of literature. Feminist, novelist, essayist, and critic, the polymath Woolf poured forth experimental fiction and opinion from the comfortable redoubt of genteel British bohemianism. As the center of the brilliant Bloomsbury Group, she was the incarnation of a literary philosophy which held that aesthetic sophistication and personal relationships were the sine qua non of a life well lived.

Born to Sir Leslie Stephen, an eminent and unorthodox Victorian father whose controlled formality did not preclude the use of emotional blackmail, and Julia Duckworth, an ethereal, slightly puritanical beauty, Woolf suffered extremes of grief and terror in her troubled childhood as well as uncontrollable rages. At the age of six, she was sexually molested by her eighteen-year-old half-brother George Duckworth, a pattern that continued into the girl's adolescence and made her permanently afraid of sex with a man. When Woolf was thirteen, her beloved mother died, leaving her devastated and haunted by Julia's voice and image well into her forties. Two years later, half-sister and surrogate mother Stella Duckworth followed their mother into the grave, and in 1904 her father, after a lingering battle with cancer, died as well. Stripped of her childhood innocence, deprived of the people who loved her most, Woolf suffered the first of her many bouts with insanity (which was also apparently a family tradition), hallucinating, among other things, that King Edward VII was screaming invective at her from the shrubbery.

Woolf's spiritual escape from the emotional turbulence that had been her family home brought her to the liberating realm of writing, where even as a child she was free to imagine another world of intense aesthetic pleasure. As a married woman few were so removed from household routine as the financially secure Woolf. This was fortunate, since few loved the creative domain as the fragile Woolf did: For her, it held the romance, the fire, and the fearlessness that life itself never could. Her vision was the twilight border of clarity between sanity and psychosis, where the humdrum daily details of life stood for life itself. Recasting plot, character, and the elements of the conventional novel, she strove for the crystal moment in which all things became focused.

After her father's death, she was free to leave the unhappy house and move to Gordon Street in Bloomsbury. Into her esoteric universe she drew others: Lytton Strachey, the homosexual aesthete who proposed to her in 1909 (to his great consternation, she accepted); her sister, the painter Vanessa; Leonard Woolf, who became her husband, supporter, and partner; E.M. Forester; Roger Fry; Clive Bell; and John Maynard Keynes. This was the nexus of the Bloomsbury Group, one of the most renowned literary circles in the history of letters, which would move English art and literature out of the Victorian era and into the modern age. In 1905, she began a long association with the *Times Literary Supplement,* providing features and criticism, and ten years later she finished her first novel, *The Voyage Out.* The strain of writing it led directly to another breakdown, and the breakdown in turn to another novel, *Night and Day* (1919). She struggled constantly with depression and the fear of madness. Two years later saw the publication of her short-story collection *Monday or Tuesday,* a harbinger of her highly imaginative mature work for its limning of the interior world of its protagonist. The next book, *Jacob's Room* (1922), was her breakthrough, with its depiction of a man through the contents of his room and the fragmented impressions of others. Three years later the stream-of-consciousness *Mrs. Dalloway* evoked the actual thought processes of its heroine. Critics would hail it as one of the most audacious novels ever written about the personal and societal transformation wrought by World War I. But it was *To the Lighthouse* (1927), with its intense portrait of a family as troubled and emotionally shackled as her own, that enthroned Woolf in the century's literary firmament.

Woolf's novels, however, were not always understood or appreciated by her fellow cognoscenti, nor did she always appreciate the revolutionary work of others. As for her opinions of her colleagues—strong, if often wrong—she too easily dismissed as lower-class her contemporary Joyce, whose work was poles apart from Woolf's dreamy and, to some critics, "rather bloodless" English drawing-room tales.

Partially as an antidote for her depression, she and Leonard founded the Hogarth Press in 1917, a single-press operation that published progressive authors of the day such as W. H. Auden, Katherine Mansfield, and Sigmund Freud. But nothing could hold her dementia at bay. Not love, though she had numerous, sometimes platonic, affairs with women, notably Vita Sackville-West. Not success in writing either: She published the highly experimental and transsexually themed *Orlando* in 1928, the classic feminist tract *A Room of One's Own* the next year, and that precursor of minimalist fiction, *The Years,* in 1937. In spite of her literary productivity and success, she was fast declining. When the Second World War began, it was as if the civilization's derangement heralded her own. No longer able to evade the stalking beast, she left a brief, loving note for her husband and led her sickness to the river.

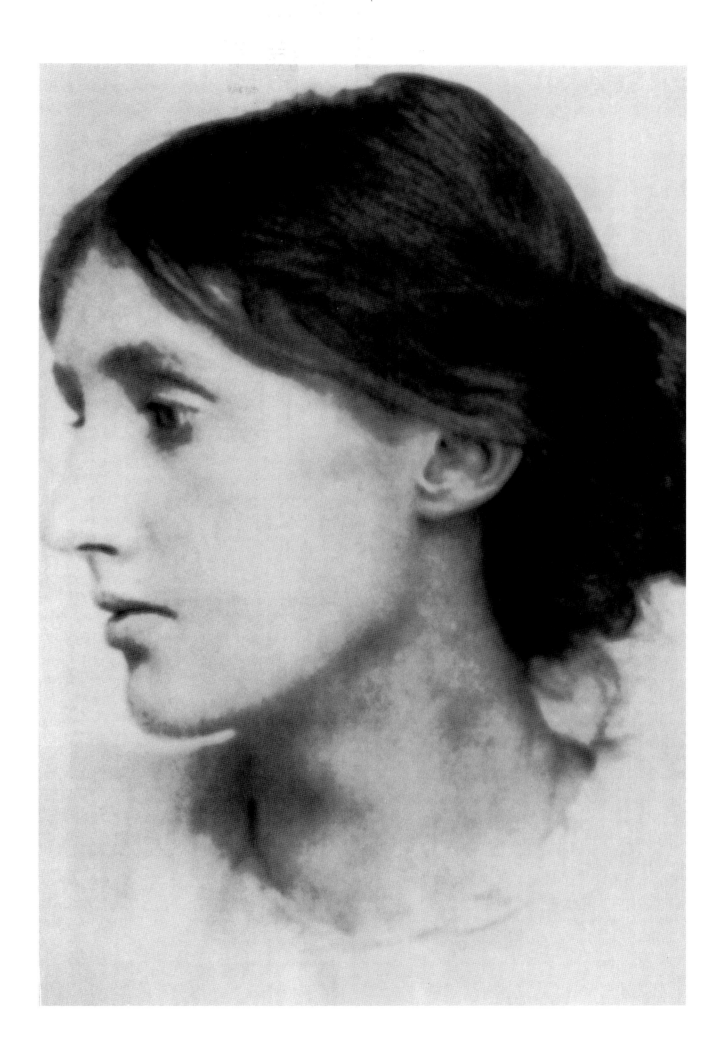

WRIGHT

FRANK LLOYD

ECCENTRICALLY CLAD IN HIS flat hat and swirling cape, Frank Lloyd Wright was a small man with a grand vision of American architecture. His work synthesized agrarian notions in ways that were both revolutionary and oddly romantic. The buildings he designed are marked by clear, crisp lines derived from the natural world as he saw it. He grew up on a farm in Richland Center, Wisconsin, long before the turn of the century. His father, William C. Wright, was a traveling preacher and musician, and Anna Lloyd-Jones, his mother, a transplanted native of Wales. Anna gave her son educational blocks to play with and watched as he created child-scale structures which foreshadowed those that would make him world famous.

Hungry for architectural training that the University of Wisconsin could not provide, he left it in 1887 after only two years. But he had learned engineering there, a skill that would stand him in good stead. As a young student, he had the horrifying experience of watching a building under construction collapse, killing several workmen. His vow that he would never be the cause of such a disaster would be severely tested in Tokyo in 1923, when one of his largest commissions, the Imperial Hotel, withstood the record-breaking tremors of the Kanto earthquake. Wright had decided not to sink the building's pilings into the unstable mud, and instead, in a brilliant innovation, he floated it *on* the mud. Some twenty years after this triumph, Wright's skills allowed him to pile six times the maximum legal weight onto a slender column for the buildings he designed for the S.C. Johnson Wax Company in Racine, Wisconsin. Here, in one of the most inspiring workplaces ever designed, Wright's imagination soared.

Leaving his home state in 1887, the ambitious twenty-year-old joined the Chicago firm, James Lyman Silsbee. When he became responsible for supporting his mother and sisters, his search for a well-paying job brought him to the prestigious firm of Adler and Sullivan—and to the right hand of the great modernist himself, Louis H. Sullivan. Sullivan, who had forged the dictum "form follows function," was the only man the irascible Wright would ever call "Master," but Wright refined the Chicagoan's credo into "form and function are one." Assigned to residential work, the junior architect began moonlighting for a growing private clientele. His "bootlegged houses," featuring asymmetrical layouts, flowing interior spaces, and sweeping roofs, meant to serve as a reminder of the house's relationship to the earth, were quietly magnificent things that established him as the primary practitioner of the "Prairie Style." The Robie House, built in 1909 in Chicago, with its flat, expansive roof, and its centrally located fireplaces, is one of the finest examples of this early design. Using prestressed concrete and other building materials in new ways, Wright's next project was the "Usonian" home—the neologism referring to the USA—a prefabricated modular edifice that for him embodied his nation's democratic ideals. His Usonian home for George D. Sturges was an ultrasleek construction of rectangles arranged with bold artistry over a steep slope.

In 1911, Wright completed the first version of his famous summer home, Taliesin, in Spring Green, Wisconsin. Designed as a home for his mistress, Mamah Borthwick Cheney—who, like Wright, was still married—it would burn down twice and each time he would rebuild it. Here he would desert one family, see another (Cheney's) murdered by a mad servant, and acquire a third. Yet these events, and even the scarcity of commissions, never deterred him from creating. He designed everything he used, from his own clothes to the napkins on his table. A social and garrulous man who fancied himself a lady-killer, Wright possessed a highly developed sense of his own pioneering importance and surrounded himself with acolytes who tilled his fields, did the laundry, and sang in the Taliesin choir in exchange for a place at the guru's feet. "They say I am the world's greatest architect," he would boast. "But who else is there? If architecture is what I conceive it to be, there has never been another architect."

As the thirties dawned, Wright found himself defending his vision against an onslaught of glass boxes marshaled by the Bauhaus refugees Walter Gropius and Ludwig Mies van der Rohe. When International Style "monstrosities" began cluttering the New York skyline, he remarked disgustedly that the Europeans were turning Manhattan into "a vast prison with glass fronts." But Wright was a lone critical voice. By the Museum of Modern Art's show of International Style architecture in 1932, he had already been written off as hopelessly rearguard. He was far from through, however. In 1936, he built the Edgar J. Kaufmann house, Fallingwater, the amazingly terrain-friendly concrete structure poised over a waterfall in Pennsylvania, then the Johnson Wax Building, and after that, in 1943, New York City's Solomon R. Guggenheim Museum. This structure, his most controversial, embodied Wright's conception of continuous space by eliminating floor levels in favor of one long spiraling ramp ascending to the domed ceiling.

Perhaps his greatest gifts were an understanding of the interweavings of man and nature and a revolutionary idea of home. To Frank Lloyd Wright, a home was "something quiet and broad and sensible and belonging where it stood," something that in its cleaving to the landscape could honor the horizon and become an organic part of its surroundings. Till the end of his ninety-one years, he devoted himself to refining the forms this sanctuary should take.

WRIGHT

WILBUR & ORVILLE

THEIR GENIUS WAS OF a peculiarly American variety—self-trained, rigorous, and daring. Together they overcame a centuries-old challenge, one that had confounded visionaries ranging from Leonardo da Vinci in the late fifteenth century to Britain's Sir George Cayley in the early nineteenth: They gave humans flight.

Wilbur Wright was born near Millville, Indiana, in 1867; his brother Orville arrived four years later, in Dayton, Ohio. The youngest sons of Milton Wright, an uncompromising bishop in the church of the United Brethren in Christ, the brothers inherited their father's confidence and sense of purpose—qualities that found a focus in 1878, when Milton Wright gave the two boys a toy helicopter designed by Alphonse Penaud, an earlier aviation pioneer. Transfixed by the rubber-band–powered device, the Wright brothers began to dream of flying machines, a shared passion that became the work of their two lifetimes.

Although the Wrights were, as their father put it, "as inseparable as twins," they were markedly different people. The handsome Orville was a mustachioed dandy who was never without a fresh collar, even in the sand and skeeters of Kitty Hawk, and who would wash his face in lemon juice to bleach away its Carolina summer tan. Wilbur, less concerned about appearance, once gave an important speech in a suit he borrowed from his brother. Prone to depression as a youth, as a man Wilbur developed an aloof self-confidence that could turn on a dime into exclusionary self-absorption. Dark, lean, and sharp-featured, he exuded an intensity that gave rise to comparisons with a hawk. Orville, volatile and so timid that he refused throughout his long life to speak in public, was in private an irredeemable tease, a practical joker, and an optimist with a quicksilver mind. His zealous conviction brought both brothers through times of doubt and despair.

The Wrights applied rigorous scientific discipline and unflagging patience to their quest. In constant correspondence with leading aeronautical researchers like the French-born Octave Chanute, who kept them abreast of developments both in Europe and the United States, they built a wind tunnel to observe the behavior of their progressively sophisticated models. In their search for aerodynamic stability, they began with box kites, then progressed to gliders, but found that the wings lacked lift. In the course of running their modest bicycle shop in Dayton, they had observed cyclists and realized that a moving vehicle does not travel in a perfectly straight line but makes a thousand small adjustments. The discovery led them to pay minute attention to an airplane's multiple axes of motion through the air. They hit upon the idea of warping the wing surface, and it worked. Cycling also made the brothers acutely aware of how the human body conspires with the wind to produce drag. They realized that they would have to lie flat on their Kitty Hawk machine.

Avid readers with the omnivorous minds of great investigators, the brothers began to construct a glider in 1900, funding their project with proceeds from their bicycle business. In October of that year, they tested the glider at the ideally windy and hilly locale of Kitty Hawk, North Carolina. The experiment was a modest success, and they returned to Dayton filled with hope. But a second, larger craft was a happy failure that yielded the Wrights' moment of illumination: "We saw that the calculations upon which all flying machines had been based were unreliable. We were driven to doubt one thing after another, 'til finally we cast all aside."

Rejecting the assumptions of the past, the Wrights solved the problem of three-torque control—pitch, roll, and yaw—that made it possible for a pilot to control the flight of his craft. Success built upon success. Developing a propeller that was as aerodynamic as a wing, they next built their own internal-combustion engine to power the revolutionary craft. In the fine, hot summer of 1903, they built a biplane and mounted it on rails to overcome the sucking sands of Kitty Hawk. And on December 14, 1903, they tossed a coin to see who would make the first flight. The winner, Wilbur, climbed into the air, stalled, and fell. He blamed himself for the mishap, and the brothers telegraphed their father: SUCCESS ASSURED. KEEP QUIET. Three days later, on December 17, the optimistic Orville saw his years of faith rewarded as he guided the self-powered flyer through the air for twelve brief seconds, traveling 120 short feet from the point it left the tracks. On the fourth flight that day, Wilbur was able to travel 852 feet, maintaining an altitude of fifteen feet, for an exhilarating fifty-nine seconds. With quiet elation, the triumphant pair telegraphed their father this time with very different news: SUCCESS. FOUR FLIGHTS THURSDAY MORNING. INFORM PRESS. HOME CHRISTMAS.

Neither Wright brother ever married. Wilbur died of typhoid fever in Dayton in 1912. Orville survived him by more than forty years, never ceasing to invent but, after 1918, flying only rarely. He lived long enough, however, to witness both the enormous benefits and unimaginable destruction that his invention brought to the modern world, a paradox he matter-of-factly compared to the dual manifestations of fire. The popular conception of the Wright brothers has been that of a pair of Yankee bumpkin geniuses—inspired bicycle tinkerers who got lucky. They were, on the contrary, deep and incisive thinkers whose minds grasped the fundamental and immutable laws of nature and then envisioned the future.

BABE DIDRIKSON

ZAHARIAS

MALE SPORTSWRITERS OF THE thirties took an ungracious delight in making sure their readers knew not only the miraculous feats that made Babe Didrikson Zaharias the greatest woman athlete the world had ever seen but also the fact that she was homely. The Babe was unfazed. She was too busy setting all-time records and training for her next event. If she worked out with a team—playing baseball, basketball, volleyball—she stayed on to practice long after the rest had left. When she was learning a new sport, she was a woman obsessed. After discovering golf, for example—the game that brought her the most renown—she would hit buckets of balls until her blistered hands began to bleed. Zaharias studied rule books, took private lessons, scrutinized the performance of other athletes, and devoted an amazing amount of effort in the pursuit of excellence—whether she was swimming, cycling, figure skating, sailing, bowling, playing tennis, shooting pool, diving, hurdling, or throwing the javelin. She gave proficient performances in all of these sports, and in 1932, as a scrappy, crop-haired twenty-one-year-old competitor in the Los Angeles Olympics, she set two world records, in the javelin throw and the eighty-meter hurdles. Her high jump would also have set a world record, but her head-first technique, now allowed, was then illegal.

Born to Norwegian immigrants in Port Arthur, Texas, Mildred Ella Didriksen was the hotshot of the Miss Royal Purples high-school basketball team in Beaumont, a nearby town to which her carpenter father and athletically inclined mother had moved when she was three. A roustabout tomboy who had no time for makeup, Mildred was soon discovered on the court by the manager of the Golden Cyclones Athletic Club of the Employers Casualty Company of Dallas. When she left home in 1930 to join the Cyclones, she was on her way not only to independence but also to a two-year stint demolishing records in women's track and field.

Her teammates found the Texas Tornado something of a braggart, but sports aficionados were too astonished at her prowess and her versatility to care. The Babe's statistics, while stunning, do not even begin to convey the excitement generated by this champion of champions. At five feet, six inches, she was a paragon of physical coordination, a poised and precise dynamo blessed with a dancer's grace and balance. By 1932 she had been named an all-American three times. Then, as a one-woman team for Employers Casualty at a double event, the Amateur Athletic Union (AAU) track-and-field national championships and the Olympic trials, she entered eight of ten events, won six of them as well as the team championship (by herself she outscored the competing team of twenty-two women), and set three world records. Eventually, Babe—who once drove 315 yards—put women's pro golf on the map and in 1947 was the first American

to win the British Women's Amateur. ("When I want to really blast one," she told her admiring galleries, "I just loosen my girdle and let 'er fly.") In baseball she could outthrow many major-league players, once lobbing a 313-foot throw from center field to home plate and another time striking out Joe DiMaggio. Grantland Rice, her friend and mentor—and the first sportswriter to call Babe the greatest athlete of all time—filmed her playing football and saw her deliver a forty-seven-yard completed pass.

Babe's triumph in the 1932 Olympic Games in Los Angeles was followed by an equally quick decline. First came the problem caused by her appearance in a Dodge automobile ad, which the AAU maintained was a breach of amateur ethics. The organization quickly reversed its decision after confirming that Babe's image was used without permission, but Babe just as promptly turned pro and began to work as a traveling vaudevillian, tap-dancing, singing, and jogging on a treadmill—complete with costume changes. She missed the sports-page headlines, however, and with no arena in which to exhibit her prodigious abilities, she took to the road with her male/female basketball team, Babe Didrikson's All-Americans.

In 1934 she entered—and won—her first golf tournament. Babe burned up the fairways, winning the 1935 Texas Women's Amateur Championship. But the United States Golf Association ruled that she was a professional and barred her from amateur competition, an action engineered by Texas country-club women who derided Babe's "mannish ways." (Officials once asked her to wear a bra during a basketball game. Her response was—"What do you think I am? A sissy?") Babe found a more tolerant milieu on the exhibition circuit. She toured with a happy-go-lucky, 225-pound professional wrestler she had married in 1938. George Zaharias adored Babe, but the marriage faltered after he gave up wrestling to manage his wife's career and his weight blossomed to almost four hundred pounds. Babe's discovery of his affair with Betty Dodd, her protégée and best friend, marked the end of their marriage.

Oddly enough, Babe's battle with cancer, starting in 1953 when she had a colostomy, brought the three together. Nourished by George and Betty's loving attention, she rallied after surgery to win the U.S. Women's Open in 1954. But the cancer had spread to the lymph nodes, and it was only a matter of time. She played in tournaments for two years, until 1955, when the malignancy spread to her spine and nothing more could be done. Her lingering death in 1956, courageous to the public, was an inspiration to a generation that had admired the Wonder Woman of world sports. Never a quitter, Babe slipped away in her sleep, at age forty-three, her golf bag leaning at the ready against her hospital-room wall.

ZAPATA

EMILIANO

BEFORE THERE WAS LENIN, there was Zapata. Mexican revolutionary Emiliano Zapata led a life of violent idealism, dying as he lived, in the service of the peasants whose cause he championed. His struggle—the first in this century to incorporate socialist ideals—predated by nearly a decade the 1917 storming of Petro-grad's Winter Palace. Most Mexican revolutions have been about the fundamental use of power; only rarely have they been about principles. Zapata combined the two: His primary aim was to give Mexican agricultural workers, who were subsisting in a state perilously close to serfdom, the right to own land. It was a program that even some of his erstwhile comrades in arms found alarming. In the end he was killed for his dedication.

Zapata came from a relatively well-off peasant family of mestizos, people of mixed Indian and Spanish heritage, in the state of Morelos, south of Mexico City. As a natural outgrowth of his surroundings, Zapata became an expert rider, roper, and gunman, so shrewd in the practice of leadership that he was made a calpuleque, or "village chief," by popular acclaim while still in his twenties. Initially, his aim was to seek redress for the lands seized from the Indians by European settlers. But as tensions grew between the communally farming Indians and their mestizos allies and the wealthy sugar planters who were expanding their holdings in Morelos, his revolutionary zeal broadened. Zapata became the organizer of the 1910 peasant uprising against the corrupt Mexican dictator Porfirio Díaz, during which the rebels occupied disputed lands by force.

A brief sojourn to Mexico City exposed Zapata to anarchist ideas that he found applicable to the plight of the campesinos. Other political activists in the country embraced the tenets of socialism, among them one of a dreary line of Mexican saviors, Francesco Madero, in whose cause Zapata conquered the south. But once Madero was installed as Mexico's president, Zapata's insistence on land reform made him and his aristocratic cabinet members and supporters uneasy. As a result, in the fluid politics of Mexican revolution, Zapata soon found himself aligned against a system Madero wanted to control, not overthrow.

In 1911, the draconian General Victoriano Huerta was sent to eliminate the upstart Zapata. While in hiding, the revolutionary drafted the sweeping agrarian land-reform Plan of Ayala, which convinced landowners that he had to be destroyed in his southern redoubt. After a few years of inconclusive battle marked by government atrocities and the Zapatistas' inability to break out of their stronghold, a desperate Zapata attempted to escalate his tactics and effect an alliance with the semicriminal insurgent Pancho Villa, who was fighting in the north.

The very picture of a Mexican revolutionary in his tight charro pants, his huge sombrero, and his enormous black mustache, the handsome Zapata was a ruthless commander of immense élan, as idolized by the peasantry as he was reviled by the rich. He recognized, however, that neither he nor Villa could last long as Robin Hoods, and their alliance fell apart in weeks. His depredations, always calculated either to extract money for the poor or to terrorize his foes, were also eroding the resources and population of his power base. Some of these lost supporters were replaced by socialist planners from Mexico City, who helped the Zapatista leadership redesign the school system and enact other reforms. In this they were opposed by a new enemy, Venustiano Carranza, the Mexican president who followed the provisional presidency of the self-exiled Huerta. Carranza, a hypocritical former lackey of Díaz, gave lip service to land reform while sending troops to suppress the south's agrarian revolution, shooting, hanging, and exiling peasants. By 1916, with Carranza's Mexican government troops encircling him, Zapata's fiery promise to "struggle against everything and everybody" had taken on the grim veracity of a recurring and inescapable nightmare.

Resorting to terrorism and sabotage, Zapata ceded properties in a last-ditch effort to maintain the debate on land reform. By 1917 he regrouped enough to abandon terror and reestablish regular military organization. But it was too late. Although the slippery Carranza, bowing to pressure to discuss agrarian reform, had withdrawn from Morelos, allowing Zapata to retake much of the territory he had lost the previous year, it was merely the last bright glow before the flame died. The revolutionary chief hung on for two years before his own cleverness undid him. In his zealous attempts to convince a government colonel to support his side of the conflict, Zapata failed to realize he was dealing with a double agent and walked straight into a trap. He was shot in the back by Carranza's agents in Morelos on April 10, 1919, his body spirited away by his enemies. To this day, no one knows where it is buried.

But Zapata's troubled spirit still hovers over Latin America. The Mexican revolutionary was a spiritual precursor of the romantic Argentinean guerrilla fighter Che Guevara, and peasant rebel armies, some ephemeral, some as seemingly deathless as Sendero Luminoso, continue to roil the political landscape of South America and the Caribbean. In 1994 an Indian uprising in the poverty-shackled Mexican state of Chiapas dubbed itself the Zapatista Army, trading the ghostly leader's sombrero for the ubiquitous ski mask of the modern terrorist. A vivid reminder of all that remains unchanged in Mexico since the fearless Zapata was lured to his death nearly eighty years earlier, the new Zapatistas fight for land for the poor, opposed by the philosophical descendants of the autocrats who had so assiduously tried to crush their namesake.

ADDAMS, JANE

ADDAMS, JANE. *Twenty Years at Hull House.* Urbana, IL: University of Illinois Press, 1990.

DAVIS, ALLEN F. *American Heroine: The Life and Legend of Jane Addams.* Oxford/NY: Oxford University Press, 1975.

—— AND MARY LYNNE MCCREE. *Eighty Years at Hull-House.* Chicago: Quadrangle Books, 1969.

DE BENEDETTI, CHARLES, ED. *Peace Heroes in Twentieth Century America.* Bloomington, IN: University of Indiana Press, 1986.

DEEGAN, MARY JO. *Women in Sociology.* Westport, NY: Greenwood, 1991.

LASCH, CHRISTOPHER. *The New Radicalism in America, 1889-1963.* NY: Knopf, 1965.

WHITMAN, ALDEN. *American Reformers.* NY: Wilson, 1985.

Amer Journ of Soc Jy '02; S '12
Journ of the Hist of Ideas Ap/Ju '61

ALI, MUHAMMAD

HAUSER, THOMAS. *Muhammad Ali: His Life and Times.* NY: Simon & Schuster, 1992.

——. *Muhammad Ali: In Perspective.* San Francisco: Collins, 1996.

MILLER, DAVIS. *The Tao of Muhammad Ali.* NY: Warner Books, 1996.

MAILER, NORMAN. *The Fight.* Boston: Little, Brown, 1975.

Ebony N '89
Ent Weekly Au 2 '96
Esquire D '83; Je '89
LA Times Je 16 '91; Ja 17 '92
NY Times Ap 28 '85; Ju 3 '91
People Ja 13 '97
Sports Illustrated Ja 13 '91; Jy 1 '91
Time F 27 '79; Mr 22 '63; Mr 6 '64

ALLEN, WOODY

ALLEN, WOODY. *On Being Funny.* NY: Charterhouse, 1975.

——. *Without Feathers.* NY: Random House, 1975.

——. *Death: A Comedy in One Act.* NY: S. French, 1975.

BRODE, DOUGLAS. *The Films of Woody Allen.* Sea-caucus, NJ: Carol Publishing, 1997.

GIRGUS, SAM B. *The Films of Woody Allen.* Cambridge: Cambridge University Press, 1993.

GROTEKE, KRISTI. *Mia & Woody: Love and Betrayal.* NY: Carroll & Graf, 1994.

GUTHRIE, LEE. *Woody Allen: A Biography.* NY: Drake Publishers, 1978.

HIRSCH, FOSTER. *Love, Sex, Death and the Meaning of Life: The Films of Woody Allen.* NY: Limelight, 1990.

LAX, ERIC. *Woody Allen: A Biography.* NY: Knopf, 1991.

MALTIN, LEONARD. *The Great Movie Comedians: From Charlie Chaplin to Woody Allen.* NY: Crown Publishers, 1978.

Christian Century S 9 '92
Downbeat O '93
GQ Ma '98
Mirabella J 11 '98
Newsweek Ap 24 '78
New York S 21 '92; O 17 '94
New Yorker F 4 '74; Ma 21 '94; D 9 '96
Paris Rev Fall '95
People D 28 '92; J 12 '98
Rolling Stone Jy 1 '76
Time Ap 30 '79, Jy 3 '72

ARAFAT, YASIR

GOWERS, ANDREW AND TONY WALKER. *Behind the Myth: Yasir Arafat and the Palestinian Revolution.* London: W. H. Allen, 1990.

HART, ALAN. *Arafat: A Political Biography.* Bloomington, IN: Indiana University Press, 1989.

RUBINSTEIN, DANNY. *The Mystery of Arafat.* South Royalton, VT: Steerforth Press, 1995.

WALLACH, JANET AND JOHN. *Arafat: In The Eyes of the Beholder.* London: Mandarin, 1991.

Newsweek My 4 '92; Ja 23 '84
People Ja 3 '94
Read Dig S '89
Time N 11 '74

ARENDT, HANNAH

ARENDT, HANNAH. *Between Friends: The Correspondence of Hannah Arendt and McCarthy: 1949-1975.* NY: Harcourt Brace, 1995.

——. *The Human Condition.* Chicago: University of Chicago Press, 1958.

——. *The Life of the Mind* (vol. 1, *Thinking;* vol. 2, *Willing*), ed. by Mary McCarthy. NY: Harcourt Brace Jovanovich, 1972.

——. *The Origins of Totalitarianism.* NY: Harcourt, Brace, 1951.

——. *Men in Dark Times.* NY: Harcourt, Brace, 1970.

DEEGAN, MARY JO. *Women in Sociology.* New York/Wesport, CT: Greenwood, 1991.

ETTINGER, ELZBIETA. *Hannah Arendt/Martin Heidegger.* New Haven: Yale University Press, 1995.

YOUNG-BRUEHL, ELISABETH. *Hannah Arendt, for Love of the World.* New Haven, CT: Yale University Press, 1982.

America Ja 31 '76
Encounter Dec '82
Harpers Sept '82
Newsweek My 3 '82
NY Rev of Books Ja 20 '66; Ja 22 '76
New Yorker D 22 '75; N 21, 28 and D 5 '77
New Rep D 27 '75
NY Times D 6 '75
Social Research Spring '77
Time Dec 15 '75
Washington Monthly Ap '83

ARMSTRONG, LOUIS

ARMSTRONG, LOUIS. *Satchmo: My Life In New Orleans.* NY: De Capo Press, 1986.

——. *Swing That Music.* NY: Da Capo Press, 1993.

GIDDINS, GARY. *Satchmo.* NY: Doubleday, 1992.

MILLER, MARC H. *Louis Armstrong: A Cultural Legacy.* Seattle, WA: University of Washington Press, 1994.

Am Her My/Je '89
Life Jy 16 '71
New Yorker Ja 16 '84
New Republic Ja 30 '84
Newsweek Jy 19 '71; O 10 '83
Read Dig D '71
Saturday Review Jy 4 '70
Time Jy 19 '71

ARMSTRONG, NEIL

ARMSTRONG, NEIL, WITH GENE FARMER AND DORA JANE-HAMBLIN. *First on the Moon: A Voyage with Neil Armstrong, Michael Collins and Edwin E. Aldrin, Jr.* Boston: Little, Brown, 1970.

——. *The First Lunar Landing: 20th Anniversary* (as told by the astronauts Neil Armstrong, Edwin Aldrin, Michael Collins). National Aeronautics and Space Administration. [1989?].

KRAMER, BARBARA. *Neil Armstrong: The First Man on the Moon.* Springfield, NJ: Enslow Publishers, 1997.

WESTMAN, PAUL. *Neil Armstrong, Space Pioneer.* Minneapolis, MN: Lerner Publications Co., 1980.

Esq D '83
News Jy 2 '79; Ag 4 '69; Jy 28 '69
Time Jy 18 '69; Jy 25 '69

ASTAIRE, FRED

ADLER, BILL. *Fred Astaire: A Wonderful Life: A Biography.* NY: Carroll and Graf, 1987.

ASTAIRE, FRED. *Steps in Time.* (New Foreword by Ginger Rogers) NY: Da Capo Press, 1981.

SATCHELL, TIM. *Astaire, The Biography.* London: Arrow Books, 1988.

THOMAS, BOB. *Astaire: The Man, the Dancer.* NY: St. Martin's Press, 1984.

Cin Journ Fall '84
Life Au 25 '41
Show O '62
Theater Arts My '37

BAKER, JOSEPHINE

BAKER, JEAN CLAUDE. *Josephine: The Hungry Heart.* NY: Random House, 1993.

BAKER, JOSEPHINE AND JO BOVILLON. *Josephine.* NY: Harper & Row, 1977.

HANEY, LYNN. *Naked at the Feast: A Biography of Josephine Baker.* NY: Dodd, Mead, 1981.

ROSE, PHYLLIS. *Jazz Cleopatra: Josephine Baker in Her Times.* NY: Doubleday, 1989.

SMITH, JESSIE CARNEY. *Epic Lives: One Hundred Black American Women Who Made a Difference.* Detroit: Gale, 1995.

——. *Notable Black American Women.* Detroit: Gale, 1995.

Am Film Oct '90
Am Her N '89
Atlantic D '64
Esq Je '74
New Rep N 6 '89
Time Oct 30 '90; Ap 21 '75

BALL, LUCILLE

ANDREWS, BART. *I Love Lucy Book.* NY: Doubleday, 1985.

—— AND THOMAS WATSON. *Loving Lucy.* NY: St. Martin's Press, 1982.

BALL, LUCILLE AND BETTY H. HOFFMAN, *Love Lucy.* NY: Putnam, 1996.

BRADY, KATHLEEN. *Lucille: The Life of Lucille Ball.* NY: Hyperion, 1994.

BROCKER, JIM. *Lucy in the Afternoon: An Intimate Memoir of Lucille Ball.* NY: Pocket, 1990.

GILBERT, TOM AND COYNE S. SANDERS. *Desilu: The Lives of Lucille Ball and Desi Arnaz.* NY: Morrow, 1993.

HARRIS, WARREN G. *Lucy and Desi: The Legendary Love Story of Television's Most Famous Couple.* NY: Simon & Schuster, 1992.

MCCLAY, MICHAEL. *I Love Lucy.* NY: Time Warner, 1955.

SANDERS, COYNE STEVEN. *Desilu: The Story of Lucille Ball and Desi Arnaz.* NY: Morrow, 1993.

Broadcasting My '89
Macleans My 8 '89
Nation My 22 '89
Newsweek My 8 '89
Read Dig Mr '90; Ja '84
Time My 8 '89

BANNISTER, ROGER

BANNISTER, ROGER. *The Four-Minute Mile.* NY: Dodd, Mead, 1981.

Sports and the National Character (proceedings of a symposium held at Grinnell College). Grinnell, IA, 1984.

Macleans Au 23 '93
Newsweek My 17 '54
NY Times My 7, D 10 '54
NY Times Book Rev N 15 '55
Runner's Word D '96
Sporting News O 2 '95
Sports Illus Ju 27 '94; Au 16 '94; S 25 '95
Time My 7 '51; My 17 '54
World Press Rev D '95

BARDOT, BRIGITTE

VADIM, ROGER. *Bardot, Deneuve, Fonda.* NewYork: Simon & Schuster, 1986.

SHIPMAN, DAVID. *The Great Movie Stars.* London: Argus & Robertson, 1972.

FRENCH, SEAN. *Bardot.* London: Pavillion, 1994.

Newsweek Ja 6 '58; Ag 28 '89
New Yorker Ja 20 '68
People N 30 '92; Au 29 '94
Time Ja 10 '83; Mr 22 '71; Ja 25 '60
Vogue N 1 '72

BARNARD, DR. CHRISTIAAN

BARNARD, CHRISTIAAN. *Christiaan Barnard: One Life.* London: Harrap, 1970.

——. *Good Life Good Death: A Doctor's Case for Euthanasia and Suicide.* Englewood Cliffs, NJ: Prentice-Hall, 1980.

DOOPER, DAVID, ED. *Chris Barnard: By Those Who Know Him.* South Africa: Vlaeberg Publishing, 1992.

HAWTHORNE, PETER. *The Transplanted Heart: The Incredible Story of the Epic Heart Transplant Operations by Professor Christiaan Barnard and His Team.* Chicago: Rand McNally, 1968.

LEIPOLD, L. EDMOND. *Dr. Christiaan N. Barnard, The Man with the Golden Hands.* Minneapolis, MN: Denison, 1971.

Life Ap 5 '68
London Observer Ja 14 '68
Nat Observer Ja 8 '68
Newsweek D 18 '67; Mar 11 '68; Ju 9 '70; Au 9 '71
NY Times D 6 '67
People Apr 17 '78; F2 '81; Apr 14 & Mar 31 '86
Sat Eve Post F 10 '68
Time Ja 5 '68; Ja 12 '68; F 23 '68; D 15 '68
Vogue S 15 '70

BEATLES, THE

BRAUN, M. *Love Me Do: The Beatles Progress.* London: Penguin, 1964.

GIULIANO, GEOFFREY. *The Beatles Album.* NY: Viking, 1991.

——. *The Lost Beatles Interviews.* NY: Dutton, 1996.

KOZINN, ALLAN. *The Beatles.* London: Phaidon Press, 1995.

MCKEEN, WILLIAM. *The Beatles.* Westport, Conn.: Greenwood, 1990.

NORMAN, P. *Shout! The Beatles in Their Generation.* NY: Fireside, 1981.

SCHAFFNER, N. *The Beatles Forever.* Harrisburg, PA: Cameron House, 1977.

PAWLOWSKI, GARETH L. *How They Became the Beatles: A Definitive History of the Early Years, 1960-1964.* NY: Dutton, 1989.

Stambler, Irvin. *The Encylopedia of Pop, Rock and Soul.* NY: St. Martin's, 1989.

Ent Weekly J 10 '92
Life Au 28 '64; Ap 24 '70
New Republic D 2 '81

Newsweek N 18 '63; F 17 '64; Je 8 '70
Time Dec 22 '80

BEN-GURION, DAVID

KURZMAN, DAN. *Ben-Gurion: Prophet of Fire.* NY: Simon & Schuster, 1983.
LIPSKY, LOUIS. *Memoirs in Profile.* Philadelphia: Jewish Publication Society, 1975.
SILVERSTEIN, HERMA. *David Ben-Gurion.* NY: Watts, 1988.

Commentary Ja '54; F '54
For Aff J '42
Jewish Dig D '72
Jewish Frontier D '56
Jewish Obs & Mid East Rev O 3 '75
Life Mr 18 '57
Nat'l Jewish Mo J '74
New Rep Je 8 '87; Je 17 '85
New Statesman D 7 '73
Newsweek D 10 '73
NY Times Mag F 6 '55; S 24 '61; O 16 '66
Time D 10 '73

BERGMAN, INGMAR

BJORKMAN, STIG AND TORSTEN MANNS, JONAS SIMA. *Bergman on Bergman: Interviews with Ingmar Bergman.* NY: De Capo Press, 1993.
COWRIE, PETER. *Ingmar Bergman: A Critical Biography.* NY: Scribner's, 1982.
BERGMAN, INGMAR. *An Artist's Journey On Stage, On Screen, In Print.* NY: Arcade Pub., 1995.
———. *Images: My Life in Film.* London: Bloomsbury, 1994.
LONG, ROBERT EMMET. *Ingmar Bergman: Film and Stage.* NY: Abrams, 1994.
MARKER, FREDERICK J. AND LISE-LONE MARKER. *Ingmar Bergman: A Life in Theatre.* Cambridge/NY: Cambridge University Press, 1992.
TORNQVIST, EGIL. *Between Stage and Screen: Ingmar Bergman Directs.* Ann Arbor, MI: University of Michigan Press, 1995.

Am Film O '88
Film Comment My/Je '83
Horizon O/N '82; N '77
Life O 15 '71
Newsweek My 3 '76
NY O 27 '80
Time Mr 14 '60; S 26 '88; F 14 '77

BERGMAN, INGRID

LEAMER, LAURENCE. *As Time Goes By: The Life of Ingrid Bergman.* NY: Harper & Row, 1986.
HARMETZ, ALJEAN. *Round Up the Usual Suspects: The Making of Casablanca——Bogart, Bergman and World War II.* NY: Hyperion, 1992.
LEWIS, AMY, ED. *American Cultural Leaders.* Santa Barbara, CA: ABC-CLIO, 1993.
MORDDEN, ETHAN. *Movie Star.* NY: St. Martin's Press, 1983.
QUIRK, LAWRENCE J. *The Films of Ingrid Bergman.* NY: Carol Publishing, 1989.
ROSS, LILLIAN. *The Player: A Profile of an Art.* NY: Simon & Schuster, 1962.

Maclean's S 13 '82; Ja 3 '83
McCalls My '82
Newsweek S 13 '82; S 15 '80
People Ja 12 '86; Ja 20 '86
Read Dig F '84
Time S 13 '80; D 25 '82

BOGART, HUMPHREY

BOGART, STEPHEN. *Bogart.* NY: Viking Penguin, 1995.
CAHILL, MARIE. *Humphrey Bogart: A Hollywood Portrait.* NY: Smithmark, 1992.
COOKE, ALISTAIR. *Six Men: Charlie Chaplin, Edward III, H. L. Mencken, Humphrey Bogart, Adlai Stevenson, Bertrand Russell.* NY: Arcade, 1995.
HEPBURN, KATHARINE. *The Making of "The African Queen" or How I Went to Africa with Bogart, Bacall and Huston and Almost Lost My Life.* NY: Knopf, 1987.
SKLAR, ROBERT. *City Boys: Cagney Bogart, Garfield.* Princeton: Princeton University Press, 1992.

Atlantic F '75
Esq S '64
Film Comment May/June '8
Newsweek Au 31 '87; N 1 '65
Vogue My '82

BRANDO, MARLON

BLY, NELLIE. *Marlon Brando: Larger Than Life.* NY: Pinnacle Books, 1994.
BRANDO, MARLON, AND ROBERT LINSEY. *Songs My Mother Taught Me.* NY: Random House, 1994.
Englund, George. *Marlon Brando: A Friend of Mine.* NY: Warner Books, 1995.

MANSO, PETER. *Brando: The Biography.* NY: Hyperion, 1994.
McCANN, GRAHAM. *Rebel Males.* New Brunswick, NJ: Rutgers University Press, 1991.
SCHICKEL, RICHARD. *Brando: A Life in Our Times.* NY: Atheneum, 1991.

Am Film Je '86
Esq N '89
Film Comment Jy/Ag '91
Newsweek Mr 13 '72
New Yorker May 31 '93
Time My 24 '76; Ja 22 '73

BRECHT, BERTOLT

BENTLY, ERIC. *The Brecht Memoir.* Evanston, IL: Northwestern University Press, 1991.
BRECHT, BERTOLT. *Bertolt Brecht, Journals 1934-1955.* NY/London: Routledge Chapman & Hall, 1993.
FUEGI, JOHN. *The Life and Lies of Bertolt Brecht.* London: Flamingo, 1994.
HAYMAN, RONALD. *Brecht: A Biography.* NY: Oxford, 1983.
LYON, JAMES K. *Bertolt Brecht in America.* Princeton: Princeton University Press, 1980.
NEEDLE, JAN, AND PETER THOMSPON. *Brecht.* Chicago: University of Chicago Press, 1987.
WILLET, JOHN. *Brecht in Context.* London/NY: Methuen, 1984.

Atlantic Ja '69
Encounter F '84
Nation S 8 '56
New Leader D 12 '83
New Republic Au 27 '56
New Yorker S 10 '90
Partisan Review '84
Time D 10 '56

BROWN, HELEN GURLEY

BROWN, HELEN GURLEY. *Helen Gurley Brown's Outrageous Opinions.* NY: Avon, 1982.
———. *Sex and the Single Girl.* NY: Geis, 1962.
———. *The Late Show: A Semiwild But Practical Survival Plan for Women Over 50.* NY: Morrow, 1993.
FALKOF, LUCILLE. *Helen Gurley Brown [Wizards of Business].* Garrett Educational Corp., 1991.
LETERMAN, EHNER G. AND T. W. CARILA. *They Dare to Be Different.* NY: Meredith, 1968.
NEWQUIST, ROY. *Conversations.* NY: Rand McNally, 1967.

Antioch Rev Fall '83
Cosmopolitan
Esq F '70
Life Ma 1 '63; O 18 '64; N 19 '65
New York S 27 '82; N 27 '95
NY Times D 31 '67; Ja 13 '97
NY Times Mag Au 11 '74
People N 1 '82
Psychol Today M '94

CALLAS, MARIA

ARDOIN, JOHN. *The Callas Legacy.* NY: Scribners Ref., 1979.
———. *The Callas Legacy: A Biography of a Career.* NY: Scribner's Ref., 1982.
CALLAS, EVANGELIA AND LAWRENCE G. BLOCHMAN. *My Daughter Maria Callas.* Andrew Farkas, ed. NY: Ayer, 1979.
JELLINEK, GEORGE. *Callas: Portrait of a Prima Donna.* NY: Dover, 1986.
RASPOU, LANFRANCO. *The Last Prima Donnas.* NY: Knopf, 1982.
SCOTT, MICHAEL. *Maria Meneghini Callas.* Boston: Northeastern University Press, 1992.

Atlantic S '81
Horizon F '81
Newsweek S 26 '77
Opera N '77
Opera Quarterly Sum '89
Time S 26 '77; Mr 23 '81

CAPONE, AL

BERGREEN, LAURENCE. *Capone: The Man and the Era.* NY: Simon & Schuster, 1994.
KOBLER, JOHN. *Capone: The Life and World of Al Capone.* NY: Da Capo Press, 1992.
MURRAY, GEORGE. *The Legacy of Al Capone.* NY: Putnam, 1975.
PASLEY, FRED. *Al Capone: The Biography of a Self-made Man.* Stratford, NH: Ayer, 1977.
SCHOENBERG, ROBERT J. *Mr. Capone.* NY: Morrow, 1992.

Am Her F '79
Life N 29 '48
Newsweek F 3 '47; F 17 '47; N 20 '39
New Yorker Mr 1 '47
Read Dig Jy '47

Sports Illustrated N 6 '72
Time F 3 '47; N 20 '39

CARSON, RACHEL

BROOKS, PAUL. *The House of Life: Rachel Carson at Work.* NY: Houghton Mifflin, 1989.
FREEMAN, MARTHA AND PAUL BROOKS. *Always Rachel: The Letters of Rachel Carson and Dorothy Freeman, 1952-1964, The Story of a Remarkable Friendship.* Boston: Beacon Press, 1994.
GARTNER, CAROL B. *Rachel Carson.* NY: Continuum, 1983.
WHITMAN, ALDEN, ED. *American Reformers.* NY: H.W. Wilson, 1985.

Audobon Jy '92
EPA Journal My/Je '92
Life O 12 '62
Newsweek Ap 27 '64

CARTIER-BRESSON, HENRI

BUNNEFOY, YVES. *Henri Cartier-Bresson: Photographer.* Boston: Little, Brown: 1979.
CARTIER-BRESSON, HENRI. *Henri Cartier-Bresson, Photographer.* London: Thames and Hudson, 1992.

American Photographer July/Aug '91
Harper's My '47; N '61
Newsweek F 17 '47
New Yorker O 23 '89; O 30 '89
NY Times Ma 13 '94; Au 20 '95; O 4 '96
Time F 17 '47

CASTRO, FIDEL

BALFOUR, SEBASTIAN. *Castro.* London: Longman, 1995.
ESCALONA, ROBERTO L. *Face to Face with Fidel Castro: A Conversation with Tomos Borge.* NY: Ocean Press, 1994.
GEYER, GEORGIE ANN. *Guerilla Prince: The Untold Story of Fidel Castro.* Boston: Little, Brown, 1991.
MINA, GIANNI. *An Encounter with Fidel: Interview with Fidel Castro.* NY: Ocean Press, 1993.
PATERSON, THOMAS G. *Contesting Castro: The United States and the Triumph of the Cuban Revolution.* Oxford/NY: Oxford University Press, 1994.
QUIRK, ROBERT E. *Fidel Castro.* NY: Norton, 1993.
SZULC, TAD. *Fidel: A Critical Portrait.* NY: Morrow, 1986.

Congressional Quarterly Researcher
Newsweek O 22 '79; Au 10 '92
New Yorker Ap 27 '92
Read Dig Je '91
Time N 2 '62; O 22 '79
US News Ju 12 '78

CHANEL, GABRIELLE "COCO"

DE LA HAYE, AMY AND SHELLY TOBIN. *Chanel: The Couturiere at Work.* NY: Overlook Press, 1996.
MADSEN, AXEL. *Chanel: A Woman of Her Own.* NY: Henry Holt, 1991.
———. *Coco Chanel: A Biography.* London: Bloomsbury, 1991.

Atlantic Ja '84
Newsweek Ja 25 '71
Time Ja 25 '71
Vogue My '77; Au '85

CHAPLIN, CHARLIE

CHAPLIN, CHARLIE. *My Autobiography.* NY: Plume, 1992.
COOKE, ALISTAIR. *Six Men: Charlie Chaplin, Edward III, H. L. Mencken, Humphrey Bogart, Adlai Stevenson, Bertrand Russell.* NY: Arcade, 1995.
DIAMOND, ARTHUR. *Charlie Chaplin.* San Diego: Lucent Books, 1995.
EPSTEIN, JERRY. *Remembering Charlie: A Pictorial Biography.* NY: Doubleday, 1989.
KAMIN, DAN. *Charlie Chaplin's One Man Show.* Carbondale, IL: Southern Illinois University Press, 1984.
LYNN, KENNETH S. *Charlie Chaplin and His Times.* NY: Simon & Schuster, 1997.
McCABE, JOHN. *Charlie Chaplin.* Garden City, NY: Doubleday, 1978.
MILTON, JOYCE. *Tramp: The Life of Charlie Chaplin.* NY: HarperCollins, 1996.
ROBINSON, DAVID. *Chaplin: His Life and Art.* NY: Da Capo, 1992.

Film Quar Ap '92
Life Ap '89
New States & Soc Ap 14 '89
Newsweek Ja 9 '78
New Yorker Au 12 '96
NY Times Book Rev F 12 '96; Jy 28 '96
People Mr 20 '89
Smithsonian O '95
Time Ja 2 '78
US News Ap 24 '89

CHRISTIE, AGATHA

CHRISTIE, AGATHA. *An Autobiography*. NY: Berkeley, 1991.

GILL, GILLIAN C. *Agatha Christie: The Woman and Her Mysteries*. NY: Free Press, 1992.

SANDERS, DENNIS AND L. LOVALL. *Agatha Christie Companion*. San Francisco: Berkeley Publications, 1989.

SMITH, LUCINDA. *Women Who Write*. Englewood Cliffs, NJ: J. Messner, 1989.

Wagoner, Mary S. *Agatha Christie*. NY: Scribner's Ref., 1986.

Encyclopedia of British Women Writers
Horizon Nov '84; Autumn '76
Newsweek Ja 26 '76
Read Dig O '85
Smithsonian S '90
Time My 27 '85; N 28 '77; Ja 26 '76

CHURCHILL, WINSTON

CHARMLEY, JOHN. *Churchill's Grand Alliance: The Anglo-American Special Relationship*. NY: Harcourt Brace, 1995.

CHARMLEY, JOHN. *Churchill: The End of Glory: A Political Biography*. San Diego: Harcourt Brace, 1992.

CHURCHILL, SIR WINSTON. *The Irrepressible Churchill: Stories, Sayings, and Impressions of Sir Winston Churchill*. Compiled by Kay Halle. NY: Facts on File, 1985.

——. *Blood, Sweat, and Tears*. NY: G.P. Putnam's Sons, 1941.

——. *The Churchill War Papers*. Comp., Martin Gilbert. NY: Norton, 1993.

——. *Memoirs of the Second World War* (An abridgment of the 6 vols.). Boston: Houghton Mifflin, 1959.

ROBERTS, ANDREW. *Eminent Churchillians*. NY: Simon & Schuster, 1995.

ROSE, NORMAN. *Churchill, The Unruly Giant*. NY: Free Press, 1995.

Hist Jour Je '96
Jour of Amer Hist Mr '96
Life Ja 29 '65
London Times Ja 25 '65
Nat Rev Mr 11 '96; Ap 8 '96; My 20 '96
New States Jy 12 '96
Newsweek F 1 '65
NY Times Book Rev S 3 '95; N 5 '95
Saturday Review Ja 24 '65
Spectator Au 12 '95
Times Lit Sup Mr 15 '96

COLETTE

DORMANN, GENEVIEVE. *Colette: A Passion for Life*. NY: Abbeville, 1985.

FLIEGER, JERRY A. *Colette and the Fantom Subject of Autobiography*. Ithaca, NY: Cornell University Press, 1992.

FRANCIS, CLAUDE. *A Charmed World: Colette, Her Life and Times*. NY: St. Martin's, 1993.

HOLMES, DIANNA. *Colette*. NY: St. Martin's, 1991.

LOTTMAN, HERBERT R. *Colette: A Life*. Boston: Little, Brown, 1991.

NORELL, DONNA M. *Colette: An Annotated Primary and Secondary Bibliography*. NY/London: Garland, 1992.

SARDE, MICHAEL. *Colette: A Biography*. NY: Morrow, 1989.

SARTORI, EV MARTIN AND DOROTHY WAYNE ZIMMERMAN, EDS. *French Women Writers*. Westport, CT: Greenwood, 1991.

STEWART. *Colette*. NY: Scribners Ref., 1996.

New Rep N 18 '91; S 6 '54
Newsweek My 9 '66; Au 16 '54
New Yorker Au 21 '54
Time Ja 1 '79; My 20 '6; Je 22 '57; Au 23 '54

LE CORBUSIER

BAKER, GEOFFREY H. *Le Corbusier: The Creative Search, The Formative Years of Charles Edouard Jeanneret*. NY: Routledge, 1995.

BLAKE, PETER. *The Master Builders*. NY: Norton, 1996.

BROOKS, H. ALLEN. *Le Corbusier's Formative Years*. Chicago: University of Chicago Press, 1997.

CURTIS, WILLIAM J. R. *Le Corbusier: Ideas and Forms*. NY: Rizzoli, 1992.

ETLIN, RICHARD. *Frank Lloyd Wright and Le Corbusier: The Romantic Legacy*. NY: St. Martin's, 1994.

PALAZZOLO, CARLO. *In the Footsteps of Le Corbusier*. NY: Rizzoli, 1991.

WEBER, HEIDI. *Le Corbusier—The Artist*. NY: Rizzoli, 1989.

Harper's Je '81
Nation Au 1-8 '87
New Rep Ja 18 '88
Newsweek S 6 '65
New Yorker My 9 '88
Time S 15 '67; S 3 '65
Vogue D '82

COUSTEAU, JACQUES

COUSTEAU, JACQUES-YVES WITH FREDERIC DUMAS. *The Silent World*. NY: Harper, 1953.

COUSTEAU, JACQUES-YVES WITH JACQUES BOURCART. *La Mer*. Paris: Larousse, 1953.

COUSTEAU, JACQUES-YVES WITH JAMES DUGAN. *The Living Sea*. NY: Harper, 1963.

——. ED., JAMES DUGAN. *World Without Sun*. NY: Harper, 1965.

MADSEN, ALEX. *Cousteau: An Unauthorized Biography*. NY: Beaufort Books, 1987.

MUNSON, RICHARD. *Cousteau: The Captain and His World*. NY: Paragon Books, 1991.

Chi Trib Ju 1 '94
E (the Environmental Magazine) Mr '96
Forbes, Mr 11 '06
LA Times Mr 31 '87
NY Times Ju 26 '97
People Ju 24 '85
Smithsonian O '86
Sports Illus Ap 30 '90
USA Today Ju 26 '97
Wash Post Ma 30 '86

CURIE, MARIE

GIROUD, FRANCOISE. *Marie Curie: A Life*. Tr., Lydia Davis. NY: Holmes and Meier, 1986.

KASS, SIMON GABRIELE. *Women of Science: Righting the Record*. Bloomington, IN: Indiana University Press, 1990.

MEADOWS, JACK. *The Great Scientists*. Oxford/NY: Oxford University Press, 1987.

OGILVIE, MARILYN BAILEY. *Women in Science: Antiquity Through the Nineteenth Century: A Biographical Dictionary with Annotated Bibliography*. Boston: MIT, 1986.

QUINN, SUSAN. *Marie Curie: A Life*. Reading, MA: Addison Wesley, 1996.

——. *Marie Curie: A Life*. NY: Simon & Schuster, 1995.

Amer Jour of Physics N '90
Chem & Engin News Ja 1 '96
Lad Home Jour N '95
L'Express Ap 20 '95
Nature S 14 '95
New Sci S 2 '95; My 18 '96
NY Times Book Rev Ap 2 '95
Physics Today Au '95
Sci Mr 24 '95
Times Lit Sup Ap 12 '96

THE DALAI LAMA

BELL, CHARLES. *Portrait of a Dalai Lama: The Life and Times of the Great Thirteenth*. Boston: Wisdom Press, 1987.

BSTAN-DZIN-RGYA-MTSHO, DALAI LAMA XIV. *My Tibet*. London: Thames and Hudson, 1990.

DALAI LAMA. *Ethics for the Next Millennium*. NY: Putnam, 1996.

——. *Path to Enlightenment*. Ithaca, NY: Snow Lion Publications, 1994.

HANZHANG, YA. *The Biographies of the Dalai Lamas*. San Francisco: Cypress Book Co., 1991.

PINBURN, SIDNEY. *Dalai Lama: A Policy of Kindness*. Ithaca, NY: Snow Lion Publications, 1993.

Harper's F '92
Maclean's O 15 '90; O 30 '80
New Republic S 29 '79; N 20 '89; N 11' 91
Newsweek S 17 '79; O 16 '89
New York S 3 '79
Time O 16 '89; Ap 11 '88; S 20 '76
Vanity Fair My '91

DALI, SALVADOR

DALI, SALVADOR. *The Secret Life of Salvador Dali*. NY: Dover, 1993.

DE LIANO, IGNACIO G. *Dali*. NY: Rizzoli, 1993.

ETHERINGTON-SMITH, MEREDITH. *The Persistence of Memory: A Biography of Dali*. NY: Random House, 1992.

FINKELSTEIN, HAIM. *Salvador Dali's Art and Writing: 1927-1942, The Metamorphoses of Narcissus*. NY: Cambridge University Press, 1996.

SWINGLENHURST, EDMUND. *Salvador Dali: Exploring the Irrational*. NY: Smithmark Publishers, 1996.

Art Am Mr '89
ARTNews Ap '89
Newsweek F 6 '89
Smithsonian O '86
Time F 6 '89

DAVIS, BETTE

HADLEIGH, BOZE. *Bette Davis Speaks*. NY: Barricade Bks., 1996.

LEAMING, BARBARA. *Bette Davis: A Biography*. NY: Ballantine, 1993.

QUIRK, LAWRENCE J. *Fasten Your Seat Belts: The Passionate Life of Bette Davis*. NY: NAL, 1990.

RIESE, RANDALL. *All About Bette: Her Life A to Z*. Chicago: Contemporary Books, 1993.

RINGGOLA, GENE. *The Films of Bette Davis*. NY: Bonanza, 1966.

SPADA, JAMES. *More Than a Woman: An Intimate Biography of Bette Davis*. London: Little, Brown, 1993.

WALKER, ALEXANDER. *Bette Davis*. NY: NAL, 1995.

Amer Spec D '89
Film Comment Mr/Ap '89; Mr '78; N/D '85.
Life Ja '90
Newsweek O 16 '89; Mr 30 '87
New Yorker Ma 21 '94
People O 23 '89
Time O 16 '89; Ap 14 '80
Utne Read S '93
Variety O 11 '89

DEAN, JAMES

ALEXANDER, PAUL. *James Dean: Boulevard of Broken Dreams*. London: Little, Brown, 1994.

DALTON, DAVID AND RON CAYEN. *James Dean: American Icon*. NY: St. Martin's 1984.

HYAMS, JOE. *James Dean: Little Boy Lost*. London: Century, 1992.

MARTINETTI, RONALD. *The James Dean Story: A Myth-Shattering Biography of an Icon*. Secausus, NJ: Carol Publishing, 1995.

RIESE, RANDALL. *The Unabridged James Dean*. NY: Wings Books, 1994.

SHROEDER, ALAN. *James Dean*. NY: Chelsea House, 1994.

STOCK, DENNIS. *James Dean Revisited*. NY: Viking, 1978.

Esq O '55; Mr '92
GQ Mr '96
Los Angeles Mag A '96
New States & Soc Je 14 '91
NY Times Book Rev Au 7 '94; Au 11 '96
People Au 7 '89; Mr 18 '91; Jy 27 '92; Jy 24 '96
Premiere S '93; My '95
Saturday Evening Post Jy/Au '85
Vogue S '88

DE BEAUVOIR, SIMONE

APPIGNANSI, LISA. *Simone de Beauvoir*. London: Penguin, 1988.

BAIR, DEIRDRE. *Simone de Beauvoir: A Biography*. NY: Summit, 1990.

Crosland, Margaret. *Simone de Beauvoir: The Woman and Her Work*. London: Heinemann, 1992.

DE BEAUVOIR, SIMONE. *Letters to Sartre*. Paris: Editions Gallimard. (Engl Transl.), 1990.

——. *The Prime of Life: The Autobiography of Simone de Beauvoir*. Tr., Peter Green. Cleveland: World Pub Co., 1962.

——. *Witness to My Life: The Letters of Jean-Paul Sartre to Simone de Beauvoir, 1926-1939*. NY: Macmillan, 1993.

FULLBROOK, KATE, AND EDWARD FULLBROOK. *Simone de Beauvoir and Jean-Paul Sartre*. NY: Knopf, 1991.

MOI, TORIL. *Simone de Beauvoir: The Making of an Intellectual Woman*. Oxford: Blackwell, 1994.

OKELY, JUDITH. *Simone de Beauvoir*. London: Virago, 1986.

Guardian F 19 '70
Nation Ap 26 '86
Newsweek F 9 '70
NY Times Jy '92
NY Times Mag Jy 11 '71
Pub Wkly S 9 '96
Time Ap 28 '86
Vogue Jy 86

DE GAULLE, CHARLES

BERNSTEIN, SERGE. *The Republic of de Gaulle, 1958-1969*. Cambridge/NY: Cambridge University Press, 1993.

COOK, DON. *Charles de Gaulle*. NY: Putnam, 1983.

CORGAN, CHARLES G. *Charles de Gaulle: A Brief History with Documents*. NY: St. Martin's, 1995.

DEBRAY, REGIS. *Charles de Gaulle: Existentialist of the Nation*. NY: Norton, 1994.

DE GAULLE, CHARLES. *The Complete War Memoirs of Charles de Gaulle*. NY: Da Capo Press, 1984.

SHENNAN, ANDREW. *De Gaulle: Profiles in Power Series*. Reading, Mass.: Addison-Wesley, 1994.

WILLIAMS, CHARLES. *The Last Great Frenchman: A Life of Charles de Gaulle*. London: Little, Brown, 1993.

Am Her O '96
Commentary Ja '93
Life N 20 '70
New States & Soc D 7 '90
Newsweek F 10 '64; D 13 '65; Ju 10 '68; N 23 '70
NY Times Book Rev N 11 '90; Au 30 '91; My 10 '92; Ap 24 '92; Ja 28, My 6 '94; Au 26 '94
Time My 31 '68
Times Lit Sup Jy 28 '95
Wkly Stand Jy 22 '96

Wilson Quar Winter '93
Wor Pol Jour Fall '96

DIANA, PRINCESS OF WALES

CAMPBELL, LADY COLIN. *Diana in Private*. London: Smith Gryphon, 1992.
DAVIS, NICHOLAS. *Diana: The Lonely Princess*. NY: Carol Publishing, 1996.
DELANO, JULIA. *Diana, Princess of Wales*. NY: Smithmark, 1993.
MORTON, ANDREW. *Diana: Her New Life*. NY: Simon & Schuster, 1994.
——. *Diana: The True Story*. NY: Simon & Schuster, 1992.
PASTERNAK, ANNA. *Princess in Love*. NY: Signet, 1994.

Chatelaine Ju '94
Ent Weekly S 19 '97
Maclean's F 5 '96; Ma 11 '96
Newsweek Ma 11 '96
NY Times S 3 '97; S 18 '97
NY Times Mag S 21 '97
NY Times International S 3 '97
People S 19 '94; O 31 '94; J 8 '96; S 15 '97; S 22 '97; O 20 '97
Read Dig Ju '83

DIETRICH, MARLENE

BACH, STEVEN. *Marlene Dietrich: Life and Legend*. NY: Morrow, 1992.
DELGAUDIO, SYBIL. *Dressing the Part: Sternberg, Dietrich, and Costume*. Rutherford, NJ: Fairleigh Dickinson University Press, 1993.
HANUT, ERYK. *I Wish You Love: Conversations with Marlene Dietrich*. Berkeley: Frog, 1996.
HIGHAM, CHARLES. *Marlene; The Life of Marlene Dietrich*. NY: Norton, 1977.
RIVA, MARIA E. *Marlene Dietrich*. NY: Random House, 1995.
SPOTO, DONALD. *Blue Angel: The Life of Marlene Dietrich*. NY: Doubleday, 1992.
STADLAR, GAYLYN. *In the Realm of Pleasure: Von Sternberg, Dietrich, and the Masochist Aesthetic*. Boulder, CO: Colorado University Press, 1993.

Daily Telegraph Ma 7 '92
NY Times My 17 '92; J 29 '93; S 26 '93
NY Times Book Rev F 7 '93
Time My 18 '92
Vanity Fair Jy '92; N '92
Vogue Jy '92

DINESEN, ISAK

DINESEN, ISAK. *Out of Africa*. NY: Random House, 1937.
DONELSON, LINDA. *Out of Isak Dinesen in Africa: The Untold Story*. Iowa City, IA: Coulsong List, 1995.
HORTON, SUSAN R. *Difficult Women, Difficult Lives: Olive Schreiner and Isak Dinesen, In and Out of Africa*. Baltimore, MD: Johns Hopkins University Press, 1995.
PELENSKY, OLGA ANASTASIA. *Isak Dinesen: The Life and Imagination of a Seducer*. Athens, OH: Ohio University Press, 1991.
PLIMPTON, GEORGE, ED. *Women Writers at Work: Paris Review Interviews*. NY: Viking Penguin, 1989.
THRUMAN, JUDITH. *Isak Dinesen: The Life of a Storyteller*.
TRZEBINSKI, ERROL. *Silence Will Speak: A Study of the Life of Denys Finch Hatton and His Relationship with Karen Blixen*. Chicago: University of Chicago Press, 1985.

Eng Lang Notes S '92
House & Gar Jy '91
Jour of Mod Lit F '88, F '90
Pub Wkly Ja 4 '91; Ap 10 '95
Scand Rev S '92
Studies in Short Fic S '90

DISNEY, WALT

ELIOT, MARC. *Walt Disney: Hollywood's Dark Prince*. London: Deutsch, 1994.
FINCH, CHRISTOPHER. *The Art of Walt Disney*. NY: Abrams, 1973.
GROVER, RON. *The Disney Touch*. Homewood: Business One, 1991.
MALTIN, LEONARD. *The Disney Films*. NY: Crown, 1984.
SCHICKEL, RICHARD. *The Disney Version*. NY: Simon & Schuster, 1968.
TAYLOR, JOHN. *Storming the Magic Kingdom*. NY: Knopf, 1987.
THOMAS, BOB. *Walt Disney: An American Original*. NY: Simon & Schuster, 1976.

Newsweek D 26 '61
Read Dig N '88
Saturday Review Ap 22 '67
Time D 23 '66; Ap 25 '88

DUNCAN, ISADORA

BOORSTIN, DANIEL. *The Creators*. NY: Random House, 1992.
DALY, ANN. *Done into Dance: Isadora Duncan in America*. Bloomington, IN: Indiana University Press, 1995.
DE MILLE, AGNES. *Portrait Gallery*. Boston: Houghton Mifflin, 1990.
DESTI, MARY. *The Untold Story: The Life of Isadora Duncan 1921-1927*. NY: Da Capo, 1981.
DUNCAN, DOREE, CAROL PRATT AND CYNTHIA SPLATT. *Life Into Art: Isadora Duncan and Her World*. NY: Norton, 1993.
DUNCAN, ISADORA. *My Life*. NY: Norton, 1995.
LOEWENTHAL, LILLIAN. *The Search for Isadora: The Legend and Legacy of Isadora Duncan*. Princeton: Princeton Book Company, 1993.

Dance Mag Jy '77; O '77; N '77; D '77; Mr '75; Je '69
Read Dig S '68
Saturday Review D 13 '75
Vogue Jy '69

DYLAN, BOB

BAULDIE, JOHN ed. *Wanted Man: In Search of Bob Dylan*. NY: Citadel Press, 1970.
COTT, JONATHAN. *Dylan*. NY: Doubleday, 1984.
HEYLIN, CLINTON. *Bob Dylan: Behind the Shades*. London: Penguin, 1992.
McGREGOR, CRAIG ED. *Bob Dylan: The Early Years: A Retrospective*. NY: Morrow, 1972.
RICHARDSON, SUSAN. *Bob Dylan*. NY: Chelsea House, 1995.
RILEY, TIM. *Hard Rain*. NY: Knopf, 1992.
SPITZ, BOB. *Dylan: A Biography*. NY: Norton, 1989.
STUESSY, JOE. *Rock and Roll*. NY: Prentice, 1990.
WILLIAMS, PAUL. *Dylan: A Man called Alias*. NY: Henry Holt, 1992.
——. *Performing Artist*. Novato, CA: Underwood, 1991.

Ent Weekly O 3 '97
Newsweek D 9 '85; Je 23 '86; O 6 '97
New Yorker Au 28 '89
NY Times S 28 '97
People N 3 '97
Phil Inquirer D 21 '97
USA Today O 9 '97

EARHART, AMELIA

BRINK, RANDALL. *Lost Star: The Search for Amelia Earhart*. London: Bloomsbury, 1994.
BUTLER, SUSAN. *East to the Dawn: The Life of Amelia Earhart*. NY: Addison-Wesley, 1997.
LOVELL, MARY S. *The Sound of Wings: The Life of Amelia Earhart*. NY: St. Martin's, 1991.
RICH, DORIS L. *Amelia Earhart: A Biography*. Washington, DC: The Smithsonian Institute, 1996.
WARE, SUSAN. *Still Missing: Amelia Earhart and the Search for Modern Feminism*. NY: Norton, 1993.

Amer Hist Ap '95
Journ of Pop Cult Winter '95
Life Ap '92
LA Times Ma 17 '92
People Ja 28 '91
Mirabella N '89; F '94
Newsweek Ja 31 '94
NY Times F 15 '94
NY Times Book Rev D 19 '93
NY Times Mag N 24 '96
Omni S '93
People Ja 28 '91
Pub Wkly N 8 '93
Time Jy '37
Times Lit Sup Ju 3 '94

EDISON, THOMAS ALVA

BALDWIN, NEIL. *Edison, Inventing the Century*. NY: Hyperion, 1995.
CONOT, ROBERT. *Thomas A. Edison: A Streak of Luck*. NY: Da Capo, 1986.
JEHL, FRANCIS. *Menlo Park Reminiscences: The Intimate Story of Thomas A. Edison*. New York: Dover, 1990.
JOSHPSON, MATHEW. *Edison: A Biography*. NY: Wiley, 1992.
MELOSIA, MARTIN. *Thomas Alva Edison and the Modernization of America*. Chicago: Scott, Foresman, 1990.

New Yorker My 28 '90
Newsweek Mr 26 '79
Rdrs Dig Jy '73
Saturday Review Ma 15 '76
Smithsonian Je '78
Time O 22 '79

EINSTEIN, ALBERT

BRIAN, DENIS. *Einstein: A Life*. NY: Wiley, 1995.
EINSTEIN, ALBERT AND MILEVA EINSTEIN MARIC. *Albert Einstein and Mileva Maric: The Love Letters*. Princeton: Princeton University Press, 1992.
EINSTEIN, ALBERT. *The Collected Papers*. Princeton: Princeton University Press, 1993.
FRENCH, A. P., ed. *Einstein: A Centenary Volume*. Cambridge, MA: Harvard University Press, 1979.
FOLSING, ALBRECH. *Einstein*. NY: Viking Penguin, 1997.
HIGHFIELD, ROGER AND PAUL CARTER. *The Private Lives of Albert Einstein*. NY: Dutton, 1994.
HOLTON, GERALD. *Einstein, History, and Other Passions: The Rebellion Against Science at the End of the Twentieth Century*. Reading, MA: Addison-Wesley, 1996.
PAIS, ABRAHAM. *Einstein Lived Here*. Oxford/NY: Oxford University Press, 1994.
SNOW, C. P. *Variety of Men*. London/Melbourne: Macmillan, 1967.
SUGIMOTO, KENJI. *Albert Einstein: a Photographic Biography*. NY: Schocken Books, 1989.
WHITE, MICHAEL. *Einstein*. UK: Dutton, 1993.
—— AND JOHN GRIBBIN. *Einstein: A Life in Science*. London: Simon & Schuster, 1993.

Cont Physics Ja '95
Discover O '96
Harper's Ja '96
New Rep N 21 '94
New Sci My 4 '96
NY Times S 18 '94; Jy 14 '95
New York O 7 '96
New Yorker Ma 10 '73; 17 '73; Jy 6 '87; D 19 '94
Phys Today D '95; My '96; S '96
Saturday Review Ap 14 '56
Sci News Je 1 '96; Je 15 '96
Sci Amer Je '96
Times Jy 24 '95
Times Lit Supp Mr 17 '95; Jy 5 '96; Jy 19 '96

EISENHOWER, DWIGHT D.

AMBROSE, STEPHEN. *Eisenhower: Soldier and President*. NY: Simon & Schuster, 1991.
BESCHLOSS, MICHAEL R. *Eisenhower: Centennial Life*. NY: HarperCollins, 1990.
BRENDON, PIERS. *Ike*. NY: Harper & Row, 1986.
FROMKIN, DAVID. *In the Time of the Americans: FDR, Truman, Eisenhower, Marshall, MacArthur—The Generation That Changed America's Role in the World*. NY: Random House, 1996.
GREENSTEIN, FRED I. *The Hidden-Hand President: Eisenhower as Leader*. Baltimore, MD: Johns Hopkins University Press, 1994.
JACOBS, WILLIAM JAY. *Dwight David Eisenhower: Soldier and Statesman*. NY: Watts, 1995.
MILLER, MERLE. *Ike: The Soldier as They Knew Him*. NY: Putnam, 1987.
PICKETT, WILLIAM. *Dwight David Eisenhower: An American Power*. Wheeling, IL: Harlan Davidson, 1995.

Am Her D '85
Esq D '83
London Times Obit.
Newsweek Ap 7 '69; My 25 '70
New Rep My 9 '81
Read Dig Mr '91
Time Ju 4 '60; Ap 4 '69
US News S 1 '86

EISENSTEIN, SERGEI

AUMONT, JACQUES. *Montage Eisenstein*. Bloomington, IN: Indiana University Press, 1987.
BERMA, YON. *Eisenstein*. Bloomington, IN: Indiana University Press, 1973.
EISENSTEIN, SERGEI M. *Immoral Memories*. Boston: Houghton Mifflin, 1983.
LERDA, JAY AND ZINA VOYHOW. *Eisenstein at Work*. NY: Pantheon/MOMA, 1982.

Drama Rev S 12 '78
Film Comment Jy/Au '91
Newsweek F 23 '48
NY Times F 12 '48; My 28 '95
Sight & Sound Summer '88
Time F 23 '48

ELIOT, T. S.

ACKROYD, PETER. *T. S. Eliot: A Life*. NY: Simon & Schuster, 1984.
BUSH, RONALD. *T. S. Eliot*. Oxford: Oxford University Press, 1984.
ELIOT, VALENE ED. *The Letters of T. S. Eliot (vol. 1)*. NY: Harcourt Brace Jovanovich, 1988.
LYNDALL, GORDON. *Eliot's Early Years*. Oxford: Oxford University Press, 1977.
MOODY, A. D. *Thomas Stearns Eliot: Poet*. Cambridge: Cambridge University Press, 1980.
TATE, ALLEN ED. *T. S. Eliot: The Man and His Work*. London: Penguin, 1971.

Amer Lit S '94
Essays in Lit Fall '93
Explicator Winter '92
Mod Age Spring '95
Nation Au 12/19 '96
Nat Rev S 30 '96
Newsweek Ja 18 '65; N 26 '84; Je 17 '96

New Yorker Mr 25 '85; N 20 '89; Je 24 '96;
    Jy 1 '96
NY Rev of Books Je 6 '96
N Amer Rev Ma '96
South Rev Winter '96
Vogue F '85

QUEEN ELIZABETH I

DUFF, DAVID. *Elizabeth of Glamis.* London: Frederick
    Muller, 1973.
LACEY, ROBERTS. *Queen Mother.* NY: Little, Brown, 1987.
LAIRD, DOROTHY. *Queen Elizabeth: The Queen Mother.*
    London: Hodder and Stoughton, 1966.
MORTIMER, PENELOPE. *Queen Elizabeth: A Life of the
    Queen Mother.* NY: St. Martin's, 1986.
McGOWAN, HELENE. *The Queen Mother.* NY: Smith-
    mark, 1992.
WAKEFORD, GEOFFREY. *Thirty Years a Queen: A Study
    of H. M. Queen Elizabeth, the Queen Mother.*
    London: Robert Hall, 1968.

New States Au 3 '90
Newsweek My 30 '60.
People Au 21 '89; Au 20 '90; Ap 22 '96
Spectator Jy 14 '90; Jy 30 '94
Time Au 18 '80; Au 11 '75
Vogue N 1 '54

QUEEN ELIZABETH II

BRADFORD, SARAH. *Elizabeth: A Biography of Britain's
    Queen.* NY: Wiley &, 1996.
CLAY, CHARLES. *Long Live the Queen.* Philadelphia:
    John Winston Co., 1953.
CATHCQUT, HELEN. *Her Majesty the Queen.* NY: Dodd,
    1962.
DAVID, NICHOLAS. *Queen Elizabeth II: A Woman Who
    Is Not Amused.* Secaucus, NJ: Carol Publishing,
    1994.
FISCHER, GRAHAM. *The Queen's Life.* London: Robert
    Hale, 1976.
HARRIS, KENNETH. *The Queen.* London: Orion, 1994.
——. *The Queen: Royalty and Reality.* NY: St. Martin's,
    1995.
HIGHAM, CHARLES. *Elizabeth and Philip: The Untold
    Story of the Queen of England and Her Prince.*
    NY: Berkeley, 1993.

Economist Ju 1 '96
Maclean's Ap 22 '96
Nat'l Law Jour O 7 '96
New States Ma 16 '97
Newsweek Jy 21 '47
New Yorker Ap 22 '96
NY Times Book Rev Ma 26 '96
People Ma 20 '96; Ju 8 '96; Ju 10 '96
Spectator F 3, S 21 '96
Time D 1 '47; O 28 '57; N 29 '48; Ap 22 '06
Times Lit Sup O 4 '96
www.royal.gov.uk (Official Website of the British
    monarchy)

ELLINGTON, DUKE

COLLIER, JAMES LINCOLN. *Duke Ellington.* NY:
    Macmillan,1991.
ELLINGTON, DUKE. *Music Is My Mistress.* NY:
    Doubleday, 1973.
GELLY, DAVE. *The Giants of Jazz.* NY: Schirmer, 1987.
HASSE, JOHN EDWARD. *Beyond Category: The Life and
    Genius of Duke Ellington.* NY: Simon & Schuster,
    1993.
JEWELL, DEREK. *Duke.* NY: Norton, 1977.
RENNERT, RICHARD, ED. *Jazz Stars.* NY: Chelsea House,
    1994.
TRAVIS, DEMPSEY J. *The Duke Ellington Primer.* Chicago:
    Urban Research Press, 1996.
TUCKER, MARK. *Ellington: The Early Years.* Chicago:
    University of Illinois Press, 1995.
—— ED. *The Duke Ellington Reader.* Oxford/NY:
    Oxford University Press, 1993.

Atlantic Ma '75
Ebony N '90; Ja '74; S '74
Esq D '83; No '73; D '75; Je '73
Read Dig N '69
New Rep Jy 11 '88
Newsweek O 12 '87; Je 3 '74; Ma 12 '69
New Yorker Je 10 '74
Time Jy 23 '73; Je 3 '74

FEDERICO FELLINI

ALPERT, HOLLIS. *Fellini, A Life.* NY: Atheneum, 1986.
BAXTER, JOHN. *Fellini.* NY: St. Martin's, 1994.
CHANDLER, CHARLOTTE. *I, Fellini.* NY: Random House,
    1995.
TORNABOUNI, LIETTA, ED. *Federico Fellini.* NY: Rizzoli,
    1995.

Amer Digest D 4 '93; My 11 '96
Am Film N '85
Film Comment My/Je '85

Film Quart Sp '94; Sp '95
Interview Ja '94
Nat Rev N 29 '93
New Rep My 25 '92; Ja 31 '94
Newsweek N 8 '93
New Yorker Je 24 '85; Mr 21 '95; D 11 '95
People Ja 18 '93; N 15 '93; D 27 '93
Premiere N '95
Sight & Sound N '92; Ap N '92; Ja '94; N '95; My '96
Time N 8 '93
Times Lit Sup Ja 21 '94; Ap 26 '96
Variety N 8 '93

FERMI, ENRICO

FERMI, LAURA. *Atoms in the Family: My Life with Enrico
    Fermi.* Chicago: University of Chicago Press, 1954.
GOTTFRIED, TED. *Enrico Fermi, Pioneer of the Atomic
    Age.* NY: Facts on File, 1992.
LATIL, PIERRE. *Enrico Fermi: The Man and: His Theories.* Tr.,
    by Len Ortzen. NY: P.S. Eriksson, 1966.
SEGRAE, EMILIO. *Enrico Fermi: Physicist.* Chicago:
    University of Chicago Press, 1970.

Nation N 27 '54
Newsweek S 7 '53; D 6 '54
New Yorker Jy 24 '54; Jy 31 '54
Time D '54

FORD, HENRY

BATCHELOR, RAY. *Henry Ford, Mass Production and
    Design.* Manchester, England: Manchester University
    Press, 1995.
FORD, HENRY J. AND SAMUEL CROWTHER. *My Life and
    Work.* NY: Ayer, 1980.
GELDERMAN, CAROL. *Henry Ford: The Wayward
    Capitalist.* NY: St. Martin's, 1989.
LACY, ROBERT. *Ford: The Men and The Machine.* NY:
    Ballantine, 1987.
STIDGER, WILLIAM L. *Henry Ford: The Man and His
    Motives.* NY: George H. Doran, [c. 1923].
WIK, RENALOD M. *Henry Ford and Grass Roots
    America.* Ann Arbor, MI: University of Michigan
    Press, 1973.

Am Her Ap '92
Am Hist Rev Je '96
Am Hist Au '96
Automotive News Je 26 '96
Graphis My '94
NY Times Mag Ap 14 '96
Sat Ev Post S '96
Times Educ Supp Mr 11 '94

FRANCO, FRANCISCO

ELLWOOD, SHEELAGH M. *Franco.* London/NY: Longman,
    1994.
FEIS, HERBERT. *The Spanish Story: Franco and the
    Nations At War.* Westport, CT: Greenwood
    Publishing, 1987.
PAYNE, STANLEY G. *Franco's Spain.* London/NY::
    Routledge, 1968.
PRESTON, PAUL. *Franco: A Biography.* NY: Basic Books,
    1994.
——. *The Politics of Revenge and Fascism and The
    Military in Twentieth Century Spain.* London/NY
    Routledge, 1995.

New Rep Au 9 '82
Newsweek N 3 '75
Time N 3 '75

FRANK, ANNE

BARNOUW, DAVID AND GERROLD VAN DER STROEM, EDS. *The
    Diary of Anne Frank.* NY: Doubleday, 1989.
FRANK, ANNE. *Diary of a Young Girl: The Definitive
    Edition.* NY: Doubleday, 1995.
GUTMAN, ISRAEL, ED. *Encyclopedia of the Holocaust.*
    NY: Macmillan, 1990.
LINDWVER, WILLY. *The Last Seven Months of Anne Frank.*
    NY: Pantheon, 1991.
TELUSHKIN, RABBI JOSEPH. *Jewish Literacy.* NY: Morrow,
    1991.

History Today Mr '85
Maclean's Ap 15 '96
Nation Mr 18 '96
New Rep Mr 4 '96
Newsweek Je 25 '79
New Yorker D 18 '89
NY Times Book Rev Jy 22 '90; Mr 5 '95
Part Rev Sum '96
People Mr 21 '94; My 13 '96
Times Educ Sup My 31 '96
Times Lit Supp Ap 13 '90
Vill Voice Mr 21 '95; N 7 '95; F 27 '96

FRANKLIN, ARETHA

BEGO, MARK. *Aretha Franklin: The Queen of Soul.* NY:
    St. Martin's, 1989.

GOURSE, LESLIE. *Aretha Franklin: Lady Soul.* NY:
    Watts, 1995.
HASKINS, JAMES. *Aretha: A Personal and Professional
    Biography of Aretha Franklin.* NY: Stein and Day,
    1986.
O'DAIR, BARBARA. *The Rolling Stone Book of Women in
    Rock.* NY: Random House, 1997.
SHAW, ARNOLD. *Black Popular Music.* NY/London:
    Shirman,1986.

Ebony Ap '95
Esq Ja '89; Mr '82
Jet O 7 '96
Ms D '87
New Yorker F 1 '88
Newsweek Au 26 '85
Time Je 28 '68
Vogue Mr '88

FREUD, SIGMUND

BADCOCK, CHRISTOPHER. *Essential Freud (2nd Edition).*
    Cambridge, MA: Blackwell Press, 1994.
EYSENCK, HANS J. *The Decline and Fall of the Freudian
    Empire.* NY: Viking, 1985.
FERGUSON, HARVIE. *The Lure of Dreams: Sigmund Freud
    and the Construction of Modernity.* London/NY:
    Routledge, 1996.
FORRESTER, JOHN. *Dispatches From The Freud Wars:
    Psychoanalysis and Its Passions.* Cambridge, MA:
    Harvard University Press, 1995.
GARCIA, EMANUEL E. *Understanding Freud: The Man and
    His Ideas.* NY: New York University Press, 1992.
GAY, PETER. *Freud: A Life for Our Time.* London: J.M.
    Dent, 1988.
HUGHES, JUDITH M. *From Freud's Consulting Rooms: The
    Unconscious in A Scientific Era.* Cambridge, MA:
    Harvard University Press, 1994.
KERR, JOHN. *A Most Dangerous Method: The Story of
    Jung, Freud, and Sabrina Spielrein.* NY: Vintage,
    1994.
ROAZEN, PAUL. *How Freud Worked: First Hand
    Accounts of Patients.* Northvale, NJ: Jason
    Aronson, 1995.
ROAZEN, PAUL. *Meeting Freud's Family.* Amherst, MA:
    University of Massachusetts Press, 1993.

Life Je '90
Newsweek N 30 '81; O 29 '90
NY Times S 3 '89
NY Times Mag Mr 17 '85
People Je 6 '88
Smithsonian Mr '90; Au '90
Time Je 26 '39

FRIEDAN, BETTY

FRIEDAN, BETTY. *Feminine Mystique.* NY: Norton, 1996.
——. *It Changed My Life: Writings on the Women's
    Movement.* NY: Dell, 1991.
——. *The Fountain of Age.* NY: Simon & Schuster, 1994.
——. *The Second Stage.* NY: Dell, 1991.
MELTZER, MILTON. *Betty Friedan: A Voice for Women's
    Rights.* NY: Viking Kestrel, 1985.

Amer Quart Mr '96
Esq D '83
Fortune O 31 '94
Life F '88
Playboy S '92
Psychol Tod N '93
Nation N 14 '81
Nat Rev F 5 '82
NY Times S 15 '93
NY Times Book Rev S 11 '88; O 3 '93
NY Times Mag Jy 5 '81; F 27 '83; N 3 '85
Yale Rev Spring '63

GAGARIN, YURI

GAGARIN, YURI AND VLADIMIR LEVEDEV. *Survival in Space.*
    Tr. Gabriella Asrael. NY: F.A. Praeger, 1969.
GAGARIN, VALENTIN ALEKSEEVICH. *My Brother Yuri: Pages
    from the Life of the First Cosmonaut.* Tr. Fainna
    Glagoleva. Moscow: Progress Publishers, 1973.
HOOPER, GORDON. *Soviet Cosmonaut Team.* Wood-
    bridge, England: GRIT Publications, 1986.
SHARPE, MICHAEL R. *Yuri Gagrin: First Man in Space.*
    Huntsville, AL: Strode Publishers, 1969.
THOMAS, SHIRLEY. *Men of Space* (vol. 3). Philadel-
    phia/NY: Chilton, 1961.
TSYMBAL, NIKOLAI, ed. *First Man in Space.* Moscow:
    Progress Publishers, 1984.
Yuri Gagarin: The First Cosmonaut. Moscow: Novosti
    Press Agency, 1977.

Newsweek Ap 24 '61; Ap 8 '68; Jy 24 '61
New Yorker Ap 29 '61
Time Ap 5 '68; Ap 21 '61; Je 30 '61

GANDHI, INDIRA

ABBAS, K. A. *That Woman: Indira Gandhi's Seven Years
    in Power.* Livingston: Orient Book Distributors, 1973.

ALEXANDER, P. *My Years with Indira Gandhi.* Columbia: South Asia Books, 1991.
FRASER, ANTONIA. *The Warrior Queens.* NY: Knopf, 1989.
GUPTE, PRANAY. *Mother India: A Political Biography of Indira Gandhi.* NY: Scribner's, 1992.
JAYAKAR, PUPUL. *Indira Gandhi: An Intimate Biography.* NY: Pantheon Books, 1993.
MALHOTRA, INDER. *Indira Gandhi: A Personal and Political Biography.* Boston: Northeastern University Press, 1991.
MASANI, Z. *Indira Gandhi: A Biography.* Miami Brown, 1976.
OPFELL, OLGA S. *Women Prime Ministers and Presidents.* Jefferson, NC: McFarland, 1993.

Christian Sci Mon Mr 25 '66
Life Mr 25 '66
NY Times Mr 27 '66
Newsweek Ap 4 '66; Jy 7 '75; N 12 '84
Time Ja 28 '66; N 12 '84

GANDHI, MOHANDAS

BROWN, JUDITH. *Gandhi: Prisoner of Hope.* New Haven, CT: Yale University Press, 1989.
CLEMENT, CATHERINE. *Gandhi: The Power of Pacifism.* NY: Abrams, 1965.
COPLEY, A. *Gandhi.* NY: Basil Blackwell, 1987.
FISCHER, LOUIS. *The Essential Gandhi.* NY: Random House, 1983.
——. *The Life of Mahatma Gandhi.* NY: Harper & Row, 1983.
GANDHI, MOHANDAS K. *Autobiography: The Story of My Experiments with Truth.* NY: Dover, 1983.
NANDA, B. R. *Gandhi and His Critics.* Oxford/NY: Oxford University Press, 1994.
——. *Mahatma Gandhi: A Biography.* London/NY: Oxford University Press, 1996.
SCHECHTER, BETTY. *The Peaceable Revolution.* NY: Houghton Mifflin, 1963.

Jour of Asian Studies F-Mr '96
New Statesman & Soc Ja 7 '94
Newsweek F 23 '48
NY Times Mag Ap14 '96
Pol Sci Quar S '97
Soc Theory & Practice F '93
Time My 3 '48
Times Lit Sup Ma 11 '94
Life F 9 '48; F 16 '48

GARBO, GRETA

BAINBRIDGE, JOHN. *Garbo.* NY: Doubleday, 1955.
CAHILL, MARIE. *Greta Garbo.* NY: Smithmark, 1992.
DAUM, RAYMOND. *Walking With Garbo: Conversations and Recollections.* NY: HarperCollins, 1992.
PARIS, BARRY. *Garbo: A Biography.* NY: Knopf, 1995.
SWENSON. *Greta Garbo: A Life Apart.* NY: Simon & Schuster, 1996.
SOUHAMI, DIANA. *Greta and Cecil.* San Francisco: Harper San Francisco, 1995.
VICKER, HUGO. *Loving Garbo: The Story of Greta Garbo, Cecil Berton, and Mercedes de Acosta.* NY: Random House, 1994.

Newsweek Ap 30 '90
NY Times Ju 6 '93
NY Times Book Rev Au 21 '94; Ap 2 '95
Time Ap 30 '90
Vogue F '95

GARCÍA MÁRQUEZ, GABRIEL

BELL, MICHAEL. *Gabriel García Márquez: Solitude and Solidarity.* NY: St. Martin's, 1993.
BELL-VILLADA, GENE H. *García Márquez: the Man and His Work.* Chapel Hill, NC: University of North Carolina Press, 1990.
BLOOM, HAROLD, ED. *Gabriel García Márquez.* NY: Chelsea House, 1989.
GARCÍA MÁRQUEZ, GABRIEL. *The Fragrance of Guava: Plinio Apuleyo Mendoza in Conversation with Gabriel García Márquez.* Tr., Ann Wright. London: Verso, 1983.
McGUIRK, BERNARD AND RICHARD CARDWELL, EDS. *Gabriel García Márquez: New Readings.* Cambridge: Cambridge University Press, 1981.
MINTA, STEPHEN. *García Márquez, Writer of Colombia.* NY: Harper & Row, 1987.
WILLIAMS, RAYMOND L. *Gabriel García Márquez.* Boston: Twayne Publishers, 1984.

Atlas Jy '79
Lat Amer Lit Rev Ja '85
Nat Rev Mr 27 '77; N 12 '82
Newsweek N 1 '82
New Yorker My 20 '85
NY Times S 26 '68; D 25 '76
Nobel Prize Winners
Saturday Review D 21 '68; D 11 '76
Time Mr 2 '83; N 1 '82
Times Lit Sup S 29 '72; Ap 15 '77

GARLAND, JUDY

EDWARDS, ANNE. *Judy Garland.* NY: Simon & Schuster, 1975.
FINCH, CHRISTOPHER. *Rainbow: The Stormy Life of Judy Garland.* NY: Grosset, 1975.
FORDIN, HUGH. *The World of Entertainment! Hollywood's Greatest Musicals.* NY: Doubleday, 1975.
FRANK, GEROLD. *Judy.* NY: Harper & Row, 1975.
FRICKE, JOHN. *Judy Garland: World's Greatest Entertainer.* NY: Henry Holt, 1992.
SHIPMAN, DAVID. *Judy Garland: The Secret Life of an American Legend.* NY: Hyperion, 1993.
TORME, MEL. *The Other Side of the Rainbow: Behind the Scenes on the Judy Garland Television Series.* NY/London: Oxford University Press, 1991.

Esq Ja '69
Lad Home Jour Au '67
Look O 7 '69
Newsweek N 4 '63; Jy 7 '69; Je 9 '75
Time Jy 4 '69

GATES, BILL

BOYD, AARON. *Smart Money: The Story of Bill Gates.* Greensboro, NC: Morgan Reynolds, 1995.
ICHBIAH, DANIEL AND SUSAN L. KNEPPER. *The Making of Microsoft.* Rocklin, CA: Prima Pub, 1992.
MANES, STEPHEN. *Gates: How Microsoft's Mogul Reinvented an Industry and Made Himself the Richest Man in America.* NY: Simon & Schuster, 1994.
WALLACE, JAMES. *Hard Drive: Bill Gates and the Making of the Microsoft Empire.* NY: Harper Business, 1992.

Bus Wk N 10 '97
Ent Weekly My 9 '97
Forbes Jy 28 '97
Fortune My 26 '97; D 8 '97
Newsweek Au 4 '97
NY Times D 11 '95; Je 12 '97; Jy 25 '97; D 30 '97; J 4 '98; J 18 '98
Time J 13, O 27 '97
USA Today O 23 '97; Mr 20 '98
Wired N '96; Ap '98

GINSBERG, ALLEN

BURROUGHS, WILLIAM S. *Letters to Allen Ginsberg: 1953-57.* NY: Full Court Press, 1982.
CASSADY, CAROLYN. *Off the Road: My Years with Cassady, Kerouac, and Ginsberg.* NY: Viking Penguin, 1991.
KRAMER, JANE. *Allen Ginsberg in America.* NY: Fromm, 1997.
MILES, BARRY. *Allen Ginsberg.* NY: Simon & Schuster, 1989.
MORGAN, BILL. *The Response to Allen Ginsberg.* Westport, CT: Greenwood Publishing Group, Inc., 1996.
——. *The Works of Allen Ginsberg, 1941-1944: A Descriptive Bibliography.* Westport, CT: Greenwood Publishing, 1995.
SCHUMACHER, MICHAEL. *Dharma Lion: A Biography.* NY: St. Martin's, 1994.

Amer Poetry Rev Jy '97
Life My; 27 '66
Maclean's N 11 '96
NY Times Mag Jy 11 '65; N 11 '84
People N 25 '96
Roll Stone My 29 '97
Vill Voice Ap 15 '97

GOODALL, JANE

GOODALL, JANE. *Through a Window: My Thirty Years with the Chimpanzees of Gombe.* Boston: Houghton Mifflin, 1992.
MONTGOMERY, SY. *Walking With the Great Apes: Jane Goodall, Dian Fossey, Birute Galdikas.* Boston: Houghton Mifflin, 1992.

Buzzworm My/Je '91
Ms Mr '88
Nation F 20 '89
Omni My '86
People My 14 '90
Pub Wkly Ja 29 '88
Science Ap 16 '93
Time N 30 '70

GORBACHEV, MIKHAIL

BUSTON, THOMAS G. *Gorbachev: A Biography.* NY: Stein and Day, 1985.
DODER, DUSKO. *Shadows and Whispers. Power Politics Inside the Kremlin from Brezhnev to Gorbachev.* NY: Random House, 1986.
—— AND LOUISE BRANSON. *Gorbachev: Heretic In the Kremlin.* NY: Viking. 1990.
GORBACHEV, MIKHAIL. *Memoirs.* NY: Doubleday, 1996.
——. *A Time for Peace.* NY: Richardson & Steirman, 1985.
McCAULEY, MARTIN. *The Soviet Union Under Gorbachev.* NY: St. Martin's, 1987.

SHEEHY, GAIL. *Why Gorbachev Happened.* Robert G. Kaiser. NY: Simon & Schuster, 1991.

Newsweek Ja 4 '88; D 4 '89; Apr 4 '91; Dec 31 '91
Time Ja 4 '88; Ja 1 '90
US News O 19 '87
Vanity Fair F '91

GRAHAM, BILLY

FRADY, MARSHALL. *Billy Graham: A Parable of American Righteousness.* Boston: Little, Brown, 1979.
GRAHAM, BILLY. *Just As I Am: The Autobiography of Billy Graham.* NY: Walker, 1997.
——. *World Aflame.* Garden City, NY, 1965.
MARTIN, WILLIAM C. *A Prophet With Honor: The Billy Graham Story.* NY: Quill, 1991.
POLLOCK, JOHN. *Billy Graham: The Authorized Biography.* NY: McGraw-Hill, 1996.
——. *To All Nations: The Billy Graham Story.* San Francisco: Harper San Francisco, 1985.
SETTEL. *Faith of Billy Graham.* NY: Random House, 1995.
WELLMAN, SAM. *Billy Graham: The Great Evangelist.* Uhrichsville, OH: Barbour & Company, 1996.

Christian Cent N 11 '92; Ap 1 '92
Newsweek My 24 '82; Ap 26 '82
New Republic Jy 7 & 14 '79
Time My 28 '90; N 14 '88; S 24 '84; My 28 '79; N 15 '93
Sat Ev Post Mr '86

GRAHAM, MARTHA

ARMITAGE, MERLE, ED. *Martha Graham: The Early Years.* NY: Da Capo Press, 1978.
DE MILLE, AGNES. *Martha.* NY: Random House, 1991.
GARFUNKEL, TRUDY. *Letter to the World: The Life and Dances of Martha Graham.* Boston: Little, Brown, 1995.
GRAHAM, MARTHA. *Blood Memory.* NY: Doubleday, 1991.
TRACY, ROBERT. *Goddess: Martha Graham's Dancers Remember.* NY: Limelight Editions, 1997.

Dance Mag Je '91; Jy '91
Life Au '91
Newsweek Ap 15 '91
Pub Wkly Ap 26 '91
Time Ap 15 '91
Vanity Fair Ag '91

GRANT, CARY

HARRIS, WARREN G. *Cary Grant: A Touch of Elegance.* Garden City, NY: Doubleday, 1987.
HIGHAM, CHARLES AND ROY MOSELEY. *Cary Grant: The Lonely Heart.* San Diego: Harcourt Brace Jovanovich, 1980.
NELSON, NANCY. *Evenings With Cary Grant: Recollections in His Own Word and by Those Who Knew Him Best.* NY: Morrow, 1991.
SCHICKEL, RICHARD. *Cary Grant: A Celebration.* Boston: Little, Brown, 1983.
WANSELL, GEOFFREY. *Haunted Idol: The Story of the Real Cary Grant.* NY: Morrow, 1984.

Arch Dig My '94
Film Comment N '89
New Yorker Mr 21 '94
People N 7 '88; Jy 26 '93
Sight & Sound My '94

GRIFFITH, D. W.

BARRY, IRIS AND EILEEN BOWSER. *D. W. Griffith: American Film Master.* NY/London: Garland, 1985.
GUNNING, TOM. *D. W. Griffith and The Origins of American Narrative Film: The Early Years at Biograph.* Champaign, IL: University of Illinois Press, 1991.
HENDERSON, ROBERT. *D. W. Griffith: His Life & Work.* NY/London: Garland Publishing, 1985.
HUNT, JAMES, ED. *The Man Who Invented Hollywood: Autobiography of D. W. Griffith.* Louisville, KY: Touchstone, 1972.
SCHICKEL, RICHARD. *D. W. Griffith: An American Life.* NY: Limelight Editions, 1996.
SIMMON, SCOTT. *The Films of D. W. Griffith.* Cambridge/NY: Cambridge University Press, 1993.
WILLIAMS, MARTIN. *Griffith: First Artist of the Movies.* Oxford/NY: Oxford University Press, 1980.

Horizon Au '79
Life Au 2 '48
Newsweek F 3 '75; Mr 8 '71
Sight & Sound Summer '73
Time Ap 9 '84

GUEVARA, CHE

ANDERSON, JON LEE. *Che Guevara: A Revolutionary Life.* NY: Grove Press, 1997.
CASTANEDA, JORGE G. *Companero: The Life and Death of Che Guevara.* Tr., Marina Castaneda. NY: Knopf, 1997.

CASTRO, FIDEL. *Che: A Memoir.* Ed., David Deutsch-mann. Melbourne/NY: Talman Co., 1994.
GADEA, HILDA. *Ernesto: A Memoir of Che Guevara.* Tr., Carmen Molina and Walter I. Bradbury. Garden City, NY: Doubleday, 1972.
GUEVARA, ERNESTO. *Episodes of the Cuban Revolutionary War, 1956-58.* NY: Pathfinder, 1996.
——. *The Motorcycle Diaries: A Journey Around South America.* Tr., Ann Wright. London/NY: Verso, 1995.
RODRIGUES, FELIX I. AND JOHN WEISMAN. *Shadow Warrior.* NY: Simon & Schuster, 1989.
TAIBO, PACO IGNACIO. *Guevara, Also Known As Che.* NY: St. Martin's, 1997.

Economist Jy 19 '97
For Aff N '97
Geogr Mag O '97
Mon Rev O '97
Newsweek Jy 21 '97; Ap 21 '97
New Yorker O 6 '97
NY Rev of Books Jy 17 '97
NY Times Mag Je 19 '60
Time Ag 8 '60
Wor Press Rev O '96

HAWKING, STEPHEN

HAWKING, STEPHEN AND MARTIN J. REES. *Before the Beginning: Our Universe and Others.* NY: Addison-Wesley, 1997.
——. *Black Holes and Baby Universes and Other Essays.* NY: Bantam, 1993.
——. *A Brief History of Time: From the Big Bang to Black Holes.* NY: Bantam, 1990.
McEVOY, J.P., OSCAR ZARATO AND RICHARD APPIGNANESI (ed.), Stephen Hawking. *Introducing Stephen Hawking.* Totem Books, 1995.
WHITE, MICHAEL AND JOHN R. GRIBBIN. *Stephen Hawking: A Life in Science.* NY: Dutton, 1992.

Astronomy Mr '93
NY Times Mag J 23 '83
Omni F '79
People Au 7 '95
The Physcis Teacher Mr '93
Science N '81
Time F 8 '88; Au 13 '90; Ju 8 '92; Jy 17 '95

HEARST, WILLIAM RANDOLPH

MILTON, JOYCE. *The Yellow Kids.* NY: Harper, 1989.
NORMAN, KENNETH. *Makers of Modern Journalism.* NY: Prentice Hall, 1952.
ROBINSON, JUDITH. *The Hearsts: An American Dynasty.* NY: Avon, 1991.
SWANBERG, W. A. *Citizen Hearst.* NY: Galahad Books, 1996.

Am Her N '92; Ap '88
New Yorker S '51
Time Au 27 '51; Au 20 '51

HEFNER, HUGH

BRADY, FRANK. *Hefner.* NY: Macmillan, 1974.
MILLER, RUSSELL. *Bunny: The Real Story of Playboy.* NY: Holt, Rinehart and Winston, 1984.

Esq Ja '92; N '84; Nov '79; D '79
Newsweek Au 4, 86; O 25 '82
Playboy ("The Playboy Philosophy": IX (D '62); X (Ja-D '63); XI (Ja-D '64); XII (N, D '65); XIII (Ja, F, Ma '65); D '56
Maclean's Ap 25 '83; Au 15 '94; Ap 22 '96
Time 3 '67

HEIFETZ, JASCHA

BROOK, DONALD. *Violinists of Today.* London: Rockliff, 1953.
SCHONBERG, HAROLD C. *The Virtuosi.* NY: Vintage, 1988.
SCHWARZ, BORIS. *Great Masters of the Violin.* NY: Simon & Schuster, 1983.

Atlantic Je '76
Life O 31 '69
Music Journ Ap '71
Nat Rev Ja 22 '88
Newsweek D 21 '87; F 11 '63; Au 21 '61
Sat Ev Post Je 4 '60
Saturday Review O 4 '75; Ap 24 '71
Time D 21 '87

HEMINGWAY, ERNEST

BAKER, CARLOS. *Ernest Hemingway: A Life Story.* NY: Scriber's, 1969.
BURGESS, ANTHONY. *Ernest Hemingway and His World.* NY: Scribner's, 1978.
DONALDSON, SCOTT. *By Force of Will.* NY: Viking, 1977.
HEMINGWAY, GREGORY H. *Papa: A Personal Memoir.* Boston: Houghton Mifflin, 1976.
HEMINGWAY, MARY WELSH. *How It Was.* NY: Knopf, 1951.
HOTCHNER, A.E. *Hemingway and His World.* NY: Vendome, 1989.

LYNN, KENNETH S. *Hemingway.* Cambridge, MA: Harvard University Press, 1995.
MELLOW, JAMES. *Hemingway: A Life Without Conse-quences.* London: Hodder and Stoughton, 1993.
MESSENT, PETER. *Ernest Hemingway.* London: Macmillan, 1992.
MEYERS, JEFFREY. *Hemingway: A Biography.* NY: Harper & Row, 1985.
REYNOLDS, MICHAEL. *Hemingway: The American Homecoming.* Cambridge, MA: Blackwell, 1992.
——. *Hemingway: The Paris Years.* Oxford, England: Blackwell, 1989.
——. *The Young Hemingway.* Oxford, England: Blackwell, 1986.

Esq D '62
Life Jy 14 '61
Newsweek Jy 10 '61
NY Times Jy 3 '61
Saturday Review Jy 29 '61

HEPBURN, KATHARINE

BERGAN, ROBERT. *Katharine Hepburn: An Independent Woman.* NY: Arcade, 1996.
BRITTON, ANDREW. *Katharine Hepburn: A Portrait of the Actress as Feminist.* NY: Continuum, 1995.
HEPBURN, KATHARINE. *The Making of "The African Queen" or How I Went to Africa with Bogart, Bacall, and Huston and Almost Lost My Life.* NY: Knopf, 1987.
——. *Me: Stories of My Life.* NY: Ballantine, 1992.
HIGHAM, CHARLES. *Kate: The Life of Katharine Hepburn.* NY: NAL, 1981.
LEAMING, BARBARA. *Katharine Hepburn.* NY: Avon, 1996.
ROBINSON, ALICE, ED. *Notable Women in American Theatre.* NY: Greenwood Press, 1989.
PRIDEAUX, JAMES. *Knowing Hepburn and Other Curious Experiences.* London: Faber, 1996.

Esq D '83
Hist Today Ap '90
Newsweek S 23 '91; Au 31 '87
Read Dig Ap '84; Ap '74
Sat Ev Post Ja/F '92
Time Je 29 '92; N 16 '81
Vogue S '91

HILLARY, SIR EDMUND AND
TENZING NORGAY

FRASER, MARY ANN. *On Top of the World: The Conquest of Mount Everest.* NY: Henry Holt, 1991.
HAKING, SUE MULLER. *Mount Everst and Beyond: Sir Edmund Hillary.* NY: Benchmark Books, 1997.
HILLARY, EDMUND, SIR. *Ascent: Two Lives Explored: The Autobiographies of Sir Edmund and Peter Hillary.* NY: Paragon House, 1991.
——. *High Adventure.* NY: Dutton, 1955.
—— AND DESMOND DOIG. *High in the Thin Cold Air: The Story of the Himalayan Expedition.* Garden City, NY: Doubleday, 1962.
——. *Nothing Venture, Nothing Win.* NY: Coward, McCann & Geoghegan, 1975.
——. *Schoolhouse in the Clouds.* NY: Penguin, 1964.
KOOP, FAITH YINGLING. *A World Explorer: Sir Edmund Hillary.* Champaign, IL: Garrard, 1970.
KRAMER, SYDELLE. *To the Top!: Climbing the World's Highest Mountain.* NY: Random House, 1993.

Far East Econ Rev My13 '93
Life Au '96
Telegraph Ma 26 '97
US News Je 7 '93
www.//everest.mountainzone.com/sherpas.stm/climbing
www.pbs.org/wgbh/nova/everest/history/norgay

HIROHITO

BEHR, EDWARD. *Hirohito: Behind the Myth.* NY: Villard, 1989.
FIELD, NORMA. *In the Realm of a Dying Emperor.* NY: Pantheon, 1991.
HOYT, EDWIN. *Hirohito: The Emperor and the Man.* NY: Praeger, 1992.
IROKAWA, DAIKICHI. *The Age of Hirohito: In Search of Modern Japan.* NY: Free Press, 1995.
LARGE, STEPHEN S. *Emperor Hirohito and Showa Japan.* London/NY: Routledge, 1992.

Hist Today Ja '82
Maclean's Ja 16 '89; N 30 '87
Nation Ja 30 '89
New States Ja 13 '89
Newsweek Ja 16 '89
NY Times O 8 '89
Time Ja 16 '89; Au 1 '83

HITCHCOCK, ALFRED

DURGNAT, RAYMOND. *The Strange Case of Alfred Hitchcock.* London: Faber, 1974.
HALEY, MICHAEL. *The Alfred Hitchcock Album.* Englewood Hills, NJ: Prentice-Hall, 1981.

KAPSIS, ROBERT E. *Hitchcock: The Making of a Reputation.* Chicago, IL: University of Chicago Press, 1992.
LaVALLEY, ALBERT J., ED. *Focus on Hitchcock.* Englewood Cliffs, NJ: Prentice-Hall, 1972.
SPOTO, DONALD. *The Art of Alfred Hitchcock: Fifty Years of His Motion Pictures.* NY: Hopkinson and Blake, 1976.
——. *The Dark Side of Genius: The Life of Alfred Hitchcock.* Boston: Little, Brown, 1993.
TRUFFAUT, FRANCOIS WITH HELEN G. SCOTT. *Hitchcock.* NY: Simon & Schuster, 1985.

America Au 4 '84; Au 11 '84
Am Film Ap '90; N '84
Esq Ap '82
Film Comment My/Je '84; Mr '79
New Rep Je 26 '80
Newsweek Mr 12 '80
Read Dig F '81
Time My 12 '80

HITLER, ADOLF

BULLOCK, ALLAN L. *Hitler: A Study in Tyranny.* NY: HarperCollins, 1991.
——. *Modern Biography: Hitler.* NY: Smithmark, 1995.
CARR, WILLIAM. *Hitler: A Study In Personality and Politics.* NY: St. Martin's, 1995.
CROSS, COLIN. *Adolf Hitler.* London: Hodder and Stoughton, 1973.
FEST, JOANCHIM C. *Hitler.* NY: Harcourt Brace, 1992.
HERZTSTEIN, ROBERT EDWIN. *The Nazis.* Alexandria, VA: Time/Life 1980.
NICHOLLS, A. J. *Weimar and The Rise of Hitler.* NY: St. Martin's, 1991.
STEINERT, MARLIS. *Hitler: A Biography.* NY: Norton, 1997.
TOLAND, JOHN. *Adolf Hitler.* NY: Doubleday, 1992.
WEINBERG, GERHARD L. *Germany, Hitler, and World War II.* NY: Cambridge/Cambridge University Press, 1995.

Hist Today S '90
Life Ap 23 '45
Newsweek My 7 '45
New Yorker My 1 '95
Time My 7 '45; Au 28 '89; Ap 6 '92

HO CHI MINH

FENN, CHARLES, CAPTAIN. *Ho Chi Minh: A Biographical Introduction.* NY: Scribner's, 1973.
HUYEN, N. KHAC. *Vision Accomplished? The Enigma of Ho Chi Minh.* NY: Macmillan, 1977.
HALBERSTAM, DAVID. *Ho.* NY: Random House, 1971.
LACOUTRE, JEAN. *Ho Chi Minh: A Political Biography.* Tr., Peter Wiles. NY: Random House, 1968.

Asian Affairs Je '85; F '92
Esq N '67
Life Mr 22 '68
Newsweek S 15 '69; S 22 '69
New York O 6 '97
Time Jy 16 '65; S 12 '69; N 6 '72

HOLIDAY, BILLIE

BURNETT, JAMES. *Billie Holiday.* NY: Hippocrene, 1984.
CHILTON, JOHN. *Billie's Bounce: The Billie Holiday Story, 1933-1959.* NY: Da Capo Press, 1989.
CLARKE, DONALD. *Wishing on the Moon: The Life and Times of Billie Holiday.* NY: Viking, 1994.
HOLIDAY, BILLIE WITH WILLIAM DUFFY. *Lady Sings the Blues.* Garden City, NY: Doubleday, 1956.
KLIMENT, BUD. *Billie Holiday.* NY: Chelsea House, 1990.
NICHOLSON, STUART. *Billie Holiday.* Boston: Northeastern University Press, 1995.
SANDBERG. *The Billie Holiday Companion.* NY: Macmillan, 1997.
WHITE, JOHN. *Billie Holiday: Her Life and Times.* NY: Universe, 1987.
New Grove Dictionary of Jazz; London: MacMillan, 1988.
Harmony Illustrated Encyclopedia of Jazz. NY: Harmony, 1987.

Downbeat F '94; Jy '94
Esq O '89; Au '94
New Yorker Mr 26 '60
NY Times Book Rev O 29 '95
Pop Music & Soc Winter '94
Saturday Review Au 29 '59
Times Lit Sup Ap 15 '94; N 17 '95

HOROWITZ, VLADIMIR

DUBAL, DAVID. *Evenings with Horowitz: A Personal Portrait.* London: Robson, 1992.
——ED. *Remembering Horowitz: 125 Pianists Recall a Legend.* NY: Schirmer Books, 1993.
KAISER, JOACHIM. *Great Pianists of Our Time.* London: George Allen, 1971.
MACH, ELYSE. *Great Pianists Speak for Themselves.* NY: Dodd, 1980.
SCHONBERG, HAROLD C. *The Great Pianists.* NY: Simon & Schuster, 1963.

——. *Horowitz: His Life and Music*. NY: Simon & Schuster, 1992.

Clavier N '92; Ja '90; O '79
Macleans N 20 '89
Nat Rev D 8 '89
New Republic N 30 '92
Newsweek N 20 '89
New Yorker Je 4 '90
Time Nov 20 '89; My 5 '86

IBARRURI, DOLORES

IBARRURI, DOLORES. *They Shall Not Pass: The Auto-biography of La Pasionaria*. NY: International, 1976.
KERN, ROBERT, ed. *Historical Dictionary of Modern Spain*. NY: Greenwood, 1989.
LOW, ROBERT. *La Pasionaria: The Spanish Firebrand*. London: Hutchinson, 1992.

Economist D 14 '85
Nat Rev D 8 '89
Newsweek My 23 '77
NY Times N 13 '89
Time My 23 '77

JACKSON, MICHAEL

ANDERSON, CHRISTOPHER P. *Michael Jackson: Unauthorized*. NY: Simon & Schuster, 1994.
CAMPBELL, LISA. *Michael Jackson: The King of Pop*. Boston: Branden Books, 1993.
GEORGE, NELSON. *The Michael Jackson Story*. NY: Dell, 1987.
TARABORRELLI, J. RANDY. *Michael Jackson: The Magic and the Madness*. NY: Ballantine, 1991.

Atlantic Ap '92
Maclean's Jy 23 '84
Newsweek Jy 16 '84
People N 29 '93
Time F 22 '93; Mr 19 '84

JAGGER, MICK

DALTON, DAVID. *The Rolling Stones: The First Twenty Years*. NY: Knopf, 1981.
HIGHWATER, JAMAKE. *Mick Jagger: The Singer, Not the Song*. NY: Curtis Books, 1973.
SANFORD, CHRISTOPHER. *Mick Jagger: Primitive Cool*. NY: St. Martin's, 1994.
SCADUTO, ANTHONY. *Mick Jagger: Everybody's Lucifer*. NY: McKay, 1974.
WELCH, CHRIS. *The Rolling Stones*. Miami Springs, FL: Carlton Books, 1994.

Esq Je '68; Ap '93
Life Jy 14 '72
Maclean's F 15 '93; Au 8 '94
Newsweek Ja 4 '71
NY Times Mag Jy 23 '72
People Au 2, 13 '93; S 12 '94
Time Jy 17 '72
Toronto Sun S 30 '97
Vanity Fair D '97
Vogue My '91

JIANG QING

BONAVIA, DAVID. *Verdict in Peking*. NY: Putnam, 1984.
CARTER, PETER. *MAO*. NY: Viking, 1979.
HAN, SUYIN. *Wind in the Tower: Mas Tsetung and the Cultural Revolution*. Boston: Little, Brown, 1976.
TERRILL, ROSS. *Madame Mao: The White Boned Demon*. NY: Simon & Schuster, 1992.

Far East Econ Rev Ju 20 '91
Jour of Asian Studs F '94
Newsweek F 20 '84; N 17 '80; Ja 12 '81; 1 '76
Punch N 13 '91
Time Mr 21 '77; D 1 '80; F 2 '81
Vanity Fair D '91

JOHN, ELTON

CLIFFORD, MIKE, CONS. ED. *The Harmony Illustrated Encyclopedia of Rock*. NY: Harmony, 1992.
CRIMP, SUSAN AND PATRICIA BURSTEIN. *The Many Lives of Elton John*. NY: Carol, 1992.
NORMAN, PHILIP. *Elton John*. NY: Simon & Schuster, 1993.

Atl Const D 30 '97
Hello D 20 '97
People S 8 '86; D 5 '88; My 2 '92; O 6 '97; D 29 '97
Roll Stone Mr 19 '92; O 16 '97
Time Mr 13 '95

POPE JOHN XXIII

COUSINS, NORMAN. *The Improbable Triumvirate: John F. Kennedy, Pope John, and Nikita Khrushev*. NY: Norton, 1984.
HATCH, ALDEN. *A Man Named John*. NY: Hawthorn, 1963.

HEBBLETHWAITE, PETER. *Pope John XXIII: Shepherd of the Modern World*. NY: Doubleday, 1987.
POPE JOHN XXIII. *Letters to His Family*. Tr., Dorothy White. NY/Toronto: McGraw-Hill, 1968.
WALCH, TIMOTHY. *John the Twenty-Third*. NY: Chelsea House, 1987.
WYNN, WILTON. *Keepers of the Keys*. NY: Random House, 1988.

Horizon Au '63
Newsweek Mr 30 '64; Je 10 '63; O 15 '62
New Rep Je 8 '63
Read Dig Ap '63
Sat Ev Post Jy 27 '63
Time Je 14 '63

JORDAN, MICHAEL

GREENE, BOB. *Hang Time: Days and Dreams with Michael Jordan*. NY: Doubleday, 1992.
JORDAN, MICHAEL. *I Can't Accept Not Trying*. San Francisco: Harper Collins, 1995.
SMITH, SAM. *The Jordan Rules*. NY: Simon & Schuster, 1992.

Newsweek My 29 '89; D 4 '89; Ja 5 '87; N 26 '84
Sports Illus Mr 13 '89; Mr 24 '86; D 10 '84; O 18 '93
Vanity Fair F '92

JOYCE, JAMES

BEJA, MORRIAS. *James Joyce: A Literary Life*. Columbus, OH: Ohio State University Press, 1992.
BENSTOCK, BERNARD. *James Joyce*. NY: Ungar, 1985.
BRUCE, BRADLEY. *James Joyce's Schooldays*. Dublin: Gill and Macmillam, 1982.
COSTELLO, PETER. *James Joyce: The Years of Growth, 1882-1915*. NY: Pantheon, 1993.
ELLMANN, RICHARD. *James Joyce*. Oxford/NY: Oxford University Press, 1989.
——, ED. *My Brother's Keeper: James Joyce's Early Years*. NY: Viking, 1958.
HART, CLIVE. *Conversations With James Joyce*. NY: Columbia University Press, 1974.
MADDOX, BRENDA. *Nora: A Biography of Nora Joyce*. London: Hamish Hamilton, 1988.
POTTS, WILLARD, ed. *Portraits of the Artist in Exile: Recollections of James Joyce by Europeans*. Seattle, WA: University of Washington Press, 1979.

Criticism Sum '91
Econ Ja 18 '92; Au 14 '93
Jour of Mod Lit Sp '96
NY Times Book Rev Ja 3 '92; Ma 20 '94; O 9 '94
Saturday Review Ja 24 '42
Smithsonian Mr '90
Studies in the Novel S '96
Time Ja 19 '42
Times Lit Sup Au 9 '91; Au 26 '94; O 11 '96
Wired Jy '96

JUNG, CARL

JUNG, C. G. *The Essential Jung*. Princeton: Princeton University Press, 1983.
KERR, JOHN. *Most Dangerous Method: The Story of Jung, Freud and Sabina Spielrein*. NY: Vintage, 1994.
McLYNN, FRANK. *Carl Gustav Jung*. NY: St. Martin's, 1997.
STEVENS, ANTHONY. *Jung*. Oxford/NY: Oxford University Press, 1994.
NOLL, RICHARD. *The Aryan Christ: The Secret Life of Carl Jung*. NY: Random House, 1997.
STORR, ANTHONY. *Jung*. London: Fontana/Collins, 1973.

New Rep Au 4 '79
Newsweek Ap 29 '74
Time Je 16 '61; D 1 '75
US News D 7 '92

KAFKA, FRANZ

BROD, MAX. *Franz Kafka: A Biography*. NY: Da Capo Press, 1995.
KARL, FREDERICK R. *Franz Kafka, Representative Man*. NY: Fromm, 1993.
NORTHEY, ANTHONY. *Kafka's Relatives: Their Lives and His Writing*. New Haven, CT: Yale University Press, 1991.
PAWEL, ERNST. *The Nightmare of Reason: A Life of Franz Kafka*. NY: Noonday, 1993.
SPANN, MENO. *Franz Kafka*. NY: Macmillan, 1976.

Encounter My '81; N '87
Newsweek S 24 '73
New Rep D 19 '88
New Yorker My 9 '83; Je 18 '84; My 29 '90
Time Ja 30 '78
Vogue Jy '83

KAHLO, FRIDA

BILLETER, ERICA, ED. *The World of Frida Kahlo: The Blue House*. Seattle, WA: University of Washington Press, 1994.

DRUCKER, MARIA. *Frida Kahlo: Torment and Triumph in Her Life*. NY: Bantam, 1991.
——. *Frida Kahlo*. Albuquerque, NM: University of New Mexico, 1995.
HARDIN, TERRI. *Frida Kahlo: A Modern Master*. NY: Smithmark, 1997.
HERRERA, HAYDEN. *Frida: A Biography of Frida Kahlo*. NY: Harper & Row, 1983.
TIBOL, RAQUEL. *Frida Kahlo: An Open Life*. Albuquerque, NM: University of New Mexico, 1993.
TURNER, ROBYN. *Frida Kahlo*. Boston: Little, Brown, 1993.

Americas Mr '80
Art Forum Mr '83; My '76
Art in Am Ja '93; Ap '83
Arts Ja '82
New Rep S 30 '91
New York Mr 28 '83
Psych Today Mr '83

KELLER, HELEN

BROOKS, VAN WYCK. *Helen Keller: Sketch for a Portrait*. NY: Dutton, 1956.
EINHORN, LOIS. *Helen Keller, Public Speaker: Sightless But Seen, Deaf But Heard*. NY: Greenwood Press, 1996.
FONER, PHILIP S. *Helen Keller: Her Socialist Years*. NY: International, 1967.
HURWITZ, JOHANNA. *Helen Keller*. NY: Random House,1997.
KELLER, HELEN. *The Story of My Life*. NY: Doubleday, 1922.
LASH, JOSEPH P. *Helen and Teacher: The Story of Helen Keller and Anne Sullivan Macy*. NY: Delacourt, 1980.

Amer Je 15 '68
Newsweek Ju 10 '68
NY Times Ju 2 '68
NY Times Mag Ju 26 '55; Ju 26 '60
Time Je 7 '68

KELLY, GRACE

HAWKINS, PETER. *Prince Rainier of Monaco*. London: William, Kimber, 1966.
LACEY, ROBERT. *Grace*. NY: Putnam, 1994.
SURCOUL, ELIZABETH GILLEN. *Grace Kelly, American Princess*. Minneapolis, MN: Lerner, 1992.

Ent Weekly Ap 14 '95
Films in Review N '78
Newsweek S 27 '82
Time S 20 '82; S 27 '82
Vanity Fair O '94

KENNEDY, JOHN F.

ANDERSON, CHRISTOPHER P. *Jack and Jackie: Portrait of an American Marriage*. NY: Morrow, 1996.
GARDNER, JOHN W., ED. *To Turn the Tide*. NY: Harper & Row, 1962.
HAMILTON, NIGEL. *Reckless Youth*. NY: Random House,1992.
HARPER, PAUL AND JOANN P. KRIEG. *JFK: The Promise Revisited*. Westport, CT: Greenwood, 1988.
McGINNISS, JOE. *The Last Brother*. NY: Simon & Schuster, 1993.
REEVES, RICHARD. *President Kennedy: Profile of Power*. NY: Simon & Schuster, 1993.
REEVES, THOMAS C. *A Question of Character: A Life of John F. Kennedy*. Rocklin, CA: Prima, 1992.
SALINGER, PIERRE. *John F. Kennedy*. NY: Viking, 1997.
SCHWARZ, URS. *JFK 1917-1963*. London: Paul Hamlyn, 1964.
SORENSON, THEODORE. *Kennedy*. NY: Harper & Row, 1965.
——. *The Kennedy Legacy*. NY: Macmillan, 1993.
——. *Modern Biography: Kennedy*. NY: Smithmark, 1995.

Ad Age Jy 15 '96
Amer His Rev Ja '96
Esq S '96
Newsweek N 28 '83; Au 19 '96; O 7 '96; O 21 '96
NY Times N 22 '92; O 8 '93; N 21 '93; N 13 '97
NY Times Book Rev Mr 10 '96
People Jy 15 '96; Au 5 '96
Time N 14 '83; O 7 '96
US News O 24 '88
Vanity Fair F '86
Vogue O '93

KEVORKIAN, DR. JACK

BETZOLD, MICHAEL. *Appointment With Dr. Death*. Troy, MI: Momentum Books, 1993.
KEVORKIAN, JACK. *Prescription: Medicide; The Goodness of Planned Death*. 1991.
LOVING, CAROL. *My Son, My Sorrow: The Tragic Tale of Dr. Kevorkian's Youngest Patient*. Far Hills, NJ: New Horizon Press, 1998.

Amer Scholar Winter '97
Brit Medical Jour (International) Ju 8 '96
Christianity Today Au 15 '94
Economist Ma 22 '93; N 13 '93; My 31 '97
Esq '97
Human Life Rev Fall '94; Winter '94; Fall '96;
  Winter '97
Humanist Ma-Ap '97
Maclean's Ju 25 '90
Nat Rev Jy 9 '90; Ap 8 '96
NY Times D 26 '93; Ju 15 '94
People Je 25 '90
Playboy Au '94
Time Ju 18 '90; D 28 '92; Ju 3 '96
US News Ju 18 '90; Ag 27 '90; D 17 '90
Van Fair My '91
Wash Times My 19 '94

KING, BILLIE JEAN

KING, BILLIE J. *The Autobiography of Billie Jean King.*
  Granada.
———. *We Have Come A Long Way.* NY: McGraw Hill,
  1989.
SANFORD, WILLIAM R. AND CARL R. GREEN. Billie Jean
  King. Crestwood House, 1993.

Esq O '74
Ms F '88; N '83
Read Dig Je '74
Sports II Ap 29 '91; N 14 '77; My 19 '75; D 25 '72;
  O 1 '73
Newsweek S 24 '73

KING, MARTIN LUTHER JR.

ALBERT, PETER J AND RONALD HOFFMAN EDS. We Shall
  Overcome: Martin Luther King Jr. and the Black
  Freedom Struggle. NY: Da Capo Press, 1993.
BRANCH, TAYLOR. Pillar of Fire: America in the King
  Years, 1963-65. NY: Simon & Schuster, 1998.
COLAIACO, JAMES A. Martin Luther King Jr.: Apostle of
  Militant Nonviolence. NY: St. Martin's, 1992.
DAVIS, LENWOOD G. I Have a Dream: The Life and
  Times of Martin Luther King Jr. Westport, CT:
  Greenwood, 1973.
KING, CORETTA S. My Life with Martin Luther King, Jr.
  NY: St Martin's, 1994.
LISCHER, RICHARD. The Preacher King: Martin Luther
  King Jr. and the Word that Moved America.
  Oxford/NY: Oxford University Press, 1995.
SCHULK, FLIP. He Had A Dream. NY: Norton, 1995.
SCHULK, FLIP, AND PENELOPE ORTNER MCPHEE. King
  Remembered. NY: Norton, 1986.
WARD, BRIAN AND TONY BADGER, EDS. The Making of
  Martin Luther King and the Civil Rights Movement.
  NY: New York University Press, 1996.

Ebony Ja '91
Life F 12 '65; Ap 12 '68
Newsweek Ap 13 '68
New Yorker Ap 13 '68
NY Times J 18 '98
Time Ja 3 '64

LANDERS, ANN AND ABIGAIL
VAN BUREN

GROSSVOGEL, DAVID I. Dear Ann Landers: Our Intimate
  and Changing Dialogue with America's Best-Loved
  Confidante. Chicago: Contemporary Books, 1987.
LANDERS, ANN. The Ann Landers Encyclopedia A to Z.
  NY: Ballantine, 1981.
———. Wake up and smell the coffee! The Best of Ann
  Landers. NY: Fawcett, 1997.
POTTKER, JANICE AND BOB SPEZIALE. Dear Ann, Dear
  Abby: The Unauthorized Biography of Ann Landers
  and Abigail Van Buren. NY: Dodd-Mead, 1987.
VAN BUREN, ABIGAIL. The Best of Dear Abby. NY:
  Andrews & McMeel, 1981.
ZASLOW, JEFFREY. Tell Me All About It: A Personal
  Look At the Advice Business by the Man Who
  Replaced Ann Landers. NY: Morrow, 1990.

Look O 18 '66; Mr 5 '68
Ny Times Book Rev F 5 '79
New Yorker D 4 '95
Newsweek Jy 14 '75
Read Dig Je '85
Time Ja 21 '57; Ja 19 '81
US News Jy 7 '96
Vogue Mr '82

LENIN, VLADIMIR

CLARK, RONALD. LENIN. NY: Harper & Row, 1988.
CONQUEST, ROBERT. V. I. Lenin. NY: Viking, 1972.
FIGES, ORLANDO. A People's Tragedy: The Russian
  Revolution, 1891-1924. NY: Viking, 1996.
HARDING, NEIL. Leninism. Durham, NC: Duke
  University Press, 1996.
PIPES, RICHARD. Russia Under the New Regime: Lenin
  and the Birth of the Totalitarian State. NY: Knopf,
  1994.

SERVICE, ROBERT. Lenin: A Political Life. Bloomington,
  IN: Indiana University Press, 1985.
VOLKOGONOV, DMITRI, HAROLD SHUKMAN (trans., ed.).
  Lenin: A New Biography. NY: Free Press, 1996.

Economist F 18 '95
Forbes O 23 '95
Nation Ja 30 '95
New Rep O 14 '96
Newsweek S 16 '96
NY Rev of Books Je 8 '95
Sci & Soc Fall '95; Spring '96
Time Ap 13 '70; Au 14 '89; F 19 '90
Times Lit Sup Ap 7 '95
Wilson Quar Autumn '96

LINDBERGH, CHARLES

AHLGREN, GREG AND STEPHEN R. MONIER. Crime of the
  Century: The Lindberg Kidnapping Hoax. Boston:
  Branden, 1993.
BEHN, NOEL. Lindbergh: The Crime. NY: NAL, 1995.
FISHER, JIM. The Lindbergh Case. Camden, NJ: Rutgers
  University Press, 1994.
KENNEDY, LUDOVIC. The Airman and the Carpenter.
  NY: Viking, 1985.
MILTON, JOYCE. Loss of Eden: A Biography of Charles
  and Anne Morrow Lindbergh. NY: HarperCollins,
  1994.

Am History My/Je '91
Newsweek My 2 '77
Read Dig My '77
Time My 23 '77

LOREN, SOPHIA

CRAWLEY, TONY. The Films of Sophia Loren. London:
  LSP Books, 1974.
HARRIS, WARREN G. Sophia Loren: A Biography. NY:
  Simon & Schuster, 1998.
HOTCHNER, H. E. Sophia: Living and Loving. NY:
  Morrow, 1979.
LEVY, ALAN. Forever, Sophia: An Intimate Portrait.
  NY: St. Martin's, 1986.
LOREN, SOPHIA. Women and Beauty. NY: Morrow, 1984.
SHAW, SAM. Sophia Loren in the Camera Eye.
  London/NY: Hamlyn,1980.

Esq Au '94
Interview O '93
McCall's My '89; O '92
Newsweek Au 15 '55; Jy 28 '55
People Ap 11 '88; Au 29 '94
Time Ap 6 '62; F 6 '56
Vanity Fair Ja '91

LUXEMBURG, ROSA

ABRAHAM, RICHARD. Rosa Luxemburg: A Life for the
  Internationale. NY: St. Martin's, 1989.
ARESTIS, PHILIP, ED. A Biographical Dictionary of
  Dissenting Economists. Hauts, England: Elgar, 1992.
BRONNER, STEPHEN. Rosa Luxemburg: A Revolutionary of
  Our Times. NY: Columbia University Press, 1987.
LUXEMBURG, ROSA. Comrade and Lover: Letters to Leo
  Jogiches. Cambridge, MA: MIT, 1979.
NETTL, J. P. Rosa Luxemburg (2 vols.). London: Oxford
  University Press, 1966.
ROWTHORN, R. Capitalism, Conflict and Inflation.
  London: Lawrence and Wishart, 1980.
SHEPARDSON, DONALD E. Rosa Luxemburg and the
  Noble Dream. NY: Lang, 1995.
WATERS, MARY ALICE, ED. Rosa Luxemburg Speaks. NY:
  Pathfinder, 1970.

Hist Today F '72
Mass Rev Spring '75
Newsweek Ja 27 '69

MACARTHUR, GENERAL DOUGLAS

CLAYTON, JAMES D. The Years of MacArthur: Vol. I,
  1880-1941. NY: Houghton Mifflin, 1970.
MACARTHUR, DOUGLAS. Reminiscences. NY: McGraw-
  Hill, 1964.
MANCHESTER, WILLIAM. American Caesar: Douglas
  MacArthur, 1880-1964. NY: Little, Brown, 1978.
PETILLO, CAROL MORRIS. Douglas MacArthur: The
  Philippine Years. Bloomington, IN: Indiana
  University Press, 1981.
SCHALLER, MICHAEL. Douglas MacArthur: The Far Eastern
  General. NY: Oxford University Press, 1989.
SPANIER, JOHN W. The Truman-MacArthur Controversy
  and the Korean War. Cambridge, MA: Belknap
  Press, 1959.
WHAN, VORIN E., JR., ed. A Soldier Speaks: Public
  Papers and Speeches of General of the Army
  Douglas MacArthur. Praeger, 1965.

Harper's N '64
Life Apr 17 '64; Ap 24 '64
Natl Rev D 15 '64
New Rep Ap 18 '64

NY Times Ap 6 '64
Time Ap 10 '64; O 2 '64
US News Ap 13 '64; Ap 20 '64
www.dmiusma.eu/voics/duty-honor-country
www.army

MADONNA

ANDERSON, CHRISTOPHER P. Madonna Unauthorized.
  NY: Simon & Schuster, 1991.
BEGO, MARK. Madonna: Blonde Ambition. NY:
  Harmony, 1992.
KING, NORMAN. Madonna: The Book. NY: Morrow,
  1991.
ROBERTSON, PAMELA. Guilty Pleasures: Feminist Camp
  from Mae West to Madonna. Durham, NC: Duke
  University Press, 1996.
THOMPSON, DOUGLAS. Madonna Revealed. London:
  Warner, 1991.
TURNER, KAY, ED. I Dream of Madonna: Dreams of
  the Goddess of Pop. London: Collins, 1993.

Am Film Jy/Au '87
New Rep Au 20 '90
Newsweek O 4 '93; N 2 '92
Time My 20 '91; D 17 '90
Vanity Fair O '92; Ap '91
Vogue O '92

MALCOLM X

Alex Haley and Malcolm X's The Autobiography of
  Malcolm X. Ed., Harold Bloom. NY: Chelsea
  House Publications, 1996.
BREITMAN, GEORGE, ED. The Last Years of Malcolm X.
  NY: Pathfinder, 1967.
———. Malcolm X Speaks. NY: Grove Press, 1995.
CLARKE, JOHN HENRIK. Malcolm X: The Man and His
  Times. Trenton, NJ: African World Press, 1990.
KING, MARTIN LUTHER. King, Malcolm, Baldwin: Three
  Interviews. Middletown, CT: Wesleyan University
  Press, 1985.
PERRY, BRUCE, ED. Malcolm X: The Last Speeches. NY:
  Pathfinder, 1986.
STRICKLAND, WILLIAM. Malcolm X: Make It Plain. (Oral
  histories selected and edited by Cheryll Greene).
  NY: Viking, 1994.

Afr Amer Rev S '97
Amer Hist Rev Ap '97
Christ Cent D 23 '92
Commonweal D 18 '92
Dissent Winter '96
Ebony F '92; F '93
Essence F '92
Forbes Ma 13 '95
Harper's D '92
Hist Today Ap '93
Life D '92
Newsweek Ja 31 '94
NY Rev of Books F 16 '95
NY Times Book Rev N 27 '94; Ma 5 '95
US News N 23 '92
Vanity Fair Ju '95

MANDELA, NELSON

BENSON, MARY. Nelson Mandela: The Man and the
  Movement. NY: Norton, 1994.
JUCKES, TIM J. Opposition in South Africa: The Leadership
  of Z. K. Matthews, Nelson Mandela and Stephen
  Biko. Westport, CT: Greenwood Press, 1995.
KATHRADA. No Bread for Mandela: The Prison Years of
  Nelson Mandela. NY: Simon & Schuster, 1997.
MANDELA, NELSON. Long Walk to Freedom. Boston:
  Little, Brown, 1994.
OTTAWAY, DAVID. Chained Together: Mandela, de
  Klerk, and the Struggle to Remake South Africa.
  NY: Times Books, 1993.

Africa Report S/O '90
New Rep Mr 1 '93
Newsweek F 19 '90; Jy 2 '90; O 25 '93
NY Times D 18 '94
NY Times Internat'l Ma 1 '94; Ma 2 '94; Au 19 '94
People D 12 '96
Time Je 14 '93
World Press Review S '86

MAO ZEDONG

CHOU, ERIC. Mao Tse-Tung: The Man and the Myth.
  NY: Stein & Day, 1982.
LAWRENCE, ALAN. Mao Zedong: A Biography.
  Westport, CT: Greenwood Publishing, 1991.
LI, ZHISUI. The Private Life of Chairman Mao. NY:
  Random House, 1994.
SALISBURY, HARRISON E. The New Emperors: China in the
  Era of Mao & Deng. NY: Little, Brown, 1992.
TERRILL, ROSS. Mao: A Biography. NY: Simon &
  Schuster, 1993.
THURSTON, ANNE F. The Private Life of Chairman Mao.
  NY: Random House, 1996.
WILSON, DICK. The People's Emperor. NY: Doubleday,
  1980.

Amer Hist Rev Je '96
Amer Pol Sci Rev D '95
Atlantic D '92
China Quart Mr '96
Far East Rev My 16 '96
Newsweek Au 14 '89; S 20 '76
New Yorker F 13 '95
NY Times Book Rev N 27 '94
NY Times Mag N 6 '94; Je 30 '96
Sci & Soc Spring '95
Time S 20 '76; S 27 '76
US News My 20 '96
World Press Review Au '96

MARX BROTHERS, THE

CHANDLER, CHARLOTTE. Hello, I Must Be Going: Groucho and His Friends. Garden City, NY: Doubleday, 1978.
GOULART, RON. Groucho Marx, Master Detective. NY: St. Martin's, 1998.
GEHRING, WES D. Grouch and W.C Fields: Huckster Comedians. University, MS: University of Mississippi Press, 1994.
———. The Marx Brothers: A Bio-bibliography. NY: Greenwood Press, 1987.
MARX, ARTHUR. My Life with Groucho: A Son's Eye View. Parkwest Publications, 1991.
MARX, GROUCHO. Groucho and Me. NY: Da Capo Press, 1995.
——— AND RICHARD J. ANOBILE. The Marx Brothers: A Scrapbook. NY: Darien House, 1989.
KARNICK, KRISTINE BRUNOVSKA AND HENRY JENKINS, EDS. Classical Hollywood Comedy. NY/London: Routledge, 1995.

Amer Schol Winter '95
Ent Weekly Ja 10 '92
NY Times Book Rev D 4 '88
People Jy 27 '92
Pub Wkly My 18 '92
TV Guide S 19 '92
Vill Voice N 19 '91

MATA HARI

HARI, MATA. Diary of Mata Hari. NY: Carroll & Graf, 1984.
OSTROVSKY, ERIKA. Eye of Dawn: The Rise and Fall of Mata Hari. NY: Dorset, 1990.
WHEELWRIGHT, JULIE. The Fatal Lover: Mata Hari and the Myth of Women in Espionage. North Pomfret: Trafalgar Square, 1993.

Horizon Spring '75
Maclean's Ap 2 '79
Ms July '74
Newsweek Oct 4 '65
Smithsonian May '86
Time Au 3 '53

MATISSE, HENRI

BERNIER, ROSAMUND. Matisse, Picasso, Miro: As I Knew Them. NY: Knopf, 1991.
ELDERFIELD, JOHN. Henri Matisse: A Retrospective. NY: MOMA, 1992.
HERRERA, HAYDEN. Matisse: A Portrait of the Man and His Art. NY: Harcourt Brace, 1993.
HOWARD, RICHARD, TR. Bonnard–Matisse: Letters Between Friends, 1925-1946. NY: Abrams, 1992.
LUCIE-SMITH, EDWARD. Lives of the Great Twentieth Century Artists. NY: Rizzoli, 1986.
MORGAN, GENEVIEVE ED. Matisse, the Artist Speaks. San Francisco: Collins, 1996.

ART News My '90
Arts Digest D 1 '54
Horizon Sum '76
New Rep Mr 16 '87
Newsweek N 15 '54; S 19 '77; S 28 '92
Smithsonian S '77
Time N 15 '54; S 19 '77
Vogue O '84; S '92

MEAD, MARGARET

BATESON, MARY C. With a Daughter's Eye: A Memoir of Gregory Bateson and Margaret Mead. NY: HarperCollins, 1994.
CASSIDY, ROBERT. Margaret Mead: A Voice for the Century. NY: Universe Books, 1982.
FOERSTEL, LEONORA AND ANGELA GILLIAM, EDS. Confronting the Margaret Mead Legacy: Scholarship, Empire and South Pacific. Philadelphia: Temple University Press, 1991.
HOWARD, JANE. Margaret Mead: A Life. NY: Simon & Schuster, 1984.
METRAUX, RHODA, ed. Margaret Mead: Some Personal Views. NY: Walker, 1979.

Life Je 4 '71
Nat Rev D 8 '78
Nat Hist Ja '79

Newsweek N 27 '78
Redbook Ja '78
Time N 27 '78

MEIR, GOLDA

MCAULEY, KAREN. Golda Meir. NY: Chelsea House, 1985.
MARTIN, RALPH G. Golda. Golda Meir: The Romantic Years. NY: Scribner's, 1988.
MEIR, GOLDA. My Life. NY: Putnam, 1975.
THACKERAY, FRANK W. Statesmen Who Changed the World. Westport, CT: Greenwood Press, 1993.
GUTMAN, ISRAEL. Encyclopedia of the Holocaust. NY: Macmillan, 1990.

Encounter N '83
New York Au 30 '82
Time S 19 '69; Je 7 '82
Wilson Q Spring '88

MONROE, MARILYN

GUILES, FRED LAWRENCE. Norma Jean: The Life of Marilyn Monroe. NY: Paragon House, 1993.
HOSPIEL, JAMES. Marilyn: Ultimate Look at the Legend. NY: Henry Holt, 1993.
———. Young Marilyn: Becoming the Legend. NY: Hyperion, 1995.
MIRACLE, BERNIECE B. AND MINA R. MIRACLE. My Sister Marilyn: A Memoir of Marilyn Manrow. Chapel Hill, NC: Algonquin Books, 1994.
MCGANN, GRAHAM. Marilyn Monroe. New Brunswick, NJ: Rutgers University Press, 1988.
SPOTO, DONALD. Marilyn Monroe: The Biography. NY: Chivers, 1993.
STRASBERG, SUSAN. Marilyn and Me. NY: Warner, 1992.

Ent Weekly Ja 10 '92; Au 7 '92
Life Ja 25 '63
Nation Au 25 '62
NY Times Jy 26 '92; D 18 '94
Newsweek Au 20 '62
Times Au 6 '62
Vanity Fair Ma '91

MONTESSORI, MARIA

HAINSTOCK, ELIZABETH. Essential Montessori. NY: NAL, 1997.
KRAMER, RITA. Maria Montessori: A Biography. NY: Putnam, 1976.
LEONE, BRUNO. Maria Montessori: Knight of the Children. St. Paul, MN: Greenhaven Press, 1978.
MONTESSORI, MARIA. From Childhood to Adolescence. NY: Schocken, 1973.
———. The Montessori Method. NY: Schocken, 1964.
OREM, R. C. AND GEORGE L. STEVENS. American Montessori Manual. College Park, MD: Orem, 1970.
RAMBUSCH, NANCY M. Women in Psychology. Eds., Agnes N. O'Connell and Nancy Felipe Russo. NY: Greenwood, 1990.
STANDING, E. M. Maria Montessori. NY: NAL, 1989.

Commentary Ju '64
Educ Dig Mr '93
School Lib Jour Ap '93
Time Ma 19 '53
Times Educ Sup Ja 20 '89

MOORE, HENRY

BERTHOUD, ROGER. The Life of Henry Moore. London: Faber, 1987.
FINN, DAVID. One Man's Henry Moore. NY: Black Swan, 1993.
GARDNER, JANE MYLUM. Henry Moore: From Bones and Stones to Sketches and Sculptures. NY: Four Winds Press, 1993.
Henry Moore: Sculpture and Environment. NY: Abrams, 1976.
Henry Moore: The Reclining Figure. Columbus, OH: Columbus Museum of Art, 1984.
JAMES, PHILIP. Henry Moore on Sculpture. NY: Da Capo, 1992.
LIEBERMAN, WILLIAM S. Henry Moore: 60 Years of His Art. NY: Thames & Hudson and the Metropolitan Museum of Art, 1983.

Horizon Ap '83
New Crit O '86
Newsweek My 23 '83; S 15 '86
Saturday Review Mr '81
Time S 15 '86

MURROW, EDWARD R.

CLOUD, STANLEY AND LYNNE OLSON. The Murrow Boys: Pioneers on the Front Lines of Broadcast Journalism. Boston: Houghton Mifflin, 1996.
FANG, IRVING E. Those Radio Commentators! Ames, IA: Iowa State University Press, 1977.
FINKELSTEIN, NORMAN H. With Heroic Truth: The Life of Edward R. Murrow. Boston: Houghton Mifflin, 1995.

PERSICO, JOSEPH. Edward R. Murrow: An American Original. NY: Dell, 1990.
SPERBER, A. M. Murrow: Life and Times. NY: Bantam, 1987.

Am Hist II Ja '94
Billboard S 25 '93
Broadcasting Jy 9 '90
Jour of Amer Cult Sp '92
Jour of Mass Med Ethics '93
Nat'l Cath Rep F 14 '92
New Rep Ja 9 '89
NY Times Book Rev Ja 15 '89; Je 2 '96
Telev Quart '89, '90
Times My 20 '96
TV Guide My 6 '89; Jy 28 '90; Ap 17 '93
Washington Monthly Jy '96

MUSSOLINI, BENITO

BLINKHORN, MARTIN. Mussolini and Fascist Italy. NY/London: Routledge, 1994.
CANNISTRARO, PHILIP V. AND BRIAN R. SULLIVAN. Il Duce's Other Woman. NY: Morrow, 1992.
HOYT, EDWIN PALMER. Mussolini's Empire: The Rise and Fall of the Fascist Vision. NY: Wiley, 1994.
LAMB, RICHARD. War in Italy 1943-1945: A Brutal Story. NY: St. Martin's, 1995.
WHITTAM, JOHN. Fascist Italy. NY: St. Martin's, 1995.

Encounter N '83
New Yorker Au 30 '82
Time Je 7 '82
Wilson Q Spring '88

NAMATH, JOE

HOLLANDER, ZANDER. Great Moments in Pro Football. NY: Random House, 1969.
LISS, HOWARD. They Changed the Game: Football's Great Coaches, Players, and Games. Philadlephia: Lippincott, 1975.
NAMATH, JOE. Chrome Hearts. (VHS Tape). Siamese Dot Press, 1992.
RALBOVSKY, MARTY. The Namath Effect. Englewood Cliffs, NJ: Prentice-Hall, 1976.
SANFORD, WILLIAM R. AND CARL R. GREEN. Joe Namath. Crestwood House, 1993.
SZOLNOKI, ROSE NAMATH. Namath: My Son Joe. Birmingham, AL: Oxmoor House, 1975.

Ad Age N 21 '88
GQ Ja '96
Life Au 20 '65
NY Her Trib Au 20 '65
People N 13 '89
Sport F '92; Mr '93
Sports Illus O 17 '66; Ja 28 '91; S 19 '94; O 31 '94; Ja 15 '96

NASSER, GAMAL ABDEL

DUBOIS, SHIRLEY GRAHAM. Gamal Abdel Nasser: Son of the Nile. NY: Joseph Okpaku Publishing, 1972.
LACOUTURE, JEAN. Nasser. NY: Knopf, 1973.
MALIK, ABDEL ANOUAR. Egypt: Military Society. NY: Vintage, 1973.
MANSFIELD, PETER. Nasser's Egypt. Middlesex, England: Penguin, 1971.
NASSER, GAMAL ABDEL. The Philosophy of the Revolution: Egypt's Liberation. Washington, DC: Public Affairs Press, 1955.
STEPHENS, ROBERT. Nasser: A Political Biography. London: Penguin, 1971.
WYNN, WILTON. Nasser of Egypt: The Search for Dignity. Cambridge: Arlington Books, 1959.

Atlantic J '71
Hist Today F '81
Newsweek O 12 '70; Ap 1 '74
NY Times Mr 30 '54; Ap 18 '54; Ap 30 '54; S 29 '70; S 30 '70; O 2 '70; D 28 '70
NY Times Mag S 19 '54
Time Mr 8 '54; Ap 26 '54; Mr 29 '63; My 16 '69; J 12 '70; O 12 '70
US News My 22 '53; Mr 5 '54; J 26 '70

NIXON, RICHARD M.

AMBROSE, STEPHEN E. Nixon. (3 vols.). NY: Simon & Schuster, 1987-91.
BERNSTEIN, CARL AND BOB WOODWARD. The Final Days. NY: Simon & Schuster, 1976.
KUTLER, STANLEY I. Abuse of Power: The New Nixon Tapes. NY: The Free Press, 1997.
MATTHEWS, CHRISTOPHER. Kennedy and Nixon. NY: Simon & Schuster, 1995.
MAZLISH, BRUCE. In Search of Nixon: A Psychohistorical Inquiry. NY: Basic Books, 1972.
MORRIS, ROGER. Richard Milhous Nixon: The Rise of an American Politician. NY: Henry Holt, 1990.
NIXON, RICHARD. The Memoirs of Richard Nixon. NY: Grosset and Dunlap, 1978.
PARMET, HERBERT S. Richard Nixon and His America. Boston: Little, Brown, 1990.

WHITE, THEODORE H. *The Making of the President*. NY: Atheneum, 1980.
WICKER, TOM. *One of Us: Richard Nixon and the American Dream*. NY: Random House, 1991.

New Leader My 9-23 '94
Newsweek Ma 19 '86
NY Times Au 9 '74; Ap 23 '94
People Ma 9 '94
Roll Stone Ju 16 '94
Time Ja 3 '72; Ma 20 '74; Ma 9 '77
US News Au 5 '74
www.chapman.edu/nixon/library/biography

NUREYEV, RUDOLF

CLARKE, MARY AND DAVID VAUGHN. *Encyclopedia of Dance and Ballet*. NY: Putnam, 1977.
COHEN-STRATYNER, BARBARA NAOMI. *Biographical Dictionary of Dance*. NY: Macmillan, 1982.
MONEY, KEITH. *Fonteyn and Nureyev: The Great Years*. London: Harvill, 1994.
NUREYEV, RUDOLF. *An Autobiography*. NY: Dutton, 1962.
STUART, OTIS. *Perpetual Motion: The Public and Private Lives of Rudolf Nureyev*. NY: Simon & Schuster, 1995.
TERRY, WALKER. *Great Male Dancers of the Ballet*. NY: Anchor, 1978.
WATSON, PETER. *Nureyev: A Biography*. London: Hodder & Stoughton, 1994.

Newsweek Ap 19 '65; Ja 18 '93
New Yorker Ja 18 '93
Time Ap 16 '65; Ja 18 '93

O'KEEFFE, GEORGIA

CASTRO, JAN GARDEN. *The Art and Life of Georgia O'Keeffe*. NY: Crown, 1995.
EISLER, BENITA. *O'Keeffe and Stieglitz: An American Romance*. NY: Penguin, 1992.
GHERMAN, BEVERLY. *Georgia O'Keeffe: The Wideness and Wonder of Her World*. NY: Collier, 1994.
HOGREFE, JEFFREY. *O'Keeffe: The Life of an American Legend*. NY: Bantam, 1984.
LISLE, LAURIE. *Portrait of an Artist: A Biography of Georgia O'Keeffe*. Albuquerque, NM: University of New Mexico, 1986.
LOENGARD, JOHN. *Georgia O'Keeffe at Ghost Ranch*. NY: Stewart, Tabori & Chang, 1995.
O'KEEFFE, GEORGIA. *Georgia O'Keeffe*. New York: Viking, 1978.
PETERS, SARAH WHITAKER. *Becoming O'Keeffe: The Early Years*. NY: Doubleday, 1991.
POLLITZER, ANITA. *A Woman on Paper: Georgia O'Keeffe*. NY: Simon & Schuster, 1988.
ROBINSON, ROZANA. *Georgia O'Keeffe*. NY: HarperCollins, 1990.
TURNER, ROBYN MONTANA. *Georgia O'Keeffe*. Boston: Little, Brown, 1991.

Art News N '77
Horizon D '77
Newsweek N 9 '87; Ja 8 '89
Read Dig My '79
Time N 29 '89
Vanity Fair Ap '91
Vogue My '86; O '87

OLIVIER, SIR LAURENCE

COTTRELL, JOHN. *Laurence Olivier*. Englewood Cliffs, NJ: Prentice-Hall, 1975.
DANIELS, ROBERT L. *Laurence Olivier, Theater and Cinema*. San Diego, CA: A.S. Barnes, 1980.
HOOPES, ROY. *When The Stars Went to War: Hollywood and World War II*. NY: Random House.
KARNEY, ROBYN. *The Movie Star Story. An Illustrated Guide to 500 of the World's Most Famous Stars of the Cinema*. Ed., Margaret Morley. Godalming: LSP Books Ltd., 1978.
O'CONNOR, GARRY, ED. *Olivier: A Celebration*. London: Hodder & Stoughton, 1987.
OLIVIER, LAURENCE. *Confessions of an Actor: An Autobiography*. NY: Simon & Schuster, 1982.
——. *On Acting*. NY: Simon & Schuster, 1986.
SILVIRIA, DALE. *Laurence Olivier and the Art of Film Making*. Rutherford, NJ: Fairleigh Dickinson University Press, 1985.

Maclean's Jy 24 '89
Newsweek Jy 24 '89
Observer Rev F 9 '69
Read Dig My '90

ONASSIS, JACQUELINE KENNEDY

ANDERSEN, CHRISTOPHER. *Jack and Jackie: Portrait of an American Marriage*. NY: Morrow, 1996.
BUCK, PEARL S. *The Kennedy Women*. NY: Cowles, 1970.
DAVIS, JOHN H. *Jacqueline Bouvier: An Intimate Memoir*. NY: Wiley, 1996.
HEYMANN, C. DAVID. *A Woman Named Jackie: An Intimate Biography*. NY: Carol Publishers, 1994.

KLEIN, EDWARD. *All Too Human: The Love Story of Jack and Jackie Kennedy*. Thorndike, ME: Thorndike Press, 1997.
KOESTENBAUM, WAYNE. *Jackie Under My Skin: Interpreting an Icon*. Farrar, Straus & Giroux, 1994.
LEAMER, LAURENCE. *The Kennedy Women*. NY: Villard, 1994.
LOWE, JACQUES. *Jacqueline Kennedy Onassis: Making of a First Lady: A Tribute*. General Publishing Group, 1996.
WATNEY, HEDDA. *Jackie O*. NY: Leisure, 1994.

Esq D '83
Life Jy '89; Jy 15 '94
New York My 30 '94; My 1 '95
NY Times F 25 '86; Ma 22 '94; Ju 12 '94
NY Times Book Rev O 9 '94
Newsweek Ja 1 '62; Ma 30 '94
People Ma 29 '95
Phil Inquirer My 20 '94
Time Ju 18 '84
Wash Post Jy 23 '89

OPPENHEIMER, J. ROBERT

DAVIS, NUEL PHARR. *Lawrence and Oppenheimer*. NY: Simon & Schuster, 1968.
GOODCHILD, PETER. *J. Robert Oppenheimer: Shatterer of Worlds*. NY: Fromm, 1985.
HOLLOWAY, RACHEL. *In the Matter of J. Robert Oppenheimer*. Westport, CT: Praeger, 1993.
KUNETKA, JAMES W. *Oppenheimer: The Years of Risk*. Prentice-Hall, 1982.
OPPENHEIMER, ROBERT. *The Open Mind*. NY: Simon & Schuster, 1955.
——. *Robert Oppenheimer: Letters and Recollections*. Eds., Alice Kimball Smith and Charles Weiner. Cambridge, MA: Harvard University Press, 1981.
——. *Science and the Common Understanding*. NY: Simon & Schuster, 1954.
RUMMEL, JADE. *Robert Oppenheimer: Dark Prince*. NY: Facts on File, 1992.
STERN, PHILLIP. *The Oppenheimer Case: Security on Trial*. NY: Harper & Row, 1969.

Amer Her O '77
Esq D '83
Nation Apr 27 '70
New Rep N 22 '69
Newsweek Je 27 '66; N 10 '69
New Yorker Mr 4 '67
NY Rev of Books Jy 2 '70
NY Times F 19 '67; N 3 '69
Saturday Review Je '80
Time F 24 '67
Times F 20 '67
Wash Post Ap 17 '70

OWENS, JESSE

BAKER, WILLIAM J. *Jesse Owens: An American Life*. NY: Free Press, 1986.
JOSEPHSON, JUDITH PINKERTON. *Jesse Owens: Track and Field Legend*. Springfield, NJ: Enslow Pub. 1997.
NEIMARK, PAUL. *Jesse: The Man Who Outran Hitler*. NY: Fawcett, 1985.
OWENS, JESSE. *Jesse: The Man Who Outran Hitler*. NY: Fawcett, 1978.
SAKIN, FRACENE. *Jesse Owens, Olympic Hero*. NY: Troll Assoc., 1986.
SCHAAP, RICHARD. *The Story of the Olympics*. NY: Knopf, 1967.

Ebony Je '80; S '88; Ap '96; Jy '96
Jet Au 26, S 16 '96
Life Au '96
Newsweek Ap 14 '80
Sporting News S 11 '88
Sat Ev Post Ja '76
Time Ap 14 '80

PANKHURST, EMMELINE

BANES, OLIVE. *Biographical Dictionary of British Feminists*. NY: New York University Press, 1985.
BRANDAN, PIERS. *Eminent Edwardians*. Boston: Houghton Mifflin, 1980.
MITCHELL, DAVID J. *The Fighting Pankhursts*. NY: Macmillan, 1959.
MITCHELL, SALLY. *Victorian Britain: An Encyclopedia*. Chicago: St. James Press, 1990.
NOBLE, IRIS. *Emmeline and Her Daughters: The Pankhurst Suffragettes*. NY: J. Messner, 1971.
SCHLUETER, JUNE, ED. *Encyclopedia of British Women Writers*. NY: Garland, 1988.

Journ of Brit Studies O '91
Journ of Mod Hist D '89
Times Educ Sup Ma 10 '96

PARKER, CHARLIE

GIDDINS, GARY. *Celebrating Bird: The Triumph of Charlie Parker*. NY: Morrow, 1987.

KOCH, LAWRENCE O. *Yardbird Suite: A Compendium of the Music and Life of Charlie Parker*. Bowling Green, OH: Bowling Green University Press, 1988.
REISNER, ROBERT GEORGE. *Bird: The Legend of Charlie Parker*. NY: Citadel, 1975.
RUSSELL, ROSS. *Bird Lives!: The High Life and Hard Times of Charlie (Yardbird) Parker*. NY: Da Capo Press, 1996.
WOIDECK, CARL. *Charlie Parker: His Music and Life*. Ann Arbor, MI: University of Michigan Press, 1996.

Bus Wk N 14 '88
Downbeat F '89; Je, F '94; Au '95; Au '97
Ebony Ja '89
Instrumentalist Ma '94
Jet S 2 '96
Ken Rev Sp '96
New Rep F 27 '89
Newsweek O 31 '88
People D 5 '88
Roll Stone D 1 '88; S 5 '91
Saturday Review Ap 30 '55; Mr 1 '56
Vill Voice Au '95; N '95

PASTERNAK, BORIS

BARNES, CHRISTOPHER. *Boris Pasternak: A Literary Biography, Vol. 1 (1890-1928)*. NY: Cambridge University Press, 1989.
CONQUEST, ROBERT. *Courage of Genius: The Pasternak Affair*. Philadelphia: Lippincott, 1962.
CORNWELL, NEIL. *Pasternak's Novel: Perspectives on "Dr. Zhivago."* England: Keele University Press, 1986.
DE MALLAC, GUY. *Boris Pasternak: His Life and His Art*. Norman, OK: University of Oklahoma Press, 1981.
FLEISHMAN, LAZAR. *Boris Pasternak: The Poet and His Politics*. Cambridge, MA: Harvard University Press, 1990.
GIFFORD, HENRY. *Pasternak: A Critical Study*. Cambridge/NY: Cambridge University Press, 1977.
HAYWARD, MAX AND MANYA HARARI, TRANS. *Dr. Zhivago*. NY: Pantheon, 1958.
HINGLEY, RONALD. *Pasternak: A Biography*. NY: Knopf, 1983.
IVINSKAYA, OLGA. *A Captive of Time*. Tr., Max Hayward. Garden City, NY: Doubleday, 1978.
MALLAC, GUY DE. *Boris Pasternak: His Life and Art*. Norman, OK: University of Oklahoma Press, 1981.
MAUROIS, ANDRÉ. *From Proust to Camus*. Garden City, NY: Doubleday, 1966.
PASTERNAK, BORIS. *I Remember: Sketch for an Autobiography*. Cambridge, MA: Harvard University Press, 1983.
——. *The Voice of Prose: Early Prose and Autobiography*. ed. Christopher Barnes. NY: Grove Press, 1987.

Amer Hist Rev D '84
Cont Sociology S '85
Downbeat F '89; Je '89; F '94; Au '95; Au '97
New Rep F 20 '89; 26 '89; Jy 6 '87
New Yorker N 25 '85
NY Times O 24 '58; D 29 '58
Saturday Review S 6 '58
Time Mr 6 '78; Je 13 '60

PAVAROTTI, LUCIANO

BONVICINI, CANDIDO. *The Tenor's Son: My Days with Pavarotti*. NY: St. Martin's, 1993.
MAYER, MARTIN AND GERALD FITZGERALD. *Grandissimo Pavarotti*. NY: Doubleday, 1986.
PAVAROTTI, ADUA. *Pavarotti: Life with Luciano*. NY: Rizzoli, 1992.
PAVAROTTI, LUCIANO AND WILLIAM WRIGHT. *Pavarotti: My World*. NY: Crown, 1995.

Esq Je 5 '79
Newsweek Mr 15 '76
New Yorker Je 21 '93
NY Times O 21 '97
Opera F '81
Opera News Mr 29 '86; D 10 '83
Read Dig Ja '80
Time S 24 '79

PAVLOVA, ANNA

FONTEYNE, DAME MARGOT. *Pavlova: Self-Portrait of a Dancer*. NY: Viking, 1984.
FRANKS, A. H. *Pavlova (1891-1931): A Biography*. NY: Da Capo Press, 1979.
——. *Pavlova: A Collection of Memoirs*. NY: Da Capo Press, 1981.
MONEY, KEITH. *Anna Pavlova: Her Life and Art*. London: Collins, 1982.
OLIVEROFF, ANDRE. *Flight of the Swan: A Memory of Anna Pavlova*. NY: Da Capo Press, 1979.

Dance Mag Ja '81; Ja '78; Ja '76; Ja '71
Horizon F '81
New Yorker D 20 '82
Read Dig F '68

PELÉ

BODO, PETER. *Pelé's New World*. NY: Norton, 1977.
NASCIMENTO, EDSON ARANTES DO AND ROBERT L. FISH (Pelé). *My Life and the Beautiful Game: The Autobiography of Pelé*. Garden City, NY: Doubleday, 1977.
THEBAUD, FRANCOIS. *Pelé*. Tr., Leo Weinstein. NY: Harper and Row, 1976.

Newsweek Je 11 '79
New Yorker Je 30 '75
Read Dig S '76; O '64
Sports Illus O 10 '77; Je 23 '75
Time S 12 '77; Ap 12 '63

PERON, EVA

BARNES, JOHN. *Evita First Lady: A Biography of Eva Peron*. NY: Grove Press, 1978.
DAIHL, LAURA. *Evita: In My Own Words*. NY: The New Press, 1996.
FRASER, NICHOLAS AND NARYSA NAVARRO. *Evita: The Real Life of Eva Peron*. NY: Norton, 1996.
MARTINEZ, TOMAS ELOY. *Santa Evita*. Trans., Helen Lane. NY: Knopf, 1996.
ORTIZ, ALICIA D. *Eva Peron*. NY: St. Martin's, 1996.
TAYLOR, J. M. *Eva Peron: The Myths of a Woman*. Chicago: University of Chicago Press, 1979.

Newsweek S 3 '51; S 10 '51; Au 4 '52
People D 16 '96
Time My 21 '51; Au 11 '51; Au 4 '52

PIAF, EDITH

BRET, DAVID. *The Piaf Legend*. Jersey City, NJ: Parkwest Publications, 1990.
CROSLAND, MARGARET. *Piaf*. NY: Fromm, 1987.
Northcutt, Wayne. *Historical Dictionary of the French Fourth and Fifth Republic, 1946-1991*. London: Greenwood, 1992.
PIAF, EDITH. *My Life*. Chester Springs: Dufour Editions, 1990.

Esquire Nov '83
Life O 6 '52; Au 11 '72
Ms My '81
New Rep N 17 '47; S 1 '47
Newsweek O 21 '63; N 10 '47; D 28 '59
New Yorker N 2 '63; N 15 '47; N 8 '47; Ja 21 '61
Time O 18 '63; O 3 '49

PICASSO, PABLO

BERGER, JOHN. *The Success and Failure of Picasso*. NY: Random House, 1993.
BERNIER, ROSAMUND. *Matisse, Picasso, Miro: As I Knew Them*. NY: Knopf, 1991.
DAIX, PIERRE. *Picasso: Life and Art*. NY: HarperCollins, 1994.
GILOT, FRANCOISE. *Metisse and Picasso*. NY: Doubleday, 1992.
JANIS, HARRIET AND SIDNEY. *Picasso*. NY: Doubleday, 1946.
LORD, JAMES. *Picasso and Dora*. NY: Farrar, Straus and Giroux, 1993.
MAILER, NORMAN. *Portrait of Picasso as a Young Man*. NY: Atlantic Monthly, 1995.
——. *Pablo and Fernande*. NY: Atlantic Monthly, 1995.
O'BRIAN, PATRICK. *Pablo Ruiz Picasso. A biography*. NY: Putnam, 1976.
RICHARDSON, JOHN. *A Life of Picasso*. NY: Random House, 1991.
STEIN, GERTRUDE. *Picasso*. NY: Dover, 1984.

Am Art S '97
Art in Am Ju '97
ARTNews S '96
Nation Au 26 '96; S 2 '96
Nat Rev F 12 '96
New Rep Jy 8 '96; Ju 2 '97
Newsweek Apr 16 '73
New York Ma 6 '96
NY Times Book Rev Ap 30 '95
People Ma 20, Ju 10 '96
Smithsonian Jy '96
Time Ap 23 '73
Times Lit Sup Jy 12 '96; Au 1 '97

PICKFORD, MARY

KATZ, EPHRAIM. *The Stars Appear*. NY: Scarecrow Press, 1992.
LYMAN, SCOTT. *Mary Pickford: America's Sweetheart*. NY: Fine, 1990.
MORDDEN, ETHAN. *Movie Skar*. NY St. Martin's, 1983.
WHITFIELD, EILEEN. *Pickford: The Woman Who Made Hollywood*. University Press of Kentucky, 1997.
WINDELER, ROBERT. *Sweetheart: The Story of Mary Pickford*. London/NY: Howard and Wyndham, 1973.

Am Her D '71
Arch Dig Ap '90

Life Spring '89
Newsweek Je 11 '79; N 28 '77; N 6 '67
People My 21 '90
Spectator Ap 25 '92
Time Je 11 '79
Vanity Fair F 25 '91

POLLOCK, JACKSON

FRANK, ELIZABETH. *Jackson Pollock*. NY: Abbeville, 1983.
FRASCINA, FRANCIS, ED. *Pollock and After: The Critical Debate*. NY: HarperCollins, 1985.
FREIDMAN, B. J. *Jackson Pollock: Energy Made Visible*. NY: Da Capo Press, 1995.
LUCIE-SMITH, EDWARD. *Lives of the Great Twentieth Century Artists*. NY: Rizzoli, 1986.
O'CONNOR, FRANCIS VALENTINE AND EUGENE THAW. *Jackson Pollock: A Catalogue Raisonne of Paintings, Drawings and Other Works*. New Haven, CT: Yale University Press.
RATCLIFF, CARTER. *The Fate of a Gesture: Jackson Pollock and Postwar American Art*. NY: Farrar, Straus and Giroux, 1997.

Amer N 24 '79
Art in Am My '67
Artforum S '65; F '67; Mr '67: Ap '67; My '67
ARTNews My '51; D '81; Ap '90
Esq D '83
Horizon F '79
Life Au 8 '49
Newsweek J 9 '61; J 8 '90
New Yorker Au 5 '50
NY Times Ag 12 '56; D 2 '82
NY Times Book Rev F 16 '97
NY Times Mag J 27 '74
Time J 20 '64; Ap 17 '67

PRESLEY, ELVIS

AGUILA, RICHARD. *That Old Time Rock & Roll*. NY: Schirmer, 1989.
CARLIN, RICHARD. *The World of Music, Rock & Roll, 1955-1970*. NY: Facts on File, 1988.
CHADWICK, VERNON ed. *In Search of Elvis: Music, Race, Art, Religion*. Boulder, CO: Westview Press, 1997.
CLAYTON, ROSE AND DICK HEARD, ed. *Elvis Up Close: In the Words of Those Who Knew Him Best*. Atlanta: Turner Publishing, 1994.
EBERSOLE, LUCINDA AND RICHARD PEABODY. *Mondo Elvis*. NY: St. Martin's, 1994.
GORDON, ROBERT. *Elvis: The King on the Road*. NY: St. Martin's Press, 1996.
GURALNICK, PETER. *Last Train to Memphis: The Rise of Elvis Presley*. Boston: Little, Brown, 1994.
MARLING, KARAL A. *Graceland: Going Home with Elvis*. Cambridge, MA: Harvard University Press, 1996.
NASH, ALANNA. *Elvis Aaron Presley*. NY: HarperCollins, 1995.
QUAIN, KEVIN, ED. *The Elvis Reader: Texts and Sources on the King of Rock 'n' Roll*. NY: St. Martin's, 1992.

Life Je '90
NY Times Au 17 '77; D 18 '94
Time Ja 20 '64; Ap 17 '67; Au 29 '77

PROUST, MARCEL

HAYMAN, RONALD. *Proust: A Biography*. Minerva, 1991.
MAUROIS, ANDRÉ. *From Proust to Camus*. Garden City, NJ: Doubleday, 1966.
PAINTER, GEORGE. *Marcel Proust: A Biography*. NY: Random, 1989.
PROUST, MARCEL. *Remembrance of Things Past* (3 vols.). Tr., Scott Moncrieff and Terence Kilmartin. London: Chatto & Windus, 1981.
SANSOM, WILLIAM. *Proust*. London: Thames and Hudson, 1986.

Amer Theater N '94
DLB, vol. 65 ("Marcel Proust" by Douglas W. Alden)
Inter Phil Quart D '94
Mod Lang Rev O '93; Ja '95
NY Times Book Rev D 23 '90
Paris Rev Winter '92
Sewanee Rev Summer '93
Time Jy 5 '71
Times Lit Sup D 4 '92; D 3 '93; Au 26 '94; Mr 24 '95; Ma 12 '95; O 4 '96
Wor Lit Today Summer '95
Vogue N '84

RAND, AYN

BERLINER, MICHAEL S. *Letters of Ayn Rand*. NY: Penguin, 1997.
BRANDEN, BARBARA. *The Passion of Ayn Rand*. NY: Doubleday, 1986.
BRANDEN, NATHANIEL. *Judgment Day: My Years with Ayn Rand*. NY: Avon, 1989.

Barron's Ja 4 '93
Humanist Ja '89

Ms S '78
Nat Rev Ap 2 '82; My 14 '82
Newsweek N 29 '76; S 16 '74
New York My 31 '93
New Yorker Jy 24 '95
NY Times Book Rev Je 25 '89; Au 6 '95
Reason Ja '89
Sports Illus Au 4 '86
Vanity Fair Je '89; S '92

REAGAN, RONALD

CANNON, LOUIS. *Reagan*. NY: Putnam, 1982.
——. *Ronald Reagan: The Role of a Lifetime*. NY: Simon & Schuster, 1991.
DAVIS, PATTI. *Angels Don't Die*. NY: HarperCollins, 1995.
DUGGER, RENNIE. *On Reagan*. NY: McGraw-Hill, 1983.
LARSEN, REBECCA. *Ronald Reagan*. NY: Watts, 1994.
REAGAN, RONALD. *An American Life*. NY: Simon & Schuster, 1990.
SANDAK, CASS R. *The Reagans*. NY: Crestwood, 1993.
VAUGHN, STEPHEN. *Ronald Reagan in Hollywood: Movies and Politics*. Cambridge/New York: Cambridge University Press, 1994.

Life O 14 '66
Nat Rev N 2 '89
Newsweek Mr 20 '67; O 31 '66; Au 22 '66; F 6 '84; Ja 9 '89
Time Ja 5 '81; N 19 '84; Jy 7 '86; N 5, 12 '90
US News Ja 9 '89

RIEFENSTAHL, LENI

ACKAR, ALLY. *Reel Women: Pioneers of the Cinema 1896–Present*. NY: Continuum, 1991.
HINTON, DAVID B. *The Films of Leni Riefenstahl*. Metuchen, NJ: Scarecrow Press, 1978.
INFIELD, GLENN B. *Leni Riefenstahl: The Fallen Film Goddess*. NY: Crowell, 1976.
RIEFENSTAHL, LENI. *Leni Riefenstahl, A Memoir*. NY: St. Martin's Press, 1993.
SMITH, SHARON. *Women Who Make Movies*. NY: Hopkinson and Blake, 1975.

Newsweek N 29 '76; S 16 '74
Sports Illus Au 4 '86
Vanity Fair S '92

ROBINSON, JACKIE

ALLEN, MAURY. *Jackie Robinson: A Life Remembered*. NY: Watts, 1987.
DINGLE, DEREK T. *First in the Field: Baseball Hero Jackie Robinson*. NY: Hyperion, 1998.
JACOBS, WILLIAM JAY. *They Shaped the Game: Ty Cobb, Babe Ruth, Jackie Robinson*. NY: Scribner's, 1994.
RAMPERSAND, ARNOLD. *Jackie Robinson: A Biography*. NY: Knopf, 1997.
ROBINSON, JACKIE. *I Never Had It Made: An Autobiography*. Hopewell, NJ: Ecco Press, 1995.
ROBINSON, SHARON. *Stealing Home: An Intimate Family Portrait by the Daughter of Jackie Robinson*. NY: Harper Perennial, 1997.

Am Her Au/S '84
Ebony Au '92; O '96; N '95
Essence N '96
Esq D '83
Nation My 15 '95
Nat Rev Ap 8 '96
NY Times Book Rev Ap 2 '95
Sport Je '88; S '96
Sporting News O 29 '90; F 13 '95; O 21 '96
Sports Illus S 16 '96
World Press Review Au '96

ROCKEFELLER, JOHN D.

ALBRIGHT, HORACE M. *Worthwhile Places: The Correspondence of John D. Rockefeller Jr. and Horace M. Albright*. NY: Fordham University Press, 1991.
ERNST, JOSEPH W. *Dear Father—Dear Son: The Correspondence of John D. Rockefeller and John D. Rockefeller Jr.*. NY: Fordham University Press, 1994.
HARR, JOHN E. AND PETER J. JOHNSON. *The Rockefeller Century*. NY: Scribner's, 1988.
ROCKEFELLER, JOHN D. *Random Reminiscences of Men and Events*. Tarrytown, NY: Sleepy Hollow Press, 1984.

Am Her Ap '70; D '64; Je '64; S '88
Christian Cent O 26 '88
Fortune S 12 '88
Nat Bus Mr '71
Pub Wkly Ma 20 '88

ROOSEVELT, ELEANOR

COOK, BLANCHE WIESEN. *Eleanor Roosevelt: Vol. 1: 1884-1933*. NY: Viking, 1992.
GOODWIN, DORIS KEARNS. *No Ordinary Time*. NY: Simon & Schuster, 1994.

HAREVEN, TAMARA K. *Eleanor Roosevelt: An American Conscience.* Chicago: Quadrangle Books, 1968.
LASH, JOSEPH P. *A World of Love: Eleanor Roosevelt and Her Friends, 1943-1962,* NY: McGraw-Hill, 1985.
ROOSEVELT, ELEANOR. *The Autobiography of Eleanor Roosevelt.* NY: Harper & Row, 1978.
——. *This is My Story.* NY: Harper & Brothers, 1937.
SCHARF, LOIS. *Eleanor Roosevelt: First Lady of American Liberalism.* Boston: Twayne, 1987.

Jour of Women's Hist Winter '95
Life Jy '97
Newsweek O 3 '94
New Yorker O 24 '94
NY Times Mag Ap 14 '96
People D 26 '94
Pol Sci Quar Sp '97
Revs in Amer Hist Ju '95
Soc Ed S '96

ROOSEVELT, FRANKLIN D.

ABBOTT, PHILIP. *The Exemplary President: Franklin D. Roosevelt and the American Political Tradition.* Amherst, MA: University of Massachusetts Press, 1990.
ALLDRITT. *Greatest of Friends: Franklin D. Roosevelt and Winston Chirchill.* NY: St. Martin's, 1995.
BUHITE, RUSSELL D. AND DAVID W. LEVY, EDS. *FDR's Fireside Chats.* Norman, OK: University of Oklahoma Press, 1992.
DAVIS, ROBERT ED. *FDR: The Beckoning of Destiny 1882-1928.* NY: Random House, 1993.
——. *FDR: The New York Years 1928-1933.* NY: Random House, 1994.
FREIDEL, FRANK. *Franklin D. Roosevelt: A Rendezvous with Destiny.* Boston: Little, Brown, 1991.
GOODWIN, DORIS KEARNS. *No Ordinary Time.* NY: Simon & Schuster, 1994.
LEUCHTENBURG, WILLIAM E. *The FDR Years: On Roosevelt and His Legacy.* NY: Columbia University Press, 1995.
MANEY, PATRICK. *Franklin D. Roosevelt.* NY: Macmillan, 1992.
VAN MINNEN, CORNELIS A. AND JOHN F. SEARS. *FDR and His Contemporaries: Foreign Perception of an American President.* NY: St. Martin's, 1992.

Am Her Ap '95; D '95
Commonweal My 5 '95
Life My 29 '44
Nation Ap 21 '45; My 15 '95
Nat Rev Mr 6 '95
Newsweek Ap 24 '95
NY Times Mag Ap 14 '96
Time Ap 23 '45; Mr 6 '95; My 20 '96
US News Ap 10 '95

ROSENBERG, ETHEL AND JULIUS

MEEROPOL, MICHAEL. *We Are Your Sons: The Legacy of Ethel and Julius Rosenberg.* Champaign, IL: University of Illinois Press, 1986.
PHILIPSON, ILENE. *Ethel Rosenberg: Beyond the Myth.* New York/Toronto: Watts, 1988.
NEVILLE, JOHN F. *The Press, the Rosenbergs and the Cold War.* Westport, CT: Greenwood Publishing, 1995.
RADOSH, RONALD. *The Rosenberg File.* New Haven, CT: Yale University Press, 1997.

Commentary O '83
Esq My '75
Maclean's Au 29 '83
Nat Rev N 25 '83
New Rev O 31 '83
Newsweek My 19 '80; Jy 2 '79; My 19 '75
New York Mr 7 '83
Time My 5 '75; F 24 '67

RUDOLPH, WILMA

BIRACREE, TOM. *Wilma Rudolph.* NY: 1988.
KRULL, KATHLEEN. *Wilma Unlimited: How Wilma Rudolph Became the World's Fastest Woman.* NY: Harcourt Brace, 1996.
RUDOLPH, WILMA. *Wilma: The Story of Wilma Rudolph.* NY: Signet Books, 1977.

Contemp. Black Biography v. 4
Ebony F '84
Life O 17 '60; S 19 '60
Newsweek F 6 '61
Notable Black Amer. Woman
Read Dig My '61
Sat Ev Post O '76
Sports Illus Ja 30 '61
Time S 19 '60; F 10 '61

RUSSELL, BERTRAND

MOOREHEAD, CAROLINE. *Bertrand Russell: A Life.* NY: Viking, 1992.
RUSSELL, BERTRAND. *Autobiography of Bertrand Russell.* NY: Routledge, 1978.

RYAN, ALAN. *Bertrand Russell: A Political Life.* Oxford/NY: Oxford University Press, 1993.

Dict of Lit Biog
London Times Obit
New Rep Au 17-24 '92
New Crit S '92
NY Rev of Books Au 13 '92
New States Soc Jy 22' 88
Newsweek Au 20 '62; Ja 19 '76; F 16 '70; O 27 '69
Time Ja 12 '76; F 16 '70

RUTH, GEORGE HERMAN "BABE"

BURLEIGH, ROBERT. *Home Run: The Story of Babe Ruth.* San Diego: Harcourt Brace, 1996.
CREAMER, ROBERT W. *Babe.* NY: Simon & Schuster, 1974.
——. *Babe: The Legend Comes to Life.* NY: Simon & Schuster, 1992.
KELLY, BRENT P. *In the Shadow of the Babe: Interviews with Baseball Players Who Played with or Against Babe Ruth.* Jefferson, VA, 1995.
RUTH, BABE. *Babe Ruth Story.* NY: NAL, 1992.
SMELSER, MARSHALL. *The Life that Ruth Built.* NY: Quadrangle, 1975.
WAGENHEIM, KAL. *Babe Ruth: His Life and Legend.* NY: Henry Holt, 1992.

Amer Her My/Je '89
Life Ja 29 '65
Newsweek F 23 '48; F 1 '65

SANGER, MARGARET

CHESLER, ELLEN. *Women of Valor: Margaret Sanger and the Birth Control Movement.* NY: Simon & Schuster, 1992.
DOUGLAS, EMILY. *Margaret Sanger.* NY: Holt, Rinehart & Winston, 1969.
FREYER, PETER. *The Birth Controllers.* London: Secker & Warburg, 1965.
GRAY, MADELINE. *Margaret Sanger.* NY: Marek, 1979.
SANGER, MARGARET. *Margaret Sanger: An auto-biography.* NY: Dover, 1971 [1938].
——. *My Fight for Birth Control.* NY: Maxwell Reproduction Co., 1969.
WINTELAW, NANCY. *Margaret Sanger: Every Child a Wanted Child.* NY: Macmillan, 1994.

Am Hist Rev O '93
Chi Trib Ju 21 '92
Hum Life Rev Sum '93
LA Times Je 28 '92
Jour of Am Hist S '93
Maclean's Au 14 '95
Nature N 2 '95
Newsweek S 19 '66
NY Times Je 17 '92; Jy 5 '92
Revs in Amer Hist Ju '93
Time S 16 '66

SARTRE, JEAN-PAUL

FULLBROOK, KATE AND EDWARD FULLBROOK. *Simone de Beauvoir and Jean-Paul Sartre.* NY: Knopf, 1991.
HAYMAN, RONALD. *Sartre: A Life.* NY: Simon & Schuster, 1987.
HOWELLS, CHRISTINA, ED. *The Cambridge Companion to Sartre.* NY/London: Cambridge University Press, 1992.
——. *Sartre.* NY: Longman, 1992.
SARTRE, JEAN-PAUL. *Quiet Moments in a War: The Letters of Jean-Paul Sartre to Simone de Beauvoir.* NY: Scribner's, 1993.
——. *Witness to My Life.* London: Hamilton, 1993.

Ethics Jy '95
Harper's My '96
Internat'l Phil Quart S '96
Journ Hist of Ideas Ja '94
Nation Je 7 '80
New Lead D 19 '94
NY Times Book Rev Ja 9 '94; Ja 23 '94; Ap 14 '96
Phil O '95
Phil Today Spring '94; Winter '95
Rev of Pol Winter '94
Theatre Res Inter Spring '95
Time Ap 28 '80
Times Lit Sup Mr 12 '93; F 24 '95; Ja 19 '96
Wor Lit Today Winter '96

SCHWEITZER, ALBERT

COUSINS, NORMAN. *Dr. Schweitzer at Lambaréné.* NY: Harper, 1960.
MARSHALL, GEORGE. *Schweitzer: A Biography.* Boston: Albert Schweitzer Fellowship, 1989.
MONTAGUE, JOSEPH FRANKLIN, M.D. *The Why of Albert Schweitzer.* NY: Hawthorne Books, 1965.
SCHWEITZER, ALBERT. *Out of My Life and Thought: An Autobiography.* NY: Henry Holt, 1991.

Am Jour of Psychiatry S '92
Humanist Mr '93
NY Times Book Rev S 27 '92
Nobel Prize Winners
Parabola Winter '90
Sat Ev Post N '94
Time S 17 '65

SHAW, GEORGE BERNARD

GANZ, ARTHUR. *George Bernard Shaw.* NY: Grove Press, 1983.
HOLROYD, MICHAEL. *Bernard Shaw.* NY: Random House, 1992.
MINNEY, R. J. *Recollections of George Bernard Shaw.* Englewood Cliffs, NJ: Prentice-Hall, 1969.
SHAW, GEORGE BERNARD AND ARCHIBALD HENDERSON. *Table-talk of G.B.S.: Conversations on Things in General, Between George Bernard Shaw and His Biographer.* NY/London: Harper & Brothers, 1925.
VALENCY, MAURICE JACQUES. *The Cart and the Trumpet: The Plays of George Bernard Shaw.* Oxford/NY: Oxford University Press, 1973.

Dict Lit Biog, vol. 57
New Crit S '93
New Rep Ag 8-15 '88; N 14 '88
New Yorker Ja 2 '89.
Nobel Prize Winners
Smithsonian N '90
Time O 10 '88

SINATRA, FRANK

BRITT, STAN. *Sinatra: A Celebration.* NY: Macmillan, 1995.
COLEMAN, RAY. *Frank Sinatra: Portrait of an Artist.* Georgia: Turner Publishing, 1995.
FRIEDWALD, WILL. *Sinatra! The Song Is You: A Singer's Art.* NY: Scribner's, 1995.
KELLEY, KITTY. *His Way: The Unauthorized Biography of Frank Sinatra.* NY: Bantam, 1986.
PETKOV, STEVEN AND LEONARD MUSTAZZA, EDS. *The Frank Sinatra Reader.* Oxford/NY: Oxford University Press, 1995.
SHAW, ARNOLD. *Sinatra: Twentieth Century Romantic.* New York: Henry Holt, 1968.
SINATRA, NANCY. *Frank Sinatra: An American Legend.* General Publishing Group, 1995.

Esq F '78
Nat Rev F 17 '92
New Rep Mr 31 '86
Newsweek D 17 '90; O 28 '63; S 6 '65
New Yorker N 3 '97
NY Times D 7 '97
Time Je 16 '86; N 3 '86
Wall St Jour S 26 '97
Vogue F '84

SOLZHENITSYN, ALEKSANDR

MOODY, CHRISTOPHER. *Solzhenitsyn.* NY: Harper & Row, 1975.
SCAMMELL, MICHAEL. *Solzhenitsyn: A Biography.* NY: Norton, 1984.
SOLZHENITSYN, ALEXANDER. *Cancer Ward.* Tr., Nicholas Bethell and David Burg. NY: Norton, 1984.
——. *The Gulag Archipelago.* Vol.1 & 2, tr., Thomas Whitney; Vol. 3, tr., Harry Willetts. NY: Harper & Row, 1974, 1975, 1978.
THOMAS, D .M. *Alexander Solzhenitsyn: A Century in His Life.* NY: St. Martin's, 1998.

Economist Ma 28 '94
Nation Mr 16 '85
Nat Rev Ap 8 '96
Newsweek Ju 6 '94
New Yorker F 14 '94; D 1 '95
NY Times D 11 '70
NY Times Book Rev N 24 '91; F 7 '93; Ja 7 '96
People My 16 '94
Pub Wkly Ma 25 '92; F 15 '93; Jy 17 '95
Spectator D9 '95
Time Mr 21 '69; Mr 12 '84; My 23 '83; Jy 24 '89; Ju 20 '94
Times Lit Sup N 16 '90; Ja 26 '96
Vir Quarterly Rev Autumn '95
Wor Lit Today Ap '96
World Press Review S '94

SPIELBERG, STEVEN

BAXTER, JOHN. *Steven Spielberg: The Unauthorized Biography.* NY: HarperCollins, 1997.
CRAWLEY, TONY. *The Steven Spielberg Story.* NY: Quill, 1983.
MCBRIDE JOSEPH. *Steven Spielberg: A Biography.* NY: Simon & Schuster, 1997.
TAYLOR, PHILIP M. *Steven Spielberg: The Man, His Movies, and Their Meaning.* NY: Continuum, 1992.

Am Film Je '88
Maclean'ss Je 4 '84

Newsweek Je 4 '84
Time Jy 15 '88; Jy 15 '85

SPOCK, DR. BENJAMIN

SPOCK, BENJAMIN. *Baby and Child Care*. NY: Pocket Books, 1945.
——AND MITCHELL ZIMMERMAN. *Dr. Spock on Vietnam*. NY: Dell, 1968.
——AND MARY MORGAN. *Spock on Spock*. NY: Pantheon, 1989.
SPOCK, MICHAEL. *My Father, Doctor Spock*. Downe Publishing, 1968.

Am Spect J '90
Nat Rev N 3'64
New Rep D 5 '94
NY Times Mag D 3 '67; Mr 17 '98
New Yorker My 20 '96
Redbook O '63
US News N 4 '96

STALIN, JOSEPH

BEREZHKOV, VALENTIN M. *At Stalin's Side: His interpreter's Memoir from the October Revolution to the Fall of the Dictator's Empire*. Seacaucus, NJ: Carol Publishing, 1994.
BOFFA, GIUSEPPE. *The Stalin Phenomenon*. Ithaca, NY: Cornell University Press, 1992.
BULLOCK, ALAN L. *Hitler and Stalin: Parallel Lives*. NY: Random House, 1993.
CAMERON, KENNETH N. *Stalin: The Man of Contradiction*. Toronto: University of Toronto Press, 1990.
CONQUEST, ROBERT. *Stalin: Breaker of Nations*. NY: Viking, 1991.
HINGLEY, RONALD. *Josef Stalin: Myth and Legend*. NY: Smithmark Publishers, 1994.
HOCHSCHILD, ADAM. *The Unquiet Ghost: Russians Remember Stalin*. NY: Viking Penguin, 1995.
MCNEAL, ROBERT. *Stalin: Man and Ruler*. NY: New York University Press, 1988.
NOVE, ALEC. *The Stalin Phenomenon*. NY: St. Martin's, 1993.
RADZINSKY, EDVARD. *Stalin: The First In-Depth Biography Based on Explosive New Documents From Russia's Secret Archives*. NY: Doubleday, 1996.
RICHARDSON, ROSAMOND. *Stalin's Shadow: Inside the Family of One of the World's Greatest Tyrants*. NY: St. Martin's, 1993.
THURSTON, ROBERT W. *Life and Terror in Stalin's Russia*. New Haven, CT: Yale University Press, 1996.
VOLKOGONOV, DMITRI. *Stalin: Triumph and Tragedy*. Rocklin, CA: Prima Publishing, 1996.
ZUBOK, VLADISLAV AND CONSTANTINE PLESHAKOV. *Inside the Kremlin's Cold War: From Stalin to Khrushchev*. Cambridge, MA: Harvard University Press, 1996.

Life Mr 16 '53; Mr 23 '53
Nation Mr 6 '89; Aug 7 '89; Au 14 '89
Newsweek Mr 16 '53
Time 61: Mr 16 '53; Je 11 '57; Ap 10 '89

STEIN, GERTRUDE

BRIDGEMAN, RICHARD. *Gertrude Stein in Pieces*. Oxford/NY: Oxford University Press, 1970.
BRINNIN, JOHN MALCOLM. *The Third Rose*. Boston: Little, Brown, 1959.
KNAPP, BETTINA L. *Gertrude Stein*. NY: Continuum, 1990.
SIMON, LINDA, ED. *Gertrude Stein Remembered*. Lincoln, NE: University of Nebraska Press, 1994.
SOUHAMI, DIANA. *Gertrude and Alice*. London: Pandora/HarperCollins, 1991.
STENDHAL, RENATE. *Gertrude Stein: In Words and Pictures*. Chapel Hill, NC: Algonquin, 1994.
WINEAPPLE, BRENDA. *Sister Brother: Gertrude and Leo Stein*. NY: Putnam, 1996.

Esq D '77
Harper's D '47
Hor N '80
Nation Au 10 '46
Newsweek Au 5 '76
New Yorker Au 10 '46; My 31'47
Time Au 5 '46

STRAVINSKY, IGOR

CRAFT, ROBERT. *Stravinsky: Glimpses of a Life*. NY: St. Martin's, 1992.
GRIFFITHS, PAUL. *Stravinsky*. NY: Scribner', 1992.
HORGAN, PAUL. *Encounter with Stravinsky*. Middletown, CT: Wesleyan University Press, 1988.
OLIVER, MICHAEL. *Igor Stravinsky*. London: Phaiden Press, 1995.
STRAVINSKY, IGOR. *An Autobiography*. NY: Simon & Schuster, 1936.
TARUSKIN, RICHARD. *Stravinsky and the Russian Traditions*. Berkeley: University of California, 1995.
WALSH, STEPHEN. *The Music of Stravinsky*. London/NY: Routledge, 1988.

Atlantic Ap 19 '71
Esq D '72
Newsweek Ap 19 '71
Saturday Review My 29 '71

BARBRA STREISAND

BLY, NELLIE. *Barbra Streisand: The Untold Story*. NY: Windsor, 1994.
BRADY, FRANK. *Barbra Streisand: An Illustrated Biography*. NY: Grosset & Dunlap, 1979.
CONSIDINE, SHAUN. *Barbra Streisand: The Woman, the Myth, the Music*.
EDWARDS, ANNE. *Streisand: A Biography*. Boston: Little, Brown, 1997.
RIESE, RANDALL. *Her Name is Barbra: An Intimate Portrait of the Real Barbra Streisand*. Secaucus, NJ: Carol Publishing, 1993.
SPADA, JAMES. *Streisand: Her Life*. NY: Crown, 1995.
——. *Streisand, the Woman and the Legend*. Garden City, NY: Doubleday, 1981.

Esq S '95
Nat Rev Mr 20 '95
New York O 24 '94; F 20 '95; O 30 '95; Ap 8 '96
NY Times N 11 '97
NY Times Book Rev N 11 '95
People Je 27 '94; F 20 '95
Time F 13 '95
USA Today Ja 28 '98
Vanity Fair N '94; Mr '94; Ap '94; S '95
Vill Voice Mr 26 '96

TAYLOR, ELIZABETH

HEYMAN, DAVID C. *Liz: An Intimate Biography of Elizabeth Taylor*. Seacaucus, NJ: Carol Publishing, 1995.
PARKER, JOHN. *Five for Hollywood: Their Friendship, Their Fame, Their Tragedies*. Seacaucus, NJ: Carol Publishing, 1991.
SHEPPARD, DICK. *Elizabeth: The life and Career of Elizabeth Taylor*. NY: Doubleday, 1974.
SPOTO, DONALD. *A Passion for Life: The Biography of Elizabeth Taylor*. NY: HarperCollins, 1995.

Film Com My/Je '86
Lad Hom Jour O '87
Newsweek My 7 '90
NY My 9 '83
Vanity Fair N '92

TEMPLE, SHIRLEY

BLACK, SHIRLEY TEMPLE. *Child Star: An Autobiography*. NY: Warner, 1989.
CALKIN, HOMER L. *Women in the Department of State: Their Role in American Foreign Affairs*. Washington, DC: Department of State # 8951, 1978.
STINEMAN, ESTHER, ED. *American Political Women: Contemporary and Historical Profiles*. Littleton, CO: Libraries Unlimited, 1980.
WINDLER, ROBERT. *Films of Shirley Temple*. 1978.
ZIEROLD, NORMAN J. *The Child Stars*. NY: Coward McCann, 1965.

Am Her M '89
Christian Sci Mon D 26 '69
Cur Biog '45; '70
Ebony Mr '76
Look Au 21 '45; N 14 '67
Newsweek S 11 '67; Je 16 '75
NY Times D 27 '66; Au 30 '67; Au 30 '69; D 12 '69
Redbook N '75
Sat Ev Post Jy 9 '38; Je 5 '65
Time Ap 27 '36; S 8 '67
US News J 19 '76; F 4' 80

MOTHER TERESA

CHAWLA, NARIN. *Mother Teresa: An Authorized Biography*. Rockport, MA: Element, 1996.
MUGGERIDGE, MALCOLM. *Something Beautiful for God: Mother Teresa of Calcutta*. London: Collins, 1971.
PORTER, DAVID. *Mother Teresa, the Early Years*. Grand Rapids: Wm. B. Eerdman's, 1986.
SEBBA, ANNE. *Mother Teresa: Beyond the Image*. NY: Doubleday, 1997.
VARDEY, LUCINDA. *Mother Teresa: A Simple Path*. NY: Ballantine, 1995.

Life Ap '88
Newsweek O 29 '79; S 22 '97
NY Times S 14 '97
People 9 29 '97
Read Dig D '87Time O 29 '79

THATCHER, MARGARET

OFFEL, OLGA. *Women Prime Ministers and Presidents*. NY: McFarland, 1993.
SMITH, GEOFFREY. *Reagan and Thatcher*. NY: Norton, 1991.
THATCHER, MARGARET. *The Downing Street Years*. NY: HarperCollins, 1993.

YOUNG, HUGO. *One of Us: A Biography of Margaret Thatcher*. London: Macmillan, 1991.

Atlantic D '91
Bus Wk Ap 1 '96
Economist S 21 '96
Jour of Am Hist Ma '96
Nation Ma 13 '96
New Yorker F 10 '86
NY Rev of Books Ma 21 '96
Newsweek D 3 '90
Parl Aff Jy '96
Pol Studies D '95
Read Dig N '87
Spect Ma 3 '97; Jy '97; S 28 '96
Vanity Fair Je '91

THORPE, JIM

BERNOTAS, BOB. *Jim Thorpe: Sac and Fox Athlete*. NY: Chelsea House, 1992.
DOCKSTADER, FREDERICK J. *Great North American Indians*. NY: Van Nostrand Reinhold, 1977.
FALL, THOMAS. *Jim Thorpe*. NY: Crowell, 1970.
HAHN, JAMES. *Thorpe! The Sports Career of Jim Thorpe*. Mankato, MN: Crestwood House, 1981.
LIPSYTE, ROBERT. *Jim Thorpe: 20th Century Jock*. NY: HarperCollins, 1993.
PAENTER, MAC. *Champions of American Sports*. NY: Abrams, 1981.
SCHOON, GENE. *The Jim Thorpe Story: America's Greatest Athlete*. NY: Messner, 1951.
SULLIVAN, GEORGE. *Professional Football's All-Time All-Star Team*. NY: Putnam, 1968.
VAN REPER, GUERNSEY. *Jim Thorpe: Indian Athlete*. Indianapolis, IN: Bobbs-Merrill, 1961.
WHELLER, ROBERT W. *Jim Thorpe: World's Greatest Athlete*. Norman, OK: University of Oklahoma Press, 1979.

Am Her Jy '92
Forbes S 12 '83
Instructor O '67
Newsweek Ap 6 '53
Sat Ev Post Mr '90
Scholastic My 7 '52
Sporting News N 20 '95
Sports Illus O 25 '82; Ap 2 '90; N 27 '95
Time Ap 6 '53

TOKYO ROSE

DUUS, MASAYO. *Tokyo Rose: Orphan of the Pacific*. Tokyo/NY: Kodansha, 1979.
HOWE, RUSSELL. *The Hunt for Tokyo Rose*. Boston: Madison, 1990.

Am Merc Ja '54
Commentary O. '83
Esquire My '69; My '75
Maclean's Au 29 '83
Nat Rev N 25 '83
New Rep O 31'83
Newsweek S 17 '45; Au 30 '48; Ja 16 '56; Mr 5 '56; My 10 '75; Ja 31 '77; Jy 2 '79; My 19 '80
New York Mr 7 '83
Time Jy 18 '49; F 24 '67; Mr 22 '67; My 5 '75; Ja 31 '77; F 16 '78

TOSCANINI, ARTURO

HOROWITZ, JOSEPH. *Understanding Toscanini: A Social History of American Concert Life*. Berkeley: University of California, 1994.
LEBRECHT, NORMAN. *The Maestro Myth: Great Conductors in the Pursuit of Power*. NY: Brich Lane Press, 1992.
SACHS, HARVEY. *Reflections on Toscanini*. NY: Grove, 1993.
——. *Toscanini*. Rocklin, CA: Prima Publishers, 1995.
SCHONBERG, HAROLD. *The Glorious Ones: Classical Music's Legendary Performers*. NY: Times Books, 1988.

Atlantic D '66
Commentary Ap '88
Newsweek Mr 2 '87; Mr 27 '67; Ap 13 '59; Ja 28 '57
New Rep Je 1 '87
Read Dig Jy '66
Time Ja 28 '57; Mr 4 '57; Mr 9 '87
Vogue Mr 1 '57

TURNER, TED

BIBB, PORTER. *It Ain't As Easy As It Looks*. NY: Crown, 1993.
GOLDBERG, ROBERT AND GERALD JAY GOLDBERG. *Citizen Turner: The Wild Rise of An American Tycoon*. NY: Harcourt Brace, 1994.
WHITTEMORE, HANK. *CNN: The Inside Story*. Little, Brown, 1990.

Atl Const Jy 17 '70; Ma 12 '73; Ja 14 '76; Je 13 '77; Au 21 '79; D 10 '89
Broadcasting Au 17 '87; Ap 9 '90; Mr 4 '91

Esq F '91
Time S 19 '77; Ja 6 '92; Ja 20 '90
Newsweek Jy 11 '75; Mr 11 '85; Ma 21 '90; Je 11
    '90; Ja 6 '92
NY Times D 9 '97
People N 12 '91; Ja 6 '92
Sail S '78
Sports Illus O 12 '77; Au 21 '78
Wall St Jour F 13 '93

VALENTINO, RUDOLPH

BOTHAM, NOEL. *Valentino: The Love God.* Miami:
    Brown Rock Co., 1976.
MORRIS, MICHAEL. *Madame Valentino: The Many Lives of
    Natacha Rambova.* NY: Abbeville, 1991.
OBERFIRST, ROBERT. *Rudolf Valentino: The Man Behind
    the Myth.* NY: Citadel, 1962.
SHULMAN, IRVING. *Valentino.* NY: Trident, 1967.
WALKER, ALAXANDER. *Rudolf Valentino.* NY: Viking,
    1977.

VON BRAUN, WERNHER

HEILBRON, J. L. *Dilemmas of an Upright Man.* Berkeley:
    University of California Press, 1986.
PISZKIEWICZ, DENNIS. *The Nazi Rocketeers: Dreams of
    Space and Crimes of War.* Wesport, MA:
    Greenwood Publishing, 1995.
STUHLINGER, ERNST. *Wernher Von Braun: Crusade for
    Space.* Melbourne: Krieger Publishing, 1996
WUSTRICH, ROBERT. *Who's Who in Nazi Germany.*
    London/NY: Routledge, 1995.

Current Biography '52
Life N 18 '57
Newsweek Je 27 '77; Je 5 '72; F 9 '70; F10 '58
New Yorker Ap 21 '51
Read Dig Ja '61; My '58
Sight&Sound Winter '60
Time Je 27 '77; Je 18 '69; F 17 '58

VREELAND, DIANA

MARTIN, RICHARD. *Diana Vreeland: Immoderate Style.*
    NY: Metropolitan Museum, 1993.
ROOSEVELT, FELICIA. *Doers and Dowagers.* NY: Dou-
    bleday, 1975,

Harper's Bazaar N '95
House&Gar My '88
Interview N '89
Ms Au '75
Newsweek My 31 '71; Ja 2 '78; S 22 '80; F 27 '89;
    S 4 '89
New York N 29 '82
New Yorker N 7 '94; S 16 '96
NY Times Mag Ap 1 '90
People D 8 '80; S 11 '89
Vanity Fair Ja '90; N '93
Vogue D '89

WALESA, LECH

BOYES, ROGER. *The Naked President: A Political Life of
    Lech Walesa.* London: Secker & Warburg, 1994.
BROLEWICZ, WALTER. *My Brother, Lech Walesa.* NY:
    Tribeca Communications, 1983.
ERINGER, ROBERT. *Strike for Freedom!: The Story of
    Lech Walesa and Polish Solidarity.* NY: Dodd,
    1982.
WALESA, LECH. *A Way of Hope.* NY: Arcade Pub., 1987.
——. *The Struggle and the Triumph.* NY: Arcade Pub.,
    1992.

Commonweal D 15 '95
Economist Ap 28 '90; D 1 '90; Jy 11'92; O 22 '94
Forbes D 18 '95
Maclean's N 26 '90; D 24 '90
Nation N 27 '95
Nat Rev Ma 5 '90; D 31 '90; J 28 '91
New Rep Jy 23 D 3 '90; Ma 18 '91
Time Ap D 19 '83; Ju 24 '85; O 17 '83; Au 28 '89
US News O 17 '83; Ju 8 '92
Wash Post Jy 5 '94

WARHOL, ANDY

ALEXANDER, PAUL. *Death & Disaster: The Rise of the
    Warhol Empire and the Race for Andy's Millions.*
    NY: Random House, 1994.
BOCKRIS, VICTOR. *Life and Death of Andy Warhol.* NY:
    Bantam, 1989.
BOURDON, MAURICE. *Warhol.* NY: Abrams, 1991.
COLACELLO, BOB. *Holy Terror: Andy Warhol Close Up.*
    NY: Harper Perennial, 1991.
FINKELSTEIN, NAT. *Andy Warhol: The Factory Years.*
    NY: St Martin's, 1989.
HACKETT, PAT. *The Andy Warhol Diaries.* NY: Warner
    Books Inc., 1991.
HONNEF, KLAUS. *Warhol.* Carson, CA: Books Nippon:
    1994.
KOCH, STEPHEN. *Stargazer: The Life, World and Films
    of Andy Warhol.* NY: Rizzoli, 1991.

MCSHINE, KYNASTON. *Andy Warhol: A Retrospective.*
    NY: Museum of Modern Art, 1991.
WARHOL, ANDY. *Popism: The Warhol Sixties.* Orlando,
    FL: Harcourt Brace, 1990.
WRENN, MIKE. *Andy Warhol: In His Own Words.* NY:
    Omnibus Press, 1991.

ARTNews My '87
Atlantic Au '89
New Rep My 18'87
Newsweek My 22 '89
New York My 29 '89; F 22 '88; Mr 7 '88
New Yorker Ap 27 '87
Time Mr 9 '87
Vogue F '89

WATSON, JAMES & FRANCIS CRICK

CRICK, FRANCIS. *What Mad Pursuit: A Personal View of
    Scientific Discovery.* NY: Basic Books, 1988.
NEWTON, DAVID E. *James Watson & Francis Crick:
    Discovery of the Double Helix and Beyond.* NY:
    Facts on File, 1992.

Time O 26 '62; O 3 '83; O 3 '88; Mr 15 '93
Newsweek O 29 '62
Smithsonian F '90
Psych Tod N '83
Life O 30 '70; N 2 '62
Biog Dict of Sci
Thinkers of the Twentieth Century

WAYNE, JOHN

HYAMS, JAY. *Life and Times of the Western Movie.* NY:
    Gallery Books, 1983.
LEVY, EMANUEL. *John Wayne: Prophet of the American
    Way of Life.* Metuchen, NJ: Scarecrow Press, 1988.
MATTHEWS, LEONARD. *History of Western Movies.* NY:
    Crescent Books, 1984.
MCGHEE, RICHARD. *John Wayne: Actor, Artist, Hero.*
    NY: McFarland, 1990.
MINSHALL, BERT AND SHARON CLARK. *On Board with the
    Duke.* Washington, DC: Seven Locks Press, 1992.
NALDO, DAN. *John Wayne.* NY: Chelsea House, 1994.
ROBERTS, RANDY AND JAMES S. OLSON. *John Wayne:
    American.* NY: The Free Press, 1995.
STACY, PAT AND BEVERLY LINET. *Duke, A Love Story.*
    Atheneum, 1983.
THOMAS, TONY. *The West That Never Was.* NY: Citadel,
    1989.
WELCH, JULIE. *Leading Men.* Villard, 1985.

Film Comment S '79
New Rep Au 4 '79
Newsweek Je 25 '79
Read Dig O '79
Sat Ev Post Jy/Ag '86

WELLES, ORSON

BRADY, FRANK. *Citizen Welles: A Biography of Orson
    Welles.* NY: Scribner's, 1989.
CALLOW, SIMON. *Orson Welles: The Road to Xanadu.*
    NY: Viking, 1996.
HIGHAM, CHARLES. *The Films of Orson Welles.*
    Berkeley: University of California Press, 1970.
——. *Orson Welles: The Rise and Fall of an American
    Genius.* NY: St. Martin's, 1985.
LEAMING, BARBARA. *Orson Welles, A Biography.* NY:
    Viking, 1985.
THOMSON, DAVID. *Rosebud.* NY: Alfred A. Knopf, 1996.

Film Comment S '96
Hist Today Mr '96
LA Times Ap'96
Nation Ma 27 '96
New Rep O 21 '85
Newsweek O 21 '85
NY Times Book Rev Ja 7 '96; Je 30 '96
Time O 21 '85; Ja 29 '96
Times Lit Sup S 20 '96
Wilson Q Summer '96

WEST, MAE

CURRY, RAMINA. *Too Much of A Good Thing: Mae
    West as Cultural Icon.* Duluth, MN: University of
    Minnesota Press, 1996.
HAMILTON, MARYBETH. *When I'm Bad, I'm Better: Mae
    West, Sex, and American Entertainment.* NY:
    HarperCollins, 1995.
LEONARD, MAURICE. *Mae West: Empress of Sex.*
    London: Collins, 1991.
STEIN, CHARLES W. *American Vaudeville as Seen by Its
    Contemporaries.* NY: Knopf, 1984.
SOCHEN, JUNE. *Mae West: She Who Laughs, Lasts.*
    Wheeling, IL: Harlan Davidson, 1992.
UNTERBRINK, MARY. *Funny Women.* NY: McFarland,
    1987.

Dict of Lit Biog vol. 44
Esq Jy '67

Film Comment My/Je '80; Ja/F '81
Time D 1 '80; My 22 '78
Vogue Je '70; F '83

WILLIAMS, HANK

FLIPPO, CHET. *Your Cheatin' Heart: A Biography of
    Hank Williams.* NY: Simon & Schuster, 1981.
RIVERS, JERRY. *Hank Williams, From Life to Legend.*
    Denver, CO: Heather Enterprises, 1967.
WILLIAMS, HANK. *Living Proof: An Autobiography.* NY:
    Putnam, 1979.
WILLIAMS, ROGER M. *Sing a Sad Song: The Life of Hank
    Williams.* Garden City, NY: Doubleday, 1970.

Guitar Player N '96
New Yorker D 28 '92
People Au 5 '96
South Atl Q Winter '95

WILLIAMS, TENNESSEE

BOXILL, ROGER. *Tennessee Williams.* NY: St. Martin's,
    1987.
HAYMAN, RONALD. *Tennessee Williams: Everyone Else
    Is an Audience.* New Haven, CT: Yale University
    Press, 1993.
LEVERICH, LYLE. *Tom: The Unknown Tennessee Williams.*
    NY: Crown, 1995.
WILLIAMS, DAKIN, AND SHEPHERD MEAD. *Tennessee
    Williams: An Intimate Biography.* NY: Arbor House,
    1983.
WINDHAM, DONALD. *Tennessee William's Letters to
    Donald Windham.* Athens, GA: University of
    Georgia Press, 1996.

Amer Mr 26 '83
Esq D '83
Harper's Baz S ' 85; S '89
Maclean's Mr 7 '83
Nation Mr 19 '83
Newsweek Mr 7 '83
Time D 26 '83

WINDSOR, DUKE AND DUCHESS OF

BLACKWOOD, CAROLINE. *The Last of the Duchess.* NY:
    Pantheon, 1995.
BLOCH, MICHAEL. *Duchess of Windsor.* NY: St.
    Martin's, 1996.
——. *Wallis and Edward—Letters 1931-1937: The
    Intimate Correspondence of the Duke and Duchess
    of Windsor.* NY: Avon, 1988.
BRYAN, JOSEPH. *The Windsor Story.* NY: Morrow, 1979.
FAIRLEY, JOSEPHINE. *The Princess and Duchess.* NY: St.
    Martin's, 1989.
GARRETT, RICHARD. *Mrs. Simpson.* NY: St. Martin's, 1979.
HIGHAM, CHARLES. *The Duchess of Windsor: The Secret
    Life.* NY: Diamond Books, 1989.
MARTIN, RALPH G. *The Woman He Loved.* NY: Simon
    & Schuster, 1973.
SPOTO, DONALD. *The Decline and Fall of the House of
    Windsor.* NY: Simon & Schuster, 1995.
VICKERS, HUGO. *The Private World of the Duke and
    Duchess of Windsor.* NY: Abbeville, 1996.
ZIEGLER, PHILIP. *King Edward VIII.* NY: Knopf, 1991.

Am Her D '91
Time N 2 '36; D 7 '36; My 5 '86
Newsweek My 5 '86

WINFREY, OPRAH

BLY, NELLIE. *Oprah!: Up Close and Down Home.* NY:
    Kensington, 1993.
BUFFALO, AUDREEN. *Meet Oprah Winfrey.* NY: Random
    House, 1993.
OTFINOSKI, STEVEN. *Oprah Winfrey: Televison Star.*
    Woodbridge, CT: Blackbirch Press, 1993.
WALDRON, ROBERT. *Oprah!* NY: St. Martin's, 1987.

Bus Wk O 2 '95
Ebony Au '97
Forbes O 16 '95; N 20 '95
Jet Ja 26 '95; O 16 '95; N 27 '95
Mirabella Jy/Au '97
People O 16 '95; S 9 '96; Ma 12 '97; Ju 23 '97
Newsweek O 7 '96
New York Times Mag N 19 '95; N 24 '96
Pub Wkly S 16 '96
Time J 17 '96
Variety O 9 '95

WOOLF, VIRGINIA

BELL, QUENTIN. *Virginia Woolf: A Biography.* NY:
    Harcourt Brace, 1972.
BLODGETT, HARRIET, ED. *Capacious Hold-All: An Antho-
    logy of English Women's Diary Writings.* Char-
    lotteseville, VA: University of Virginia Press, 1991.
DUNN, JANE. *A Very Close Conspiracy.* Boston: Little,
    Brown, 1991.
GORDON, LYNDALL. *Virginia Woolf: A Writer's Life.* NY:
    Norton, 1984.

KING, JAMES. *Virginia Woolf*. London: Norton, 1995.
LEE, HERMIONE. *Virginia Woolf*. NY: Knopf, 1997.
MEPHAM, JOHN. *Virginia Woolf: A Literary Life*. NY: St. Martin's, 1991.
RAITT, SUZANNE. *Vita and Virginia*. Oxford/NY: Oxford University Press, 1993.
SCHLUETER, PAUL AND JANE, EDS. *An Encyclopedia of British Women Writers*. NY: Garland, 1998.
WOOLF, VIRGINIA. *Moments of Being*. NY: Harcourt Brace, 1985.

Horizon S '75
New Republic Ja 31 '87
Newsweek N 17 '75; O 15 '84
New Yorker F 3 '73; F 25 '85; N 6 '89
Time N 20 '72; N 29 '76

WRIGHT, FRANK LLOYD

ALOFSIN, ANTHONY. *Frank Lloyd Wright: The Lost Years 1910-1922*. Chicago: University of Chicago Press, 1994.
GOSSEL, PETER. *Frank Lloyd Wright*. Carson, CA: Books Nippan, 1994.
GUERRERO, PEDRO E. *Picturing Wright: An Album from Frank Lloyd Wright's Photographer*. San Francisco: Pomegranate Artbooks, 1994.
HERTZ. *Frank Lloyd Wright*. NY: Macmillan, 1995.
HOFFMAN, DONALD. *Understanding Frank Lloyd Wright's Architecture*. NY: Dover, 1995.
HOPPEN, DONALD W. *The Seven Ages of Frank Lloyd Wright: A New Appraisal*. Santa Barbara: Capra Press, 1992.
KAUFMAN, EDGAR. *Frank Lloyd Wright*. NY: NAL, 1989.
MEEHAN, PATRICK J. *Truth Against the World*. NY: Wiley, 1987.
NASH, ERIC P. *Frank Lloyd Wright of Nature*. NY: Smithmark Publishers, 1996.
PFEIFFER, BRUCE BROOKS. *Frank Lloyd Wright: The Masterworks*. NY: Rizzoli, 1993.
RUBIN, SUSAN GOLDMAN. *Frank Lloyd Wright*. NY: Abrams, 1994.
SECREST, MERYLE. *Frank Lloyd Wright*. NY: Knopf, 1993.
STORRER, WILLIAM ALLEN. *The Frank Lloyd Wright Companion Book*. Chicago: University of Chicago Press, 1994.
WRIGHT, FRANK LLOYD. *Collected Writings, Vol. 1, 1894-1930*. NY: Rizzoli, 1992.

Life Ap 27 '59
Newsweek Ap 20 '59
Saturday Review N 7 '59
Time F 9 '48; Ap 20 '59

WRIGHT, WILBUR & ORVILLE

BILSTEIN, ROGER. *Flight in America*. Baltimore, MD: Johns Hopkins, 1984.
CROUCH, TOM D. *The Bishop's Boys*. NY: Norton, 1989.
DEGEN, PAULA. *Wind and Sand: The Story of the Wright Brothers at Kitty Hawk*. NY: Abrams, 1988.
HALLION, RICHARD P. *The Wright Brothers*. DC: Smithsonian, 1978.
HOWARD, FRED. *Wilbur & Orville: A Biography of the Wright Brothers*. NY: Ballantine, 1988.
WRIGHT, WILBUR. *Miracle at Kitty Hawk: The Letters of Wilbur and Orville Wright*. NY: Da Capo Press, 1996.

Time F 9 '48
Newsweek F 9 '48

ZAHARIAS, BABE DIDRIKSON

CAYLEFF, SUSAN E. *Babe: The Life and Legend of Babe Didrikson Zaharias*. Urbana, IL: University of Illinois Press, 1995.
DAVIS, MAC. *100 Greatest Sports Heroes*. NY: Grossett, 1991.
GRIMSLEY, WILL. *Gold: Its History, People and Events*. Englewood Cliffs, NJ: Prentice, Hall, 1966.
GUTTMAN, ALLEN. *Women's Sports: A History*. NY: Columbia University Press, 1991.

Newsweek O 8 '56
Read Dig Ja '57
Sports Illus O 6 '75; O 13 '75; O 20 '75

ZAPATA, EMILIANO

ADAMS, JEROME R. *Liberators and Patriots of Latin America*. Jefferson, NC/London: McFarland, 1991.
BRUNK, SAMUEL. *Revolution and Betrayal in Mexico: A Life of Emiliano Zapata*. Albuquerque: University of New Mexico Press, 1995.
NEWLON, CHARLIE. *The Men Who Made Mexico*. NY: Dodd, Mead, 1973.
WOMACK, JOHN. *Zapata and the Mexican Revolution*. NY: Knopf, 1969.

Americas S '68
Life F 25 '52
New Rep F 25 '52

Newsweek F 10 '69; F 4 '52
New Yorker F 16 '52
Time F 11 '53; F 7 '69

GENERAL

ARMS, THOMAS S. *Encyclopedia of the Cold War*. NY: Facts on File, 1994.
BAECHLER, LEA AND A. WALTON LITZ, GEN. EDS. *American Writers: A Collection of Literary Biographies*. (4 vols.). NY: Scribner's, 1974 and Supplement 11, Pt. 1, 1981.
The Biographical Dictionary of Scientists. NY: Helicon Publishers, 1994.
BERGMAN, RONALD. *The United Artists Story*. NY: Crown, 1986.
CHARMLEY, JOHN. *Churchill's Grand Alliance: The Anglo-American Special Relationship, 1940-57*. NY: Harcourt Brace, 1995.
Chronicle of the Cinema. London: Dorling Kindersley, 1995.
COLLINS, BUD AND ZANDER HOLLANDER, EDS. *Bud Collins' Modern Encyclopedia of Tennis*.
Contemporary Authors: A Bio-Bibliographical Guide to Current Writers in Fiction.
DANIEL, CLIFTON, ED. *Chronicle of the Twentieth Century*. NY: Chronicles, 1987.
DE CURTIS, ANTHONY AND JAMES HENKE, EDS. *The Rolling Stone Illustrated History of Rock & Roll*. NY: Random House, 1992.

NONFICTION, POETRY, JOURNALISM, DRAMA, MOTION PICTURES, TELEVISION, AND OTHER

Crystal, David. *The Cambridge Biographical Encyclopedia*. Cambridge/NY: Cambridge University Press, 1994.
Current Biography. (1940-1997) NY: Wilson Co. Detroit: Visible Ink Press, 1994.
DEEGAN, MARY JO. *Women in Sociology*. NY/Westport, CT: Greenwood, 1991.
DEVINE, ELIZABETH, ED. *Thinkers of the Twentieth Century*. Detroit: Gale, 1984.
EAMES, JOHN DOUGLAS. *The MGM Story*. NY: Crown, 1976.
DREXEL, JOHN, GEN. ED. *The Facts on File Encyclopedia of the Twentieth Century*. NY: Facts on File, 1991.
——. *The Paramount Story*. NY: Crown, 1985.
FEATHER, LEONARD. *The Encyclopedia of Jazz*. NY: Bonanza Books, 1960. HarperCollins, 1995.
FINDLING, JOHN E. *Dictionary of American Diplomatic History*. NY/London: Greenwood, 1989.
FINLER, JOEL W. *The Hollywood Story*. NY: Crown, 1988.
FLEISCHMAN, WOLFGANG. *Encyclopedia of World Literature in the Twentieth Century*. NY: Frederick Unger, 1967.
GARRATY, JOHN A. AND JEROME L. STERNSTEIN. *Encyclopedia of American Biography*. NY: H
GLANVILLE, BRIAN. *The Story of the World Cup*. London: Faber, 1993.
GRAFF, HENRY F., ED. *The Presidents: A Reference History*. (2nd ed.). NY: Scribner's, 1996.
Great Events of the Twentieth Century. NY: Time Books, 1997.
HART-DAVIS. *Hitler's Games: the 1936 Olympics*. NY/London: Harper & Row, 1986.
HIRSCHHORN, CLIVE *The Columbia Story*. NY: Crown, 1990.
——. *The Hollywood Musical*. NY: Crown, 1981.
——. *The Universal Story*. NY: Crown, 1983.
——. *The Warner Bros. Story*. NY: Crown, 1979.
HOCHMAN, STANLEY AND ELEANOR HOCHMAN. *Contemporary American History: 1945 to the Present*. NY: Penguin, 1997.
HOOPES, ROY. *When the Stars Went to War: Hollywood and World War II*. NY: Random House, 1994.
JAMES, EDWARD. *Notable American Women, 1607-1950*. (Vol. 1). London: Oxford University Press, 1971.
JANSON. H.W. *History of Art: A Survey of the Major Visual Arts from the Dawn of History to the Present Day*. (2nd ed.). Engelwood Cliffs, N.J. and NY: Prentice-Hall and Abrams, 1977.
JEWELL, RICHARD B. WITH VERNON HARBIN. *The RKO Story*. NY: Arlington House, 1982.
KARNEY, ROBYN. *The Movie Stars Story*. NY: Crescent Books, 1984.
KARSH, YOUSUF. *Portraits of Greatness*. NY: Nelson, 1961.
KATZ, EPHRAIM. *The Film Encyclopedia*. NY: Harper Perennial, 1990.
KERN, ROBERT. *Historical Dictionary of Modern Spain*. NY: Greenwood, 1990.
KUHN, ANNETEE, ED., WITH SUSANNAH RADSTONE. *Women in Film: An International Guide*. NY: Fawcett Columbine, 1990.
LEYDA, JAY. *Voices of Film Experience: 1984 to the Present*. NY: Macmillan, 1977.

Life Legends: The Century's Most Unforgettable Faces. Ed., Killian Jordan. NY: Life Books, 1997.
Life Special Issue. The Seventies: The Decade in Pictures. December, 1979.
Life Special Report. Remarkable American Women: 1776-1996. 1976.
Life Special Double Issue. Ed., Robert Friedman. *The Millennium*. Fall, 1997.
MANCHESTER, WILLIAM. *The Glory and the Dream: A Narrative History of America, 1932-72*. NY: Bantam, 1990.
MARKS, CHARLES. *World Artists, 1950-1986*. NY: Wilson, 1984.
McGraw-Hill Encyclopedia of Science and Technology. (8th ed., 20 vols.). NY: McGraw-Hill, 1997.
MELTON, J. GORDON. *Religious Leaders of America*. Detroit: Gale, 1991.
McGUIRE, PAULA. *American Political Leaders from Colonial Times to the Present*. Santa Barbara, CA: ABC-CLIO, 1991.
MITCHELL, JAMES, ED-IN-CHIEF. *The Random House Encyclopedia*. NY: Random House, 1977.
MOREHEAD, PHILIP D., ED. *The New International Dictionary of Music*. NY: NAL, 1992.
MUNRO, ELENAOR. *Originals: American Women Artists*. NY: Simon & Schuster, 1982.
MUNSTERBERG, HUGO. *A History of Women Artists*. NY: Crown, 1975.
Nobel Laureates in Literature. NY: Garland, 1990.
Nobel Prize Winners. NY: Wilson, 1992.
PARK, JAMES. *Icons: An A-Z Guide to the People Who Shaped Our Time*. NY: Collier, 1991.
PARRY, MELANIE, ED. *Chambers Biographical Dictionary of Women*. Edinburgh: Chambers, 1996.
People Weekly Special Collector's Edition: The Most Intriguing People of the Century. NY: People Books, 1997.
QUINLAN, DAVID. *Quintan's Illustrated Directory of Film Comedy Directors*. NY: Henry Holt, 1992.
Random House Webster's Dictionary of Scientists. NY: Random House, 1997.
The Random House International Encyclopedia of Golf. Random House: 1991.
REES, DAFYDD AND LUKE CRAMPTON. *Encyclopedia of Rock Stars*. London: DK Publishing, 1996.
REICH, BERNARD. *Political Leaders of the Contemporary Middle East and North Africa*. NY: Greenwood, 1990.
RHODES, RICHARD. *The Making of the Atomic Bomb*. NY: Touchstone, 1988.
SCHLUETER, PAUL AND JANE., EDS. *An Encyclopedia of British Women Writers*. NY: Garland, 1988.
SHAW, ARNOLD. *Black Popular Music in America*. NY: Schirmer, 1986.
SIEGEL, SCOTT AND BARBARA SIEGEL. *The Encyclopedia of Hollywood*. NY: Avon, 1990.
SLIDE, ANTHONY. *The American Film Industry: A Historical Dictionary*. NY: Greenwood Press, 1986.
SINGER, MICHAEL, COMP. AND ED. *Film Directors: a Complete Guide*. Beverly Hills, CA: Lone Eagle Publishing, 1990.
SLATKIN, WENDY. *Women Artists in History*. Englewood Cliffs, NY: Prentice-Hall, 1990.
SMITH, JESSIE CARNEY. *Epic Lives: One Hundred Black American Women Who Made a Difference*. Detroit: Gale, 1995.
SOMMER, ROBIN LANGLEY. *Hollywood: The Glamour Years (1919-1941)*. NY: Gallery Books, 1987.
STAMBLER, IRWIN AND GRELUN LANDON. *Country Music: The Encyclopedia*. NY: St. Martin's, 1997.
SULZBERGER, C. L. *The American Heritage Picture History of World War II*. NY: American Heritage/Bonanza Books, 1966.
The Sunday Times. 1000 Makers of the Twentieth Century. Initiating ed., Susan Raven, ed., Hannah Charlton. London: Times Newspapers Ltd., 1991.
THOMAS, TONY AND AUBREY SOLOMAN. *The Films of 20th Century Fox: A Pictorial History*. Secaucus, NY: Citadel Press, 1979.
WAKEMAN, JOHN. *World Film Directors: 1890-1945*. NY: Wilson, 1987.
WALLACE, IRVING AND AMY WALLACE, DAVID WALLECHINSKY AND SYLVIA WALLACE. *The Intimate Sex Lives of Famous People*. NY: Delacourt, 1981.
WALLENCHINSKY, DAVID. *The Complete Book of the Olympics*. Boston: Little, Brown, 1992.
Webster's New Biographical Dictionary. Springfield, MS: Mirriam-Webster, 1988.
Who's Who in America With World Notables. New Providence, NJ: Marquis' Who's Who.
Who's Who in the World. New Providence, NJ: Marquis' Who's Who, 1994.
Who's Who of American Women. New Providence, NJ: Marquis' Who's Who.
WISTRICH, ROBERT. *Who's Who in Nazi Germany*. London/NY: Routledge, 1995.
WOLFF, RICH, ED. DIR. *The Baseball Encyclopedia*. (9th ed.). NY: Macmillan, 1993.
ZILBOORG, CAROLINE, ED. *Women's Firsts*. Detroit: Gale, 1996.

CREDITS

ADDAMS, JANE — *ARCHIVE PHOTOS*
ALI, MUHAMMAD — *PAUL SLADE/PARIS MATCH*
ALLEN, WOODY — *CHESTER HIGGINS/N. YTIMES/ARCHIVE PHOTOS*
ARAFAT, YASIR — *RENE BURRI/MAGNUM*
ARENDT, HANNAH — *UPI/CORBIS/BETTMANN*
ARMSTRONG, LOUIS — *DR*
ARMSTRONG, NEIL — *ARCHIVE PHOTOS*
ASTAIRE, FRED — *ARCHIVE PHOTOS*
BAKER, JOSEPHINE — *ROGER VIOLLET*
BALL, LUCILLE — *THE McCLAY ARCHIVES*
BANNISTER, ROGER — *ARCHIVE PHOTOS*
BARDOT, BRIGITTE — *WALTER CARONE*
BARNARD, DR. CHRISTIAAN — *ARCHIVE PHOTOS*
BEATLES, THE — *ROGER VIOLLET*
BEN-GURION, DAVID — *HORST TAPPE/ARCHIVE PHOTOS*
BERGMAN, INGMAR — *UPI/CORBIS/BETTMANN*
BERGMAN, INGRID — *ARCHIVE PHOTOS*
BOGART, HUMPHREY — *POPPERFOTO/ARCHIVE PHOTOS*
BRANDO, MARLON — *PHOTOFEST*
BRECHT, BERTOLT — *AGENCE BERNAND*
BROWN, HELEN GURLEY — *UPI/CORBIS/BETTMANN*
CALLAS, MARIA — *AGIP*
CAPONE, AL — *ARCHIVE PHOTOS*
CARSON, RACHEL — *ERICH HARTMANN/MAGNUM*
CARTIER-BRESSON, HENRI — *MARTIN FRANCK/MAGNUM*
CASTRO, FIDEL — *FRANCOIS PAGES/PARIS MATCH*
CHANEL, GABRIELLE "COCO" — *ROGER SCHALL*
CHAPLIN, CHARLIE — *PHOTOFEST*
CHRISTIE, AGATHA — *HUBERT DE SEGONZAC/PARIS MATCH*
CHURCHILL, WINSTON — *UPI/CORBIS/BETTMANN*
COLETTE — *HARLINGUE/ROGER VIOLLET*
LE CORBUSIER — *ROBERT DOISNEAU/RAPHO*
COUSTEAU, JACQUES — *PHILIPPE LE TELLIER/PARIS MATCH*
CURIE, MARIE — *KEYSTONE*
DALAI LAMA — *BENJAMIN AUGER/PARIS MATCH*
DALI, SALVADOR — *PHOTOFEST*
DAVIS, BETTE — *PHOTOFEST*
DEAN, JAMES — *PHOTOFEST*
DE BEAUVOIR, SIMONE — *ROBERT DOISNEAU/RAPHO*
DE GAULLE, CHARLES — *DR*
DIANA, PRINCESS OF WALES — *EXPRESS NEWSPAPERS/ARCHIVE PHOTOS*
DIETRICH, MARLENE — *PHOTOFEST*
DINESEN, ISAK — *NORDISK PRESSEFOTO/ARCHIVE PHOTOS*
DISNEY, WALT — *ARCHIVE PHOTOS*
DUNCAN, ISADORA — *IMAPRESS*
DYLAN, BOB — *PHOTOFEST*
EARHART, AMELIA — *UPI/CORBIS/BETTMANN*
EDISON, THOMAS — *UPI/CORBIS/BETTMANN*
EINSTEIN, ALBERT — *PHOTO RESEARCHERS*
EISENHOWER, DWIGHT D. — *CAMERA PRESS*
EISENSTEIN, SERGEI — *PHOTOFEST*
ELIOT, T. S. — *UPI/CORBIS/BETTMANN*
ELIZABETH, QUEEN I — *REX FEATURES*
ELIZABETH, QUEEN II — *CAMERA PRESS*
ELLINGTON, DUKE — *FRANK DRIGGS COLLECTION/ARCHIVE PHOTOS*
FELLINI, FEDERICO — *ROMA PRESS PHOTO/ARCHIVE PHOTOS*
FERMI, ENRICO — *ARCHIVE PHOTOS*
FORD, HENRY — *ARCHIVE PHOTOS*
FRANCO, FRANCISCO — *ARCHIVE PHOTOS*
FRANK, ANNE — *UPI/CORBIS/BETTMANN*
FRANKLIN, ARETHA — *PHOTOFEST*
FREUD, SIGMUND — *ARCHIVE PHOTOS*
FRIEDAN, BETTY — *GERALD DAVIS/ARCHIVE PHOTOS*
GAGARIN, YURI — *ARCHIVE PHOTOS*
GANDHI, INDIRA — *UPI/CORBIS/BETTMANN*
GANDHI, MOHANDAS — *SUPI/CORBIS/BETTMANN*
GARBO, GRETA — *DR*
GARCÍA MÁRQUEZ, GABRIEL — *HELMUT NEWTON/ SYGMA*
GARLAND, JUDY — *PHOTOFEST*
GATES, BILL — *REUTERS/SUE OGROCKI/ARCHIVE PHOTOS*
GINSBERG, ALLEN — *CAMERA PRESS/ARCHIVE PHOTOS*
GOODALL, JANE — *UPI/CORBIS/BETTMANN*
GORBACHEV, MIKHAIL — *SHONE/GAMMA*
GRAHAM, BILLY — *PHOTOFEST*
GRAHAM, MARTHA — *PHOTOFEST*
GRANT, CARY — *PHOTOFEST*
GRIFFITH, D.W. — *ARCHIVE PHOTOS*
GUEVARA, CHE — *ARCHIVE PHOTOS*
HAWKING, STEPHEN — *REUTERS/MARTIN LANGFIELD/ARCHIVE PHOTOS*
HEARST, WILLIAM RANDOLPH — *ARCHIVE PHOTOS*
HEFNER, HUGH — *ARCHIVE PHOTOS*
HEIFETZ, JASCHA — *PHOTOFEST*
HEMINGWAY, ERNEST — *PHOTOFEST*
HEPBURN, KATHARINE — *ARCHIVE PHOTOS*
HILLARY, EDMUND SIR & TENZING NORGAY — *UPI/CORBIS/BETTMANN*
HIROHITO, EMPEROR — *KEYSTONE*
HITCHCOCK, ALFRED — *ARCHIVE PHOTOS*
HITLER, ADOLPH — *DR*
HO CHI MINH — *ROGER PIC*
HOLIDAY, BILLIE — *HERMAN LEONARD*
HOROWITZ, VLADIMIR — *PHOTOFEST*
IBARRURI, DOLORES — *LAPI/ROGER VIOLLET*
JACKSON, MICHAEL — *ARCHIVE PHOTOS*
JAGGER, MICK — *PHOTOFEST*
JIANG QING (MADAME MAO) — *BRUNO BARBEY/MAGNUM*
JOHN, ELTON — *TIM BOXER/ARCHIVE PHOTOS*
POPE JOHN XXIII — *PHOTOFEST*
JORDAN, MICHAEL — *UPI/CORBIS/BETTMANN*
JOYCE, JAMES — *FABER & FABER/PARIS MATCH*
JUNG, CARL — *HENRI CARTIER BRESSON/MAGNUM*

KAFKA, FRANZ — *KEYSTONE*
KAHLO, FRIDA — *ARCHIVE PHOTOS*
KELLER, HELEN — *UPI/CORBIS/BETTMANN*
KELLY, GRACE — *IZIS/PARIS MATCH*
KENNEDY, JOHN F. — *AMERICAN STOCK/ARCHIVE PHOTOS*
KEVORKIAN, DR. JACK — *REUTERS/JEFF KOWALSKY/ARCHIVE PHOTOS*
KING, BILLIE JEAN — *ARCHIVE PHOTOS*
KING, MARTIN LUTHER, JR. — *ARCHIVE PHOTOS*
ANN LANDERS/ABIGAIL VAN BUREN — *ARCHIVE PHOTOS/PHOTOFEST*
LENIN, VLADIMIR — *NOVOSTI PRESS AGENCY*
LINDBERGH, CHARLES — *ARCHIVE PHOTOS*
LOREN, SOPHIA — *UPI/CORBIS/BETTMANN*
LUXEMBURG, ROSA — *UPI/CORBIS/BETTMANN*
MACARTHUR, GENERAL DOUGLAS — *ARCHIVE PHOTOS*
MADONNA — *PHOTOFEST*
MALCOLM X — *PHOTOFEST*
MANDELA, NELSON — *ARCHIVE PHOTOS*
MAO ZEDONG — *ARCHIVE PHOTOS*
MARX BROTHERS, THE — *ARCHIVE PHOTOS*
MATA HARI — *DR*
MATISSE, HENRI — *ARCHIVE PHOTOS*
MEAD, MARGARET — *UPI/CORBIS/BETTMANN*
MEIR, GOLDA — *DR*
MONROE, MARILYN — *MICHAEL OCHS*
MONTESSORI, MARIA — *UPI/CORBIS/BETTMANN*
MOORE, HENRY — *SABINE WEISS/ RAPHO*
MURROW, EDWARD R. — *ARCHIVE PHOTOS*
MUSSOLINI, BENITO — *ARCHIVE PHOTOS*
NAMATH, JOE — *ARCHIVE PHOTOS*
NASSAR, GAMAL ABDEL — *POPPERFOTO/ARCHIVE PHOTOS*
NIXON, RICHARD M. — *ARCHIVE PHOTOS*
NUREYEV, RUDOLPH — *PHOTOFEST*
O'KEEFFE, GEORGIA — *UPI/CORBIS/BETTMANN*
OLIVIER, SIR LAURENCE — *AMERICAN STOCK/ARCHIVE PHOTOS*
ONASSIS, JACQUELINE KENNEDY — *MOLLY THAYER COLLECTION/ MAGNUM*
OPPENHEIMER, J. ROBERT — *HENRI CARTIER BRESSON/MAGNUM*
OWENS, JESSE — *BARNABY'S/ARCHIVE PHOTOS*
PANKHURST, EMMELINE — *ILN/ARCHIVE PHOTOS*
PARKER, CHARLIE — *FREDDIE PATTERSON/ARCHIVE PHOTOS*
PASTERNAK, BORIS — *CORNELL CAPA/MAGNUM*
PAVAROTTI, LUCIANO — *DAVID LEES/ARCHIVE PHOTOS*
PAVLOVA, ANNA — *PHOTOFEST*
PELÉ — *ARCHIVE PHOTOS*
PERON, EVA — *DR*
PIAF, EDITH — *IZIS/PARIS MATCH*
PICASSO, PABLO — *ROBERT CAPA/MAGNUM*
PICKFORD, MARY — *PHOTOFEST*
POLLOCK, JACKSON — *POLLOCK-KRASNER/HANS NAMUTH*
PRESLEY, ELVIS — *PHOTOFEST*
PROUST, MARCEL — *MARTINIE/ROGER VIOLLET*
RAND, AYN — *UPI/CORBIS/BETTMANN*
REAGAN, RONALD — *PHOTOFEST*
RIEFENSTAHL, LENI — *EXPRESS NEWSPAPERS/ARCHIVE PHOTOS*
ROBINSON, JACKIE — *UPI/CORBIS/BETTMANN*
ROCKEFELLER, JOHN D. — *PHOTOFEST*
ROOSEVELT, ELEANOR — *PHILIPPE HALSMAN*
ROOSEVELT, FRANKLIN D. — *ROGER VIOLLET*
ROSENBERG, ETHEL & JULIUS — *ARCHIVE PHOTOS*
RUDOLPH, WILMA — *EXPRESS NEWSPAPERS/ARCHIVE PHOTOS*
RUSSEL, BERTRAND — *ARCHIVE PHOTOS*
RUTH, GEORGE HERMAN "BABE" — *AMERICAN STOCK/ARCHIVE PHOTOS*
SANGER, MARGARET — *HACKETT/ARCHIVE PHOTOS*
SARTRE, JEAN-PAUL — *MARC RIBOUD*
SCHWEITZER, ALBERT — *ARCHIVE PHOTOS*
SHAW, GEORGE BERNARD — *LAPI/ROGER VIOLLET*
SINATRA, FRANK — *PHOTOFEST*
SOLZHENITSYN, ALEKSANDR — *UPI/CORBIS/BETTMANN*
SPIELBERG, STEVEN — *PHOTOFEST*
SPOCK, DR. BENJAMIN — *ARCHIVE PHOTOS*
STALIN, JOSEPH — *PHOTOFEST*
STEIN, GERTRUDE — *UPI/CORBIS/BETTMANN*
STRAVINSKY, IGOR — *PHOTOFEST*
STREISAND, BARBRA — *PHOTOFEST*
TAYLOR, ELIZABETH — *BURT GLINN/MAGNUM*
TEMPLE, SHIRLEY — *STILLS*
TERESA, MOTHER — *RAGHU RAI/MAGNUM*
THATCHER, MARGARET — *PHOTOGRAPHERS INT/ARCHIVE PHOTOS*
THORPE, JIM — *BRANGER/ ROGER VIOLLET*
TOKYO ROSE — *ARCHIVE PHOTOS*
TOSCANINI, ARTURO — *UPI/CORBIS/BETTMANN*
TRUMAN, HARRY S. — *ARCHIVE PHOTOS*
TURNER, TED — *REUTERS/MARK CARDWELL/ARCHIVE PHOTOS*
VALENTINO, RUDOLPH — *PHOTOFEST*
VON BRAUN, WERNHER — *UPI/CORBIS/BETTMANN*
VREELAND, DIANA — *CECIL BEATON/SOTHEBY'S*
WALESA, LECH — *IMAPRESS/ARCHIVE PHOTOS*
WARHOL, ANDY — *PHOTOFEST*
WATSON & CRICK — *ARCHIVE PHOTOS*
WAYNE, JOHN — *PHOTOFEST*
WELLES, ORSON — *ARCHIVE PHOTOS*
WEST, MAE — *ARCHIVE PHOTOS*
WILLIAMS, HANK — *ARCHIVE PHOTOS*
WILLIAMS, TENNESSEE — *ARA GULER/MAGNUM*
WINDSOR, DUKE & DUCHESS OF — *PHOTOFEST*
WINFREY, OPRAH — *TERRY THOMPSON/SIPA*
WOOLF, VIRGINIA — *CAMERA PRESS/ARCHIVE PHOTOS*
WRIGHT, FRANK LLOYD — *AMERICAN STOCK/ARCHIVE PHOTOS*
WRIGHT, WILBUR & ORVILLE — *UPI/CORBIS/BETTMANN*
ZAHARIAS, BABE DIDRIKSON — *UPI/CORBIS/BETTMANN*
ZAPATA, EMILIANO — *UPI/CORBIS/BETTMANN*